EYEWITNES

ROME

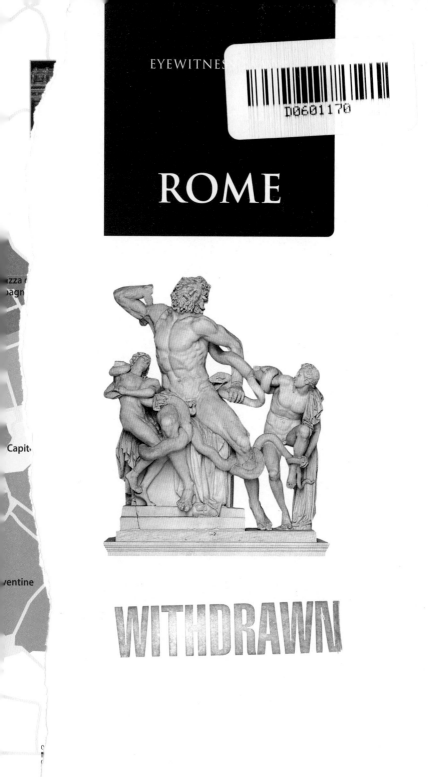

WITHDRAWN

azza
agn

Capit

entine

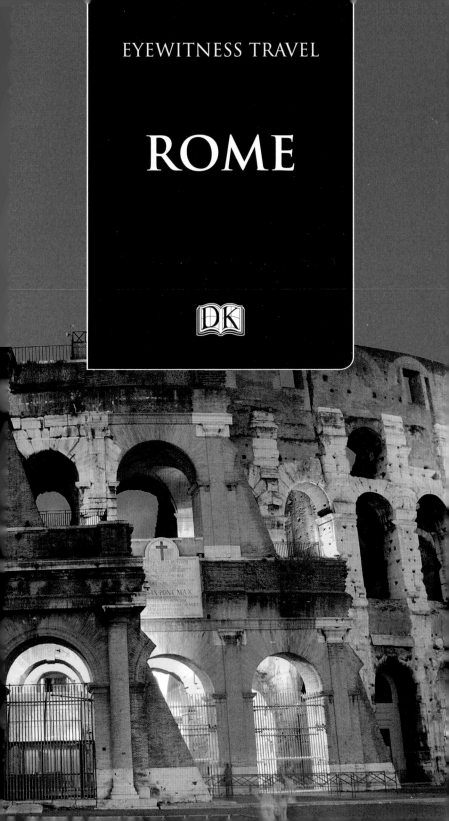

EYEWITNESS TRAVEL

ROME

DK

LONDON, NEW YORK,
MELBOURNE, MUNICH AND DELHI
www.dk.com

Project Editor Fiona Wild
Art Editor Annette Jacobs
Editors Ferdie McDonald, Mark Ronan, Anna Streiffert
Designer Lisa Kosky
Design Assistant Marisa Renzullo
Picture Research Catherine O'Rourke
Research in Rome Sam Cole
DTP Editor Siri Lowe

Main Contributors
Olivia Ercoli, Ros Belford, Roberta Mitchell

Photographers
John Heseltine, Mike Dunning, Kim Sayer

Illustrators
Studio Illibill, Kevin Jones Associates, Martin Woodward, Robbie Polley

This book was produced with the assistance of
Websters International Publishers.

Printed and bound by South China Printing Co. Ltd., China

First American edition 1993
14 15 16 17 10 9 8 7 6 5 4 3 2 1

Published in the United States by DK Publishing,
345 Hudson Street, New York, New York 10014

Reprinted with revisions
2001, 2002, 2003, 2004, 2005, 2006, 2007, 2008, 2009,
2010, 2011, 2012, 2013, 2014

Copyright 1993, 2014 © Dorling Kindersley Limited, London
A Penguin Random House Company

All rights reserved. Without limiting the rights under copyright reserved above,
no part of this publication may be reproduced, stored in or introduced into a retrieval
system, or transmitted, in any form, or by any means (electronic, mechanical,
photocopying, recording, or otherwise), without the prior written permission of both
the copyright owner and the above publisher of this book.

Published in Great Britain by Dorling Kindersley Limited.
A catalog record for this book is available from the Library of Congress.
ISSN: 1542-1554
ISBN: 978-1-46541-054-2

Floors are referred to throughout in accordance with American usage;
i.e., the "first floor" is the floor at ground level.

MIX
Paper from
responsible sources
FSC™ C018179
www.fsc.org

**The information in this
DK Eyewitness Travel Guide is checked annually.**
Every effort has been made to ensure that this book is as up- to-date as possible at
the time of going to press. Some details, however, such as telephone numbers,
opening hours, prices, gallery hanging arrangements and travel information, are
liable to change. The publishers cannot accept responsibility for any consequences
arising from the use of this book, nor for any material on third party websites, and
cannot guarantee that any website address in this book will be a suitable source of
travel information. We value the views and suggestions of our readers very highly.
Please write to: Publisher, DK Eyewitness Travel Guides, Dorling Kindersley,
80 Strand, London WC2R 0RL, UK, or email: travelguides@dk.com.

Front cover main image: Ponte Sant'Angelo and St. Peter's Basilica

◀ The Colosseum by night

Contents

Colosseum

Introducing Rome

Moses by Michelangelo in
San Pietro in Vincoli

Fresco in Villa Farnesina

Rome Area by Area

The Tempietto

Arch of Titus

Travelers' Needs

Mosaic in Santa Prassede

Survival Guide

Outdoor café in
Santa Maria in Trastevere

The basilica of St. Peter's
in Vatican City

HOW TO USE THIS GUIDE

This Eyewitness Travel Guide helps you get the most from your stay in Rome with the minimum of practical difficulty. The opening section, *Introducing Rome*, locates the city geographically, sets modern Rome in its historical context, and explains how Roman life changes through the year. *Rome at a Glance* is an overview of the city's attractions. The main sightseeing section, *Rome Area by Area*, starts on page 64. It describes all the important sights with maps, photographs, and detailed illustrations. In addition, nine planned walks take you to parts of Rome you might otherwise miss.

Carefully researched tips for hotels, shops and markets, restaurants and cafés, sports and entertainment are found in *Travelers' Needs*, and the *Survival Guide* has advice on everything from mailing a letter to catching the Metro.

Finding Your Way Around the Sightseeing Section

Each of the sixteen sightseeing areas in the city is color-coded for easy reference. Every chapter opens with an introduction to the part of Rome it covers, describing its history and character, followed by a Street-by-Street map illustrating the heart of the area. Finding your way around each chapter is made simple by the numbering system used throughout. The most important sights are covered in detail in two or more full pages.

Each area has color-coded thumb tabs.

A locator map shows where you are in relation to other areas in the center of the city.

Locator map

1 Area Map
For easy reference, the sights in each area are numbered and marked on an area map. To help the visitor, this map also shows Metro stations. The area's key sights are listed by category, such as Churches and Temples, Museums and Galleries, and Ancient Sites.

A suggested route takes in some of the most interesting and attractive streets in the area.

2 Street by Street Map
This gives a bird's-eye view of interesting and important parts of each sightseeing area. The numbering of the sights ties in with the area map and the fuller description of the entries on the pages that follow.

Stars indicate the sights that no visitor should miss.

Rome Area Map

The colored areas shown on this map (see inside front cover) are the sixteen main sightseeing areas of Rome – each covered in a full chapter in Rome Area by Area (pp64–257). They are highlighted on other maps throughout the book. In Rome at a Glance (pp44–59), for example, they help locate the top sights. They are also used to help you find the locations of the nine guided walks (p275).

Numbers refer to each sight's location on the area map and its place in the chapter.

Practical information provides everything you need to know to visit each sight. Map references pinpoint the sight's location on the *Street Finder* map (see pp388–411).

The facade of each major sight is shown to help you spot it quickly.

The visitors' checklist gives all the practical information needed to plan your visit.

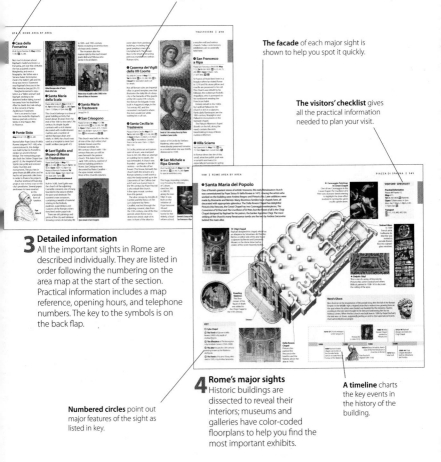

3 Detailed information
All the important sights in Rome are described individually. They are listed in order following the numbering on the area map at the start of the section. Practical information includes a map reference, opening hours, and telephone numbers. The key to the symbols is on the back flap.

4 Rome's major sights
Historic buildings are dissected to reveal their interiors; museums and galleries have color-coded floorplans to help you find the most important exhibits.

Numbered circles point out major features of the sight as listed in key.

A timeline charts the key events in the history of the building.

INTRODUCING ROME

GREAT DAYS IN ROME

Rome is a city packed with treasures and wonderful things to see and do. Its history can be traced in the crumbling columns of the ancient empire, the medieval alleys, Renaissance palaces, Baroque fountains, and elegant piazzas. Whether here for several days or just wanting a flavor of this great city, you need to make the most of your time. Over the following pages, you'll find itineraries for some of the best of Rome's attractions, arranged first by theme, and then by length of stay. Price guides on pages 10–11, include travel, food and admission for two adults, while family prices are for two adults and two children.

Teatro di Marcello and the trio of standing columns

Ancient Rome

Two adults allow at least €150

- **Explore the Republic**
- **Lunch in medieval ambience**
- **Absorb Imperial grandeur**
- **See how the Caesars lived**

Morning
Cram highlights of the 1,000-year history of ancient Rome's Republic and Empire into one very full day. Start at its heart, the **Roman Forum** (see pp78–93), then spend an hour or so perusing some of its treasures inside the **Capitoline Museums** (see pp70–3). Stroll over to Largo della Torre Argentina to gaze upon the remains of three Republican-era temples and the crumbling brick steps of the 55 BC Baths of Pompey, where Julius Caesar was murdered, ending the Republican era. The Baths of Pompey complex included a theater that has now vanished, but some of its vaults survive in the foundations of the Campo de' Fiori area's medieval buildings – including the basement rooms of **Ristorante Da Pancrazio** (see p312), which serves excellent pasta.

Afternoon
Return to the core of ancient Rome past the Teatro di Marcello – model for the Colosseum – and the two tiny **Temples of the Forum Boarium** (see p205) in Piazza della Bocca della Verità. Go up Via del Velabro and skirt around the edge of the Forum. Head to the dank **Mamertine Prison** (see p93) to see where enemies of Rome were held and executed. Next, explore the ruins of Rome's Imperial era – the **Market and Forum of Trajan** (see pp90–91), and look down on the **Forums of Caesar**, **Augustus**, and **Nerva** (see pp92–3). At the end, you can admire the **Colosseum** (see pp94–5), built over Nero's former artificial lake. Stroll up the Via Sacra to roam the **Palatine Hill** (see pp99–103; entry for this and the Colosseum is included on the Forum ticket), peppered with original palatial homes.

Christian Rome

Two adults allow €140

- **The Vatican Museums**
- **Picnic on the Piazza**
- **Mosaics and a Mithraic temple**
- **Holy (dinner) orders**

Morning
Exploring the **Vatican Museums** (see pp232–45) can easily occupy a full morning. When you're hungry, leave the museum and walk four streets up Via Tunisi to shop for goodies at the outdoor market on Via Andrea Doria. Take them back to picnic on Piazza San Pietro.

Afternoon
Pop into **St. Peter's Basilica** (see pp228–31) to marvel at this capital of Christendom, then admire the glittering mosaics of **Santa Maria Maggiore** (see pp174–5). Afterward, visit **San Clemente** (see pp188–9), a gorgeous 12th-century church built atop a 4th-century one, which stands on an ancient Mithraic temple. You will find important works by Raphael, Bernini, Caravaggio, and Bramante in the church of **Santa Maria del Popolo** (see pp140–41).

Detail of the mosaics in Santa Maria Maggiore

Dolce & Gabbana store window in Piazza di Spagna

Enjoy the evening *passeggiata* (Rome's see-and-be-seen stroll along the Via del Corso) with a drink at one of the busy cafés flanking the piazza. Finish off by eating in a hearty trattoria **Al Duello** *(see p311)*, or the sophisticated seafood restaurant **La Pallacorda** *(see p313)*.

Art and Shopping

Two adults
allow at least €30

- Fountains and piazzas
- National Gallery treasures
- Temples and boutiques
- Spanish Steps and the Trevi Fountain

Morning

Start at the fruit and flower market of **Campo de' Fiori** *(see pp145–55)*, located around a statue of Giordano Bruno, who was burned at the stake in the Middle Ages. **Piazza Navona** *(see p118–29)*, with its Baroque fountains and excellent cafés, owes its oval shape to the ancient stadium beneath (a fragment is visible at its north end). Visit the collections of the National Gallery in the **Palazzo Altemps** *(see p129)*. Peek into the church of **San Luigi dei Francesi** *(see p124)* for the early Caravaggios, then duck into Corso del Rinascimento 40 to

see the hidden fantasy facade on **Sant'Ivo alla Sapienza** *(see p124)*. Do not miss Rome's **Pantheon** *(see pp114–15)*, an ancient temple (now church), and **Santa Maria sopra Minerva** *(see p112)*, for its art. Try the cappuccinos at **Caffè Sant'Eustachio** *(see p322)*.

Afternoon

Cross the Via del Corso, and enjoy an afternoon's shopping in the chic boutiques of **Via Condotti** *(see p135)* and its tributaries fanning out from the base of the **Spanish Steps** *(see pp136–7)*. To end the day, treat yourself to some of Rome's best ice cream at **San Crispino** *(see p322)*, and wander over to the nearby **Trevi Fountain** *(see p161)* before it melts.

A Family Day

Family of 4 allow at least €200

- Cycle in Villa Borghese park
- See puppets, creatures, and creepy crypts
- Cross the Tiber for medieval alleys and panoramic views

Morning

Rent bikes in **Villa Borghese** park *(see pp260–61)* where, as well as exploring, you can visit the Etruscan Museum in **Villa**

Giulia *(see pp264–5)* or the excellent **Galleria Borghese** *(see pp262–3;* book ahead). If the kids need less art and more fun, take in Rome's zoo, the **Bioparco** *(see p261)*. If it's a Sunday, stop at **Pincio Gardens** *(see pp138–9)* for an open-air carousel and the San Carlino, one of Rome's few remaining puppet theaters, which puts on *Pulcinella* shows from 11am.

Afternoon

Return the bikes and stroll past the top of the **Spanish Steps** *(see pp136–7)* down Via Gregoriana, looking for the Palazzetto Zuccari at number 28, whose windows and doors are shaped into hideous creatures. Below Via Veneto's **Santa Maria della Concezione** *(see p256)* lies the creepy Capuchin Crypts, which are covered in mosaics made from the bones of monks. (Cappuccino coffee was named after the color of these friars' robes.)

At Piazza della Bocca della Verità, on the porch of **Santa Maria in Cosmedin** *(see p204)*, sits the Mouth of Truth, an ancient drain cover carved as a monstrous face. The story goes that if you tell a lie with your fingers in the mouth, it will bite them off. Head across the river to **Trastevere** *(see pp209–15)*, an area of twisting medieval alleys. Climb **Janiculum Hill** *(see pp217–19)* to enjoy the sweeping views of the city. Descend to Trastevere for a pizza at **Pizzeria Ivo** *(see p320)*.

View of Via Condotti from the top of the Spanish Steps

2 days in Rome

- Marvel at the treasures in the Vatican Museums
- See the sites of the ancient city, from the Colosseum to the Palatine
- Watch the world go by from the Spanish Steps

Day 1
Morning Buy tickets online to avoid the lines at the **Vatican Museums** (*pp232–45*), the largest art collection in the world. Admire Michelangelo's masterpieces in the **Sistine Chapel** (*pp242–5*), then head to the vast, ornate basilica, **St. Peter's** (*pp228–31*).

Afternoon Cross the river via the Ponte Vittorio Emanuele II to the heart of the historic downtown. A brisk walk takes in all the major sights, from the Baroque splendor of **Piazza Navona** (*p122*) to the architectural marvel of the ancient **Pantheon** (*pp114–15*). Be sure to also visit the **Trevi Fountain** (*p161*) and the **Spanish Steps** (*pp136–7*).

Day 2
Morning Take a trip to the **Colosseum** (*pp94–7*), Rome's spectacular amphitheater, then take a stroll through the **Forum** (*pp80–89*), once the beating heart of the Empire. One ticket (buy at the entrance to the Forum) grants access to both

sites, as well as the **Palatine** (*pp100–103*), where Rome's emperors had their palaces. Don't miss the beautiful 2,000-year-old frescoes in the **House of Livia** (*p103*).

Afternoon Take the glass elevator to the top of the **Victor Emmanuel Monument** (*p76*) for some of the best views in town. From here, an easy walk will lead you via the ancient **Portico of Octavia** (*p154*) to **Campo de' Fiori** (*p148*) for some people-watching. Cross **Ponte Sisto** (*p212*) to the picturesque neighborhood of **Trastevere** (*pp208–215*) for dinner and a pleasant evening stroll.

3 days in Rome

- Be awed by the magificent interiors of the Pantheon
- Admire the art collection of the Borghese family
- Make a wish and throw a coin in the Trevi Fountain

Day 1
Morning A lifetime is not enough to see everything in the **Vatican Museums** (*pp232–45*), so focus on highlights such as awe-inspiring ancient sculpture the *Laocoön* (*p237*), and the Renaissance treasures in the **Raphael Rooms** (*pp240–41*). Finish your visit with the magnificent **Sistine Chapel** (*pp242–45*) and the grand basilica of **St. Peter's** (*pp228–31*).

Baroque Trevi Fountain, one of the most familiar sights of Rome

Afternoon A short walk from the Vatican is the imposing **Castel Sant'Angelo** (*pp250–51*). Cross Ponte Sant'Angelo to browse the antique shops lining **Via dei Coronari** (*p128*), then continue on to Rome's loveliest square, **Piazza Navona** (*p122*). Visit the **Pantheon** (*pp114–15*) for stunning architecture, before moving on to **Sant'Ignazio di Loyola** (*p108*) to see the *trompe l'oeil* paintings housed within.

Day 2
Morning Relive Rome's glorious past by roaming through the ancient paths, grandiose arches, and solitary columns of the **Forum** (*pp80–89*). Explore the **Palatine** (*pp100–103*), and if you have time, climb the terraces of the **Colosseum** (*pp94–7*).

Afternoon See layers of history at **San Clemente** (*pp188–9*), then walk across the **Circus Maximus** (*p207*) to the beautifully simple church **Santa Maria in Cosmedin** (*p204*). Bustling **Campo de' Fiori** (*p148*) and lively **Trastevere** (*pp208–215*) are a pleasant stroll away.

Day 3
Morning Reserve in advance to visit the magnificent **Museo e Galleria Borghese** (*pp262–3*), with its masterpieces by Bernini. Afterward, make your way to **Piazza del Popolo** (*p139*) with its towering obelisk and fantastic churches. Join the crowds on the **Spanish Steps** (*pp136–7*), then throw a coin in the **Trevi Fountain** (*p161*).

The Colosseum, where deadly gladiatorial combat and wild animal fights were once staged

Afternoon Stroll to the Capitol to visit the world's first public museum, **Palazzo Nuovo**, *(pp70–71)* for Greek and Roman sculpture, and the **Palazzo dei Conservatori** *(pp72–3)* for paintings by great artists such as Titian, Veronese, Rubens, and Caravaggio. Stop off at the nearby **Victor Emmanuel Monument** *(p76)* for some truly magnificent views of the city.

5 days in Rome

- View Michelangelo's stunning *Pietà* in St. Peter's
- Bike along the monument-lined Via Appia Antica
- Delight in Tivoli's ancient and Renaissance villas

Santa Maria in Trastevere, with its 12th-century apse mosaic of the Coronation of the Virgin

Day 1

Morning Walk in the footsteps of popes through the art-filled **Vatican Museums** *(pp232–45)* to the **Sistine Chapel** *(pp242–5)*. Take in the wonders of **St. Peter's** *(pp228–31)*, with Michelangelo's famous sculpture *Pietà*, his soaring dome, and Bernini's bronze masterpiece *baldacchino*. Take a tour of the Necropolis where St. Peter is buried.

Afternoon Visit the ancient, medieval, and Renaissance site of **Castel Sant'Angelo** *(pp250–51)*, before crossing the river to the French national church **San Luigi dei Francesi** *(p124)*, where three Caravaggio masterworks are on display.

Day 2

Morning Take the elevator to the top of the **Victor Emmanuel Monument** *(p76)* for wonderful views, and to check out the layout of the ruins of the **Forum** *(pp80–89)*, the **Palatine** *(pp100–103)*, and the **Colosseum** *(pp94–7)*. Then head down to see the ancient remains of these amazing historic sites close up.

Afternoon Marvel at the sheer enormity of the **Circus Maximus** *(p207)*. Just around the corner, find the Bocca della Verità in **Santa Maria in**

Cosmedin *(p204)*, and visit the well-preserved **Temples of the Forum Boarium** *(p205)*. Explore the much-recycled **Theater of Marcellus** *(p153)* and finish with a visit to the **Ghetto and Synagogue** *(p154)*. Look for a hidden gem, **Fontana delle Tartarughe** *(p152)*, nearby.

Day 3

Morning Stroll through leafy **Villa Borghese** *(p260)* to work up an appetite for the glorious art at the **Museo e Galleria Borghese** *(pp262–3)*. Check out the panoramic view from the **Pincio Gardens** *(p138)* before winding down to **Piazza del Popolo** *(p139)*. Explore the square's famous church, **Santa Maria del Popolo** *(pp140–41)*, with works by Caravaggio and Raphael. The elegant Rococo **Spanish Steps** *(pp136–7)* are just around the corner.

Afternoon Treat yourself to ice cream en route to the iconic **Trevi Fountain** *(p161)*. Continue your walk at a leisurely pace to the **Pantheon** *(pp114–15)* to explore its airy interiors. Next, visit the historic square **Campo de' Fiori** *(p148)* and walk over **Ponte Sisto** *(p212)* to gaze at medieval mosaics in **Santa Maria in Trastevere** *(p214–15)*.

Day 4

Morning Visit the lowest level of **San Clemente** *(pp188–9)*, where the ancient rites of Mithraism were practiced. Not far away, the **Baths of Caracalla** *(p199)* give an idea of ancient Roman bathing facilities.

Afternoon Ride a bike or take a walk along the **Via Appia Antica** *(p267)*, with sights along the way including the **Tomb of Cecilia Metella** *(p268)* and lots of spine-chilling catacombs.

Day 5

Morning Take a trip out of the city and explore the historic hill town of **Tivoli** *(p270)* and the surrounding area. Be sure to visit Renaissance **Villa d'Este** *(p270)*, with its world-famous gardens bursting with fountains and water features, sculptures and manicured hedges.

Afternoon
Wander the sprawling ruins of **Hadrian's Villa** *(p271)*, 4 miles (6 km) southwest of Tivoli, the emperor's 2nd-century AD summer retreat. It boasts pools, theaters, baths, libraries, and gymnasiums. The grounds of the villa are great for a picnic.

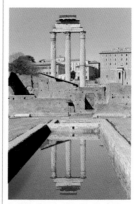

Corinthian columns of the Temple of Castor and Pollux, rebuilt in AD 6, in the Forum

Putting Rome on the Map

Since its foundation over 2,760 years ago on seven hills near the banks of the Tiber River, Rome has grown into a city of 3 million people covering 580 square miles (1,500 sq km) of central Italy. Within this area is the independent Vatican City State. Rome was made capital of the newly united Italy in 1870. It is about 17 miles (28 km) from the sea and has good rail and road links to nearby historic Italian towns and cities.

Key

≡≡≡ Freeway
━━ Major road
≡ ≡ Road under construction
━━ Other road
---- Train line
━━ Regional border

Rome and Environs

0 kilometers 10
0 miles 5

See next page

ROME

Olbia, Arbatax, Cagliari ↓   ↘ Palermo

Arbatax, Cagliari, C Porto-Vec

Labaro
Tomba di Nerone
Monte Sacro
Flaminio
Casalotti
Primavalle
Centocelle
Case Rosse
Torre Angela
Massimina
Ostiense
Cinecittà
Trullo
EUR
Cecchignola
Ciampino
Fiumicino Airport
Tevere
Ciampino Airport
Acilia
Fiumicino
Ostia Antica
Spinaceto

Emilia-Romagna
Bologna
Pontremoli
Sasso Marconi
Aulla
La Spezia
Massa
Forte dei Marmi
Pistoia
Viareggio
Lucca
Prato
Pisa
Cascina
Empoli
Firenze (Florence)
Livorno
Collesalvetti
Certaldo
Isola di Gorgona
Rosignano Marittimo
Volterra
Cecina
Siena
Toscana
Massa Marittima
Roccastrac
Isola Capraia
Piombino
Follonica
Portoferraio
Isola d'Elba
Grosseto
Isola Pianosa
Mare Tirreno
Orbetello
Isola di Montecristo
Isola del Giglio
Monte Argentario
L'Ile-Rousse
St-Florent
Bastia
Calvi
Corsica
Corte
Caterragio
Ajaccio

Central Rome

This book divides central Rome into 16 areas and has further sections for sights on the outskirts of the city, including some day trips, as well as some suggested walks. Each of the main areas has its own chapter and contains a selection of sights that convey some of its history and distinctive character. The Forum will give you a glimpse of ancient Rome, while the Capitol, Piazza della Rotonda, and Piazza Navona represent the historic center. If you are interested in Renaissance palaces, make a point of visiting the fine examples in Campo de' Fiori. In Piazza di Spagna, you can find designer shops and hints of the Grand Tour, with its array of Renaissance, and Baroque art. A stop at the Vatican will reveal the impressive St. Peter's at the heart of Roman Catholicism.

Pantheon
Fronted by lofty granite columns, the Pantheon was built as a Roman temple of "all the gods" (see pp114–15).

Vatican Museums
This vast complex of buildings holds one of the world's greatest collections of Classical and Renaissance art (see pp232–45).

Key to Symbols see back flap

Colosseum
One of Rome's most famous landmarks, the Colosseum *(see pp94–7)* was the venue for gladiatorial and animal fights. These provided a gory spectacle for Rome's citizens, up to 55,000 of whom would cram into the amphitheater at one time.

Capitoline Museums
These fine collections *(see pp70–73)* include both Classical sculpture and Renaissance art, including this Greek statue of a discus thrower.

St. Peter's
The magnificent dome of St. Peter's *(see pp228–31)* was designed by Michelangelo and is visible on the Rome skyline.

THE HISTORY OF ROME

One of the most ancient cities in Europe, Rome was founded over 2,760 years ago. Since then it has been continuously inhabited, and, as the headquarters first of the Roman Empire and then of the Catholic Church, it has had an immense impact on the world. Many European languages are based on Latin; many political and legal systems follow the ancient Roman model; and buildings all around the world utilize styles and techniques perfected in ancient Rome. The city itself retains layers of buildings spanning over two millennia. Not surprisingly, all this history can seem a little overwhelming.

Rome began as an Iron Age hut village, founded in the mid-8th century BC. In 616, the Romans' sophisticated Etruscan neighbors seized power, but were ousted in 509, when Rome became a Republic. It conquered most of the rest of Italy, then turned its attentions overseas, and by the 1st century BC ruled Spain, North Africa, and Greece. The expansion of the Empire provided opportunities for power-hungry individuals, and the clashing of egos led to the collapse of democracy. Julius Caesar ruled for a time as dictator, and his nephew Octavian became Rome's first emperor, assuming the title Augustus. During the reign of Augustus, Christ was born, and though Christians were persecuted until the 4th century AD, the new religion took hold and Rome became its main center.

Even though it was the seat of the papacy, during the Middle Ages Rome went into decline. The city recovered spectacularly in the mid-15th century, and for over 200 years was embellished by the greatest artists of the Renaissance and the Baroque. Finally, in 1870, Rome became the capital of the newly unified Italy.

15th-century map of Rome from the north

◀ Detail from 2nd-century AD Roman mosaic from the Temple of Fortune in Palestrina

Rome's Early Development

According to the historian Livy, Romulus founded Rome
in 753 BC. Some time later, realizing his tribe was short
of females, he invited the neighboring Sabines to a
festival, and orchestrated the mass abduction of their
women. Although Livy's account is pure legend, there is
evidence that Rome was founded around the middle of
the 8th century BC, and that the Romans and Sabines
united shortly afterward. Historical evidence also gives
some support to Livy's claim that after Romulus's death,
Rome was ruled by a series of kings, and that in the 7th
century BC it was conquered by the Etruscans and ruled
by the Tarquin family. Last of the dynasty was Tarquinius
Superbus (Tarquin the Proud). His despotic rule led to
the expulsion of the Etruscansand the founding of a
Republic run by two annually elected consuls. The
uprising was led by Lucius Junius Brutus, the model
of the stern, patriotic Roman Republican.

Extent of the City

☐ 750BC   ☐ Today

Ceremonial trumpets

Capitoline   Quirinal   Viminal

Palatine

Aventine   Celian   Esquiline

The Seven Hills of Rome
By the 8th century BC, shepherds and farmers lived on
four of Rome's seven hills. As the population grew,
huts were built in the marshy valley later occupied by
the Forum.

Iron Age Hut
Early settlers lived
in wattle-and-
daub huts.
Traces of their
foundations have
been found on
the Palatine.

Augur, digging
foundation

Temple of Jupiter
This Renaissance painting by Perin del Vaga
shows Tarquinius Superbus founding the
Temple of Jupiter on the Capitol, the sacred
citadel of Rome.

750 BC Tarpeia
betrays city to the
Sabines

700 BC Approximate
beginning of Etruscan
period

*Etruscan jug
(7th century BC)*

750

700

650

*Romulus
and Remus*

753 BC Legendary
founding of Rome
by Romulus, first of
seven kings

715–713 BC King Numa
Pompilius establishes
12-month calendar

659 BC Romans
destroy rival city,
Alba Longa

The Legend of the She-Wolf
The evil king of Alba threw his baby nephews, Romulus and Remus, into the Tiber, but they were washed ashore and nursed by a she-wolf.

Apollo of Veio
Etruscan culture and religion were influenced by the Greeks. This 5th- or 6th-century statue of the Greek god Apollo comes from Veio and is in the Villa Giulia museum (see pp264–5).

Raven, guardian of the citadel

King Tarquin, holding stone worshipped as a thunderbolt

The Legend of Aeneas
Some Roman legends make the Trojan hero Aeneas the grandfather of Romulus and Remus.

Where to see Etruscan Rome

The Cloaca Maxima sewer still functions, but there are few other traces of Etruscan Rome. Most finds come from Etruscan sites outside Rome. like Tarquinia, with its tomb paintings of sumptuous banquets (see p273), but there are major collections in the Villa Giulia (pp264–5) and Vatican Museums (p236). The most famous object, however, is a bronze statue of the legendary she-wolf in the Capitoline Museums (p73). The Antiquarium Forense (p89) displays objects from the necropolis that once occupied the site of the Roman Forum.

Funeral urns shaped like huts were used for cremation from the mid-8th century BC.

Etruscan jewelry, like this 7th-century BC gold filigree brooch, was lavish. Treasures of this kind have given the Etruscans a reputation for luxurious living.

600 BC Possible date of construction of Cloaca Maxima sewer

565 BC Traditional date of the Servian Wall around Rome's seven hills

534 BC King Servius murdered

510 BC Temple of Jupiter consecrated on the Capitoline hill

Statue of Jupiter

600   **550**   **500**

578 BC Servius Tullius Etruscan king

509 BC L. J. Brutus expels Etruscans from Rome and founds the Republic
L. J. Brutus

507 BC War against Etruscans. Horatius defends wooden bridge across Tiber

616 BC Tarquinius Priscus, first Etruscan king. Forum and Circus Maximus established

Kings, Consuls, and Emperors

Rome had over 250 rulers in the 1,200 years between its foundation by Romulus and AD 476, when the last emperor was deposed by the German warrior Odoacer. Romulus was the first of seven kings, overthrown in 509 BC when Rome became a Republic. Authority was held by two annually elected consuls, but provision was made for the appointment of a dictator in times of crisis. In 494 BC, the office of Tribune was set up to protect the plebeians from injustice at the hands of their patrician rulers. Roman democracy, however, was always cosmetic. It was discarded completely in 27 BC, when absolute power was placed in the hands of the emperor.

Romulus, his twin Remus, and the she-wolf who nursed them

205 BC Scipio Africanus

218 BC Quintus Fabius Maximus

456 BC Lucius Quintus Cincinnatus

c. **753–715 BC** Romulus

800 BC	700	600	500	400	300	2(
SEVEN KINGS			REPUBLIC			
800 BC	700	600	500	400	300	2(

c. **715–673 BC** Numa Pompilius

c. **673–641 BC** Tullus Hostilius

c. **641–616** BC Ancus Marcius

616–579 BC Tarquinius Priscus

c. **579–534 BC** Servius Tullius

c. **534–509 BC** Tarquinius Superbus

c. **509 BC** Lucius Junius Brutus and Horatius Pulvillus

396 BC Marcus Furius Camillus

Tarquinius Priscus consulting an augur

Julius Caesar, whose rise to power marked the end of the Roman Republic

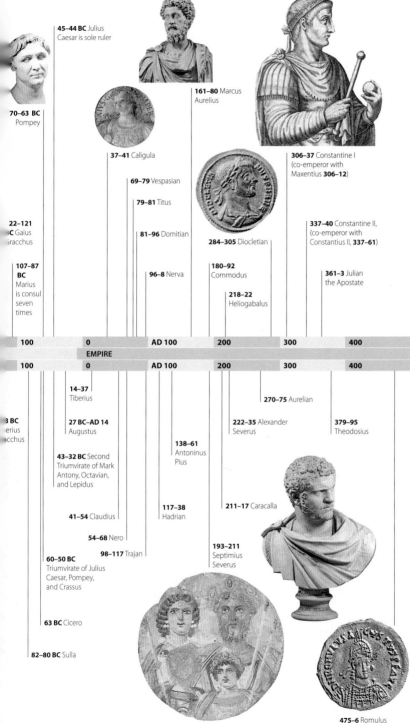

45–44 BC Julius Caesar is sole ruler

70–63 BC Pompey

161–80 Marcus Aurelius

37–41 Caligula

306–37 Constantine I (co-emperor with Maxentius **306–12**)

69–79 Vespasian

79–81 Titus

22–121 BC Gaius Gracchus

337–40 Constantine II, (co-emperor with Constantius II, **337–61**)

81–96 Domitian

284–305 Diocletian

107–87 BC Marius is consul seven times

96–8 Nerva

180–92 Commodus

361–3 Julian the Apostate

218–22 Heliogabalus

100	0	AD 100	200	300	400

EMPIRE

100	0	AD 100	200	300	400

14–37 Tiberius

270–75 Aurelian

3 BC Tiberius Gracchus

27 BC–AD 14 Augustus

222–35 Alexander Severus

379–95 Theodosius

138–61 Antoninus Pius

43–32 BC Second Triumvirate of Mark Antony, Octavian, and Lepidus

117–38 Hadrian

211–17 Caracalla

41–54 Claudius

54–68 Nero

193–211 Septimius Severus

98–117 Trajan

60–50 BC Triumvirate of Julius Caesar, Pompey, and Crassus

63 BC Cicero

82–80 BC Sulla

Septimius Severus and family

475–6 Romulus Augustulus

The Roman Republic

By the mid-2nd century BC, Rome controlled the western Mediterranean, policing and defending it with massive armies. The troops had more loyalty to the generals than to distant politicians, giving men like Marius, Sulla, Pompey, and Caesar the muscle to seize political power. Meanwhile, peasants, whose land had been destroyed during the invasion of Hannibal in 219 BC, had flooded into Rome. They were followed by slaves and freedmen from conquered lands such as Greece, swelling the population to half a million. There was plenty of work for immigrants, constructing roads, aqueducts, markets, and temples, financed by taxes on Rome's expanding trade.

Extent of the City

◻ 400 BC   ◼ Today

Arch spanning road

The gradient of an aqueduct was about 1 in 1,000.

Covered water channels

Cut stone blocks

How an Aqueduct Worked
Water from a spring in the hills was collected in a reservoir to build up pressure and ensure a steady supply to the city.

High ground

Cleaning vent

Reservoir

Underground water channel

Arches carrying water across low ground

Cicero Denounces Catiline
In 62 BC Catiline planned a coup. Cicero discovered the plot and persuaded the Senate to condemn the conspirators to death.

Via Appia

499 BC Battle against Latin tribes; Temple of Castor and Pollux built to commemorate the victory

380 BC Servian Wall rebuilt

396 BC Definitive victory over rival Etruscan city, Veio

312 BC Construction of Via Appia and Rome's first aqueduct, the Aqua Appia

500 BC   **450 BC**   **400 BC**   **350 BC**   **300 BC**

Relief of Capitoline geese

390 BC Rome invaded by Celtic Gauls: quacking geese on Capitoline hill warn of impending attack

Roman Street
In the 1st century BC, most buildings in Rome were made from brick and concrete. Only a few public buildings used marble.

Where to see Republican Rome

This fresco depicting a gang of slaves building a wall can be seen at the Museo Nazionale Romano (see p165).

Aqueduct (2nd Century BC)
Rome owed much of its prosperity to its skilled civil engineers. When the city's wells were no longer sufficient, aqueducts were built to bring water from surrounding hills. Some aqueducts were more than 50 miles (80 km) long.

Arches for maintaining a constant gradient over low-lying land

Temple of Juno
The ruins of this 197 BC temple are embedded in the church of San Nicola in Carcere (see p153). Romans consulted their gods before all important ventures.

The Temple of Saturn, first built in 497 BC, now consists of eight majestic columns overlooking the Forum at the end of the Via Sacra (see p85).

Rome's loveliest Republican buildings are the two Temples of the Forum Boarium (see p205). Four more temples can be seen in the Area Sacra of Largo Argentina (p152). Most monuments from this period, however, lie underground. Only a few, like the Tomb of the Scipios (p197), have been excavated. One of the bridges leading to Tiber Island (p155), the Ponte Fabricio, dates from the 1st century BC and is still used by pedestrians.

Scipio Africanus
In 202 BC the Roman general Scipio defeated Hannibal. Rome replaced Carthage as master of the Mediterranean.

Ponte Fabricio, built in 62 BC

220 BC Via Flaminia built, linking Rome to the Adriatic coast

168 BC Victory in Macedonian War completes Roman conquest of Greece

133–120 BC Gracchi brothers killed for trying to introduce land reforms

51 BC Caesar conquers Gaul

250 BC   **200 BC**   **150 BC**   **100 BC**

…4–241 BC st Punic …ar (against …rthage)

218–202 BC Second Punic War; Scipio Africanus defeats Carthaginians

Hannibal

149–146 BC Third Punic War; Carthage destroyed

71 BC Spartacus's slave revolt crushed by Crassus and Pompey

60 BC Rome has three joint rulers: Pompey, Crassus, and Caesar

Imperial Rome

In 44 BC Caesar became dictator for life, only to be assassinated a month later. The result was 17 years of civil war, which ended only in 27 BC when Augustus became Rome's first emperor. The Empire expanded in fits and starts, but by the late 3rd century was so huge that Diocletian decided to share it between four emperors. Thanks to trade and taxes from its vast domains, Rome was the most magnificent city in the world, studded with the lavish buildings of emperors eager to advertise their civic munificence and military triumphs.

Extent of the City

☐ AD 250 ▦ Today

Cross-vaulted ceiling with mosaic decoration

Natatio (swimming pool)

Apotheosis of Augustus
The first and perhaps the greatest Roman emperor, Augustus ruled for 27 years and was deified by the Senate after his death.

ROMA CAPVT MVNDI

The baths could hold up to 3,000 people. They met to gossip in the central *frigidarium* (cold room).

Area for exercise and gymnastics

The Roman Empire under Trajan
By the 2nd century AD, the Roman Empire stretched from Britain to Syria, and Rome was known as the Caput Mundi, the head of the world.

49 BC Caesar crosses the Rubicon and takes Rome

27 Augustus becomes first emperor

Emperor Nero

64 Fire during Nero's rule destroys much of city

65 First persecution of Christians under Nero

72 Colosseum begun

| 50 BC | 0 | AD 50 | 100 |

44 Caesar becomes dictator for life, and is murdered by Brutus and Cassius

AD 42 St. Peter the Apostle comes to Rome

13 Ara Pacis is erected to celebrate the peace Augustus has secured in the Empire

67 St. Peter is crucified and St. Paul executed in Rome

Statue of St. Peter in San Paolo fuori le Mura

125 Hadria redesigns th Pantheo

Roman Revelry
Banquets could last for up to 10 hours, with numerous courses, between which guests would retire to a small room to relax.

Where to see Imperial Rome

There are relics of Imperial Rome throughout the central city, some hidden below churches and palazzi, others, like the Forum (see pp78–89), the Palatine (pp99–103) and the Imperial Fora (pp90–3), fully excavated. The magnificence of the era, however, is best conveyed by the Pantheon (pp114–15) and the Colosseum (pp94–7).

Baths of Diocletian (AD 298)

Rome's public baths were not just places to keep clean. They also had bars, libraries, barber shops, brothels, and sports facilities.

The Arch of Titus (p89), erected in the Forum in AD 81, commemorates Emperor Titus's sack of Jerusalem in AD 70.

Tepidarium (warm room)

Virgil (70–19 BC)
Virgil was Rome's greatest epic poet. His most famous work is the *Aeneid*, the story of the Trojan hero Aeneas's journey to the future site of Rome.

A relief of Mithras, a popular Persian god (3rd century AD), can be seen beneath the church of San Clemente (pp188–9).

164–180 Plague rages in Roman Empire

212 Citizenship granted to virtually all inhabitants of the Empire

Section of Aurelian Wall

270 Aurelian Wall begun

150

200

250

216 Baths of Caracalla completed

247 Rome's Millennium is celebrated

284 Empire divided into West and East

Mosaic from the Baths of Caracalla

Early Christian Rome

In the 1st century AD, during the reign of Tiberius, a rebellious pacifist was crucified in a distant corner of the Empire. This was nothing unusual, but within a few years Jesus Christ and his teachings became notorious in Rome, his followers were perceived as a threat to public order, and many were executed. This was no deterrent, and the new religion spread through all levels of Roman society. When the Apostles Peter and Paul arrived in Rome, there was already a small Christian community, and in spite of continued persecution by the state, Christianity flourished. In AD 313 the Emperor Constantine issued an edict granting freedom of worship to Christians, and soon after founded a shrine on the site of St. Peter's tomb. This secured Rome's position as a center of Christianity, but in the 5th century the political importance of Rome declined and the city fell to Goths and other invaders.

Extent of the City
☐ AD 395 ☐ Today

Youthful, beardless representation of Christ

St. Paul

Classical-style border decorated with fruit

Santo Stefano Rotondo
This 17th-century engraving shows how a Roman temple *(top)* might have been transformed *(above)* into the 5th-century round church of Santo Stefano *(see p187)*.

4th-Century Mosaic, Santa Costanza
Beautiful mosaics, often with palm trees and other oriental motifs suggesting Jerusalem, helped spread the message of early Christianity.

The Good Shepherd
The pagan image of a shepherd sacrificing a lamb became a Christian symbol.

c. **320** Building of first St. Peter's

356 Legendary founding of Santa Maria Maggiore

Gold solidus of Theodosius

410 Rome sacked by Alaric's Goths

455 Rome sacked again by Vandals

300 | **350** | **400** | **450**

312 Control of Empire won by Constantine after battle at Milvian Bridge

Battle of the Milvian Bridge

380 Emperor Theodosius makes Christianity the official religion of the Roman Empire

395 Division of the Empire between Ravenna and Constantinople

422 Founding of Santa Sabina

Epigraph of Peter and Paul
This is one of hundreds of early Christian graffiti housed in the Lapidary Gallery of the Vatican (see p239).

Where to see Early Christian Rome

There are traces of early Christianity all over Rome. Many ancient churches were built over early Christian meeting places and sites of martyrdoms: among them San Clemente (see pp188–9), Santa Pudenziana (p173), and Santa Cecilia (p213). Outside the walls of the old city are miles of underground catacombs (pp267–8), many decorated with Christian frescoes, while the Vatican's Pio-Christian Museum (p238) has the best collection of early Christian art.

Crucifixion, Santa Sabina
This 5th-century panel on the door of Santa Sabina (see p206) is one of the earliest known representations of the Crucifixion. Interestingly, Christ's cross is not actually shown.

This figurine, carved out of bone, is embedded in the rock of the Catacombs of San Panfilo, just off the Via Salaria (see p56).

St. Peter receiving peace from the Savior

Lambs symbolizing the Christian flock

Constantine's Cross
Constantine's vision of the True Cross during the Battle of the Milvian Bridge made him convert to Christianity.

The Cross of Justin, in the Treasury of St. Peter's (p230), was given to Rome by the Emperor Justin II in AD 578.

A Byzantine image of St. Paul

609 Pantheon is consecrated as a Christian church

500

550

600

496 Anastasius II is first pope to assume title Pontifex Maximus

590–604 Pope Gregory the Great strengthens the papacy

630 Sant'Agnese fuori le Mura is built in Roman Byzantine style

475 Fall of Western Roman Empire; Byzantium becomes seat of Empire

The Papacy

The Pope is considered Christ's representative on earth, claiming his authority from St. Peter, the first Bishop of Rome. Though some popes have been great thinkers and reformers, the role has rarely been purely spiritual. In the Middle Ages, many popes were involved in power struggles with the Holy Roman Emperor. Renaissance popes like Julius II and Leo X, the patrons of Raphael and Michelangelo, lived as luxuriously as any secular prince. The popes listed here include all those who exercised significant political or religious influence, up as far as the end of the Counter-Reformation, when the power of the papacy began to wane.

St. Ludovic Kneels before Boniface *VIII* by Simone Martini

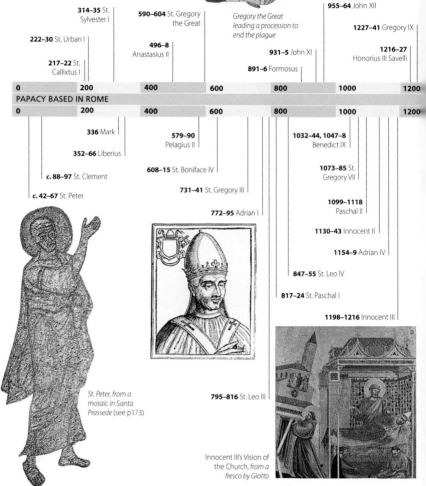

314–35 St. Sylvester I

590–604 St. Gregory the Great

Gregory the Great leading a procession to end the plague

955–64 John XII

1227–41 Gregory IX

222–30 St. Urban I

496–8 Anastasius II

931–5 John XI

1216–27 Honorius III Savelli

217–22 St. Callixtus I

891–6 Formosus

0	200	400	600	800	1000	1200

PAPACY BASED IN ROME

0	200	400	600	800	1000	1200

336 Mark

352–66 Liberius

579–90 Pelagius II

1032–44, 1047–8 Benedict IX

608–15 St. Boniface IV

1073–85 St. Gregory VII

***c.* 88–97** St. Clement

731–41 St. Gregory III

1099–1118 Paschal II

***c.* 42–67** St. Peter

772–95 Adrian I

1130–43 Innocent II

1154–9 Adrian IV

847–55 St. Leo IV

817–24 St. Paschal I

1198–1216 Innocent III

St. Peter, from a mosaic in Santa Prassede (see p173)

795–816 St. Leo III

Innocent III's Vision of the Church, from a fresco by Giotto

Portrait of Gregory XIII
by Lavinia Fontana

1560–65 Pius IV Medici

1555–9 Paul IV

1523–34
Clement VII Medici

1513–21 Leo X Medici

1492–1503
Alexander
VI Borgia

1572–84 Gregory XIII Boncompagni

1294–1303
Boniface VIII

1484–92 Innocent
VIII Cybo

1670–76 Clement X Altieri

1667–9 Clement IX

1471–84 Sixtus IV della Rovere

1655–67 Alexander VII
Chigi

1464–71 Paul II Barbo

1605 Leo XI
Medici

1700–21 Clement XI

1458–64 Pius II
Piccolomini

1300	1400	1500	1600	1700

AVIGNON	PAPACY AGAIN BASED IN ROME

1300	1400	1500	1600	1700

1417–31 Martin V
Colonna

1644–55 Innocent X Pamphilj

1447–55
Nicholas V

1585–90
Sixtus V

1623–44 Urban VIII Barberini

Nicholas V Receiving a Book,
*illustration from a
contemporary manuscript*

1592–1605
Clement VIII
Aldobrandini

1503–13 Julius II della Rovere

1605–21 Paul V
Borghese

Urban VIII Approving a Building
Project *in the Vatican's Gallery of
Tapestries (see p239)*

Raphael's portrait of Julius II

1534–49 Paul III Farnese

Paul III Gives His Approval to the
Capuchin Order *by Sebastiano Ricci*

Medieval Rome

Supplanted by Constantinople as capital of the Empire in the 4th century, Rome was reduced to a few thousand inhabitants by the early Middle Ages, its power just a memory. In the 8th and 9th centuries, the growing importance of the papacy revived the city and made it once more a center of power. But continual conflicts between the pope and the Holy Roman Emperor soon weakened the papacy. The 10th, 11th, and 12th centuries were among the bleakest in Roman history: violent invaders left Rome poverty-stricken, and the constantly warring local barons tore apart what remained of the city. Despite this, the first Holy Year was declared in 1300 and thousands of pilgrims arrived in Rome. But by 1309 the papacy was forced to move to Avignon, leaving Rome to slide into further squalor and strife.

Extent of the City

☐ *1300*   ☐ *Today*

Charlemagne Crowned in St. Peter's
On Christmas Day in 800, Charlemagne was made "emperor of the Romans," ruler of a new Christian dominion to replace that of ancient Rome.

Trajan's Column

Column of Marcus Aurelius

Madonna and Child Mosaic
The Chapel of St. Zeno (817–24) in the church of Santa Prassede *(see p173)* has some of the best examples of Byzantine mosaics in Rome.

San Giovanni in Laterano

Aurelian Wall

Medieval Plan of Rome
Maps like this one, illustrating the principal features of the city, were produced for pilgrims, the tourists of the Middle Ages.

725 King Ine of Wessex founds the first hostel for pilgrims in the Borgo

852 The Vatican is fortified with walls following a raid by Saracens

Emperor Otto I

961 King Otto the Great of Germany becomes first Holy Roman Emperor

700

800

900

1000

778 Charlemagne, King of the Franks, conquers Italy

800 Charlemagne crowned emperor in St. Peter's

880–932 Rome is ruled by two women, Theodora and then her daughter, Marozia

Stefaneschi Triptych (1315)
Giotto and his pupils painted this triptych for Cardinal Stefaneschi as an altarpiece for St. Peter's. It is now in the Vatican Museums *(see p238).*

Where to see Medieval Rome

Among the most interesting churches of the period are San Clemente, with a fine apse mosaic and Cosmati floor *(see pp188–9)*, Santa Maria in Trastevere *(pp214–15)* and Santa Maria sopra Minerva, Rome's only Gothic church *(p112)*. Santa Cecilia in Trastevere *(p213)* has a Cavallini fresco, and there is fine Cosmati work in Santa Maria in Cosmedin *(p204)*.

Colosseum   Capitol   Pyramid of Caius Cestius

Pantheon   Castel Sant'Angelo   Old St. Peter's

Charlemagne's Dalmatic in the Treasury of St. Peter's *(p230)* was supposedly worn by the emperor at his coronation in 800. In fact. the richly embroidered vestment probably dates from the 14th century.

Cosmati Tabernacle
Marblework by the Cosmati family, like this tabernacle in Santa Sabina *(see p206)*, decorates many of Rome's medieval churches.

Santa Sabina *(p206)* on the Aventine Hill has a medieval bell tower.

1084 Rome is attacked by Normans

1108 San Clemente is rebuilt

1200 Rome is an independent commune under Arnaldo di Brescia

1309 Pope Clement V moves the papacy to Avignon

1300 First Holy Year proclaimed by Pope Boniface VIII

1348 Black Death strikes Rome

1100   **1200**   **1300**

1140 Santa Maria in Trastevere is restored

Mosaic facade, Santa Maria in Trastevere (pp214–15)

1232 Cloister of San Giovanni in Laterano completed

Cola di Rienzo

1347 Cola di Rienzo – an Italian patriot – tries to restore the Roman Republic

Renaissance Rome

Pope Nicholas V came to the throne in 1447 determined to make Rome a city fit for the papacy. Among his successors, men like Julius II and Leo X eagerly followed his lead, and the city's appearance was transformed. The Classical ideals of the Renaissance inspired artists, architects and craftsmen, such as Michelangelo, Bramante, Raphael and Cellini, to build and decorate the churches and palaces of a newly confident Rome.

Extent of the City
☐ 1500   ☐ Today

Hemispherical dome

Balustrade of small columns

Classical colonnade of 16 Doric columns

School of Athens by Raphael
In this fresco *(see p241)* Raphael complimented many of his peers by representing them as ancient Greek philosophers. The building shown is based on a design by Bramante.

The Tempietto
The Tempietto (1502) at San Pietro in Montorio *(see p223)* was one of Bramante's first works in Rome. A simple, perfectly proportioned miniature Classical temple, it is a model of High Renaissance architecture.

Cosmati-style mosaic floor

Palazzo Caprini
Bramante's design had a strong influence on later Renaissance palazzi. Parts of the building survive in Palazzo dei Convertendi *(see p247)*.

1377 Papacy returns to Rome from Avignon under Pope Gregory XI

1409–15 Papacy moves to Pisa

1444 Birth of Bramante

1417 Pope Martin V ends the Great Schism in the papacy

1452 Demolition of old St. Peter's basilica begins

350   **1400**   **1450**

1378–1417 The Great Schism, a division in the papacy in Avignon

Pope Martin V, reigned 1417–31

Sack of Rome
In 1527, the unruly troops of Charles V of Spain pillaged the city, destroying countless works of art. Pope Clement VII took refuge in Castel Sant'Angelo.

Pope Nicholas V
Nicholas ordered the demolition of the old St. Peter's.

Statue of St. Peter, believed to have been crucified on this site

Underground chapel

Where to see Renaissance Rome

The Campo de' Fiori area (see pp144–55) is full of grand Renaissance palazzi, especially along Via Giulia (pp278–9). Across the river stands the delightful Villa Farnesina (pp220–21). The most typical church of the period is Santa Maria del Popolo (pp140–41), and the best collection of Renaissance art is in the Vatican Museums (pp232–45). These include the Sistine Chapel (pp242–5) and the Raphael Rooms (pp240–41).

The Madonna di Foligno by Raphael (1511–12) is one of the fine Renaissance paintings in the Vatican Pinacoteca (p239).

The Pietà, commissioned for St. Peter's in 1501, was one of Michelangelo's first sculptures executed in Rome (p231).

1483 Birth of Raphael

1486 Building of Palazzo della Cancelleria

1519 Frescoes completed in Villa Farnesina

1527 Troops of Emperor Charles V sack Rome

Emperor Charles V

1500

1550

5 Birth of helangelo

1508 Michelangelo begins painting the Sistine Chapel ceiling

1506 Pope Julius II orders start of work on new St. Peter's

1547 Pope Paul III appoints Michelangelo architect of St. Peter's

Cumaean Sibyl, Sistine Chapel

Baroque Rome

By the 16th century, the Catholic Church had become immensely rich – one of the chief criticisms of the Protestant reformers. The display of grandeur and extravagance by the papal court contrasted sharply with the poverty of the people, and wealthy Roman society was characterized by sumptuous luxury and a ceaseless round of entertainment. To make the Catholic faith more appealing than Protestantism, scores of churches were built and monuments and fountains were erected to glorify the Holy See. The finest architects in the ornate, dramatic style of the Baroque were Bernini and Borromini.

Extent of the City
☐ 1645 ☐ Today

Ceiling portraying heavenly scenes

Monument to Pope Alexander VII
This Bernini tomb in St. Peter's *(pp228–31)* includes a skeleton brandishing an hourglass.

Gian Lorenzo Bernini (1598–1680)
The favorite artist of the papacy, Bernini transformed Rome with his churches, palaces, statues, and fountains.

Tapestry of Pope Urban VIII
Bernini's most devoted patron, Pope Urban VIII Barberini (1623–44), is shown here receiving the homage of the nations.

Holy Family fresco

Pozzo Corridor
The use of perspective to create an illusion of depth and space was a favorite Baroque device. Andrea Pozzo painted this illusionistic corridor in the 1680s in the Rooms of St. Ignatius near the Gesù (*see pp110–11*).

1568 The Jesuits build the Gesù, prototypical church of the early Baroque

Altar carving from the Gesù

1595 Annibale Carracci begins to fresco Palazzo Farnese

1624 Bernini's sculpture of *Apollo and Daphne*

1626 Work on St. Peter's is completed

550 | **1575** | **1600** | **1625**

1585 Pope Sixtus V plans new streets

1600 Philosopher Giordano Bruno is burned at the stake for heresy

1571 Birth of Caravaggio

Galileo

1633 Galileo condemned to house arrest for heresy

Illusionistic beams in ceiling

Chapel painted on flat slanting wall

Figures painted to be viewed from an angle

Queen Christina of Sweden
In a coup for Catholicism, Christina renounced Protestantism and abdicated her throne. In 1655 she moved to Rome, where she became the center of a lively literary and scientific circle.

St. Ignatius, founder of the Jesuits

Francesco Borromini (1599–1667)
In the many churches he built in Rome, Borromini made use of revolutionary geometric forms.

A marble rose marks the best place to stand to appreciate the illusion of space created by the artist.

San Carlo alle Quattro Fontane
One of Borromini's most influential designs was this tiny oval church (see p159) on the Quirinal hill.

1651 Bernini redesigns much of Piazza Navona

Bernini's Fontana dei Fiumi in Piazza Navona

1694 Palazzo di Montecitorio is completed

1735 Spanish Steps are designed

1732 Work starts on the Trevi Fountain

1650   **1675**   **1700**   **1725**

1657 Borromini completes Sant'Agnese in Agone

Bonnie Prince Charlie, pretender to the throne of England

1721 Bonnie Prince Charlie is born in Rome

1734 Clement XII makes Palazzo Nuovo world's first public museum

1656 Work starts on Bernini's colonnade for St. Peter's Square

Understanding Rome's Architecture

The architecture of Imperial Rome kept alive the Classical styles of ancient Greece, at the same time developing new, uniquely Roman forms based on the arch, the vault, and the dome. The next important period was the 12th century, when many Romanesque churches were built. The Renaissance saw a return to Classical ideals, inspired by the example of Florence, but in the 17th century Rome found a style of its own again in the flamboyance of the Baroque.

The entablature above these columns has both straight and arched sections (Hadrian's Villa).

Classical Rome

Most Roman buildings were of concrete faced with brick, but from the 1st century BC, the Romans started to imitate earlier Greek models, using marble to decorate temples and other public buildings.

Corinthian capital · Plain frieze · Triangular pediment · Cornice (projecting section along facade) · Architrave (horizontal section resting on columns) · Fluted column shaft · Podium · Cella (inner sanctuary) · Colonnade enclosing portico

Caryatids were sculpted columns, usually in the form of a female figure. Roman caryatids, like this one in the Forum of Augustus, were often copied in detail from earlier Greek examples.

Roman temples were usually built on a raised dais or podium, to make them prominent. Many were fronted by a portico, a roofed porch with columns.

The orders of Classical architecture were building styles, each based on a different column design. The three major orders were borrowed by the Romans from the Greeks.

Doric order · Ionic order · Corinthian order

Aedicules were small shrines, framed by two pillars, usually containing a statue of a god.

Coffers were decorative sunken panels that reduced the weight of domed and vaulted ceilings.

Early Christian and Medieval Rome

The first Christian churches in Rome were based on the basilica: oblong, with three naves, each usually ending in an apse. From the 10th to the 13th centuries, most churches were built in the Romanesque style, which used the rounded arches of ancient Rome.

Basilicas in Rome have, in most cases, kept their original rectangular shape. The nave of San Giovanni in Laterano retains its 4th-century floorplan.

The triumphal arch divides the nave of a church from the apse. Here, in San Paolo fuori le Mura, it is decorated with mosaics.

Renaissance and Baroque Rome

Renaissance architecture (15th–16th centuries) drew its inspiration directly from Classical models. It revived the use of strict geometric proportions. The Baroque age (late 16th–17th centuries) broke many established rules, favoring grandiose decoration over pure Classical forms.

A tabernacle is used to house the Sacrament for the mass. This 13th-century Gothic wall tabernacle is in San Clemente.

A baldacchino is a canopy, supported on columns, rising over the main altar. This Baroque example is in St. Peter's.

Putti were a popular decorative feature in the Baroque. A putto is a painting or a sculpture of a child like a Cupid or cherub.

A loggia is an open-sided gallery or arcade. It may be a separate structure or part of a building, as here at San Saba.

Rusticated masonry decorates the exterior of many Renaissance palazzi. It consists of massive blocks divided by deep joints.

Cosmatesque Sculpture and Mosaics

The Cosmati family, active in Rome during the 12th and 13th centuries, have given their name to a particularly Roman style of decoration. They worked in marble, producing all kinds of fixtures for churches, including cloisters, episcopal thrones, tombs, pulpits, fonts, and candlesticks. These were often decorated with bands of colorful mosaic. They also left many fine floor mosaics, usually of white marble with an inlay of red and green porphyry. Ancient Roman columns were cut up to provide the materials. Several other families of stonemasons used a similar style, and their work is also described as Cosmatesque.

Cosmatesque floor, Santa Maria in Cosmedin

Rome During Unification

Under Napoleon, Italy had a brief taste of unity, but by 1815 it was once more divided into many small states and papal rule was restored in Rome. Over the next 50 years, patriots, led by Mazzini, Garibaldi, and others, struggled to create an independent, unified Italy. In 1848 Rome was briefly declared a Republic, but Garibaldi's forces were driven out by French troops. The French continued to protect the pope, while the rest of Italy was united as a kingdom under Vittorio Emanuele of Savoy. In 1870, troops stormed the city, and Rome became capital of Italy.

Extent of the City
☐ 1870   ▨ Today

Allegory of Italy's Liberty
This patriotic poster from 1890 shows the king, his chief minister Cavour, Garibaldi, and Mazzini. The woman in red represents Italy.

Porta Pia

Tricolored flag of the new Italian kingdom

Plumed hat of the Bersaglieri, crack troops from Savoy

Vittorio Emanuele II
Vittorio Emanuele of Savoy became the first King of Italy in 1861.

Royalists Storm Porta Pia
On September 20, 1870, troops of the kingdom of Italy put an end to the papal domination of Rome. They breached the city walls near Porta Pia; the pope retreated and Rome was made the Italian capital.

1751 Piranesi's *Views of Rome* revive interest in Classical ruins

1762 Trevi Fountain is completed

Napoleon Bonaparte

1799 Napoleon expelled from Italy by Austrians and Russians

1797 Napoleon captures Rome

1807 Birth of Garibaldi

1750

1775

1800

1792 Canova creates the Tomb of Pope Clement XIII, St. Peter's

Piranesi etching of Trajan's Forum

1800–1 Napoleon takes Italy again

Garibaldi and Rome
The charismatic leader Giuseppe Garibaldi had taken much of Italy from foreign rule by 1860. Rome still remained a crucial problem. Here he declares "O Roma o morte" (Rome or Death).

Villa Paolina

Giuseppe Verdi
(1813–1901)
Verdi, the opera composer, supported unification and in 1861 became a member of Italy's first national parliament.

Breach in Aurelian Wall

Victor Emmanuel Monument
A vast monument to Italy's first king *(see p76)* stands in Piazza Venezia.

S · P · Q · R ·
VRBE · ITALIAE · VINDICATA
INCOLIS · FELICITER · AVCTIS
GEMINOS · FORNICES · CONDIDIT

A Freed City
This marble plaque was set up at Porta Pia to commemorate the liberation of Rome.

Fountain in Piazza del Popolo

1816 Work begins on Piazza del Popolo

1848 Nationalist uprising in Rome. Pope flees and a Republic is formed

1849 Pope is restored to power, protected by a French garrison

1870 Royalist troops take Rome, completing the unification of Italy

1825

1850

1821 English poet Keats dies in Piazza di Spagna

1820 Revolts throughout Italy

Pope Pius IX

1860 Garibaldi and his 1,000 followers take Sicily and Naples

1861 Kingdom of Italy founded with capital in Turin

Modern Rome

The Fascist dictator Mussolini dreamed of recreating the immensity, order, and power of the old Roman Empire: "Rome," he said, "must appear wonderful to the whole world." He began to build a grandiose new complex, EUR, in the suburbs, and razed 15 churches and many medieval houses to create space for wide new roads. Fortunately, most of the old center has survived, leaving the city with one of Europe's most picturesque historic cores. To mark the Holy Year and the new millennium, many crumbling churches, buildings, and monuments were given a thorough facelift.

Extent of the City
☐ 1960s   ◼ Today

Mussolini's Plans for Rome
This propaganda poster reflects Mussolini's grandiose projects such as Via dei Fori Imperiali in the Forum area *(see p78)* and EUR *(p268)*.

Pope Francis
After the resignation of Pope Benedict XVI in 2013, the Argentinian cardinal Jorge Mario Bergoglio was elected Pope Francis. The Pope exerts a huge influence on the lives of the world's Catholics.

Jubilee celebrations
Jubilee Years are usually celebrated every quarter of a century. Millions of Catholics visited Rome to celebrate the year 2000.

1911 Victor Emmanuel Monument is completed

1929 Lateran Treaty creates a separate Vatican state

1926 Opposition parties banned

1944 Allies liberate Rome from Germans

1960 Olympic Games are held in Rome

1946 National referendum establishes Italy as a republic; King Umberto II exiled

1900   **1915**   **1930**   **1945**   **1960**

1915 Italy enters World War I

1922 Fascists march on Rome. Mussolini becomes prime minister

Poster for EUR

1940 Italy enters World War II; work begins on EUR zone

1957 Treaty of Rome initiates European Common Market

1962 Second Vatican Council brings about Church reforms

Three Tenors Concert (1990)
Combining Italy's love of music and soccer, this opera recital at the Baths of Caracalla was broadcast live during the World Cup.

Poster for La Dolce Vita
In the 1950s and 1960s, Rome was Europe's Hollywood. *Ben-Hur*, *Quo Vadis?*, and *Cleopatra* were made at the Cinecittà studios, as well as Italian films like Fellini's *La Dolce Vita*.

Valentino Model
While not as important as Milan for fashion, Rome is still home to some of the industry's leading designers.

Downtown Traffic
Rome's streets are congested, and many buildings have been damaged by pollution. There are plans to close the historic central city to traffic. Mayor Ignazio Marino closed a stretch of Via dei Fori Imperiali to cars and scooters in 2013.

1978 Premier Aldo Moro kidnapped, then killed, by Red Brigades; Karol Wojtyla is elected Pope John Paul II

2004 EU constitution signed in Rome

2005 Pope John Paul II dies in Rome; he is succeeded by Benedict XVI

2009 Rome hosts the World Swimming Championships

1990 Rome hosts soccer World Cup finals

1975	1990	2005	2020

1981 Assassination attempt on Pope John Paul II in St. Peter's Square

1993 Francesco Rutelli becomes Rome's first elected mayor

2000 Rome enters the 21st century with millions of pilgrims celebrating the Holy Year – the Jubilee

2013 Pope Benedict XVI resigns and Pope Francis is elected; Ignazio Marino is elected mayor

2011 Rome celebrates 150 years of the Italian state

ROME AT A GLANCE

From its early days as a settlement of shepherds on the Palatine hill, Rome grew to rule a vast empire stretching from northern England to North Africa. Later, after the empire had collapsed, Rome became the center of the Christian world, and artists and architects flocked to work for the popes. The legacy of this history can be seen all over the city. The following pages are a time-saving summary of some of the best Rome has to offer. There are sections on churches, museums and galleries, fountains and obelisks, and celebrated artists and writers in Rome. Listed below are the top attractions that no visitor should miss.

Rome's Top Tourist Attractions

Capitoline Museums
See pp70–73.

Colosseum
See pp94–97.

Sistine Chapel
See pp242–245.

Spanish Steps
See p136.

Raphael Rooms
See pp242–243.

Trevi Fountain
See p159.

Castel Sant'Angelo
See pp250–251.

Pantheon
See pp114–115.

St. Peter's
See pp228–231.

Roman Forum
See pp80–89.

Piazza Navona
See p122.

◀ *The Last Judgment* by Michelangelo on the altar wall of the Sistine Chapel, Vatican

Rome's Best: Churches and Temples

As the center of Christianity, Rome has a vast wealth of beautiful and interesting churches. These range from magnificent great basilicas, built to assert the importance of the medieval and Renaissance Catholic church, to smaller, humbler buildings where the first Christians gathered, often in secret. Among the most fascinating early churches are those converted from ancient Roman temples. Additions to these over the years have resulted in some intriguing, many-layered buildings. A more detailed historical overview of Rome's churches is on pages 48–9.

Pantheon
This monumental 2,000-year-old building is one of the largest surviving temples of ancient Rome.

St. Peter's
At 450 ft (136 m) high, Michelangelo's dome is the tallest in the world. The artist died before seeing his work completed.

Piazz
Spac

Vatican

Piazza
della
Rotond

Piazza
Navona

Campo
de' Fiori

Janiculum

Santa Maria in Trastevere
Built over a very early Christian foundation, this church is famous for its ornate mosaics.

Trastevere

Avent

Santa Maria in Cosmedin
The decorations in this 6th-century church are 12th-century and earlier. A restored painting in the apse shows the Virgin, Child, and saints.

Santa Cecilia in Trastevere
This statue of Cecilia, showing her as she lay when her tomb was uncovered, was sculpted in 1599 by Stefano Maderno.

Sant'Andrea al Quirinale
Bernini made maximum use of strong, dynamic curves in this oval interior (1658–70), creating a small masterpiece of the Roman Baroque.

Santa Maria Maggiore
Rich mosaics and relics contrast with the sober interior form of Santa Maria Maggiore. Among its treasures are vestments bearing the Borghese coat of arms.

Santa Prassede
Magnificent Byzantine mosaics cover the walls and ceilings of this 9th-century church. This Christ with Angels is in the Chapel of St. Zeno.

Via Veneto

Quirinal

0 meters 500
0 yards 500

Esquiline

rum

atine

Lateran

Santa Croce in Gerusalemme
Saints adorn the facade of Santa Croce. Inside are relics of the Cross, brought from Jerusalem by St. Helena.

Caracalla

San Clemente
Different archaeological layers lie beneath the 12th-century church. This sarcophagus dates from the 4th century.

San Giovanni in Laterano
The original church was built by Constantine, the first Christian emperor. The Chapel of St. Venantius mosaics include the figure of St. Venantius himself.

Exploring Churches and Temples

There are more churches in Rome than there are days of the year, so you'll have to be selective. Catholic pilgrims have always been drawn to the seven major basilicas: **St. Peter's**, the heart of the Roman Catholic church, **San Giovanni in Laterano**, **San Paolo fuori le Mura**, **Santa Maria Maggiore**, **Santa Croce in Gerusalemme**, **San Lorenzo fuori le Mura**, and **San Sebastiano**. These have a wealth of relics, tombs, and magnificent works of art from many different periods. Smaller churches can be equally fascinating, especially those where the original character is preserved.

13th-century fresco by Pietro Cavallini in Santa Cecilia

Ancient Temples

One pagan temple survives virtually unaltered since it was erected in the 2nd century AD. The **Pantheon**, "Temple of all the Gods," has a domed interior quite different in structure from any other church in Rome. It was reconsecrated as a Christian church in the 7th century.

Other Roman temples have been incorporated into Christian churches at various times. Two of these are in the Forum; **Santi Cosma e Damiano** was established in the Temple of Romulus in 526, while San Lorenzo in Miranda was built on to the ruins of the

Temple of Antoninus and Faustina in the 11th century. The Baroque facade, built in 1602, looms behind the columns of the temple.

Another church that clearly shows its ancient Roman origins is **Santa Costanza**, built as a mausoleum for Constantine's daughter. It is a round church with some splendid 4th-century mosaics.

Early Christian and Medieval Churches

Some early basilicas – the 5th-century **Santa Maria Maggiore** and **Santa Sabina**, for example – retain much of their original structure. Other, even earlier, churches such as the 4th-century **San Paolo fuori le Mura** and **San Giovanni in Laterano** still preserve their original basilica shape. San Paolo was rebuilt after a fire in 1823 destroyed the original building, and the San Giovanni of today dates from a 1646 reconstruction by Borromini. Both these churches still have their medieval cloisters. **Santa Maria in Trastevere** and **Santa Cecilia in Trastevere**

The impressive domed interior of the Pantheon, which became a church in 609

were built over houses where the earliest Christian communities met and worshipped in secret to avoid persecution. One church where the different layers of earlier structures can clearly be seen is **San Clemente**. At its lowest level, it has a Mithraic temple of the 3rd century AD. Other early churches include **Santa Maria in Cosmedin**, with its impressive Romanesque bell tower, and the fortified convent of **Santi Quattro Coronati**. Many Roman churches, most notably **Santa Prassede**, contain fine early Christian and medieval mosaics.

Cloister of San Giovanni in Laterano

Unusual Floor plans

The design of Rome's first churches was based on the ancient basilica, a rectangular building divided into three naves. Since then there have been many bold departures from this plan, including round churches, square churches based on the shape of the Greek cross, as in Bramante's plan for St. Peter's, and, in the Baroque period, even oval and hexagonal ones.

Pantheon (2nd century)

Santa Costanza (4th century)

Renaissance

The greatest undertaking of the Renaissance popes was the rebuilding of **St. Peter's**. Disagreements on the form it should take meant that, although work started in 1506, it was not completed until well into the 17th century. Fortunately, this did not prevent the building of Michelangelo's great dome. As well as working on St. Peter's, Michelangelo also provided the **Sistine Chapel** with its magnificent frescoes.

On a completely different scale, another key work of Renaissance architecture is Bramante's tiny **Tempietto** (1499) on the Janiculum. **Santa Maria della Pace** has a Bramante cloister, some frescoes by Raphael and a charming portico by Pietro da Cortona. Also of interest is Michelangelo's imaginative use of the great vaults of the Roman Baths of Diocletian in the church of **Santa Maria degli Angeli**.

There are other churches worth visiting for the sake of their outstanding paintings and sculptures. **Santa Maria del**

Michelangelo's dramatic dome crowning the interior of St. Peter's

Popolo, for example, has two great paintings by Caravaggio, the Chigi Chapel designed by Raphael, and a series of 15th-century frescoes by Pinturicchio. **San Pietro in Vincoli**, besides having the chains with which St. Peter was bound in prison, also has Michelangelo's awe-inspiring statue of Moses, while **San Luigi dei Francesi** has three Caravaggios depicting St. Matthew and frescoes by Domenichino.

Interior of Rosati's dome in San Carlo ai Catinari (1620)

Baroque

The Counter-Reformation inspired the exuberant, lavish style of churches such as the **Gesù** and **Sant' Ignazio di Loyola**. The best-loved examples of Roman Baroque are the later works associated with Bernini, such as the great colonnade and baldacchino he built for **St. Peter's**. Of the smaller churches he designed, perhaps the finest is **Sant' Andrea al Quirinale**, while **Santa Maria della Vittoria** houses his truly astonishing Cornaro Chapel with its sculpture of the *Ecstasy of St. Teresa*. The late Baroque was not all Bernini, however. You should also look for churches such as **San Carlo ai Catinari** with its beautiful dome by Rosato Rosati

and the many churches by Bernini's rival, Borromini. **Sant'Agnese in Agone** and **San Carlo alle Quattro Fontane** are famed for the dramatic concave surfaces of their facades, while the complex structure of **Sant'Ivo alla Sapienza** makes it one of the miniature masterpieces of the Baroque.

Where to find the Churches

Bramante's St. Peter's (1503)

Sant'Andrea al Quirinale (1658)

Sant'Ivo alla Sapienza (1642)

Rome's Best: Museums and Galleries

The museums of Rome are among the richest in the world; the Vatican alone contains incomparable collections of Egyptian, Etruscan, Greek, Roman, and early Christian artifacts, as well as frescoes by Michelangelo and Raphael, priceless manuscripts, and jewels. Excavations in the 19th century added treasures from ancient Rome, which are now on display in museums throughout the city. The finest Etruscan collections in the world can be enjoyed in the Villa Giulia. More details of Rome's museums and galleries are given on pages 52–5.

Villa Giulia
Etruscan treasures from Rome's early history are displayed in this beautiful Renaissance villa.

| 0 meters | 500 |
| 0 yards | 500 |

Vatican Museums
The galleries and long corridors hold priceless artifacts such as this 9th-century mosaic showing scenes from the life of Christ.

Vatican

Piazza Navona

Janiculum

Campo de' Fiori

Trastevere

Galleria Spada
This collection's strength lies in its 17th- and 18th-century paintings. Earlier works include a *Visitation* by Andrea del Sarto (1486–1530).

Palazzo Corsini
Included here are works by Caravaggio, Rubens, and Van Dyck, as well as a painting of the Baroque sculptor Bernini – a rare portrait by Il Baciccia (1639–1709).

Galleria Doria Pamphilj
Most of the great names of the Renaissance are represented on this gallery's crowded walls. Titian (1485–1576) painted Salome early in his career.

Museo e Galleria Borghese
The ground-floor museum houses ancient Greek and Roman sculpture as well as early Bernini masterpieces such as his David (1619). Upstairs are paintings by Titian, Rubens, and other masters.

Palazzo Barberini
The works of art here date mainly from the 13th to the 16th centuries. This figure of Providence comes from Pietro da Cortona's *The Triumph of Divine Providence* (1633–9).

Via Veneto

Quirinal

Esquiline

tol

Forum

Palatine

Lateran

Caracalla

Museo Nazionale Romano
This fresco, from Livia's Villa (1st century AD) outside Rome, is one of a huge collection of finds from archaeological sites throughout the city.

Palazzo Venezia
The highlights of Rome's most important museum of decorative arts are its Byzantine and medieval collections, including this Byzantine enamel of Christ dating from the 13th century.

Capitoline Museums: Palazzo dei Conservatori
Pietro da Cortona's *Rape of the Sabine Women* (1629) is one of many Baroque paintings in the picture gallery.

Capitoline Museums: Palazzo Nuovo
Among the sculptures is this head of Giulia Domna (wife of Septimius Severus) from the 2nd century AD.

Exploring Museums and Galleries

Rome's museums and galleries have two major strengths: Greek and Roman archaeological treasures, and paintings and sculptures of the Renaissance and the Baroque periods. The Vatican Museums have superb collections of both, as do, on a smaller scale, the Capitoline Museums. Fine paintings can also be found scattered throughout Rome in museums, galleries, and churches (see pp48–9).

Centurion's breastplate, Museo della Civiltà Romana

figurines, and artifacts are relics of the Faliscans, Latins, and other tribes who inhabited central Italy before the Romans.

The Gregorian Etruscan Museum in the **Vatican Museums** was opened in 1837 to house Etruscan finds from tombs on Church-owned land. The Museo Barracco in the **Piccola Farnesina** has statues from the much older civilizations of ancient Egypt and Assyria.

5th-century BC Etruscan gold plate with inscription, Villa Giulia

Etruscan Artifacts

The Etruscans inhabited an area stretching from Florence to Rome from the 8th century BC, and ruled Rome from the late 7th century BC (see pp20–21). It was the Etruscan custom to bury the dead along with their possessions, and as a result, Etruscan artifacts have been excavated from tombs all over central Italy. Three main collections can be seen in Rome. The **Villa Giulia** has been the home of the Museo Nazionale Etrusco since 1889. The villa, designed by Vignola for Pope Julius III for summer outings, is one of Rome's prettiest Renaissance buildings. Its gardens contain a reconstructed Etruscan temple. Not all objects here are Etruscan, however; some of the pottery,

Victory banner, Museo della Civiltà Romana

Ancient Roman Art

The archaeological zone in Rome forms a huge open-air museum of evidence of ancient Roman life, while the porticoes and cloisters of the city's churches are filled with ancient sarcophagi and fragments of statuary. The largest important collection can be seen in the **Museo Nazionale Romano** at the Baths of Diocletian and the Palazzo Massimo. The museum's many ancient artifacts include, most notably, a sarcophagus from Livia's Villa at Prima Porta just north of Rome. Also on display are some wonderfully well-preserved mosaics. The museum's great collection of Roman statues is now housed in the **Palazzo Altemps**. The most important statues are in the **Vatican Museums**, which also have the best of the great Greek works, such as the Laocoön, brought to Rome around the 1st century AD. It had tremendous influence on the subsequent development of Roman art. Splendid copies of Greek originals can be seen in the **Capitoline Museums**.

In the Forum, occupying two floors of the church of Santa Francesca Romana, is the **Antiquarium Forense** with restored finds from the excavations. For those who enjoy history, the large-scale model at the **Museo della Civiltà Romana** in EUR gives an excellent idea of what ancient Rome looked like in the 4th century AD.

Muses in Raphael's Parnassus (1508–11), Vatican Museums

Art Galleries

In the past, many of Rome's great aristocratic families owned magnificent private collections of paintings and sculpture. Some of these are still housed in ancestral palazzi, which are open to the public. One is the **Galleria Doria Pamphilj**, which has the greatest concentration of paintings of any palazzo in Rome. It's well worth searching through the various rooms to find the pearls of the collection, which include works by Raphael, Filippo Lippi, Caravaggio, Titian, and Claude

Lorrain, and a portrait of Pope Innocent X Pamphilj by the Spanish artist Velázquez. The **Galleria Spada** collection, begun by Bernardino Spada in 1632, is still housed in the fine original gallery built for it. The paintings

Hellenistic faun, Museo Borghese

demonstrate 17th-century Roman taste and include works by Rubens, Guido Reni, Guercino, and Jan Brueghel the Elder. The **Galleria Colonna** contains a collection of art dating from the same period.

Other old family residences are now showcases for state art collections. The Galleria Nazionale d'Arte Antica is divided between **Palazzo Barberini** and **Palazzo Corsini**. Palazzo Barberini, built between 1625 and 1633 by Bernini and others for the Barberini family, houses paintings from the 13th to the 16th centuries. Pietro da Cortona painted the stunning *Triumph of Divine Providence* on the ceiling of the Grand Salon. Palazzo Corsini, on the south side of the Tiber, is famed for its collection of 16th–17th-century art. Another wonderful private

collection was that of the Borghese family, also now managed by the state. The sculpture collection of the **Museo e Galleria Borghese** includes the amazing *Apollo and Daphne* by Bernini and the famous statue of Pauline Borghese by Canova. On the first floor is the picture collection with paintings by Titian, Correggio, and others.

The **Capitoline Museums** hold collections that were gifts of the popes to the people of Rome. The Pinacoteca (art gallery) in the **Palazzo dei Conservatori** contains works by Titian, Guercino, and Van Dyck. There is an art gallery at the **Vatican Museums**, but lovers of Renaissance art will head straight for the Sistine Chapel and the Raphael Rooms. Rome's main modern art collection is in the **Galleria Nazionale d'Arte Moderna**, though modern art is displayed in the Zaha Hadid–designed **MAXXI** museum.

Smaller Museums

The most important of the smaller collections is the beautifully laid out medieval museum in **Palazzo Venezia,** with exhibits ranging from ceramics to sculpture. Rome has a wealth of specialty museums like the **Museum of Musical Instruments**, the **Museo di Roma in Trastevere**, with tableaux showing life in Rome during the last century, and the **Burcardo Theater Museum**. For those with an interest in the English Romantic poets who lived in Rome in the 19th century, there is the **Keats-Shelley Memorial House**, a museum in the house where John Keats died. Focusing on the French Empire, the **Museo Napoleonico** has relics and paintings

Laocoön (1st century AD) in the Vatican's Pio-Clementine Museum

of Napoleon and members of his family, many of whom came to live in Rome.

Portrait of Pauline Borghese painted by Kinson (*c.* 1805), now in the Museo Napoleonico

Where to find the Museums and Galleries

The Deposition (1604) by Caravaggio, Vatican museums

Rome's Best: Fountains and Obelisks

Rome has some of the loveliest fountains in the world. Many of them are the work of the greatest Renaissance and Baroque sculptors. Some fountains are flamboyant displays, others restful trickles of water. Many are simply drinking fountains, while a few cascade from the sides of buildings. Obelisks date from far earlier in the city's history. Although some of them were commissioned by Roman emperors, many are even older and were brought to Rome by conquering armies. A more detailed overview of Rome's fountains and obelisks is on pages 56–7.

Piazza San Pietro
Twin fountains give life to the splendid monumental piazza of St. Peter's. Maderno designed the one on the Vatican side in 1614; the other was later built to match.

Piazza del Popolo
Nineteenth-century marble lions and fountains surround an ancient obelisk in the center of the piazza.

Piazz
Spac

Vatican

Pia
de
Roto

Piazza
Navona

Campo
de' Fiori

Fontana dei Quattro Fiumi
The fountain of the four rivers is the work of Bernini. The four figures represent the Ganges, the Plate, the Danube, and the Nile.

Janiculum

Trastevere

**Obelisk of Santa
Maria sopra Minerva**
The Egyptian obelisk, held up by Bernini's marble elephant, dates from the 6th century BC.

Fontana delle Tartarughe
One of Rome's more secret fountains, this jewel of Renaissance sculpture shows youths helping tortoises into a basin.

Fontana della Barcaccia
This elegant fountain of 1627 is probably the work of Pietro Bernini, father of the more famous Gian Lorenzo.

Trevi Fountain
The Trevi, inspired by Roman triumphal arches, was designed by Nicola Salvi in 1732. Tradition has it that a coin thrown into the water guarantees a visitor's return to Rome.

```
0 meters        500
0 miles         500
```

Via Veneto

Quirinal

itol

Esquiline

Forum

Palatine

Lateran

entine

Caracalla

Fontana delle Naiadi
When this fountain was unveiled in 1901, the realistically sensual bronze nymphs caused a storm of protest.

Piazza della Bocca della Verità Fountain
In this 18th-century fountain, built by Carlo Bizzaccheri for Pope Clement XI, water spills over a craggy rock formation where two Tritons hold aloft a large shell.

Obelisk of Piazza San Giovanni in Laterano
The oldest obelisk in Rome dates from the 14th century BC. It came to Rome in AD 357, brought here on the orders of Constantine II.

Exploring Fountains and Obelisks

The popes who restored the ancient Roman aqueducts used to build fountains to commemorate their deeds of munificence. As a result, fountains of all sizes and shapes punctuate the city, drawing grateful crowds on hot summer days. Ancient obelisks provide powerful reminders of the debt Roman civilization owed to the Egyptians. Architects have learned to incorporate them into Roman piazzas in fascinating ways.

The Pantheon Fountain

Fountains

The Trevi fountain is one of the most famous of all. It is a *mostra*, a monumental fountain built to mark the end of an aqueduct – in this case the Acqua Vergine, built by Marcus Agrippa in 19 BC, although the Trevi itself was only completed in 1762. Other *mostre* are the **Fontana dell'Acqua Paola**, built for Pope Paul V in 1612 on the Janiculum, and the **Moses Fountain**, commemorating the opening of the Acqua Felice by Pope Sixtus V in 1587.

Almost all Rome's famous piazzas have fountains. In **Piazza San Pietro** there is a matching pair of powerful fountains. Piazza Navona has Bernini's wonderful Baroque **Fontana dei Quattro Fiumi** (fountain of the four rivers) as its main attraction. The fountain's four figures each represent one of the principal rivers of the four continents then known. To the south of this is the smaller **Fontana del Moro** (the Moor), also by Bernini, showing an Ethiopian struggling with a dolphin. At the north end, Neptune wrestles with an octopus on a

19th-century fountain. In Piazza Barberini is the magnificent Bernini creation of 1642–3: the **Fontana del Tritone** with its sea god blowing through a shell.

More recently, large piazzas have been redesigned around fountains. Valadier's great design for **Piazza del Popolo** (1816–20) has marble lions and fountains surrounding the central obelisk plus two more fountains on the

Fountain of the four tiaras located behind St. Peter's

east and west sides of the square. The early 20th century saw the opening of the **Fontana delle Naiadi** (nymphs) in Piazza della Repubblica; its earthy figures caused great scandal at the time. The highly original **Fountain of the Amphorae** (**map** 8 D2) was erected in Piazza dell'Emporio during the 1920s. The same designer, Pietro Lombardi, also created the **Fountain of the Four Tiaras** (**map** 3 C3) behind the colonnade of St. Peter's.

The city also has a number of smaller, and often very charming, fountains. At the foot of the Spanish Steps is the **Fontana della Barcaccia** (the leaking boat) of 1627; the **Fontana delle Tartarughe** (the tortoise fountain) has been in

The Trevi Fountain

Appropriately for a fountain resembling a stage set, the theatrical Trevi has been the star of many movies set in Rome, including romantic films like *Three Coins in a Fountain* and *Roman Holiday*, but also *La Dolce Vita*, Fellini's satirical portrait of Rome in the 1950s. Whatever liberties Anita Ekberg took then, wading in the fountains of Rome is now forbidden, however tempting it could be in the summer heat.

Anita Ekberg in *La Dolce Vita* (1960)

Fontana dei Cavalli Marini

the tiny Piazza Mattei since 1581, and by Santa Maria in Domnica is the **Fontana della Navicella** (little boat), created out of an ancient Roman sculpture in the 16th century. In the forecourt of **Santa Sabina** (**map** 8 D2) water gushes from a huge mask set in an ancient basin. The **Pantheon Fountain** (**map** 4 F4), from 1575, is by Jacopo della Porta. **Le Quattro Fontane** (four fountains) have stood at the Quirinal hill crossroads since 1593.

Fountains in parks and gardens include the **Galleon Fountain** (1620–21) at the Vatican, and the **Fontana dei Cavalli Marini** (seahorses), of 1791, at Villa Borghese. The somewhat decayed 16th-century terraced gardens of the **Villa d'Este**, with their display of over 500 fountains, are still worth a trip.

Piazza Navona with Fontana dei Quattro Fiumi, by Pannini (1691–1765)

The Ovato fountain at Villa d'Este

Obelisks

The most ancient and tallest of Rome's obelisks is the **Obelisk of Piazza di San Giovanni in Laterano**. Built of red granite, 100 ft (31 m) high, it came from the Temple of Amon at Thebes, erected in the 14th century BC. It was brought to Rome in AD 357 by the order of Constantine II and put up in the Circus Maximus. It was rediscovered in 1587, broken into three pieces, and reerected in the following year. Next in age is the obelisk in **Piazza del Popolo**, from the 13th or 12th century BC. It was brought to Rome in the time of Augustus and also erected in the Circus Maximus.

The slightly smaller **Obelisk of Piazza Montecitorio** was another of Augustus's trophies. The bronze ball and spike at the top recall its past use as a gnomon for a sundial of vast proportions. Other obelisks, such as the one at the top of the Spanish Steps, are Roman imitations of Egyptian originals. The **Obelisk of Piazza dell' Esquilino** and the one in **Piazza del Quirinale** (**map** 5 B4) first stood at the entrance to the Mausoleum of Augustus. When reerected, most obelisks were mounted on decorative bases, often with statues and fountains at their foot. Others became parts of sculptures. Bernini was the creator of the marble

Obelisk in Piazza del Popolo

elephant balancing the Egyptian **Obelisk of Santa Maria sopra Minerva** on its back, and the **Fontana dei Fiumi**, with an obelisk from the Circus of Maxentius. Another obelisk was added to the remodeled Pantheon Fountain in 1711. The obelisk in **Piazza San Pietro** is Egyptian but does not have the usual hieroglyphics.

Wall fountain at Villa d'Este

Where to find the Fountains and Obelisks

Artists and Writers Inspired by Rome

Artists and writers have been attracted to Rome since Classical times. Many came to work for the emperors; the poets Horace, Virgil, and Ovid, for example, all enjoyed the patronage of Emperor Augustus. Later on, especially in the Renaissance and Baroque periods, the greatest artists and architects came to Rome to compete for commissions from the popes. However, patronage was not the only magnet. Since the Renaissance, Rome's Classical past and its picturesque ruins have drawn artists, architects, and writers from all over Italy and abroad.

Self-portrait by the 18th-century artist Angelica Kauffmann, *c.* 1770

Diego Velázquez, one of many great 17th-century artists to visit Rome

Painters, Sculptors, and Architects

In the early 16th century, artists and architects were summoned from all parts of Italy to realize the grandiose building projects of the popes. From Urbino came Bramante (1444–1514) and Raphael (1483–1520); from Perugia, Perugino (1450–1523); from Florence, Michelangelo (1475–1564) and many others. They worked in the Vatican, on the new St. Peter's and the decoration of the Sistine Chapel. Artists were often well rewarded, but they also lived in dangerous times. Florentine sculptor and goldsmith Benvenuto Cellini (1500–71) helped defend Castel Sant' Angelo (*see pp250–51*) during the Sack of Rome (1527), but was later imprisoned there and made a dramatic escape. His memoirs tell the story.

Toward the end of the 16th century, Church patronage was generous to the Milanese-born Caravaggio (1571–1610) despite his violent character and unruly

life. The Carracci family from Bologna also flourished – especially brothers Annibale (1560–1609) and Agostino (1557–1602).

The work of Gian Lorenzo Bernini (1598–1680) can be seen all over Rome. He succeeded Carlo Maderno (1556–1629) as architect of St. Peter's, and created its great bronze baldacchino, the splendid colonnade (*see pp228–9*), and numerous fountains, churches and sculptures. His rival for the title of leading architect of the Roman Baroque was Francesco Borromini (1599–1667), whose highly original genius can be appreciated in many Roman churches and palazzi.

In the 17th century it became more common for artists from outside Italy to come and work in Rome. Diego Velázquez (1599–1660), King Philip IV of Spain's court painter, came in 1628 to study the art treasures of the Vatican. Rubens (1577–

1640) came from Antwerp to study, and carried out various commissions. The French artists Nicolas Poussin (1594–1665) and Claude Lorrain (1600–82) lived here for many years.

The Classical revival of the 18th century attracted artists to Rome in unprecedented numbers. From Britain came the Scottish architect Robert Adam (1728–92) and the Swiss artist Angelica Kauffmann (1741–1807), who settled here and was buried with great honor in Sant'Andrea delle Fratte. After the excesses of the Baroque, sculpture also turned to the simplicity of Neo-Classicism. A leading exponent of this movement was Antonio Canova (1757–1821). Sculptors from all over Europe were influenced by him, including the Dane Bertel Thorvaldsen (1770–1844), who lived in Rome for many years.

Claude Lorrain's view of the Forum, painted in Rome in 1632

Writers

Dante (1262–1321) visited Rome during his exile from Florence and in the *Inferno* describes the great influx of pilgrims for the first Holy Year (1300). The poet Petrarch (1304–74), born in Arezzo, was crowned with laurels on the Capitol in 1341. The poet Torquato Tasso (1544–95), from Sorrento, was invited to receive a similar honor, but died soon after his arrival. He is buried in Sant'Onofrio *(see p223)* on the Janiculum. Two of the first writers from abroad to visit Rome were the French essayist Montaigne (1533–92) and English poet John Milton (1608–74). Then, by the early 18th century, writers seemed to flock to Rome.

Torquato Tasso

Edward Gibbon (1737–94) was inspired to write *Decline and Fall of the Roman Empire* when he heard the monks singing the Angelus outside Santa Maria in Aracoeli *(see p75)*. German visitors included J. J. Winckelmann (1717–68), who wrote studies of ancient art, and poet J. W. von Goethe (1749–1832).

In the Romantic period, Rome teemed with English writers: Keats, Shelley, and Byron, followed by the Brownings and Charles Dickens. Travel writers in the 19th century included Augustus Hare (1834–1903) and the German historian Ferdinand Gregorovius (1821–91). Much of *The Portrait of a Lady* by American Henry James (1843–1916) is set in Rome.

Modern life in Rome is brilliantly captured by the Roman writer Alberto Moravia (1907–90), whose residence is sometimes open to visitors (www.fondo albertomoravia.it).

Portrait of the poet John Keats painted by his friend Joseph Severn in 1819

Musicians

Giovanni Pierluigi da Palestrina (1525–94), from the town of that name, became choirmaster and organist to the Vatican and composed some of the greatest unaccompanied choral music ever written. In 1770 the 14-year-old Mozart heard Gregorio Allegri's unpublished *Miserere* in the Sistine Chapel and wrote it down from memory. Arcangelo Corelli (1653–1713), the great violinist and composer of the Baroque age, worked in Rome under the patronage of Cardinal Ottoboni. One of his first commissions was to provide a festival of music for Queen Christina of Sweden.

During the 19th century, the Prix de Rome brought many French musicians to study here at the Villa Medici *(see p137)*. Hector Berlioz (1803–69) owed the inspiration for his popular *Roman Carnival*, the overture to his opera *Benvenuto Cellini*, to his two-year stay in Rome. Georges Bizet (1838–75) and Claude Debussy (1862–1918) were also Prix de Rome winners. Franz Liszt (1811–86), after his 50th year, settled in Rome, took minor orders, and became known as Abbé Liszt. He wrote *Fountains of the Villa d'Este* while staying at the villa in Tivoli.

Giacomo Puccini

Twentieth-century musical associations with Rome include two popular works by Ottorino Respighi (1870–1936), *The Fountains of Rome* and *The Pines of Rome*, while Giacomo Puccini (1858–1924) used Roman settings when creating his dramatic, tragic opera *Tosca*.

Roman Cinema

The Cinecittà studios, built in 1937 just outside Rome, are most famous for the films made here in the 1940s – classics of Italian Neo-Realism such as Roberto Rossellini's *Roma Città Aperta* and Vittorio De Sica's *Sciuscià* and *Ladri di Biciclette*. The director most often linked with Roman cinema is Federico Fellini, through films like *La Dolce Vita* (1960) and *Roma* (1972). However, perhaps the most famous artist associated with Rome is the controversial writer-turned-film-maker Pier Paolo Pasolini (1922–75), widely known for his films *Teorema* (1968) and *Il Decamerone* (1971).

Since the 1950s, Rome and Cinecittà have also been much used for foreign films: from *Ben-Hur* and *Spartacus* in the 1950s through to *Gladiator* and Woody Allen's *To Rome with Love*.

Pier Paolo Pasolini

ROME THROUGH THE YEAR

The best times to visit Rome are spring and fall, when the weather is usually warm, and sometimes even hot enough to sunbathe and swim at the beaches and lakes outside the city. In the winter months, the weather tends to be gray and wet, while in high summer, most people (including Romans, who leave the city in droves) find the heat unbearable. Easter and Christmas are obviously very special in Rome, but there are other religious festivals worth seeing at other times of the year, as well as some enjoyable secular events like the Festa de' Noantri in Trastevere and the Flower Festival in Genzano. In villages outside Rome, local celebrations are held to welcome new crops such as strawberries and beans in the spring, and grapes and truffles in the fall.

Spring

Easter, falling in March or April, marks the official beginning of the tourist season in Rome. Catholics from all over the world flock into the city to make their pilgrimages to the main basilicas and to hear the Pope's Easter Sunday address outside St. Peter's, while the less devout come simply to take advantage of the mild weather. Meanwhile, Romans pile into their cars and head for the coast and countryside, so you can expect the roads, beaches, and restaurants of the Castelli Romani and Lake Bracciano to be busy.

Temperatures tend to be around 66°F (18°C), but can hit 82°F (28°C), so by mid-May it is usually possible to picnic or dine outside. However, there can still be sudden downpours and temperature swings, so do bring warm clothes and an umbrella.

Crowds gathering in St. Peter's Square at Easter

In April, tubs of colorful azaleas are set out on the Spanish Steps and along Via Veneto, and once the roses start to flower in the city's Rose Garden overlooking the Circus Maximus, it is opened to the public.

For two weeks from mid-May, Via dei Coronari is lit by candles, lined with plants, and hung with banners for the street's antique fair, while Via Margutta hosts an outdoor art show. In the first week of May the International Horse Show is held in the Villa Borghese. Also usually in May, many world-class tennis players flock to Rome to compete in the International Tennis Championships held annually at the Foro Italico.

Events

Festa di Santa Francesca Romana (March 9), Santa Francesca Romana. Blessing of the city's vehicles (see p89).
Festa di San Giuseppe (19 March), in the Trionfale area. St. Joseph's (and Father's) Day celebrated in the streets.
Rome Marathon (late March), through the city (see p359).
Festa della Primavera (March/April), Spanish Steps and Trinità dei Monti. Azaleas in the street and concerts.
Good Friday (March/April), Colosseum. Procession of the Cross at 9pm led by the Pope.
Easter Sunday (March/April), St. Peter's Square. Address made by the Pope (see p229).
Rome's Birthday (April 21), Piazza del Campidoglio and elsewhere.
Beni Culturali Week (April). Free entry to most galleries.
Art exhibition (April/May), Via Margutta (see p345).
International Horse Show (early May), Villa Borghese.
International Tennis Championships (usually May), Foro Italico (see p358).

International Horse Show in Villa Borghese in May

Average Daily Hours of Sunshine

Hours

Jan Feb Mar Apr May Jun Jul Aug Sep Oct Nov Dec

Sunshine Chart
Rome is famous for its light. June is the sunniest month, but it is also very dry, and without a shower or two, the heat can feel intense. In fall, Rome's southerly position means that the sun can still be enjoyably warm at midday.

Summer

In June, a season of concerts begins, with performances in some of the city's most beautiful palaces, churches. and courtyards. In July and August, opera and drama are staged at Ostia Antica (see pp272–3) and in various outdoor locations. During the summer there are also contemporary cultural events – film, music of all kinds, dance, and theater. On midsummer evenings there are stands and amusements on the Tiber embankments by Castel Sant'Angelo, while in the last two weeks of July, Trastevere becomes an open-air party as the Noantri festival is celebrated with trinket stands, dining in the street, and fireworks. The sales (saldi) begin in mid-July, and the Alta Moda Fashion Show is usually held mid- to late July at the Spanish Steps.

Many Romans leave the city at the end of June, when schools close, but since June and July are peak tourist months, hotels, cafés, restaurants, and all the main places of interest and

Flower-carpeted streets in Genzano

other attractions are packed. In August, when the temperature often soars to over 104°F (40°C), virtually all Romans flee the city for the seaside, meaning that many cafés, shops, and restaurants are closed for the entire month.

Events

Flower Festival (June, the Sunday after Corpus Domini), Genzano, Castelli Romani, south of Rome. Streets are carpeted with flowers.
Festa di San Giovanni (June 23–24), Piazza di Porta San Giovanni. Celebrated with meals of snails in tomato sauce, suckling pig, fair and fireworks display.
Festa dei Santi Pietro e Paolo (June 29), many churches. Celebrations mark the feast of saints Peter and Paul.

Tevere Village (end June–mid-July), along the Tiber. Crafts, food and wine, music, and fireworks (see p345).
Festa de' Noantri (last two weeks in July), the streets of Trastevere. Food and entertainment (see p345 and p347).
Alta Moda Fashion Show (usually mid- to late July), Spanish Steps (see p345).
Estate Romana (July/August), Villa Ada, Ostia Antica, in parks, by the Tiber. Opera, concerts, drama, dance, and film (see p347).
Festa della Madonna della Neve (August 5), Santa Maria Maggiore. Fourth-century snowfall reenacted with white flower petals (see p174).
Ferragosto (August 15), Santa Maria in Trastevere. Midsummer holiday; almost everything closes down. Celebrations are held for the Feast of the Assumption.

The heat of an August afternoon in front of St. Peter's

Display of Roberto Cavalli's fashion collection on the Spanish Steps

Average Monthly Rainfall

Rainfall Chart
Fall is Rome's rainiest season, with heavy downpours, sometimes lasting for days, especially in November. Rain in summer tends to come in violent – but often extremely refreshing – storms. In winter and early spring expect a few gray, drizzly days.

Fall

September and October are the best – and among the most popular – months to visit Rome. The fiery heat of July and August will have cooled a little, but midday can be very hot, and you can still eat and drink outside without feeling chilly until late at night. Visiting Rome in November is not recommended: it is the wettest month of the year and Roman rainstorms are often very strong and heavy.

At the beginning of October, an artisans' fair is held on Via dell'Orso and adjacent streets, while nearby the antiques galleries of Via dei Coronari hold an open house. There are also October antiques fairs in Orvieto and Perugia, two of the loveliest Umbrian hill towns, which are about an hour's drive north of Rome. In November, there's yet another prestigious antiques fair at the papal palace of Viterbo, 40 miles (65 km) north of Rome *(see p273)*. Fall is the season of harvest festivals, so head out to the small towns around Rome to sample delicacies such as local cheeses, sausages, chestnuts, and mushrooms. Another reason for taking a trip out of Rome is the wine festival in Marino, in the Castelli Romani, south of the city. There are many opportunities to sample the wines of this region that was once the home to luxurious

A roast chestnut stall in fall

16th- and 17th-century country residences but now is renowned particularly for its white wines.

Throughout the fall and winter in Rome, freshly roasted chestnuts can be bought from vendors on street corners, and occasionally there is a stand on Campo de' Fiori where you can sample *vino novello*, the new season's wine. On All Saints' and All Souls' Days, which fall on November 1 and 2, respectively, Romans make pilgrimages to place chrysanthemums on the tombs of relatives who are buried in the two main cemeteries of Prima Porta and Verano. On a happier note, the classical concert and opera seasons begin again in October and November. Details of performances can be found in listings magazines such as *Trova Roma* and *Where Rome (see p346)*, in daily newspapers, such as *La Repubblica (see p375)*, and on posters around the city.

Events

RomaEuropa *(fall)*. Films, dance, theater, and concerts around Rome *(see p347)*.
Art fair *(September)*, Via Margutta *(see p345)*.

Craft fair *(last week September/first week October)*, Via dell'Orso *(see p345)*.
International Festival of Cinema *(October)*. New screenings and stars aplenty *(see p352)*.
Marino Wine Festival *(first Sunday in October)*, Marino. Celebrations include tastings and street entertainment.
Antique Fair *(mid-October)*, Via dei Coronari *(see p345)*.
Festival di Musica e Arte Sacra *(Oct/Nov)*. Concerts by the world's leading choirs and orchestras take place in Rome's most important churches.
All Saints' and All Souls' Days *(November 1, 2)*, Prima Porta and Verano cemeteries. The Pope usually celebrates Mass in the Verano cemetery.
Festa di Santa Cecilia *(November 22)*, Santa Cecilia in Trastevere and Catacombs of San Callisto.

Fall in the Villa Doria Pamphilj park

Average Monthly Temperature

Temperature Chart
The chart shows the average minimum and maximum monthly temperatures. July and August can be unbearably hot, making sightseeing a chore. The fresher days of spring and fall are ideal to visit Rome, but there are some cloudy and rainy spells.

Winter

During the winter, Rome is bracingly chilly but the temperature rarely drops below freezing. Not all buildings are centrally heated, so if you are staying in a small hotel, bring warm clothes and request extra blankets as soon as you arrive, as they can be in short supply. Warm up in cafés with hot chocolate and cappuccino.

The Christmas season is great fun in Rome, especially if you have children. Manger scenes, *presepi*, are set up in many churches, piazzas, and public places, and from mid-December to Twelfth Night, Piazza Navona hosts a market where you can buy manger scenes, decorations, and toys. Unless you have friends in Rome, Christmas itself can be rather lonely, as it is very much a family event. On New Year's Eve, however, everyone is out on the street to drink sparkling wine and set off fireworks.

La Befana, on January 6, is a traditional holiday when a witch, called La Befana, delivers candy to children.

The Carnival season runs from late January to February, celebrated largely by children with costume parties and parades along Via Nazionale, Via

Rome during one of its rare snowfalls

Cola di Rienzo, and the Pincio. Keep out of the way of teenagers with shaving-cream spray cans and water balloons.

Events

Festa della Madonna Immacolata *(December 8)*, Piazza di Spagna. In the Pope's presence, firemen climb up a ladder to place a wreath on the statue of the Virgin Mary.
Christmas Market *(mid-December– January 6)*, Piazza Navona. Christmas and children's market *(see p118)*.
Nativity scenes *(mid-December –mid-January)*, many churches. Life-size scene in St. Peter's Square, collection at Santi Cosma e Damiano.
Midnight Mass *(December 24)*, at most churches.
Christmas Day *(December 25)*, St. Peter's Square. Blessing by the Pope.
New Year's Eve *(December 31)*, all over city. Fireworks displays, furniture thrown out.
La Befana *(January 6)*, all over city. Parties for children.

Public Holidays

New Year's Day (Jan 1)
Epiphany (Jan 6)
Easter Monday Liberation Day (Apr 25)
Labor Day (May 1)
Republic Day (Jun 2)
SS Peter & Paul (Jun 29)
Ferragosto (Aug 15)
All Saints' Day (Nov 1)
Immaculate Conception (Dec 8)
Christmas Day (Dec 25)
Santo Stefano (Dec 26)

Via Condotti at Christmas

Market on Piazza Navona

View of St. Peter's Basilica, Vatican ▶

ROME AREA BY AREA

CAPITOL

The temple of Jupiter on the Capitol, the southern summit of the Capitoline hill, was the center of the Roman world. Reached by a zigzag path up from the Forum, the temple was the scene of all the most sacred religious and political ceremonies. The hill and its temple came to symbolize Rome's authority as *caput mundi*, head of the world, and the Capitol gave its name to the seat of the US Congress. Throughout the city's history, the Capitol (Campidoglio) has remained the seat of municipal government. Today's city council, the Comune di Roma,

meets in the Renaissance splendor of Palazzo Senatorio. The Capitol also serves as Rome's Registry Office. Rome's position as a modern capital is forcefully expressed in the enormous Victor Emmanuel Monument, which unfortunately blots out the view of the Capitol from Piazza Venezia. The present arrangement on the hill dates from the 16th century, when Michelangelo created a beautiful piazza reached by a flight of steps, the Cordonata. Two of the buildings around the piazza now house the Capitoline Museums.

Sights at a Glance

Churches and Temples
7 Santa Maria in Aracoeli
8 Temple of Jupiter
12 San Marco

Museums and Galleries
1 Capitoline Museums: Palazzo Nuovo pp70–71
2 Capitoline Museums: Palazzo dei Conservatori pp72–3
11 Palazzo Venezia and Museum

Historic Buildings
5 Roman *Insula*

Historic Streets and Piazzas
3 Piazza del Campidoglio
4 Cordonata
6 Aracoeli Staircase

Ancient Sites
9 Carpeian Rock

Monuments
10 Victor Emmanuel Monument

See also Street Finder maps 5, 12

◀ The God of the Nile River in front of the Roman City Hall, Piazza del Campidoglio

For map symbols see back flap

Street by Street: The Capitol and Piazza Venezia

The Capitol, citadel of ancient Rome, is a must for every visitor. A broad flight of steps (the Cordonata) leads up to Michelangelo's spectacular Piazza del Campidoglio. This is flanked by the Palazzo Nuovo and Palazzo dei Conservatori, housing the Capitoline Museums with their fine collections of sculptures and paintings. The absence of cars makes the hill a welcome retreat from the squeal of brakes below, but you should brave the traffic to visit Palazzo Venezia and its museum.

❿ Victor Emmanuel Monument
This huge white marble monument to Italy's first king was completed in 1911.

PIAZZA VENEZIA

PIAZZA VENEZIA

VIA DEL TEATRO DI MARCELLO

⓬ San Marco
The church of the Venetians in Rome has a fine 9th-century apse mosaic.

⓫ Palazzo Venezia
The museum's finest exhibits, such as this 13th-century gilded angel decorated with enamel, date from the late Middle Ages.

❺ Roman *Insula*
This is a ruined apartment block dating from Imperial Rome.

❻ Aracoeli Staircase
When it was built in 1348, the staircase became a center for political debate.

❹ Cordonata
Michelangelo's great staircase changed the orientation of the Capitol toward the west.

Key

— Suggested route

0 meters		75
0 yards		75

❷ ★ Palazzo dei Conservatori
In this part of the Capitoline Museums, a fine series of reliefs from the Temple of Hadrian *(see p108)* is displayed in the courtyard.

7 Santa Maria in Aracoeli
The treasures hidden behind the church's brick facade include this 15th-century fresco of the Funeral of St. Bernardino by Pinturicchio.

Locator Map
See Central Rome Map pp16–17

1 ★ Palazzo Nuovo
This bust of Augustus in the Hall of the Emperors is one of many fine Classical sculptures in the Capitoline Museums.

Palazzo Senatorio was used by the Roman Senate from about the 12th century. It now houses the offices of the mayor.

Palazzo dei Conservatori

3 ★ Piazza del Campidoglio
Michelangelo designed both the geometric paving and the facades of the buildings.

9 Tarpeian Rock
In ancient Rome, traitors were thrown to their death from this cliff on the Capitol.

8 Temple of Jupiter
This artist's impression shows the gold and ivory statue of Jupiter that stood in the temple.

❶ Capitoline Museums: Palazzo Nuovo

A collection of Classical statues has been kept on the Capitoline hill since the Renaissance. The first group of bronze sculptures was given to the city by Pope Sixtus IV in 1471 and more additions were made by Pope Pius V in 1566. The Palazzo Nuovo was designed by Michelangelo as part of the renovation of the Piazza del Campidoglio, and after its completion in 1655, a number of the statues were transferred here. In 1734 Pope Clement XII Corsini decreed that the building be turned into the world's first public museum.

★ **Capitoline Venus**
This marble statue of Venus dating from around AD 100–150 is a Roman copy of the original carved in the 4th century BC by the Greek sculptor Praxiteles. The statue is prized for its striking beauty.

Museum Guide

The Palazzo Nuovo is devoted chiefly to sculpture, and most of its finest works, such as the Capitoline Venus, are Roman copies of Greek masterpieces. For visitors eager to identify the philosophers and poets of ancient Greece and the rulers of ancient Rome, there are collections of busts assembled in the 18th century. Admission price also includes entry to the Palazzo dei Conservatori opposite. A gallery below Piazza del Campidoglio links the two buildings.

Portrait of a Flavian Lady
The woman wears the fanciful and elaborate hairstyle popular among the female aristocracy of the 1st century AD.

47

46

48   49   50

First floor

Courtyard

Ground floor

Hall of the Philosophers
The hall contains a rich mix of portraits of Greek politicians, scientists, and literary figures.

The facade of Palazzo Nuovo
was designed by Michelangelo, but the work was actually finished in 1655 by the brothers Carlo and Girolamo Rainaldi.

Key to Floor plan

▨ Non-exhibition space

☐ Exhibition space

Mosaic of the Doves
This charming, naturalistic mosaic once decorated the floor of Hadrian's Villa at Tivoli *(see p271)*. It shows doves drinking water from a vase.

★ Discobolus
The twisted torso was part of a Greek statue of a discus thrower. An 18th-century French sculptor, Monnot, made the additions that turned him into a wounded warrior.

VISITORS' CHECKLIST

Practical Information
Musei Capitolini, Piazza del Campidoglio.
Map 5 A5 & 12 F5.
Tel 06-0608.
🌐 museicapitolini.org
Open 9am–8pm Tue–Sun (last adm 7pm).
Closed Jan 1, May 1, Dec 25.
🎫 Tickets are valid for the whole complex. Note that the main entrance is through Palazzo dei Conservatori. 🏛 🎟 📷 🏪 ♿

Transportation
🚌 63, 70, 75, 81, 87, 160, 170, 204, 628, 716 and many other routes to Piazza Venezia.

Red Faun
Found at Tivoli, the famous red marble satyr is a 2nd-century AD version of a Greek original – an example of Hadrian's fondness for all things Greek.

Stairs to ground floor

Stairs to galleries below the Senate and connecting with Palazzo dei Conservatori

Stairs to first floor

★ Dying Galatian
Great compassion is conveyed in this Roman copy of an original Greek work of the 3rd century BC.

Alexander Severus as Hunter
In this marble of the 3rd century AD, the emperor's pose is a pastiche of Perseus, holding up the head of Medusa the Gorgon after he killed her in her sleep.

Exit

❷ Capitoline Museums: Palazzo dei Conservatori

The Palazzo dei Conservatori was the seat of the city's magistrates during the late Middle Ages. Its frescoed halls are still used occasionally for political meetings, and the ground floor houses the municipal register office. The palazzo was built by Giacomo della Porta, who carried out Michelangelo's designs for the Piazza del Campidoglio in the mid-16th century. While much of the palazzo is given over to sculpture, the art galleries on the third floor hold works by Veronese, Guercino, Tintoretto, Rubens, Caravaggio, Van Dyck, and Titian.

Burial and Glory of St. Petronilla
This huge Baroque altarpiece was painted in 1622–3 by Guercino to hang in St. Peter's.

Third-floor art gallery

Stairs to third floor

Stairs to second floor

★ St. John the Baptist
Painted in 1595–6, Caravaggio's sensual portrait of the young saint presents a highly unorthodox image of the forerunner of Christ.

Museum Guide

The second-floor rooms have original 16th- and 17th-century decoration and Classical statues. The third-floor gallery holds paintings and a porcelain collection. Rooms 13 and 14 are used as temporary exhibition space.

The Horatii and Curatii
D'Arpino's fresco was painted in 1613 and depicts a duel taken from early Roman legend.

Main entrance

Tickets

Facade of Palazzo dei Conservatori
Work began on this Michelangelo design in 1563, the year before his death.

Key to Floor Plan

☐ Exhibition space
▨ Non-exhibition space

Endymion
The youth doomed to sleep forever by the goddess Diana was painted by Pier Francesco Mola (1612–66), who studied under Cavalier d'Arpino.

VISITORS' CHECKLIST
See p71.

Constantine I
The head of a colossal 4th-century AD statue of the emperor has survived, along with a hand and other odd fragments.

Portico of Marcus Aurelius

Second floor

Medusa
This bust by Bernini of the mythological Medusa is in Room 11.

★ Spinario
This is a charming bronze sculpture from the 1st century BC of a boy trying to remove a thorn from his foot.

★ She-Wolf
The Etruscan bronze of the wolf dates from the early 5th century BC. The legendary twins Romulus and Remus (see pp20–21) were probably added in the 15th century.

❸ Piazza del Campidoglio

Map 5 A5 & 12 F5. 🚌 40, 62, 63, 64, 95, 110, 170.

When Emperor Charles V visited Rome in 1536, Pope Paul III Farnese was so embarrassed by the muddy state of the Capitol that he asked Michelangelo to draw up plans for repaving the piazza, and for renovating the facades of the Palazzo dei Conservatori and Palazzo Senatorio.

Michelangelo proposed adding the Palazzo Nuovo to form a piazza in the shape of a trapezium, embellished with Classical sculptures chosen for their relevance to Rome. Building started in 1546 but progressed so slowly that Michelangelo only lived to oversee the double flight of steps at the entrance of Palazzo Senatorio. The piazza was completed in the 17th century, the design remaining largely faithful to the original. Pilasters two stories high and balustrades interspersed with statues link the buildings thematically. The piazza faces west toward St. Peter's, the Christian equivalent of the Capitol. At its center stands a replica of a statue of Marcus Aurelius. The original is in the Palazzo dei Conservatori *(see pp72–3)*.

Statue of Marcus Aurelius on Piazza del Campidoglio

❹ Cordonata

Map 5 A5 & 12 F5. 🚌 40, 62, 63, 64, 95, 110, 170.

From Piazza Venezia, the Capitol is approached by a gently rising, subtly widening ramp – the Cordonata. At the foot is a pair of granite Egyptian lions, and on the left a 19th-century monument to Cola di Rienzo, close to where the dashing 14th-century tyrant was executed. The top of the ramp is guarded by Classical statues of the Dioscuri – Castor and Pollux.

❺ Roman *Insula*

Piazza d'Aracoeli. **Map** 5 A5 & 12 F4. **Tel** 06-0608. 🚌 40, 62, 63, 64, 95, 110, 170. **Open** by appt only: call first.

Two thousand years ago, the urban poor of Rome used to make their homes in *insulae* – apartment blocks. These were often badly maintained by landlords, and expensive to rent in a city where land costs were high. This 2nd-century AD tenement block, of barrel-vault construction, is the only survivor in Rome from that era. The fourth, fifth, and part of the sixth story remain above current ground level.

In the Middle Ages, a section of these upper stories was converted into a church; its bell tower and 14th-century Madonna in a niche are visible from the street.

During the Fascist years, the area was cleared, and three lower floors emerged. Some 380 people may have lived in the tenement, in the squalid conditions described by the 1st-century AD satirical writers Martial and Juvenal. The latter mentions that he had to climb 200 steps to reach his garret.

This *insula* may once have had more stories. The higher you lived, the more dismal the conditions, as the cramped spaces of the building's upper levels testify.

The Dioscuri twins looking onto the Cordonata leading up to the Piazza del Campidoglio

❻ Aracoeli Staircase

Piazza d'Aracoeli. **Map** 5 A5 & 12 F4.
🚌 40, 62, 63, 64, 95, 110, 170.

The Aracoeli Staircase numbers 124 marble steps (122 if you start from the right) and was completed in 1348, some say in thanks for the passing of the Black Death, but probably in honor of the 1350 Holy Year.

The 14th-century tribune-turned-tyrant Cola di Rienzo used to harangue the masses from the Aracoeli Staircase; in the 17th century, foreigners used to sleep on the steps, until Prince Caffarelli, who lived on the hill, scared them off by rolling barrels filled with stones down them.

Popular belief has it that by climbing the steps on your knees you can win the Italian national lottery. From the top there is a good view of Rome, with the domes of Sant' Andrea della Valle and St. Peter's slightly to the right.

Aracoeli Staircase

❼ Santa Maria in Aracoeli

Piazza d'Aracoeli (entrances via Aracoeli Staircase and door behind Palazzo Nuovo). **Map** 5 A5 & 12 F4.
Tel 06-6976 38 39. 🚌 40, 62, 63, 64, 95, 110, 170. **Open** summer: 9am–6:30pm daily; winter: 9am–5:30pm daily.

Dating from at least the 6th century, the church of Santa Maria in Aracoeli, or St. Mary of the Altar in the Sky, stands on the northern summit of the Capitoline, on the site of the

Ceiling commemorating Battle of Lepanto in Santa Maria in Aracoeli

ancient temple to Juno. Its 22 columns were taken from various ancient buildings; the inscription on the third column to the left tells us that it comes *"a cubiculo Augustorum"* – from the bedroom of the emperors.

The church of the Roman senators and people, Santa Maria in Aracoeli has been used to celebrate many triumphs over adversity. Its ceiling, with naval motifs, commemorates the Battle of Lepanto (1571), and was built under Pope Gregory XIII Boncompagni, whose family crest, the dragon, can be seen toward the altar end.

Many other Roman families and individuals are honored by memorials in the church. To the right of the entrance door, the tombstone of archdeacon Giovanni Crivelli, rather than being set into the floor of the church, stands eternally at attention, partly so that the signature "Donatelli" (by Donatello) can be read at eye level.

The frescoes in the first chapel on the right, painted by Pinturicchio in the 1480s in the beautifully clear style of the early Renaissance, depict St. Bernardino of Siena. On the left wall, the perspective of *The Burial of the Saint* slants to the right, taking into account the position of the viewer just outside the chapel.

The church is most famous, however, for an icon with apparently miraculous powers, the *Santo Bambino*, a 15th-century olive-wood figure of the Christ Child that was carved out of a tree from the garden of Gethsemane. Its powers are said to include resurrecting the dead, and it is sometimes summoned to the bedsides of the gravely ill. The original figure was stolen in 1994 but has been replaced by a replica.

At Christmas the Christ Child takes its place in the center of a picturesque crib (second chapel to the left) but is usually to be found in the sacristy, as is the panel of the *Holy Family* from the workshop of Giulio Romano.

The miraculous olive-wood Christ Child at Santa Maria in Aracoeli

❽ Temple of Jupiter

Via del Tempio di Giove. **Map** 5 A5 & 12 F5. 🚌 40, 62, 63, 64, 95, 110, 170.

The temple of Jupiter, the most important in ancient Rome, was founded in honor of the king of the gods around 509 BC on the southern summit of the Capitoline hill. From the few traces that remain, archaeologists have been able to reconstruct the rectangular, Greek appearance of the temple as it once stood. In places, you can see remnants of its particularly Roman feature, the podium. Most of this lies beneath the Museo Nuovo wing of the Palazzo dei Conservatori *(see pp72–3)*.

By walking around the site, from the podium's south-western corner in Via del Tempio di Giove to its south-eastern corner in Piazzale Caffarelli, you can see that the temple was about the same size as the Pantheon.

Ancient coin showing the Temple of Jupiter

❾ Tarpeian Rock

Via di Monte Caprino and Via del Tempio di Giove. **Map** 5 A5 & 12 F5. 🚌 40, 62, 63, 64, 95, 110, 170.

The southern tip of the Capitoline is called the Tarpeian Rock (Rupe Tarpea), after Tarpeia, the young daughter of Spurius Tarpeius, defender of the Capitol in the 8th-century-BC Sabine War.

The Sabines, bent on vengeance for the rape of their women by Romulus and his

Sabine soldiers crushing the treacherous Tarpeia with their shields

men, bribed Tarpeia to let them up onto the Capitol. As the Augustan historian Livy records, the Sabines used to wear heavy gold bracelets and jeweled rings on their left hands, and Tarpeia's reward for her treachery was to be "what they wore on their shield-arms."

The Sabines kept to the letter of the bargain if not to its spirit – they repaid Tarpeia not with their jewelry but by crushing her to death between their shields. Tarpeia was possibly the only casualty of her act of treachery – as the invading warriors met the Roman defenders, the Sabine women leapt between the two opposing armies, forcing a reconciliation. Traitors and other condemned criminals were subsequently executed by being thrown over the sheer face of the rock.

The site has been considered dangerous and used to be fenced off, but restoration work is now under way.

❿ Victor Emmanuel Monument

Piazza Venezia. **Map** 5 A5 & 12 F4. **Tel** 06-678 0664. 🚌 40, 62, 63, 64, 95, 110, 170. **Open** 9:30am–4pm daily (summer: to 5pm). 🖥

Known as Il Vittoriano, this monument was begun in 1885 and inaugurated in 1911 in honor of Victor Emmanuel II of Savoy, the first king of a unified Italy. The king is depicted here in a gilt bronze equestrian statue, oversized like the monument itself – the statue is 39 ft (12 m) long.

The edifice also contains a museum of the Risorgimento, the events that led to unification *(see pp40–41)*. Built in white Brescian marble, the "wedding cake" (one of its many nicknames) will never mellow into the ocher tones of surrounding buildings. It is widely held to be the epitome of self-important, insensitive architecture, though the views it offers are spectacular. A glass elevator at the back takes visitors to the very top.

Victor Emmanuel Monument in Piazza Venezia

⓫ Palazzo Venezia and Museum

Via del Plebiscito 118. **Map** 5 A4 & 12 E4. **Tel** 06-6999 4388. 🚌 40, 62, 63, 64, 95, 110, 170. **Open** 8:30am–7pm Tue–Sun (last adm: 30 min before closing). **Closed** Jan 1, May 1, Dec 25. 🏛 🚻 Temporary exhibitions.

Palazzo Venezia with Mussolini's balcony in the center

The arched windows and doors of this Renaissance civic building are so harmonious that the facade was once attributed to the great Humanist architect Leon Battista Alberti (1404–72). It was more probably built by Giuliano da Maiano, who is known to have carved the fine doorway onto the piazza. Palazzo Venezia was built in 1455–64 for the Venetian cardinal Pietro Barbo, who later became Pope Paul II. It was at times a papal residence, but it also served as the Venetian Embassy to Rome before passing into French hands in 1797. Since 1916 it has belonged to the state; in the Fascist era, Mussolini used Palazzo Venezia as his headquarters and addressed crowds from the central balcony.

Pope Paul II

The interior is best seen by visiting the Museo del Palazzo Venezia, Rome's most underrated museum. It holds first-class collections of early Renaissance painting; painted wood sculptures and Renaissance chests from Italy; tapestries from all of Europe; majolica; silver; Neapolitan ceramic figurines; Renaissance bronzes; arms and armor; Baroque terra-cotta sculptures by Bernini, Algardi, and others; and 17th- and 18th-century Italian painting. There is a marble screen from the Aracoeli convent, destroyed to make way for the Victor Emmanuel Monument, and a bust of Paul II, showing him to rank with Martin V and Leo X among the fattest-ever popes. The building also hosts major temporary exhibitions.

⓬ San Marco

Piazza San Marco 48. **Map** 5 A4 & 12 F4. **Tel** 06-679 52 05. 🚌 40, 62, 63, 64, 95, 110, 170. **Open** 4–7pm Mon; 7:30am–12:30pm, 4–7pm Tue–Sun. ✝

The church of San Marco was founded in 336 by Pope Mark, in honor of St. Mark the Evangelist. The Pope's relics lie under the altar. The church was restored by Pope Gregory IV in the 9th century – the magnificent apse mosaics date from this period.

Further major rebuilding took place in 1455–71, when Pope Paul II Barbo made San Marco the church of the Venetian community in Rome.

Coat of arms of Pope Paul II

The blue and gold coffered ceiling is decorated with Pope Paul's heraldic crest, the lion rampant, recalling the lion of St. Mark, patron saint of Venice. The appearance of the rest of the interior, with its colonnades of Sicilian jasper, was largely the creation of Filippo Barigioni in the 1740s. Complemented by an interesting array of funerary monuments in the aisles, the style is typical of the late Roman Baroque.

Leon Battista Alberti, whose name is also mentioned tentatively in connection with Palazzo Venezia, may have been the architect of the elegant travertine arcade and loggia of the facade.

San Marco's apse mosaic of Christ, with Gregory IV on the far left

FORUM

The Forum was the center of political, commercial, and judicial life in ancient Rome. The largest buildings were the basilicas, where legal cases were heard. According to the playwright Plautus, the area teemed with "lawyers and litigants, bankers and brokers, shopkeepers and strumpets, good-for-nothings waiting for a tip from the rich."

As Rome's population boomed, the Forum became too small. In 46 BC, Julius Caesar built a new one, setting a precedent that was followed by emperors from Augustus to Trajan. Emperors also erected triumphal arches to themselves, and just to the east, Vespasian built the Colosseum, center of entertainment after the business of the day was done.

See also Street Finder maps 5, 8, 9, 12

Sights at a Glance

Churches and Temples
5 Temple of Saturn
8 Temple of Castor and Pollux
9 Temple of Vesta
11 Temple of Antoninus and Faustina
12 Temple of Romulus and Santi Cosma e Damiano
14 Santa Francesca Romana
17 Temple of Venus and Rome

Historic Buildings
1 Basilica Aemilia
2 Curia
7 Basilica Julia
10 House of the Vestal Virgins
13 Basilica of Constantine and Maxentius
18 *Trajan's Markets pp90–91*
20 Torre delle Milizie

21 Casa dei Cavalieri di Rodi
24 Mamertine Prison
27 *Colosseum pp94–7*

Museums
15 Antiquarium Forense

Arches and Columns
4 Arch of Septimius Severus
6 Column of Phocas
16 Arch of Titus
19 Trajan's Column
26 Arch of Constantine

Ancient Sites
3 Rostra
22 Forum of Augustus
23 Forum of Caesar
25 Forum of Nerva

Restaurants
see pp310–11
1 Enoteca Provincia Romana

◀ Ancient ruins at the Roman Forum

For map symbols *see back flap*

A Tour of the Roman Forum: West

To appreciate the layout of the Forum before visiting its confusing patchwork of ruined temples and basilicas, it is best to view the whole area from above, from the back of the Capitol. From there you can make out the Via Sacra (the Sacred Way), the route followed through the Forum by religious and triumphal processions toward the Capitol. Up until the 18th century, when archaeological excavations began, the Arch of Septimius Severus and the columns of the Temple of Saturn lay half-buried underground. Excavation of the Forum continues, and the ruins uncovered date from many different periods of Roman history.

The Temple of Vespasian was the point from where Piranesi made this 18th-century engraving of the Forum. Its three columns were then almost completely buried.

Temple of Concord

Portico of the Dii Consentes

5 **Temple of Saturn**
The eight surviving columns of this temple stand close to the three columns of the Temple of Vespasian.

Arch of Septimius Severus

3 **Rostra**
These are the ruins of the platform used for public oratory in the Forum.

7 **Basilica Julia**
Named after Julius Caesar, who ordered its construction, the basilica housed important law courts.

6 **Column of Phocas**
One of the very last monuments erected in the Forum, this single column dates from AD 608.

4 ★ Arch of Septimius Severus
A 19th-century engraving shows the arch after the Forum was first excavated.

Santi Luca e Martina was an early medieval church, but was rebuilt in 1635–64 by Pietro da Cortona.

The Forum included the area under Via dei Fori Imperiali. More parts have now been made public.

Locator Map
See Central Rome Map pp16–17

Key

— Suggested route

| 0 meters | 75 |
| 0 yards | 75 |

2 Curia
This 3rd-century rebuilding of the Curia was greatly restored in 1937.

1 Basilica Aemilia
This large meeting hall was razed to the ground in the 5th century AD.

VIA DEI FORI IMPERIALI

VIA DELLA SALARA VECCHIA

DELLA CURIA

A SACRA

Entrance to Forum

The Temple of Julius Caesar was erected in his memory by Augustus on the spot where Caesar's body was cremated after his assassination in 44 BC.

Julius Caesar

To Roman Forum: East
See pp82–3

8 Temple of Castor and Pollux
A temple to the twin brothers (of whom only Pollux was fathered by Jupiter) stood on this spot from the 5th century BC. This section of cornice and its supporting columns date from the rebuilding of AD 6.

A Tour of the Roman Forum: East

The eastern end of the Roman Forum is dominated by the massive barrel-vaulted ruins of the Basilica of Constantine. To picture the building as it was in the 4th century AD, you must imagine marble columns, floors, and statues, and glittering tiles of gilt bronze. The remains of the other important buildings are scant, though the garden and ponds in the center of the House of the Vestal Virgins make it a very attractive spot. The two churches in this part of the Forum cannot be reached from within the archaeological area, but are accessible from the road outside.

The Regia was the office of the Pontifex Maximus, the chief priest of ancient Rome.

⓫ Temple of Antoninus and Faustina
The portico of this temple, built in AD 141, has been incorporated in the church of San Lorenzo in Miranda.

To Forum entrance

VIA SACRA

An early Iron Age necropolis was found here in 1902. Finds from it, such as this burial urn, are on view in the Antiquarium.

➒ Temple of Vesta
Partly reconstructed, this tiny temple to the goddess of the hearth was one of ancient Rome's most sacred shrines.

➓ ★ House of the Vestal Virgins
The priestesses who tended the sacred flame in the Temple of Vesta lived here. The house was a large rectangular building around a central garden.

⓬ Temple of Romulus
This domed building from the 4th century AD has survived as part of the church of Santi Cosma e Damiano.

⑬ ★ Basilica of Constantine and Maxentius
The stark remains of the basilica's huge arches and ceilings give some idea of the original scale and grandeur of the Forum's public buildings.

Locator Map
See Central Rome Map pp16–17

⑭ Santa Francesca Romana
The church takes its name from a saint who cared for the Roman poor in the 15th century.

⑮ Antiquarium Forense
A small museum houses archaeological finds made in the Forum. They include this frieze of *Aeneas and the Founding of Rome* from the Basilica Aemilia.

VIA DEI FORI IMPERIALI

Colonnade surrounding Temple of Venus and Rome

VIA SACRA

⑰ Temple of Venus and Rome
These extensive ruins are of a magnificent temple, built here in AD 121 by the Emperor Hadrian, largely to his own design.

Ruined Baths

To the Palatine

⑯ Arch of Titus
This 19th-century reconstruction shows how the arch may have looked when it spanned the flagstone roadway of the Via Sacra.

Key
— Suggested route

0 meters 75
0 yards 75

❶ Basilica Aemilia

See Visitors' Checklist.

Originally this building was a rectangular colonnaded hall, with a multicolored marble floor and a bronze-tiled roof. It was built by the consuls Marcus Aemilius Lepidus and Marcus Fulvius Nobilor in 179 BC. The two consuls, who were elected annually, exercised supreme power over the Republic.

Basilicas in ancient Rome served no religious purpose; they were meeting halls for politicians, moneylenders, and *publicani* (businessmen contracted by the state to collect taxes). A consortium agreed to hand over a specified sum to the state, but its members were allowed to collect as much as they could and keep the difference. This is why tax collectors in the Bible were so loathed.

The basilica was rebuilt many times; it was finally burned down when the Visigoths sacked Rome in AD 410. Business seems to have continued until the last moment, for the pavement is splashed with tiny lumps of coins that melted in the fire.

Melted coins embedded in the floor of the Basilica Aemilia

The Curia, or the Court of Rome, as rebuilt by Diocletian in the 3rd century

❷ Curia

See Visitors' Checklist.

A modern restoration now stands over the ruins of the hall where Rome's Senate (chief council of state) used to meet. The first Curia stood on the site now occupied by the church of Santi Luca e Martina, but after the building was destroyed by fire in 52 BC, Julius Caesar built a new Curia at the edge of the Forum. This was restored by Domitian in AD 94 and, after another fire, rebuilt by Diocletian in the 3rd century. The building you see today is a 1937 restoration of Diocletian's Curia. Inside are two relief panels commissioned by Trajan to decorate the Rostra. One shows Trajan destroying records of unpaid taxes to free citizens from debt; in the other he sits on a throne receiving a mother and child.

❸ Rostra

See Visitors' Checklist.

Speeches were delivered from this dais, the most famous – thanks to Shakespeare – being Mark Antony's "Friends, Romans, Countrymen" oration after the assassination of Julius Caesar in 44 BC. Caesar himself had just reorganized the Forum, and this speech was made from the newly sited Rostra, where the ruins now stand. In the following year the head and hands of Cicero were put on display here after he had been put to death by the second Triumvirate (Augustus, Mark Antony, and Marcus Lepidus). Fulvia, Mark Antony's wife, stabbed the great orator's tongue with a hairpin. It was also here that Julia, Augustus's daughter, was said to have played the prostitute – one of many scandalous acts that led to her banishment.

The dais took its name from the ships' prows (*rostra*) with which it was decorated. Sheathed in iron (for ramming enemy vessels), these came from ships captured at the Battle of Antium in 338 BC.

❹ Arch of Septimius Severus

See Visitors' Checklist.

This triumphal arch, one of the most striking and best preserved monuments of the Forum, was erected in AD 203 to celebrate the tenth anniversary of the accession of

Rostra
This reconstruction shows the platform for public speaking in the Forum, as it looked in Imperial times.

Honorary statue

Relief panel in balustrade, showing Trajan's acts of charity

Prows of ships (*rostra*)

Septimius Severus. The relief panels – largely eroded – celebrate the emperor's victories in Parthia (modern-day Iraq and Iran) and Arabia. Originally, the inscription along the top of the arch was to Septimius and his two sons, Caracalla and Geta, but after Septimius died, Caracalla murdered Geta and had his brother's name removed. Even so, the holes into which the letters of his name were pegged are still visible.

During the Middle Ages, the central arch, half buried in earth and debris, was used to shelter a barber shop.

Ionic capitals on the surviving columns of the Temple of Saturn

Triumphal arch of the Emperor Septimius Severus

❺ Temple of Saturn

See Visitors' Checklist.

The most prominent of the ruins in the fenced-off area between the Forum and the Capitoline Hill is the Temple of Saturn. It consists of a high platform, eight columns, and a section of entablature. There was a temple dedicated to Saturn here as early as 497 BC, but it had to be rebuilt many times, and the current remains date only from 42 BC.

Saturn was the mythical god-king of Italy, said to have presided over a prosperous and peaceful Golden Age from which slavery, private property, crime, and war were absent. As such, he appealed particularly to the lower and slave classes. Every year,

between December 17 and December 23, Saturn's reign was remembered in a week of sacrifices and feasting, known as the Saturnalia.

As long as the revels lasted, the normal social order was turned upside down. Slaves were permitted to drink and dine with (and sometimes even be served by) their masters. Senators and other high-ranking Romans would abandon the aristocratic togas that they usually wore to distinguish themselves from the lower classes and wear more democratic, loose-fitting gowns. During the holidays, all the courts of law and schools in the city were closed. No prisoner could be punished, and no war could be declared.

People also celebrated the Saturnalia in their own homes: they exchanged gifts, in particular special wax dolls and wax tapers, and played light-hearted gambling games, the stakes usually being nuts, a symbol of fruitfulness. Much of the spirit and many of the rituals of the festival have been preserved in the Christian celebration of Christmas.

❻ Column of Phocas

See Visitors' Checklist.

This column, 44 ft (13.5 m) high, is one of the few to have remained upright since the day it was put up. Until 1816, when an inquisitive Englishwoman, Lady Elizabeth Foster, widow of the

fifth Duke of Devonshire, decided to excavate its pedestal, nobody knew what it was. It turned out to be the youngest of the Forum's monuments, erected in AD 608 in honor of the Byzantine emperor, Phocas, who had just paid a visit to Rome. The column may have been placed here as a mark of gratitude to Phocas for giving the Pantheon to the pope *(see pp114–15).*

VISITORS' CHECKLIST

Practical Information
Entrance: Via della Salara Vecchia 5/6. **Map** 5 B5 & 8 F1. **Tel** 06-3996 7700. **Open** 8:30am–approx 1 hour before sunset daily (last adm: 1 hour before closing). **Closed** Jan 1, Dec 25. (includes entry to Colosseum and Palatine).

Transportation
Ⓜ Colosseo. 75, 85, 87, 117, 175, 186, 810. 3.

Slender, fluted Column of Phocas

Remains of the Basilica Julia, a Roman court of civil law

❼ Basilica Julia

See Visitors' Checklist, p85.

This immense basilica, which occupied the area between the temple of Saturn and the temple of Castor and Pollux, was begun by Julius Caesar in 54 BC and completed after his death by his great-nephew Augustus. It was damaged by fire almost immediately afterward in 9 BC, but was subsequently repaired and dedicated to the emperor's grandsons, Gaius and Lucius.

After numerous sackings and pilferings, only the steps, pavement, and column stumps remain. Nevertheless, the ground plan is fairly clear. The basilica had a central hall, measuring 260 ft by 59 ft (80 m by 18 m), surrounded by a double portico. The hall was on three floors, while the outer portico had only two.

The Basilica Julia was the seat of the *centumviri*, a body of 180 magistrates who tried civil law cases. They were split into four chambers of 45 men, and unless a case was particularly complicated, they would all sit separately.

The four courts were, however, divided only by screens or curtains, and the voices of lawyers and cheers and boos of spectators in the upper galleries echoed through the building. Lawyers hired crowds of spectators, who would applaud every time the lawyer who was paying them made a point and jeer at his opponents. The clappers and booers must have had a good deal of time on their hands: scratched into the steps are checkerboards where they played dice and other gambling games to while away the time between cases.

Corinthian columns of the Temple of Castor and Pollux

❽ Temple of Castor and Pollux

See Visitors' Checklist, p85.

The three slender fluted columns of this temple form one of the Forum's most beautiful ruins. The first temple here was probably dedicated in 484 BC in honor of the mythical twins and patrons of horsemanship Castor and Pollux. During the battle of Lake Regillus (499 BC) against the ousted Tarquin kings, the Roman dictator Postumius promised to build a temple to the twins if the Romans were victorious. Some said the twins appeared on the battlefield, helped theRomans to victory, and then materialized in the Forum – the temple marks the spot – to announce the news.

The temple, like most buildings in the Forum, was rebuilt many times. The three surviving columns date from the last occasion on which it was rebuilt – by the future Emperor Tiberius after a fire in AD 6. For a long period, the temple housed the city's office of weights and measures, and it was also used at times by a number of bankers.

❾ Temple of Vesta

See Visitors' Checklist, p85.

The Forum's most elegant temple, a circular building originally surrounded by a ring of 20 fine fluted columns, dates from the 4th century AD, though there had been a temple on the site for far longer. It was partially reconstructed in 1930.

The cult of the Vestals was one of the oldest in Rome, and centered on six Vestal Virgins, who were required to keep alight the sacred flame of Vesta, the goddess of the hearth.

Cella (sacred inner chamber)

Sacred flame

Ring of Corinthian columns

The Temple preserved the shape of an original primitive structure made of wooden posts with a thatched roof.

This responsibility was originally entrusted to the daughters of the king, but it then passed to the Vestals, the only group of women priests in Rome. It was no easy task, as the flame was easily blown out. Any Vestal who allowed the flame to die was whipped by the high priest (Pontifex Maximus) and dismissed.

The girls, who had to belong to noble families, were selected when they were between 6 and 10 years old. They served for 30 years: the first ten were spent learning their duties, the next ten performing them and the final ten teaching novices. They enjoyed high status and financial security, but had to remain virgins. The penalty for transgressing was to be buried alive, although only ten Vestals are recorded as ever having suffered this fate. The men involved were whipped to death. When Vestals retired, they were free to live the rest of their lives as ordinary citizens. If they wished, they could marry, but few ever did.

Another of the Vestals' duties was to guard the Palladium, a sacred statue of the goddess Pallas Athenae. The irreverent Emperor Heliogabalus burgled the temple in the 3rd century AD. He thought he had succeeded in stealing the Palladium, but the Vestals had been warned of his intention and had replaced it with a replica.

Central courtyard of the House of the Vestal Virgins

⑩ House of the Vestal Virgins

See Visitors' Checklist, p85.

Honorary statue of a Vestal Virgin

As soon as a girl became a Vestal, she came to live in the House of the Vestal Virgins. This was once an enormous complex with about 50 rooms on three stories. The only remains today are some of the rooms around the central courtyard. This space is perhaps the most evocative part of the Forum. Overlooking ponds of water lilies and goldfish is a row of eroded, and mostly headless, statues of senior Vestals, dating from the 3rd, and 4th centuries AD. The better-preserved examples are in the Museo Nazionale Romano (see p165). On one of the pedestals the inscription has been removed because the disgraced Vestal in question may have been a certain Claudia, known to have betrayed the cult by converting to Christianity.

Though many of the rooms surrounding the courtyard are well preserved – some even retain flights of steps – entry is not allowed. If you peek into the series of rooms along the south side, however, you might be able to see the remains of a mill, used for grinding the grain with which the Vestals made a special sacrificial cake. The bakery was next door.

⑪ Temple of Antoninus and Faustina

See Visitors' Checklist, p85.

One of the Forum's oddest sights is the Baroque facade of the church of San Lorenzo in Miranda rising above the porch of a Roman temple. First dedicated in AD 141 by the Emperor Antoninus Pius to his late wife Faustina, the temple was rededicated to them both on the death of the emperor. In the 11th century it was converted into a church because it was believed that San Lorenzo (St. Lawrence) had been condemned to death there. The current church dates from 1601.

Temple of Antoninus and Faustina

Restored section of Temple of Vesta

⓬ Temple of Romulus and Santi Cosma e Damiano

See Visitors' Checklist, p85. Santi Cosma e Damiano: **Tel** 06-692 0441. **Open** 9am–1pm, 3–7pm daily. Crib: **Closed** Mon–Thu. Donation for crib. 🕀 ♿

No one is sure to whom the Temple of Romulus was dedicated, but it was probably to the son of Emperor Maxentius, and not to Rome's founder.

The temple is a circular brick building, topped by a cupola, with two rectangular side rooms and a concave porch. The heavy, dull bronze doors are original.

Since the 6th century the temple has acted as a vestibule to the church of Santi Cosma e Damiano, which itself occupies an ancient building – a hall in Vespasian's Forum of Peace. The entrance to the church is on Via dei Fori Imperiali. The beautiful carved figures of its 18th-century Neapolitan *presepio* (crib or Nativity scene) are on view, and the church has a vivid Byzantine apse mosaic with Christ pictured against orange clouds.

Roof of the Temple of Romulus

⓭ Basilica of Constantine and Maxentius

See Visitors' Checklist, p85.

The basilica's three vast, coffered barrel vaults are powerful relics of what was the largest building in the Forum. Work began in AD 308 under the Emperor Maxentius. When he was deposed by Constantine after the Battle of the Milvian Bridge in AD 312, work on the massive project continued under the new regime. The building, which, like other Roman basilicas, was used for the administration of justice and for carrying out business, is often referred to simply as the Basilica of Constantine.

The area covered by the basilica was roughly 330 ft by 215 ft (100 m by 65 m). It was originally designed to have a long nave and aisles running from east to west, but Constantine switched the axis around to create three short broad aisles with the main entrance in the center of the long south wall. The height of the building was 115 ft (35 m). In the apse at the western end, where it could be seen from all over the building, stood a 39-ft (12-m) statue of the emperor, made partly of wood and partly of marble. The giant head, hand, and foot are on display in the courtyard of the Palazzo dei Conservatori *(see pp72–3)*. The roof of the basilica glittered with gilded tiles until the 7th century, when they were stripped off to cover the roof of the old St. Peter's.

The three barrel-vaulted aisles of the basilica were used as law courts.

The octagonal coffers in the vaulted ceiling were originally faced with marble.

The roof was supported by eight massive Corinthian columns. One now stands in Piazza Santa Maria Maggiore *(see p175).*

The main entrance was added by Constantine in AD 313.

⓮ Santa Francesca Romana

Piazza di Santa Francesca Romana.
Map 5 B5. **Tel** 06-679 5528. 🚌 85, 87,
117, 175, 810. 🚋 3. Ⓜ Colosseo.
Open 10:30am–noon, 3–5pm daily
(times may vary). 🚩 🗺

Every year on March 9, devout
Roman drivers try to park as
close as possible to this Baroque
church with a Romanesque bell
tower. The aim of their
pilgrimage is to have their
vehicles blessed by Santa
Francesca Romana, the patron
saint of motorists. During the
15th century, Francesca of
Trastevere founded a society of
pious women devoted to
helping the less fortunate. After
her canonization in 1608 the
church, originally named Santa
Maria Nova, was rededicated
to Francesca.

The most curious sight inside
the church is a flagstone with
what are said to be the imprints
of the knees of St. Peter and
St. Paul. A magician,
Simon Magus, decided to
prove that his powers
were superior to those of
the Apostles by levitating
above the Forum. As
Simon was in mid-air,
Peter and Paul
fell to their knees
and prayed
fervently for God
to humble him,
and Simon
immediately
plummeted to
his death.

**Bell tower of
Santa Francesca**

⓯ Antiquarium Forense

See Visitors' Checklist, p85.

The former convent of Santa
Francesca Romana is now
occupied by the offices in
charge of the excavations
of the Forum and a small
museum. The latter is
currently being
reorganized and the
rooms are being restored.
They contain Iron Age
burial urns, graves, and
their skeletal occupants,
along with some ancient

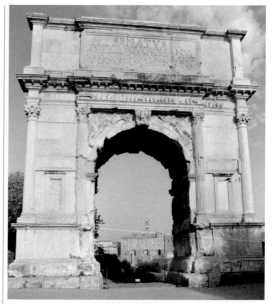

Dedication to Titus and Vespasian on the Arch of Titus

bric-a-brac exhumed from the
Forum's drains. When the
reorganization is complete, you
should be able to see fragments
of statues, capitals, friezes, and
other architectural decoration
taken from the Forum's buildings.

⓰ Arch of Titus

See Visitors' Checklist, p85.

This triumphal arch was erected
in AD 81 by the Emperor
Domitian in honor of the
victories of his brother, Titus,
and his father, Vespasian, in
Judaea. In AD 66, the Jews,
weary of being exploited by
unscrupulous Roman officials,
rebeled. A bitter war broke out;
ending four years later in the
fall of Jerusalem and the
Jewish Diaspora.

Although the reliefs inside the
arch are badly eroded, you can

Frieze of Aeneas in the Antiquarium Forense

make out a triumphant
procession of Roman soldiers
carrying off spoils from the
Temple of Jerusalem. The
booty includes the altar, silver
trumpets, and a golden seven-
branched candelabrum.

⓱ Temple of Venus and Rome

See Visitors' Checklist, p85.

The emperor Hadrian designed
this temple to occupy what had
been the vestibule to Nero's
Domus Aurea *(see p177)*. Many
of the columns have been
reerected, and though there is
no access, there is a good view
as you leave the Forum and
from the upper tiers of the
Colosseum. The temple, the
largest in Rome, was dedicated
to Roma, the personification of
the city, and to Venus because
she was the mother of Aeneas,
father of Romulus and Remus.
Each goddess had her own *cella*
(shrine). When the architect
Apollodorus pointed out that
the seated statues in the niches
were too big (had they tried to
"stand," their heads would have
hit the vaults), Hadrian had him
put to death.

⓲ Trajan's Markets

Originally considered among the wonders of the Classical world, Trajan's Markets now show only a hint of their former splendor. Emperor Trajan and his architect, Apollodorus of Damascus, built this visionary new complex of 150 shops and offices (probably used for administering the corn dole) in the early 2nd century AD. It was the ancient Roman equivalent of the modern shopping center, selling everything from silks, and spices imported from the Middle East to fresh fish, fruit, and flowers.

The Markets Today
Above the facade stands the 13th-century Torre delle Milizie, built for defensive purposes.

Main Hall
Twelve shops were built on two floors, and the grain dole was shared out on the upper story. This was a free grain ration given to Roman men to prevent hunger.

KEY

① Staircase

② Small semicircle of shops

③ Cross vaulting

④ **Market shops** were built with arched entrances, with jambs and lintels creating rectangular portals and windows. A wooden mezzanine was used for storage.

⑤ **The terrace** over the archway spanning Via Biberatica has a good view of the Forum of Trajan below.

⑥ **Large hall with semidomed ceiling**

⑦ **Forum of Trajan**, built in front of the markets in AD 107–113, was flanked by the Basilica Ulpia. The basilica, measuring 558 ft by 197 ft (170 m by 60 m), was the largest in Rome. A small portion of the Forum has been excavated; unfortunately, however, the rest of it remains buried beneath modern Rome's busy city streets.

⑧ **Wall dividing market area from Forum of Trajan**

Trajan
The emperor was a benevolent ruler and a successful general.

Via Biberatica
The main street that runs through the market is named after the drinking inns that once lined it.

The Markets in the 16th Century
This fanciful fresco depicts a gladiatorial combat taking place in front of the partly buried remains of Trajan's Markets.

VISITORS' CHECKLIST

Practical Information
Mercati Traianei,
Via IV Novembre 94. **Map** 5 B4.
Tel 06-0608.
Open 9am–7pm daily.
Last adm: 1 hour before closing.
Closed Jan 1, Dec 25.

Transportation
64, 70, 170, and many routes to Piazza Venezia.

Upper Corridor
Shops on this upper level are thought to have sold wine and oil, since a number of storage jars were discovered here.

④
⑤
③
⑥
⑦

Market Shopping

Shops opened early, and closed about noon. The best ones were decorated with mosaics of the goods they sold. Almost all the shopping was done by men, though women visited the dressmaker and cobbler. The tradesmen were almost all male. In employment records for the period AD 117–193, the only female shop-keepers mentioned are three wool-sellers, two jewelers, a green-grocer, and a fishwife.

Fish mosaic

AD 100–112 Building of Trajan's Markets	**472** Invasion by Ricimer the Suevian. Some of his Germanic troops stationed here	**1200s** Torre delle Milizie built on top of the markets	**1572** Convent of Santa Caterina da Siena built over part of markets	**1924** Many medieval houses demolished / **1911–14** Convent demolished
AD 0	**AD 390**	**780**	**1170**	**1560**
AD 117 Death of Trajan / **AD 98** Trajan succeeds Nerva as emperor	**552** Byzantine takeover of Rome. Markets occupied and fortified by the army	**1300s** Annibaldi and Caetani families vie for control of the area	**1828** First tentative excavations, but value of site not recognized / **1930–33** Markets finally excavated	

Detail of Trajan's Column

⓳ Trajan's Column

Via dei Fori Imperiali. **Map** 5 A4 & 12 F4. *See Visitors' Checklist for Trajan's Markets, p91.*

This elegant marble column was inaugurated by Trajan in AD 113, and celebrates his two campaigns in Dacia (Romania) in AD 101–3 and AD 107–8. The column, base, and pedestal are 131 ft (40 m) tall – precisely the same height as the spur of Quirinal Hill that was excavated to make room for Trajan's Forum.

Spiralling up the column are minutely detailed scenes from the campaigns, beginning with the Romans preparing for war and ending with the Dacians being ousted from their homeland. The column is pierced with small windows to illuminate its internal spiral staircase (closed to the public). If you wish to see the reliefs in detail, there is a complete set of casts in the Museo della Civiltà Romana in EUR *(see p268).*

When Trajan died in AD 117, his ashes, along with those of his wife Plotina, were placed in a golden urn in the column's hollow base. The column's survival was largely thanks to the intervention of Pope Gregory the Great (reigned 590–604). He was so moved by a relief showing Trajan helping a woman whose son had been killed that he begged God to release the emperor's soul from hell. God duly appeared to the pope to say that Trajan had been rescued, but asked him not to pray for the souls of any more pagans.

According to legend, when Trajan's ashes were exhumed, his skull and tongue were not only intact, but his tongue told of his release from hell. The land around the column was then declared sacred and the column itself was spared. The statue of Trajan remained on top of the column until 1587, when it was replaced with one of St. Peter.

⓴ Torre delle Milizie

Mercati Traianei, Via IV Novembre. **Map** 5 B4. **Tel** 06-679 0048. **Closed** to the public.

For centuries this massive brick tower was thought to have been the one in which Nero stood watching Rome burn, after he had set it alight to clear the city's slums. It is uncertain whether arson was among Nero's crimes, but it is certain that he did not watch the fire from this tower – it was built in the 13th century.

㉑ Casa dei Cavalieri di Rodi

Piazza del Grillo 1. **Map** 5 B5. **Tel** 06-0608. 🚌 85, 87, 117, 175, 186, 810. **Open** Tue am, Thu am (by appt only, well in advance).

Since the 12th century the crusading order, the Knights of St. John, also known as the Knights of Rhodes (Rodi) or Malta, have had their priorate in this medieval house above the Forum of Augustus. If you are lucky enough to get inside, ask to see the beautiful Cappella di San Giovanni (Chapel of St. John).

㉒ Forum of Augustus

Piazza del Grillo 1. **Map** 5 B5 & 12 F5. *See Trajan's Markets' Visitors' Checklist, p91.* **Tel** 06-0608. **Open** by appt.

The Forum of Augustus was built to celebrate Augustus's victory over Julius Caesar's assassins, Brutus and Cassius, at the Battle of Philippi in 41 BC. The temple in its center was dedicated to Mars the Avenger. The forum stretched from a high wall at the foot of the seedy Suburra quarter to the edge of the Forum of Caesar. At least half of it is now concealed below Mussolini's Via dei Fori Imperiali. The temple is easily identified, with its cracked steps and four Corinthian columns. Originally it had a statue of Mars that looked very much like Augustus. In case anyone failed to notice the resemblance, a giant statue of Augustus himself was placed against the Suburra wall.

㉓ Forum of Caesar

Via del Carcere Tulliano. **Map** 5 A5. **Tel** 06-0608. 🚌 85, 87, 175, 186, 810. 850. **Open** to research scholars by appt only.

The first of Rome's Imperial fora was built by Julius Caesar. He spent a fortune – most of it booty from his conquest of Gaul – buying up and demolishing houses on the site. Taking center stage was a temple dedicated in 46 BC to the goddess Venus Genetrix, from whom Caesar claimed descent. The temple contained statues of Caesar and Cleopatra as well as of Venus. All that remains of this temple to vanity is a platform

View of the Temple of Mars, Forum of Augustus

and three Corinthian columns. The forum was enclosed by a double colonnade that sheltered a row of shops, but this burned down in AD 80 and was rebuilt by Domitian, and Trajan. Trajan also added the Basilica Argentaria and a heated public lavatory.

The forum is only open to the public by appointment, but parts are visible from above in Via dei Fori Imperiali.

17th-century view of the ruined Forum of Nerva

㉕ Forum of Nerva

Piazza del Grillo 1 (reached through Forum of Augustus). **Map** 5 B5. **Tel** 06-0608. 85, 87, 175, 186, 810. **Open** by appt only.

The Forum of Nerva was begun by his predecessor, Domitian, and completed in AD 97. Little more than a long corridor with a colonnade along the sides, and a Temple of Minerva at one end, it was also known as the Forum Transitorium because it lay between the Forum of Peace built by the Emperor Vespasian in AD 70 and the Forum of Augustus. Vespasian's forum is almost completely covered by Via dei Fori Imperiali, as is much

of the Forum of Nerva itself. Excavations have unearthed Renaissance shops, and taverns, but only part of the forum can be seen, including the base of the temple and two columns that were part of the original colonnade. These support a relief of Minerva above a frieze of young girls learning to sew, and weave.

㉖ Arch of Constantine

Between Via di San Gregorio and Piazza del Colosseo. **Map** 8 F1. 75, 85, 87, 175, 673, 810. 3. Colosseo.

This triumphal arch was dedicated in AD 315 to celebrate Constantine's victory three years before over his co-emperor, Maxentius. Constantine claimed he owed his victory to a vision of Christ, but there is nothing Christian about the arch – in fact, most of the medallions, reliefs, and statues were scavenged from earlier monuments. There are statues of Dacian prisoners taken from Trajan's Forum and reliefs of Marcus Aurelius, including one where he distributes bread to the poor. Inside the arch are reliefs of Trajan's victory over the Dacians. These were probably by the artist who worked on Trajan's Column.

Medallion on the Arch of Constantine

19th-century engraving of guards visiting prisoners in the Mamertine

㉔ Mamertine Prison

Clivo Argentario 1. **Map** 5 A5. **Tel** 06-698 961. 85, 87, 175, 186, 810. **Open** 9am–7pm daily (until 5pm in winter). every 20 minutes.

Below the 16th-century church of San Giuseppe dei Falegnami (St. Joseph of the Carpenters) is a dank dungeon in which, according to Christian legend, St. Peter was imprisoned. He is said to have caused a spring to bubble up into the cell and used the water to baptize his guards.

The prison, also known as Tullianum, was in an old cistern with access to the city's main sewer (the Cloaca Maxima). The lower cell was used for executions, and bodies were thrown into the sewer. Among the enemies of Rome executed here was the Gaulish leader Vercingetorix, defeated by Julius Caesar in 52 BC.

North side of the Arch of Constantine, facing the Colosseum

㉗ Colosseum

Rome's greatest amphitheater was commissioned by the Emperor Vespasian in
AD 72 on the marshy site of a lake in the grounds of Nero's palace, the Domus Aurea
(see p177). Deadly gladiatorial combats and wild animal fights were staged free of
charge by the emperor and wealthy citizens for public viewing. The Colosseum was
built to a practical design, with its 80 arched entrances allowing easy access for
55,000 spectators, but it is also a building of great beauty. The drawing here shows
how it looked at the time of its opening in AD 80. It was one of several similar
amphitheaters built in the Roman Empire, and some survive at El Djem
in North Africa, Nîmes and Arles in France, and Verona in
northern Italy. Despite being damaged over the years by
neglect and theft, it remains a majestic sight.

KEY

① **The bollards** anchored the velarium.

② **The outer walls** are made of travertine. Stone plundered from the facade in the Renaissance was used to build several palaces, bridges, and parts of St. Peter's.

③ **The vomitorium** was the exit used from each numbered section.

④ **Brick** formed the inner walls.

⑤ **Entry routes** to take the spectators to their seats were reached by means of staircases to the various levels of the amphitheater.

⑥ **The podium** was a large terrace where the emperor and the wealthy upper classes had their seats.

⑦ **The velarium** was a huge awning that shaded spectators from the sun. Supported on poles attached to the upper story of the building, it was then hoisted into position with ropes anchored to bollards outside the stadium.

⑧ **Corinthian**

⑨ **Ionic columns**

⑩ **Doric columns**

⑪ **Arched entrances,** 80 in total, were all numbered to let in the vast crowds that attended the fights.

72 Emperor Vespasian begins work on the Colosseum			**1312** Emperor Henry VII gives Colosseum to the Senate and people of Rome
230 Colosseum restored by Alexander Severus	**248** Thousandth anniversary celebration of founding of Rome by Romulus and Remus	*A gladiator's shield*	
	442 Building damaged in an earthquake		

A gladiator's shield

0	400	800	1200

81–96 Amphitheater completed in reign of Domitian

523 Wild animal fights banned

1200s Frangipane family turns Colosseum into a fortress

404 Gladiatorial combats banned

15th–16th centuries Ruins used as quarry. Travertine blocks recycled by popes

80 Vespasian's son, Titus, stages inaugural festival in the amphitheater. It lasts 100 days

Internal Corridors
These were designed to allow the large and often unruly crowd to move freely and to be seated within 10 minutes of arriving at the Colosseum.

VISITORS' CHECKLIST

Practical Information
Piazza del Colosseo.
Map 9 A1.
Tel 06-3996 7700.
Open 8:30am–approx 1 hour before sunset daily (last adm: 1 hr before closing).
Closed Jan 1, Dec 25. (inc Palatine & Forum). Additional fees for upper tier and guided tours of underground areas. limited.
Beware of "gladiators" who charge for photos.

Transportation
75, 81, 85, 87, 117, 175, 673, 810. 3 to Piazza del Colosseo. Colosseo.

Colossus of Nero
The Colosseum may have acquired its name from this huge gilt bronze statue that stood near the amphitheater.

The Founder of the Colosseum
Vespasian was a professional soldier who became emperor in AD 69, founding the Flavian dynasty.

1870 All vegetation removed

1600

1893–6 Structure below arena revealed

49 Colosseum dedicated to ssion of Jesus

Flora of the Colosseum

By the 19th century the Colosseum was heavily overgrown. Different microclimates in various parts of the ruin had created an impressive variety of herbs, grasses, and wild flowers. Several botanists were inspired to study, and catalog them, and two books were published, one listing 420 different species.

Borage, an herb

How Fights Were Staged in the Arena

The emperors held shows here that often began with animals performing circus tricks. Then came the gladiators, who fought each other to the death. When one was killed, attendants dressed as Charon, the mythical ferryman of the dead, carried his body off on a stretcher, and sand was raked over the blood to prepare for the next bout. A badly wounded gladiator would surrender his fate to the crowd. The "thumbs up" sign from the emperor meant he could live, "thumbs down" that he died, and the victor became an instant hero. Animals were brought here from as far away as North Africa and the Middle East. The games held in AD 248 to mark the thousandth anniversary of Rome's founding saw the death of a host of lions, elephants, hippos, zebras, and elks.

Beneath the Arena
Late 19th-century excavations exposed the network of underground rooms where the animals were kept.

Interior of the Colosseum
The amphitheater was built in the form of an ellipse, with tiers of seats around a vast central arena.

Emperor's box

Emperor's entrance

Underground passages

Gladiators' entrance

Tiers of seats

Consul's box

Consul's entrance

KEY

① **A complex** of rooms, passages, and elevators lies underneath the arena.

② **Metal fencing** kept animals penned in, while archers stood by just in case any escaped.

③ **Seating** was tiered, and different social classes were segregated.

④ **A winch** brought the animal cages up to arena level when they were due to fight.

⑤ **A ramp and trap door** allowed the animal to reach the arena after walking along a corridor.

⑥ **Cages** were three-sided elevators that went up to the next level, where the animals were released.

Dramatic Entrances
Below the sand was a wooden floor through which animals, men, and scenery appeared in the arena.

Roman Gladiators
These were usually slaves, prisoners of war, or condemned criminals. Most were men, but there were a few female gladiators.

The Colosseum by Antonio Canaletto
This 18th-century view of the Colosseum shows the Meta Sudans fountain (now demolished). Water "sweated" from a metal ball on top of its brick cone.

Sea Battles in the Arena

The historian Dion Cassius, writing in the 4th century AD, relates how, 150 years earlier, the Colosseum's arena was flooded to stage a mock sea battle. Scholars now believe that he was mistaken. The spectacle probably took place in the Naumachia of Augustus, a water-filled arena situated across the Tiber in Trastevere.

PALATINE

According to legend, Romulus and Remus were brought up here by a wolf in a cave. Traces of Iron Age huts, dating from the 9th century BC, have been found on the Palatine Hill, providing archaeological support for the area's legendary links with the founding of Rome. The Palatine was a very desirable place to live, becoming home to some of the city's most famous inhabitants. The great orator Cicero had a house here, as did the lyric poet Catullus. Augustus was born on the hill and continued to live here in very modest circumstances even when he became emperor. The two buildings identified as the House of Augustus and the House of Livia, his wife, are among the best preserved. The first emperor's example of frugality was ignored by his successors, Tiberius, Caligula, and Domitian, who all built extravagant palaces here. The ruins of Tiberius's palace lie beneath the 16th-century Farnese Gardens. The most extensive ruins are those of the Domus Augustana and Domus Flavia, the two wings of Domitian's palace, and the later extension built by Septimius Severus.

Sights at a Glance

Temples
❼ Temple of Cybele

Historic Buildings
❶ Domus Flavia
❸ Domus Augustana
❺ House of Livia
❻ House of Augustus

Ancient Sites
❷ Cryptoporticus
❹ Stadium
❽ Huts of Romulus

Parks and Gardens
❾ Farnese Gardens

See also Street Finder map 8

PALATINE

0 meters   200
0 yards   200

◀ Scenic view of umbrella pine trees on the Palatine Hill   **For map symbols** *see back flap*

A Tour of the Palatine

Shaded on its lower slopes with pines, and scattered in spring with wild flowers, the Palatine is the most pleasant and relaxing of the city's ancient sites. You can reach the hill by walking up from the Roman Forum *(see pp78–9)*. The area is dominated by the ruins of the Domus Flavia and the Domus Augustana, two parts of Domitian's huge palace built at the end of the 1st century AD. What you are able to see depends on where excavations are taking place at the time.

To Farnese Gardens *see p103*

❼ Temple of Cybele
Also known as the Temple of the Magna Mater, this was the center of an important fertility cult.

❽ Huts of Romulus
These are traces of a 9th-century BC village on the Palatine.

❻ ★ House of Augustus
Splendid frescoes, painted in about 30 BC, can be seen in four rooms here.

❺ ★ House of Livia
Many of the wall paintings have survived in the house where Augustus lived with his wife Livia.

| 0 meters | 75 |
| 0 yards | 75 |

Key

— Suggested route

❶ ★ Domus Flavia
This oval fountain was designed to be seen from the dining hall of the palace.

❸ Domus Augustana
The Roman emperors lived in this part of the palace, while the Domus Flavia was used for public functions.

2 Cryptoporticus
In this long underground tunnel, built by Nero, the stuccoes that decorated the walls and vault have been replaced with copies.

Locator Map
See Central Rome Map pp16–17

Octagonal fountain of the Domus Flavia

The Palatine Museum is inside a former convent, and houses artifacts from ancient Rome.

4 Stadium
Part of the Imperial palace, this enclosure may have been used by the emperors as a private garden.

Via San Gregorio entrance

The exedra of the Stadium may have housed a balcony for emperors to view races.

Baths of Septimius Severus

The Palace of Septimius Severus (reigned AD 193–211) was an extension of the Domus Augustana. It projected beyond the hillside, requiring enormous arched supports.

Substructure of palace

Marble pavement in the courtyard of the Domus Flavia

❶ Domus Flavia

See Visitors' Checklist.

In AD 81, Domitian, the third of the Flavian dynasty of emperors, decided to build a splendid new palace on the Palatine hill. But the western peak, the Germalus, was covered with houses and temples, while the eastern peak, the Palatium, was very steep. So the emperor's architect, Rabirius, flattened the Palatium and used the soil to fill in the cleft between the two peaks, burying (and preserving) a number of Republican-era houses.

The palace had two wings – one official (the Domus Flavia), the other private (the Domus Augustana). It was the main Imperial palace for 300 years. At the front of the Domus Flavia, the surviving stubs of columns and fragments of walls trace the shapes of three adjoining rooms. In the first of these, the Basilica, Domitian dispensed his personal brand of justice.

The central Aula Regia was a throne room decorated with 12 black basalt statues. The third room (now covered with corrugated plastic) was the Lararium, a shrine for the household gods known as Lares (usually the owner's ancestors). It may have been used for official ceremonies or by the palace guards.

Fearing assassination, Domitian had the walls of the courtyard covered with shiny marble slabs designed to act as mirrors so that he could see anyone lurking behind him. In the end, he was assassinated in his bedroom, possibly on the orders of his wife, Domitia. The courtyard is now a pleasant place to pause;

the flower beds in the center follow the maze pattern of a sunken fountain pool.

❷ Cryptoporticus

See Visitors' Checklist.

The Cryptoporticus, a series of underground corridors, was built by Nero to connect his Domus Aurea *(see p177)* with the palaces of earlier emperors on the Palatine. A further branch leading to the Palace of Domitian was added later. Its vaults are decorated with delicate stucco reliefs – copies of originals now kept in the Palatine's museum.

❸ Domus Augustana

See Visitors' Checklist.

This part of Domitian's palace was called the Domus Augustana because it was the private residence of the "august" emperors. On the upper level, a high brick wall remains, and you can make out the shape of its two courtyards. The far better-preserved lower level is closed to the public, though you can look down on its sunken courtyard with the geometric foundations of a fountain in its center. Sadly, you can't see the stairs linking the two levels (once lit by sunlight falling on a mirror-paved pool), nor the surrounding rooms, paved with colored marble.

❹ Stadium

See Visitors' Checklist.

The Stadium on the Palatine was laid out at the same time as the Palace of Domitian. It is not

clear whether it was a public stadium, a private track for exercising horses, or simply a large garden. The alcove in the eastern wall looks as though it may have held a box from which the emperor could have watched races. It is, however, known that the Stadium was used for foot races by the Ostrogothic king, Theodoric, in the 6th century – he added the small oval-shaped enclosure at the southern end of the site.

Stadium viewed from the south

❺ House of Livia

See Visitors' Checklist. If closed, apply to custodian.

This house dating from the 1st century BC is one of the best preserved on the Palatine. It was probably part of the house in which the Emperor Augustus and his wife Livia lived. Compared with later Imperial palaces, it is a relatively modest home. According to Suetonius, the biographer of Rome's early emperors, Augustus slept in

Remains of the Domus Augustana and the Palace of Septimius Severus

the same small bedroom for 40 years on a low bed that had "a very ordinary coverlet."

A flight of steps leads down to a mosaic-paved corridor into a courtyard. Its imitation-marble wall frescoes have been detached in order to preserve them, but they still hang in place. They are faded, but you can make out the veining patterns nonetheless. Off the courtyard are three small reception rooms. The frescoes in the central one include a faded scene of Hermes coming to the rescue of Zeus's beloved Io, who is guarded by the 100-eyed Argos. In the left-hand room are frescoed figures of griffins, and other beasts, while the decor in the right-hand room includes landscapes, and cityscapes.

Vaulted ceiling painting in the House of Augustus

Statue of the goddess Cybele

the Temple of Cybele, a popular fertility goddess imported to Rome from Asia. The priests of the cult castrated themselves in the belief that if they sacrificed their own fertility, they would guarantee that of the natural world. The annual festival of Cybele, in early spring, culminated with frenzied eunuch-priests slashing their bodies to offer up their blood to the goddess, and the ceremonial castration of novice priests.

❻ House of Augustus

See Visitors' Checklist.

Painted in about 30 BC, the frescoes in the House of Augustus are among the most impressive existing examples of Roman wall paintings, similar in quality to those found in Pompeii and Herculaneum. In vivid shades of red, blue, and ocher, they include various *trompe l'oeil* effects, including a room with walls painted to resemble a stage with side doors, and a garden vista.

Although the frescoes are impressive, the house itself is modest. This is where Augustus (or Octavian, as he was then known) lived before assuming supreme power as Rome's first emperor. Only a few visitors are allowed in at any one time.

❼ Temple of Cybele

See Visitors' Checklist.

Other than a platform with a few column stumps and capitals, there is little to see of

❽ Huts of Romulus

See Visitors' Checklist.

According to legend, after killing his brother Remus, Romulus founded a village on the Palatine. In the 1940s a series of holes was found, and archaeologists deduced that these must originally have held the supporting poles of three Iron Age huts – the first foundations of Rome *(see pp20–21).*

❾ Farnese Gardens

See Visitors' Checklist.

In the mid-1500s, Cardinal Alessandro Farnese, grandson of Pope Paul III, bought the ruins of Tiberius's palace on the Palatine. He filled in the ruined building and had the architect Vignola design a garden. The result was one of the first botanical gardens in Europe, its terraces linked by steps stretching from the House of Vestal Virgins in the Forum to the Palatine's Germalus peak. The gardeners introduced a number of plants to Italy and Europe, among them *Acacia farnesiana.* Farnese was at the center of a glittering set that included a number of courtesans, so the parties here are likely to have been somewhat unholy.

The area was dug up during the excavation of the Palatine and re-landscaped. The tree-lined avenues, rose gardens, and glorious views make it an ideal place to unwind.

VISITORS' CHECKLIST

Practical Information
Entrances & ticket kiosks: Via di San Gregorio 30. **Map** 8 E1–8 F1. **Tel** 06-3996 7700. **Open** 8:30am–approx 1 hour before sunset daily; last adm: 1 hour before closing. **Closed** Jan 1, Dec 25. ⬛ (includes entry to the Palatine Museum, the Forum & the Colosseum *see pp94–7).* ⬛⬛⬛

Transportation
⬛ 75, 85, 87, 117, 175, 186, 810, 850 to Via dei Fori Imperiali. ⬛ 3. Ⓜ Colosseo.

Farnese pavilions, relics of the age when the Palatine was a private garden

PIAZZA DELLA ROTONDA

The Pantheon, one of the great buildings in the history of European architecture, has stood at the heart of Rome for nearly 2,000 years. The historic area around it has seen uninterrupted economic and political activity throughout that time. Palazzo di Montecitorio, built for Pope Innocent XII as a papal tribunal in 1694, is now the Italian parliament, and many nearby buildings are government offices. This is also the main financial district of Rome, with banking headquarters and the stock exchange. Not many people live here, but in the evenings, Romans stroll in the narrow streets and fill the lively restaurants and cafés that make this a focus for the city's social life.

Sights at a Glance

Churches and Temples
1 Temple of Hadrian
3 Sant'Ignazio di Loyola
9 Gesù pp110–11
11 Santa Maria sopra Minerva
13 Pantheon pp114–15
14 Sant'Eustachio
15 La Maddalena
18 Santa Maria in Campo Marzio
20 San Lorenzo in Lucina

Historic Streets and Piazzas
2 Piazza di Sant'Ignazio
7 Via della Gatta

Historic Buildings
4 Palazzo del Collegio Romano
6 Palazzo Doria Pamphilj
8 Palazzo Altieri
17 Palazzo Baldassini
19 Palazzo Borghese
21 Palazzo di Montecitorio
24 Palazzo Capranica

Columns, Obelisks, and Statues
10 Pie' di Marmo
12 Obelisk of Santa Maria sopra Minerva
22 Obelisk of Montecitorio
23 Column of Marcus Aurelius

Fountains
5 Fontanella del Facchino

Cafés and Restaurants
16 Caffè Giolitti

Restaurants
see pp311–15
1 Al Duello
2 Armando al Pantheon
3 Clemente alla Maddalena
4 Enoteca Capranica
5 Il Bacaro
6 La Pallacorda
7 La Rosetta
8 Maccheroni
9 Osteria del Sostegno
10 Pantha Rei
11 Vitti

See also Street Finder maps 4, 5, 12

0 meters 200
0 yards 200

◀ Fountain outside the Pantheon at night

For map symbols see back flap

Street-by-Street: Piazza della Rotonda

If you wander through this area, sooner or later you will emerge into Piazza della Rotonda with its jumble of open-air café tables in front of the Pantheon. The refreshing splash of the fountain makes it a welcome resting place. In this warren of narrow streets, it can be hard to realize just how close you are to some of Rome's finest sights. The magnificent art collection of Palazzo Doria Pamphilj and the Baroque splendor of the Gesù are just a few minutes' walk from the Pantheon. At night there is always a lively buzz of activity, as people dine in style or enjoy the coffee and ice cream for which the area is famous.

❷ Piazza di Sant'Ignazio
The square is a rare example of stylish domestic architecture from the early 18th century.

❶ Temple of Hadrian
The columns of this Roman temple now form the facade of the stock exchange.

La Tazza d'Oro enjoys a reputation for the wonderful coffee consumed on its premises, as well as for its freshly ground coffee to take out. *(See p322.)*

❸ ★ Pantheon
The awe-inspiring interior of Rome's best-preserved ancient temple is only hinted at from the outside.

PIAZZA DI SANT'IGNAZIO

VIA DI SANT'IGNAZIO

VIA DEL SEMINARIO

PIAZZA DELLA ROTONDA

PIAZZA DELLA MINERVA

⓫ Santa Maria sopra Minerva
The rich decoration of Rome's only Gothic church was added in the 19th century.

⓬ Obelisk of Santa Maria sopra Minerva
In 1667 Bernini dreamed up the idea of mounting a recently discovered obelisk on the back of a marble elephant.

Locator Map
See Central Rome Map pp16–17

❸ ★ Sant'Ignazio di Loyola
Andrea Pozzo painted this glorious
Baroque ceiling (1685) to celebrate
St. Ignatius and the Jesuit order.

❺ Fontanella del Facchino
The water in this small
16th-century fountain spurts
from a barrel held by a porter.

**❹ Palazzo del
Collegio Romano**
Up until 1870, the
college educated many
leading figures in the
Catholic Church.

❻ ★ Palazzo Doria Pamphilj
Among the masterpieces
in the art gallery of this magnificent
family palazzo is this portrait of Pope
Innocent X by Velázquez (1650).

❼ Via della Gatta
The street is named
after the statue of a cat.

❽ Palazzo Altieri
This enormous 17th-century
palazzo is decorated with the
arms of Pope Clement X.

Key

— Suggested route

0 meters 75
0 yards 75

❿ Pie' di Marmo
This marble foot is a stray
fragment from a gigantic
Roman statue.

❾ ★ Gesù
The design of the first-ever Jesuit
church had a great impact on
religious architecture.

❶ Temple of Hadrian

La Borsa, Piazza di Pietra. **Map** 4 F3 & 12 E2. 🚌 117, 119, 492 and routes along Via del Corso or stopping at Piazza S. Silvestro. **Open** for exhibitions.

This temple honors the emperor Hadrian as a god, and was dedicated by his son, and successor Antoninus Pius in AD 145. The remains of the temple are visible on the southern side of Piazza di Pietra, incorporated into a 17th-century building. This was originally a papal customs house, completed by Carlo Fontana and his son in the 1690s. Today the building houses the Roman stock exchange (La Borsa).

Eleven marble Corinthian columns 49 ft (15 m) high stand on a base of *peperino*, a volcanic rock quarried from the Alban hills to the south of Rome. The columns decorated the northern flank of the temple enclosing its inner shrine, the *cella*. The *peperino* wall of the *cella* is still visible behind the columns, as is part of the coffered portico ceiling.

A number of reliefs from the temple, representing conquered Roman provinces, are now in the courtyard of the Palazzo dei Conservatori (*see pp72–3*). They reflect the mostly peaceful foreign policy of Hadrian's reign.

Remains of Hadrian's Temple

❷ Piazza di Sant'Ignazio

Map 4 F4 & 12 E3. 🚌 117, 119, 492 and routes along Via del Corso or stopping at Piazza S. Silvestro.

One of the major works of the Roman Rococo, the piazza (1727–8) is Filippo Raguzzini's

Illusionistic ceiling in the crossing of Sant'Ignazio

masterpiece. It offsets the imposing facade of the church of Sant'Ignazio with the intimacy of the houses belonging to the bourgeoisie. The theatrical setting, the curvilinear design, and the playful forms of its windows, balconies, and balusters mark the piazza as one of a highly distinct group of structures. Along with Palazzo Doria Pamphilj (1731), the facade of La Maddalena (1735), and the aristocratic Spanish Steps (1723), it belongs to the moment when Rome's bubbly Rococo triumphed over conservative Classicism.

❸ Sant'Ignazio di Loyola

Piazza di Sant'Ignazio. **Map** 4 F4 & 12 E3. **Tel** 06-679 4406. 🚌 117, 119, 492 and along Via del Corso. **Open** 7:30am–7pm daily (9am Sun). 🚹 🚻

The church was built by Pope Gregory XV in 1626 in honor of St. Ignatius of Loyola, founder of the Society of Jesus, and the man who most embodied the zeal of the Counter-Reformation.

Together with the Gesù (*see pp110–11*), Sant'Ignazio forms the center of the Jesuit area in Rome. Built in Baroque style, its vast interior, lined with

precious stones, marble, stucco, and gilt, creates a sense of theater. The church has a Latin-cross plan, with an apse and many side chapels. A cupola was planned but never built, so the space it would have filled was covered by a fake perspective painting. The piers built to uphold the cupola support the observatory of the Collegio Romano.

❹ Palazzo del Collegio Romano

Piazza del Collegio Romano. **Map** 5 A4 & 12 E3. 🚌 117, 119, 492 and along Via del Corso or stopping at Piazza Venezia. **Closed** to the public.

On the same block as the church of Sant'Ignazio is the palazzo used by Jesuits as a college where many future bishops, cardinals, and popes studied. The college was confiscated in 1870 and turned into an ordinary school. The portals bear the coat of arms of its founder, Pope Gregory XIII of Boncompagni (reigned 1572–85). The facade is also adorned with a bell, a clock, and two sundials. On the right is a tower built in 1787 as a meteorological observatory. Until 1925 its time signal regulated all the clocks within the city.

❺ Fontanella del Facchino

Via Lata. **Map** 5 A4 & 12 E3. 🚌 64, 81, 85, 117, 119, 492 and many other routes.

Il Facchino (the Porter), once in the Corso, now set in the wall of the Banco di Roma, was one of Rome's "talking statues" like Pasquino *(see p126)*. Created around 1590, the fountain may have been based on a drawing by painter Jacopino del Conte. The statue of a man holding a barrel most likely represents a member of the Università degli Acquaroli (Fraternity of Water-carriers), though it is also said to be of Martin Luther, or of the porter Abbondio Rizzio, who died carrying a barrel.

The Facchino drinking fountain

❻ Palazzo Doria Pamphilj

Via del Corso 305. **Map** 5 A4 & 12 E3. **Tel** 06-679 7323. 🚌 64, 81, 85, 117, 119, 492 and many other routes. **Open** 10am–5pm daily. **Closed** Jan 1, Easter Sun, Dec 25. 🚫 ♿ 📷 for private apartments. 🔲 📷 🔲 Concerts. 🌐 **dopart.it**

Palazzo Doria Pamphilj is a great island of stone in the heart of Rome, the oldest parts dating from 1435. Through the Corso entrance you can see the 16th-century porticoed courtyard with the coat of arms of the della Rovere family. The Aldobrandini were the next owners. Between 1601 and 1647 the mansion acquired a second courtyard and flanking wings at the expense of a public bath that stood nearby.

When the Pamphilj family took over, they completed the Piazza del Collegio Romano facade and the Via della Gatta

The facade of the Rococo palace building, Palazzo Doria Pamphilj

wing, a splendid chapel, and a theater inaugurated by Queen Christina of Sweden in 1684.

In the first half of the 1700s, Gabriele Valvassori created the gallery above the courtyard, and a new facade along the Corso, using the highly decorative style of the period known as the *barocchetto*, which now dominates the building. The stairways, and salons, the Mirror Gallery, and the picture gallery all radiate a sense of light and space.

The family collection in the Doria Pamphilj gallery has over 400 paintings dating from the 15th to the 18th centuries, including the famous portrait of Pope Innocent X Pamphilj by Velázquez. There are also works by Titian, Caravaggio, Lorenzo Lotto, and Guercino. The rooms in the private apartment still have many of their original furnishings, including splendid

Brussels and Gobelin tapestries. Occasionally, the gallery hosts concerts and evening visits of the collection.

❼ Via della Gatta

Map 5 A4 & 12 E3. 🚌 62, 63, 64, 70, 81, 87, 186, 492 & routes along Via del Plebiscito & Corso Vittorio Emanuele II.

This narrow street runs between the Palazzo Doria Pamphilj and the smaller Palazzo Grazioli. The ancient marble sculpture of a cat *(gatta)* that gives the street its name is on the first cornice on the corner of Palazzo Grazioli.

❽ Palazzo Altieri

Via del Gesù 49. **Map** 4 F4 & 12 E3. 🚌 46, 62, 63, 64, 70, 81, 87, 186, 492 and routes along Via del Plebiscito and Corso Vittorio Emanuele II. 🚋 8. **Closed** to the public.

The Altieri family is first mentioned in Rome's history in the 9th century. This palazzo was built by the last male heirs, the brothers Cardinal Giambattista di Lorenzo Altieri and Cardinal Emilio Altieri, who later became Pope Clement X (reigned 1670–76). Many surrounding houses had to be demolished, but an old woman called Berta refused to leave, so her hovel was incorporated in the palazzo. Its windows are still visible on the west end of the building.

Caravaggio's *Rest during the Flight into Egypt* in Palazzo Doria Pamphilj

⑨ Gesù

Dating from between 1568 and 1584, the Gesù was the first Jesuit church to be built in Rome. Its design epitomizes Counter-Reformation Baroque architecture, and has been much imitated throughout the Catholic world. The layout proclaims the church's two major functions: a large nave with side pulpits for preaching to great crowds, and a main altar as the centerpiece for the celebration of the Mass. The illusionistic, decoration in the nave and dome was added a century later. Its message is clear, and confident: faithful Catholic worshippers will be joyfully uplifted into the heavens while Protestants, and other heretics are flung into the fires of Hell.

★ Chapel of Sant'Ignazio
Above its altar is a statue of the saint, framed by gilded lapis lazuli columns. The chapel was built in 1696–1700 by Andrea Pozzo, a Jesuit artist.

Triumph of Faith Over Idolatry
This vivid Baroque allegory sculpted by Théudon illustrates the great ambition of Jesuit theology.

St. Ignatius and the Jesuit Order

Spanish soldier Ignatius Loyola (1491–1556) joined the Church after being wounded in battle in 1521. He came to Rome in 1537 and founded the Jesuits, sending missionaries, and teachers all over the world to win souls for Catholicism.

Main entrance

Allegorical Figures
Antonio Raggi made these stuccoes, which were designed by Il Baciccia to complement the figures on his own nave frescoes.

KEY

① **The Chapel of St. Francis Xavier** is a memorial to the great missionary who died alone on an island off China in 1552.

Madonna della Strada
This 15th-century image, the Madonna of the Road, was originally displayed on the facade of Santa Maria della Strada, which once stood on this site.

VISITORS' CHECKLIST

Practical Information
Piazza del Gesù.
Map 4 F4 & 12 E4.
Tel 06- 697 001. **Open**
7am–12:30pm (8am–1pm Sun),
4–7:45pm daily.

Transportation
H, 46, 62, 64, 70, 81, 87, 186, 492, 628, 810 and other routes.
8.

★ Monument to San Roberto Bellarmino
Bernini captured the forceful personality of this anti-Protestant theologian, who died in 1621.

★ Nave Ceiling Decorations
The figures in Il Baciccia's astonishing fresco of the *Triumph of the Name of Jesus* spill out on to the coffered vaulting of the nave.

Cupola Frescoes
The cupola was completed by della Porta to Vignola's design. The frescoes, by Il Baciccia, feature Old Testament figures.

1540 Founding of the Society of Jesus (the Jesuits)

1571 Giacomo della Porta's design chosen for the facade

1584 Church's consecration

1696–1700 The Chapel of Sant'Ignazio is designed by Andrea Pozzo, a Jesuit artist

1622 Ignatius Loyola is canonized

1773 Pope Clement XIV orders the suppression of the Jesuit order

1500 | **1600** | **1700**

1545–63 Council of Trent defines the new Catholic orthodoxy

1556 Ignatius Loyola dies

1568–71 Vignola builds the church up to the crossing under the patronage of Cardinal Alessandro Farnese

1670–83 Giovanni Battista Gaulli (Il Baciccia) paints the nave vault, dome, and apse

Marble foot from a Roman statue

⓾ Pie' di Marmo

Via Santo Stefano del Cacco. **Map** 4 F4 & 12 E3. 🚌 62, 63, 64, 70, 81, 87, 116, 186, 492 and other routes along Via del Corso, Via del Plebiscito, and Corso Vittorio Emanuele II.

It was popularly believed in the Middle Ages that half the population of ancient Rome was made up of bronze and marble statues. Fragments of these giants, usually gods or emperors, are scattered over the city. This piece, a marble foot *(pie' di marmo)*, comes from an area dedicated to the Egyptian gods Isis and Serapis and was probably part of a temple statue. Statues were painted and covered with jewels and clothes given by the faithful – a great fire risk with unattended burning tapers.

⓫ Santa Maria sopra Minerva

Piazza della Minerva 42. **Map** 4 F4 & 12 E3. **Tel** 06-679 3926. 🚌 116 and along Via del Corso, Via del Plebiscito, and Corso Vittorio Emanuele II. **Open** 7:10am–7pm Mon–Sat; 8am–noon, 4–7pm Sun. Cloister: **Open** call for details. 🏛 📷 Concerts.

Few other churches display such a complete and impressive record of Italian art. Dating from the 13th century, the Minerva is one of the few examples of Gothic architecture in Rome. It was the traditional stronghold of the Dominicans, whose anti-heretical zeal earned them the nickname of *Domini Canes* (the hounds of the Lord).

Built on ancient ruins, supposed to have been the Temple of Minerva, the simple T-shaped vaulted building acquired rich chapels and works of art by which its many patrons wished to be remembered.

Note the Cosmatesque 13th-century tombs, and the exquisite works of 15th-century Tuscan and Venetian artists. Local talent of the period can be admired in Antoniazzo Romano's *Annunciation*, featuring Cardinal Juan de Torquemada, uncle of the infamous Spanish Inquisitor.

The more monumental style of the Roman Renaissance is well represented in the tombs of the 16th-century Medici popes, Leo X and his cousin Clement VII, and in the richly decorated Aldobrandini Chapel. Near the steps of the choir is the celebrated sculpture of the *Risen Christ*, started by Michelangelo but completed by Raffaele da Montelupo in 1521. There are also splendid works of art from the Baroque period, including a tomb, and a bust by Bernini.

The church is also visited because it contains the tombs of many famous Italians: St. Catherine of Siena, who died here in 1380; the Venetian sculptor Andrea Bregno (died 1506); the Humanist cardinal Pietro Bembo (died 1547); and Fra Angelico, the Dominican friar and painter, who died in Rome in 1455.

⓬ Obelisk of Santa Maria sopra Minerva

Piazza della Minerva. **Map** 4 F4 & 12 D3. 🚌 116 and routes along Via del Corso, and Corso Vittorio Emanuele II.

Originally meant to decorate Palazzo Barberini as a joke, this exotic elephant and obelisk sculpture is typical of Bernini's inexhaustible imagination. (The elephant was actually sculpted by Ercole Ferrata to Bernini's design.) When the ancient obelisk was found in the garden of the monastery of Santa Maria sopra Minerva, the friars wanted the monument erected in their piazza. The elephant was provided with its enormous saddle-cloth because of a friar's insistence that the gap under the animal's abdomen would undermine its stability. Bernini knew better: you need only look at the Fontana dei Quattro Fiumi *(see p122)* to appreciate his use of empty space. The elephant, an ancient symbol of intelligence and piety, was chosen as the embodiment of the virtues on which Christians should build true wisdom.

Bernini's Egyptian obelisk and marble elephant

Nave of Santa Maria sopra Minerva

⓭ Pantheon

See pp114–15.

⓮ Sant'Eustachio

Piazza Sant'Eustachio. **Map** 4 F4 & 12 D3. **Tel** 06-686 5334. 🚌 116, and routes along Corso Vittorio Emanuele II. **Open** 9am–noon, 4–7:30pm daily. ⛪

The origins of this church date to early Christian times, when it offered relief to the poor. In medieval times, many charitable brotherhoods elected Sant'Eustachio as their patron, and had chapels here.

The Romanesque bell tower is one of the few surviving remains of the medieval church, which was completely redecorated in the 17th and 18th centuries.

Nearby is the excellent Caffè Sant'Eustachio *(see p322)*.

Bell tower of Sant'Eustachio

⓯ La Maddalena

Piazza della Maddalena. **Map** 4 F3 & 12 D2. **Tel** 06-899 281. 🚌 116, and many routes along Via del Corso, and Corso Vittorio Emanuele II. **Open** 8:30–11:30am, 5–6:30pm Mon–Fri, Sun; 8:30–11:30am Sat. ⛪

Situated in a small piazza near the Pantheon, the Maddalena's Rococo facade, built in 1735, epitomizes the love of light and movement of the late Baroque. Its curves are reminiscent of Borromini's San Carlo alle Quattro Fontane *(see p163)*. The facade has been lovingly restored, although diehard Neo-Classicists dismiss its painted stucco as "icing sugar."

The small size of the Maddalena did not deter the

The old-fashioned *salone* of the Caffè Giolitti

17th- and 18th-century decorators who filled the interior with ornaments from the floor to the top of the elegant cupola. The organ loft and choir are particularly powerful examples of the Baroque desire to fire the imagination of the faithful.

Many of the paintings, and sculptures adopt the Christian imagery of the Counter-Reformation. In the niches of the nave, the statues are personifications of virtues such as Humility and Simplicity. There are also scenes from the life of San Camillo, who died in the adjacent convent in 1614. The church belonged to his followers, the Camillians, a preaching order active in Rome's hospitals. Like the Jesuits, they commissioned powerful works of art to convey the force of their religious message.

La Maddalena's stuccoed facade

⓰ Caffè Giolitti

Via degli Uffici del Vicario 40. **Map** 4 F3 & 12 D2. **Tel** 06-699 1243. 🚌 116, and many routes along Via del Corso, and Corso Rinascimento. **Open** 7am–1am daily.

Founded in 1900, the Caffè Giolitti is the heir to the *Belle Époque* cafés that lined the nearby Via del Corso in Rome's first days as capital of the new Italian state. Its *salone* holds tourists in summer and Roman families on weekends, and on weekdays is frequented by local workers. Its ice cream is especially good.

⓱ Palazzo Baldassini

Via delle Coppelle 35. **Map** 4 F3 & 12 D2. **Tel** 06-684 0421. 🚌 116, and many routes along Via del Corso, and Corso Rinascimento. **Open** 9:30am–noon Sat (reservations required).

Melchiorre Baldassini commissioned Antonio da Sangallo the Younger to build his home in Florentine Renaissance style in 1514–20. With its cornices marking the different floors and wrought-iron window grilles, this is one of the best examples of an early-16th-century Roman palazzo. It stands in the part of Rome still known as the Renaissance Quarter, which flourished around the long straight streets, such as Via di Ripetta and Via della Scrofa, built at the time of Pope Leo X (reigned 1513–21).

⓭ Pantheon

In the Middle Ages, the Pantheon, the Roman temple of "all the gods," became a church; in time, this magnificent building with its awe-inspiring domed interior became a symbol of Rome itself. The rectangular portico screens the vast hemispherical dome: only from inside can its true scale and beauty be appreciated. The rotunda's height and diameter are equal: 142 ft (43.3 m). The hole at the top of the dome, the *oculus*, provides the only light. We owe this marvel of Roman engineering to the emperor Hadrian, who designed it (AD 118–125) to replace an earlier temple built by Marcus Agrippa, son-in-law of Augustus. The shrines that now line the wall of the Pantheon range from the Tomb of Raphael to those of the kings of modern Italy.

★ **Interior of the Dome**
The dome was cast by pouring concrete mixed with tufa and pumice over a temporary wooden framework.

Floor Patterning
The marble floor, restored in 1873, preserves the original Roman design.

The portico, enclosed by granite columns

KEY

① **The immense portico** is built on the foundations of Agrippa's temple.

② **The walls of** the drum supporting the dome are 19 ft (6 m) thick.

③ **Oculus**

④ **Constructing the dome** from hollow decorative coffers reduced its weight.

Bell Towers
This 18th-century view by Bernardo Bellotto shows Bernini's much-ridiculed turrets, which were removed in 1883.

Raphael and La Fornarina

Raphael, at his own request, was buried here when he died in 1520. He had lived for years with his model, La Fornarina (see p212), seen here in a painting by Giulio Romano, but she was excluded from the ceremony of his burial. On the right of his tomb is a memorial to his fiancée, Maria Bibbiena, niece of the artist's patron, Cardinal Dovizi di Bibbiena.

VISITORS' CHECKLIST

Practical Informationn
Piazza della Rotonda.
Map 4 F4 & 12 D3.
Tel 06-6830 0230.
Open 8.30am–7.30pm Mon–Sat, 9am–6pm Sun, 9am–1pm public hols.
Closed Jan 1, May 1, Dec 25.

Transportation
🚍 116 and routes along Via del Corso, Corso Vittorio Emanuele II & Corso del Rinascimento.

Relieving Arches
Brick arches embedded in the structure of the wall act as internal buttresses, distributing the weight of the dome.

★ **Tomb of Raphael**
The artist's body rests below a Madonna by Lorenzetto (1520).

27–25 BC Marcus Agrippa builds first Pantheon

MAGRIPPA
Inscription on pediment

735 Gregory III roofs the Pantheon in lead

1309–77 While papal seat is in Avignon, Pantheon is used as a fortress and poultry market

50 BC **0** **AD 600** **1200** **1800**

118–25 Hadrian builds new Pantheon

609 Pope Boniface IV consecrates Pantheon as church of Santa Maria ad Martyres

663 Byzantine Emperor Constans II strips gilded tiles from the roof

1632 Urban VIII melts down bronze from portico for Bernini's baldacchino in St. Peter's

1888 Tomb of King Vittorio Emanuele II completed

Bernini's curving southern facade of Palazzo di Montecitorio

⑱ Santa Maria in Campo Marzio

Piazza di Campo Marzio 45. **Map** 4 F3 & 12 D2. **Tel** 06-679 4973. 🚌 116 and many routes on Via del Corso and Corso Rinascimento. **Open** only for services (10:30am Sun, and usually 4–7pm Mon–Fri).

Around the courtyard through which you enter the church, there are fascinating remnants of medieval houses. The church itself was rebuilt in 1685 by Antonio de Rossi, using a square Greek-cross plan with a cupola. Above the altar is a 12th-century painting of the Madonna, after which the church is named.

⑲ Palazzo Borghese

Largo della Fontanella di Borghese. **Map** 4 F3 & 12 D1. 🚌 81, 117, 492, 628. **Closed** to the public.

The palazzo was acquired in about 1605 by Cardinal Camillo Borghese, just before he became Pope Paul V. Flaminio Ponzio was hired to enlarge the building and give it the grandeur appropriate to the residence of the pope's family. He added a wing overlooking Piazza Borghese and the delightful porticoed courtyard inside. Subsequent enlargements included the building and decoration of a great *nymphaeum* known as the Bath of Venus. For more than two centuries this palazzo housed the Borghese family's renowned collection of paintings, which was bought by the Italian state in 1902 and transferred to the Galleria Borghese (see pp262–3).

Pope Paul V, who commissioned Palazzo Borghese for his family

⑳ San Lorenzo in Lucina

Via in Lucina 16A. **Map** 4 F3 & 12 E1. **Tel** 06-687 1494. 🚌 81, 117, 492, 628. **Open** 8am–8pm daily. 🕇

The church is one of Rome's oldest Christian places of worship, and was probably built on a well sacred to Juno, protector of women. It was rebuilt during the 12th century, and today's external appearance is quite typical of the period, featuring a portico with reused Roman columns crowned by medieval capitals, a plain triangular pediment, and a Romanesque bell tower with colored marble inlay.

The interior was totally rebuilt in 1856–8. The old basilical plan was destroyed and the two side naves were replaced by Baroque chapels. Do not miss the fine busts in the Fonseca Chapel, designed by Bernini, or the *Crucifixion* by Guido Reni above the main altar. There is also a 19th-century monument honoring French painter Nicolas Poussin, who died in Rome in 1655 and was buried in the church.

㉑ Palazzo di Montecitorio

Piazza di Montecitorio. **Map** 4 F3 & 12 E2. **Tel** 06-676 01. 🚌 116 and all routes along Via del Corso or stopping at Piazza S. Silvestro. **Open** 10am–3:30pm, usually 1st Sun each month (except Aug). Last adm: 3:30pm. 🆆 camera.it

The palazzo's first architect, Bernini, got the job after he presented a silver model of his design to the wife of his patron, Prince Ludovisi. The building was completed in 1694 by Carlo Fontana and became the Papal Tribunal of Justice. In 1871 it was chosen to be Italy's new Chamber of Deputies and by 1927 it had doubled in size with a second grand facade. The 630 members of parliament are elected by a majority system with proportional representation.

The church of San Lorenzo in Lucina

Emperor Augustus's obelisk

㉒ Obelisk of Montecitorio

Piazza di Montecitorio. **Map** 4 F3 & 12 E2. 116 and routes along Via del Corso or to Piazza S. Silvestro.

The measurement of time in ancient Rome was always a rather hit-or-miss affair: for many years the Romans relied on an imported (and therefore inaccurate) sundial, a trophy from the conquest of Sicily. In 10 BC the Emperor Augustus laid out an enormous sundial in the Campus Martius. Its center was roughly in today's Piazza di San Lorenzo in Lucina. The shadow was cast by a huge granite obelisk that Augustus brought back from Heliopolis in Egypt. Unfortunately, this sundial too became inaccurate after only 50 years, possibly due to settling of the ground.

The obelisk was still in the piazza in the 9th century, but then disappeared until it was rediscovered lying under medieval houses in the reign of Pope Julius II (1503–13). The Pope was intrigued, because Egyptian hieroglyphs were thought to hold the key to the wisdom of Adam before the Fall, but it was only under Pope Benedict XIV (reigned 1740–58) that the obelisk was finally unearthed. It was erected in its present location in 1792 by Pope Pius VI.

㉓ Column of Marcus Aurelius

Piazza Colonna. **Map** 5 A3 & 12 E2. 116 and routes along Via del Corso or to Piazza S. Silvestro.

Clearly an imitation of the Column of Trajan *(see p92)*, this monument was erected after the death of Marcus Aurelius in AD 180 to commemorate his victories over the barbarian tribes of the Danube. The 80-year lapse between the two works produced a great artistic change: the wars of Marcus Aurelius are rendered with simplified pictures in stronger relief, sacrificing Classical proportions for the sake of clarity and immediacy. The spirit of the work is more akin to the 4th-century Arch of Constantine *(see p93)* than to Trajan's monument. Gone are the heroic qualities of the Roman soldiers, by now mostly barbarian mercenaries, and a sense of respect for the vanquished. A new emphasis on the supernatural points to the end of the Hellenistic tradition and the beginning of Christianity.

Composed of 28 drums of marble, the column was restored in 1588 by Domenico Fontana on the orders of Pope Sixtus V. The emperor's statue on the summit was replaced by a bronze of St. Paul. The 20 spirals of the low relief chronicle the German war of AD 172–3, and (above) the Sarmatic War of AD 174–5. The column is almost 100 ft (30 m) high and 12 ft (3.7 m) in diameter. An internal spiral staircase leads to the top. The easiest way to appreciate the sculptural work, however, is to visit the Museo della Civiltà Romana at EUR *(see p268)* and study the casts of the reliefs.

Windows of Palazzo Capranica

㉔ Palazzo Capranica

Piazza Capranica 101. **Map** 4 F3 & 12 D2. 116 and routes along Via del Corso or to Piazza S. Silvestro. **Closed** to the public.

One of Rome's small number of surviving 15th-century buildings, the palazzo was commissioned by Cardinal Domenico Capranica both as his family residence and as a college for higher education. Its fortress-like appearance is a patchwork of subsequent additions, not unusual in the late 15th century, when Rome was still hovering between medieval and Renaissance taste. The Gothic-looking windows on the right of the building show the cardinal's coat of arms and the date 1451 is inscribed on the doorway underneath. The palazzo now houses a conference center.

Relief of the emperor's campaigns on the Column of Marcus Aurelius

PIAZZA NAVONA

The foundations of the buildings surrounding the elongated oval of Piazza Navona were the ruined grandstands of the vast Stadium of Domitian. The piazza still provides a dramatic spectacle today, with the obelisk of the Fontana dei Quattro Fiumi in front of the church of Sant'Agnese in Agone as its focal point.

The predominant style of the area is Baroque, many of its finest buildings dating from the reign of Innocent X Pamphilj (1644–55), patron of Bernini and Borromini. Of special interest is the complex of the Chiesa Nuova, headquarters of the Filippini, the order founded by San Filippo Neri, the 16th-century "Apostle of Rome."

Sights at a Glance

Churches and Temples
4 Sant'Agnese in Agone
5 Santa Maria dell'Anima
6 Santa Maria della Pace
7 San Luigi dei Francesi
9 Sant'Ivo alla Sapienza
10 Sant'Andrea della Valle
15 Chiesa Nuova
16 Oratorio dei Filippini
20 San Salvatore in Lauro

Museums
12 Palazzo Braschi
21 Museo Napoleonico

Historic Buildings
3 Palazzo Pamphilj
8 Palazzo Madama
11 Palazzo Massimo alle Colonne
17 Torre dell'Orologio
18 Palazzo del Banco di Santo Spirito
23 Palazzo Altemps

Fountains and Statues
1 Fontana dei Quattro Fiumi
13 Pasquino

Historic Streets and Piazzas
2 Piazza Navona
14 Via del Governo Vecchio
19 Via dei Coronari

Restaurants
22 Hostaria dell'Orso

☐ Restaurants
see pp311–15
1 Baffetto
2 Cantina e Cucina
3 Capricci Siciliani
4 Casa Bleve
5 Cul de Sac
6 Enoteca Il Piccolo
7 Hostaria dell'Orso
8 Il Convivio-Troiani
9 Il Corallo
10 La Campana
11 Montevecchio
12 Old Bear
13 Osteria del Gallo
14 Osteria del Pegno
15 Terra di Siena
16 The Library
17 Sangallo ai Coronari

Street by Street: Piazza Navona

No other piazza in Rome can rival the theatricality of Piazza Navona. Day or night, there is always something going on in the pedestrian area around its three flamboyant fountains. The Baroque is also represented in many of the area's churches. To discover an older Rome, walk along Via del Governo Vecchio to admire the façades of its Renaissance buildings, and browse in the fascinating antique shops.

⑯ Oratorio dei Filippini
The musical term oratorio comes from this place of informal worship.

⑰ Torre dell' Orologio
This clock tower by Borromini (1648) is part of the Convent of the Filippini.

VIA DEL CORALLO

VIA DEL GOVERNO VECCHIO

VIA DI PARIONE

⑮ Chiesa Nuova
This church was rebuilt in the late 16th century for the order founded by San Filippo Neri.

To Corso Vittorio Emanuele II

⑭ Via del Governo Vecchio
This street preserves a large number of fine Renaissance houses.

CORSO VITTORIO EMANUELE II

PIAZZA DI PASQU

❻ Santa Maria della Pace
This medallion shows Pope Sixtus IV who reigned 1471–84, and under whose orders the church was built.

⑬ Pasquino
Romans hung satirical verses and dialogues on this weather-beaten statue.

❸ Palazzo Pamphilj
This grand town house was built for Pope Innocent X and his family in the mid-17th century.

PIAZZA DI SAN PANTALEO

⑪ Palazzo Massimo alle Colonne
The magnificent curving colonnade (1536) is by Baldassarre Peruzzi.

⑫ Palazzo Braschi
A late 18th-century building with a splendid balcony, the palazzo houses the Museo di Roma.

Key

— Suggested route

| 0 meters | 75 |
| 0 yards | 75 |

5 Santa Maria dell'Anima
For four centuries this has been the German church in Rome.

Locator Map
See Central Rome Map pp16–17

Santa Maria della Pace

4 Sant'Agnese in Agone
Borromini's startling concave facade (1657) dominates one side of Piazza Navona.

2 ★ Piazza Navona
This unique piazza owes its shape to a Roman racetrack, and its stunning decor to the genius of the Roman Baroque.

7 ★ San Luigi dei Francesi
An 18th-century statue of St. Louis stands in a niche in the facade.

1 Fontana dei Quattro Fiumi
This fountain supporting an Egyptian obelisk was designed by Bernini.

8 Palazzo Madama
A spread-eagled stone lion skin decorates the central doorway of the palazzo, now the Italian Senate.

The Fontana del Moro was remodeled in 1653 by Bernini, who designed the central sea god.

9 Sant'Ivo alla Sapienza
This tiny domed church is one of Borromini's most original creations. He worked on it between 1642 and 1650.

10 ★ Sant'Andrea della Valle
The church, with its grandiose facade by Carlo Rainaldi (1665), has gained fame outside Rome as the setting of the first act of Puccini's *Tosca*.

To Campo de' Fiori

❶ Fontana dei Quattro Fiumi

Piazza Navona. **Map** 4 E4 & 11 C3. 🚌 46, 62, 64, 70, 81, 87, 116, 492, 628.

Built for Pope Innocent X Pamphilj, this magnificent fountain in the center of Piazza Navona was unveiled in 1651. The pope's coat of arms, the dove, and the olive branch decorate the pyramid rock formation supporting the Roman obelisk, which once stood in the Circus of Maxentius on the Appian Way. Bernini designed the fountain, which was paid for by means of taxes on bread and other staples. The great rivers – the Ganges, the Danube, the Nile, and the Plate – are represented by four giants. The Nile's veiled head symbolizes the river's unknown source, but there is also a legend that the veil conveys Bernini's dislike for the nearby Sant'Agnese in Agone, designed by his rival Borromini. Similarly, the athletic figure of the Plate, cringing with arm upraised, is supposed to express Bernini's fear that the church will collapse. Sadly, these widely believed stories can have no basis in fact: Bernini had completed the fountain before Borromini started work on the church.

Palazzo Pamphilj, the largest building in Piazza Navona

❷ Piazza Navona

Map 4 E3 & 11 C2. 🚌 46, 62, 64, 70, 81, 87, 116, 492, 628.

The most beautiful Baroque piazza in the city follows the shape of Domitian's Stadium, which once stood on this site – some of its arches are still visible below the church of Sant'Agnese in Agone. The *agones* were athletic contests held in the 1st-century stadium, which could seat as many as 33,000 people. The word "Navona" is thought to be a corruption of *in agone*. The piazza's unique appearance and atmosphere were created

in the 17th century with the addition of the Fontana dei Quattro Fiumi. The other fountains date from the previous century but have been altered several times since. The basin of the Fontana di Nettuno, at the northern end, was built by Giacomo della Porta in 1576, while the statues of Neptune and the Nereids date from the 19th century. The Fontana del Moro, at the southern end, was also designed by della Porta, though Bernini altered it later, adding a statue of a Moor fighting a dolphin.

Up until the 19th century, Piazza Navona was flooded during August by plugging the fountain outlets. The rich would splash around in carriages, while street urchins paddled after them. Today, with its numerous shops and cafés, the piazza is a favorite in all seasons. In summer it is busy with street entertainers, while in winter it fills with colorful stands selling toys and sweets for the feast of the Befana.

Family dove and olive branch on facade of Palazzo Pamphilj

❸ Palazzo Pamphilj

Piazza Navona. **Map** 4 E4 & 11 C3. 🚌 46, 62, 64, 70, 81, 87, 116, 492, 628. **Closed** to the public.

In 1644 Giovanni Battista Pamphilj became Pope Innocent X. During his 10-year reign, he heaped riches on his own family, especially his domineering sister-in-law, Olimpia Maidalchini. The "talking statue" Pasquino *(see p126)* gave her the nickname "Olim-Pia," Latin for "formerly virtuous." She lived in the grand Palazzo Pamphilj, which has frescoes by Pietro da Cortona and a gallery by Borromini. The building is now the Brazilian embassy and cultural center.

Bernini's Fontana dei Quattro Fiumi in Piazza Navona

❹ Sant'Agnese in Agone

Piazza Navona. **Map** 4 E4 & 11 C3.
Tel 06-6819 2134. ▇ 46, 62, 64, 70,
81, 87, 116, 492, 628. **Open** 9:30am–
12:30pm, 3:30–7pm Mon–Sat;
9am–1pm, 4–8pm Sun. 🔁 ♿

This church is believed to have
been founded on the site of the
brothel where, in AD 304, the
young St. Agnes was exposed
naked to force her to renounce
her faith. A marble relief in the
crypt shows the miraculous
growth of her hair, which fell
around her body to protect
her modesty. She was martyred
on this site and is buried in
the catacombs that bear
her name along the Via
Nomentana (see p266).

Today's church was
commissioned by Pope
Innocent X in 1652. The first
architects were father and son
Girolamo and Carlo Rainaldi, but
they were replaced by Borromini
in 1653. He stuck more
or less to the Rainaldi
plan except for the
concave facade
designed to
emphasize the
dome. A statue
of St. Agnes on
the facade is said
to be reassuring
the Fontana dei
Quattro Fiumi's
statue of the Plate
River that the
church is stable.

**Statue of St. Agnes
on facade of Sant'
Agnese in Agone**

Carlo Saraceni's *Miracle of St. Benno and the Keys of Meissen Cathedral*

Peruzzi in Santa Maria dell'
Anima. It stands to the right of
Giulio Romano's damaged
altarpiece and is redolent of
the pagan Renaissance
spirit the pope had so
condemned during his
brief, rather gloomy
reign, when patronage
of the arts ground to a
halt. Santa Maria dell'
Anima is the German
church in Rome and
some of its paintings,
such as the *Miracle of St.
Benno* by Carlo Saraceni
(1618), illustrate events
connected with the
history of Germany.

❺ Santa Maria dell'Anima

Via Santa Maria dell'Anima 66.
Map 4 E4 & 11 C2. **Tel** 06-682 8181.
▇ 46, 62, 64, 70, 81, 87, 116, 492, 628.
Open 9am–12:45pm, 3–7pm daily
(times may vary). 🔁 ♿

Pope Adrian VI (reigned 1522–3),
son of a shipbuilder from
Utrecht, was the last non-Italian
pope before John Paul II. He
would have disapproved of his
superb tomb by Baldassarre

❻ Santa Maria della Pace

Vicolo dell'Arco della Pace 5. **Map** 4 E3
& 11 C2. **Tel** 06-686 1156. ▇ 46, 62,
64, 70, 81, 87, 116, 492, 628. **Open**
9am–noon Mon, Wed, Sat. 🔁 ♿ 2
steps. Exhibitions, concerts.

A drunken soldier allegedly
pierced the breast of a painted
Madonna on this site, causing it
to bleed. Pope Sixtus IV della

Rovere (reigned 1471–84)
placated the Virgin by ordering
Baccio Pontelli to build her a
church if she would bring the
war with Turkey to an end.
Peace was restored and the
church was named Santa Maria
della Pace (St. Mary of Peace).

The cloister was added by
Bramante in 1504. As in his
famous Tempietto (see p223), he
scrupulously followed Classical
rules of proportion and
achieved a monumental effect
in a relatively small space. Pietro
da Cortona may have had
Bramante's Tempietto in mind
when he added the church's
charming semicircular portico
in 1656. The interior, a short
nave ending under an
octagonal cupola, houses
Raphael's famous frescoes of
four *Sibyls*, and four *Prophets* by
his pupil Timoteo Viti, painted
for the banker Agostino Chigi in
1514. Baldassarre Peruzzi also
did some work in the church
(fresco in the first chapel on the
left), as did the architect
Antonio da Sangallo the
Younger, who designed the
second chapel on the right.

❼ San Luigi dei Francesi

Piazza di San Luigi dei Francesi 5.
Map 4 F4 & 12 D2. **Tel** 06-688 271.
🚌 70, 81, 87, 116, 186, 492, 628.
Open 10am–12:30pm, 3–7pm daily.
Closed Thu pm. 🚪 📷 📧 ♿

The French national church was founded in 1518, but it took until 1589 to complete, with contributions by Giacomo della Porta and Domenico Fontana. The church serves as a last resting place for many illustrious French people, including Chateau-briand's lover Pauline de Beaumont.

Three Caravaggios hang in the fifth chapel on the left, all dedicated to St. Matthew. Painted between 1597 and 1602, these were Caravaggio's first great religious works: the *Calling of St. Matthew*, the *Martyrdom of St. Matthew*, and *St. Matthew and the Angel*. The first version of this last painting was rejected because of its vivid realism; never before had a saint been shown as a tired old man with dirty feet. All three works display a highly dramatic use of light.

Shield linking symbols of France and Rome on façade of San Luigi

St. Matthew and the Angel by Caravaggio, San Luigi dei Francesi

❽ Palazzo Madama

Corso del Rinascimento. **Map** 4 F4 & 12 D3. **Tel** 06-670 61. 🚌 70, 81, 87, 116, 186, 492, 628. **Open** 10am–6pm generally first Sat of month (exc Aug). Tickets available from 8:30am on day of visit. 🖥 senato.it

This 16th-century palazzo was built for the Medici family. It was the residence of Medici cousins Giovanni and Giuliano, both of whom became popes: Giovanni as Leo X and Giuliano as Clement VII. Caterina de' Medici, Clement VII's niece, also lived here before she was married to Henry, son of King Francis I of France, in 1533.

The palazzo takes its name from Madama Margherita of Austria, illegitimate daughter of Emperor Charles V, who married Alessandro de' Medici and, after his death, Ottavio Farnese. Thus part of the art collection of the Florentine Medici family was inherited by the Roman Farnese family.

The spectacular façade was built in the 17th century by Paolo Maruccelli. He gave it an ornate cornice and whimsical decorative details on the roof. Since 1871 the

Cornice of Palazzo Madama

palazzo has been the seat of the upper house of the Italian parliament.

❾ Sant'Ivo alla Sapienza

Corso del Rinascimento 40.
Map 4 F4 & 12 D3. **Tel** 06-361 2562.
🚌 40, 46, 64, 70, 81, 87, 116, 186, 492, 628. **Open** 9am–noon Sun. 🚪

The church's lantern is crowned with a cross on top of a dramatic twisted spiral – a highly distinctive landmark from Rome's roof terraces. No other Baroque church is quite like this one, made by Borromini. Based on a ground design of astonishing geometrical complexity, the walls are a breathtaking combination of concave and convex surfaces. The church stands in the small courtyard of the Palazzo della Sapienza, seat of the old University of Rome from the 15th century until 1935.

Dome of Sant'Andrea della Valle

⑩ Sant'Andrea della Valle

Piazza Sant'Andrea della Valle. **Map** 4 E4 & 12 D4. **Tel** 06-686 1339. 🚌 H, 40, 46, 62, 64, 70, 81, 87, 116, 186, 492, 628. 🚋 8. **Open** 7:30am–12:30pm, 4–7:30pm daily. ✝

The church is the scene of the first act of Puccini's opera *Tosca*, though opera fans will not find the Attavanti chapel a poetic invention. The real church has much to recommend it – the impressive facade shows the flamboyant Baroque style at its best. Inside, a golden light filters through high windows, showing off the gilded interior. Here lie the two popes of the Sienese Piccolomini family: on the left of the central nave is the tomb of Pius II, the first Humanist pope (reigned 1458–64); Pope Pius III lies opposite – he reigned for less than a month in 1503.

The church is famous for its beautiful dome, the largest in Rome after St. Peter's. It was built by Carlo Maderno in 1622–5 and was painted with splendid frescoes by Domenichino and Giovanni Lanfranco. The latter's extravagant style, to be seen in the dome fresco *Glory of Paradise*, won him most of the commission, and the jealous Domenichino is said to have tried to kill his colleague. He failed, but Domenichino's jealousy was unnecessary, as shown by his two beautiful paintings of scenes from the life of St. Andrew around the apse, and altar. In the Strozzi Chapel, built in the style of Michelangelo, the altar has copies of *Leah* and *Rachel* by Michelangelo in San Pietro in Vincoli *(see p172)*.

Roman column, Palazzo Massimo

⑪ Palazzo Massimo alle Colonne

Corso Vittorio Emanuele II 141. **Map** 4 F4 & 11 C3. 🚌 40, 46, 62, 64, 70, 81, 87, 116, 186, 492, 628. Chapel: **Open** 7am–noon Mar 16.

During the last two years of his life, Baldassarre Peruzzi built this palazzo for the Massimo family, whose home had been destroyed in the 1527 Sack of Rome. Peruzzi displayed great ingenuity in dealing with an awkwardly shaped site. The previous building had stood on the ruined Theater of Domitian, which created a curve in the great processional Via Papalis. Peruzzi's convex colonnaded facade follows the line of the street. His originality is also evident in the small square upper windows, the courtyard, and the stuccoed vestibule. The Piazza de' Massimi entrance has a Renaissance-style, frescoed facade. A single column from the theater has been set up in the piazza.

The Massimo family traced its origins to Quintus Fabius Maximus, conqueror of Hannibal in the 3rd century BC, and their coat of arms is borne by an infant Hercules. Over the years the family produced many great Humanists, and in the 19th century, it was a Massimo who negotiated peace with Napoleon. On March 16 each year, the family chapel opens to the public to commemorate young Paolo Massimo's resurrection from the dead by San Filippo Neri in 1538.

⑫ Palazzo Braschi

Piazza San Pantaleo 10. **Map** 4 E4 & 11 C3. **Tel** 06-0608. 🚌 40, 46, 62, 64, 70, 81, 87, 116, 186, 492, 628. **Open** 10am–8pm Tue–Sun (ticket office closes at 7pm). ♿ 🎧 📷 🎁 🛗

On one side of Piazza San Pantaleo is the last Roman palazzo to be built for the family of a pope. Palazzo Braschi was built in the late 18th century for Pope Pius VI Braschi's nephews by the architect Cosimo Morelli. He gave the building its imposing facade, which looks out on to the piazza.

The palazzo now houses the municipal Museo di Roma. It holds collections of pictures, drawings, and everyday objects illustrating life in Rome from medieval times to the 19th century.

Angel with raised wing by Ercole Ferrata, flanking the facade of Sant'Andrea della Valle sayings of the "talking statue" (renamed Pasquino) were part of popular culture up until the 19th century. Other statues started to "talk" in the same vein; Pasquino used to conduct dialogues with the statue Marforio in Via del Campidoglio (now in the courtyard of Palazzo Nuovo, *see pp70–71*) and with the Babuino in Via del Babuino (*see p137*). Pasquino still speaks on occasion, and Rome's English-language movie theater is named after him (*see p353*).

⑭ Via del Governo Vecchio

Map 4 E4 & 11 B3. 🚌 40, 46, 62, 64.

The street takes its name from Palazzo del Governo Vecchio, the seat of papal government in the 17th and 18th centuries. Once part of the Via Papalis, which led from the Lateran to St. Peter's, the street is lined with 15th- and 16th-century houses and small workshops. Particularly interesting are those at No. 104 and No. 106. The small palazzo at No. 123 was once thought to have been the home of Bramante.

Opposite is Palazzo del Governo Vecchio. It is also known as Palazzo Nardini, from the name of its founder, which is inscribed on the first-floor windows, with the date 1477.

Pasquino, the most famous of Rome's satirical "talking statues"

⑬ Pasquino

Piazza di Pasquino. **Map** 4 E4 & 11 C3. 🚌 40, 46, 62, 64, 70, 81, 87, 116, 492, 628.

This rough chunk of marble is all that remains of a Hellenistic group, probably representing the incident in Homer's *Iliad* in which Menelaus shields the body of the slain Patroclus. For years it lay as a stepping stone in a muddy medieval street, until it was erected on this corner in 1501, near the shop of an outspoken cobbler named Pasquino. Freedom of speech was not encouraged in papal Rome, so the cobbler wrote out his satirical comments on current events and attached them to the statue.

Other Romans followed suit, hanging their maxims and verses on the statue by night to escape punishment. Despite the wrath of the authorities, the

Facade of the Chiesa Nuova

⑮ Chiesa Nuova

Piazza della Chiesa Nuova. **Map** 4 E4 & 11 B3. **Tel** 06-687 52 89. 🚌 40, 46, 62, 64. **Open** 7:30am–noon, 4:30–7pm daily. 🚹

San Filippo Neri (St. Philip Neri) is the most appealing of the Counter-Reformation saints. A highly unconventional reformer, he required his noble Roman followers to humble themselves in public. He made aristocratic young men parade through the streets of Rome in rags or even with a fox's tail tied behind them, and set noblemen to work as laborers building his church. With the help of Pope Gregory XIII, his church was built in place of an old medieval church, Santa Maria in Vallicella, and it has been known ever since as the Chiesa Nuova (new church).

Begun in 1575 by Matteo da Città di Castello and continued by Martino Longhi the Elder, it was consecrated in 1599 (although the facade, by Fausto Rughesi, was only finished in 1606). Against San Filippo's wishes, the interior was decorated after his death; Pietro da Cortona frescoed the nave, dome, and apse, taking nearly 20 years. There are also three paintings by Rubens: *Madonna and Angels* above the altar, *Saints Domitilla, Nereus and Achilleus* on the right of the altar, and *Saints Gregory, Maurus, and Papias* on the left. San Filippo is buried in his own chapel, to the left of the altar.

Via del Governo Vecchio

Borromini's facade of the Oratorio

🔟 Oratorio dei Filippini

Piazza della Chiesa Nuova. **Map** 4 E4 & 11 B3. **Tel** 06-6710 8100. 🚌 46, 62, 64. **Closed** to the public.

With the adjoining church and convent, the oratory formed the center of Filippo Neri's religious order, which was founded in 1575. Its members are commonly known as Filippini. The musical term "oratorio" (a religious text sung by solo voices and chorus) derives from the services that

were held here. Filippo Neri came to Rome at age 18 to work as a tutor. The city was undergoing a period of religious strife and an economic slump after the Sack of Rome in 1527. There was also an outbreak of the plague. It was left to newcomers like Neri and Ignazio di Loyola to revive the spiritual life of the city.

Neri formed a brotherhood of laymen who worshipped together and helped pilgrims and the sick *(see Santissima Trinità dei Pellegrini p145)*. He founded the Oratory as a center for religious discourse. Its conspicuous curving brick facade was built by Borromini in 1637–43.

🔟 Torre dell' Orologio

Piazza dell'Orologio. **Map** 4 E4 & 11 B3. 🚌 40, 46, 62, 64.

Borromini built this clock tower to decorate one corner of the Convent of the Oratorians of San Filippo Neri in 1647–9. It is typical of Borromini in that the front and rear are concave and the sides convex. The mosaic of

the Madonna beneath the clock is by Pietro da Cortona, while on the corner of the building is a small tabernacle to the Madonna flanked by angels in the style of Bernini.

Pietro da Cortona (1596–1669)

🔟 Palazzo del Banco di Santo Spirito

Via del Banco di Santo Spirito. **Map** 4 D4 & 11 A2. 🚌 40, 46, 62, 64. **Open** normal banking hours.

Formerly the mint of papal Rome, this palazzo is often referred to as the Antica Zecca (old mint). The upper stories of the facade, built by Antonio da Sangallo the Younger in the 1520s, are in the shape of a Roman triumphal arch. Above it stand two Baroque statues symbolizing Charity, and Thrift, and in the center of the arch above the main entrance an inscription records the founding of the Banco di Santo Spirito by Pope Paul V Borghese in 1605.

Pope Paul was a very shrewd financier, and he encouraged Romans to deposit their money at the bank by offering the vast estates of the Hospital of Santo Spirito *(see p246)* as security. The system catered only to the rudimentary banking requirements of the population, but business was brisk as people deposited money here, safe in the knowledge that they could get it out simply by presenting a chit. The hospital coffers also gained from the system. The Banco di Santo Spirito still exists, but is now part of the Banca di Roma.

Facade of the Banco di Santo Spirito, built to resemble a Roman arch

Cloister, San Salvatore in Lauro

⓳ Via dei Coronari

Map 4 D3 & 11 B2. 🚌 40, 46, 62, 64, 70, 81, 87, 116, 186, 280, 492.

Large numbers of medieval pilgrims making their way to St. Peter's walked along this street to cross over the Tiber at Ponte Sant'Angelo. Of the businesses that sprang up to try to part the pilgrims from their money, the most enduring was the selling of rosaries, and the street is still named after the rosary sellers *(coronari)*. The street followed the course of the ancient Roman Via Recta (straight street), which originally ran from today's Piazza Colonna to the Tiber.

Making one's way through the vast throng of people in Via dei Coronari could be extremely hazardous. In the Holy Year of 1450, some 200 pilgrims died, crushed by the crowds or drowned in the Tiber. Following the tragedy, Pope Nicholas V demolished the Roman triumphal arch that stood at the entrance to Ponte Sant'Angelo. In the late 15th century, Pope Sixtus IV encouraged the building of private houses and palaces along the street.

Although the rosary sellers have been replaced by antique dealers, the street still has many original buildings from the 15th and 16th centuries. One of the earliest, at Nos. 156–7, is known as the House of Fiammetta, the mistress of Cesare Borgia.

⓴ San Salvatore in Lauro

Piazza San Salvatore in Lauro 15. **Map** 4 E3 & 11 B2. **Tel** 06-687 5187. 🚌 70, 81, 87, 116, 186, 280, 492. **Open** 4:30–7pm Mon–Sat; 8am–1pm, 4:30–7pm Sun. 🚹

Named "in Lauro" after the laurel grove that grew here in ancient times, this church was built at the end of the 16th century by Ottaviano Mascherino. The bell tower and sacristy were 18th-century additions by Nicola Salvi, famous for the Trevi Fountain *(see p161)*.

The church contains the first great altarpiece by the 17th-century artist Pietro da Cortona, *The Birth of Jesus*, in the first chapel to the right.

The adjacent convent of San Giorgio, to the left, has a pretty

Facade of San Salvatore in Lauro

Renaissance cloister, a frescoed refectory, and the monument to Pope Eugenius IV (reigned 1431–47) moved here when the old St. Peter's was pulled down. An extravagant Venetian, Eugenius would willingly spend thousands of ducats on his gold tiara, but requested a "simple, lowly burial place" near his predecessor Pope Eugenius III. His portrait, painted by Salviati, hangs in the refectory.

In 1669 San Salvatore in Lauro became the seat of a pious association, the Confraternity of the Piceni, who were inhabitants of the Marche region. Fanatically loyal to the pope, the Piceni were traditionally employed as papal soldiers and tax collectors.

㉑ Museo Napoleonico

Piazza di Ponte Umberto 1. **Map** 4 E3 & 11 C1. **Tel** 06-0608. 🚌 70, 81, 87, 116, 186, 280, 492. **Open** 10am–6pm Tue–Sun. **Closed** Jan 1, May 1, Dec 25. 🎫 🎥 📷 📱

This museum contains memorabilia and portraits of Napoleon Bonaparte and his family. Personal relics of Napoleon himself include an Indian shawl he wore during his exile on St. Helena.

After his death in 1821, the pope allowed many of Bonaparte's family to settle in Rome, including his mother, Letizia, who lived in Palazzo Misciattelli on Via del Corso, and his sister Pauline, who married the Roman Prince Camillo Borghese. The museum has a cast of her right breast, made by Canova in 1805 as a study for his statue of her as a reclining Venus, now in the Museo Borghese *(see p263)*. Portraits and personal effects of other members of the family are on display, including uniforms, court dresses, and a penny-farthing bicycle that belonged to Prince Eugène, the son of Emperor Napoleon III.

The last male of the Roman branch of the family was Napoleon Charles, portrayed in a late 19th-century painting by Guglielmo de Sanctis. The collection was assembled in 1927 by the Counts Primoli, the sons of Charles's sister, Carlotta Bonaparte.

The palace next door, in Via Zanardelli, houses the Racolta Praz, an impressive selection of over a thousand *objets d'art*, paintings, and pieces of furniture. Dating from the 17th and 18th centuries, they were collected by the art historian and literary critic Mario Praz.

Side relief of the Ludovisi Throne, Palazzo Altemps

Entrance to Museo Napoleonico

㉒ Hostaria dell'Orso

Via dei Soldati 25. **Map** 4 E3 & 11 C2. 🚌 70, 81, 87, 116, 186, 204, 280, 492, 628. **Open** 8pm–2am Mon–Sat.

This ancient inn *(see p314)* has a 15th-century portico and loggia built with columns from Roman ruins. Visitors to the inn included the 16th-century French writers Rabelais and Montaigne. Dante is also said to have stayed here.

㉓ Palazzo Altemps

Piazza Sant'Apollinare 46. **Map** 4 E3 & 11 C2. **Tel** 06-3996 7700. 🚌 70, 81, 87, 116, 280, 492, 628. **Open** 9am–7:45pm Tue–Sun (last adm: 1 hour before closing.) **Closed** Jan 1, Dec 25. ♿ ♿ ♿ ♿

An extraordinary collection of Classical sculpture is housed in this branch of the Museo Nazionale Romano. Restored as a museum during the 1990s, the palazzo was originally built for Girolamo Riario, nephew of Pope Sixtus IV in 1480. The Riario coat of arms can still be seen in the janitor's room. In the popular uprising that followed the pope's death in 1484, the building was sacked, and Girolamo fled the city.

In 1568 the palazzo was bought by Cardinal Marco Sittico Altemps. His family was of German origin – the name is an Italianization of Hohenems – and influential in the church. The palazzo was renovated by Martino Longhi the Elder in the 1570s. He added the great belvedere, crowned with obelisks, and a marble unicorn.

The Altemps family were ostentatious collectors; the courtyard, and its staircase are lined with ancient sculptures. These form part of the museum's collection, together with the Ludovisi collection of ancient sculptures, which was previously housed in the Museo Nazionale Romano in the Baths of Diocletian *(see p161)*. Located on the ground floor is the Greek statue of Athena Parthenos and the Dionysius group, a Roman copy of the Greek original. On the first floor, at the far end of the courtyard, visitors can admire the Painted Loggia, dating from 1595. The Ludovisi throne, a Greek original carved in the 5th century BC, is on the same floor. It is decorated with reliefs, one of which shows a young woman rising from the sea, thought to represent Aphrodite. In the room known as the Salone del Camino is the powerful statue *Galatian's Suicide*, a marble copy of a group originally made in bronze. Nearby is the Ludovisi Sarcophagus, dating from the 3rd century AD.

Galatian's Suicide in the Palazzo Altemps

PIAZZA DI SPAGNA

By the 16th century, the increase in numbers of visiting pilgrims and ecclesiastics was making life in Rome's already congested medieval center unbearable. A new triangle of roads was built, still in place today, to help channel pilgrims as quickly as possible from the city's north gate, the Porta del Popolo, to the Vatican. By the 18th century, hotels had sprung up all over the district. Today this attractive area offers much more: the superb works of Renaissance and Baroque art in Santa Maria del Popolo and Sant' Andrea delle Fratte, the magnificent reliefs of the restored Ara Pacis, art exhibitions in the Villa Medici, fine views of the city from the Spanish Steps, and the Pincio Gardens, and Rome's most famous shopping streets, centered on Via Condotti.

Sights at a Glance

Churches
1 Sant'Andrea delle Fratte
10 Trinità dei Monti
12 All Saints
14 Santa Maria dei Miracoli and Santa Maria in Montesanto
17 *Santa Maria del Popolo pp140–41*
21 San Rocco
22 Santi Ambrogio e Carlo al Corso

Museums and Galleries
7 Keats-Shelley Memorial House
13 Casa di Goethe

Historic Buildings
2 Palazzo di Propaganda Fide
11 Villa Medici

Arches, Gates, and Columns
3 Colonna dell'Immacolata
18 Porta del Popolo

Historic Streets and Piazzas
4 Via Condotti
6 Piazza di Spagna
9 Spanish Steps
16 Piazza del Popolo

Monuments and Tombs
19 Ara Pacis
20 Mausoleum of Augustus

Parks and Gardens
15 Pincio Gardens

Cafés and Restaurants
5 Antico Caffè Greco
8 Babington's Tea Rooms

Restaurants
see pp315–17
1 Babette
2 Canova-Tadolini Museum Atelier
3 'Gusto
4 Hamasei
5 Il Palazzetto Wine Bar
6 Imàgo
7 Le Jardin de Russie
8 Osteria Margutta
9 Rhome
10 Tati' al 28

See also Street Finder maps 4, 5

◄ The church of Trinità dei Monti, Piazza di Spagna

For map symbols *see back flap*

Street by Street: Piazza di Spagna

The network of narrow streets between Piazza di Spagna, and Via del Corso is one of the liveliest areas in Rome, drawing throngs of tourists and Romans to its discreet and elegant shops. In the 18th century the area was full of hotels for frivolous English aristocrats doing the Grand Tour, but there were also artists, writers, and composers, who took the city's history and culture more seriously.

Spagna station

8 Babington's Tea Rooms
English tourists are catered for in the style of the 1890s.

PIAZZA DI SPAGNA

6 ★ Piazza di Spagna
For almost three centuries, the square with its curious Barcaccia fountain in the center has been the chief meeting place for visitors to Rome.

VIA VITTORIA

VIA DELLA CROCE

VIA DELLA BOCCA DI LEONE

VIA DELLA CARROZZE

5 Antico Caffè Greco
Busts and portraits recall the café's former artistic patrons.

VIA DEL CORSO

Via delle Carrozze took its name from the carriages of wealthy tourists that used to line up here for repairs.

VIA DELLA CONDOTTI

VIA BORGOGNONA

VIA FRATT

4 Via Condotti
This shadowy, narrow street has the smartest shops in one of the smartest shopping areas in the world.

Bulgari sells very expensive jewelry behind an austere shopfront in Via Condotti.

| 0 meters | | 75 |
| 0 yards | | 75 |

Key

— Suggested route

Ⓜ Metro station

9 ★ Spanish Steps
Even obscured by crowds, the steps are one of the glories of late Baroque Rome.

Locator Map
See Central Rome Map pp16–17

3 Colonna dell'Immacolata
A Roman column supports a statue of the Virgin Mary.

10 Trinità dei Monti
This 16th-century church has a spectacular setting, and some of the finest views in Rome.

1 Sant'Andrea delle Fratte
Pasquale Marini painted *The Redemption* to decorate the interior of Borromini's high dome in 1691.

2 Palazzo di Propaganda Fide
This facade (1665) was one of the last works of the great Francesco Borromini.

7 ★ Keats-Shelley Memorial House
The library is part of the small museum established in the house where the English poet Keats died in 1821.

➊ Sant'Andrea delle Fratte

Via Sant'Andrea delle Fratte 1. **Map** 5 A3. **Tel** 06-679 3191. 🚌 116, 117. Ⓜ Spagna. **Open** 6:30am–12:30pm, 4–7:30pm daily (to 8pm Sun). ✝

When Sant'Andrea delle Fratte was built in the 12th century, this was the northernmost edge of Rome. Though the church is now firmly embedded in the city, its name (*fratte* means thickets) recalls its original setting.

The church was completely rebuilt in the 17th century, partly by Borromini. His bell tower and dome, best viewed from the higher ground farther up Via Capo le Case, are remarkable for the complex arrangement of concave and convex surfaces. The bell tower is particularly fanciful, with angel caryatids, flaming torches, and exaggerated scrolls like semi-folded hearts supporting a spiky crown.

In 1842, the Virgin Mary appeared in the church to a Jewish banker, who promptly converted to Christianity and became a missionary. Inside, the chapel of the Miraculous Madonna is the first thing you notice. The church is better known, however, for the angels that Borromini's rival, Bernini, carved for the Ponte Sant'Angelo. Pope Clement IX declared they were too lovely to be exposed to the weather, so they remained with Bernini's family until 1729, when they were moved to the church.

➋ Palazzo di Propaganda Fide

Via di Propaganda 1. **Map** 5 A2. **Tel** 06-6987 9299. **Fax** 06-6988 0266. 🚌 116, 117. Ⓜ Spagna. Museum **Open** 2–6pm Mon, Wed, Fri.

The powerful Jesuit Congregation for the Propagation of the Faith was founded in 1622. Although Bernini had originally been commissioned to create their headquarters, Innocent X, who became pope in 1644, preferred the style of Borromini, who was asked to continue. His extraordinary west facade, completed in 1662, is striped with broad pilasters, between which the first-floor windows bend in, and the central bay bulges. A rigid band divides its floors, and the cornice above the convex central bay swerves inward. The more you look at it, the more restless it seems; a sign perhaps of the increasing unhappiness of the architect, who committed suicide in 1667. The building houses the Vatican's missionary museum.

Angel by Bernini, Sant'Andrea delle Fratte

Entrance to the Jesuit College

➌ Colonna dell'Immacolata

Piazza Mignanelli. **Map** 5 A2. 🚌 116, 117. Ⓜ Spagna.

Inaugurated in 1857, the column commemorates Pope Pius IX's proclamation of the doctrine of the Immaculate Conception, holding that the Virgin Mary was the only human being ever to have been born "without the stain of original sin." The column itself dates from ancient, pagan Rome but is crowned with a statue of the Virgin Mary.

On December 8, the Pope, assisted by the fire department, places a wreath around the head of the statue (*see p63*).

Portrait of Pope Pius IX (reigned 1846–78)

4 Via Condotti

Map 5 A2. 🚌 81, 116, 117, 119,
492 and many routes along via del
Corso or stopping at Piazza S. Silvestro.
Ⓜ Spagna. *See Shops and Markets
pp325–37.*

Named after the conduits that
carried water to the Baths of
Agrippa near the Pantheon, Via
Condotti is now home to the
most traditional of Rome's
designer clothes shops. Stores
selling shoes and other leather
goods are also well represented.
The street is extremely popular
for early evening strolls, when
elegant Italians mingle with
tourists in shorts and T-shirts.

Laura Biagiotti and the
Fendi sisters have shops on
the parallel Via Borgognona,
while Valentino and Giorgio
Armani both have shops on Via
Condotti itself. Valentino has a
second branch on Via Bocca di
Leone, which crosses Via
Condotti just below Piazza di
Spagna, and Versace also has a
shop here. Giorgio Armani has a
second store on nearby Via del
Babuino, among the discreet art
galleries, exclusive antique
shops, and furnishing stores.

Crowds strolling along the chic Via Condotti,
lined with designer clothes shops

5 Antico Caffè Greco

Via Condotti 86. **Map** 5 A2. **Tel** 06-67
91 700. 🚌 81, 116, 117, 119, 492.
Ⓜ Spagna. **Open** 9am–8pm daily.
Closed Jan 1, Aug 14 & 15. ♿

This café was opened by a
Greek (hence *greco*) in 1760,
and throughout the 18th
century it was a favorite

Antico Caffè Greco, over 240 years old

meeting place for foreign artists.
Writers such as Keats,
Byron, and Goethe and
composers like Liszt,
Wagner, and Bizet all
breakfasted and drank
here. So did Casanova,
and mad King Ludwig
of Bavaria. Today,
Italians stand in the
crowded foyer to sip a
quick espresso, and
foreigners sit in a cozy
back room whose
walls are studded with
portraits of the café's illustrious
customers.

Pope Urban VIII's arms, with
the Barberini bees

6 Piazza di Spagna

Map 5 A2. 🚌 116, 117, 119.
Ⓜ Spagna.

Shaped like a crooked bow
tie and surrounded by tall,
shuttered houses painted in
muted shades of ocher, cream,
and russet, Piazza di Spagna
(Spanish Square) is crowded all
day and (in summer) most of
the night. It is the most famous
square in Rome, and has long
been the haunt of foreign
visitors and expatriates.

In the 17th century, Spain's
ambassador to the Holy See had
his headquarters on the square,
and the area around it was
deemed to be Spanish territory.
Foreigners who unwittingly
trespassed were liable to be
dragooned into the Spanish
army. In the 18th and 19th
centuries, Rome was almost as
popular with visitors as it is

today, and the square stood at
the heart of the city's main
hotel district. Some of the
travelers came in search of
knowledge and artistic
inspiration, but most were
more interested in gambling,
collecting ancient statues, and
conducting love affairs with
Italian women.

Not surprisingly, the wealthy
travelers attracted hordes of
beggars, who were usually
supplied with tear-jerking letters
by scribes who worked in
the square.

The Fontana della Barcaccia in
the square is the least showy
of Rome's Baroque fountains,
and it is often completely
screened from
view by people
resting on its
rim. It was
designed either
by the famous
Gian Lorenzo
Bernini or by
his father Pietro.
Because the
pressure from
the aqueduct
that feeds the
fountain is
extremely low, there are no
spectacular cascades or spurts
of water. Instead, Bernini
constructed a leaking boat –
barcaccia means useless, old
boat – that lies half submerged
in a shallow pool.

The bees and suns that
decorate the Fontana della
Barcaccia are taken from the
family coat of arms of Pope
Urban VIII Barberini, who
commissioned the fountain.

The Fontana della Barcaccia at the foot
of the Spanish Steps

Bust of Shelley by Moses Ezekiel

● Keats-Shelley Memorial House

Piazza di Spagna 26. **Map** 5 A2. **Tel** 06-678 4235. 🚌 116, 117, 119. Ⓜ Spagna. **Open** 10am–1pm, 2–6pm Mon–Fri; 11am–2pm, 3–6pm Sat. **Closed** Dec 8, Dec 24–Jan 1. 🎫 📷 book in advance. 🏠 Ⓦ **keats-shelley-house.org**

In November 1820 the English poet John Keats came to stay with his friend, the painter Joseph Severn, in a dusty pink house, the Casina Rossa, on the corner of the Spanish Steps. Suffering from consumption, Keats had been sent to Rome by his doctor, in the hope that the mild, dry climate would help the young man's recovery. Depressed because of scathing criticism of his work and tormented by his love for a young girl named Fanny Brawne, Keats died the following February at age 25.

His death inspired fellow poet Percy Bysshe Shelley to write the poem *Mourn not for Adonais*. In July 1822 Shelley himself was drowned in a boating accident in the Gulf of La Spezia off the coast of Liguria. Keats, Shelley, and Severn are all buried in Rome's Protestant Cemetery (*see p207*).

In 1906 the house was bought by an Anglo-American association and preserved as a memorial and library in honor of English Romantic poets. The relics include a lock of Keats's hair, some fragments of Shelley's bones in a tiny urn, and a garish carnival mask picked up by Lord Byron as a souvenir of a trip to Venice. You can visit the room where Keats died, though all the original furniture was burned after his death, on papal orders.

● Babington's Tea Rooms

Piazza di Spagna 23. **Map** 5 A2. **Tel** 06-678 6027. 🚌 116, 117, 119. Ⓜ Spagna. **Open** 10am–9:30pm daily. **Closed** Dec 25. ♿

These august, old-fashioned tea rooms were opened in 1896 by two Englishwomen, Anna Maria and Isabel Cargill Babington, to serve homesick British tourists with scones, jam, and pots of Earl Grey tea. The food remains homey – shepherd's pie and chicken supreme for lunch, muffins and cinnamon toast for tea – although these days the menu offers pancakes with maple syrup for breakfast as well as the traditional bacon and eggs.

Purveyors of English breakfasts to homesick exiles since 1896

● Spanish Steps

Scalinata della Trinità dei Monti, Piazza di Spagna. **Map** 5 A2. 🚌 116, 117, 119. Ⓜ Spagna.

In the 17th century the French owners of Trinità dei Monti decided to link the church with Piazza di Spagna by building a magnificent new flight of steps. They also planned to place an equestrian statue of King Louis XIV at the top. Pope Alexander VII Chigi was not happy at the prospect of erecting a

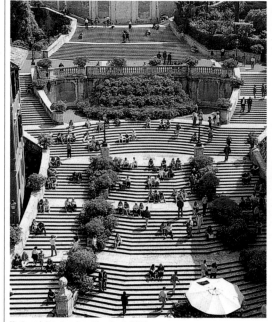

The Spanish Steps in spring with azaleas in full bloom

statue of a French monarch in the papal city, and the arguments continued until the 1720s, when an Italian architect, Francesco de Sanctis, produced a design that satisfied both parties. The steps, completed in 1726, combine straight sections, curves, and terraces to create one of the city's most dramatic and distinctive landmarks.

When the Victorian novelist Charles Dickens visited Rome, he reported that the Spanish Steps were the meeting place for artists' models, who would dress in colorful traditional costumes, hoping to catch the attention of a wealthy artist. The steps are now a popular place to sit, write postcards, take photos, flirt, busk, or watch the passers-by, but eating here is not allowed.

Trinità dei Monti's bell towers

❿ Trinità dei Monti

Piazza della Trinità dei Monti. **Map** 5 A2. **Tel** 06-679 4179. 🚌 116, 117, 119. Ⓜ Spagna. **Open** 6:30am–8pm Tue–Sun (to midnight Thu). 🚹

The views of Rome from the platform in front of the twin bell-towered facade of Trinità dei Monti are so beautiful that the church itself is often ignored. It is, however, unusual for Rome, for it was founded by the French in 1495, and although it was later badly damaged, there are still traces of attractive late Gothic latticework in the vaults of the transept. The interconnecting side chapels are decorated with Mannerist paintings, including two fine works by Daniele da Volterra.

19th-century engraving of the inner facade of the Villa Medici

A pupil of Michelangelo, Volterra had to paint clothes on the nudes in the *Last Judgment* in the Sistine Chapel in response to the objections of Pope Pius IV.

Michelangelo's influence is obvious in the powerfully muscled bodies shown in the *Deposition* (second chapel on the left). The circles of gesturing figures and dancing angels surrounding the Virgin Mary in the *Assumption* (third chapel on the right) have more in common with the graceful style of Raphael.

⓫ Villa Medici

Accademia di Francia a Roma, Viale Trinità dei Monti 1. **Map** 5 A2. **Tel** 06-676 11. 🚌 117, 119. Ⓜ Spagna. **Open** for exhibitions, and concerts. Gardens: **Open** Tue–Sun (four to six guided visits daily; in English at noon). 🅿️ 🎫 🖥️ 🔳 villamedici.it

Superbly positioned on the Pincio hill above Piazza di Spagna, this 16th-century villa has kept the name it assumed when Cardinal Ferdinando de' Medici bought it in 1576. From the terrace you can look across the city to Castel Sant'Angelo, from where Queen Christina of Sweden is said to have fired the large cannonball that now sits in the basin of the fountain.

The villa is home to the French Academy. This was founded by Louis XIV in 1666 to give a few select painters the chance to study in Rome. Nicolas Poussin

was one of the first advisers to the Academy, Ingres was a director and ex-students include Jean-Honoré Fragonard and François Boucher.

After 1803, when the French Academy moved to the Villa Medici, musicians were also admitted; both Berlioz and Debussy came to Rome as students of the Academy.

⓬ All Saints

Via del Babuino 153B. **Map** 4 F2. **Tel** 06-3600 1881. 🚌 117, 119. **Open** 8am–4pm daily. 🚹

In 1816 the Pope gave English residents, and visitors the right to hold Anglican services in Rome, but it wasn't until the early 1880s that they acquired a site to build their own church. The architect was G. E. Street, best known in Britain for his Neo-Gothic churches, and the London Law Courts. All Saints is also built in Victorian Neo-Gothic, and the interior, though splendidly decorated with different colored Italian marbles, has a very English air. Street also designed St. Paul's-within-the-Walls in Via Nazionale, whose interior is a jewel of British Pre-Raphaelite art.

The street on which All Saints stands got its name from the statue on Fontana del Sileno, known as Babuino (baboon) due to the sad condition in which it was found.

Fontana del Sileno, on Via del Babuino since 1957

⑬ Casa di Goethe

Via del Corso 18. **Map** 4 F1. **Tel** 06-3265 0412. 🚌 117, 119, 490, 495, 628, 926. 🚋 2. Ⓜ Flaminio. **Open** 10am–6pm Tue–Sun. 🅿️ ♿ 🎥 📷
w casadigoethe.it

The German poet, dramatist, and novelist Johann Wolfgang von Goethe (1749–1832) lived in this house from 1786 until 1788 and worked on a journal that eventually formed part of his travel book *The Italian Journey*. Rome's noisy street life irritated him, especially during Carnival time. He was a little perturbed by the number of murders in his neighborhood, but Rome energized him and his book became one of the most influential ever written about Italy.

⑭ Santa Maria dei Miracoli and Santa Maria in Montesanto

Piazza del Popolo. **Map** 4 F1.
🚌 117, 119, 490, 495, 628, 926.
🚋 2. Ⓜ Flaminio. Santa Maria dei Miracoli: **Tel** 06-361 0250. **Open** 7am–12:30pm, 4–7:30pm daily. 🔔
♿ Santa Maria in Montesanto: **Tel** 06-361 0594. **Open** 7am–8pm Mon–Fri, 10:30am–1:30pm Sun.

The two churches at the south end of Piazza del Popolo were designed by the architect Carlo Rainaldi (1611–91), proof that he could be as ingenious as his peers, Bernini and Borromini. To provide a focal point for the piazza, the churches had to appear symmetrical, but the site on the left was narrower. So Rainaldi gave

Portrait of Goethe in the Roman countryside by Tischbein (1751–1821)

Santa Maria dei Miracoli (on the right) a circular dome and Santa Maria in Montesanto an oval one to squeeze it into the narrower site, while keeping the sides of the supporting drums that face the piazza identical.

⑮ Pincio Gardens

Il Pincio. **Map** 4 F1. 🚌 117, 119, 490, 495, 628, 926. 🚋 2. Ⓜ Flaminio.

The Pincio Gardens lie above Piazza del Popolo on a hillside that has been so skillfully terraced, and richly planted with trees that, from below, the zig-zagging road climbing to the gardens is virtually invisible. In ancient Roman times, there were magnificent gardens on the Pincio hill, but the present gardens were designed in the early 19th century by Giuseppe Valadier (who also redesigned the Piazza del Popolo). The broad avenues, lined with umbrella pines, palm trees, and evergreen oaks,

The Pincio Gardens water clock

soon became a fashionable place to stroll, and even in the 20th century such diverse characters as Gandhi and Mussolini, Richard Strauss and King Farouk of Egypt patronized the Casina Valadier, an exclusive café, and restaurant in the grounds.

From the Pincio's main square, Piazzale Napoleone I, the panoramic views of Rome stretch from the Monte Mario to the Janiculum. For full effect, approach the gardens from the grounds of Villa Borghese *(see pp260–61)* above the Pincio, or along Viale della Trinità dei Monti. The panorama is particularly beautiful at sunset,

The twin churches of Santa Maria in Montesanto (left) and Santa Maria dei Miracoli in a 19th-century view of Piazza del Popolo he traditional time for tourists to take a stroll in the gardens.

One of the most striking eatures of the park itself is an gyptian-style obelisk that mperor Hadrian erected on he tomb of his favorite, the peautiful male slave Antinous. After the slave's premature death according to some accounts, he died saving the emperor's life), Hadrian deified him.

The 19th-century water clock on Via dell'Orologio was designed by a Dominican monk. t was displayed at the Paris Exhibition of 1889.

The Casina Valadier restaurant in the Pincio Gardens

⑯ Piazza del Popolo

Map 4 F1. 🚌 117, 119, 490, 495, 926. 🚃 2. Ⓜ Flaminio.

A vast cobbled oval standing at the apex of the triangle of roads known as the Trident, Piazza del Popolo forms a grand symmetrical antechamber to the heart of Rome. Twin Neo-Classical facades stand on either side of the Porta del Popolo; an Egyptian obelisk rises in the center; and the matching domes and porticoes of Santa Maria dei Miracoli and Santa Maria in Montesanto flank the beginning of Via del Corso.

Although it is now one of the most unified squares in Rome, Piazza del Popolo evolved gradually over the centuries. In 1589 the great town-planning pope, Sixtus V, had the obelisk erected in the center by Domenico Fontana. Over 3,000

Traditional carnival band in Piazza del Popolo

years old, the obelisk was originally brought to Rome by Augustus to adorn the Circus Maximus after the conquest of Egypt. Almost a century later, Pope Alexander VII commissioned Carlo Rainaldi to build the twin Santa Marias.

In the 19th century the piazza was turned into a grandiose oval by Giuseppe Valadier, the designer of the Pincio Gardens. He also encased Santa Maria del Popolo in a Neo-Classical shell to make its south facade fit in better with the overall appearance of the piazza.

In contrast to the piazza's air of ordered rationalism, many of the events staged here were barbaric. In the 18th and 19th centuries, public executions were held in Piazza del Popolo, often as part of the celebration of Carnival. Condemned men were sometimes hammered to death by repeated blows to the temples. The last time a criminal was executed in this way was in 1826, even though the guillotine had by then been adopted as a more efficient means of execution.

The riderless horse races from the piazza down Via del Corso were scarcely more humane: the performance of the runners was enhanced by feeding the horses stimulants, wrapping them in nail-studded ropes, and letting off fireworks at their heels.

⑰ Santa Maria del Popolo

See pp140–41.

⑱ Porta del Popolo

Between Piazzale Flaminio and Piazza del Popolo. **Map** 4 F1. 🚌 117, 119, 490, 495, 926. 🚃 2. Ⓜ Flaminio.

The Via Flaminia, built in 220 BC to connect Rome with Italy's Adriatic coast, enters the city at Porta del Popolo, a grand 16th-century gate built on the orders of Pope Pius IV Medici. The architect, Nanni di Baccio Bigio, modeled it on a Roman triumphal arch. The outer face has statues of St. Peter and St. Paul on either side and a huge Medici coat of arms above.

A century later, Pope Alexander VII commissioned Bernini to decorate the inner face to celebrate the arrival in Rome of Queen Christina of Sweden. Lesser visitors were often held up while customs officers rifled through their luggage. The only way to speed things up was with a bribe.

Porta del Popolo's central arch

⓱ Santa Maria del Popolo

One of Rome's greatest stores of artistic treasures, this early Renaissance church was commissioned by Pope Sixtus IV della Rovere in 1472. Among the artists who worked on the building were Andrea Bregno, and Pinturicchio. Later additions were made by Bramante and Bernini. Many illustrious families have chapels here, all decorated with appropriate splendor. The Della Rovere Chapel has delightful Pinturicchio frescoes, the Cerasi Chapel has two Caravaggio masterpieces, *The Conversion of St. Paul*, and *The Crucifixion of St. Peter*, but the finest of all is the Chigi Chapel designed by Raphael for his patron, the banker Agostino Chigi. The most striking of the church's many Renaissance tombs are the two by Andrea Sansovino behind the main altar.

★ Chigi Chapel
Raphael designed this chapel, which has an altarpiece by Sebastiano del Piombo. Niches on either side of the altar house sculptures by Bernini and Lorenzetto. Mosaics in the dome show God as creator of the seven heavenly bodies.

Kneeling Skeleton
This floor mosaic of the figure of death was added to the Chigi Chapel in the 17th century.

Entrance

KEY

① **Cybo Chapel**

② **The Tomb** of Giovanni della Rovere (1483) is by pupils of Andrea Bregno.

③ **The altarpiece** of *The Assumption* is by Annibale Carracci (1540–1609).

④ **The altar** houses the 13th-century painting known as the *Madonna del Popolo*.

⑤ **The Tomb** of Ascanio Sforza, who died in 1505, is by Andrea Sansovino.

Della Rovere Chapel
Pinturicchio painted the frescoes in the lunettes and the Nativity above the altar in 1490.

★ Caravaggio Paintings in Cerasi Chapel

One of two Caravaggios in the Cerasi Chapel, *The Crucifixion of St. Peter* uses dramatic foreshortening to highlight the sheer effort involved in turning the saint's crucifix upside down.

VISITORS' CHECKLIST

Practical Information
Piazza del Popolo 12.
Map 4 F1.
Tel 06-361 0836. **M** Flaminio.
Open 7am–noon, 4–7pm Mon–Sat; 7:30am–1:30pm, 4:30–7:30pm Sun. 🕇 ⚅

Transportation
🚌 117, 119, 490, 495, 926.
🚋 2.

Stained Glass
In 1509 French artist Guillaume de Marcillat was invited to provide Rome's first two stained-glass windows.

★ Delphic Sibyl

This is one of a series of frescoes by Pinturicchio, some Classical and others Biblical, painted in 1508–10 to decorate the ceiling of the apse.

Nero's Ghost

Nero lived on in the imagination of the people long after the fall of the Roman Empire. In the Middle Ages a legend arose that a walnut tree growing here on the spot where his ashes were buried was haunted by the emperor. Ravens roosting in the tree were thought to be demons tormenting him for his hideous crimes. When the first church was built here in 1099 by Pope Paschal II, the tree was cut down, supposedly putting an end to the supernatural events that had terrified local people.

1213–27 Church enlarged under Gregory IX

Pinturicchio (c. 1454–1513)

1485–9 Della Rovere Chapel painted by Pinturicchio

1513–16 Raphael designs, and executes Chigi Chapel

1050	1200	1350	1500

1099 Paschal II builds chapel over tombs of the Domitia family (which included Nero) in honor of the Madonna

Pope Paschal II (reigned 1099–1118)

1472–8 Sixtus IV builds church (one of the first Renaissance churches in Rome)

1473 Main altar built

1530–34 Chigi Chapel altarpiece built by Sebastiano del Piombo

🕦 Ara Pacis

Lungotevere in Augusta. **Map** 4 F2.
Tel 06-0608. 🚌 70, 81, 117, 119, 186,
628. **Open** 9am–7pm Tue–Sun (last
adm: 6pm). **Closed** Jan 1, Dec 25. 🔊
🔳 🏠 🕸 **arapacis.it**

Reconstructed at considerable
expense over many years, the
Ara Pacis (Altar of Peace) is
one of the most significant
monuments of ancient Rome. It
celebrates the peace created
throughout the Mediterranean
area by Emperor Augustus after
his victorious campaigns in Gaul
and Spain. The monument was
commissioned by the Senate in
13 BC and completed four years
later. It was positioned so that
the shadow of the huge obelisk
sundial on Campus Martius
(see p117) would fall upon it on
Augustus's birthday. It is a

Frieze on south wall showing procession with the family of Augustus

square enclosure on a low
platform with the altar in the
center. All surfaces are
decorated with magnificent
friezes, and reliefs carved in
Carrara marble. The reliefs
on the north and south walls
depict a procession that took
place on July 4, 13 BC, in which
the members of the emperor's
family can be identified, ranked
by their position in the
succession. At the time the heir
apparent was Marcus Agrippa,
husband of Augustus's
daughter Julia. All the portraits
in the relief are carved with
extraordinary realism, even

the innocent toddler clinging
to his mother's skirts.
   The tale of the rediscovery of
the Ara Pacis dates back to the
16th century, when the first
panels were unearthed. One
section ended up in Paris,
another in Florence. Further
discoveries were made in
the late 19th century, when
archaeologists finally realized
just what they had found. What
we see today has all been
pieced together since 1938, in
part original, in part facsimile. In
1999 the architect Richard Meier
designed a building to house
the monument.

Marcus Agrippa (right)

The altar was used once
a year for a sacrifice on
the anniversary of the
monument's
inauguration.

Augustus's young
grandson, Lucius

East wall

South wall

West wall

North wall

An acanthus frieze
runs around the
lower half of the
outside wall.

⓴ Mausoleum of Augustus

Piazza Augusto Imperatore. **Map** 4 F2. **Tel** 06-0608. 🚌 81, 117, 492, 628, 926. **Closed** for restoration.

Now just a weedy mound ringed with cypresses, and sadly strewn with litter, this was once the most prestigious burial place in Rome. Augustus had the mausoleum built in 28 BC, the year he became sole ruler, as a tomb for himself and his descendants. The circular building was 285 ft (87 m) in diameter with two obelisks (now in Piazza del Quirinale and Piazza dell'Esquilino) at the entrance.

Inside were four concentric passageways linked by corridors where the urns containing the ashes of the Imperial family were placed. The first to be buried here was Augustus's favorite nephew, Marcellus, who had married Julia, the emperor's daughter. He died in 23 BC, possibly poisoned by Augustus's second wife Livia, who felt that her son, Tiberius, would make a more reliable emperor. When Augustus died in AD 14, his ashes were placed in the mausoleum, Tiberius duly became emperor, and dynastic poisonings continued to fill the family vault with urns.

This sinister monument was later used as a medieval fortress, a vineyard, a private garden, and even, in the 18th century, as an auditorium and theater.

Augustus, the first Roman emperor

Madonna, San Rocco, and Sant'Antonio with Victims of the Plague by Il Baciccia (1639–1709)

㉑ San Rocco

Largo San Rocco 1. **Map** 4 F2. **Tel** 06-689 6416. 🚌 81, 117, 492, 628, 926. **Open** 7:30–9:15am, 4:30–8pm Mon–Sat; 8:30am–1pm, 4:30–8pm Sun. **Closed** Aug 17–31. 🕆

This church, with a restrained Neo-Classical facade by Giuseppe Valadier, the designer of Piazza del Popolo, began life as the chapel of a 16th-century hospital with beds for 50 men – San Rocco was a healer of the plague-stricken. A maternity wing was added for the wives of Tiber bargees to save them from having to give birth in the unsanitary conditions of a boat. The hospital came to be used by unmarried mothers, and one section was set aside for women who wished to conceal their identities. They were even permitted to wear a veil for the duration of their stay. Unwanted children were sent to an orphanage, and if any mothers or children died, they were buried in anonymous graves. The hospital was abandoned in the early 20th century, and demolished in the 1930s during the excavation of the Mausoleum of Augustus.

The church sacristy is an interesting Baroque altarpiece (c. 1660) by Il Baciccia, the artist who decorated the ceiling of the Gesù (see pp110–11).

㉒ Santi Ambrogio e Carlo al Corso

Via del Corso 437. **Map** 4 F2. **Tel** 06-682 8101. 🚌 81, 117, 492, 628, 926. **Open** 7am–7pm daily. 📷

This church belonged to the Lombard community in Rome, and is dedicated to two canonized bishops of Milan, Lombardy's capital. In 1471, Pope Sixtus IV gave the Lombards a church, which they dedicated to Sant'Ambrogio, who died in 397. Then, in 1610, when Carlo Borromeo was canonized, the church was rebuilt in his honor. Most of the new church was the work of father and son Onorio and Martino Longhi, but the fine dome is by Pietro da Cortona. The altarpiece by Carlo Maratta (1625–1713) is the *Gloria dei Santi Ambrogio e Carlo*. An ambulatory leads behind the altar to a chapel housing the the heart of San Carlo in a richly decorated reliquary.

Statue of San Carlo by Attilio Selva (1888–1970) behind the apse of Santi Ambrogio e Carlo

CAMPO DE' FIORI

Between Corso Vittorio Emanuele II, and the Tiber, the city displays many distinct personalities. The open-air market of Campo de' Fiori preserves the lively, bohemian atmosphere of the medieval inns that once flourished here, while the area also contains Renaissance palazzi, such as Palazzo Farnese, and Palazzo Spada, where powerful Roman families built their fortress-like houses near the route of papal processions. Close by, overlooking the picturesque Tiber Island, lies the former Jewish Ghetto, where many traces of daily life from past centuries can still be seen. The Portico of Octavia and the Theater of Marcellus are spectacular examples of the city's many-layered history, built up over the half-ruined remains of ancient Rome.

Sights at a Glance

Churches and Temples
5 Santissima Trinità dei Pellegrini
7 Santa Maria dell'Orazione e Morte
9 San Girolamo della Carità
10 Sant'Eligio degli Orefici
11 Santa Maria in Monserrato
18 San Carlo ai Catinari
20 Santa Maria in Campitelli
21 San Nicola in Carcere
29 San Giovanni dei Fiorentini

Museums and Galleries
6 Palazzo Spada
14 Piccola Farnesina
15 Burcardo Theatre Museum

Historic Buildings
2 Palazzo Pio Righetti
3 Palazzo del Monte di Pietà
8 Palazzo Farnese
12 Palazzo Ricci
13 Palazzo della Cancelleria
25 Casa di Lorenzo Manilio
26 Palazzo Cenci

Fountains
19 Fontana delle Tartarughe

Historic Streets and Piazzas
1 Campo de' Fiori
24 Ghetto and Synagogue
27 Tiber Island
28 Via Giulia

Famous Theaters
16 Teatro Argentina

Ancient Sites
4 Sotterranei di San Paolo alla Regola
17 Area Sacra dell'Argentina
22 Theater of Marcellus
23 Portico of Octavia

Restaurants
see pp311–15
1 Acchiappafantasmi
2 Angolo Divino
3 Al Bric
4 Ba'Ghetto Milky
5 Camponeschi
6 Da Pancrazio
7 Enoteca il Goccetto
8 Giggetto
9 Il Sanlorenzo
10 Nonna Betta
11 Open Baladin
12 Pagliaccio
13 Percento
14 Pierluigi
15 Piperno
16 Polese
17 Roscioli
18 Settimio al Pellegrino
19 Sora Lella
20 Sora Margherita
21 Vinando
22 Vino e Camino

See also Street Finder maps 4, 8, 11, 12

0 meters 300
0 yards 300

◀ Theater of Marcellus

For map symbols see back flap

Street by Street: Campo de' Fiori

This fascinating part of Renaissance Rome is also an exciting area for shopping and nightlife, centered on the market square of Campo de' Fiori. Its stands supply many nearby restaurants, and young people shop for clothes in Via dei Giubbonari. Popular restaurants keep the area alive late into the night, when overcrowding and drunks can become problems. By day there are great buildings to admire, though few are open to the public. Two exceptions are the Piccola Farnesina, with its collection of Classical statues, and Palazzo Spada, home to many important paintings.

🔟 **Sant'Eligio degli Orefici**
A small Renaissance church designed by Raphael is concealed behind a later facade.

⓬ **Palazzo Ricci**
Painted Classical scenes were a favorite form of decoration for the facades of Renaissance houses.

9️⃣ **San Girolamo della Carità**
The chief attraction of this church is Borromini's fabulous Spada Chapel.

⓫ **Santa Maria in Monserrato**
This church, which has strong connections with Spain, houses a Bernini bust of Cardinal Pedro Foix de Montoya.

8️⃣ **Palazzo Farnese**
Michelangelo and other great artists helped create this monumental Renaissance palazzo.

Key

— Suggested route

0 meters	75
0 yards	75

7️⃣ **Santa Maria dell'Orazione e Morte**
A pair of dramatic winged skulls flank the doorway to this church dedicated to the burial of the dead.

❶ ★ Campo de' Fiori
This colourful market makes Piazza Campo de' Fiori one of Rome's most entertaining squares.

Locator Map
See Central Rome Map pp16–17

⓭ Palazzo della Cancelleria
The papal administration ran the affairs of the Church from this vast building.

⓮ Piccola Farnesina
This plaque honors Giovanni Barracco. His sculpture collection is housed in the palazzo.

❷ Palazzo Pio Righetti
Heraldic eagles stare down from the pediments of the palazzo's windows.

❻ ★ Palazzo Spada
The picture gallery houses a collection started by two wonderfully eccentric 17th-century cardinals.

❺ Santissima Trinità dei Pellegrini
The principal role of this church was one of charity, caring for poor pilgrims arriving in Rome.

❹ Sotterranei di San Paolo alla Regola
Remains of a Roman house have survived in the basement of an old palace.

❸ Palazzo del Monte di Pietà
This was a papal institution, where the poor pawned their possessions in order to borrow small sums of money.

❶ Campo de' Fiori

Piazza Campo de' Fiori. **Map** 4 E4 & 11 C4. 🚌 116 and routes to Largo di Torre Argentina or Corso Vittorio Emanuele II. *See Markets p344.*

The Campo de' Fiori (field of flowers), once a meadow, occupies the site of the open space facing the Theater of Pompey. Cardinals and noblemen used to rub shoulders with fishmongers and foreigners in the piazza's market, making it one of the liveliest areas of medieval and Renaissance Rome. Today's market retains much of the traditional lively atmosphere.

In the center of the square is a statue of the philosopher Giordano Bruno, burned at the stake for heresy here in 1600. The hooded figure is a grim reminder of the executions that were held here.

The piazza was surrounded by inns for pilgrims and other travelers. Many of these were once owned by the successful 15th-century courtesan Vannozza Catanei, mistress of Pope Alexander VI Borgia. On the corner between the piazza and Via del Pellegrino you can see Catanei's shield, which she had decorated with her own coat of arms and those of her husband, and her lover, the Borgia pope.

❷ Palazzo Pio Righetti

Piazza del Biscione 89. **Map** 4 E5 & 11 C4. 🚌 116 and routes to Largo Torre Argentina or Corso Vittorio Emanuele II. **Closed** to the public.

The vast 17th-century Palazzo Pio Righetti was built over the ruined Theater of Pompey. The windows of the palazzo are decorated with lions and pine cones from the coat of arms of the Pio da Carpi family, who lived here.

The curve of the Theater of Pompey, completed in 55 BC, is followed by Via di Grotta Pinta. Rome's first permanent theater was built of stone and concrete, and in the basement of the Pancrazio restaurant you can see early examples of *opus*

Window pediment with heraldic lion and pine cones, Palazzo Pio Righetti

reticulatum – small square blocks of tufa (porous rock) set diagonally as a facing for a concrete wall.

❸ Palazzo del Monte di Pietà

Piazza del Monte di Pietà 33. **Map** 4 E5 & 11 C4. **Tel** 06-8782 0112. 🚌 116 and routes to Largo di Torre Argentina or Corso Vittorio Emanuele II. 🚋 8. Chapel: **Open** by appt. Call ahead.

The Monte, as it is known, is a public institution, founded in 1539 by Pope Paul III Farnese as a pawn shop to staunch the usury then rampant in the city. The building still has offices and auction rooms for the sale of unclaimed goods. The stars with diagonal bands on the huge central plaque decorating the facade are the coat of arms of Pope Clement VIII Aldobrandini, added when Carlo Maderno enlarged the palace in the 17th century. The clock on the left was added later.

Within, the chapel is a jewel of Baroque architecture, adorned with gilded stucco, marble paneling, and reliefs. The decoration makes a perfect setting for the sculptures by Domenico Guidi – a bust of San Carlo Borromeo and a relief of the *Pietà*. There are also splendid reliefs by Giovanni Battista Théudon and Pierre Legros of biblical scenes illustrating the charitable nature of the institution.

❹ Sotterranei di San Paolo alla Regola

Via di San Paolo alla Regola. **Map** 11 C5. **Tel** 06-0608. 🚌 23, 116, 280 and routes to Largo di Torre Argentina. 🚋 8. **Open** by appt only, with permit.

An old palace hides the perfectly conserved remains of an ancient Roman house, dating from the 2nd–3rd centuries. Restoration works are being

Relief by Théudon of *Joseph Distributing Grain to the Egyptians* in Palazzo del Monte di Pietà

carried out in order to open this site to the public, but at present it is only possible to visit by special arrangement.

A ramp leads down well below today's street level, to reveal the locations of shops of the time. One level above is the Stanza della Colonna, at one time an open courtyard, with traces of frescoes and mosaics on its walls.

Guido Reni's *Holy Trinity*, in Santissima Trinità dei Pellegrini

❺ Santissima Trinità dei Pellegrini

Via dei Pettinari 36A. **Map** 4 E5 & 11 C5. **Tel** 06-686 8451. 23, 116, 280 and routes to Largo di Torre Argentina. 8. **Open** 4–8pm Mon–Sat; 8am–1pm, 4–8pm Sun.

The church was donated in the 16th century to a charitable organization founded by San Filippo Neri to care for the poor and sick, in particular the thousands of paupers who flocked in pilgrimage to Rome during the special holy years known as Jubilees. The 18th-century facade has niches with statues of the Evangelists by Bernardino Ludovisi. The interior, with Corinthian columns, ends in a horseshoe vault and apse, dominated by Guido Reni's striking altarpiece of the Holy Trinity (1625). The frescoes in the lantern are also by Reni. Other interesting paintings include *St. Gregory the Great Freeing Souls from Purgatory*, by Baldassarre Croce (third chapel to the left); Cavalier d'Arpino's *Virgin and*

Saints (second chapel to the left); and a painting by Borgognone (1677) of the Virgin and recently canonized saints, including San Filippo Neri. In the sacristy are depictions of the nobility washing the feet of pilgrims, a custom started by San Filippo.

❻ Palazzo Spada

Piazza Capo di Ferro 13. **Map** 2 F5. **Tel** 06-686 1158 (Palazzo) or 06-683 2409 (Galleria). 23, 116, 280 and routes to Largo di Torre Argentina. 8. Galleria Spada: **Open** 8:30am–7:30pm Tue–Sun (last adm: 7pm). **Closed** Jan 1, Dec 25.

This majestic palazzo, built around 1550 for Cardinal Capo di Ferro, has an elegant stuccoed courtyard and facade decorated with reliefs evoking Rome's glorious past.

Cardinal Bernardino Spada, who lived here in the 17th century with his brother Virginio (also a cardinal), hired architects Bernini and Borromini to work on the building. The brothers' whimsical delight in false perspectives resulted in a colonnaded gallery by Borromini that appears four times longer than it really is.

The cardinals also amassed a superb private collection of paintings, which is now on display in the Galleria Spada. The collection features a wide range of artists, including Rubens, Dürer, and Guido Reni. The most important works on display include *The Visitation* by Andrea del Sarto (1486–1530), *Cain and Abel* by Giovanni Lanfranco (1582–1647), and *The Death of Dido* by Guercino (1591–1666).

❼ Santa Maria dell'Orazione e Morte

Via Giulia 262. **Map** 4 E5 & 11 B4. **Tel** 339-3484 378. 23, 116, 280. **Open** 10am–12.15pm, 4–6.30pm Mon–Fri; 4–6:30pm Sat; 10am–12:30pm, 4–7pm Sun.

A pious confraternity was formed here in the 16th century to collect the bodies of the

Offertory box in Santa Maria dell'Orazione e Morte

unknown dead and give them a Christian burial. The theme of death is stressed in this church, dedicated to St. Mary of Prayer and Death. The doors and windows of Ferdinando Fuga's dramatic Baroque facade are decorated with winged skulls. Above the central entrance there is a *clepsydra* (an ancient hourglass) – symbolic of death.

❽ Palazzo Farnese

Piazza Farnese. **Map** 4 E5 & 11 B4. 23, 116, 280 and routes to Corso Vittorio Emanuele II. **Open** for guided tours only (3, 4 & 5pm Mon, Wed & Fri).

The prototype for numerous princely palaces, the imposing Palazzo Farnese was originally built for Cardinal Alessandro Farnese (who became Pope Paul III in 1534). He commissioned the greatest artists to work on it, starting with Antonio da Sangallo the Younger as architect in 1517. Michelangelo, who took over after him, contributed the great cornice and central window of the main facade, and the third level of the courtyard.

Michelangelo had a plan for the Farnese gardens to be connected by a bridge to the Farnese home in Trastevere, Villa Farnesina *(see pp220–21)*. The elegant arch spanning Via Giulia belongs to this unrealized scheme. The palazzo was completed in 1589, on a less ambitious scale, by Giacomo della Porta. It is now the home of the French Embassy, which moved in as early as 1635.

Spada Chapel in San Girolamo

❾ San Girolamo della Carità

Via di Monserrato 62A. **Map** 4 E5 & 11 B4. **Tel** 06-687 9786. 🚌 23, 40, 46, 62, 64, 116, 280. **Open** 10:30am–12:30pm Sun & public hols. 🔟

The church was built on a site incorporating the home of San Filippo Neri, the 16th-century saint from Tuscany who renewed Rome's spiritual and cultural life by his friendly, open approach to religion. He would have loved the frolicking putti shown surrounding his statue, in his chapel, reminding him of the Roman urchins he had cared for during his lifetime.

The breathtaking Spada Chapel was designed by Borromini, and is unique both as a work of art and as an illustration of the spirit of the Baroque age. All architectural elements are concealed so that the space of the chapel's interior is defined solely by decorative marblework and statues. Veined jasper and precious multicolored marbles are sculpted to imitate flowery damask and velvet hangings. Even the altar rail is a long swag of jasper drapery held up by a pair of kneeling angels with wooden wings.

Although there are memorials to former members of the Spada family, oddly, there is no indication as to which of the Spadas was responsible for endowing the chapel. It was probably art-lover Virgilio Spada, a follower of San Filippo Neri.

❿ Sant'Eligio degli Orefici

Via di Sant'Eligio 8A. **Map** 4 D4 & 11 B4. **Tel** 06-686 8260. 🚌 23, 40, 46, 62, 64, 116, 280. **Open** 9:30am–1pm Mon–Fri (stop first at Via di Sant'Eligio 7). **Closed** Aug. 🔟

The name of the church still records the fact that it was commissioned by a rich corporation of goldsmiths (*orefici*) in the early 16th century. The original design was by Raphael, who, like his master Bramante, had acquired a sense of the grandiose from the remains of Roman antiquity. The influence of some of Bramante's works, such as the choir of Santa Maria del Popolo (*see pp140–41*), is evident in the simple way the arches and pilasters define the structure of the walls.

The cupola of Sant' Eligio is attributed to Baldassarre Peruzzi, while the facade was added in the early 17th century by Flaminio Ponzio. Among the various 16th-century painters who decorated the interior was Taddeo Zuccari, who worked on Palazzo Farnese (*see p149*).

Statue of San Filippo Neri by Pierre Legros

An early bust by Bernini of Cardinal Pedro Foix de Montoya

⓫ Santa Maria in Monserrato

Via di Monserrato. **Map** 4 E4 & 11 B3. **Tel** 06-686 5865. 🚌 23, 40, 46, 62, 64, 116, 280. **Open** 5–7pm Sat; 10am–1pm, 5–7pm Sun. To arrange a visit Mon–Fri, call 06-688 9651. 🔟

The origins of the Spanish national church in Rome go back to 1506, when a hospice for Spanish pilgrims was begun by a brotherhood of the Virgin of Montserrat in Catalonia. Inside is Annibale Carracci's painting *San Diego de Alcalà* and, in the third chapel on the left, a copy of a Sansovino statue of St. James. Some beautiful 15th-century tombs by Andrea Bregno and Luigi Capponi are in the courtyard and side chapels. Don't miss Bernini's bust of Pedro Foix de Montoya, the church's benefactor, in the annex.

San Diego by Annibale Carracci

⓬ Palazzo Ricci

Piazza de' Ricci. **Map** 4 D4 & 11 B4.
🚌 23, 40, 46, 62, 64, 116, 280, 870.
Closed to the public.

Palazzo Ricci was famous for its frescoed facade – now rather faded – originally painted in the 16th century by Polidoro da Caravaggio, a follower of Raphael.

In Renaissance Rome it was common to commission artists to decorate the outsides of houses with heroes of Classical antiquity. A fresco by a leading artist such as Polidoro, reputedly the inventor of this style of painting, was a conspicuous status symbol, in the nobility's attempts to outshine each other with their palazzi.

⓭ Palazzo della Cancelleria

Piazza della Cancelleria. **Map** 4 E4 & 11 C3. **Tel** 06-6988 7566. 🚌 40, 46, 62, 64, 70, 81, 87, 116, 492. **Open** 7:30am–2pm, 4–8pm Mon–Sat (Sala Riaria: Tue pm & Sat am).

The palazzo, a supreme example of the confident architecture of the Early Renaissance, was begun in 1485. It was financed partly with the gambling winnings of Cardinal Raffaele Riario. Roses, the emblem of the Riario family, adorn the vaults and capitals of the beautiful Doric courtyard. The palazzo's interior was decorated after the Sack of Rome in 1527. Giorgio Vasari boasted that he had completed work on one enormous room in just 100 days; Michelangelo allegedly retorted, "It looks like it." Other Mannerist artists, Perin del Vaga and Francesco Salviati, frescoed the rooms of the cardinal in charge of the Papal Chancellery, the office that gave the palazzo its name when it was installed here by Pope Leo X. On the right of the main entrance is the unobtrusive and rather quaint church of San Lorenzo in Damaso, founded by Pope Damasus (reigned 366–84). It was reconstructed in 1495, and although Bernini made

Courtyard of Palazzo della Cancelleria

alterations to the transept and apse in 1638, it was later restored to its 15th-century lines. Its porticoes housed libraries for the first Papal Archives.

⓮ Piccola Farnesina

Corso Vittorio Emanuele II 168.
Map 4 E4 & 11 C3. **Tel** 06-0608. 🚌 40, 46, 62, 64, 70, 81, 87, 116, 492. **Open** 9am–7pm Tue–Sun.
🌐 **museobarracco.it**

This delightful miniature palazzo acquired its name from the lilies decorating its cornices. These were mistakenly identified as part of the Farnese family crest. In fact they were part of the coat of arms of a French clergyman, Thomas Le Roy, for whom the palazzo was built in 1523.

The entrance is in a facade built to overlook Corso Vittorio Emanuele II when the road was

Inner courtyard, Piccola Farnesina

constructed at the start of the 20th century. The original facade on the left of today's entrance is attributed to Antonio da Sangallo the Younger. Note the asymmetrical arrangement of its windows and ledges. The elegant central courtyard also retains its original appearance. The Piccola Farnesina now houses the Museo Barracco, a collection of ancient sculpture assembled during the last century by the politician Baron Giovanni Barracco. A bust of the baron can be seen in the courtyard. The collection includes an ancient Egyptian relief of the scribe Nofer, some Assyrian artifacts, and, among the Etruscan exhibits, a delicate ceramic female head. On the first floor is the Greek collection with a head of Apollo.

⓯ Burcardo Theater Museum

Via del Sudario 44. **Map** 4 F4 & 12 D4. **Tel** 06-6819 471. 🚌 40, 46, 62, 64, 70, 81, 186, 492. 🚋 8. Museum: **Open** 9:15am–4:30pm Tue & Thu. **Closed** Aug. 📷 🌐 **burcardo.org**

This late-15th-century house once belonged to Johannes Burckhardt, chamberlain to Pope Alexander VI Borgia, and author of a diary of Rome under the Borgias. His house now holds Rome's most complete collection of theater literature, plus Chinese puppets and comic masks from the various regions of Italy.

Detail of facade, Teatro Argentina

⑯ Teatro Argentina

Largo di Torre Argentina 52. **Map** 4 F4
& 12 D4. **Tel** 06-684 000 311. 🚌 40, 46,
62, 64, 70, 81, 87, 186, 492, 810. 🚋 8.
Open 10am–2pm, 3–7pm Tue–Sat.
Plays performed Oct–Jun. *See Entertainment pp352–3*. 🆆 teatrodiroma.net

One of the city's most important
theaters was founded by the
powerful Sforza Cesarini family
in 1732, though the facade
dates from a century later. Many
famous operas, including those
of Verdi, were first performed
here. In 1816, the theater saw
the ill-fated debut of Rossini's
Barber of Seville, during which
the composer insulted the
unappreciative audience, who
then pursued him, enraged,
through the streets of Rome.

⑰ Area Sacra dell'Argentina

Largo di Torre Argentina. **Map** 4 F4 &
12 D4. 🚌 40, 46, 62, 64, 70, 81, 87,
186, 492, 810. 🚋 8. **Open** by appt
only (call 06-0608).

The remains of four temples
were discovered here in
the 1920s. Dating from the
Republican era, they are among
the oldest in Rome. They are
known as A, B, C, and D. The
oldest (temple C) dates from the
early 3rd century BC. It was
placed on a high platform
preceded by an altar and is
typical of Italic plans. Temple A is
from later in the 3rd century BC.
In medieval times the church of
San Nicola de' Cesarini was built
over its podium: remains of its
two apses are still visible. The
north column stumps belonged
to a great portico, the Hecato-
stylum (portico of 100 columns).

In Imperial times two marble
lavatories were built here – the
remains of one is visible behind
temple A. Behind temples B
and C are remains of a great
platform of tufa blocks
identified as part of the Curia
of Pompey – a rectangular
building with a statue of
Pompey. It was here that the
Senate met and Julius Caesar
was murdered on March 15, 44
BC. At the southwest corner of
the site is a cat sanctuary, home
to Rome's abandoned felines
(open afternoons).

⑱ San Carlo ai Catinari

Piazza B Cairoli. **Map** 4 F5 & 12 D4.
Tel 06-6880 3554. 🚌 see Area Sacra.
🚋 8. **Open** 4–7pm daily, also
7:30am–noon Mon–Sat & 9.30am–
m12.30pm Sun. ✝ No visits during
services.

In 1620, Rome's Milanese
congregation decided to honor
Cardinal Carlo Borromeo with
this great church. It was called
"ai Catinari" on account of the

San Carlo at Prayer by Guido Reni

bowl-makers' *(catinari)* shops
in the area. The solemn
travertine facade was
completed in 1638 by the
Roman architect Soria. The
16th-century basilican plan
is flanked by chapels. The
St. Cecilia chapel was designed
and decorated by Antonio
Gherardi, who added a family
portrait. The church's paintings
and frescoes by Pietro da
Cortona and Guido Reni are
mature works of the Counter-
Reformation, depicting the life
and acts of the recently
canonized San Carlo.

The ornate crucifix on
the sacristy altar, inlaid with
marble and mother-of-pearl,
is by the 16th-century
sculptor Algardi.

Sacristy altar, San Carlo ai Catinari

⑲ Fontana delle Tartarughe

Piazza Mattei. **Map** 4 F5 & 12 D4.
🚌 46, 62, 63, 64, 70, 87, 186, 492,
810. 🚋 8.

The delightful Fontana delle
Tartarughe (*tartarughe* are
tortoises) was commissioned by
the Mattei family to decorate
"their" piazza between 1581
and 1588. The design was by
Giacomo della Porta, but the
fountain owes much of its
charm to the four bronze youths
each resting one foot on the
head of a dolphin, sculpted by
Taddeo Landini. Nearly a

Della Porta's graceful Fontana delle Tartarughe

century after the fountain was built, an unknown sculptor added the struggling tortoises to complete the composition.

⑳ Santa Maria in Campitelli

Piazza di Campitelli 9. **Map** 4 F5 & 12 E5. **Tel** 06-6880 3978. ▣ 40, 46, 62, 63, 64, 70, 87, 186, 780, 810. **Open** 7:30am–noon, 3:30–7:30pm daily. ⬆ ♿

In 17th-century Rome the plague could still strike fiercely, and there were no reliable, effective remedies. Many Romans simply prayed for a cure to a sacred medieval icon of the Virgin, the Madonna del Portico. When a particularly lethal outbreak of plague abated in 1656, popular gratitude was so strong that a new church was built to house the icon.

Lavish altar tabernacle in Santa Maria in Campitelli

The church, designed by a pupil of Bernini, Carlo Rainaldi, was completed in 1667. The main elements of the lively Baroque facade are the graceful columns, symbolizing the supporters of the true faith.

Inside the church stands a fabulously ornate, gilded altar tabernacle with spiral columns, which was designed by Giovanni Antonio de Rossi to contain the image of the Virgin. The side chapels are decorated by some of Rome's finest Baroque painters: Sebastiano Conca, Giovanni Battista Gaulli (known as Il Baciccia), and Luca Giordano.

Facade and medieval bell tower of San Nicola in Carcere

㉑ San Nicola in Carcere

Via del Teatro di Marcello 46. **Map** 5 A5 & 12 E5. **Tel** 06-6830 7198. ▣ 44, 63, 81, 160, 170, 628, 780, 781. **Open** 10am–5pm daily. ⬛ of excavations. ⬛ for tours. ⬆

The medieval church of San Nicola in Carcere stands on the site of three Roman temples of the Republican era that were converted into a prison *(carcere)* in the Middle Ages. The temples of Juno, Spes, and Janus faced a city gate leading from the Forum Holitorium, the city's vegetable and oil market, to the road down to the port on the Tiber. The columns embedded in the walls of the church belonged to two flanking temples whose platforms are

now marked by grass lawns. The church was rebuilt in 1599 and restored in the 19th century, but the bell tower and Roman columns are part of the original design.

The Theater of Marcellus by Thomas Hartley Cromek (1809–73)

㉒ Theater of Marcellus

Via del Teatro di Marcello. **Map** 4 A5 & 12 E5. **Tel** 06-0608. ▣ 44, 63, 81, 160, 170, 628, 780, 781. **Open** 9am–6pm (to 7pm in summer) daily.

The curved outer wall of this vast amphitheater has supported generations of Roman buildings. It was built by the Emperor Augustus (27 BC–AD 14), who dedicated it to Marcellus, his nephew and son-in-law, who had died at age 19 in 23 BC.

The Middle Ages were a turbulent time of invasions and local conflicts *(see p32)*, and by the 13th century the theater had been converted into the fortress of the Savelli family. In the 16th century Baldassarre Peruzzi built a great palace on the theater ruins for the Orsini family. This included a garden that faced the Tiber. The lower arches were later occupied by humble dwellings and workshops.

Close to the theater stand three beautiful Corinthian columns and a section of frieze. These are from the Temple of Apollo, which housed many great works of art that the Romans plundered from Greece in the 2nd century BC.

㉓ Portico of Octavia

Via del Portico d'Ottavia. **Map** 4 F5 &
12 E5. 🚌 46, 62, 63, 64, 70, 87, 186,
780, 810.

Built in honor of Octavia (the
sister of Augustus and the
abandoned wife of Mark
Antony), this is the only surviving
portico of what used to be the
monumental piazza of Circus
Flaminius. The rectangular
portico enclosed temples
dedicated to Jupiter and Juno,
decorated with bronze statues.
The part we see today is the
great central atrium originally
covered by marble facings.

In the Middle Ages a great fish
market and a church, Sant'Angelo
in Pescheria, were built in the
ruins of the portico. As the
church was associated with the
fishing activities of the nearby
river port, aquatic flora and fauna
feature in many of its inlays.
Links with the Tiber are also
apparent in the stucco facade
on the adjacent Fishmonger's
Oratory, built in 1689. The church
has a fresco of the Madonna
and angels by the school of
Benozzo Gozzoli.

㉔ Ghetto and Synagogue

Synagogue, Lungotevere dei Cenci.
Map 4 F5 & 12 E5. **Tel** 06-6840 0661.
🚌 23, 63, 280, 780 and routes to
Largo di Torre Argentina. 🚋 8.
Museum: Open mid-Jun–mid-Sep:
10am–7pm Sun–Thu, 10am–4pm Fri;
mid-Sep–mid-Jun: 10am–5pm Sun–
Thu, 9am–2pm Fri. **Closed** on Jewish
public hols. 🚻 📷 🛒 📷
W museoebraico.roma.it Ghetto:
main street is Via del Portico d'Ottavia.

The first Jews came to Rome as
traders in the 2nd century BC,
and there has been a Jewish
community in Rome ever since.
Jews were much appreciated
for their financial and medical
skills during the time of the
Roman Empire.

Systematic persecution began
in the 16th century. From July 25,
1556, all of Rome's Jews were
forced to live inside a high-walled
enclosure erected on the orders
of Pope Paul IV. The Ghetto was
in an unhealthy part of Rome.

Inhabitants were only allowed
out during the day, and on
Sundays they were driven into
the Church of Sant'Angelo in
Pescheria to listen to Christian
sermons – a practice abolished
only in 1848.

Persecution started again
in 1943 with the German
occupation. Although many Jews
were helped to escape or hidden
by Roman citizens, thousands
were deported to German
concentration camps.

Today many Jews still live
in the former Ghetto, and the
medieval streets retain much
of their old character. The
Synagogue on Lungotevere was
completed in 1904 and houses
a Jewish museum that describes
the history of the community
through plans, Torahs, and
other artifacts.

㉕ Casa di Lorenzo Manilio

Via del Portico d'Ottavia 1D. **Map** 4 F5
& 12 D5. 🚌 46, 62, 63, 64, 70, 87,
186, 780, 810. **Closed** to the public.

Before the Renaissance, most
Romans had only vague ideas
of their city's past, but the
15th-century revival of interest
in the philosophy, and arts of
antiquity inspired some to build
houses recalling the splendor of
ancient Rome. In 1468 a certain
Lorenzo Manilio built a great
house for his family, decorating
it with an elegant Classical
plaque. The Latin inscription
dates the building according to
the ancient Roman method –
2,221 years after the foundation
of the city – and gives the
owner's name. Original reliefs

are embedded in the facades,
as well as a fragment of an
ancient sarcophagus. The Piazza
Costaguti facade's windows are
inscribed *Ave Roma* (Hail Rome).

Balcony of Palazzo Cenci

㉖ Palazzo Cenci

Vicolo dei Cenci. **Map** 4 F5 & 12 D5.
🚌 *See Ghetto and Synagogue.*
Closed to the public.

Palazzo Cenci belonged to the
family of Beatrice Cenci, who
was accused, together with
her brothers and stepmother,
of witchcraft, and the murder
of her tyrannical father. She
was condemned to death, and
beheaded at Ponte Sant'Angelo
in 1599.

Most of the original medieval
palazzo has been demolished,
and the building you see today

Row of Roman busts decorating the Casa di Lorenzo Manilio

Tiber Island, with Ponte Cestio linking it to Trastevere

㉙ San Giovanni dei Fiorentini

Via Acciaioli 2. **Map** 4 D4 & 11 A2. **Tel** 06-6889 2059. ▥ 23, 40, 46, 62, 64, 116, 280, 870. **Open** 7am–noon, 5–7pm daily. ✝

dates back to the 1570s, though its rather forbidding appearance seems medieval. Heraldic half-moons decorate the main facade on Via del Progresso, while pretty balconies open on the opposite side where a medieval arch joins the palace to Palazzetto Cenci, designed by Martino Longhi the Elder. Inside is a traditional courtyard with an Ionic-style loggia; many of the rooms retain the original 16th-century decoration that the unfortunate Beatrice would have known as a child.

㉗ Tiber Island

Isola Tiberina. **Map** 8 D1 & 12 D5. ▥ 23, 63, 280, 780. ▥ 8.

In ancient times, the island, which lay opposite the city's port, had large structures of white travertine at either end built to resemble the stern and prow of a ship.

Since 293 BC, when a temple was dedicated here to Aesculapius, the god of healing and protector against the plague, the island has been associated with the sick, and there is still a hospital here.

San Bartolomeo all'Isola, the church in the island's central piazza, was built on the ruins of the Temple of Aesculapius in the 10th century. Its Romanesque bell tower is clearly visible from across the river.

From the Ghetto area you can reach the island by a footbridge, the Ponte Fabricio. The oldest original bridge over the Tiber still in use, it was built in 62 BC. In medieval times, the Pierleoni, and then the Caetani, two powerful families, controlled this strategic point by means of

a tower, still in place. The other bridge to the island, the Ponte Cestio, is inscribed with the names of the Byzantine emperors associated with its restoration in AD 370.

Mask fountain in Via Giulia

㉘ Via Giulia

Map 4 D4 & 11 A3. ▥ 23, 116, 280, 870.

This picturesque street was laid out by Bramante for Pope Julius II della Rovere. Lined with 16th–18th century aristocratic palazzi, as well as fine churches and antique shops, Via Giulia makes a fascinating walk *(see pp278–9)*.

The church of St. John of the Florentines was built for the large Florentine community living in this area. Pope Leo X wanted it to be an expression of the cultural superiority of Florence over Rome. Started in the early 16th century, the church took over a century to build. The principal architect was Antonio da Sangallo the Younger, but many others contributed before Carlo Maderno's elongated cupola was finally completed in 1620. The present facade was added in the 18th century.

The church was decorated mainly by Tuscan artists. One interesting exception is the 15th-century statue of San Giovannino by the Sicilian Mino del Reame in a niche above the sacristy. The spectacular high altar houses a marble group by Antonio Raggi, the *Baptism of Christ*. The altar itself is by Borromini, who is buried in the church along with Carlo Maderno.

This and San Lorenzo in Lucina *(see p116)* are the only churches in Rome that admit animals: the faithful can bring their pets, and an Easter lamb-blessing takes place.

Antonio Raggi's *Baptism of Christ* in San Giovanni dei Fiorentini

QUIRINAL

One of the original seven hills of Rome, the Quirinal was a largely residential area in Imperial times. To the east of the hill were the vast Baths of Diocletian, still standing in front of what is now the main train station. Abandoned in the Middle Ages, the district returned to favor in the late 16th century. The prime site was taken by the popes for Palazzo del Quirinale. Great families such as the Colonna and the Aldobrandini had their palazzi lower down the hill. With the end of papal rule in 1870, the surrounding area, especially Via Nazionale, was redeveloped as the Quirinal became the residence of the kings of Italy, then of the Italian president.

Sights at a Glance

Churches
- ❹ Santi Apostoli
- ❺ San Marcello al Corso
- ❼ Santa Maria in Trivio
- ❾ Santi Vincenzo e Anastasio
- ⓫ Sant'Andrea al Quirinale
- ⓬ San Carlo alle Quattro Fontane
- ⓯ Santa Maria degli Angeli e dei Martiri
- ⓴ Santa Maria dei Monti
- ㉑ Sant'Agata dei Goti
- ㉓ Santi Domenico e Sisto

Museums and Galleries
- ❽ Accademia Nazionale di San Luca
- ❿ Scuderie del Quirinale
- ⓰ Museo Nazionale Romano (Palazzo Massimo)
- ⓳ Palazzo delle Esposizioni

Historic Piazzas
- ⓲ Piazza della Repubblica

Historic Buildings
- ❷ Palazzo del Quirinale
- ❸ Palazzo Colonna
- ⓱ Baths of Diocletian

Fountains and Statues
- ❶ Castor and Pollux
- ❻ Trevi Fountain
- ⓭ Le Quattro Fontane
- ⓮ Moses Fountain

Parks and Gardens
- ㉒ Villa Aldobrandini

Restaurants
see pp315–17
1. Abruzzi ai SS Apostoli
2. Ai Tre Scalini
3. Antica Birreria Peroni
4. Asmara
5. Cavour 313
6. Colline Emiliane
7. Doozo
8. Il Baccano
9. La Carbonara
10. L'Asino d'Oro
11. Open Colonna
12. Pipero al Rex
13. Taverna dei Fori Imperiali
14. Trimani il Wine Bar
15. Urbana 47
16. Vineria Il Chianti
17. Vivendo

See also Street Finder maps 5, 6, 12

Street-by-Street: The Quirinal Hill

Even though Palazzo del Quirinale is usually closed to the public, it is well worth walking up the hill to the palace to see the giant Roman statues of Castor and Pollux in the piazza and enjoy fine views of the city. Come down the hill by way of the narrow streets and stairways that lead to one of Rome's unforgettable sights, the Trevi Fountain. Many small churches lie hidden away in the back streets. Toward Piazza Venezia there are grand palazzi, including that of the Colonna, one of Rome's most ancient and powerful families.

Santa Maria in Via is famous for its medieval well and miraculous 13th-century icon of the Madonna.

❼ Santa Maria in Trivio
The attractive facade of this tiny church conceals a rich Baroque interior.

❽ Accademia Nazionale di San Luca
The art academy has works by famous former members, such as Canova and Angelica Kauffmann.

❻ ★ Trevi Fountain
Rome's grandest and best-known fountain almost fills the tiny Piazza di Trevi.

❾ Santi Vincenzo e Anastasio
The grand facade of this small Baroque church is on a corner facing the Trevi Fountain.

❺ San Marcello al Corso
This stark *Crucifixion* by Van Dyck hangs in the sacristy of the church.

Palazzo Odescalchi has a Bernini facade from 1664, with a balustrade and richly decorated cornice. The building faces Santi Apostoli.

To Piazza Venezia

I Giardini del Quirinale
The magnificent gardens of
the presidential palace are
open to visitors just once a
year, on June 2.

Locator Map
See Central Rome Map pp16–17

2 Palazzo del Quirinale
The old papal palace is now the
home of the president of Italy.
Palace guards in colorful dress
uniform can often be seen outside.

1 Castor and Pollux
The statues are grouped
with an obelisk and a
fountain.

**Piazza della
Pilotta** is
dominated by the
imposing facade
of the Gregorian
University.

3 Palazzo Colonna
One of the art
gallery's finest
Old Masters is
Annibale Carracci's
The Bean Eater.

4 Santi Apostoli
The figures of Christ
and the Apostles on
the balustrade were
added by Carlo
Rainaldi in 168.

Museo delle Cere, a
wax museum opened
in 1953, places its
emphasis on horror.

Key

— Suggested route

0 meters		75
0 yards		75

Quirinal fountain and obelisk with Roman statues of Castor and Pollux

❶ Castor and Pollux

Piazza del Quirinale. **Map** 5 B4. 🚌 H, 40, 64, 70, 170 and many routes along Via del Tritone.

Castor and Pollux – the patrons of horsemanship – and their prancing horses stand in splendor in the Piazza del Quirinale. Over 18 ft (5.5 m) high, these statues are huge Roman copies of 5th-century BC Greek originals. They once stood at the entrance to the nearby Baths of Constantine. Pope Sixtus V had them restored and placed here in 1588. Formerly known as the "horse tamers," they gave the square its familiar name of Monte Cavallo (horse hill).

The obelisk that stands between them was brought here in 1786 from the Mausoleum of Augustus. In 1818 the composition was completed by the addition of a massive granite basin, once a cattle trough in the Forum.

❷ Palazzo del Quirinale

Piazza del Quirinale. **Map** 5 B3. **Tel** 06-469 91. 🚌 H, 40, 64, 70, 170 and many routes along Via del Tritone. **Open** usually 8:30am–noon Sun (call ahead). **Closed** pub hols & late Jun–mid-Sep. 🚫 🖼 **quirinale.it**

By the 1500s, the Vatican had a reputation as an unhealthy location because of the high incidence of malaria, so Pope Gregory XIII chose this site on the highest of Rome's seven hills

as a papal summer residence. Work began in 1573. Piazza del Quirinale has buildings on three sides, while the fourth is open, with a splendid view of the city. Many great architects worked on the palace before it assumed its present form in the 1730s. Domenico Fontana designed the main facade, Carlo Maderno the huge chapel, and Bernini the narrow wing on Via del Quirinale.

Following the unification of Italy in 1870, it became the official residence of the king, then, in 1947, of the president of the republic.

The immaculately manicured palace gardens are open to the public only once a year, on Republic Day (June 2).

❸ Palazzo Colonna

Via della Pilotta 17. **Map** 5 A4 & 12 F3. **Tel** 06-678 4350. 🚌 H, 40, 64, 70, 170 and many routes to Piazza Venezia. **Open** 9am–1:15pm Sat only or by appt. **Closed** Aug & public hols. 🚫 🖼 🖼 **galleriacolonna.it**

Pope Martin V Colonna (reigned 1417–31) began building the palazzo, but most of the structure dates from the 18th century. The art gallery, built by Antonio del Grande between 1654 and 1665, is the only part open to the public. The pictures are numbered but unlabeled, so pick up a guide on the way in. Go up the stairs and through the antechamber leading to a series of three gleaming marble rooms with prominent yellow

Palazzo del Quirinale, official residence of the president of Italy

Canova's monument to Pope Clement XIV in Santi Apostoli, with figures of Humility and Modesty

columns, the Colonna family emblem (*colonna* means column).

The ceiling frescoes celebrate Marcantonio Colonna's victory over the Turks at the Battle of Lepanto (1571). On the walls are 16th- to 18th-century paintings, including Annibale Carracci's *The Bean Eater (see p159)*. The room of landscape paintings, many by Poussin's brother-in-law Gaspare Dughet, reflects the 18th-century taste of Cardinal Girolamo Colonna. Beyond is a room with a ceiling fresco of *The Apotheosis of Martin V*. The throne room has a chair reserved for visiting popes and a copy of Pisanello's portrait of Martin V. The gallery also offers a fine view of the private palace garden, site of the ruined Temple of Serapis.

❹ Santi Apostoli

Piazza dei Santi Apostoli. **Map** 5 A4 & 12 F3. **Tel** 06-699 571. 🚌 H, 40, 64, 70, 170 and many other routes to Piazza Venezia. **Open** 7:30am–noon, 4–7pm daily. ✝

The original 6th-century church on this site was rebuilt in the 15th century by Popes Martin V Colonna and Sixtus IV della Rovere, whose oak-tree crest decorates the capitals of the late 15th-century portico. Inside the portico on the left is Canova's 1807 memorial to the engraver Giovanni Volpato. The church itself contains a much larger monument by Canova, his Tomb of Clement XIV (1789).

The Baroque interior by Francesco and Carlo Fontana was completed in 1714. Note the 3-D effect of Giovanni Odazzi's painted *Rebel Angels*, who really look as though they are falling from the sky. A huge 18th-century altarpiece by Domenico Muratori shows the martyrdom of the Apostles James and Philip, whose tombs are in the crypt.

Detail of Triton and "sea horse" at Rome's grandest fountain, the Trevi

❺ San Marcello al Corso

Piazza San Marcello 5. **Map** 5 A4 & 12 F3. **Tel** 06-6993 0221. 🚌 62, 63, 81, 85, 117, 119, 160, 175, 492, 628. **Open** 7:30am–noon, 4–7pm daily (from 9:30am Sun). 🔓

This church was originally one of the first places of Christian worship in Rome, which were known as *tituli*. A later Romanesque building burned down in 1519, and was rebuilt by Jacopo Sansovino with a single nave and many richly decorated private chapels on either side. The imposing travertine facade was designed by Fontana in late Baroque style.

The third chapel on the right has fine frescoes of the Virgin Mary by Francesco Salviati. The decoration of the next chapel was interrupted by the Sack of Rome in 1527. Raphael's follower Perin del Vaga fled, leaving the ceiling frescoes to be completed by Daniele da Volterra and Pellegrino Tibaldi when peace returned to the city. In the nave stands a splendid Venetian-style double tomb by Sansovino, a memorial to Cardinal Giovanni Michiel (victim of a Borgia poisoning in 1503) and his nephew, Bishop Antonio Orso.

❻ Trevi Fountain

Fontana di Trevi. **Map** 5 A3 & 12 F2. 🚌 52, 53, 61, 62, 63, 71, 80, 116, 119 and many other routes along Via del Corso and Via del Tritone.

Most visitors gathering around the coin-filled fountain assume that it has always been here, but by the standards of the Eternal City, the Trevi is a fairly recent creation. Nicola Salvi's theatrical design for Rome's largest and most famous fountain (*see p56*) was completed only in 1762. The central figures are Neptune flanked by two Tritons. One struggles to master a very unruly "sea horse," the other leads a far more docile animal. These symbolize the two contrasting moods of the sea.

The site originally marked the terminal of the Aqua Virgo aqueduct built in 19 BC. One of the first-story reliefs shows a young girl (the legendary virgin after whom the aqueduct was named) pointing to the spring from which the water flows.

Chapel in San Marcello al Corso, decorated by Francesco Salviati

Facade of Santa Maria in Trivio

❼ Santa Maria in Trivio

Piazza dei Crociferi 49. **Map** 5 A3 & 12 F2. **Tel** 06-678 9645. 🚌 52, 53, 61, 62, 63, 71, 80, 116, 119. **Open** 8am–noon, 4–8pm daily. 🕀

It has been said that Italian architecture is one of facades, and nowhere is this clearer than in the 1570s facade of Santa Maria in Trivio, delightfully stuck on to the building behind it. Note the false windows. There is illusion inside too, particularly in the ceiling frescoes, which show scenes from the New Testament by Antonio Gherardi (1644–1702).
The name of the tiny church probably means "St. Mary-at-the-meeting-of-three-roads."

❽ Accademia Nazionale di San Luca

Piazza dell'Accademia di San Luca 77. **Map** 5 A3 & 12 F2. **Tel** 06-679 8850. 🚌 52, 53, 61, 62, 63, 71, 80, 116, 119 and many routes along Via del Corso and Via del Tritone. **Open** 10am–12:30pm Mon–Sat. 🌐 accademiasanluca.it

St. Luke is supposed to have been a painter, hence the name of Rome's academy of fine arts. Appropriately, the gallery contains a painting of *St. Luke Painting a Portrait of the Virgin* by Raphael and his followers. The academy's heyday was in the 17th and 18th centuries, when many members gave their

work to the collection. Canova donated a model for his famous marble group, *The Three Graces*.
Of particular interest are three fascinating self-portraits painted by women: the 17th-century Italian Lavinia Fontana; the 18th-century Swiss Angelica Kauffmann, whose painting is copied from a portrait of her by Joshua Reynolds; and Elisabeth Vigée-Lebrun, the French painter of the years before the 1789 Revolution.

❾ Santi Vincenzo e Anastasio

Vicolo dei Modelli 73. **Map** 5 A3 & 12 F2. **Tel** 331-284 5596. 🚌 52, 53, 61, 62, 63, 71, 80, 116, 119. **Open** 9am–8pm daily. 🕀 (Bulgarian Orthodox services).

Overlooking the Trevi Fountain *(see p161)* is one of the most over-the-top Baroque facades in Rome. Its thickets of columns are crowned by the huge coat of arms of Cardinal Raimondo Mazzarino, who commissioned Martino Longhi the Younger to build the church in 1650. The female bust above the door is of one of the cardinal's

famous nieces, either Louis XIV's first love, Maria Mancini (1639–1715), or her younger sister, Ortensia. In the apse, memorial plaques record the popes whose *praecordia* (a part of the heart) are enshrined behind the wall. This gruesome tradition was started at the end of the 16th century by Pope Sixtus V and continued until Pius X stopped it in the early 20th century.

❿ Scuderie del Quirinale

Via 24 Maggio 16. **Map** 5 B4. **Tel** 06-3996 7500. 🚌 H, 40, 60, 64, 70, 170. **Open** for exhibitions 10am–8pm Sun–Thu, 10am–10:30pm Fri & Sat. 🎨 ♿ 🖥 📷 🌐 scuderiequirinale.it

The Scuderie started life as stables for the nearby Palazzo del Quirinale. Built in the early 1700s by Ferdinando Fuga over the remains of the ancient Temple of Serapis, the stables were remodeled by Gae Aulenti at the end of the 20th century and now house some of the best temporary art exhibitions in the country.

Self-portrait by Lavinia Fontana in the Accademia Nazionale di San Luca

Interior of Bernini's oval Sant'Andrea al Quirinale

⓫ Sant'Andrea al Quirinale

Via del Quirinale 29. **Map** 5 B3. **Tel** 06-474 0807. 116, 117 and routes to Via del Tritone. **Open** 8:30am–noon, 3:30–7pm Mon–Sat; 9am–noon, 4–7pm Sun.

Known as the "Pearl of the Baroque" because of its beautiful roseate marble interior, Sant'Andrea was designed by Bernini and executed by his assistants between 1658 and 1670. It was built for the Jesuits, hence the many IHS emblems (*Iesus Hominum Salvator* – Jesus Savior of Mankind).

The site for the church was wide but shallow, so Bernini pointed the long axis of his oval plan not toward the altar, but toward the sides; he then leads the eye around to the altar end. Here Bernini ordered works of art in various media that function not in isolation, but together. The crucified St. Andrew (Sant'Andrea) of the altarpiece looks up at a stucco

version of himself, who in turn ascends toward the lantern and the Holy Spirit.

The many rooms of St. Stanislas Kostka in the adjacent convent should not be missed. The quarters of the Jesuit novice, who died in 1568 at age 19, reflect not only his own spartan taste, but also the richer style of the 17th-century Jesuits. The Polish saint has been brilliantly immortalized in an exquisite marble piece created by Pierre Legros (1666–1719).

⓬ San Carlo alle Quattro Fontane

Via del Quirinale 23. **Map** 5 B3. **Tel** 06-488 3109. 116, 117 & routes to Piazza Barberini. Ⓜ Barberini. **Open** 10am–1pm, 3–6pm Mon–Fri; 10am–1pm Sat & Sun.

In 1634, the Trinitarians, a Spanish order whose role was to pay the ransom of Christian hostages to the Arabs, commissioned Borromini to design a church and convent at the Quattro Fontane crossroads. The church, so small it would fit inside one of the piers of St. Peter's, is also known as "San Carlino."

Although dedicated to Carlo Borromeo, the 16th-century Milanese cardinal canonized in 1620, San Carlo is as much a monument to Borromini. Both facade and interior employ bold curves that give light and life to a small, cramped site. The oval dome and tiny lantern are particularly ingenious. The undulating lines of the facade are decorated with angels and a statue of San Carlo. Finished in 1667, the facade is one of Borromini's very last works.

There are further delights in the playful inverted shapes in the cloister and the stucco work in the refectory (now the sacristy), which houses a painting of San Carlo by Orazio Borgianni (1611).

In a small room off the sacristy hangs a portrait of Borromini himself wearing the Trinitarian cross. Borromini committed suicide in 1667, and in the crypt (which is now open to the public) a small curved chapel reserved for him remains empty.

Dome of San Carlo alle Quattro Fontane, lit by concealed windows

Fountain of Strength (or Juno)

⓭ Le Quattro Fontane

Intersection of Via delle Quattro Fontane and Via del Quirinale. **Map** 5 B3. 🚌 Routes to Piazza Barberini or Via Nazionale. Ⓜ Barberini.

These four small fountains are attached to the corners of the buildings at the intersection of two narrow, busy streets. They date from the great redevelopment of Rome in the reign of Sixtus V (1585–90). Each fountain has a statue of a reclining deity. The river god accompanied by the she-wolf is clearly the Tiber; the other male figure may be the Arno. The female figures represent Strength and Fidelity or the goddesses Juno and Diana.

The crossroads is at the highest point of the Quirinal hill and commands splendid views of three distant landmark obelisks: those placed by Sixtus V in front of Santa Maria Maggiore and Trinità dei Monti, and the one that stands in Piazza del Quirinale.

⓮ Moses Fountain

Fontana dell'Acqua Felice, Piazza San Bernardo. **Map** 5 C2. 🚌 36, 60, 61, 62, 84, 175, 492. Ⓜ Repubblica.

Officially known as the Fontana dell'Acqua Felice, this fountain owes its popular name to the grotesque statue of Moses in the central niche. The massive structure with its three elegant arches was designed by Domenico Fontana to mark the terminal of the Acqua Felice aqueduct, so called because it was one of the many great improvements commissioned by Felice Peretti, Pope Sixtus V. Completed in 1587, it brought clean piped water to this quarter of Rome for the first time.

The notorious statue of Moses striking water from the rock is larger than life and the proportions of the body are obviously wrong. Sculpted either by Prospero Bresciano or Leonardo Sormani, it is a clumsy attempt at recreating the awesome appearance of Michelangelo's Moses in the church of San Pietro in Vincoli (see p172). As soon as it was unveiled, it was said to be frowning at having been brought into the world by such an inept sculptor. The side reliefs also illustrate water

Fontana's Moses Fountain

stories from the Old Testament: Aaron leading the Israelites to water and Joshua pointing the army toward the Red Sea. The fountain's four lions are copies of Egyptian originals (now in the Vatican Museums), which Sixtus V had put there for the public's "convenience" and "delight."

Gold coin with head of the Emperor Diocletian (AD 285–305)

⓯ Santa Maria degli Angeli e dei Martiri

Piazza della Repubblica. **Map** 5 C3. **Tel** 06-488 0812. 🚌 36, 60, 61, 62, 64, 84, 90, 116, 170, 492, 910. Ⓜ Repubblica, Termini. **Open** 7am– 6:30pm Mon–Sat, 7:30am–7:30pm Sun. ✝ ♿ 📷

Parts of the ruined Baths of Diocletian (right) provided building material and setting for this church, constructed by Michelangelo in 1563. The church was so altered in the 18th century that it has lost most of its original character.

An exhibition in the sacristy gives a detailed account of Michelangelo's original design.

Fidelity (or Diana) with her attendant dog, one of the Quattro Fontane

Part of the Museo Nazionale Romano in the Baths of Diocletian

⑯ Museo Nazionale Romano (Palazzo Massimo)

Palazzo Massimo, Largo di Villa Peretti 1. **Map** 6 D3. **Tel** 06-480 201. 🚌 36, 38, 40, 64, 86, 170, 175, H and other routes to Piazza dei Cinquecento. Ⓜ Repubblica, Termini. **Open** 9am–7:45pm Tue–Sun (last adm: 6:45pm). **Closed** Jan 1, Dec 25. 🎫 (the biglietto cumulativo gives entry to the museum's five branches). ♿ 🛍 🎪 📷

Founded in 1889, the Museo Nazionale Romano holds most of the antiquities found in Rome since 1870 as well as preexisting collections, and is one of the world's leading museums of Classical art. It now has five branches: its original site, occupying part of the Baths of Diocletian; the Palazzo Massimo; the Palazzo Altemps *(see p129)*; the Aula Ottagona (near the Baths of Diocletian); and Crypta Balbi at Via delle Botteghe Oscure 31, excavated from the foyer of the theater of Balbus (1st century BC) and housing findings from medieval Rome. The Palazzo Massimo, built in

1883–7 on the site of a villa that belonged to Sixtus V, used to be a Jesuit college. In 1981–97 it was restored to house a significant proportion of the museum's collections. The exhibits, contained on four floors, are originals dating from the 2nd century BC to the end of the 4th century AD.

The basement contains an excellent display of ancient coins, precious artifacts, and the only mummified child to be found in the ancient city. The ground floor is devoted to Roman statuary, with funeral monuments in Room 2 and Emperor Augustus in Pontifex Maximus guise in Room 5. Upstairs there are statues from Nero's summer villa in Anzio and Roman copies of famous Greek originals, such as the *Discobolos Ex-Lancellotti*. The real joy of the museum, however, is on the second floor, where entire rooms of wall paintings have been brought in from various villas excavated in and around Rome. The most incredible frescoes are from Livia's Villa at Prima Porta. Her triclinium (dining room) was decorated with an abundance of trees, plants, and fruit, painted in a totally naturalistic style to fool guests that they were eating alfresco, rather than indoors.

Oaks, pine trees, cypresses, oleanders, roses, poppies, and irises are all clearly distinguishable. Other marvels include rooms brought from the first Villa Farnesina: the children's room has a predominantly white design, while the adults' bedroom is red, complete with erotic paintings. Equally impressive is the museum's display of mosaics on the same floor.

⑰ Baths of Diocletian

Terme di Diocleziano, Viale E de Nicola 79. **Map** 6 D3. **Tel** 06-3996 7700. 🚌 36, 60, 61, 62, 84, 90. Ⓜ Repubblica, Termini. **Open** 9am–7:45pm Tue–Sun (last adm: 6:45pm). **Closed** Jan 1, Dec 25.

Built in AD 298–306 under the infamous Emperor Diocletian, who murdered thousands of Christians, the baths *(see pp26–7)* were the most extensive in Rome and could accommodate up to 3,000 bathers at a time.

Part of the Museo Nazionale Romano, the complex houses a vast collection of Roman statues and inscriptions and incorporates the former Carthusian monastery of Santa Maria degli Angeli, which has a beautiful cloister designed by Michelangelo.

One of the Quattro Aurighe mosaics, Museo Nazionale Romano

⓲ Piazza della Repubblica

Map 5 C3. 🚌 36, 60, 61, 62, 64, 84, 90, 170, 175, 492, 646, 910. Ⓜ Repubblica.

Romans often refer to the piazza by its old name, Piazza Esedra, so called because it follows the shape of an *exedra* (a semicircular recess) that was part of the Baths of Diocletian. The piazza was part of the great redevelopment undertaken when Rome became capital of a unified Italy. Under its sweeping 19th-century colonnades there were once elegant shops, but they have been ousted by banks, travel agencies, and cafés.

In the middle of the piazza stands the Fontana delle Naiadi. Mario Rutelli's four naked bronze nymphs caused something of a scandal when they were unveiled in 1901. Each reclines on an aquatic creature symbolizing water in its various forms: a sea horse for the oceans, a water snake for rivers, a swan for lakes, and a curious frilled lizard for subterranean streams. The

Piazza della Repubblica and the Fontana delle Naiadi

figure in the middle, added in 1911, is of the sea god Glaucus, who represents man victorious over the hostile forces of nature.

⓳ Palazzo delle Esposizioni

Via Nazionale 194. **Map** 5 B4. **Tel** 06-3996 7500. 🚌 40, 60, 64, 70, 116T, 170. **Open** 10am–8pm Tue–Thu & Sun, 10am–10:30pm Fri & Sat. 🎟 ♿ ♿ from Via Piacenza or Via Milano 13 entrance. ✎ ▢ 🖼 🕸 **palaexpo.it**

Facade of the Palazzo delle Esposizioni

This grandiose building, with wide steps, Corinthian columns, and statues, was designed as an exhibition center by the architect Pio Piacentini and built by the city of Rome in 1882 during the reign of Umberto I. The main entrance looks like a triumphal arch.

The restored palazzo is still used to house high-profile exhibitions of contemporary art. The exhibitions are changed every three to six months and include a variety of sculpture and paintings. Live performances, films, and lectures also take place here *(see p352)*. Foreign films are usually shown in the original language.

⓴ Santa Maria dei Monti

Via Madonna dei Monti 41. **Map** 5 B4. **Tel** 06-48 55 31. 🚌 75, 84, 117. Ⓜ Cavour. **Open** 7am–12:30pm, 4:30–7:30pm daily. ✝ ♿

Designed by Giacomo della Porta, this church, dating from 1580, has a particularly splendid dome. Over the high altar is a stunning medieval painting of the Madonna, patroness of this quarter of Rome. The altar in the left transept houses the tomb and effigy of the unworldly French saint Benoît-Joseph Labre, who died here in 1783, having spent his life as a solitary pilgrim. He slept rough in the ruins of the Colosseum, gave away any charitable gifts he received, and came regularly to Santa Maria dei Monti to worship. His faith could not sustain his body: still in his mid-thirties, he collapsed and died outside the church. The foul rags he wore are preserved.

One of the bronze nymphs of the fountain in Piazza della Repubblica

㉑ Sant'Agata dei Goti

Via Mazzarino 16 and Via Panisperna 29. **Map** 5 B4. **Tel** 06-4879 3531. 🚌 40, 60, 64, 70, 71, 117, 170. **Open** 7–9am, 4–7pm Mon–Fri; 10am–noon, 4–6pm Sat & Sun. ✝ ♿

The Goths (*Goti*) who gave their name to this church occupied Rome in the 6th century AD. They were Aryan heretics who denied the divinity of Christ. The church was founded between AD 462 and 470, shortly before the main Gothic invasions, and the beautiful granite columns date from this period. The main altar has a well-preserved 12th-century Cosmatesque tabernacle, but the most delightful part of the church is the charming 18th-century courtyard built around an ivy-draped well.

18th-century courtyard of Sant'Agata dei Goti

㉒ Villa Aldobrandini

Via Panisperna. Entrance to gardens: Via Mazzarino 1. **Map** 5 B4. 🚌 40, 60, 64, 70, 71, 117, 170. Gardens: **Open** dawn–dusk daily. Villa: **Closed** to the public.

Built in the 16th century for the Dukes of Urbino and acquired for his family by Pope Clement VIII Aldobrandini (reigned 1592–1605), the villa is now government property and houses an international law library.

The villa itself, decorated with the family's six-starred coat of arms, is closed to the public, but the gardens and terraces, hidden behind a high wall that runs along Via Nazionale, can be reached through an iron gate in Via Mazzarino. Steps lead up past 2nd-century AD ruins into the gardens, highly recommended as an oasis of tranquillity in the center of the city. Gravel paths lead between formal lawns and clearly marked specimen trees, and benches are provided for the weary. Since the garden is raised some 30 ft (10 m) above street level, the views are excellent.

㉓ Santi Domenico e Sisto

Largo Angelicum 1. **Map** 5 B4. **Tel** 06-670 2201. 🚌 40, 60, 64, 70, 71 117, 170. **Open** 3–6pm Sat.

The church has a tall, slender Baroque facade rising above a steep flight of steps. This divides into two curving flights that sweep up to the terrace in front of the entrance. The pediment of the facade is crowned by eight flaming candlesticks.

The interior has a vaulted ceiling with a large fresco of *The Apotheosis of St. Dominic* by Domenico Canuti (1620–84). The first chapel on the right was decorated by Bernini, who may also have designed the sculpture of Mary Magdalene meeting the risen Christ in the Garden of Gethsemane. This fine marble group was executed by Antonio Raggi (1649). Above the altar is a 15th-century terra-cotta plaque of the Virgin and Child. On the left over a side altar is a large painting of the Madonna from the same period, attributed to Benozzo Gozzoli (1420–97), a pupil of Fra Angelico.

Chapel in Santi Domenico e Sisto

The imposing facade of Villa Aldobrandini

ESQUILINE

The Esquiline is the largest and highest of Rome's seven hills. In Imperial Rome, the western slopes overlooking the Forum housed the crowded slums of the Suburra. On the eastern side there were a few villas belonging to wealthy citizens like Maecenas, patron of the arts and adviser to Augustus. The essential character of the place has persisted through two millennia; it is still one of the poorer quarters of the city. The area is now heavily built up, except for a rather seedy park on the Colle Oppio, a smaller hill to the south of the Esquiline, where you can see the remains of the Baths of Titus, the Baths of Trajan, and Nero's Domus Aurea. The area's main interest, however, lies in its churches. Many of these were founded on the sites of private houses where Christians met to worship secretly in the days when their religion was banned.

Sights at a Glance

Churches
1. San Martino ai Monti
2. San Pietro in Vincoli
3. Santa Pudenziana
4. *Santa Maria Maggiore pp174–5*
5. Santa Prassede
7. Santa Bibiana

Museums
9. Museo Nazionale d'Arte Orientale

Historic Piazzas
8. Piazza Vittorio Emanuele II

Ancient Sites
10. Auditorium of Maecenas
11. Sette Sale
12. Domus Aurea

Arches
6. Arch of Gallienus

See also Street Finder maps 5, 6

Restaurants
see pp310–11
1. Agata e Romeo
2. Cuoco e Camicia
3. Da Danilo
4. Hang Zhou
5. La Gallina Bianca
6. Tempio di Iside
7. Trattoria Monti

| 0 meters | | 300 |
| 0 yards | | 300 |

◀ Detail from the apse mosaic at Santa Maria Maggiore

For map symbols *see back flap*

Street-by-Street: The Esquiline Hill

The sight that draws most people to this rather scruffy part of
Rome is the great basilica of Santa Maria Maggiore. But it is also
well worth searching out some of the smaller churches on the
Esquiline: Santa Pudenziana and Santa Prassede with
their celebrated mosaics, and San Pietro in Vincoli,
home to one of Michelangelo's most famous sculptures.
To the south, in the Colle Oppio park, are the scattered
remains of the Baths of Trajan.

❸ **Santa Pudenziana**
The apse of this
ancient church
has a magnificent
4th-century mosaic of
Christ surrounded by
the Apostles.

Piazza dell'Esquilino was
furnished with an obelisk in
1587 by Pope Sixtus V. This
helped to guide pilgrims
coming from the north to
the important church of
Santa Maria Maggiore.

❷ ★ **San Pietro
in Vincoli**
The church's
treasures include
Michelangelo's
Moses and the
chains that bound
St. Peter.

To the
Colosseum

**The Baths of
Trajan** (AD 109)
were the first to be
built on the
massive scale later
used in the Baths
of Diocletian and
of Caracalla.

**The Torre
dei Capocci**, a
restored medieval tower,
is one of the area's most
distinctive landmarks.

❹ ★ Santa Maria Maggiore
This imposing rear facade was added by Baroque architect Carlo Rainaldi in 1673. Santa Maria's interior is one of the most richly decorated in Rome.

Locator Map
See Central Rome Map pp16–17

The Tomb of Pius V (died 1572) by Domenico Fontana stands in this less-well-known Sistine Chapel, under the northeast dome of Santa Maria Maggiore.

To Vittorio Emanuele Metro

DELL' ESQUILINO

PIAZZA DI SANTA MARIA MAGGIORE

VIA CARLO ALBERTO

VIA MERULANA

❻ Arch of Gallienus
This was built in the 3rd century AD to replace an entrance in the old Servian Wall.

❺ ★ Santa Prassede
The 9th-century mosaics in the Chapel of San Zeno are among the finest in Rome.

❶ San Martino ai Monti
The frescoes include 17th-century Roman landscapes and scenes from the life of Elijah by Gaspare Dughet.

Key
— Suggested route

| 0 meters | | 75 |
| 0 yards | | 75 |

Fresco of old San Giovanni in Laterano in San Martino ai Monti

❶ San Martino ai Monti

Viale del Monte Oppio 28. **Map** 6 D5. **Tel** 06-478 4701. 🚌 16, 714. Ⓜ Cavour, Vittorio Emanuele. **Open** 7:30am–noon, 4–7pm daily. 🛉 ♿

Christians have been worshipping on the site of this church since the 3rd century, when they used to meet in the house of a man named Equitius. In the 4th century, after Constantine had legalized Christianity, Pope Sylvester I built a church, one of very few things he did during his pontificate. In fact, he was so insignificant that in the 5th century a more exciting life was fabricated for him – which included tales of him converting Constantine, curing him of leprosy, and forcing him to close all pagan temples. Pope Sylvester's fictional life was further enhanced in the 8th century, with the forgery of a document in which Constantine offered him the Imperial crown.

Pope Sylvester's church was replaced in about AD 500 by St. Symmachus, rebuilt in the 9th century, and then transformed completely in the 1630s. The only obvious signs of its age are the ancient Corinthian columns dividing the nave and aisles. The most interesting interior features are a series of frescoed landscapes of the countryside around Rome (*campagna*

romana) by the 17th-century French artist Gaspare Dughet, Poussin's brother-in-law, in the right aisle. The frescoes by Filippo Gagliardi, at either end of the left aisle, show old St. Peter's and the interior of San Giovanni in Laterano before Borromini's redesign. If you can find the sacristan, you can go beneath the church to see the remains of Equitius's house.

❷ San Pietro in Vincoli

Piazza di San Pietro in Vincoli 4A. **Map** 5 C5. **Tel** 06-9784 4950. 🚌 75, 84, 117. Ⓜ Cavour, Colosseo. **Open** 8am–12:30pm, 3–7pm (Oct–Mar: 6pm) daily. 🛉 ♿ 📷

According to tradition, the two chains (*vincoli*) used to shackle St. Peter while he was being held in the depths of

Reliquary with St. Peter's chains

the Mamertine Prison (*see p93*) were subsequently taken to Constantinople. In the 5th century, Empress Eudoxia deposited one in a church in Constantinople and sent the other to her daughter Eudoxia in Rome. She in turn gave hers to Pope Leo I, who had this church built to house it. Some years later the second chain was brought to Rome, where it linked miraculously with its partner.

The chains are still here, displayed below the high altar, but the church is now best known for Michelangelo's *Tomb of Pope Julius II*. When it was commissioned in 1505, Michelangelo spent eight months searching for perfect blocks of marble at Carrara in Tuscany, but Pope Julius became more interested in the building of a new St. Peter's and the project was laid aside. After the pope's death in 1513, Michelangelo resumed work on the tomb, but had only finished the statues of *Moses* and *The Dying Slaves* when Pope Paul III persuaded him to start work on the Sistine Chapel's *Last Judgment*. Michelangelo had planned a vast monument with over 40 statues, but the tomb that was built – mainly by his pupils – is simply a facade with six niches for statues. *The Dying Slaves* are in Paris and Florence, but the tremendous bearded *Moses* is here. The horns on Moses' head should really be beams of light – they are the result of the original Hebrew from the Old Testament being wrongly translated.

Michelangelo's *Moses* in San Pietro

❸ Santa Pudenziana

Via Urbana 160. **Map** 5 C4. **Tel** 06-481 4622. 🚌 16, 75, 84, 105, 714. Ⓜ Cavour. **Open** 8:30am–noon (from 9am Sun), 3–6pm daily. 🔲

Churches tend to be dedicated to existing saints, but in this case, the church, through a linguistic accident, created a brand new saint. In the 1st century AD a Roman senator called Pudens lived here, and, according to legend, allowed St. Peter to lodge with him. In the 2nd century a bath house was built on this site and in the 4th century a church was established inside the baths, known as the *Ecclesia Pudentiana* (the church of Pudens). In time it was assumed that "Pudentiana" was a woman's name, and a life was created for her – she became the sister of Prassede and was credited with caring for Christian victims of persecution. In 1969, both saints were declared invalid, though their churches both kept their names.

The 19th-century facade of the church retains an 11th-century frieze depicting both Prassede and Pudenziana dressed as crowned Byzantine empresses. The apse has a remarkable 4th-century mosaic, clearly influenced by Classical pagan art in its use of subtle colors. The Apostles are represented as Roman

Apse mosaics in Santa Prassede, showing the saint with St. Paul

senators in togas, but a clumsy attempt at restoration in the 16th century destroyed two of the Apostles and left other figures without legs.

❹ Santa Maria Maggiore

See pp174–5.

❺ Santa Prassede

Via Santa Prassede 9A. **Map** 6 D4. **Tel** 06-488 2456. 🚌 16, 70, 71, 75, 714. Ⓜ Vittorio Emanuele. **Open** 7:30am–noon, 4–6:30pm daily (from 8am Sun; Aug: pm only). 🔲 ♿

The church was founded by Pope Paschal II in the 9th century, on the site of a 2nd-century oratory. Although the interior has been altered and rebuilt, the structure of the original design of the 9th-century church is clearly visible. Its three aisles are separated by rows of granite columns. In the central

Facade of the 19th-century church, Santa Pudenziana

nave, there is a round stone slab covering the well where, according to legend, St. Prassede buried the remains of 2,000 martyrs.

Artists from Byzantium decorated the church with glittering, jewel-colored mosaics. Those in the apse and choir depict stylized white-robed elders, the haloed elect looking down from the gold and blue walls of heaven, spindly legged lambs, feather-mop palm trees, and bright red poppies.

In the apse, Santa Prassede and Santa Pudenziana stand on either side of Christ, with the fatherly arms of St. Paul and St. Peter on their shoulders. Beautiful mosaics of saints, the Virgin, and Christ and the Apostles also cover the walls and vault of the Chapel of St. Zeno, built as a mausoleum for Pope Paschal's mother, Theodora. Part of a column brought back from Jerusalem, allegedly the one to which Christ was bound and flogged, also stands here.

❹ Santa Maria Maggiore

Of all the great Roman basilicas, Santa Maria has the most successful blend of different architectural styles. Its colonnaded nave is part of the original 5th-century building. The Cosmatesque marble floor and delightful Romanesque bell tower, with its blue ceramic roundels, are medieval. The Renaissance saw a new coffered ceiling, and the Baroque gave the church twin domes and its imposing front and rear facades. The mosaics are Santa Maria's most famous feature. From the 5th century come the biblical scenes in the aisle and the spectacular mosaics on the triumphal arch. Medieval highlights include a 13th-century enthroned Christ in the loggia.

Obelisk in Piazza dell'Esquilino
The Egyptian obelisk was erected by Pope Sixtus V in 1587 as a landmark for pilgrims.

★ **Cappella Paolina**
Flaminio Ponzio designed this richly decorated chapel (1611) for Pope Paul V Borghese.

Coffered Ceiling
The gilded ceiling, possibly by Giuliano da Sangallo, was a gift of Alexander VI Borgia at the end of the 15th century. The gold is said to be the first brought from America by Columbus.

356 Virgin appears to Pope Liberius

Pope Gregory VII

1347 Cola di Rienzo crowned Tribune of Rome in Santa Maria

1673 Carlo Rainaldi rebuilds apse

300 AD — **600** — **900** — **1200** — **1500** — **1**

432–40 Sixtus III completes church

420 Probable founding date

1075 Pope Gregory VII kidnapped by opponents while saying Christmas mass in Santa Maria

Coat of arms of Gregory VII

1288–92 Nicholas IV adds apse and transepts

1743 Ferdinando Fuga adds main facade on orders of Benedict XIV

★ Coronation of the Virgin Mosaic

This is the central image of a series of wonderful apse mosaics of the Virgin by Jacopo Torriti (1295).

VISITORS' CHECKLIST

Practical Information
Piazza di Santa Maria Maggiore.
Map 6 D4.
Tel 06-6988 6800.
Open 7am–6:45pm daily.
🕆 ⛪ 📷

Transportation
🚌 16, 70, 71, 714. 🚋 14.
Ⓜ Termini, Cavour.

Baldacchino (1740s)
Its columns of red porphyry and bronze were the work of Ferdinando Fuga.

★ Tomb of Cardinal Rodriguez

The Gothic tomb (1299) contains magnificent Cosmatesque marblework.

★ Cappella Sistina

This Sistine Chapel was built for Pope Sixtus V (1584–87) by Domenico Fontana and houses his tomb.

Column in Piazza Santa Maria Maggiore

A bronze of the Virgin and Child was added to this ancient marble column in 1615. The column came from the Basilica of Constantine in the Forum.

Legend of the Snow

In 356, Pope Liberius had a dream in which the Virgin told him to build a church on the spot where he found snow. When it fell on the Esquiline, on the morning of August 5, in the middle of a baking Roman summer, he naturally obeyed. The miracle of the snow is commemorated each year by a service during which thousands of white petals float down from the ceiling of Santa Maria. Originally roses were used, but nowadays the petals are more usually taken from dahlias.

❻ Arch of Gallienus

Via Carlo Alberto. **Map** 6 D4. 🚌 16, 71, 714. Ⓜ Vittorio Emanuele.

Squashed between two buildings just off Via Carlo Alberto is the central arch of an originally three-arched gate erected in memory of Emperor Gallienus, who was assassinated by his Illyrian officers in AD 262. It was built on the site of the old Esquiline Gate in the Servian Wall, parts of which are visible nearby.

National monument of Vittorio Emanuele II, built in honor of unified Italy's first king

Arch erected in memory of Emperor Gallienus

❼ Santa Bibiana

Via Giovanni Giolitti 154. **Map** 6 F4. **Tel** 06-446 5235. 🚌 71. 🚊 5, 14. Ⓜ Vittorio Emanuele. **Open** 7:30–10am, 4:30–7:30pm Mon–Sat; 7:30am–12:30pm, 4.30–7:30pm Sun. 🚻 ♿

The deceptively simple facade of Santa Bibiana was Bernini's first foray into architecture. It is a clean, economic design with superimposed pilasters and deeply shadowed archways. The church itself was built on the site of the palace belonging to Bibiana's family. This is where the saint was buried after being flogged to death with leaded cords during the brief persecution of the Christians in the reign of Julian the Apostate (361–3). Just inside the church is a small column against which Bibiana is said to have been whipped. Her remains, along with those of her mother Dafrosa and her sister Demetria, who also suffered martyrdom, are preserved in an alabaster urn below the altar. In a niche above the altar stands a statue of Santa Bibiana by Bernini – the first fully clothed figure he ever sculpted. He depicts her standing beside a column, holding the cords with which she was whipped, apparently on the verge of a deadly swoon.

Early sculpture by Bernini of the martyr Santa Bibiana (1626)

❽ Piazza Vittorio Emanuele II

Map 6 E5. 🚌 4, 9, 71. 🚊 5, 14. Ⓜ Vittorio Emanuele. *See Markets p344.*

Piazza Vittorio, as it is called for short, was once one of the city's main open-air food markets, though now it has moved around the corner to new, covered premises. The arcaded square was built in the urban development undertaken after the unification of Italy in 1870. It was named after Italy's first king, but there is nothing regal about its appearance today.

However, the garden area in the center of the square has been restored. It contains a number of mysterious ruins, including a large mound, part of a Roman fountain from the 3rd century AD, and the Porta Magica, a curious 17th-century doorway inscribed with alchemical signs and formulae.

❾ Museo Nazionale d'Arte Orientale

Via Merulana 248. **Map** 6 D5. **Tel** 06-4697 4832. 🚌 16, 70, 71, 714. Ⓜ Vittorio Emanuele. **Open** 9am–2pm Tue, Wed & Fri; 9am–7:30pm Thu, Sat & Sun. 🚗♿ 🅦 museorientale. beniculturali.it

The museum occupies part of the late 19th-century Palazzo Brancaccio, home of the Italian Institute of the Middle and Far East since 1957. The collection ranges from prehistoric Iranian ceramics to sculpture from Afghanistan, Nepal, Kashmir, and India to 18th-century Tibetan paintings on vellum.

From East Asia there are collections of Japanese screen paintings and Chinese jade.

The most unusual exhibits are the finds from the Italian excavation of the ancient civilization of Swat in northeast Pakistan. This fascinating Gandhara culture lasted from the 3rd century BC to about the 10th century AD. Its wonderfully exotic, sensual reliefs show an unusual combination of Hellenistic, Buddhist, and Hindu influences.

Nepalese Bodhisattva in the Museo Nazionale d'Arte Orientale

❿ Auditorium of Maecenas

Largo Leopardi 2. **Map** 6 D5. **Tel** 06-0608. 🚌 16, 714. Ⓜ Vittorio Emanuele. **Open** by appt; phone in advance. 🚫 🔊

Maecenas, a dandy, gourmet, and patron of the arts, was also an astute adviser and colleague of the Emperor Augustus. Fabulously rich, he created a fantastic villa and gardens on the Esquiline hill, most of which has long disappeared beneath the modern city. The partially reconstructed auditorium, isolated on a traffic island, is all that remains.

Inside, a semicircle of tiered seats suggests that it may have been a place for readings and performances. If it was, then Maecenas would have been entertained here by his protégés, the lyric poet Horace and Virgil, author of the *Aeneid*, reading their latest works. However,

water ducts have also been discovered and it may well have been a *nympheum* – a kind of summerhouse – with fountains. Traces of frescoes remain on the walls: you can make out garden scenes and a procession of miniature figures – including one of a characteristically drunken Dionysus (the Greek god of wine) being propped upright by a satyr.

⓫ Sette Sale

Via delle Terme di Traiano. **Map** 5 C5. **Tel** 06-0608. 🚌 85, 87, 117, 186, 810, 850. 🚋 3. Ⓜ Colosseo. **Open** by appt; phone in advance.

Not far from Nero's Domus Aurea is the cistern of the Sette Sale. It was built here to supply the enormous quantities of water needed for the Baths of Trajan. These were built for Emperor Trajan in AD 104 on parts of the Domus Aurea that had been damaged by a fire.

A set of stairs leads down into the cistern, well below street level. There is not much to see here now, but a walk through the huge, echoing cistern where light rays illuminate the watery surfaces is still an evocative experience. The nine sections, 98 ft (30 m) long and 16 ft (5 m) wide, had a capacity of 2 million gallons (8 million liters).

⓬ Domus Aurea

Viale della Domus Aurea. **Map** 5 C5. **Tel** 06-0608. 🚌 85, 87, 117, 186, 810, 850. 🚋 3. Ⓜ Colosseo. **Closed** to the public (call for further information). 🚫 🔊 🏠 🔊

After allegedly setting fire to Rome in AD 64, Nero decided to build himself an outrageous new palace. The Domus Aurea (sometimes called Nero's Golden House) occupied part of the Palatine and most of the Celian and Esquiline hills – an area approximately 25 times the size of the Colosseum. The vestibule on the Palatine side of the complex contained a colossal gilded statue of Nero. There was an artificial lake, with gardens and woods

where imported wild beasts were allowed to roam free. According to Suetonius in his life of Nero, the palace walls were adorned with gold and mother-of-pearl, rooms were designed with ceilings that showered guests with flowers or perfumes, the dining hall rotated, and the baths were fed with both sulfurous water and seawater.

Tacitus described Nero's debauched garden parties, with banquets served on barges and lakeside brothels serviced by aristocratic women, though since Nero killed himself in AD 68, he did not have long to enjoy his new home.

Nero's successors, anxious to distance themselves from the monster-emperor, did their utmost to erase all traces of palace. Vespasian drained the lake and built the Colosseum *(see pp94–7)* in its place, Titus and Trajan each erected a complex of baths over the palace, and Hadrian placed the Temple of Venus and Rome *(see p89)* over the vestibule.

Rooms from one wing of the palace have survived, buried beneath the ruins of the Baths of Trajan on the Oppian hill. Excavations have revealed large frescoes and mosaics that are thought to be a panorama of Rome from a bird's-eye perspective.

Following a structural collapse, the Domus Aurea is closed to the public for repairs.

Frescoed room in the ruins of the Domus Aurea

LATERAN

In the Middle Ages, the Lateran Palace was the residence of the popes, and the Basilica of San Giovanni beside it rivaled St. Peter's in splendor. After the return of the popes from Avignon at the end of the 14th century, the area declined in importance. Pilgrims still continued to visit San Giovanni and Santa Croce in Gerusalemme, but the area remained sparsely inhabited. Ancient convents were situated amid gardens and vineyards until Rome became capital of Italy in 1870 and a network of residential streets was laid out here to house the influx of newcomers. Archaeological interest lies chiefly in the Aurelian Wall and the ruins of the Aqueduct of Nero.

Sights at a Glance

Churches
1. San Giovanni in Laterano pp182–3
5. Santa Croce in Gerusalemme
11. Santi Quattro Coronati
12. San Clemente pp188–9
13. Santo Stefano Rotondo

Shrines
2. Scala Santa and Sancta Sanctorum

Arches and Gates
3. Porta Asinaria
7. Porta Maggiore

Ancient Sites
4. Amphiteatrum Castrense
8. Baker's Tomb
9. Aqueduct of Nero and the Freedmen's Tombs

Museums
6. Museum of Musical Instruments
10. Museo Storico della Liberazione di Roma

Restaurants
see pp310–11
1. Aroma
2. Bibenda
3. Charly's Saucière
4. I Clementini
5. Il Pentagrappolo
6. La Tavena dei 40
7. Maud

See also Street Finder maps 6, 9, 10

◀ The impressive interior of the Basilica of San Clemente

For map symbols see back flap

Street by Street: Piazza di San Giovanni

Both the Basilica of San Giovanni and the Lateran Palace look out over a huge open area, the Piazza di San Giovanni, laid out at the end of the 16th century with an Egyptian obelisk, the oldest in Rome, in the center. Unfortunately, the traffic streaming in and out of the city through Porta San Giovanni tends to detract from its grandeur. Across the square is the building housing the Scala Santa (the Holy Staircase), one of the most revered relics in Rome and the goal for many pilgrims. The area is also a venue for political rallies, and the feast of St. John on June 24 is celebrated with a fair at which Romans consume roast *porchetta (see p61).*

The Chapel of Santa Rufina, originally the portico of the baptistry, has a 5th-century mosaic of spiraling foliage in the apse.

VIA DI SAN STEFANO ROTOI

VIA DELL'AMBA ARADAM

VIA DEI LATERANI

The Cloister of San Giovanni fortunately survived the two fires that destroyed the early basilica. A 13th-century masterpiece of mosaic work, the cloister now houses fragments from the medieval basilica.

Key

— Suggested route

0 meters   75
0 yards   75

The Chapel of San Venanzio is decorated with a series of 7th-century mosaics on a gold background. This detail from the apse shows one of the angels flanking the central figure of Christ. San Venanzio was an accomplished 6th-century Latin poet.

Piazza di San Giovanni in Laterano boasts an ancient obelisk, and parts of Nero's Aqueduct. This 18th-century painting by Canaletto shows how the piazza once looked.

Locator Map
See Central Rome Map pp16–17

The Lateran Palace, residence of the popes until 1309, was rebuilt by Domenico Fontana in 1586.

1 ★ **San Giovanni in Laterano**
Borromini's interior dates from the 17th century, but the grand facade by Alessandro Galilei, with its giant statues of Christ, and the Apostles, was added in 1735.

2 **Scala Santa**
This door at the top of the Holy Staircase leads to the Sancta Sanctorum.

The Triclinio Leoniano is a piece of wall, and a mosaic from the dining hall of 8th-century Pope Leo III.

3 **Porta Asinaria**
This minor gateway, no longer in use, is as old as the Aurelian Wall, dating back to the 3rd century AD.

❶ San Giovanni in Laterano

Early in the 4th century, the Laterani family were disgraced, and their land taken by Emperor Constantine to build Rome's first Christian basilica. Today's church retains the original shape, but has been destroyed by fire twice and rebuilt several times. Borromini undertook the last major rebuild of the interior in 1646, and the main facade is an 18th-century addition. Before the pope's move to Avignon in 1309, the adjoining Lateran Palace was the official papal residence, and until 1870 all popes were crowned in the church. This is the city's main cathedral, and the seat of the Bishop of Rome, the Pope, who celebrates Maundy Thursday Mass here and attends the annual blessing of the people.

★ Baptistry
Though much restored, the domed baptistry dates back to Constantine's time. It assumed its present octagonal shape in AD 432 and the design has served as the model for baptistries throughout the Christian world.

Entrance to museum

KEY

① Apse

② **The Cappella di San Venanzio** chapel is attached to the baptistry, and is decorated with 7th-century mosaics.

③ **The original Lateran Palace** was almost destroyed by the fire of 1308, which devastated San Giovanni. Pope Sixtus V commissioned Fontana to replace it in 1586.

④ **Statues of Christ and the Apostles**

⑤ **A side door** is opened every Holy Year.

⑥ **The main entrance's** bronze doors originally came from the Curia (see p84).

Papal Altar
Only the Pope can celebrate mass at this altar. The Gothic *baldacchino*, decorated with frescoes, dates from the 14th century.

★ Cloisters
Built by the Vassalletto family in about 1220, the cloisters are remarkable for their twisted twin columns and inlaid marble mosaics.

North Facade
This was added by Domenico Fontana in 1586. The pope gives his blessing from the upper loggia.

Boniface VIII Fresco
This fragment showing the pope proclaiming the Holy Year of 1300 is attributed to Giotto.

VISITORS' CHECKLIST

Practical Information
Piazza di San Giovanni in Laterano 4. **Map** 9 C2.
Tel 06-6988 6433.
Cathedral: **Open** 7am–6:30pm daily. Cloister: **Open** 9am–6pm daily. Museum: **Open** 10am–5:30pm daily. Baptistry: **Open** 7am–12:30pm, 4–6:30pm daily. 🏛 for museum, and cloister. 🎫 📷

Transportation
🚌 16, 81, 85, 87, 186, 650, 850 and other routes to Piazza San Giovanni. Ⓜ San Giovanni. 🚊 3.

Corsini Chapel
This chapel was built in the 1730s for Pope Clement XII. The altarpiece is a mosaic copy of Guido Reni's painting of Sant'Andrea Corsini.

Trial of a Corpse

Fear of rival factions led the early popes to extraordinary lengths. An absurd case took place at the Lateran Palace in 897 when Pope Stephen VI tried the corpse of his predecessor, Formosus, for disloyalty to the Church. The corpse was found guilty, its right hand was mutilated, and it was thrown into the Tiber.

Pope Formosus

AD 313 Constantine gives Laterani site to Pope Melchiades for a church	**1144** Church dedicated to San Giovanni in Laterano	**1360** Church burned down for second time **1309** Papacy moves to Avignon	**1586** Domenico Fontana builds north facade
314-18 Five-aisled basilical church is built	**896** Church damaged in earthquake		**1646** Borromini rebuilds interior
AD 300 **600**	**900**	**1200**	**1500**
324 Basilica consecrated by Pope Sylvester I, and dedicated to the Redeemer	**1300** First Holy Year proclaimed		**1730-40** Alessandro Galilei constructs main facade
904-911 Church rebuilt under Pope Sergius III	**1308** Church destroyed by fire		**1377** Return of popes from Avignon

Devout Christians climbing the Scala Santa on their knees

❷ Scala Santa and Sancta Sanctorum

Piazza di San Giovanni in Laterano 14. **Map** 9 C1. **Tel** 06-772 6641. ▣ 16, 81, 85, 87, 186 and other routes to Piazza di San Giovanni in Laterano. 🚊 3. Ⓜ San Giovanni. **Open** 6:30am–noon, 3–5pm daily (3:30–6pm in summer). ✝

On the east side of Piazza di San Giovanni in Laterano, a building designed by Domenico Fontana (1589) houses two surviving parts of the old Lateran Palace. One is the Sancta Sanctorum, the other the holy staircase, the Scala Santa. The 28 steps, said to be those that Christ ascended in Pontius Pilate's house during his trial, are supposed to have been brought from Jerusalem by St Helena, mother of the Emperor Constantine. This belief, however, cannot be traced back any earlier than the 7th century.

The steps were moved to their present site by Pope Sixtus V (reigned 1585–90) when the old Lateran Palace was destroyed. No foot may touch the holy steps, so they are covered by wooden boards. They may only be climbed by the faithful on their knees, a penance that is performed especially on Good Friday. In the vestibule there are various 19th-century sculptures including an *Ecce Homo* by Giosuè Meli (1874).

The Scala Santa and two side stairways lead to the Chapel of St Lawrence or Sancta

Sanctorum (Holy of Holies), built by Pope Nicholas III in 1278. Decorated with fine Cosmatesque marble-work, the chapel contains many important relics, the most precious being an image of Jesus – the *Acheiropoeton* or "picture painted without hands", said to be the work of St Luke, with the help of an angel. It was taken on procession in medieval times to ward off plagues.

On the walls and in the vault, restoration work has revealed 13th-century frescoes which for 500 years had been covered by later paintings. The frescoes, representing the legends of St Nicholas, St Lawrence, St Agnes and St Paul, show signs of the style that would characterize the frescoes of Giotto in Assisi, made a few years later.

❸ Porta Asinaria

Between Piazza di Porta San Giovanni and Piazzale Appio. **Map** 10 D2. ▣ 16, 81, 85, 87. 🚊 3. Ⓜ San Giovanni. *See Markets p345.*

The Porta Asinaria (Gate of the Donkeys) is one of the minor gateways in the Aurelian Wall *(see p198)*. Twin circular towers were added and a small enclosure built around the entrance; the remains are still visible. From outside the walls you can see the gate's white

Porta Asinaria from inside the wall

travertine facade and two rows of small windows, giving light to two corridors built into the wall above the gateway. In AD 546, treacherous barbarian soldiers serving in the Roman army opened this gate to the hordes of the Goth Totila, who mercilessly looted the city. In 1084 the Holy Roman Emperor Henry IV entered Rome via Porta Asinaria with the antipope Guibert to oust Pope Gregory VII. The gate was badly damaged in the conflicts that followed.

The area close to the gate, especially in the Via Sannio, is the home of a popular flea market *(see p345)*.

Shopping for bargain clothes at the Via Sannio flea market

❹ Amphiteatrum Castrense

Between Piazza di Santa Croce in Gerusalemme and Viale Castrense. **Map** 10 E1. ▣ 649. 🚊 3. **Open** by appt; call 06-0608.

This small 3rd-century amphitheater was used for games and baiting animals. It owes its preservation to the fact that it was incorporated in the Aurelian Wall *(see p198)*, which included several existing high buildings in its fortifications. The graceful arches framed by brick semicolumns were blocked up. The amphitheater is best seen from outside the walls, from where there is also a good view of the bell tower of Santa Croce in Gerusalemme.

Discovery and Triumph of the Cross, attributed to Antoniazzo Romano, in Santa Croce in Gerusalemme

❺ Santa Croce in Gerusalemme

Piazza di Santa Croce in Gerusalemme 12. **Map** 10 E1. **Tel** 06-7061 3053. 16, 81, 649, 810. 3. **Open** 7am–12:45pm, 3:30–7:30pm daily.

Emperor Constantine's mother St. Helena founded this church in AD 320 in the grounds of her private palace. Although the church stood at the edge of the city, the relics of the Crucifixion that St. Helena had brought back from Jerusalem made it a center of pilgrimage. Most important were the pieces of Christ's Cross (*croce* means cross) and part of Pontius Pilate's

18th-century statue of St. Helena on the facade of Santa Croce

inscription in Latin, Hebrew and Greek: "Jesus of Nazareth King of the Jews."

In the crypt is a Roman statue of Juno, found at Ostia (*see pp272–3*), transformed into a statue of St. Helena by replacing the head and arms and adding a cross. The 15th-century apse fresco shows the medieval legends that arose around the Cross. Helena is shown holding it over a dead youth and restoring him to life. Another episode shows its recovery from the Persians by the Byzantine Emperor Heraclitus after a bloody battle. In the center of the apse is a magnificent tomb by Jacopo Sansovino made for Cardinal Quiñones, Emperor Charles V's confessor (died 1540).

❻ Museum of Musical Instruments

Museo degli Strumenti Musicali, Piazza di Santa Croce in Gerusalemme 9a. **Map** 10 E1. **Tel** 06-701 4796. 16, 81, 649, 810. 3. **Open** 9am –7pm Tue–Sun. **Closed** Jan 1, Dec 25. **w museostrumentimusicali.it**

One of Rome's lesser-known museums, the building stands on the site of the Sessorianum, the great Imperial villa belonging to Empress St. Helena, later included in the Aurelian Wall.

Opened in 1974, the museum has a collection of more than 3,000 outstanding musical instruments from all over the world, including instruments typical of the various regions of Italy, and wind, string, and percussion instruments of all ages (including ancient Egyptian, Greek, and Roman). There are also sections dedicated to church and military music. The greater part of the collection is composed of Baroque instruments: don't miss the gorgeous Barberini harp, remarkably well-preserved, on the first floor in Room 13. There are spinets, harpsichords, and clavichords, and one of the first pianos ever made, dating from 1722.

Art Nouveau entrance to the Museum of Musical Instruments

❼ Porta Maggiore

Piazza di Porta Maggiore. **Map** 6 F5.
🚌 105. 🚃 3, 5, 14, 19.

Originally the two arches of
Porta Maggiore were not part
of the city wall, but part of an
aqueduct built by the Emperor
Claudius in AD 52. They carried
the water of the Aqua Claudia
over the Via Labicana and Via
Prenestina, two of ancient
Rome's main southbound roads.
You can still see the original
roadway beneath the gate. In
the large slabs of basalt – a hard
volcanic rock used in all old
Roman roads – note the great
ruts created by generations of
cart wheels. On top of the arches,
separate conduits carried the
water of two aqueducts: the
Aqua Claudia, and its offshoot,
the Aqueduct of Nero. They
bear inscriptions from the time
of the Emperor Claudius and
also from the reigns of Vespasian
and Titus, who restored them in
AD 71 and AD 81, respectively.
In all, six aqueducts from
different water sources entered
the city at Porta Maggiore.

The Aqua Claudia was
43 miles (68 km) long, with over
9 miles (15 km) above ground.
Its majestic arches are a
notable feature of the Roman
countryside, and a popular
mineral water bears its name.
One stretch of the Aqua Claudia
had its arches bricked up
when it was incorporated
into the 3rd-century Aurelian
Wall (see p198).

Relief showing breadmaking on the tomb of the baker Eurysaces

❽ Baker's Tomb

Piazzale Labicano. **Map** 6 F5. 🚌 105.
🚃 3, 5, 14, 19.

In the middle of the streetcar
intersection near Porta Maggiore
stands the tomb of the rich baker
Eurysaces and his wife Atistia,
built in 30 BC. Roman
custom forbade
burials within city walls,
and the roads leading
out of cities became
lined with tombs, and
monuments for the
middle and upper
classes. This tomb is
shaped like a baking
oven: a low-relief
frieze at the top
shows Eurysaces
presiding over his
slaves in the various phases of
breadmaking. The inscription
proudly asserts his origins, and
reveals him as a freed slave,
probably of Greek origin. Many
men like him saved money from
their meager slave salaries to
earn their freedom and set up
businesses, becoming the
backbone of Rome's economy.

Relief on the Tomb of
the Statilii freedmen

❾ Aqueduct of Nero and the Freedmen's Tombs

Intersection of Via Statilia and Via di
Santa Croce in Gerusalemme. **Map** 10
D1. 🚌 105, 649. 🚃 3, 5, 14, 19. **Open**
by appt only: call 06-0608.

The aqueduct was built by Nero
in the 1st century AD as an
extension of the Aqua Claudia
to supply Nero's Golden House
(see p177). It was later extended
to the Imperial residences on
the Palatine. Partly incorporated
into later buildings, the imposing arches make their way via
the Lateran to the Celian hill.
Along the first section of the
aqueduct, in Via Statilia, is a
small tomb in the
shape of a house,
dating from the
1st century BC,
bearing the names
and likenesses of a
group of freed slaves.
Their name, Statilii,
indicates that they
had been freed by the
Statilii, the family of
Claudius's notorious
wife Messalina.
Servants of families
often pooled funds in this way
to pay for a dignified burial in a
common resting place.

Porta Maggiore, a city gate formed by the
arches of an aqueduct

Well-preserved section of Nero's Aqueduct
near San Giovanni

❿ Museo Storico della Liberazione di Roma

Via Tasso 145. **Map** 9 C1. **Tel** 06-700 3866. Ⓜ Manzoni, San Giovanni. 🚌 3. **Open** 3:30–7:30pm Tue, Thu & Fri; 9:30am–12:30pm Tue–Sun.

This museum, dedicated to the resistance to the Nazi occupation of Rome, is housed in the ex-prison of the Gestapo. The makeshift cells with bloodstained walls make a strong impact (see p268).

⓫ Santi Quattro Coronati

Via Santi Quattro Coronati 20. **Map** 9 B1. **Tel** 06-7047 5427. 🚌 85, 117. 🚋 3. **Open** 6:30am–12:30pm, 3:30–7:45pm daily. Cloister, St. Sylvester **Open** 10–11:45am (until 10:30am Sun) 4–5:45pm. 🚻 ♿

The name of this fortified convent (Four Crowned Saints) refers to four Christian soldiers martyred after refusing to worship a pagan god. For centuries it was the bastion of the pope's residence, the Lateran Palace. Its high apse looms over the houses below, while a Carolingian tower dominates the entrance. Erected in the 4th century AD, it was rebuilt after the invading Normans set fire to the neighborhood in 1084. Hidden within is the garden of the delightful inner cloister (admission on request), one of the earliest of its kind, built c. 1220.

The remains of medieval frescoes can be seen in the Chapel of Santa Barbara, but the convent's main feature is the Chapel of St. Sylvester – its remarkable frescoes (1246) recount the legend of the conversion to Christianity of the Emperor Constantine by Pope Sylvester I (reigned 314–35), then living as a hermit on Monte Soratte, north of Rome.

Stricken by the plague, Constantine is prescribed a bath in children's blood, to the horror of the matrons of Rome. Unable to bring himself to obey, Constantine is visited in a dream by St. Peter and St. Paul. They advise him to find Sylvester, who cures him and baptizes him. The final scene shows the emperor kneeling before the pope. The implied idea of the pope as heir to the Roman Empire would affect the whole course of medieval European history.

⓬ San Clemente

See pp188–9.

⓭ Santo Stefano Rotondo

Via di Santo Stefano Rotondo 7. **Map** 9 B2. **Tel** 06-42 11 99. 🚌 81, 117, 673. **Open** 9:30am–12:30pm, 3–6pm (2–5pm winter) Tue–Sun. 📷

One of Rome's earliest Christian churches, Santo Stefano Rotondo was constructed between 468 and 483. It has an unusual circular plan with four chapels

Distinctive circular outline of Santo Stefano Rotondo

in the shape of a cross. The round inner area was surrounded by concentric corridors with 22 Ionic supporting columns. The high drum in the center is 72 ft (22 m) high and just as wide. It is lit by 22 high windows, a few of them restored or blocked by restorations carried out under Pope Nicholas V (reigned 1447–55), who consulted the Florentine architect Leon Battista Alberti. The archway in the center may have been added during this period.

In the 16th century the church walls were frescoed by Niccolò Pomarancio, with particularly gruesome illustrations of the martyrdom of innumerable saints. Some of the medieval decor remains: in the first chapel to the left of the entrance is a 7th-century mosaic of Christ with San Primo, and San Feliciano.

Fresco of St. Sylvester and Constantine in Santi Quattro Coronati

⑫ San Clemente

San Clemente provides an opportunity to travel back through three layers of history. At street level, there is a 12th-century church; underneath this lies a 4th-century church; and below that are ancient Roman buildings, including a Temple of Mithras. Mithraism, an all-male cult imported from Persia in the 1st century BC, was a rival to Christianity in Imperial Rome.

The upper levels are dedicated to St. Clement, the fourth pope, who was exiled to the Crimea and martyred by being tied to an anchor and drowned. His life is illustrated in some of the frescoes in the 4th-century church. The site was taken over in the 17th century by Irish Dominicans, who still continue the excavating work begun by Father Mullooly in 1857.

★ Cappella di Santa Caterina
The restored frescoes by the 15th-century Florentine artist Masolino da Panicale show scenes from the life of the martyred St. Catherine of Alexandria.

18th-century Facade
Twelfth-century columns were used in the arcade.

Piscina
This deep pit was discovered in 1967. It could have been used as a font or fountain.

★ 11th-century Frescoes
Commissioned by the de Rapiza family, one shows the story of a boy found alive in St. Clement's tomb beneath the Black Sea.

Catacomb
Discovered in 1938 and dating from the 5th or 6th century, it contains 16 wall tombs known as *loculi*.

KEY

① **1st–3rd-century temple and buildings**

② **4th-century church**

③ **12th-century church**

④ **Entrance** to the church is through a door in Via di San Giovanni in Laterano.

⑤ **Temple of Mithras**

★ Apse Mosaic
The 12th-century *Triumph of the Cross* includes beautifully detailed animals and acanthus leaves.

VISITORS' CHECKLIST

Practical Information
Via di San Giovanni in Laterano.
Map 9 B1.
Tel 06-774 0021.
Open 9am–12:30pm, 3–6pm
Mon–Sat; noon–6pm Sun. Last
adm: 20 min before closing.
🚫 to excavations. 🚻 ♿ 📷
🌐 **basilicasanclemente.com**

Transportation
🚌 85, 87, 117, 186, 810, 850.
🚃 3. Ⓜ Colosseo.

Schola Cantorum
The 6th-century enclosure for the choir was retained for the new church, built in 1108.

Paschal Candlestick
This 12th-century spiraling candlestick, striped with glittering mosaic, is a magnificent example of Cosmati work.

★ Triclinium and Altar of Mithras
The altar, with a relief of Mithras slaying the bull, stands in the *triclinium*, a room used for ritual banquets.

2nd century Site possibly used for secret Christian worship

Late 2nd century Temple of Mithras built

867 Reputed transfer of remains of San Clemente to Rome

1108 New church built over 4th-century church

1857 Original 4th-century church rediscovered by Father Mullooly

| 0 | 500 | 1000 | 1500 | 2000 |

8-97 Papacy t. Clement

4th century First church built over courtyard of earlier Roman building

1667 Church and convent given to Irish Dominicans

4 Nero's fire oys area

1084 Church destroyed during Norman invasion led by Robert Guiscard

1861 Church is excavated. Roman ruins discovered

CARACALLA

The Celian Hill overlooks the Colosseum, and takes its name from Caelius Vibenna, the legendary hero of Rome's struggle against the Tarquins *(see pp20–21)*. In Imperial Rome, this was a fashionable place to live, and some of its vanished splendor is still apparent in the vast ruins of the Baths of Caracalla. Today, thanks to the Archaeological Zone established at the beginning of the 20th century, it is a peaceful area, a green wedge from the Aurelian Wall to the heart of the city. Through it runs the cobbled Via di Porta San Sebastiano, part of the old Via Appia. This road leads to Porta San Sebastiano, one of the best-preserved gates in the ancient city wall.

Sights at a Glance

Churches
1 Santi Giovanni e Paolo
2 San Gregorio Magno
4 Santa Maria in Domnica
6 San Sisto Vecchio
7 Santi Nereo e Achilleo
8 San Cesareo
9 San Giovanni a Porta Latina
10 San Giovanni in Oleo
16 Santa Balbina

Arches and Gates
3 Arch of Dolabella
13 Arch of Drusus
14 Aurelian Wall and Porta San Sebastiano
15 Sangallo Bastion

Historic Buildings
17 Baths of Caracalla

Tombs
11 Columbarium of Pomponius Hylas
12 Tomb of the Scipios

Parks and Gardens
5 Villa Celimontana

See also Street Finder maps 8, 9

0 meters 300
0 yards 300

◀ The Baths of Caracalla

For map symbols *see back flap*

Street-by-Street: The Celian Hill

In the course of a morning's exploration of the green slopes of the Celian hill, you will see a fascinating assortment of archaeological remains and beautiful churches. A good starting point is the church of San Gregorio Magno, from where the Clivo di Scauro leads up to the top of the hill. The steep, narrow street passes the ancient porticoed church of Santi Giovanni e Paolo with its beautiful Romanesque bell tower soaring above the surrounding medieval monastery buildings. Of the parks on the hill, the best kept and most peaceful is the Villa Celimontana with its formal walks and avenues. It is a good place for a picnic, since there are few bars or restaurants in the area.

Clivo di Scauro, the Roman *Clivus Scauri*, leads up to Santi Giovanni e Paolo, passing under the flying buttresses that support the church.

VIA DI SAN GREGORIO

CLIVO DI SCAURO

La Vignola is a delightful Renaissance pavilion, reconstructed here in 1911 after it was demolished during the creation of the Archaeological Zone around the Baths of Caracalla.

To Circo Massimo Metro

❷ San Gregorio Magno
A monastery and chapel were founded here by Pope Gregory the Great at the end of the 6th century.

❶ ★ Santi Giovanni e Paolo
The nave of the church, lit by a blaze of chandeliers, has been restored many times, assuming its present appearance in the 18th century.

❺ ★ Villa Celimontana
The beautiful 16th-century villa built for the Mattei family is now the center of a public park.

Streetcars passing over the Celian hill from the Colosseum rumble up a narrow, picturesque track through the Parco del Celio.

Locator Map
See Central Rome Map pp16–17

Ruins of the Temple of Claudius are visible over a large area of the Celian hill. These travertine blocks have been incorporated in the base of the bell tower of Santi Giovanni e Paolo.

❸ Arch of Dolabella
Built in the 1st century AD, probably as an entrance to the city, this archway was later incorporated in Nero's aqueduct to the Palatine.

The gateway of San Tommaso in Formis is decorated with a wonderful 13th-century mosaic showing Christ with two freed slaves, one white, one black.

❹ ★ Santa Maria in Domnica
This church is famed for its 9th-century mosaics. These Apostles appear on the triumphal arch above the apse, flanking a medallion containing the figure of Christ.

Key

— Suggested route

0 meters   75
0 yards   75

❶ Santi Giovanni e Paolo

Piazza Santi Giovanni e Paolo 13. **Map** 9 A1. **Tel** 06-772 711. 🚌 75, 81, 117, 175, 673. 🚊 3. Ⓜ Colosseo or Circo Massimo. Church: **Open** 8:30am–noon, 3:30–6pm daily. Roman houses: **Tel** 06-7045 4544. **Open** 10am–1pm, 3–6pm Thu–Mon. 🔼 ♿ church only. 🌐 **caseromane.it**

Santi Giovanni e Paolo is dedicated to two martyred Roman officers whose house originally stood on this site. Giovanni (John) and Paolo (Paul) had served the first Christian emperor, Constantine. When they were later called to arms by the pagan emperor Julian the Apostate, they refused and were beheaded and buried in secret in their own house in AD 362.

Built toward the end of the 4th century, the church retains many elements of its original structure. The Ionic portico dates from the 12th century, and the apse and bell tower were added by Nicholas Breakspeare, the only English pope, who reigned as Adrian IV (1154–9). The base of the superb 13th-century Romanesque bell tower was part of the Temple of Claudius that stood on this site. The interior, which was remodeled in 1718, has granite piers and columns. A tomb slab in the nave marks the burial place of the martyrs, whose relics are preserved in an urn under the high altar. In a tiny room near the altar, a magnificent 13th-century fresco depicts the figure of Christ flanked by his Apostles (ask the sacristan, who will be able to unlock the door).

Excavations beneath the church have revealed two 2nd- and 3rd-century Roman houses used as a Christian burial place. These are well worth a visit. The two-story construction, with 20 rooms and a labyrinth of corridors, has well-preserved pagan and Christian paintings. The arches to the left of the church were part of a 3rd-century street of shops.

Facade of San Gregorio Magno

❷ San Gregorio Magno

Piazza di San Gregorio. **Map** 8 F2. **Tel** 06-700 8227. 🚌 75, 81, 117, 175, 673. 🚊 3. Ⓜ Circo Massimo. **Open** 9am–1pm, 3:30–7pm daily. 🔼

To the English, this is one of the most important churches in Rome, for it was from here that St. Augustine was sent on his mission to convert England to

Marble throne of Gregory the Great from the 1st century BC

Christianity. The church was founded in AD 575 by San Gregorio Magno (St. Gregory the Great), who turned his family home on this site into a monastery. It was rebuilt in medieval times and restored in 1629–33 by Giovanni Battista Soria. The church is reached via a flight of steps from the street.

The forecourt contains some interesting tombs. To the left is that of Sir Edward Carne, who came to Rome several times between 1529 and 1533 as King Henry VIII's envoy to gain the pope's consent to the annulment of Henry's marriage to Catherine of Aragon.

The interior, remodeled by Francesco Ferrari in the mid-18th century, is Baroque, apart from the fine mosaic floor and some ancient columns. At the end of the right aisle is the chapel of St. Gregory. Leading off it, another small chapel, believed to have been the saint's own cell, houses his episcopal throne – a Roman chair of sculpted marble. The Salviati Chapel on the left contains a picture of the Virgin said to have spoken to St. Gregory.

Outside, amid the cypresses to the left of the church, stand three small chapels, dedicated to St. Andrew, St. Barbara and St. Sylvia (Gregory the Great's mother). The chapels contain frescoes by Domenichino and Guido Reni.

Fresco of Christ and the Apostles in Santi Giovanni e Paolo

❸ Arch of Dolabella

Via di San Paolo della Croce. Map 9
A2. 🚌 81, 117, 673. 🚃 3. Ⓜ
Colosseo.

The arch was built in AD 10 by
consuls Caius Junius Silanus and
Cornelius Dolabella, possibly on
the site of one of the old Servian
Wall's gateways. It was made of
travertine blocks and later used
to support Nero's extension of
the Claudian aqueduct, built to
supply the Imperial Palace on
the Palatine Hill.

The restored Arch of Dolabella

❹ Santa Maria in Domnica

Piazza della Navicella 12. Map 9 A2. Tel
06-7720 2685. 🚌 81,117, 673. 🚃 3.
Ⓜ Colosseo. Open 9am–noon, 3:30–
7pm (to 6pm in winter) daily. 🚻 ♿

The church overlooks the Piazza
della Navicella (little boat) and
takes its name from the
16th-century fountain. Dating
from the 7th century, the
church was probably built on
the site of an ancient Roman
firemen's barracks, which later
became a meeting place for
Christians. In the 16th century
Pope Leo X added the portico
and the coffered ceiling.

In the apse behind the
modern altar is a superb
9th-century mosaic commissioned by Pope Paschal I.
Wearing the square halo of the
living, the pope appears at the
feet of the Virgin and Child. The
Virgin, surrounded by a throng
of angels, holds a handkerchief
like a fashionable lady at a
Byzantine court.

❺ Villa Celimontana

Piazza della Navicella. Map 9 A2.
🚌 81, 117, 673. Park: Open 7am–
dusk daily.

The Dukes of Mattei bought this
land in 1553 and transformed the
vineyards that covered the
hillside into a formal garden. As
well as palms and other exotic
trees, the garden has its own
Egyptian obelisk. Villa Mattei, built
in the 1580s and now known as
Villa Celimontana, houses the
Italian Geographical Society.

The Mattei family used to
open the park to the public on
the day of the Visit of the Seven
Churches, an annual event
instituted by San Filippo Neri in
1552. Starting from the Chiesa
Nuova (see p126), Romans went
on foot to the city's seven major
churches and, on reaching Villa
Mattei, were given bread, wine,
salami, cheese, an egg, and two
apples. The garden, now owned
by the city of Rome, still makes
an ideal place for a picnic. In
summer it hosts an excellent
jazz festival (see p350).

Park of Villa Celimontana

❻ San Sisto Vecchio

Piazzale Numa Pompilio 8. Map 9 A3.
Tel 06-7720 5174. 🚌 160, 628, 671,
714. Open 9–11am, 3–5:30pm daily.
📧

This small church is of great
historical interest as it was
granted to St. Dominic in 1219
by Pope Honorius III. The
founder of the Dominican
order soon moved his own
headquarters to Santa Sabina
(see p206), San Sisto becoming
the first home of the order of
Dominican nuns. The church,
with its 13th-century bell tower
and frescoes, is also a popular
place for weddings.

Apse mosaic of the Virgin and Child in Santa Maria in Domnica

Fresco by Niccolò Pomarancio of the *Martyrdom of St. Simon* in Santi Nereo e Achilleo

➐ Santi Nereo e Achilleo

Via D. Terme di Caracalla 28. **Map** 9 A3. **Fax** 06 687 3124. 160, 628, 671, 714. **Open** 10am–noon, 4–6pm Thu–Mon (timings may vary).

According to legend, St. Peter, after escaping from prison, was fleeing the city when he lost a bandage from his wounds. The original church was founded here in the 4th century on the spot where the bandage fell, but it was later rededicated to the 1st-century AD martyrs St. Nereus and St. Achilleus.

Detail of mosaic, Santi Nereo e Achilleo

Restored at the end of the 16th century, the church has retained many medieval features, including some fine 9th-century mosaics on the triumphal arch. A magnificent pulpit rests on an enormous porphyry pedestal that was found nearby in the Baths of Caracalla. The walls of the side aisles are decorated with grisly 16th-century frescoes by Niccolò Pomarancio, showing in clinical detail how each of the Apostles was martyred.

➑ San Cesareo

Via di Porta San Sebastiano. **Map** 9 A3. **Tel** 06-5823 0140. 218, 628. **Open** 9am–noon Sun & by appt.

This splendid old church was built over Roman ruins of the 2nd century AD. You can still admire Giacomo della Porta's fine Renaissance facade, but by calling ahead to schedule a visit, you can also see Cosmatesque mosaic work, and carving to rival that of any church in Rome. The episcopal throne, altar, and pulpit are decorated with delightful birds and beasts. The church was restored in the 16th century by Pope Clement VIII, whose coat of arms decorates the ceiling.

➒ San Giovanni a Porta Latina

Via di San Giovanni a Porta Latina. **Map** 9 B3. **Tel** 06-7740 0032. 218, 360, 628. **Open** 7:30am–12.30pm, 3–7pm daily.

The church of "St. John at the Latin Gate" was founded in the 5th century, rebuilt in 720, and restored in 1191. This is one of the most picturesque of the old Roman churches.

Classical columns support the medieval portico, and the 12th-century bell tower is superb. A tall cedar tree shades an ancient well standing in the forecourt. The interior has been restored, but it preserves the rare simplicity of its early origins with ancient columns of varying styles lining the aisles. Traces of early medieval frescoes can still be seen within the church. There are 12th-century frescoes showing 46 different biblical scenes, from both the Old and New testaments, which are among the finest of their kind in Rome.

➓ San Giovanni in Oleo

Via di Porta Latina. **Map** 9 C4. **Tel** 06-7740 0032. 628. ask at S. Giovanni a Porta Latina.

The name of this charming octagonal Renaissance chapel means "St. John in Oil." The tiny building marks the spot where, according to legend, St. John was boiled in oil – and came out unscathed, or even refreshed. An earlier chapel is said to have existed on the site; the present one was built in the early 16th century. The design has been attributed to Baldassare Peruzzi or Antonio da Sangallo the Younger. It was restored by Borromini, who altered the roof, crowning it with a cross supported by a sphere decorated with roses. He also added a terra-cotta frieze of roses, and palm leaves. The wall paintings inside the chapel include one of St. John in a cauldron of boiling oil.

Fresco, San Giovanni a Porta Latina

Niches for funerary urns in the Columbarium of Pomponius Hylas

⓫ Columbarium of Pomponius Hylas

Via di Porta Latina 10. **Map** 9 B4.
Tel 06-0608. 218, 360, 628. **Open**
Guided tours only; phone ahead.

Known as a columbarium
because it resembles a
dovecote (*columba* is the Latin
word for dove), this kind of
vaulted tomb was usually built
by rich Romans to house the
cremated remains of their
freedmen. Many similar tombs
have been uncovered in this
part of Rome, which up until the
3rd century AD lay outside the
city wall. This one, excavated in
1831, dates from the 1st century
AD. An inscription informs
us that it is the tomb of
Pomponius Hylas and his wife,

Mosaic inscription in the Columbarium of
Pomponius Hylas

Pomponia Vitalinis. Above her
name is a "V" that indicates
that she was still living when
the inscription was made.
The tomb was probably a
commercial venture. Niches
in the interior walls of the
columbarium were sold to
people who could not afford to
build vaults of their own.

⓬ Tomb of the Scipios

Via di Porta San Sebastiano 9.
Map 9 B4. **Tel** 06-0608. 218, 360,
628. **Open** Guided tours only;
call ahead.

The Scipios were a family of
conquering generals. Southern
Italy, Corsica, Algeria, Spain, and
Asia Minor all fell to their
victorious Roman armies. The
most famous of these generals
was Publius Cornelius Scipio
Africanus, who defeated the
great Carthaginian general
Hannibal at the Battle of Zama
in 202 BC *(see p25)*. Scipio
Africanus himself was not
buried here in the family
tomb, but at Liternum near
Naples, where he owned a
favorite villa.
   The Tomb of the Scipios was
discovered in 1780. It contained
various sarcophagi, statues, and

niches with terra-cotta burial
urns. Many of the originals have
now been moved to the Vatican
Museums and copies stand in
their place.
   The earliest sarcophagus
was that of Cornelius Scipio
Barbatus, consul in 298 BC, for
whom the tomb was built.
Members of his illustrious family
continued to be buried here up
to the middle of the 2nd century
BC. Excavations in the area have
revealed a columbarium similar
to that of Pomponius Hylas, a
Christian catacomb, and a three-
story house dating from the 3rd
century AD, which was built
over the Tomb of the Scipios.

⓭ Arch of Drusus

Via di Porta San Sebastiano. **Map** 9 B4.
218, 360.

Once mistakenly identified as a
triumphal arch, the so-called
Arch of Drusus merely
supported the branch aqueduct
that supplied the Baths of
Caracalla. It was built in the
3rd century AD, so it had no
connection with Drusus, a
stepson of the Emperor
Augustus. Its monumental
appearance was due to the fact
that it carried the aqueduct
across an important route, Via
Appia. The arch still spans the
old cobbled road, just 160 ft
(50 m) short of the gateway
Porta San Sebastiano.

Arch of Drusus, part of the Aqua
Antoniniana aqueduct

⓮ Aurelian Wall and Porta San Sebastiano

Museo delle Mura, Via di Porta San Sebastiano 18. **Map** 9 B4. 218, 360. **Tel** 06-0608. **Open** 9am–2pm Tue–Sun. Last adm: 30 min before closing. **Closed** Jan 1, May 1, Dec 25. W museodellemuraroma.it

Most of the Aurelian Wall, begun by the emperor Aurelian (AD 270–75) and completed by his successor Probus (AD 276–82), has survived. Aurelian ordered its construction as a defense against Germanic tribes, whose raids were penetrating deeper and deeper into Italy. Some 11 miles (18 km) around, with 18 gates and 381 towers, the wall took in all the seven hills of Rome. It was raised to almost twice its original height by Maxentius (AD 306–12).

The wall was Rome's main defense until 1870, when it was breached by Italian artillery near Porta Pia, close to today's British Embassy. Many of the gates are still in use, and although the city has spread, most of its noteworthy historical and cultural sights still lie within the walls.

Porta San Sebastiano, the gate leading to the Via Appia Antica (see p286), is the largest and best-preserved gateway in the Aurelian Wall. It was rebuilt by Emperor Honorius in the 5th century AD. Originally the Porta Appia, in Christian times it gradually became known as the Porta San Sebastiano, because the Via Appia led to the

Basilica and Catacombs of San Sebastiano, which were popular places of pilgrimage.

It was at this gate that the last triumphal procession to enter the city by the Appian Way was received in state – that of Marcantonio Colonna after the victory of Lepanto over the Turkish fleet in 1571. Today the gate's towers house a museum with prints, and models showing the walls' history. From here you can take a short walk along the restored walls. The views are spectacular.

Pope Paul III Farnese

⓯ Sangallo Bastion

Viale di Porta Ardeatina. **Map** 9 A4. 160. **Closed** for restoration.

Haunted by the memory of the Sack of Rome in 1527 and fearing attack by the Turks, Pope Paul III asked Antonio da Sangallo the Younger to reinforce the Aurelian Wall. Work on the huge projecting bastion began in 1537. For the moment its massive bulk can only be admired from outside.

The high altar of Santa Balbina

⓰ Santa Balbina

Piazza di Santa Balbina 8. **Map** 8 F3. **Tel** 06-578 0207. 160. 3. M Circo Massimo. **Open** 10:30–11:30am Sun.

Overlooking the Baths of Caracalla, this isolated church is dedicated to Santa Balbina, a 2nd-century virgin martyr. It is one of the oldest in Rome, dating back to the fifth century, and was built on the remains of a Roman villa. Consecrated by Pope Gregory the Great, in the Middle Ages Santa Balbina was a fortified monastery, and over time it has changed in appearance several times, regaining its Romanesque aspect in the 1920s.

From the piazza in front of the church, a staircase leads up to a three-arched portico. Inside, light streams in from a series of high windows along the length of the nave. The remains of St. Balbina and her father, St. Quirinus, are in an urn at the high altar, though the church's real treasure is situated in the far right-hand corner: the magnificent sculpted and inlaid tomb of Cardinal Stefanis de Surdis by Giovanni di Cosma (1303).

Other features worth noting are a 13th-century episcopal throne and various fragments of frescoes. These include a lovely *Madonna and Child*, an example of the school of Pietro Cavallini, in the second chapel on the left. Fragments of first-century Roman mosaics were also discovered in the 1930s. Depicting birds and signs of the zodiac, these are now set in the church floor.

Fortified gateway of Porta San Sebastiano

⑰ Baths of Caracalla

Viale delle Terme di Caracalla 52. **Map**
9 A3. **Tel** 06-3996 7700. 🚌 160, 628.
🚋 3. Ⓜ Circo Massimo. **Open**
9am–2pm Mon, 9am–approx 1hr
before sunset Tue–Sun. **Closed** Jan 1,
Dec 25. 🅿 ♿ 🏛 ♿

Completed by Emperor
Caracalla in AD 217, the baths
functioned for about 300 years,
until the plumbing was
destroyed by invading Goths.
Over 1,600 bathers at a time
could enjoy the facilities. A
Roman bath was a serious
business, beginning with a sort
of Turkish bath, followed by a
spell in the *caldarium*, a large
hot room with pools
of water to provide
humidity. Then came
the lukewarm
tepidarium, a visit to
the large central
meeting
place known as the
frigidarium, and
finally a plunge into

Part of one of the gymnasia in the Baths of Caracalla

the *natatio*, an open-air
swimming pool. For the rich,
this was followed by a rub-
down with scented woolen
cloth. As well as the
baths, there were
spaces for exercise,
libraries, art galleries,
and gardens – a true
leisure center. Most of
the rich marble
decorations were
removed by the Farnese
family in the 16th

Fragment of mosaic pavement

century to adorn the interior of
Palazzo Farnese *(see p149)*. Open-
air operas, mostly Verdi or Puccini,
are performed in these settings
in the summer months and are
very well attended.

Key
▦ Caldarium (very hot)
▢ Tepidarium (lukewarm)
▦ Frigidarium (cold)
▢ Natatio (pool)
▢ Garden

Conference and meeting rooms · Original front entrance · Changing rooms · Gymnasia · Storage room for oils and perfumes · Conference and meeting room · Gymnasium · Stadium · Water tanks · Greek and Latin libraries

AVENTINE

This is one of the most peaceful areas within the walls of the city. Although it is largely residential, there are some unique historic sights. From the top of the Aventine Hill, crowned by the magnificent basilica of Santa Sabina, there are fine views across the river to Trastevere and St. Peter's.

At the foot of the hill, ancient Rome is preserved in the two tiny temples of the Forum Boarium and the Circus Maximus. The liveliest streets are in Testaccio, which has shops, restaurants, and clubs, while to the south, beside Rome's solitary pyramid, the Protestant Cemetery is another oasis of calm.

Sights at a Glance

Churches and Temples
1 Santa Maria in Cosmedin
3 San Giorgio in Velabro
4 San Teodoro
5 Santa Maria della Consolazione
7 San Giovanni Decollato
9 Temples of the Forum Boarium
10 Santa Sabina
11 Santi Bonifacio e Alessio
16 San Saba

Historic Buildings
8 Casa dei Crescenzi

Arches
2 Arch of Janus

Historic Streets and Piazzas
12 Piazza dei Cavalieri di Malta

Ancient Sites
6 Area Archeologica di Sant'Omobono
13 Ponte Testaccio
17 Circus Maximus

Monuments and Tombs
14 Protestant Cemetery
15 Pyramid of Caius Cestius

Restaurants
see pp310–11
1 0,75
2 Angelina a Testaccio
3 Checchino dal 1887
4 Da Oio a Casa Mia
5 Da Remo
6 Felice a Testaccio
7 Flavio al Velavevodetto
8 Oasi della Birra
9 Perilli

See also Street Finder maps 7, 8, 12

◀ Mask fountain in courtyard of Santa Sabina

For map symbols *see back flap*

Street-by-Street: Piazza della Bocca della Verità

The area attracts visitors eager to place their hands inside the Bocca della Verità (the Mouth of Truth) in the portico of Santa Maria in Cosmedin. There are many other sights to see in this quiet corner of the city beside the Tiber, which was the site of ancient Rome's first port and its busy cattle market. Substantial Classical remains include two small temples from the Republican age and the Arch of Janus from the later Empire. In the 6th century the area became home to a Greek community from Byzantium, who founded the churches of San Giorgio in Velabro and Santa Maria in Cosmedin.

❽ **Casa dei Crescenzi**
This 11th-century building used columns and capitals from ancient Roman temples.

Key

— Suggested route

0 meters

0 yards   75

❻**Sant'Omobono**, a late-16th-century church, now stands in isolation in the middle of an important archaeological site. The remains of sacrificial altars and two temples from the 6th century BC have been discovered.

Ponte Rotto, as this forlorn ruined arch in the Tiber is called, means simply "broken bridge." Built in the 2nd century BC, its original name was Pons Aemilius.

❾ ★ **Temples of the Forum Boarium**
The tiny round Temple of Hercules and its neighbor, the Temple of Portunus, are the best preserved of Rome's Republican temples.

The Fontana dei Tritoni by Carlo Bizzaccheri was built here in 1715. The style shows the powerful influence of Bernini.

⑤ Santa Maria della Consolazione
This 16th-century church used to serve a hospital nearby.

④ San Teodoro
The 15th-century portal of this ancient round church is decorated with the insignia of Pope Nicholas V.

Locator Map
See Central Rome Map pp16–17

⑦ San Giovanni Decollato
The plain Renaissance facade was completed in about 1504.

VIA DEI FIENILI

VIA DI SAN TEODORO

③ San Giorgio in Velabro
The simple 12th-century portico of Ionic columns was destroyed by a bomb in 1993 but has been restored.

The Arco degli Argentari, dedicated to the Emperor Septimius Severus in AD 204, is decorated with scenes of religion and war.

PIAZZA DELLA BOCCA DELLA VERITÀ

② Arch of Janus
This square structure with arches on each side dates from the 4th century AD.

COLLATO

VIA DEI CERCHI

DELLA GRECA

① ★ Santa Maria in Cosmedin
This medieval church has a fine marble mosaic floor and a Gothic baldacchino.

❶ Santa Maria in Cosmedin

Piazza della Bocca della Verità 18.
Map 8 E1. **Tel** 06-678 1419. 🚌 23, 44, 81, 160, 170, 280, 628, 715, 716.
Open summer: 9:30am–6pm daily (to 5pm winter). 🚹 ♿ 📷

This beautiful unadorned church was built in the 6th century on the site of the ancient city's food market. The elegant Romanesque bell tower and portico were added during the 12th century. In the 19th century a Baroque facade was removed and the church restored to its original simplicity. It contains many fine examples of Cosmati work, in particular the mosaic pavement, the raised choir, the bishop's throne, and the canopy over the main altar.

Set into the wall of the portico is the Bocca della Verità (Mouth of Truth). This may have been a drain cover, dating back to before the 4th century BC. Medieval tradition had it that the formidable jaws would snap shut over the hand of those who told lies – a useful trick for testing the faithfulness of spouses.

Bocca della Verità at Santa Maria in Cosmedin

❷ Arch of Janus

Via del Velabro. **Map** 8 E1. 🚌 23, 44, 63, 81, 160, 170, 280, 628, 715, 716, 780.

Probably dating from the reign of Constantine, this imposing four-faced marble arch stood at the crossroads on the edge of the Forum Boarium, near the ancient docks. Merchants did business in its shade. On the keystones above the four arches you can see small figures of the goddesses Roma, Juno, Ceres, and Minerva. In medieval times the arch formed the base of a tower fortress. It was restored to its original shape in 1827.

San Giorgio in Velabro after its restoration in 1999

❸ San Giorgio in Velabro

Via del Velabro 19. **Map** 8 E1.
Tel 06-6979 7536. 🚌 23, 44, 63, 81, 95, 160, 170, 280, 628, 715, 716, 780.
Open 10am–12:30pm, 4–6:30pm Tue, Fri & Sat.

In the hollow of the street named after the Velabrum, the swamp where Romulus and Remus are said to have been found by the she-wolf, is a small church dedicated to St. George, whose bones lie under the altar.

The 7th-century basilica has suffered over time from periodic floods, and in 1993 a bomb damaged the front of the church. Careful restoration has, however, returned it to its original appearance.

A double row of granite and marble columns (taken from ancient Roman temples) divides the triple nave. The austerity of the gray interior is relieved by golden frescoes in the apse (attributed to Pietro Cavallini, 1295). The facade and the bell tower date from the 12th century.

❹ San Teodoro

Via di San Teodoro 7. **Map** 8 E1.
Tel 06-678 6624. 🚌 23, 44, 81, 95, 160, 170, 280, 628, 715, 716.
Open 9:30am–12:30pm Sun–Fri.

This small, round 6th-century church at the foot of the Palatine features breathtaking 6th-century mosaics in the apse, and a Florentine cupola dating from 1454. The fetching outer courtyard was designed by Carlo Fontana in 1705. Greek Orthodox services are held here on Sunday mornings.

❺ Santa Maria della Consolazione

Piazza della Consolazione 94. **Map** 5 A5. **Tel** 06-678 4654. 🚌 23, 44, 63, 81, 160, 170, 280, 628, 715, 716, 780.
Open 6:30am–6:30pm Mon–Sat; 10am–6:30pm Sun. 🚹 ♿

The church stands near the foot of the Tarpeian Rock, the site of public execution of traitors since the time of the Sabine War *(see p76)*.

In 1385, Giordanello degli Alberini, a condemned noble-

The Arch of Janus, where cattle dealers sheltered from the midday sun

Facade of Santa Maria della Consolazione

man, paid two gold florins for an image of the Virgin Mary to be placed here, to provide consolation to prisoners in their final moments before execution. Hence the name of the church that was built here in 1470. It was reconstructed between 1583 and 1600 by Martino Longhi, who provided the early Baroque facade at the same time.

The church's 11 side-chapels are owned by noble families and local crafts guild members. Taddeo Zuccari is responsible for the 1556 frescoes depicting scenes from the Passion (first chapel on the right), while the Mannerist artist Niccolò Circignani painted the scenes from the life of Mary and Jesus housed in the fifth chapel. In the presbytery is the image of Mary, attributed to Antoniazzo Romano.

❻ Area Archeologica di Sant'Omobono

Vico Jugario 4. **Map** 5 A5. **Tel** 06-0608. 🚌 23, 44, 63, 81, 160, 170, 280, 628, 715, 716, 780.

Unearthed in 1937, this important archaeological area opened to the public in 2013. The remains of the temple Mater Matuta, dating from the 6th century BC, have been attributed to the time of King Tullius. The excavations have also revealed traces of a pre-Roman cult.

❼ San Giovanni Decollato

Via di San Giovanni Decollato 22. **Map** 8 E1. **Tel** 06-679 1890. 🚌 23, 44, 63, 81, 160, 170, 280, 628, 715, 716, 780. **Open** around the feast of St. John (Jun 24).

Giorgio Vasari's *The Beheading of St. John* (1553), from which the church takes its name, dominates the main altar. In 1490 Pope Innocent VIII gave this site to build a church for a Florentine confraternity. Clad in black robes and hoods, they would encourage prisoners to repent and give them a decent burial after they had been hanged. In the cloisters there are seven manholes, which received the bodies. The confraternity still exists, with church funds assisting prisoners' families.

The oratory holds a cycle of frescoes by Florentine Mannerists Francesco Salviati and Jacopino del Conte depicting events in the life of St. John the Baptist.

❽ Casa dei Crescenzi

Via Luigi Petroselli. **Map** 8 E1. 🚌 23, 44, 63, 81, 160, 170, 280, 628, 715, 716, 780.

Studded with archaeological fragments, the house is what remains of an 11th-century tower fortress. The powerful Crescenzi family built it to keep an eye on the docks (now the site of the Public Records Office) and on the bridge where they collected a toll.

❾ Temples of the Forum Boarium

Piazza della Bocca della Verità. **Map** 8 E1. 🚌 23, 44, 81, 160, 170, 280, 628, 715, 716.

These incredibly well-preserved Republican temples date from the 2nd century BC and were saved for posterity when they were reconsecrated as Christian churches in the Middle Ages. They offer rare examples of combined elements from Greek and Roman architecture.

The rectangular temple (formerly known as the Temple of Fortuna Virilis) was dedicated to Portunus, god of rivers and ports – a reference to the nearby port of ancient Rome. Set on a podium, it has four Ionic travertine columns and 12 half-columns, embedded in the tufa wall of the *cella* – the room that housed the image of the god. Nearby is the small circular Temple of Hercules, its slender Corinthian columns surrounding the central *cella*. Built around 120 BC, the temple is thought to be the earliest Roman marble edifice to have survived to the present day. It is often referred to as the Temple of Vesta due to its similarity to the one in the Forum.

Ancient Roman fragments in the Casa dei Crescenzi

Luminous interior of Santa Sabina

⓾ Santa Sabina

Piazza Pietro d'Illiria 1. **Map** 8 E2. **Tel** 06-579 401. 🚌 23, 280, 716. Ⓜ Circo Massimo. **Open** 8:15am–12:30pm, 3:30–6pm daily. ♿

High on the Aventine stands an early Christian basilica, founded by Peter of Illyria in AD 425, and restored to its original simplicity in the early 20th century. Light filters through 9th-century windows upon a wide nave framed by white Corinthian columns supporting an arcade decorated with a marble frieze. Over the main door is a 5th-century blue and gold mosaic dedicatory inscription. The pulpit, carved choir, and bishop's throne date from the 9th century.

The church was given to the Dominicans in the 13th century and in the nave is the magnificent mosaic tombstone of one of the first leaders of the order, Muñoz de Zamora (died 1300).

The side portico has 5th-century paneled doors carved from cypress wood, representing scenes from the Bible, including one of the earliest Crucifixions in existence.

⓫ Santi Bonifacio e Alessio

Piazza di Sant'Alessio 23. **Map** 8 D2. **Tel** 06-574 3446. 🚌 23, 280, 716. Ⓜ Circo Massimo. **Open** for wedding services only. ♿

The church is dedicated to two early Christian martyrs, whose remains lie under the main altar.

Legend has it that Alessio, son of a rich senator living on the site, fled to the East to avoid an impending marriage, and became a pilgrim. Returning home after many years, he died as a servant, unrecognized, under the stairs of the family entrance hall, clutching the manuscript of his story for posterity.

The original 5th-century church has undergone many changes over time. Noteworthy are the 18th-century facade with its five arches, the restored Cosmati doorway, and pavement, and the magnificent Romanesque five-story bell tower (1217).

An 18th-century Baroque chapel by Andrea Bergondi houses part of the famous staircase. Other relics include the well from Alessio's family home and the glowing Byzantine Madonna of the Intercession brought from Damascus to Rome at the end of the 10th century.

⓬ Piazza dei Cavalieri di Malta

Map 8 D2. 🚌 23, 280, 716. Ⓜ Circo Massimo.

Surrounded by cypress trees, this ornate walled piazza decorated with obelisks, and military trophies was designed by Piranesi in 1765. It is named after the Order of the Knights of Malta (Cavalieri di Malta), whose priory (at No. 3) is famous for the bronze keyhole through which there is a miniature view of St. Peter's, framed by a tree-lined avenue. The priory church, Santa Maria del Priorato, was restored in Neo-Classical style by Piranesi in the 18th century. To visit the church, ask permission in person at the Order's building at 48 Via Condotti. At the

southwest corner of the square is Sant'Anselmo, the international Benedictine church, where Gregorian chant may be heard on Sundays (see p348).

Doorway of the Priory of the Knights of Malta

⓭ Monte Testaccio

Via Galvani. **Map** 8 D4. Ⓜ Piramide. 🚌 23, 63, 719. 🚋 3. **Open** by appt only; call 06-0608.

From about 140 BC to AD 250 this hill was created by dumping millions of *testae* (hence Testaccio) – pieces of the amphorae used to carry goods to nearby warehouses. The full archaeological significance of this 118-ft- (36-m-) high artificial hill was not realized until the late 18th century.

Facade of Santi Bonifacio e Alessio

⓮ Protestant Cemetery

Cimitero Acattolico, Via Caio Cestio 6.
Map 8 D4. **Tel** 06-574 1900. 🚌 23,
280, 716. 🚊 3. Ⓜ Piramide. **Open**
9am–5pm Mon–Sat; 9am–1pm Sun
(last adm: 30 min before closing).
Donation expected. ♿

The peace of this well-tended
cemetery beneath the Aurelian
Wall is profoundly moving.
Non-Catholics, mainly
English, and German,
have been buried
here since 1738. In
the oldest part are
the graves of John
Keats (died 1821),
whose epitaph
reads: "Here lies
One Whose Name
was writ in Water,"
and his friend
Joseph Severn
(died 1879); not far
away are the ashes
of Percy Bysshe Shelley (died
1822). Goethe's son Julius is also
buried here.

Tombstone of John Keats

Memorial pyramid of Caius Cestius

⓯ Pyramid of Caius Cestius

Piazzale Ostiense. **Map** 8 E4. 🚌 23,
280, 716. 🚊 3. Ⓜ Piramide. **Open** for
guided tours only.

Caius Cestius, a wealthy *praetor*
(senior Roman magistrate), died
in 12 BC. His one claim to fame is
his tomb, an imposing pyramid
faced in white marble set in the
Aurelian Wall near Porta San
Paolo. It stands 118 ft (36 m)
high and, according to an
inscription, took 330 days
to build. Unmistakable as a
landmark, it must have looked
almost as incongruous when it
was built as it does today.

Detail of carving on sarcophagus in the
portico of San Saba

⓰ San Saba

Via di San Saba. **Map** 8 F3. **Tel** 06-
6458 0140. 🚌 75, 175, 673. 🚊 3.
Open 8am–noon, 4–7pm Mon–Sat;
9:30am–1pm, 4–7:30pm Sun. 🚻

Tucked away in a residential
street on the Little Aventine hill,
San Saba began life as an
oratory for Palestinian monks
fleeing from Arab invasions in
the 7th century. The existing
church dates from the 10th
century, and has undergone
much restoration. The portico
houses a fascinating collection
of archaeological remains.
    The church has three naves in
the Greek style and a short
fourth 11th-century nave to the
left with vestiges of 13th-century
frescoes of the life of St. Nicholas
of Bari. Particularly intriguing is
a scene of three naked young
ladies lying in bed, who are
saved from penury by the gift

of a bag of gold from St.
Nicholas, the future Santa
Claus. The beautiful marble
inlay in the main door, the
floor, and the remains of the
choir are all 13th-century
Cosmati work.

⓱ Circus Maximus

Via del Circo Massimo. **Map** 8 F2.
🚌 81, 160, 628, 715. 🚊 3.
Ⓜ Circo Massimo.

What was once ancient Rome's
largest stadium is today little
more than a long grassy
esplanade. Set in the valley
between the Palatine, and
Aventine hills, the Circus
Maximus was continually
embellished and expanded
from the 4th century BC until
AD 549, when the last races
were held. The grandstands
held some 300,000 spectators,
cheering wildly at the horse,
and chariot races, athletic
contests, and wild animal fights,
betting furiously throughout.
    The Circus had a central
dividing barrier *(spina)* with
seven large egg-shaped objects
on it used for counting the laps
of a race. These were joined in
33 BC by seven bronze dolphins
that served a similar purpose.
In 10 BC, Augustus built the
Imperial box under the Palatine
and decorated the *spina* with
the obelisk that now stands in
the center of Piazza del Popolo
(see p139). A second obelisk,
which was added in the 4th
century by Constantine II, is
now in Piazza di San Giovanni in
Laterano *(see pp180–81)*.

Reconstruction of the Circus Maximus in its heyday

TRASTEVERE

The proud and aggressively independent inhabitants of Trastevere, the area "across the Tiber," consider themselves the most authentic of Romans. In one of the most picturesque old quarters of the city, it is still possible to glimpse scenes of everyday life that seem to belong to bygone centuries. There are, however, signs that much of the earthy, proletarian character of the place may soon be destroyed by the proliferation of fashionable clubs, restaurants, and boutiques. Some of Rome's most fascinating medieval churches lie hidden away in the patchwork of narrow, cobbled backstreets, the only clue to their location an occasional glimpse of a Romanesque bell tower. Of these, Santa Cecilia was built on the site of the martyrdom of the patron saint of music; San Francesco a Ripa commemorates St. Francis of Assisi's visit to Rome; and Santa Maria in Trastevere is the traditional center of the spiritual and social life of the area.

Sights at a Glance

Churches
3 Santa Maria della Scala
5 Santa Maria in Trastevere pp214–15
6 San Crisogono
8 Santa Cecilia in Trastevere
10 San Francesco a Ripa

Museums and Galleries
4 Sant'Egidio and Museo di Roma in Trastevere

Historic Buildings
1 Casa della Fornarina
7 Caserma dei Vigili della VII Coorte
9 San Michele a Ripa Grande

Bridges
2 Ponte Sisto

Parks and Gardens
11 Villa Sciarra

See also Street Finder maps 4, 7, 8, 11

Restaurants
see pp317–19
1 Bir & Fud
2 Da Gildo
3 Da Lucia
4 Dar Poeta
5 Da Teo
6 Fish Market
7 Glass
8 Il Capriccio
9 In Vino Veritas
10 Ivo a Trastevere
11 La Gensola
12 Meridionale
13 Pizzeria L'Obitorio Panattoni
14 Rajdhani
15 Roma Sparita
16 Spirito Divino
17 Taverna Trilussa

0 meters 300
0 yards 300

Street by Street: Trastevere

Trastevere is a major attraction both for its restaurants, clubs, and movie theaters, and for its picturesque maze of narrow cobbled alleyways. On summer evenings the streets are packed with jostling groups of pleasure-seekers, especially during the noisy local festival, the Festa de' Noantri (see p61). Everywhere café and restaurant tables spill out over sidewalks, especially around Piazza di Santa Maria in Trastevere and outside the pizzerias along Viale di Trastevere. There are also kiosks selling slices of watermelon and *grattachecca*, a mixture of syrup and grated ice. It is usually easier to appreciate the antique charm of Trastevere's narrow streets in the more tranquil atmosphere of the early morning.

1 Casa della Fornarina
Raphael's beautiful mistress is said to have lived here. There is now a flourishing restaurant in the back garden.

The church of Santa Maria dei Sette Dolori
(1643) is a minor work by Borromini.

3 Santa Maria della Scala
The church's unassuming facade conceals a rich Baroque interior.

4 Sant'Egidio and Museo di Roma in Trastevere
This 17th-century fresco of Sant' Egidio by Pomarancio decorates the left-hand chapel in the church. The convent next door is a museum of Roman life and customs.

Vicolo del Piede is one of the picturesque narrow streets lined with restaurant tables leading off Piazza di Santa Maria in Trastevere.

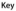

5 ★ Santa Maria in Trastevere
The church is famous for its mosaics by Pietro Cavallini, but it also has earlier works such as this mosaic of the prophet Isaiah to the left of the apse.

Key

— Suggested route

| 0 meters | 75 |
| 0 yards | 75 |

The fountain of Piazza di Santa Maria in Trastevere by Carlo Fontana (1692) is a popular meeting place. At night it is floodlit and dozens of young people sit on the steps around its octagonal base.

2 Ponte Sisto
This bridge was built on the orders
of Sixtus IV in 1474 to link
Trastevere to central Rome.

Locator Map
See Central Rome Map pp16–17

**The Torre degli
Anguillara** (13th century)
is the only survivor of the
many medieval towers
that once dominated the
Trastevere skyline.

Piazza Belli is named after Giuseppe Gioacchino
Belli (1791–1863), who wrote satirical sonnets in
Roman dialect rather than academic Italian.
At the center of the piazza stands a statue of
the poet (1913).

**7 Caserma dei
Vigili della VII
Coorte**
The courtyard of this
antique Roman fire
station still stands.

6 San Crisogono
The Romanesque bell tower
dates from the early 12th century.
The plain portico is a later addition
(1626), but is in keeping with the spirit
of this ancient church.

❶ Casa della Fornarina

Via di Santa Dorotea 20. **Map** 4 D5 &
11 B5. 🚌 23, 280.

Not much is known about
Raphael's model and lover, La
Fornarina, yet over the centuries
she has acquired a name,
Margherita, and even a
biography. Her father was a
Sienese baker (*la fornarina*
means the baker's girl), and his
shop was here in Trastevere
near Raphael's frescoes in the
Villa Farnesina (*see pp220–21*).

Margherita earned a repu-
tation as a "fallen woman,"
and Raphael, wishing to be
absolved before dying, turned
her away from his deathbed.
After his death she took refuge
in the convent of Santa
Apollonia in Trastevere.

She is assumed to have
been the model for Raphael's
famous portrait *La Donna
Velata* in the Palazzo Pitti
in Florence.

❷ Ponte Sisto

Map 4 E5 & 11 B5. 🚌 23, 280.

Named after Pope Sixtus IV della
Rovere (reigned 1471–84), who
commissioned it, this bridge
was built by Baccio Pontelli to
replace an ancient Roman
bridge. The enterprising pope
also built the Sistine Chapel
(*see pp242–5*), the Hospital of
Santo Spirito (*see p246*), and
restored many churches, and
monuments. This caused him
great financial difficulties and he
had to sell personal collections
in order to finance his projects.

Another method of financing
projects was to levy a tax on the
city's prostitutes. Several popes
are known to have resorted
to this
unpopular
form of
taxation.

Pope
Sixtus IV

Gilded Baroque altar of Santa
Maria della Scala

❸ Santa Maria della Scala

Piazza della Scala 23. **Map** 4 D5 & 11
B5. **Tel** 06-580 6233. 🚌 23, 280. **Open**
9am–noon, 3:30–6pm daily. 🕇

This church belongs to a time
of major building activity that
lasted about 30 years from the
end of the 16th to the early
17th century. Its simple facade
contrasts with a rich interior
decorated with multicolored
marbles, and a number of
spirited Baroque altars, and
reliefs. In 1849, the church was
used as a hospital to treat Garibaldi's soldiers (*see pp40–41*).

❹ Sant'Egidio and Museo di Roma in Trastevere

Piazza Sant'Egidio 1. **Map** 7 C1.
🚌 H, 23, 280. 🚃 8. Church:
Tel 06-589 5945. **Closed** for
restoration. Museo di Roma in
Trastevere: **Tel** 06-0608. **Open**
10am–8pm Tue–Sun (last adm: 7pm).
♿ 🌐 museodiromaintrastevere.it

Built in 1630, Sant'Egidio was
the church of the adjoining
Carmelite convent, one of many
founded in the area to shelter
the poor and destitute. The
convent is now a museum,
containing a wealth of material
relating to the festivals,
pastimes, superstitions, and
customs of the Romans when
they lived under papal rule.

There are old paintings and
prints of the city and tableaux
showing scenes of everyday life
in 18th- and 19th-century
Rome, including reconstructions
of shops and a tavern.

The museum also has
manuscripts by the much-loved
poets Belli and Trilussa, who
wrote in local dialect.

Watercolor of public scribe (1880) in the
Museo di Roma in Trastevere

❺ Santa Maria in Trastevere

See pp214–15.

❻ San Crisogono

Piazza Sonnino 44. **Map** 7 C1. **Tel**
06-5810 0076. 🚌 H, 23, 280, 780. 🚃
8. **Open** 7:30–11:30am, 4–7:30pm
Mon–Sat; 8:30am–1pm, 4:15–7:30pm
Sun. 🔦 for excavations. 🕇 ♿

This church was built on the site
of one of the city's oldest *tituli*
(private houses used for
Christian worship). An
8th-century church with 11th-
century frescoes can still be
seen beneath the present
church. This dates from the
early 12th century, a period of
intense building activity in
Rome. San Crisogono was
decorated by Pietro Cavallini –
the apse mosaic remains.
Most of the church's columns

Apse mosaic in San Crisogono

were taken from previous buildings, including the great porphyry ones of a triumphal arch. The mosaic floor is the result of recycling precious marble from various Roman ruins.

❼ Caserma dei Vigili della VII Coorte

Via della VII Coorte 9. **Map** 7 C1. **Tel** 06-0608. H, 23, 280, 780. 8. **Closed** for restoration work; call for details.

Not all Roman ruins are Imperial villas or grand temples; one that illustrates the daily life of a busy city is the barracks of the guards of the VII Coorte (7th Cohort), the Roman fire department. It was built in Augustus's reign, in the 1st century AD, and the excavated courtyard is where the men would rest while waiting for a callout.

❽ Santa Cecilia in Trastevere

Piazza di Santa Cecilia. **Map** 8 D1. **Tel** 06-589 9289. H, 23, 44, 280. 8. **Open** 9:30am–1pm, 4–6:30pm daily. for excavations. Cavallini fresco can be seen 10am–12:30pm Mon–Sat.

St. Cecilia, aristocrat, and patron saint of music, was martyred here in AD 230. After an attempt at scalding her to death, she was beheaded. A church was founded – perhaps in the 4th century – on the site of her house. (The house, beneath the church with the remains of a Roman tannery, is well worth a visit.) Her body turned up in the Catacombs of San Callisto (see p267), and was buried here in the 9th century by Pope Paschal I, who rebuilt the church. A fine apse mosaic survives from this period.

The altar canopy by Arnolfo di Cambio and the fresco of The Last Judgment by Pietro Cavallini, reached through the adjoining convent, date from the 13th century, one of the few periods when Rome had a distinctive artistic style of its own. In front of the altar is a

Detail of 13th-century fresco by Pietro Cavallini in Santa Cecilia

statue of St. Cecilia by Stefano Maderno, who used her miraculously preserved remains as a model when she was briefly disinterred in 1599.

❾ San Michele a Ripa Grande

Via di San Michele 25. **Map** 8 D2. **Tel** 06-6723 1440. 23, 44, 75, 280. **Open** for special exhibitions only.

This huge, imposing complex, now housing the Ministry of Culture, stretches 985 ft (300 m) along the Tiber River. It was built on the initiative of Pope Innocent XII and contained a home for the elderly, a boys' reform school, a woolen mill, and various chapels. Today, contemporary exhibitions are occasionally held here.

❿ San Francesco a Ripa

Piazza San Francesco d'Assisi 88. **Map** 7 C2. **Tel** 06-581 9020. H, 23, 44, 75, 280. 8. **Open** 7:30am–1pm, 2–7pm daily.

St. Francis of Assisi lived here in a hospice when he visited Rome in 1219, and his stone pillow and crucifix are preserved in his cell. The church was rebuilt by his follower, the nobleman Rodolfo Anguillara, who is portrayed on his tombstone wearing the Franciscan habit.

Entirely rebuilt in the 1680s by Cardinal Pallavicini, the church is rich in sculptures. Particularly flamboyant are the 18th-century Rospigliosi and Pallavicini monuments in the transept chapel.

The Paluzzi-Albertoni chapel (fourth on the left, along the nave) contains Bernini's breathtaking Ecstasy of Beata Ludovica Albertoni.

⓫ Villa Sciarra

Via Calandrelli 35. **Map** 7 B2. 44, 75. Park: **Open** 9am–sunset daily.

In Roman times the site of this small, attractive public park was a nymph's sanctuary. It is especially picturesque in spring when its wisterias are in full bloom. The paths through the park are decorated with Romantic follies, fountains, and statues, and there are splendid views over the bastions of the Janiculum.

Bernini's Ecstasy of Beata Ludovica Albertoni (1674) in San Francesco a Ripa

❺ Santa Maria in Trastevere

Probably the first official Christian place of worship to be built in Rome, this basilica became the focus of devotion to the Virgin Mary. According to legend, the church was founded by Pope Callixtus I in the 3rd century, when Christianity was still a minority cult. Today's church is largely a 12th-century building, remarkable for its mosaics, in particular those by Pietro Cavallini. The 22 granite columns in the nave were taken from the ruins of ancient Roman buildings. Despite some 18th-century Baroque additions, Santa Maria has retained its medieval character. This friendly church has strong links with the local community.

Piazza Santa Maria in Trastevere
The piazza in front of the church is the traditional heart of Trastevere. Today it is surrounded by lively bars and restaurants. Carlo Fontana built the octagonal fountain in the late 17th century.

★ **Facade Mosaics**
The 12th-century mosaic shows Mary feeding the baby Jesus and ten women holding lamps. Eight of the lamps are lit, symbolizing virginity; the veiled women whose lamps have gone out are probably widows.

Modest Donors

Many of Rome's mosaics include a portrait of the pope or cardinal responsible for the building of the church. Often the portrait is dwarfed by the rest of the picture, which glorifies the saint to whom the church is dedicated. On the facade of Santa Maria, two tiny unidentified figures kneel at the Virgin's feet. Were they to stand up, the men would barely reach her knees.

Facade mosaic, detail

KEY

① **The portico** was remodeled in 1702 by Carlo Fontana. Statues of four popes decorate the balustrade above.

② **The bell tower** was built in the 12th century. At the top is a small mosaic of the Virgin.

③ **The floor**, relaid in the 1870s, is a recreation of the Cosmatesque mosaic floor of the 13th century.

④ **15th-century wall tabernacle** by Mino del Reame.

Front entrance

Apse Mosaic
The 12th-century mosaic in the basin of the apse shows the Coronation of the Virgin. She sits on Christ's right hand, surrounded by saints.

VISITORS' CHECKLIST

Practical Information
Via della Paglia 14c, Piazza Santa Maria in Trastevere.
Map 7 C1.
Tel 06-581 9443.
Open 7:30am–9pm daily. ⛪
9am & 5:30pm daily. ♿ 📷

Transportation
🚌 H & 780 to Piazza S. Sonnino, 23 & 280 along Lungotevere Sanzio. 🚊 8 from Largo Argentina.

Madonna della Clemenza
The life-size icon probably dates from the 7th century. A replica is displayed above the altar of the Cappella Altemps.

★ Cavallini Mosaics
The details in the six mosaics of the Life of the Virgin (1291) display a touching realism.

Tomb of Cardinal Pietro Stefaneschi
The last of his line, Pietro Stefaneschi died in 1417. His tomb is by an otherwise unknown sculptor called Paolo.

AD 217–22 Church founded by Pope Callixtus I

Pope Innocent II

1291 Pietro Cavallini adds mosaics of scenes from the life of the Virgin for his patron, Bertoldo Stefaneschi

1866–77 Church restored by Virginio Vespignani

50 BC	0	600	1200	1800

38 BC Jet of mineral oil spouts from the ground on this site. Later interpreted as a portent of the coming of Christ

c. 1138 Pope Innocent II starts rebuilding the church

1580 Martino Longhi the Elder restores church and builds family chapel for Cardinal Marco Sittico Altemps

1702 Pope Clement XI has portico rebuilt

1617 Domenichino designs coffered ceiling with octagonal panel of the Assumption of the Virgin

JANICULUM

Overlooking the Tiber on the Trastevere side of the river, the Janiculum Hill has often played its part in the defense of the city. The last occasion was in 1849, when Garibaldi held off the attacking French troops. The park at the top of the hill is filled with monuments to Garibaldi and his men. A popular place for walks, the park provides a welcome escape from the densely packed streets of Trastevere. You will often come

across puppet shows and other children's amusements. In medieval times, most of the hill was occupied by monasteries and convents. Bramante built his miniature masterpiece, the Tempietto, in the convent of San Pietro in Montorio. The Renaissance also saw the development of the riverside area along Via della Lungara, where the rich and powerful built beautiful houses such as the Villa Farnesina.

Sights at a Glance

Churches and Temples
6 Sant'Onofrio
7 San Pietro in Montorio
8 Tempietto

Museums and Galleries
2 Palazzo Corsini and Galleria Nazionale d'Arte Antica

Historic Buildings
1 Villa Farnesina pp220–21

Fountains
9 Fontana dell'Acqua Paola

Monuments
5 Garibaldi Monument

Arches and Gates
3 Porta Settimiana

Parks and Gardens
4 Botanical Gardens

See also Street Finder maps 3, 4, 7, 11

Restaurants
see pp317–19
1 Antica Pesa
2 Antico Arco
3 Isole di Sicilia
4 Lo Scarpone

A Tour of the Janiculum

The long hike to the top of the Janiculum is rewarded by wonderful views over the city. The park's monuments include a lighthouse and statues of Garibaldi and his wife Anita. There is also a cannon that is fired at noon each day. In Via della Lungara, between the Janiculum and the Tiber, stand Palazzo Corsini with its national art collection and the Villa Farnesina, decorated by Raphael for his friend and patron, the fabulously wealthy banker Agostino Chigi.

Tasso's Oak is a memorial to the poet Torquato Tasso, who liked to sit here in the days before he died in 1595. The tree was struck by lightning in 1843.

VIALE AL DO FABRIZI

PIAZZALE GIUSEPPE GARIBALDI

The Manfredi Lighthouse, built in 1911, was a gift to the city of Rome from Italians in Argentina.

The Monument to Anita Garibaldi by Mario Rutelli was erected in 1932. The great patriot's Brazilian wife lies buried beneath the statue.

The view from Villa Lante, a beautiful Renaissance summer residence, gives a magnificent panorama of the whole city.

ROMA O MORTE

⑤ **Garibaldi Monument**
The inscription on the base of the equestrian statue says "Rome or Death."

❹ Botanical Gardens
These were established in 1883 when part of the grounds of Palazzo Corsini was given to the University of Rome.

❶ ★ Villa Farnesina
The suburban villa of the banker Agostino Chigi is celebrated for its frescoes by Raphael, Baldassarre Peruzzi, and other Renaissance masters.

Locator Map
See Central Rome Map pp16–17

❷ ★ Palazzo Corsini
This 15th-century triptych by Fra Angelico hangs in the Galleria Nazionale d'Arte Antica.

Key

— Suggested route

| 0 meters | 75 |
| 0 yards | 75 |

❸ Porta Settimiana
Looking through this Renaissance gateway from Via della Lungara, you catch a glimpse of Trastevere's warren of narrow streets.

● Villa Farnesina

The wealthy Sienese banker Agostino Chigi, who had established the headquarters of his far-flung financial empire in Rome, commissioned the villa in 1508 from his compatriot Baldassare Peruzzi. The simple, harmonious design, with a central block and projecting wings, made this one of the earliest true Renaissance villas. The decoration was carried out between 1510 and 1519, and this has been restored. Peruzzi frescoed some of the interiors himself. Later, Sebastiano del Piombo, Raphael, and his pupils added more elaborate works. The frescoes illustrate Classical myths, and the vault of the main hall, the Sala di Galatea, is adorned with astrological scenes showing the position of the stars at the time of Chigi's birth. Artists, poets, cardinals, princes, and the pope himself were entertained here in magnificent style by their wealthy and influential host. In 1577 the villa was bought by Cardinal Alessandro Farnese. Since then, it has been known as the Villa Farnesina.

North Facade
The Loggia of Cupid and Psyche looks out on formal gardens that were used for parties and putting on plays.

The Wedding of Alexander and Roxanne by Sodoma
Cherubs are shown helping the bride Roxanne to prepare for her marriage.

Entrance

★ Triumph of Galatea by Raphael
The beautiful sea nymph Galatea was one of the 50 daughters of the god Nereus.

The Architect

Baldassare Peruzzi, painter and architect, arrived in Rome from Siena in 1503 at age 20 and became Bramante's chief assistant. Although his architectural designs were typical of Classicism, his painting owes more to Gothic influences, as his figurework is very highly stylized. On Raphael's death, he became Head of Works at St. Peter's, but was captured in the Sack of Rome (see p35), exiled to Siena until 1535, and died in 1536.

Baldassare Peruzzi

Frescoes in the Room of Galatea
Perseus beheads Medusa in a scene from one of Peruzzi's series of mythological frescoes.

★ **Salone delle Prospettive**
Peruzzi's frescoes create the illusion of looking out at views of 16th-century Rome through a marble colonnade.

VISITORS' CHECKLIST

Practical Information
Via della Lungara 230. **Map** 4 D5 & 11 A5. **Tel** 06-6802 7268.
Open 9am–2pm Mon–Sat and second Sun of every month.
Closed Aug. ♿ 🚫 🏠 ♿
W **villafarnesina.it**

Transportation
🚌 23, 280 to Lungotevere Farnesina.

Fresco from the Salone delle Prospettive
This scene shows the Torre delle Milizie *(see p92)* as it looked in the 1500s.

★ **Loggia of Cupid and Psyche**
The model for the figure on the left in Raphael's painting of *The Three Graces* was Agostino Chigi's mistress, the courtesan Imperia.

Lunette in the Room of Galatea
This giant monochrome head by Peruzzi was once attributed to Michelangelo.

Queen Christina's bedroom in the Palazzo Corsini

❷ Palazzo Corsini and Galleria Nazionale d'Arte Antica

Via della Lungara 10. **Map** 4 D5 & 11 A5. **Tel** 06-6880 2323. 🚌 23, 280.
Open 8:30am–7:30pm Tue–Sun.
Closed Jan 1, Dec 25. 🎫 🎟 🏛 ♿
📷 🌐 **galleriacorsini.beniculturali.it**

The history of Palazzo Corsini is intimately entwined with that of Rome. Built for Cardinal Domenico Riario in 1510–12, it has boasted among its many distinguished guests Bramante, the young Michelangelo, Erasmus, and Queen Christina of Sweden, who died here in 1689. The old palazzo was completely rebuilt for Cardinal Neri Corsini by Ferdinando Fuga in 1736. Via della Lungara is too narrow for a good frontal view, so Fuga designed the facade so it could be seen from an angle.

Palazzo Corsini houses the Galleria Nazionale d'Arte Antica, also known as Galleria Corsini. This outstanding collection includes paintings by Rubens, Van Dyck, Murillo, Caravaggio, and Guido Reni, together with 17th- and 18th-century Italian regional art. The palazzo is also home to the Accademia dei Lincei, a learned society founded in 1603, which once included Galileo among its members.

In 1797 Palazzo Corsini was the backdrop to momentous events: French General Duphot (the fiancé of Napoleon's sister Pauline) was killed here in a skirmish between papal troops and Republicans. The consequent French occupation of the city, and the deportation of Pope Pius VI led to the proclamation of a short-lived Roman Republic (1798–99).

❸ Porta Settimiana

Between Via della Scala and Via della Lungara. **Map** 4 D5 & 11 B5.
🚌 23, 280.

This gate was built in 1498 by Pope Alexander VI Borgia to replace a minor passageway in the Aurelian Wall. The Porta Settimiana marks the start of Via della Lungara, a long, straight road built in the early 16th century.

❹ Botanical Gardens

Largo Cristina di Svezia 24, off Via Corsini. **Map** 4 D5. **Tel** 06-4991 7108.
🚌 23, 280. **Open** Apr–Sep: 9:30am–6:30pm Mon–Sat (Oct–Mar: to 5:30pm). **Closed** public hols. 📷 🎫 (call to book).

Sequoias, palm trees, and collections of orchids and bromeliads are housed in Rome's Botanical Gardens (Orto Botanico). These tranquil gardens contain more than 7,000 plant species from all over the world. Indigenous and exotic species are grouped to illustrate their botanical families and their adaptation to different climates and ecosystems.

There are also plants such as the ginkgo that have survived virtually unchanged from earlier eras. The gardens were originally part of the Palazzo Corsini, but since 1983 have belonged to the University of Rome.

Base of the Garibaldi Monument

❺ Garibaldi Monument

Piazzale Giuseppe Garibaldi.
Map 3 C5. 🚌 870.

This huge equestrian statue is part of a commemorative park, recalling the heroic events witnessed on the Janiculum when the French army attacked the city in 1849. Garibaldi's Republicans fended off the greatly superior French forces for weeks, until the Italians were overwhelmed. Garibaldi and his men escaped. The monument, erected in 1895, was the work of Emilio Gallori. Around the pedestal are four smaller sculptures in bronze showing battle scenes and allegorical figures.

Steps and tiered fountains at the Botanical Gardens

Courtyard of Sant'Onofrio

❻ Sant'Onofrio

Piazza di Sant'Onofrio 2. **Map** 3 C4.
Tel 06-686 4498. 🚌 870. **Open**
9am–1pm Mon–Sat. **Closed** Aug. 🚹
Museum **Open** by appt only.
Tel 06-687 7341 (call 4–6pm Tue).

Beato Nicola da Forca Palena, whose tombstone guards the entrance, founded this church in 1419 in honor of the hermit Sant'Onofrio. It retains the flavor of the 15th century in the simple shapes of the portico and the cloister. In the early 17th century the portico was decorated with frescoes by Domenichino.

The monastery next to the church houses a small museum dedicated to the 16th-century Italian poet Torquato Tasso, who died there.

❼ San Pietro in Montorio

Piazza San Pietro in Montorio 2.
Map 7 B1. **Tel** 06-581 39 40. 🚌 44, 75.
Open 8am–noon daily, 3–4pm
(4–6pm summer) Mon–Fri. If closed,
ring bell at door to right of church. 🚹

San Pietro in Montorio – the church of St. Peter on the Golden Hill – was founded in the Middle Ages near the spot where St. Peter was presumed to have been crucified. It was rebuilt by order of Ferdinand and Isabella of Spain at the end of the 15th century, and decorated by outstanding artists of the Renaissance.

The facade is typical of a time when clean, geometric shapes derived from Classical architecture were in vogue. The single nave ends in a deep apse that once contained Raphael's *Transfiguration*, now in the Vatican. Two wide chapels, one on either side of the nave, were decorated by some of Michelangelo's most famous pupils. The left-hand chapel was designed by one of the few artists Michelangelo openly admired, Daniele da Volterra, also responsible for the altar painting, *The Baptism of Christ*. The chapel on the right was the work of Giorgio Vasari, who included a self-portrait (in black, on the left) in his altar painting, *The Conversion of St. Paul*.

The first chapel to the right of the entrance contains a powerful *Flagellation*, by the Venetian artist Sebastiano del Piombo (1518); Michelangelo is said to have provided the original drawings. Work by Bernini and his followers can be seen in the second chapel on the left and in the flanking De Raymondi tombs.

❽ Tempietto

Piazza San Pietro in Montorio (in
courtyard). **Map** 7 B1. **Tel** 06-581
280 806. 🚌 44, 75. **Open** 9:30am–
12:30pm, 2–4:30pm Tue–Sat.
See The History of Rome pp34–5.

Around 1502, Bramante completed what many consider to be the first true Renaissance building in Rome: the Tempietto. The name means simply "little temple." Its circular shape echoes early Christian *martyria*, chapels built on the site of a saint's martyrdom. This was believed to be the place where St. Peter was crucified.

Bramante chose the Doric order for the 16 columns surrounding the domed chapel. Above the columns is a Classical frieze and a delicate balustrade. Though the scale of the Tempietto is tiny, Bramante's masterly use of Classical proportions creates a satisfyingly harmonious whole. The Tempietto illustrates the great Renaissance dream that the city of Rome would once again relive its ancient glory.

Fontana dell'Acqua Paola

❾ Fontana dell'Acqua Paola

Via Garibaldi. **Map** 7 B1. 🚌 44, 75.

This monumental fountain commemorates the reopening in 1612 of an aqueduct originally built by Emperor Trajan in AD 109. The aqueduct was renamed the "Acqua Paola" after Paul V, the Borghese pope who ordered its restoration. When it was first built, the fountain had five small basins, but in 1690 Carlo Fontana altered the design, adding the huge basin you can see today. Despite many laws intended to deter them, generations of Romans used this convenient pool of fresh water for bathing and washing their vegetables.

Bramante's round chapel, the Tempietto

VATICAN

As the site where St. Peter was martyred and buried, the Vatican became the residence of the popes who succeeded him. Decisions made here have shaped the destiny of Europe, and the great Basilica of St. Peter's draws pilgrims from all over the Christian world. The papal palaces beside St. Peter's house the Vatican Museums. With the added attractions of Michelangelo's Sistine Chapel and the Raphael Rooms, their wonderful collections of Classical sculpture make them the finest museums in Rome. The Vatican's position as a state within a state was guaranteed by the Lateran Treaty of 1929, marked by the building of a new road, the Via della Conciliazione. This leads from St. Peter's to Castel Sant'Angelo, a monument to a far grimmer past. Built originally as the Emperor Hadrian's mausoleum, this papal fortress and prison has witnessed many fierce battles for control of the city.

Sights at a Glance

Churches and Temples
1 St. Peter's pp228–9
4 Santo Spirito in Sassia
9 Santa Maria in Traspontina

Museums and Galleries
2 Vatican Museums pp232–9

Historic Buildings
5 Hospital of Santo Spirito
6 Palazzo del Commendatore
7 Palazzo dei Convertendi
8 Palazzo dei Penitenzieri
12 Palazzo Torlonia
13 Castel Sant'Angelo pp250–51
14 Palazzo di Giustizia

Gates
3 Porta Santo Spirito

Historic Streets and Piazzas
10 The Borgo
11 Vatican Corridor

Restaurants
see pp317–19

1 Arlù
2 Da Benito e Gilberto
3 Da Cesare
4 Taverna Angelica
5 Velando
6 Veranda

0 meters 300
0 yards 300

See also Street Finder
maps 3, 4

◄ The statue of St. Peter, St. Peter's Square

For map symbols see back flap

A Tour of the Vatican

The Vatican, a center of power for Catholics all over the world and a sovereign state since February 1929, is ruled by the pope. About 1,000 people live here, staffing the Vatican's facilities. These include a post office and shops; Vatican radio, broadcasting to the world in over 20 languages; a daily newspaper (*L'Osservatore Romano*); Vatican offices; and a publishing house.

The Madonna of Guadalupe shows the miraculous image of the Madonna that appeared on the cloak of a Mexican Indian in 1531.

Papal heliport

The Grotto of Lourdes is a replica of the grotto in the southwest of France, where in 1858 the Virgin appeared to St. Bernadette.

Radio Vatican is broadcast from this tower, part of the Leonine Wall built in 847.

The Vatican Train Station, opened in 1930, connects with the line from Rome to Viterbo, but is now used only for freight.

The Papal Audience Chamber, by Pier Luigi Nervi, was opened in 1971. It seats up to 12,000.

The information office gives details of tours of the Vatican Gardens.

❶ ★ St. Peter's
The Chapel of St. Peter is in the Grottoes under the basilica. The rich marble decoration was added by Clement VIII at the end of the 16th century.

PIAZZA DEL SANT'UFFIZIO

Piazza San Pietro was laid out by Bernini between 1656 and 1667. The narrow space in front of the church opens out into an enormous ellipse flanked by colonnades.

Key

 — Suggested route

0 meters	75
0 yards	75

The Eagle Fountain was built to celebrate the arrival of water from the Acqua Paola aqueduct at the Vatican. The eagle is the Borghese crest.

Locator Map
See Central Rome Map pp16–17

The Casina of Pius IV is a delightful summer house in the Vatican Gardens built by Pirro Ligorio in the mid-16th century.

Entrance to Vatican Museums

❷ ★ Vatican Museums
Raphael's *Madonna of Foligno* (1513) is just one of the Vatican's many Renaissance masterpieces.

The Galleon Fountain is a perfect scale model of a 17th-century ship in lead, brass, and copper. It was made by a Flemish artist for Pope Paul V.

VIA DI PORTA ANGELICA

PIAZZA SAN PIETRO

PIAZZA PIO XII

The obelisk was erected here in 1586 with the help of 150 horses and 47 winches.

To Via della Conciliazione

The Cortile della Pigna is mostly the work of Bramante. The niche for the pine cone, once a Roman fountain, was added by Pirro Ligorio in 1562.

❶ St. Peter's

The center of the Roman Catholic faith, St. Peter's draws pilgrims from all over the world. Few are disappointed when they enter the sumptuously decorated basilica beneath Michelangelo's vast dome.

A shrine was erected on the site of St. Peter's tomb in the 2nd century, and the first great basilica, ordered by the Emperor Constantine, was completed around AD 349. By the 15th century it was falling down, so in 1506 Pope Julius II laid the first stone of a new church. It took more than a century to build, and all the great architects of the Roman Renaissance and Baroque had a hand in its design.

★ **Dome of St. Peter's**
Designed by Michelangelo, though not finished in his lifetime, the spectacular cupola, 448 ft (136.5 m) high, gives unity to the majestic interior of the basilica.

Papal Altar
The present altar dates from the reign of Clement VIII (1592–1605). The plain slab of marble found in the Forum of Nerva stands under Bernini's baldacchino, overlooking the well of the *confessio,* the crypt where St. Peter's body is reputedly buried.

Baldacchino
This magnificent canopy of gilded bronze, supported on spiral columns 66 ft (20 m) high, was designed by Bernini in the 17th century.

KEY

① **The nave's** total length is 715 ft (218 m).

② **The two minor cupolas** at the corners of the transept are by Vignola.

③ **Facade by Carlo Maderno** (1614)

④ **Stairs to the dome**

Pope Urban VIII's Keys
At the base of the columns of the baldacchino, the coat of arms of Pope Urban VIII features the keys to the Kingdom of Heaven.

★ **View from the Dome**
The superb symmetry of Bernini's colonnade can be appreciated from the dome.

Piazza San Pietro
On Sundays and religious occasions, the Pope blesses the crowds from his balcony above the square.

Entrance

Filarete Door
Finished in 1445, Antonio Averulino's bronze door came from the original basilica.

VISITORS' CHECKLIST

Practical Information
Piazza San Pietro **Map** 3 B3.
Tel 06-6988 3712 (sacristy), 06-6988 1662 (tourist information).
Basilica: **Open** 7am–7pm (Oct–Mar: 6:30pm).
Treasury: **Open** 8am–6:50pm (Oct–Mar: 5:50pm).
Vatican Grottoes: **Open** 9am–6:40pm (Oct–Mar: to 5:40pm).
Dome: **Open** 8am–5:45pm daily (Oct–Mar: 4:45pm). Treasury and Dome. Pre-Constantinian Necropolis by appt; fax 06-6987 3017, email scavi@fsp.va, or visit Excavations Office on right of colonnade.
Papal audiences: Public audiences, usually Wed at 10:30am in Papal Audience Chamber or Piazza San Pietro. Ring 06-6988 3114, fax 06-6988 5863 or check (free) ticket availability at office through bronze doors on right of colonnade (9am–1pm). Appearances also at noon on Sundays at library window to bless the crowd. No bare knees or shoulders.

Transportation
62 to Via della Conciliazione. 23, 49, 81, 492, 990 to Piazza del Risorgimento. 64 to Largo di Porta Cavalleggeri.

AD 61 Burial of St. Peter
324 Constantine builds basilica
1452 Nicholas V plans restoration
1506 Julius II lays first stone
1547 Michelangelo named as chief architect of St. Peter's
1593 Dome completed
1626 New basilica of St. Peter's consecrated

AD 60 — 800 — 1500 — 1550 — 1600

200 Altar built marking grave of St. Peter
800 Charlemagne crowned Emperor of Romans in St. Peter's
1503 Pope Julius II chooses Bramante as architect for new basilica
1538 Antonio da Sangallo the Younger made director of works
1514 Raphael director of works
1606 Carlo Maderno extends basilica
1564 Death of Michelangelo
1614 Maderno finishes the facade

A Guided Tour of St. Peter's

The vast basilica's 615-ft- (187-m-) long, marble-encrusted interior contains 11 chapels and 45 altars and a wealth of precious works of art. Some were salvaged from the original basilica and others commissioned from late Renaissance and Baroque artists, but much of the elaborate decoration is owed to Bernini's mid-17th-century work. The two side aisles are 250 ft (76 m) long and converge under Michelangelo's enormous dome. The building's central focus is the Papal Altar beneath Bernini's great baldacchino, filling the space between the four piers that support the dome. From the basilica you can visit the Grottoes, where the late Pope John Paul II is buried, the Treasury and St. Peter's Sacristy, or the terrace for panoramic views.

⑤ Baldacchino by Bernini
Commissioned by Pope Urban VIII in 1624, the extravagant Baroque canopy dominates the nave and crowns the Papal Altar, at which only the pope may celebrate mass.

Bernini's Monument to
Urban VIII

④ Throne of St. Peter in Glory
In the domed apse, look up to the window above Bernini's Baroque sculpture of 1656–65. It lights the image of the Holy Spirit, shown as a dove amid clouds, rays of sunlight, and flights of angels.

Entrance to Treasury
and Sacristy

Entrance to
Necropolis

Historical Plan of the Basilica of St. Peter's

St. Peter was buried *c.* AD 64 in a necropolis near his crucifixion site at the Circus of Nero. Constantine built a basilica on the burial site in AD 324. In the 15th century the old church was found to be unsafe and had to be demolished. It was rebuilt in the 16th and 17th centuries. By 1614 the facade was ready, and in 1626 the new church was consecrated.

Key
- Circus of Nero
- Constantinian
- Renaissance
- Baroque

③ **Monument to Pope Alexander VII**
Bernini's last work was finished in 1678 and is in an alcove on the left of the transept. The pope sits among the figures of Truth, Justice, Charity, and Prudence.

② **Monument to Leo XI**
On the left beneath the aisle arch is Alessandro Algardi's white marble 1650 monument to Leo XI, whose reign as pope lasted only 27 days.

Key
 — Tour route

⑥ **Angelo della Navicella**
A fragment of Giotto's beautiful 13th-century mosaic, salvaged from the old basilica, is now in the Grottoes. A later copy of the entire mosaic of Jesus and St. Peter fishing on Lake Tiberias decorates the atrium.

⑦ **St. Peter**
This famous 13th-century statue, now attributed to Arnolfo di Cambio, was once thought to be a late Roman work. Situated at the end of the nave, it is sculpted in bronze with a delicate filigree halo.

Entrance to Grottoes

The Tabernacle by Bernini is made of gilt bronze in the shape of a temple.

The Porta Santa (Holy Door) is opened only in Holy Years. The Pope knocks on it with a bronze hammer, it is unlocked, and it then remains open throughout the Holy Year.

Chapel of St. Sebastian

Stuart Monument by Canova

⑧ **Pietà**
This famous marble sculpture was finished in 1499 when Michelangelo was only 25. It stands in a chapel to one side of the nave, protected by glass since being damaged in 1972.

Filarete Door

Navicella Mosaic

Atrium by Carlo Maderno

① **Tomb of Maria Clementina Sobieski**
Near the entrance is Filippo Barigioni's sentimentally expressive 18th-century monument to Maria Clementina, the wife of James Stuart, the Old Pretender.

❷ Vatican Museums

The buildings that house one of the world's finest art collections were once papal palaces built for Renaissance popes such as Sixtus IV, Innocent VIII, and Julius II. The long courtyards and galleries, linking Innocent VIII's Belvedere Palace to the other buildings, are by Donato Bramante and were commissioned for Julius II in 1503. Most of the later additions to the buildings were made in the 18th century, when priceless works of art were first put on display. This complex of museums also houses the Sistine Chapel and the Raphael Rooms, and should not be missed. Note that no bare knees or shoulders are allowed.

★ **Atrium of the Four Gates**
Built by Camporese in 1792–3, this vast domed edifice was the original entrance to the Vatican Museums.

★ **Cortile della Pigna**
This huge bronze pine cone, part of an ancient Roman fountain, once stood in the courtyard of old St. Peter's. Its niche was designed by Pirro Ligorio.

KEY

① **Cortile di San Damaso**

② **Raphael Loggia**

③ **Borgia Apartment**

④ **Borgia Tower**

⑤ **Sistine Chapel**

⑥ **Apartment of Pius V**

⑦ **Cortile del Belvedere**

⑧ **Cortile della Biblioteca**

⑨ **Braccio Nuovo**

⑩ **The Belvedere Palace** was commissioned in the late 15th century by Pope Innocent VIII.

Spiral Ramp
The spectacular stairway leading down from the museums to the street was designed by Giuseppe Momo in 1932.

Entrance

VISITORS' CHECKLIST

Practical Information
Città del Vaticano. Entrance in Viale Vaticano. **Map** 3 B2. **Tel** 06-6988 3860. **Open** 9am–6pm (last adm: 4pm) Mon–Sat, 9am–2pm (last adm: 12:30pm) last Sun of each month. Also occasionally 7–11pm Fri (book in adv). **Closed** public & relig hols. Special permit needed for Raphael Loggia, Vatican Library, Lapidary Gallery & Vatican Archives. 🆆 **mv.vatican.va** (free last Sun of month). 🔲 🔷 special routes. 🔲 Temp exhibitions, lectures. 🔲 🔲 🔲 🔲 Gardens & tours: 06-6988 3712.

Transportation
🚌 49 to entrance, 23, 81, 492, 990 to Piazza del Risorgimento or 62 to St. Peter's. Ⓜ Cipro Musei Vaticani, Ottaviano S. Pietro.

Simonetti Stairway
Built in the 1780s with a vaulted ceiling, the stairs were part of the conversion of the Belvedere Palace into the Pio-Clementine Museum.

★ Bramante Stairway
Pope Julius II built the spiral staircase within a square tower as an entrance to the palace. The staircase could be ridden up on horseback in case of emergency.

Cortile Ottagonale
The inner court of the Belvedere Palace was given its octagonal shape in 1773.

1198 Innocent III creates papal palace	**1503** Bramante lays out Belvedere Courtyard		**1756** Foundation of Christian Museum	**1800–23** Chiaramonti Museum founded	**1837** Etruscan Museum founded
	1509 Raphael begins work on Rooms	**1655** Bernini designs Scala Regia			
1000	**1500**	**1600**	**1700**	**1800**	**1900**
1473 Pope Sixtus IV builds Sistine Chapel	**1503–13** Pope Julius II starts Classical sculpture collection	*Bramante (1444–1514)*	**1758** Museum of Pagan Antiquities founded / **1776–84** Pius VI enlarges museum	**1822** Braccio Nuovo is opened	**1970** Pope Paul VI opens Gregorian Museum of Pagan Antiquities

Exploring the Vatican Museums

Four centuries of papal patronage and connoisseurship have resulted in one of the world's great collections of Classical and Renaissance art. The Vatican houses many of the great archaeological finds of central Italy, including the *Laocoön* group, discovered in 1506 on the Esquiline, the *Apollo del Belvedere*, and the Etruscan bronze known as the *Mars of Todi*. During the Renaissance, parts of the museums were decorated with wonderful frescoes commissioned for the Sistine Chapel, the Raphael Rooms, and the Borgia Apartment.

Gallery of the Candelabra
Once an open loggia, this gallery of Greek and Roman sculpture has a fine view of the Vatican Gardens.

Room •
the Big

Gallery of Tapestries

Siege of Malta
The Gallery of Maps is an important record of 16th-century history, and cartography.

Upper floor

Raphael Rooms

Raphael Loggia

Sistine Chapel

Gallery Guide

Visitors have to follow a one-way system. It is best to concentrate on a single collection or to choose one of the four suggested itineraries. These are color-coded so that you can follow them through the museums. They vary in length from 90 minutes to 5 hours. If you are planning a long visit, make sure you allow plenty of time for resting. Conserve your stamina for the Sistine Chapel and Raphael Rooms; they are 20–30 minutes' walk from the entrance, without allowing for any viewing time along the way.

Sala dei Misteri
This is one of the rooms of the Borgia Apartment, richly decorated with Pinturicchio frescoes.

Gregorian Profane Museum

Christian Museum

St. Jerome
Leonardo da Vinci's unfinished work, lost then rediscovered in the 19th century, shows the artist's mastery of anatomy.

Entrance

Round Room

Pinacoteca

Pio-Clementine Museum

Greek Cross Room

Stairs up

Room of the Busts
This contains portraits of emperors, and other notable Romans.

Stairs down

Braccio Nuovo

Chiaramonti Museum

Vatican Library

Lapidary Gallery

Lower floor

Laocoön
This 1st-century AD marble group depicts the Trojan priest Laocoön and his sons struggling with two serpents.

Room of the Animals
Roman mosaics, like these delightful ducks, decorate the walls and floor of this room of animal sculptures.

Apollo del Belvedere
This Roman copy of a Greek statue of the sun god Apollo perfectly embodies the ideals of Classical beauty.

Key to Floorplan

- Egyptian and Assyrian art
- Greek and Roman art
- Etruscan and Italic art
- Early Christian and medieval art
- 15th- to 19th-century art
- Modern Religious art
- Non-exhibition space
- Open by special permit only

Exploring the Vatican's Collections

The Vatican's greatest treasures are its Greek and Roman antiquities. These have been on display since the 18th century. The 19th century saw the addition of exciting discoveries from Etruscan tombs and excavations in Egypt. In the Pinacoteca (art gallery) there is a small, choice collection of paintings, including works by Raphael, Titian and Leonardo. Works by great painters and sculptors are also on view throughout the older parts of the museums in the form of sumptuous decorations commissioned by the Renaissance popes.

Coloured bas-relief from an Egyptian tomb (c.2400 BC)

Egyptian and Assyrian Art

The Egyptian collection contains finds from 19th and 20th-century excavations in Egypt and statues which were brought to Rome in Imperial times. There are also Roman imitations of Egyptian art from Hadrian's Villa (see p271) and from the Campus Martius district of ancient Rome. Egyptian-style statuary from Hadrian's Villa was used to decorate the Greek Cross Room, the entrance to the new wing built in 1780 by Michelangelo Simonetti.

The genuine Egyptian works, exhibited on the lower floor of the Belvedere Palace, include statues, mummies, mummy cases and funerary artifacts. There is also a large collection of documents written on papyrus, the paper the ancient Egyptians made from reeds. Among the main treasures is a colossal granite statue of Queen Tuia, the mother of Rameses II, found on the site of the Horti Sallustiani gardens (see p253) in 1714. The statue, which dates from the 13th century BC, may have been brought to Rome by the Emperor Caligula (reigned AD 37–41), who had an unhealthy interest in pharaohs and in his own mother, Agrippina.

Also noteworthy are the head of a statue of Montuhotep IV (21st century BC), the beautiful mummy case of Queen Hetepheres, and the tomb of Iri, the guardian of the Pyramid of Cheops (26th century BC).

The Assyrian Stairway is decorated with fragments of reliefs from the palaces of the kings of Nineveh (8th century BC). These depict the military exploits of King Sennacherib and his son Sargon II, and show scenes from Assyrian and Chaldean mythology.

Etruscan and Pre-Roman Art

This collection comprises artifacts from pre-Roman civilizations in Etruria and Latium, from Neolithic times to the 1st century BC, when these ancient populations were assimilated into the Roman state. Pride of place in the Gregorian Etruscan Museum goes to the objects found in the Regolini-Galassi tomb, excavated in 1836 at the necropolis of Cerveteri (see p273). The tomb was found intact and yielded numerous everyday household objects, plus a throne, a bed and a funeral cart, all cast in bronze, dating from the 7th century BC. Beautiful black vases, delightful terracotta figurines and bronze statues such as the famous *Mars of Todi*, displayed in the Room of the Bronzes, show the Etruscans to have been a highly civilized, sophisticated people.

A number of Greek vases that were found in Etruscan tombs are on display in the Vase Collection. The Room of the Italiot Vases contains only vases produced locally in the Greek cities of Southern Italy and in Etruria itself. These date from the 3rd to the 1st century BC.

Etruscan gold clasp (fibula) from the 7th century BC

Head of an athlete in mosaic from
the Baths of Caracalla

Greek and Roman Art

The greater part of the Vatican
Museums is dedicated to
Greek and Roman art. Exhibits
line connecting corridors and
vestibules; walls and floors
display fine mosaics; and
famous sculptures decorate
the main courtyards.

The first serious organization
of the collection took place in
the reign of Julius II (1503–13)
around Bramante's Belvedere
Courtyard. The prize pieces
form the nucleus of the
18th-century Pio-Clementine
Museum. In the pavilions of
the Octagonal Courtyard and
in the surrounding rooms are
sculptures considered among
the greatest achievements of
Western art. The *Apoxyomenos*
(an athlete wiping his body
after a race) and the *Apollo
del Belvedere* are high-
quality Roman copies of
Greek originals of
about 320 BC. The
magnificent *Laocoön*,
sculpted by three
artists from Rhodes,
had long been known
to exist from a
description by Pliny the
Elder. It was rediscov-
ered near the ruins of
the Domus Aurea *(see
p177)* in 1506. Classical
works such as these
had a profound
influence on Michel-
angelo and other
Renaissance artists.

The much smaller Chiaramonti
Museum, named after Pope
Pius VII Chiaramonti, was laid
out by Canova in the early
19th century. It includes a
striking colossal head of the
goddess Athene. The Braccio
Nuovo, an extension of the
Chiaramonti, decorated with
Roman floor mosaics, contains
a statue of Augustus from the
villa of his wife Livia at Prima
Porta. Its pose is based on the
famous *Doryphoros* by the
Greek sculptor Polyclitus, of
which there is a Roman copy
on display opposite.

Exhibits in the Vase Rooms
range from the Greek
geometric style (8th century
BC) to black-figure vases
from Corinth, such as the
famous vase by Exekias, with
Achilles and Ajax playing
a game similar to
draughts (530 BC), and
the later red-figure type,
such as the *kylix* (a wide
shallow cup) with Oedipus
and the Sphinx from the
5th century BC. A stairway
links this section to the
Gallery of the
Candelabra and the
Room of the Biga (a
two-horse chariot).
The horses and
harness were
added in the 18th
century.

The Gregorian
Profane Museum
charts the
evolution
of Roman art from

The *Doryphoros* or spear-carrier, a
Roman copy in marble of an
original Greek bronze

dependence upon Greek
models to a recognizably
Roman style. Original Greek
works include large marble
fragments from the
Parthenon in Athens. There is
also a Roman copy of *Athene
and Marsyas* by Myron, which
was part of the decoration of
the Parthenon. Totally Roman
in character are two reliefs
known as the *Rilievi della
Cancelleria*, because they
were discovered beneath
the Palazzo della Cancelleria
(see p151) in the 1930s. They
show military parades of the
Emperor Vespasian and his
son Domitian. This section also
has fine Roman floor mosaics.
There are two from the
Baths of Caracalla
(see p199), depicting
athletes and referees.
They date from the
3rd century AD.
Most striking of all is
a mosaic that
creates the impression
of an unswept floor,
covered with debris
after a meal.

Away from the
main Classical
collections, in one
of the rooms of the
Vatican Library, is the
Aldobrandini Wedding,
a beautiful
Roman fresco
of a bride being
prepared for her
marriage, dating
from the 1st
century AD.

Floor mosaic from the Baths of Otricoli in Umbria, in the Chiaramonti Museum

Detail from Giotto's *Stefaneschi Triptych*

Early Christian and Medieval Art

The main collection of early Christian antiquities is in the Pio-Christian Museum, founded in the last century by Pope Pius IX and formerly housed in the Lateran Palace. It contains inscriptions and sculpture from catacombs and early Christian basilicas. The sculpture consists chiefly of reliefs decorating sarcophagi, though the most striking work is a freestanding 4th-century statue of the *Good Shepherd*. The sculpture's chief interest lies in the way it blends Biblical episodes with pagan mythology. Christianity adopted Classical images so that its doctrines could be understood in clear visual terms. The idealized pastoral figure of the shepherd, for example, became Christ himself, while bearded philosophers turned into the Apostles. At the same time, Christianity laid its claim as the spiritual and cultural heir of the Roman Empire.

The first two rooms of the Pinacoteca are dedicated to late medieval art, mostly tempera-painted wooden panels that served as altarpieces. The outstanding work is Giotto's altarpiece dating from about 1300, known as the *Stefaneschi Triptych*. It expresses much the same theme as the early Christian works: the continuity between the Classical world of the Roman Empire and the new order of Christian Europe. The crucifixion of St. Peter takes place between two landmarks of ancient Rome, the Pyramid of Caius Cestius *(see p207)*, and the pyramid known in the Middle Ages as the Tomb of Romulus, which stood near the Vatican. The triptych, which decorated the main altar of old St. Peter's, includes portraits of Pope St. Celestine V (reigned 1294), and of the donor, Cardinal Jacopo Stefaneschi, shown offering the triptych to St. Peter.

The Vatican Library has a number of medieval treasures exhibited rather haphazardly in showcases; these include woven and embroidered cloths, reliquaries, enamels, and icons. One of the aims of the 18th-century reorganization of the Vatican collections was to glorify Christian works by contrasting them with earlier pagan creations. In the long Lapidary Gallery over 3,000 stone tablets with Christian and pagan inscriptions are displayed on opposite walls. The world's greatest collection of its kind, it may be visited only with special permission.

15th- to 19th-Century Art

The Renaissance popes, many of whom were cultured connoisseurs of the arts, considered it their duty to sponsor the leading painters, sculptors, and goldsmiths of the

Pietà by the Venetian artist Giovanni Bellini (1430–1516)

Raphael's Last Painting

When Raphael died in 1520, the *Transfiguration* was found in his studio, almost complete. The wonderful luminous work was placed at the head of the bier where the great artist's body lay. It depicts the episode in the Gospels in which Christ took three of the Apostles to the top of a mountain, where he appeared to them in divine glory. In the detail shown here, Christ floats above the ground in a halo of ethereal light.

Modern Religious Art

Modern artists exhibited in the Vatican Museums face daunting competition from the great works of the past. Few modern works are displayed conspicuously, the exceptions being Momo's spiral staircase of 1932, which greets visitors as they enter the museums, and Giò Pomodoro's abstract sculpture in the center of the Cortile della Pigna.

In 1973 a contemporary art collection was inaugurated by Pope Paul VI. Housed in the Borgia Apartment, it includes over 800 exhibits by modern artists from all over the world, donated by collectors or the artists themselves. Works in a great variety of media show many contrasting approaches to religious subjects. There are paintings, drawings, engravings and sculpture by 19th- and 20th-century artists, as well as mosaics, stained glass, ceramics, and tapestries. Well-known modern painters such as Georges Braque, Paul Klee, Edvard Munch, and Graham Sutherland are all represented. There are also drawings by Henry Moore, ceramics by Picasso, and stained glass by Fernand Léger. Projects for modern church ornaments include Matisse's decorations for the church of St. Paul de Vence, Luigi Fontana's models for the bronze doors of Milan cathedral, and Emilio Greco's panels for the doors of Orvieto cathedral.

age. The galleries around the Cortile del Belvedere were all decorated by great artists between the 16th and the 19th centuries. The Gallery of Tapestries is hung with tapestries woven in Brussels to designs by students of Raphael; the Apartment of Pope Pius V has beautiful 15th-century Flemish tapestries; and the Gallery of Maps is frescoed with 16th-century maps of ancient and contemporary Italy. When you go to visit the Raphael Rooms (see pp240–41), you should not overlook the nearby Room of the Chiaroscuri and Pope Nicholas V's tiny private chapel, frescoed by Fra Angelico between 1447, and 1451. Similarly, before reaching the Sistine Chapel (see pp242–5), visit the Borgia Apartment, frescoed in a decorative, flowery style by Pinturicchio and his students in the 1490s. The contrast with Michelangelo's Sistine Chapel ceiling, begun in 1508, could hardly be greater. Another set of fascinating frescoes decorates the Loggia of Raphael, but this requires special permission to visit.

Many important works by Renaissance masters are on display in the Pinacoteca (art gallery). Highlights among the works by 15th-century painters are a fine *Pietà* by the Venetian Giovanni Bellini, and Leonardo da Vinci's unfinished *St. Jerome*. Of the great 16th-century works, do not miss the fine altarpiece by Titian, the *Crucifixion of St. Peter* by Guido Reni, the *Deposition* by Caravaggio, and the *Communion of St. Jerome* by Domenichino. Raphael has a whole room dedicated to his work. It contains the beautiful *Madonna of Foligno* and the *Transfiguration* as well as eight tapestries made to his designs.

Lunette of the *Adoration of the Magi* by Pinturicchio in the Room of the Mysteries in the Borgia Apartment

Town with Gothic Cathedral by Paul Klee (1879–1940)

Raphael Rooms

Pope Julius II's private apartments were built above those of his hated predecessor, Alexander VI, one of the Borgias, who died in 1503. Julius was impressed with Raphael's work, and chose him to redecorate the four rooms *(stanze)*. Raphael and his pupils began the task in 1508, replacing existing

Cortile del Belvedere

works by several better-known artists, including Raphael's own teacher, Perugino. The work took over 16 years and Raphael himself died before its completion. The frescoes express the religious and philosophical ideals of the Renaissance. They quickly established Raphael's reputation as an artist in Rome, putting him on a par with Michelangelo, then working on the ceiling of the Sistine Chapel.

Detail from *The Expulsion of Heliodorus from the Temple*, showing Pope Julius II watching the scene from his litter

Key to Floorplan

① Hall of Constantine

② Room of Heliodorus

③ Room of the Segnatura

④ Room of *The Fire in the Borgo*

① Hall of Constantine

The frescoes in this room were started in 1517, three years before Raphael's death, but Raphael himself probably had little hand in their execution. As a result they are not held in the same high regard as those in the other rooms. The work was completed in 1525 in the reign of Pope Clement VII by Giulio Romano, and two other former pupils of Raphael, Giovanni Francesco Penni, and Raffaellino del Colle.

The theme of the decoration is the triumph of Christianity over paganism. The four major frescoes show scenes from the life of Constantine, and include his *Vision of the Cross,* and his victory over his rival Maxentius at *The Battle of the Milvian Bridge*, for which Raphael had provided a preparatory sketch. In both *The Baptism of Constantine* and *The Donation of Constantine*, the figure of Pope Sylvester *(see p172)* was given the features of Clement VII.

② Room of Heliodorus

This private antechamber was decorated by Raphael between 1512 and 1514. The main frescoes show the miraculous protection granted to all the Church's ministers, doctrines, and property. The room's name refers to the fresco on the right, *The Expulsion of Heliodorus from the Temple*. This shows a story from Jewish history, in which a thief called Heliodorus is felled by a horseman as he tries

Swiss guards waiting with papal chair in *The Mass at Bolsena*

to make off with the treasure from the Temple of Jerusalem. The scene is witnessed by the pope, borne on a litter by courtiers. The incident is also a thinly veiled reference to Julius II's success in driving foreign armies out of Italy. In *The Meeting of Leo I and Attila* Raphael pays a similar compliment to the pope's political skill. Pope Leo was originally given the face of Julius II, but after his death, Raphael substituted the features of Julius's successor, Leo X.

The Mass at Bolsena depicts a miracle that occurred in 1263. A priest who doubted that the

The Battle of the Milvian Bridge, completed by one of Raphael's assistants

The Liberation of St Peter, a three-part composition, shows the saint asleep in his cell in the middle section, led out of prison by an angel on the right, while, on the left, the prison guards cower in terror.

The most famous, *The Fire in the Borgo*, was painted from Raphael's designs, and reflects his maturity as an artist. It celebrates the miracle that took place in 847, when Pope Leo IV extinguished a fire raging in the Borgo (see p248) by making the sign of the cross. The incident is likened to the flight of Aeneas from Troy described by Virgil. The figure of Aeneas appears in the foreground carrying his father on his back. This borrowing of an event from Classical legend shows a new willingness to experiment on the part of Raphael. Sadly, his pupils did not always follow his designs faithfully and this, combined with some poor restoration, has spoilt the work.

bread, and wine really were the body and blood of Christ suddenly saw the host bleed while he was celebrating mass. Julius II appears in this fresco, accompanied by a colorful group of Swiss guards.

Julius appears yet again as St Peter in *The Liberation of St Peter*. This fresco is remarkable for its dramatic lighting effects, achieved despite the painting's awkward shape and its position above a window.

③ Room of the Segnatura

The name is derived from a special council which met in this room to sign official documents. The frescoes here were completed between 1508 and 1511. The scheme Raphael followed was dictated by Pope Julius II. It reflects the Humanist belief that there could be perfect harmony between Classical culture and Christianity in their mutual search for truth.

The Dispute over the Holy Sacrament, the first fresco completed by Raphael for Pope Julius, represents the triumph of religion, and spiritual truth. The consecrated host is shown at the center of the painting. This links the group of learned scholars, who discuss its significance, to the Holy Trinity, and the saints floating on clouds up above.

On the opposite wall, *The School of Athens (see p34)* is a bustling scene centered around the debate on the search for

truth between Greek philosophers Plato and Aristotle. It also features portraits of many of Raphael's contemporaries, including Leonardo da Vinci, Bramante and Michelangelo. The other works include a portrait of the bearded Pope Julius II, who in 1511 vowed not to shave until he managed to rid Italy of all usurpers.

④ Room of *The Fire in the Borgo*

This was originally the dining room, but when the decoration was completed under Pope Leo X, it became a music room. All the frescoes exalt the reigning pope by depicting events in the lives of his namesakes, the 9th-century popes Leo III and IV. The main frescoes were finished by two of Raphael's assistants between 1514, and 1517, following their master's own plans.

Detail from *The Fire in the Borgo*, showing Aeneas, the Trojan hero, with his father on his back, fleeing from the fire

The Dispute over the Holy Sacrament, the first fresco completed in the Raphael Rooms

Sistine Chapel: The Walls

The massive walls of the Sistine Chapel, the main chapel in the Vatican Palace, were frescoed by some of the finest artists of the 15th and 16th centuries. The 12 paintings on the side walls, by artists including Perugino, Ghirlandaio, Botticelli, and Signorelli, show parallel episodes from the lives of Moses and Christ. The decoration of the chapel walls was completed between 1534 and 1541 by Michelangelo, who added the great altar wall fresco, *The Last Judgment*.

Key to the Frescoes: Artists and Subjects

The Last Judgment

☐ Perugino   ☐ Botticelli   ☐ Ghirlandaio
☐ Rosselli   ☐ Signorelli   ☐ Michelangelo

1 Baptism of Christ in the Jordan
2 Temptations of Christ
3 Calling of St. Peter and St. Andrew
4 Sermon on the Mount
5 Handing Over the Keys to St. Peter
6 Last Supper
7 Moses's Journey into Egypt
8 Moses Receiving the Call
9 Crossing of the Red Sea
10 Adoration of the Golden Calf
11 Punishment of the Rebels
12 Last Days of Moses

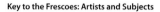

The Last Judgment by Michelangelo

Revealed in 1993 after a year's restoration, *The Last Judgment* is considered to be the masterpiece of Michelangelo's mature years. It was commissioned by Pope Paul III Farnese, and required the removal of earlier frescoes and two windows over the altar. A new wall was erected that slanted inward to stop dust from settling on it. Michelangelo worked alone on the fresco for seven years, until its completion in 1541.

The painting depicts the souls of the dead rising up to face the wrath of God, a subject that is rarely used for an altar decoration. The pope chose it as a warning to Catholics to adhere to their faith in the turmoil of the Reformation. In fact, the work conveys the artist's own tormented attitude to his faith. It offers neither the certainties of Christian orthodoxy nor the ordered view of Classicism.

In a dynamic, emotional composition, the figures are caught in a vortex of motion. The dead are torn from their graves and hauled up to face Christ the Judge, whose athletic, muscular figure is the focus of all the painting's movement. Christ shows little sympathy for the agitated saints around him, clutching the instruments of their martyrdom. Neither is any pity shown for the damned, hurled down to the demons in hell. Here, Charon, pushing people off his boat into the depths of Hades, and the infernal judge Minos, are taken from Dante's *Inferno*. Minos has ass's ears, and is a portrait of courtier Biagio da Cesena, who had objected to the nude figures in the fresco. Michelangelo's self-portrait is on the skin held by the martyr St. Bartholomew.

Souls meeting the wrath of Christ in Michelangelo's *Last Judgment*

Wall Frescoes

Detail from Botticelli's fresco
Temptations of Christ

When the Sistine Chapel was built, the papacy was a strong political power with vast accumulated wealth. In 1475 Pope Sixtus IV was able to summon some of the greatest painters of his day to decorate the chapel. Among the artists employed were Perugino, who was Raphael's master and is often credited with overseeing the project; Sandro Botticelli; Domenico Ghirlandaio; Cosimo Rosselli; and Luca Signorelli. Their work on the chapel's frescoes took from 1481 to 1483.

Although frequently overlooked by visitors who concentrate on Michelangelo's work, the frescoes along the side walls of the chapel include some of the finest works of 15th-century Italian art. The two cycles of frescoes represent scenes from the lives of Moses and Christ. Above them in the spaces between the windows are portraits of the earliest popes, painted by various artists, including Botticelli.

The fresco cycles start at the altar end of the chapel, with the story of Christ on the right-hand wall and that of Moses on the left. Originally there were two paintings, *The Birth of Christ* and *The Finding of Moses*, on the wall behind the altar, but these were both destroyed to make way for Michelangelo's *Last Judgment*. The final paintings of the two

cycles are also lost. They were on the entrance wall, which collapsed during the 16th century. When the wall was restored, they were replaced with poor substitutes.

As was customary at the time, each fresco contains a series of scenes, linked thematically to the central episode. Hidden meanings and symbols connect each painting with its counterpart on the opposite wall, and there are also many allusions to contemporary events.

The elaborate architectural details in the frescoes include familiar Roman monuments. The Arch of Constantine *(see p93)* provides the backdrop for the *Punishment of the Rebels* by Botticelli, the fifth panel in the cycle of Moses, in which the artist himself appears as the second-last figure on the right. Two similar arches appear in the painting opposite, Perugino's *Handing Over the Keys to St. Peter*.

Moses was both spiritual and temporal leader of his people. He called down the wrath of God on those who challenged his decisions, thus setting a precedent for the power

The crowd of onlookers in the *Calling of St. Peter and St. Andrew* by Ghirlandaio

exercised by the pope. In *Handing Over the Keys to St. Peter*, Christ confers spiritual and

temporal authority on St. Peter by giving him the keys to the kingdoms of Heaven and Earth. The golden-domed building in the center of the vast piazza represents both the Temple of Jerusalem and the Church, as founded by Peter, the first pope. The fifth figure on the right is thought to be a self-portrait by Perugino.

The central episode in Botticelli's
Punishment of the Rebels

Botticelli's *Temptations of Christ* includes a view of the Hospital of Santo Spirito, rebuilt in 1475 by Sixtus IV *(see p246)*. Here the devil is disguised in the habit of a Franciscan monk. Portraits of both Botticelli and Filippino Lippi are visible in the left hand corner. A portrait of the pope's nephew, Girolamo Riario, appears in the painting of the *Crossing of the Red Sea* by Rosselli, in which the sea is literally red. This painting also commemorates the papal victory at Campomorto in 1482.

Perugino's *Handing Over the Keys to St. Peter*

Sistine Chapel: The Ceiling

Michelangelo frescoed the ceiling for Pope Julius II between 1508 and 1512, working on specially designed scaffolding. The main panels, which chart the Creation of the World and Fall of Man, are surrounded by subjects from the Old and New Testaments – except for the Classical Sibyls, who are said to have foreseen the birth of Christ. In the 1980s the ceiling was restored, revealing colors of an unsuspected vibrancy.

Libyan Sibyl
The pagan prophetess reaches for the Book of Knowledge. Like most female figures Michelangelo painted, the beautiful Libyan Sibyl was probably modeled on a man.

Creation of the Sun and Moon
Michelangelo depicts God as a dynamic but terrifying figure commanding the sun to shed light on

Key to Ceiling Panels

KEY

① **Illusionistic architecture**

② **The lunettes** are devoted to frescoes of the ancestors of Christ, like Hezekiah.

③ **The Ignudi** are athletic male nudes whose significance is uncertain.

Genesis: 1 God Dividing Light from Darkness; **2** Creation of the Sun and Moon; **3** Separating Waters from Land; **4** Creation of Adam; **5** Creation of Eve; **6** Original Sin; **7** Sacrifice of Noah; **8** The Deluge; **9** Drunkenness of Noah.

Ancestors of Christ: 10 Solomon with Mother; **11** Parents of Jesse; **12** Rehoboam with Mother; **13** Asa with Parents; **14** Uzziah with Parents; **15** Hezekiah with Parents; **16** Zerubbabel with Parents; **17** Josiah with Parents.

Prophets: 18 Jonah; **19** Jeremiah; **20** Daniel; **21** Ezekiel; **22** Isaiah; **23** Joel; **24** Zechariah.

Sibyls: 25 Libyan Sibyl; **26** Persian Sibyl; **27** Cumaean Sibyl; **28** Erythrea Sibyl; **29** Delphic Sibyl.

Old Testament Scenes of Salvatio
30 Punishment of Haman; **31** Moses and the Brazen Serpent; **32** David an Goliath; **33** Judith and Holofernes.

Original Sin
This shows Adam and Eve tasting the forbidden fruit from the Tree of Knowledge, and their expulsion from Paradise. Michelangelo represents Satan as a snake with the body of a woman.

Restoration of the Sistine Ceiling

Restorers used computers, photography, and spectral analysis to inspect the fresco before cleaning began. They were therefore able to detect and remove the changes previous restorers had made to Michelangelo's original work. Analysis showed that the ceiling had been cleaned with materials ranging from bread to retsina wine. The restoration then revealed the familiarly dusky, eggshell-cracked figures to have creamy skins and lustrous hair and to be dressed in brightly colored, luscious robes: "a Benetton Michelangelo," mocked one critic, claiming that a layer of varnish that the artist had added to darken the colors had been removed. However, after examining the work, most experts agreed that the new colors probably matched those painted by Michelangelo.

A restorer cleaning the Libyan Sibyl

❸ Porta Santo Spirito

Via dei Penitenzieri. **Map** 3 C3. 🚌 23, 34, 46, 62, 64, 98, 870, 881, 982.

This gate is situated at what was the southern limit of the "Leonine City," the area enclosed within walls by Pope Leo IV as a defense against the Saracens, who had sacked Rome in AD 845. The walls measure 2 miles (3 km) in circumference.

Work on the walls started in AD 846. Pope Leo personally supervised the army of laborers, and thanks to his encouragement, the job was completed in 4 years. He then consecrated his massive feat of construction.

Since the time of Pope Leo, the walls have needed much reinforcement and repair. The gateway visible today at Porta Santo Spirito was built by the architect Antonio da Sangallo the Younger in 1543–4. It is framed by two huge bastions that were added in 1564 by Pope Pius IV Medici. Sangallo's design for a monumental entrance to the Vatican was never completed; the principal columns come to an end abruptly in a modern covering of cement.

Nave of Santo Spirito in Sassia

❹ Santo Spirito in Sassia

Via dei Penitenzieri 12. **Map** 3 C3. **Tel** 06-687 9310. 🚌 23, 34, 46, 62, 64, 98, 870, 881, 982. **Open** 7:30am–noon, 3–6:30pm daily (from 9:30am Sun). 🚻 ♿

Built on the site of a church erected by King Ine of Wessex, who died in Rome in the 8th century, the church is the work of Antonio da Sangallo the Younger. It was rebuilt (1538–44) after the Sack of Rome left it in ruins in 1527.

Sixtus V's arms over door of Santo Spirito

The facade was added under Pope Sixtus V (1585–90). The nave and side chapels are decorated with a series of light, lively frescoes. The pretty bell tower is earlier, dating from the reign of Sixtus IV (1471–84). It was probably the work of the pope's architect, Baccio Pontelli, who also built the Hospital of Santo Spirito, and the Ponte Sisto (see p212) farther down the Tiber River.

❺ Hospital of Santo Spirito

Borgo Santo Spirito 2. **Map** 3 C3. 🚌 23, 34, 46, 62, 64. Complex & chapel: **Open** for tours; call 06-683 51. ♿

The oldest hospital in Rome, this is said to have been founded as a result of a nightmare experienced by Pope Innocent III (1198–1216). In the dream, an angel showed him the bodies of Rome's unwanted babies dredged up from the Tiber River in fishing nets. As a result, the pope hastened to build a hospice for sick paupers. In 1475 the hospital was reorganized by

Fresco of an angel in the octagonal chapel of the Hospital of Santo Spirito

Pope Sixtus IV to care for the poor pilgrims expected for the Holy Year. Sixtus's hospital was a radical building. Cloisters divided the different types of patients; one area is still reserved for orphans, and their nurses.

Unwanted infants were passed through a revolving barrel-like contraption called the *rota*, still visible to the left of the central entrance in Borgo Santo Spirito, to guarantee anonymity. Martin Luther, who visited in 1511, was shocked by the number of abandoned children he saw, believing them to be "the sons of the pope himself."

In the center, under the hospital's conspicuous drum, is an octagonal chapel, where mass was said for patients. This room can be visited while the rest of the building still functions as a hospital.

Rusticated doorway of the Palazzo dei Convertendi

The *rota* of Santo Spirito, where mothers left unwanted babies

❻ Palazzo del Commendatore

Borgo Santo Spirito 3. **Map** 3 C3. 23, 34, 46, 62, 64. **Open** courtyard by appointment; call 06-6835 2353.

As director of the Hospital of Santo Spirito, the Commendatore not only oversaw the running of the hospital, he was also responsible for its estates and revenues. This important post was originally given to members of the pope's family.

The palazzo, built next door to the hospital, has a spacious 16th-century frescoed loggia appropriate to the dignity and sobriety of its owners. The frescoes represent the story of the founding of the Hospital of

Santo Spirito. To the left of the entrance is the Spezieria, or Pharmacy. This still has the wheel used for grinding the bark of the cinchona tree to produce the drug quinine, first introduced here in 1632 by Jesuits from Peru as a cure for malaria.

Above the courtyard is a splendid clock (1827). The dial is divided into six; it was not until 1846 that the familiar division of the day into two periods of 12 hours was introduced in Rome by Pope Pius IX.

Della Rovere arms

❼ Palazzo dei Convertendi

Via della Conciliazione 43. **Map** 3 C3. 23, 34, 62, 64. **Closed** to the public.

With the building of Via della Conciliazione in the 1930s, Palazzo dei Convertendi was taken down and later moved to this new site nearby. The house, partly attributed to the architect Bramante, is where the artist Raphael died in 1520.

❽ Palazzo dei Penitenzieri

Via della Conciliazione 33. **Map** 3 C3. **Tel** 06-6989 2930. 23, 34, 62, 64. **Open** 2:30–5pm Mon–Fri, by appt only. (donation) for groups.

The palazzo owes its name to the fact that the place was once home to the confessors *(penitenzieri)* of St. Peter's. Now partly housing the Hotel Columbus, it was originally built by Cardinal Domenico della Rovere in 1480. The palazzo still bears the family's coat of arms, the oak tree *(rovere* means oak), on its graceful courtyard wellhead. On the cardinal's death, the palazzo was acquired by Cardinal Francesco Alidosi, Pope Julius II della Rovere's favorite. Suspected of treason, the cardinal was murdered in 1511 by the pope's nephew, the Duke of Urbino, who took over the palazzo. A few of the rooms of the palazzo still contain beautiful frescoes.

View of the Tiber and the Borgo between Castel Sant'Angelo and St. Peter's by Gaspare Vanvitelli (1653–1736)

❾ Santa Maria in Traspontina

Via della Conciliazione 14. **Map** 3 C3.
Tel 06-6880 6451. 🚌 23, 34, 62, 64.
Open 7:30am–noon, 4:30–7pm daily.
🕇 ♿

The church occupies the site of an ancient Roman pyramid, believed in the Middle Ages to have been the Tomb of Romulus. The pyramid was destroyed by Pope Alexander VI Borgia, but representations of it survive in the bronze doors at the entrance to St. Peter's and in a Giotto triptych housed in the Vatican Pinacoteca *(see p238).*

The present church was begun in 1566 to replace an earlier one that had been in the

The facade of the Carmelite church of Santa Maria in Traspontina

line of fire of the cannons defending Castel Sant'Angelo during the Sack of Rome in 1527. The papal artillery officers insisted that the dome of the new church should be as low as possible, so it was built without a supporting drum. The first chapel to the right is dedicated to the gunners' patron saint, Santa Barbara, and is decorated with warlike motifs. In the third chapel on the left are two columns, popularly thought to be the ones that saints Peter and Paul were bound to before going to their martyrdom nearby.

❿ The Borgo

Map 3 C3. 🚌 23, 34, 40, 62.

The Borgo's name derives from the German *burg*, meaning town. Rome's Borgo is where the first pilgrims to St. Peter's were housed in hostels, and hospices, often for quite lengthy periods. The first of these foreign colonies, called "schools," was founded in AD 725 by a Saxon, King Ine of Wessex, who wished to live a life of penance and to be buried near the Tomb of St. Peter. These days, hotels, and hostels have made the Borgo a colony of international pilgrims once again. Much of

the area's character was lost after redevelopment in the 1930s, but it is still enjoyable to stroll the old narrow streets on either side of Via della Conciliazione.

Clement VII, who used the Vatican Corridor to evade capture in 1527

⓫ Vatican Corridor

Castel Sant'Angelo to the Vatican.
Map 3 C3. 🚌 23, 34, 40, 62. **Closed** to the public except for special events; call 06-0608 for information.

Locally known as the Passetto (small corridor), this long passageway was built into the fortifications during medieval times. Intended as a link between the Vatican and Castel Sant'Angelo, it constituted a fortified escape route that could also be used to control the strategic Borgo area. Arrows and other missiles could be fired from its bastions onto the streets and houses below. The corridor was used in 1494 by Pope Alexander VI Borgia when Rome was invaded by King Charles VIII of France. In 1527 it enabled Pope Clement VII to take refuge in Castel Sant'Angelo, as the troops commanded by the Constable of Bourbon began the Sack of Rome.

Palazzo Torlonia (1496), unaffected by changes to the surrounding area

⓬ Palazzo Torlonia

Via della Conciliazione 30. **Map** 3 C3.
23, 34, 40, 62, 64. **Closed** to the public.

The palazzo was built in the late 15th century by the wealthy Cardinal Adriano Castellesi, in a style closely resembling Palazzo della Cancelleria (see p151). The cardinal was a much-traveled rogue who collected vast revenues from the bishopric of Bath, and Wells, which he was given by his friend King Henry VII of England. In return, he gave Henry his palazzo for use as the seat of the English ambassador to the Holy See. Castellesi was finally stripped of his cardinalate by Pope Leo X Medici, and disappeared from history.

Pope Leo X

Since then, the palazzo has had many owners and tenants. In the 17th century it was rented for a time by Queen Christina of Sweden. The Torlonia family, who acquired the building in 1820, owed its fortune to the financial genius of shopkeeper-turned-banker Giovanni Torlonia. He lent money to the impoverished Roman nobility and bought up their property during the Napoleonic Wars.

⓭ Castel Sant'Angelo

See pp250–51.

⓮ Palazzo di Giustizia

Piazza Cavour. **Map** 4 E3. 34, 49, 70, 87, 186, 280, 492, 913, 926, 990. **Closed** to the public.

The monumental Palazzo di Giustizia (Palace of Justice) was built between 1889 and 1910 to house the national law courts.

Its riverside facade is crowned with a bronze chariot and fronted by giant statues of the great men of Italian law.

The building was supposed to embody the new order replacing the injustices of papal rule, but it has never endeared itself to the Romans. It was soon dubbed the Palazzaccio (roughly, "the ugly old palazzo") both for its appearance and for the nature of its business. By the 1970s the building was collapsing under its own weight, but it has now been restored.

The ornate travertine facade of the Palazzo di Giustizia

⑬ Castel Sant'Angelo

The massive fortress of Castel Sant'Angelo takes its name from the vision that Pope Gregory the Great had of the Archangel Michael on this site. It began life in AD 139 as Emperor Hadrian's mausoleum. Since then, it has had many roles: as part of Emperor Aurelian's city wall, as a medieval citadel and prison, and as the residence of the popes in times of political unrest. From the dank cells in the lower levels to the fine apartments of the Renaissance popes above, a 58-room museum covers all aspects of the castle's history.

Mausoleum of Hadrian
This artist's impression shows the tomb before Aurelian fortified its walls in AD 270–75.

Courtyard of Honor
Heaps of stone cannonballs decorate the courtyard, once the castle's ammunition store.

KEY

① **The spiral ramp** was the entrance to the mausoleum.

② **The Rooms of Clement VIII** are inscribed with the family crest of the Aldobrandini pope (1592–1605).

③ **Loggia of Paul III**

④ **Hall of the Library**

⑤ **Hall of the Columns**

⑥ **The Treasury** was probably the original site of Hadrian's burial chamber.

⑦ **The Round Hall** houses the original model from which Verschaffelt's angel was cast.

⑧ **The Hall of Justice** is decorated with a fresco of *The Angel of Justice* by Domenico Zaga (1545).

⑨ **Hall of Apollo** The room is frescoed with scenes from mythology attributed to the pupils of Perin del Vaga (1548).

⑩ **Ventilation shaft**

⑪ **Bridge**

⑫ **The Chamber of the Urns** housed the ashes of members of Hadrian's family.

★ **View from Terrace**
The castle's terrace, scene of the last act of Puccini's *Tosca*, offers splendid views in every direction.

Protecting the Pope

The Vatican Corridor leads from the Vatican Palace to Castel Sant'Angelo. It was built in 1277 to provide an escape route when the pope was in danger. The pentagonal ramparts built around the castle during the 17th century improved its defenses in times of siege.

■ Walls and fortifications
□ Vatican Corridor

Bronze Angel
The gigantic statue of the
Archangel Michael is by
the 18th-century Flemish
sculptor Pieter Verschaffelt.

VISITORS' CHECKLIST

Practical Informationn
Lungotevere Castello 50. **Map** 4 D3
& 11 A1. **Tel** 06-681 9111.
Open 9am–7:30pm (last adm:
6:30pm) Tue–Sun.
Closed Jan 1, Dec 25. 🖔 📷 🛗
♿ 📷 📷 Exhibitions.
ⓦ castelsantangelo.
beniculturali.it

Transportation
🚌 23, 40, 62 to Lungotevere
Vaticano; 34, 49, 87, 280, 492, 926,
990 to Piazza Cavour.

★ Sala Paolina
The illusionistic
frescoes by Perin del
Vaga and Pellegrino
Tibaldi (1546–8)
include one of a
courtier entering the
room through a
painted door.

**★ Staircase of
Alexander VI**
This staircase cuts right
through the heart
of the building.

Facade of Castel Sant'Angelo

AD 139 Mausoleum completed by Antoninus Pius

590 Legendary date of appearance of Archangel Michael above the castle

1493 Pope Alexander VI restores Vatican Corridor

1390 Pope Boniface IX remodels the castle

AD 100 — **500** — **1000** — **1500**

271 Tomb is incorporated into Aurelian Wall and fortified

Cannonballs in the Courtyard of Honor

1527 Castle withstands siege during Sack of Rome

1542–49 Sala Paolina and apartments built for Pope Paul III

1557 Ramparts built to protect the castle

1870 Castle used as barracks, and military prison

AD 130 Hadrian begins family mausoleum

VIA VENETO

In Imperial Rome, this was a suburb where rich families owned luxurious villas and gardens. Ruins from this era can be seen in the excavations in Piazza Sallustio, named after the most extensive gardens in the area, the Horti Sallustiani. After the Sack of Rome in the 5th century, the area reverted to open countryside. Not until the 17th century did it recover its lost splendor, with the building of Palazzo Barberini and the now-vanished Villa Ludovisi. When Rome became capital of Italy in 1870, the Ludovisi sold their land for development. They kept one lot for a new house, but tax on the profits from the sale was so high, they had to sell that too. By 1900, Via Veneto had become a street of chic modern hotels and cafés. It featured prominently in Fellini's 1960 film *La Dolce Vita*, a scathing satire on the lives of movie stars and the idle rich, but since then it has lost its position as the meeting place of the famous.

Sights at a Glance

Churches and Temples

3 Santa Maria della Concezione and Capuchin Crypt
7 Santa Susanna
8 Santa Maria della Vittoria

Historic Buildings

2 Casino dell'Aurora
6 Palazzo Barberini

Famous Streets

1 Via Veneto

Fountains

4 Fontana delle Api
5 Fontana del Tritone

Restaurants
see pp315–17

1 Edoardo
2 Gaetano Costa
3 Harry's Bar
4 La Terrazza
5 L'Olimpo
6 Mirabelle
7 Papà Baccus
8 San Marco

See also Street Finder map 5

The magnificent interior of Santa Maria della Vittoria

For map symbols *see back flap*

Street by Street: Via Veneto

The streets around Via Veneto, though within the walls of ancient Rome, contain little dating from before the unification of Italy in 1870. With its hotels, restaurants, bars, and travel agencies, the area is the center of 21st-century tourism in the way that Piazza di Spagna was the hub of the tourist trade in the Rome of the 18th-century Grand Tour. However, glimpses of the old city can be seen among the modern streets. These include Santa Maria della Concezione, the church of the Capuchin friars, whose convent once stood in its own gardens. In the 17th century, Palazzo Barberini was built here for the powerful papal family. Bernini's Fontana del Tritone and Fontana delle Api have stood in Piazza Barberini since it was the meeting place of cart tracks entering the city from surrounding vineyards.

3 Santa Maria della Concezione and Capuchin Crypt
This church is best known for the macabre collection of bones in its crypt.

4 Fontana delle Api
Bernini's drinking fountain is decorated with bees, emblem of his Barberini patrons.

Barberini station

PIAZZA BARBERINI

VIA VENETO

VIA DI SAN BA

VIA DI SAN NICOLA DA TOLENTINO

VIA BARBERINI

5 Fontana del Tritone
Bernini's muscular sea god has been spouting water skyward for 350 years.

VIA XX SETTEMBRE

6 ★ Palazzo Barberini
Pietro da Cortona worked on his spectacular ceiling fresco *The Triumph of Divine Providence* between 1633 and 1639.

The Porta Pinciana was built in AD 403. Only the central arch of white travertine is original.

Locator Map
See Central Rome Map pp16–17

② Casino dell'Aurora
A pavilion is all that remains of the great Ludovisi estate that once occupied most of this quarter of Rome.

① Via Veneto
Built during the redevelopment of Rome at the end of the 19th century, this street of chichotels and spacious sidewalk cafés enjoyed its heyday during the 1950s and 1960s.

Key

— Suggested route

0 meters 75
0 yards 75

⑦ Santa Susanna
This church is dedicated to a martyr executed during Diocletian's persecution of Christians in the 3rd century AD.

⑧ ★ Santa Maria della Vittoria
The highlight of this Baroque church is the Cornaro Chapel, designed to resemble a theater. The center of the stage is occupied by Bernini's thrilling sculpture of *The Ecstasy of St. Teresa.*

Sidewalk café in Via Veneto

❶ Via Veneto

Map 5 B1. 🚌 52, 53, 63, 80, 116, 119, 160 and many routes to Piazza Barberini. Ⓜ Barberini.

Via Veneto descends in a lazy curve from the Porta Pinciana to Piazza Barberini, lined in its upper reaches with exuberant late 19th-century hotels and canopied sidewalk cafés. It was laid out in 1879 over a large estate sold by the Ludovisi family in the great building boom of Rome's first years as capital of Italy. Palazzo Margherita, intended to be the new Ludovisi family palazzo, was completed in 1890. It now houses the American embassy.

In the 1960s this was the most glamorous street in Rome, its cafés patronized by movie stars and plagued by paparazzi. Most of the people drinking in the cafés today are tourists, since celebrities now seem to prefer the bohemian atmosphere of Trastevere or the luxury of the Parioli neighborhood.

❷ Casino dell'Aurora

Via Lombardia 46. **Map** 5 B2. **Tel** 06-8346 7000. 🚌 52, 53, 63, 80, 116, 119. Ⓜ Barberini. **Open** First day of every month (except Jan) 10am–noon, 3–5pm or by appt. Call above number, then email: aurorapallavicini@saita.it.

The Casino (a stately country residence) was a summer-house on the grounds of the Ludovisi Palace. It was built by Cardinal Ludovisi in the 17th century, and frescoed by Guido Reni. The ceiling fresco makes it seem as if the Casino has no roof, but lies open to a cloudy sky, across which horses pull the carriage of Aurora, the goddess of dawn, from darkness toward light.

❸ Santa Maria della Concezione and Capuchin Crypt

Via Veneto 27. **Map** 5 B2. **Tel** 06-8880 3695. 🚌 52, 53, 61, 62, 63, 80, 116, 119, 175. Ⓜ Barberini. Capuchin Crypt and Museum: **Open** 9am–7pm daily. **Closed** some religious holidays. 📷 ✝

Pope Urban VIII's brother, Antonio Barberini was a cardinal and a Capuchin friar. In 1626 he founded this plain church at what is now the foot of the Via Veneto. When he died, he was buried not in a grand marble sarcophagus, like most cardinals, but below a simple flagstone near the altar, with the bleak epitaph in Latin: "Here lies dust, ashes, nothing."

The grim reality of death is illustrated even more graphically in the crypt beneath the church, where generations of Capuchin friars decorated the walls of the five vaulted chapels with the bones and skulls of their departed brethren. In all, some 4,000 skeletons were used over about 100 years to create this macabre *memento mori* started in the late 17th century. Some of the bones are wired together to form Christian symbols such as crowns of thorns, sacred hearts, and crucifixes. There are also some complete skeletons, including one of a Barberini princess who died as a child. At the exit, an inscription in Latin reads: "What you are, we used to be. What we are, you will be."

❹ Fontana delle Api

Piazza Barberini. **Map** 5 B2. 🚌 52, 53, 61, 62, 63, 80, 116, 119, 175. Ⓜ Barberini.

The fountain of the bees – *api* are bees, symbol of the Barberini family – is one of Bernini's more modest works. Tucked away in a corner of Piazza Barberini, it is quite easy to miss. Dating from 1644, it pays homage to Pope Urban VIII Barberini, and features crablike bees that appear to be sipping the water as it dribbles down into the basin. A Latin inscription informs us that the water is for the use of the public and their animals.

Bernini's Fontana delle Api

❺ Fontana del Tritone

Piazza Barberini. **Map** 5 B3. 🚌 52, 53, 61, 62, 63, 80, 116, 119, 175. Ⓜ Barberini.

In the center of busy Piazza Barberini is one of Bernini's liveliest creations, the Triton Fountain. It was created for Pope Urban VIII Barberini in 1642, shortly after the completion of his palace on the ridge above. Acrobatic dolphins stand on their

Pope Urban VIII

The Triton and his conch shell in Bernini's Fontana del Tritone

heads, twisting their tails together to support a huge scallop shell on which the sea god Triton kneels, blowing a spindly column of water up into the air through a conch shell. Entwined artistically among the dolphins' tails are the papal tiara, the keys of St. Peter, and the Barberini coat of arms.

❻ Palazzo Barberini

Via delle Quattro Fontane 13. **Map** 5 B3. **Tel** 06-482 4184. 🚌 52, 53, 61, 62, 63, 80, 116, 175, 492, 590. Ⓜ Barberini. **Open** 8:30am–7pm Tue–Sun (last adm: 6pm). **Closed** Jan 1, Dec 25. 🌐 **galleriabarberini.beniculturali.it**

When Maffeo Barberini became Pope Urban VIII in 1623, he decided to build a grand palace for his family on the fringes of the city, overlooking a ruined temple. The architect, Carlo Maderno, designed it as a typical rural villa, with wings extending into the surrounding gardens. Maderno died in 1629 and Bernini took over, assisted by Borromini. The peculiar pediments on some of the top floor windows, and the oval staircase inside, are almost certainly by Borromini.

Of the many sumptuously decorated rooms, the most striking is the Gran Salone, with a dazzling illusionistic ceiling fresco by Pietro da Cortona. The palazzo also houses

paintings from the 13th to the 16th centuries, part of the Galleria Nazionale d'Arte Antica, with important works by Filippo Lippi, El Greco, and Caravaggio. There is also a Holbein portrait of King Henry VIII of England dressed for his wedding to Anne of Cleves. Of greater local significance are Guido Reni's *Beatrice Cenci*, the young woman executed for planning her father's murder (see p154), and La *Fornarina*, traditionally identified as a portrait of Raphael's mistress (see p212), although not necessarily painted by him.

Facade of Santa Susanna

❼ Santa Susanna

Via XX Settembre 14. **Map** 5 C2. **Tel** 06-4201 4554. 🚌 60, 61, 62, 84, 175, 492, 910. Ⓜ Repubblica. **Open** 9am–noon, 4–7pm daily. 🚹

Santa Susanna's most striking feature is its vigorous Baroque facade by Carlo Maderno, finished in 1603. Christians have worshipped on the site since at least the 4th century. In the nave, there are four huge frescoes by Baldassarre Croce (1558–1628), painted to resemble tapestries. These depict scenes from the life of Susanna, an obscure Roman saint who was martyred here, and the rather better-known life of the Old Testament Susanna, who was spotted bathing in her husband's garden by two lecherous judges.

Santa Susanna is the Catholic church for Americans in Rome and holds services in English every day.

❾ Santa Maria della Vittoria

Via XX Settembre 17. **Map** 5 C2. **Tel** 06-4274 0571. 🚌 60, 61, 62, 84, 492, 910. Ⓜ Repubblica. **Open** 8:30am–noon, 3:30–7pm daily. 🚹

Santa Maria della Vittoria is an intimate Baroque church with a lavishly decorated candlelit interior. It contains one of Bernini's most ambitious sculptural works, *The Ecstasy of St. Teresa* (1646), centerpiece of the Cornaro Chapel, built to resemble a miniature theater. It even has an audience: sculptures of the chapel's benefactor, Cardinal Federico Cornaro, and his ancestors sit in boxes, as if watching and discussing the scene occurring in front of them.

Visitors may be shocked or thrilled by the apparently physical nature of St. Teresa's ecstasy. She lies on a cloud, her mouth half open, and her eyelids closed, with rippling drapery covering her body. Looking over her with a smile, which can from different angles can appear either tender or cruel, is a curly-haired angel holding an arrow with which he is about to pierce the saint's body for a second time. The marble figures are framed and illuminated by rays of divine light materialized in bronze.

Bernini's astonishing *Ecstasy of St. Teresa*

FARTHER AFIELD

The more inquisitive visitor to Rome may wish to try a few excursions to the large parks and some of the more isolated churches on the outskirts of the city. With a day to spare, you can explore the villas of Tivoli and the ruins of the ancient Roman port of Ostia. Traditional haunts of the Grand Tour (see p132), such as the catacombs, and the ruined aqueducts of Parco Appio Claudio, still offer glimpses of the rapidly vanishing Campagna, the countryside around Rome. More modern sights include the suburb of EUR, built in the Fascist era, and the memorial at the Fosse Ardeatine.

Sights at a Glance

Towns and Areas
15 EUR
19 Tivoli

Historic Roads
9 Via Appia Antica

Churches
6 Santa Costanza
7 Sant'Agnese fuori le Mura
8 San Lorenzo fuori le Mura
16 San Paolo fuori le Mura

Museums and Galleries
2 Museo e Galleria Borghese pp262–3

3 Villa Giulia pp264–5
4 MAXXI
5 Museo d'Arte Contemporanea di Roma (MACRO)
17 Centrale Montemartini

Ancient Sites
22 Hadrian's Villa
23 Ostia Antica

Parks and Gardens
1 Villa Borghese
18 Villa Doria Pamphilj

20 Villa d'Este
21 Villa Gregoriana

Tombs and Catacombs
10 Catacombs of San Callisto
11 Catacombs of San Sebastiano
12 Catacombs of Domitilla
13 Fosse Ardeatine
14 Tomb of Cecilia Metella

Key

- Main sightseeing areas
- Freeway
- Main road
- Train line

0 kilometers   2
0 miles   1

Sights Outside Rome

Sights Outside Central Rome

ROME

◀ A picturesque waterfall in the grounds of Villa d'Este

For map symbols see back flap

❶ Villa Borghese

Map 2 E5. 🚌 52, 53, 88, 95, 116, 490, 495. 🚊 3, 19. Park: **Open** dawn to sunset. Bioparco: Viale del Giardino Zoologico 20. **Map** 2 E4. **Tel** 06-360 8211. 🚌 52. 🚊 3, 19. **Open** daily. **Closed** Dec 25. ♿ 🚻 🖥 📷 🅆 **bio parco.it**. Galleria Nazionale d'Arte Moderna: Viale delle Belle Arti 131. **Map** 2 D4. **Tel** 06-3229 8221. 🚊 3, 19. **Open** 8:30am–7:30pm Tue–Sun (last adm: 6:45pm). **Closed** Jan 1, May 1, Dec 25. ♿ 🚻 🚻 🖥 📷 Museo Carlo Bilotti: Viale F. La Guardia. **Map** 2 D5. **Open** Oct–May: 10am–4pm; Jun–Sep: 1–7pm Mon–Fri, 10am–7pm Sat–Sun. **Closed** Jan 1, May 1, Dec 25. 🚻 📷

The villa and its park were designed in 1605 for Cardinal Scipione Borghese, nephew of Pope Paul V. The park was the first of its kind in Rome. It contained 400 newly-planted pine trees, garden sculpture by Bernini's father, Pietro, and dramatic waterworks built by Giovanni Fontana. The layout of the formal gardens was imitated by other prominent Roman families at Villa Ludovisi and Villa Doria Pamphilj.

In the early 19th century, Prince Camillo Borghese assembled the family's magnificent art collection in the Casino Borghese, now the home of the Galleria and Museo Borghese.

British School at Rome, designed by Edwin Lutyens in 1911

In 1901 the park became the property of the Italian state. Within its 4-mile (6-km) circumference there are now museums and galleries, foreign academies and schools of archaeology, a zoo, a riding school, a grassy amphi-theater, an artificial lake, an aviary, and an array of summer houses, fountains, Neo-Classical statuary, and exotic follies.

There are several ways into the park, including a monumental entrance on Piazzale Flaminio, built for Prince Camillo Borghese in 1825 by Luigi Canina. Other conveniently sited entrances are at Porta Pinciana at the end of Via Veneto and from the Pincio Gardens (see p138). Piazza di Siena, a pleasantly open, grass-covered amphitheater surrounded by tall umbrella pines, was the inspiration for Ottorino Respighi's famous symphonic poem The Pines of Rome, written in 1924. Near Piazza di Siena are the so-called Casina di Raffaello, said to have been owned by Raphael, and the 18th-century Palazzetto dell' Orologio. These were summerhouses from which people enjoyed the beautiful vistas across the park.

Statue of the English poet Byron by Thorvaldsen

Many buildings in the park were originally surrounded by formal gardens: the Casino Borghese and the nearby 17th-century Casino della Meridiana and its aviary (uccelliera) have both kept their geometric flowerbeds. Throughout the park, the intersections of paths, and avenues are marked by fountains, and statues. West of Piazza di Siena is the Fontana dei Cavalli Marini (the Fountain of the Seahorses), added during the villa's 18th-century remodeling. Walking through the park you will encounter statues of Byron, Goethe, and Victor Hugo, and a gloomy equestrian King Umberto I.

Dotted around the park are picturesque temples made to look like ruins, including a circular Temple of Diana between Piazza di Siena, and Porta Pinciana, and a Temple of Faustina, wife of Emperor Antoninus Pius, on the hill north of Piazza di Siena. The nearby medieval-looking Fortezzuola by Canina contains the works of the sculptor Pietro Canonica, who lived in the building, and died there in 1959. In the garden stands Canonica's Monument to the Alpino and his Mule, which honors the humblest protagonists in Italy's alpine battles against Austria in World War I.

Neo-Classical Temple of Diana

Ionic temple dedicated to Aesculapius, built on the lake island

In the center of the park is the Giardino del Lago, its main entrance marked by an 18th-century copy of the Arch of Septimius Severus. The garden has an artificial lake complete with an Ionic temple to Aesculapius, the god of healing, by the 18th-century architect Antonio Asprucci. Rowboats, and ducks make the lake a favorite with children, banana trees, and bamboo grow around the shore, and clearings are studded with sculptures.

Surrounded by flowerbeds south of the lake is the Art Nouveau Fontana dei Fauni, one of the garden's prettiest sculptures. In a clearing close to the entrance on Viale Pietro Canonica are the original Tritons of the Fontana del Moro in Piazza Navona *(see p122)* – they were moved here and replaced by copies in the 19th century.

From the northwest, the park is entered by the Viale delle Belle Arti, where the Galleria Nazionale d'Arte Moderna houses a good collection of 19th- and 20th-century paintings. The Art Nouveau character of the area dates from the International Exhibition held here in 1911, for which pavilions were built by many nations, the most impressive being Edwin Lutyens' British School at Rome, with a facade adapted from the upper west portico of St. Paul's Cathedral in London. It is now a research institute for Classical studies, history, and the visual arts. Nearby statues include one of Simón Bolívar, and other liberators of Latin America.

In the northeastern corner of the park lie the Museo Zoologico and a small zoo, the Bioparco, where the emphasis is on conservation. Nearby, the pretty 16th-century Villa Giulia houses a world-famous collection of Etruscan and other pre-Roman remains. Another Renaissance building of importance is the Palazzina of Pius IV, designed by the architect Vignola in 1552. It now houses the Italian embassy to the Holy See.

Named after its principal benefactor, the Museo Carlo Bilotti is situated in the center of the Villa Borghese. This former orangery has been transformed into a modern art gallery boasting works by Giorgio de Chirico, Andy Warhol, and Gino Severini.

❷ Museo e Galleria Borghese
See pp262–3.

❸ Villa Giulia
See pp264–5.

❹ MAXXI (National Museum of 21st Century Arts)

Via Guido Reni 4A. **Map** 1 A2. **Tel** 06-3996 7350. 53, 217, 225, 910. 2. **Open** 11am–7pm Tue–Sun (to 10pm Sat). **Closed** May 1, Dec 25. (free up to age 14). **fondazionemaxxi.it**

Along with the nearby Parco della Musica *(see p350)*, MAXXI, the National Museum of 21st Century Arts, has put Rome on the contemporary arts map. Located in a stunning building designed by architect Zaha Hadid, it showcases emerging Italian, and international artists. An impressive amount of space is also dedicated to architecture.

MAXXI, the National Museum of 21st Century Arts, designed by Zaha Hadid

❷ Museo e Galleria Borghese

The villa and park were laid out by Cardinal Scipione Borghese, favorite nephew of Paul V, who had the house designed for pleasure, and entertainment. The hedonistic cardinal was also an extravagant patron of the arts, and he commissioned sculptures from the young Bernini that now rank among his most famous works. Scipione also opened his pleasure park to the public. Today the villa houses the superb private Borghese collection of sculptures, and paintings in the Museo and Galleria Borghese.

Facade of the Villa Borghese
This painting (1613) by the villa's Flemish architect Jan van Santen shows the highly ornate facade of the original design.

Rear entrance

4

5

6

7

Sleeping Hermaphrodite
This is a marble Roman copy of the Greek original by Polycles, dated around 150 BC. The head and mattress were added by Andrea Bergondi in the 17th century.

The Egyptian Room
Frescoes show episodes in Egyptian history and Egyptian motifs.

★ **Rape of Proserpine**
One of Bernini's finest works shows Pluto (Hades) abducting his bride. The sculptor's amazing skill with marble can be seen clearly in the twisting figures.

Gladiator Mosaic
The floor is decorated with the fragments of a 4th-century AD mosaic from a villa in Torrenova.

1613 15-year-old Bernini sculpts *Aeneas and Anchises*	**Early 1800s** Statues, and reliefs are considered too ornate and stripped from the villa's facade	**1902** Villa, grounds, and collection bought by the state
1622–25 Bernini sculpts *The Rape of Proserpine*		**1809** Much of the collection is sold by Prince Camillo Borghese to France and goes to Louvre
1610	**1710**	**1810**
1622–25 Bernini sculpts *Apollo and Daphne*	**1805** Canova sculpts the seminude, reclining Pauline Borghese	
1613–15 The Flemish architect Jan van Santen designs, and builds Villa Borghese	*Daphne's fingers turning into leaves*	**Early 1900s** Balustrade around the forecourt is bought by Lord Astor for the Cliveden estate in England

★ Apollo and Daphne

Bernini's most famous masterpiece depicts the nymph Daphne fleeing the sun god Apollo at the moment of Daphne's dramatic transformation into a tree.

VISITORS' CHECKLIST

Practical Information
Villa Borghese, Piazzale Scipione Borghese 5.
Map 2 F5.
Tel 06-328 10 (reservations).
Open 8:30am–7:30pm Tue–Sun (last adm: 6:45pm).
Closed Jan 1, Dec 25.
Advance booking recommended weekdays and obligatory Sat, Sun & for special exhibitions.
W galleriaborghese.it

Transportation
52, 53, 116, 910 to Via Pinciana. 3, 19 to Viale delle Belle Arti.

3

2

1

★ Galleria Borghese
The gallery has Old Master paintings, such as Titian's *Sacred and Profane Love* (detail) dating from 1514.

★ Pauline Borghese
Napoleon's sister Pauline posed as Venus for this sculpture. Once the statue was finished, her husband locked it away, even from its sculptor Canova.

Front entrance

Key to Floor plan

☐ Exhibition space

▦ Non-exhibition space

Museum Guide

The museum is divided into two sections: the sculpture collection (Museo Borghese) occupies the entire ground floor and the picture gallery (Galleria Borghese) is on the upper floor. The museum also hosts wonderful temporary exhibitions.

David
This sculpture, by Bernini (1624), captures the moment just before David attacks Goliath with a rock. Bernini modeled David's face on his own.

❸ Villa Giulia

This villa was built as a country retreat for Pope Julius III, and was designed for entertaining rather than as a permanent home. It once housed an impressive collection of statues – 160 boatloads were sent to the Vatican after the pope died in 1555. The villa, gardens, pavilions, and fountains were designed by exceptional architects: Vignola (designer of the Gesù), Vasari, and the sculptor Ammannati. Michelangelo also contributed. The villa's main features are its facade, the courtyard, and garden, and the *nymphaeum*. Since 1889 Villa Giulia has housed the Museo Nazionale Etrusco, with its outstanding collection of pre-Roman antiquities from central Italy.

★ Ficoroni Cist
Engraved and beautifully illustrated, this fine bronze marriage coffer dates from the 4th century BC.

★ Sarcophagus of the Spouses
This 6th-century BC masterpiece, from Cerveteri, shows a dead couple at the eternal banquet.

Votive Offering
The religious Etruscans made artifacts, such as this model of a boy feeding a bird, in their gods' honor.

Museum Guide

This is the most important Etruscan museum in Italy, housing artifacts from most of the major excavations in Tuscany and Lazio. Rooms 1–13b and 31–37 are arranged by site and include Vulci, Todi, Veio, and Cerveteri, while private collections are in rooms 14–24.

1550 Work begins on Villa Giulia under Pope Julius III		**Late 1700s** First large-scale studies of Etruscan artifacts		
	Late 1500s First chance finds of Etruscan artifacts raise some scholarly interest		**1889** Etruscan museum founded	**1919** Castellani private collection donated to museum
1550	**1650**	**1750**	**1850**	**1950**
	1655 Queen Christina of Sweden stays in villa as Vatican guest		**1908** Barberini private collection bought by the state	
1555 Villa completed		*Corner decoration of bronze chariot used to burn incense*		**1972** Pesciotti private collection bought by the state

Facade
The villa's facade dates from 1551. The entrance is designed in the form of a triumphal arch.

VISITORS' CHECKLIST

Practical Information
Piazzale di Villa Giulia 9.
Map 1 C4.
Tel 06-322 6571.
Open 8:30am–7:30pm Tue–Sun (last adm: 6:30pm).
Closed Jan 1, Dec 25. 🎫 🖼 🎦 with seven days' notice. 🏛 🛍 🖼 🦽 📷 It is also possible to visit the museum's additional collections at the nearby Villa Poniatowski, 9am–1:45pm Tue–Sat.

Transportation
🚌 52, 926 to Viale Bruno Buozzi, 88, 95, 490, 495 to Viale Washington. 🚊 3, 19 to Piazza Thorvaldsen.

Chigi Vase
Battle and hunting scenes adorn this Corinthian vase from the 6th century BC.

Faliscan Crater of the Dawn
This ornate vase, painted in the free style of the 4th century BC, shows Dawn rising in a chariot.

★ Reconstruction of an Etruscan Temple
Count Adolfo Cozza built the Temple of Alatri here in 1891. He based his design on the accounts of Vitruvius and 19th-century excavations.

Main entrance

Key to Floor plan

- ▨ Lower ground floor
- ▨ Ground floor
- ▨ First floor
- ▢ Non-exhibition space

Nymphaeum
Literally, the "area dedicated to the nymphs," this is a sunken courtyard decorated with Classical mosaics, statues, and fountains.

➎ Museo d'Arte Contemporanea di Roma (MACRO)

Via Cagliari (corner Via Nizza). **Map** 6 E1. **Tel** 06-671 070 400; 06-0608. 36, 60, 84, 90. **Open** 11am–7pm Tue–Sun (until 10pm Sat) Also at: Piazza Giustiniani 4 (Testaccio). **Map** 7 C4. 23, 95, 280, 719. **Open** for exhibitions 4–10pm Tue–Sun.
w museomacro.org

The historic Peroni beer factory is now home to the MACRO gallery of contemporary art. Apart from a permanent collection of late 20th-century art, featuring artists such as Carla Accardi and Mario Schifano, there are interesting exhibitions – both here and at the Testaccio outpost – show-casing the latest on the local, and national scene.

Interior of Santa Costanza

➏ Santa Costanza

Via Nomentana 349. **Tel** 06-8620 5456. 36, 60, 84, 90. Annibaliano. **Open** 9am–noon, 4–6pm Mon–Sat; 4–6pm Sun.

The round church of Santa Costanza was first built as a mausoleum for Emperor Constantine's daughters Constantia and Helena, in the early 4th century. The dome and its drum are supported by a circular arcade resting on 12 magnificent pairs of granite columns. The ambulatory that runs around the outside of the

Part of the 4th-century mosaic in the ambulatory of Santa Costanza

central arcade has a barrel-vaulted ceiling decorated with wonderful 4th-century mosaics of flora and fauna and charming scenes of a Roman grape harvest. In a niche on the far side of the church from the entrance is a replica of Constantia's ornately carved porphyry sarcophagus. The original was moved to the Vatican Museums in 1790.

Constantia's sanctity is debatable – she was described by the historian Marcellinus as fury incarnate, constantly goading her equally unpleasant husband Hannibalianus to violence. Her canonization was probably the result of some confusion with a saintly nun of the same name.

➐ Sant'Agnese fuori le Mura

Via Nomentana 349. **Tel** 06-8620 5456. 36, 60, 84, 90. Annibaliano. **Open** 7:30am–noon, 4–7:30pm daily. to catacombs.

The church of Sant'Agnese stands among a group of early Christian buildings that includes the ruins of a covered cemetery, some

extensive catacombs, and the crypt where the 13-year-old martyr St. Agnes was buried in AD 304. Agnes was exposed naked by order of Emperor Diocletian, furious that she should have rejected the advances of a young man at his court, but her hair miraculously grew to protect her modesty *(see p123)*.

The church is said to have been built at the request of the Emperor Constantine's daughter, Constantia, after she had prayed at the Tomb of St. Agnes for delivery from leprosy.

Though much altered over the centuries, the form, and much of the structure of the 4th-century basilica remain intact. In the 7th-century apse mosaic St. Agnes appears as a bejeweled Byzantine empress in a stole of gold, and a violet robe. According to tradition, she appeared like this eight days after her death holding a white lamb. Every year on January 21, two lambs are blessed on the church altar, and a vestment called the *pallium* is woven from their wool. Every newly appointed archbishop is sent a *pallium* by the pope.

Apse mosaic in Sant'Agnese, showing the saint flanked by two popes

Cloister, San Lorenzo fuori le Mura

❽ San Lorenzo fuori le Mura

Piazzale del Verano 3. **Tel** 06-49 15 11. 🚌 71, 492. 🚋 3, 19. **Open** summer: 7:30am–12:30pm, 4–8pm daily; winter: 7:30am–12:30pm, 3:30–7pm daily. ♿

Just outside the eastern wall of the city stands the church of San Lorenzo. Roasted slowly to death in AD 258, San Lorenzo was one of the most revered of Rome's early Christian martyrs. The first basilica erected over his burial place by Constantine was largely rebuilt in 576 by Pope Pelagius II. Close by stood a 5th-century church dedicated to the Virgin Mary. The intriguing two-level church we see today is the result of these two churches being merged into one. This process, started in the 8th century, was completed in the 13th century by Pope Honorius III, when the nave, the portico, and much of the decoration were added. The remains of San Lorenzo are in the choir of the 6th-century church (beneath the 13th-century high altar).

Romanesque bell tower of San Lorenzo

❾ Via Appia Antica

🚌 118, 218. 🌐 **parcoappiaantica.it**
See Walks pp286–7.

The first part of the Via Appia was built in 312 BC by the Censor Appius Claudius Caecus. When it was extended to the ports of Benevento, Taranto, and Brindisi in 190 BC, the road became Rome's link with its expanding empire in the East. It was the route taken by the funeral processions of the dictator Sulla (78 BC) and Emperor Augustus (AD 14) and it was along this road that St. Paul was led a prisoner to Rome in AD 56. Gradually abandoned during the Middle Ages, the road was restored by Pope Pius IV in the mid-16th century. It is lined with ruined family tombs and collective burial places known as columbaria. Beneath the fields on either side lies a vast maze of catacombs. Today the road starts at Porta San Sebastiano (see p198). Major Christian sights include the church of Domine Quo Vadis, built where St. Peter is said to have met Christ while fleeing from Rome, and the Catacombs of San Callisto and San Sebastiano. The tombs lining the road include those of Cecilia Metella (see p268) and Romulus (son of Emperor Maxentius) who died in 309. The ancient Villa dei Quintili is nearby, at Via Appia Nuova 1092 (phone 06-3996 7700).

❿ Catacombs of San Callisto

Via Appia Antica 126. **Tel** 06-5130 1580. 🚌 118, 218. **Open** 9am–noon, 2–5pm Thu–Tue. **Closed** Jan 1, late Jan–late Feb, Easter Sun & Dec 25. 🎧 🚻 ♿ 📷 🅿 📖 🌐 **catacombe.roma.it**

In burying their dead in underground cemeteries outside the city walls, the early Christians were obeying the laws of the time: it was not because of persecution. So many saints were buried that the catacombs became shrines and places of pilgrimage.

The vast Catacombs of San Callisto are on four different levels and only partly explored. The rooms and connecting passageways are hewn out of volcanic tufa. The dead were placed in niches, known as *loculi*, which held two or three bodies. The most important rooms were decorated with stucco and frescoes. The area that can be visited includes the Crypt of the Popes, where many of the early popes were buried, and the Crypt of Santa Cecilia, where the saint's body was discovered in 820 before being moved to her church in Trastevere (see p213).

⓫ Catacombs of San Sebastiano

Via Appia Antica 136. **Tel** 06-785 0350. 🚌 118, 218. **Open** 10am–4:30pm Mon–Sat. **Closed** Jan 1, late Nov–late Dec, Dec 25. 🎧 🚻 📷 🅿 🌐 **catacombe.org**

The 17th-century church of San Sebastiano, above the catacombs, occupies the site of a basilica. Preserved at the entrance to the catacombs is the *triclia*, a building that once stood above ground, and was used by mourners for taking funeral refreshments. Its walls are covered with graffiti invoking St. Peter and St. Paul, whose remains may have been moved here during one of the periods of persecution.

Cypresses lining part of the Roman Via Appia Antica

⓬ Catacombs of Domitilla

Via delle Sette Chiese 282. **Tel** 06-511 0342. 🚌 218, 716. **Open** 9am–noon, 2–5pm Wed–Mon (summer: 5:30pm). **Closed** mid-Dec–mid-Jan, Easter Sun. 🚫 ♿ 📷 W domitilla.soverdi.eu

This network of catacombs is the largest in Rome. Many of the tombs from the 1st and 2nd centuries AD have no Christian connection. In the burial chambers there are frescoes of both Classical and Christian scenes, including one of the earliest depictions of Christ as the *Good Shepherd*. Above the catacombs stands the basilica of Santi Nereo e Achilleo. After rebuilding and restoration, little remains of the original 4th-century church.

Bronze entrance gates to the Fosse Ardeatine by Mirko Basaldella

⓭ Fosse Ardeatine

Via Ardeatina 174. **Tel** 06-513 6742. 🚌 218, 716. **Open** 8:15am–3:15pm Mon–Fri, 8:15am–4:30pm Sat & Sun. **Closed** public hols.

On the evening of March 24, 1944, Nazi forces took 335 prisoners to this abandoned quarry south of Rome, and shot them at point-blank range. The execution was in reprisal for a bomb attack that had killed 32 German soldiers. The victims included various political prisoners, 73 Jews, and 10 other civilians, among them a priest and a 14-year-old boy. The Germans blew up the tunnels where the massacre had taken place, but a local peasant had witnessed the scene, and later helped find the corpses. The site is now a memorial to the values of the Resistance against the Nazi occupation, which gave birth to the modern Italian Republic *(see p187)*. A forbidding bunker-like monument houses the rows of identical tombs containing the victims.

Beside it is a museum of the Resistance. Interesting works of modern sculpture include *The Martyrs*, by Francesco Coccia, and the gates shaped like a wall of thorns by Mirko Basaldella.

⓮ Tomb of Cecilia Metella

Via Appia Antica, km 3. **Tel** 06-3996 7700. 🚌 118, 660. **Open** 9am–approx 1 hr before sunset Tue–Sun.

One of the most famous landmarks on the Via Appia Antica is the huge tomb built for the noblewoman Cecilia Metella. Her father, and husband were rich patricians, and successful generals of late Republican Rome, but hardly anything is known about the woman herself. Byron muses over her unknown destiny in his poem *Childe Harold*.

In 1302 Pope Boniface VIII donated the tomb to his family, the Caetani. They incorporated it in a fortified castle that blocked the Via Appia, allowing them to control the traffic on the road and exact high tolls. The marble facing of the tomb was pillaged by another pope, Sixtus V, at the end of the 16th century.

On the opposite side of the road stands what remains of the early 14th-century church of San Nicola.

Fragments of marble relief on the Tomb of Cecilia Metella

EUR's Palazzo della Civiltà del Lavoro, the "Square Colosseum"

⓯ EUR

🚌 170, 671, 714 and other routes. Ⓜ EUR Fermi, EUR Palasport. Museo della Civiltà Romana: Piazza G. Agnelli 10. **Tel** 06-5422 0919. **Open** 9am–2pm Tue–Sun; last adm: 1 hr before closing. **Closed** Jan 1, May 1, Dec 25. ♿

The Esposizione Universale di Roma (EUR), a suburb south of the city, was built for an international exhibition, a kind of "Work Olympics," that was planned for 1942, but never took place because of the war. The architecture was intended to glorify Fascism, and the style of the public buildings is very overblown, and rhetorical. The eerie shape of the Palazzo della Civiltà del Lavoro (The Palace of the Civilization of Work) is an unmistakable landmark for people arriving from Fiumicino airport.

The plan was completed in the 1950s. In terms of town planning, EUR has been quite successful, and people are still eager to live here. The great marble halls house several government offices, and museums.

The Museo della Civiltà Romana displays a vast scale model of Rome at the time of Constantine and casts of the reliefs on Trajan's Column. These, and the interesting planetarium, make the museum worth a visit.

To the south is a lake, and park, and the huge domed Palazzo dello Sport built for the 1960 Olympics.

⑯ San Paolo fuori le Mura

Via Ostiense 186. **Tel** 06-6988 0800.
🚌 23, 128, 170, 670, 707, 761, 769.
Ⓜ San Paolo. **Open** 7am–6:30pm daily. Cloister and museum: **Open** 9am–6pm daily. 🔼 ♿ 📷

Today's church is a faithful reconstruction of the great 4th-century basilica destroyed by fire on July 15, 1823. Few fragments of the original church survived. The triumphal arch over the nave is decorated on one side with restored 5th-century mosaics. On the other side are mosaics by Pietro Cavallini, originally on the facade. The splendid Venetian apse mosaics (1220) depict the figures of Christ with St. Peter, St. Andrew, St. Paul, and St. Luke.

The fine marble canopy over the high altar is signed by the sculptor Arnolfo di Cambio (1285) "together with his partner Pietro," who may have been Pietro Cavallini. Below the altar is the *confessio*, the tomb of St. Paul. To the right is an impressive Paschal candlestick by Nicolò di Angelo and Pietro Vassalletto.

The cloister of San Paolo, with its pairs of colorful inlaid

19th-century mosaic on facade of San Paolo fuori le Mura

columns supporting the arcade, was spared completely by the fire. Completed around 1214, it is considered one of the most beautiful in Rome.

⑰ Centrale Montemartini

Via Ostiense 106. **Tel** 06-0608.
🚌 23, 769. **Open** 9am–7pm Tue–Sun (last adm: 6:30pm). **Closed** Jan 1, May 1, Dec 25. 🎫 📷 ♿ 🛍 ✔

An enormous old industrial site has been restored to house the ACEA art center. Originally, the building was used as Rome's first power station, and its two huge generators still occupy the central machine room, creating quite an intriguing contrast to the exhibitions. On display are Roman statues and artifacts belonging to the Capitoline Museums *(see pp70–73)*. Many of the statues were discovered during excavations in the late 19th and early 20th centuries, including some from the Area Sacra di Largo Argentina *(see p152)*.

Casino del Bel Respiro, summer residence in Villa Doria Pamphilj

⑲ Villa Doria Pamphilj

Via di San Pancrazio. 🚌 31, 44, 75, 710, 870. Park: **Open** dawn–dusk daily.

One of Rome's largest public parks, the Villa Doria Pamphilj was laid out in the mid-17th century for Prince Camillo Pamphilj. His uncle, Pope Innocent X, paid for the magnificent summer residence, the Casino del Bel Respiro, and the fountains and summerhouses, some of which still survive.

Statue in Centrale Montemartini, former power plant turned art center

Day Trips around Rome

Tivoli, a favorite place to escape the heat of the Roman summer

⑲ Tivoli

Town is 20 miles (31 km) northeast of Rome. **FS** from Tiburtina. **COTRAL** COTRAL from Ponte Mammolo (on Metro line B).

Tivoli has been a popular summer resort since the days of the Roman Republic. Among the famous men who owned villas here were the poets Catullus and Horace, Caesar's assassins Brutus and Cassius, and the Emperors Trajan and Hadrian. Tivoli's main attractions were its clean air and beautiful situation on the slopes of the Tiburtini hills, its healthy sulfur springs, and the waterfalls of the Aniene – the Emperor Augustus said these had cured him of insomnia. The Romans' luxurious lifestyle was revived in Renaissance times by the owners of the Villa d'Este, the town's most famous sight.

In the Middle Ages, Tivoli suffered frequent invasions; its position made it an ideal base for an advance on Rome. In 1461 Pope Pius II built a fortress here, the Rocca Pia, declaring: "It is easier to regain Rome while possessing Tivoli, than to regain Tivoli while possessing Rome." After suffering heavy bomb damage in 1944, Tivoli's main buildings and churches were speedily restored.

The town's cobbled streets are still lined with medieval houses. The Duomo (cathedral) houses a beautiful 13th-century life-size wooden group representing the *Deposition from the Cross*.

⑳ Villa d'Este

Piazza Trento 5, Tivoli. **Tel** 0774-332 920. **COTRAL** COTRAL from Ponte Mammolo (on Metro line B). **Open** 8:30am–approx 1 hr before sunset Tue–Sun. **Closed** Jan 1, Dec 25. **W** villadestetivoli.info

The villa occupies the site of an old Benedictine convent. In the 16th century the estate was developed by Cardinal Ippolito d'Este, son of Lucrezia Borgia. A palace was designed by Pirro Ligorio to make the most of its hilltop situation, but the villa's fame rests more on the terraced gardens and fountains laid out by Ligorio and Giacomo della Porta.

The gardens have suffered neglect in the past, but the grottoes and fountains still give a vivid impression of the great luxury that the princes of the church enjoyed. From the great loggia of the palace you descend through the privet-lined paths to the Grotto of Diana and Bernini's Fontana del Bicchierone. Below to the right is the Rometta (little Rome), a model of Tiber Island with allegorical

Detail of Fontana dell'Organo at Villa d'Este

figures and the legendary she-wolf. The Rometta is at one end of the Viale delle Cento Fontane, 100 fountains in the shapes of grotesques, obelisks, ships, and the eagles of the d'Este coat of arms. Other fountains are now being restored to their former glory. The Fontana dell'Organo is a water-organ, in which the force of the water pumps air through the pipes. The garden's lowest level has flower beds and fountains as well as some splendid views out over the plain below.

Terrace of 100 Fountains in the gardens of Villa d'Este

㉑ Villa Gregoriana

Largo Sant'Angelo, Tivoli. **FS** Tivoli, then short walk. **Tel** 06-3996 7701; 0774 332 650. **Open** 10am–6:30pm Tue–Sun (to 4pm Mar, Oct 16–Nov 30). Last adm: 1 hour before close. **Closed** Dec–Feb.

The main attractions of this steeply sloping park are the waterfalls and grottoes created by the Aniene River. The park is named after Pope Gregory XVI, who in the 1830s ordered the building of a tunnel to protect against flooding. This tunnel created a new waterfall, called the Grande Cascata, which plunges 525 ft (160 m) into the valley behind the town.

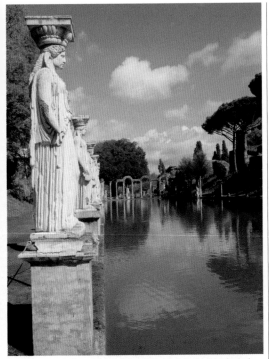

The Canopus, extensively restored, with replicas of its original caryatids lining the canal

㉒ Hadrian's Villa

Villa Adriana, Via Tiburtina. Site is 4 miles (6 km) southwest of Tivoli. **Tel** 0774-38 27 33. **FS** Tivoli, then local bus No. 4. **COTRAL** from Ponte Mammolo (on Metro line B). **Open** 9am–approx 1 hr before sunset daily (last adm: 1 hour before). **Closed** Jan 1 , May 1, Dec 25.
W villaadriana.beniculturali.it

Built as a private summer retreat between AD 118 and 134, Hadrian's Villa was a vast open-air museum of the finest architecture of the Roman world. The grounds of the Imperial Palace covered an area of 300 acres (120 hectares) and were filled with full-scale reproductions of the emperor's favorite buildings from Greece and Egypt. Although excavations on this site began in the 16th century, many of the ruins lying scattered in the surrounding fields have yet to be identified with any certainty. The grounds of the villa make a very picturesque site for a picnic, with scattered fragments of columns lying among olive trees and cypresses.

For an idea of how the whole complex would have looked in its heyday, study the scale model in the building by the parking lot. The most important buildings are signposted, and several have been partially restored or reconstructed. One of the most impressive is the so-called Maritime Theater. This is a round pool with an island in the middle, surrounded by

Pair of Ionic columns in the vaulted baths of Hadrian's Villa

columns. The island, reached by means of a swing bridge, was probably Hadrian's private studio, where he withdrew from the cares of the Empire to indulge in his two favorite pastimes, painting, and architecture. There were also theaters, Greek, and Latin libraries, two bathhouses, extensive housing for guests, and the palace staff, and formal gardens with fountains, statues, and pools.

Hadrian also loved Greek philosophy. One part of the gardens is thought to have been Hadrian's reproduction of the Grove of Academe, where Plato lectured to his students. He also had a replica made of the Stoà Poikile, a beautiful painted colonnade in Athens, from which the Stoic philosophers took their name. This copy enclosed a great piazza with a central pool. The so-called Hall of the Philosophers close to the Poikile was probably a library.

The most ambitious of Hadrian's replicas was the Canopus, a sanctuary of the god Serapis near Alexandria. For this, a canal 130 yd (119 m) long was dug and Egyptian statues were imported to decorate the temple and its grounds. This impressive piece of engineering has been restored, and the banks of the canal are lined with caryatids.

Another picturesque spot in the grounds is the Vale of Tempe, the legendary haunt of the goddess Diana, with a stream representing the Peneios River. Below ground the emperor even built a fanciful recreation of the underworld, Hades, reached through underground tunnels, of which there were many linking the various parts of the villa.

Plundered by barbarians who camped here in the 6th and 8th centuries, the villa fell into disrepair. Its marble was burned to make lime for cement, and Renaissance antiquarians contributed even further to its destruction. Statues unearthed in the grounds are on display in museums around Europe. The Vatican's Egyptian Collection (see p236) has many fine works that were found here.

㉓ Ostia Antica

Viale dei Romagnoli 717. Site is 16 miles (25 km) southwest of Rome. **Tel** 06-5635 8033. Ⓜ Piramide, then train from Porta San Paolo station. **Excavations and museum: Open** 8.30am–7pm Tue–Sun (to 5pm Nov–Feb, to 6pm Mar). Last adm: 1 hour before closing. **Closed** Jan 1, May 1, Dec 25. ♿ 🏛 💻 🚻 ♿
Ⓦ archeoroma.beniculturali.it

Ruins of shops, offices, and houses near Ostia's theater

In Republican times, Ostia was Rome's main commercial port and a military base defending the coastline and the mouth of the Tiber. The port continued to flourish under the Empire, despite the development of Portus, a new port slightly to the northwest, in the 2nd century AD. Ostia's decline began in the 4th century, when a reduction in trade was combined with the gradual silting up of the harbor. Then malaria became endemic in the area, and the city, whose population may have been nearly 100,000 at its peak, was totally abandoned.

Buried for centuries by sand, the city is remarkably well preserved. The site is less spectacular than Pompeii or Herculaneum because Ostia died a gradual death, but it gives a more complete picture of life under the Roman Empire. People of all social classes and from all over the Mediterranean lived and worked here.

Visitors can understand the layout of Ostia's streets almost at a glance. The main road through the town, the Decumanus Maximus, would have been filled with hurrying slaves and citizens, avoiding the jostling carriages and carts, while tradesmen pursued their

business under the porticoes lining the street. The floorplans of the public buildings along the road are very clear. Many were bathhouses, such as the Baths of the Cisiarii (carters) and the grander Baths of Neptune, named after their fine black-and-white floor mosaics. Beside the theater, three large masks, originally part of the decoration of the stage, have been mounted on large blocks of tufa. Beneath the great brick arches that supported the semicircular tiers of seats were taverns and shops. Classical plays are put on here in the summer.

The Tiber's course has changed considerably since Ostia was the port of Rome. It once flowed past just to the north of Piazzale delle Corporazioni, the square behind

Mask decorating the theater

the theater. The corporations were the guilds of the various trades involved in equipping and supplying ships: tanners and rope-makers, ship-builders and timber merchants, ships' chandlers, and grain weighers. There were some 60 or 70 offices around the square. Mosaics showing scenes of everyday life in the port and the names, and symbols of the corporations can still be seen. There were also offices used by ship owners and their agents from places as far apart as Tunisia, and southern France, Sardinia, and Egypt. In one office, belonging to a merchant from the town of Sabratha in North Africa, there is a delightful mosaic of an elephant.

The main cargo coming into Rome was grain from Africa. Much of this was distributed free to prevent social unrest. Although only men received this *annona*, or grain dole, at times over 300,000 were eligible. In the center of the square was a temple, probably dedicated to Ceres, goddess of the harvest. Among the

Mural from Ostia of merchant ship being loaded with grain

buildings excavated are many large warehouses in which grain was stored before it was shipped on to Rome.

The Decumanus leads to the Forum and the city's principal temple, erected by Hadrian in the 2nd century AD, and dedicated to Jove, Juno, and Minerva. In this rather romantic, lonely spot, it is hard to imagine the Forum as a bustling center, where justice was dispensed and officials met to discuss the city's affairs. In the 18th century

Floor mosaic of Nereid and sea monster in the House of the Dioscuri

Detail of floor mosaic in the Piazzale delle Corporazioni

it was used as a sheepfold. Away from the main street are the buildings where Ostia's inhabitants lived. The great majority were housed in rented apartments in blocks three or four stories high known as

insulae. These varied considerably in their comfort and decoration. The House of Diana was one of the better ones, with a balcony around the second floor, a private bathhouse, and a central courtyard with a cistern where tenants came to get their water.

Around the ground floor of the block were shops, taverns, and bars selling snacks and drinks. In the bar at the House of Diana you can see the marble counter used by customers buying their sausages and hot wine sweetened with honey.

For the wealthy there were detached houses (*domus*) such as the House of the Dioscuri, which has fine mosaics, and the House of Cupid and Psyche, named after a statue there. This is now in the site's Museo Ostiense, near the Forum, along with other sculptures and reliefs found in Ostia.

Among the houses and shops there are other fascinating buildings, including a laundry and the firemen's barracks. The religions practiced in Ostia reflect the cosmopolitan nature of the port. There are also no fewer than 18 temples dedicated to the Persian god Mithras, as well as a Jewish synagogue dating from the 1st century AD, and a Christian basilica. A plaque records the death of St. Augustine's mother in a hotel here in AD 387.

Also Worth Seeing

Anagni FS from Termini (60 min), then local bus (infrequent) or long walk.
Picturesque hill-town with papal palace, and famous cathedral.

Bracciano FS from Ostiense (about 70 min). 🚌 from Saxa Rubra, reached by train from Roma Nord (bus 90 min).
Volcanic lake with villages and wooded hills. Nice for walks or a visit to Orsini Castle. Swimming in summer.

Cerveteri FS from Termini, Tiburtina or Ostiense to Cerveteri-Ladispoli, then local bus (70 min). 🚌 from Cornelia, on Metro line A (bus 80 min).
One of the greatest Etruscan cities. Necropolis with complete streets, and houses.

Nemi 🚌 from Anagnina, on Metro line A (bus 75 min); may need to change at Genzano.
Charming village at volcanic lake in the Castelli Romani. Famous for its wine, and strawberries.

Palestrina 🚌 from Anagnina, on Metro line A (bus 70 min).
Impressive Roman sanctuary to goddess Fortuna. Museum, and the Mosaic of the Nile.

Pompeii FS from Termini to Naples, then local train (130 min). 🚌 Special tours from tourist agents.
Excavations of the wealthy and bustling Roman city where busy daily life was put to a sudden end by the eruption of Vesuvius in AD 79.

Subiaco 🚌 from Ponte Mammolo, on Metro line B (bus about 100 min).

Birthplace of St. Benedict. Two monasteries to visit.

Tarquinia FS from Termini or Ostiense plus local bus (100 min). 🚌 from Lepanto, on Metro line A. Change at Civitavecchia (150 min).
Outstanding collection of Etruscan objects and frescoes from Tarquinia's necropolis.

Viterbo FS from Ostiense (115 min) or train from Roma Nord, Piazzale Flaminio, on Metro line A (120 min). 🚌 from Saxa Rubra reached by the train above (bus 90 min).
Medieval quarter, papal palace, and archaeological museum within 13th-century walls.

NINE GUIDED WALKS

Rome is an excellent city for walking. The distances between major sights in the historic downtown are easily covered on foot, and many streets are pedestrianized. When you get tired, stop at one of the sidewalk cafés in lovely settings, such as Piazza Navona and Campo de' Fiori. If you are interested in archaeology, then a walk across the Forum (see pp78–89), and over the Palatine (see pp98–103) takes you away from the roaring traffic of modern Rome to a different world of scattered ruins and shady pine trees.

The first of the nine suggested walks takes in picturesque quarters on either side of the Tiber. The second walk, along the perfectly straight Via Giulia, gives a vivid impression of the Renaissance city. The next three walks

each follow a particular theme. You can savor the glory of ancient Rome through the triumphal arches of the emperors, tour early Christian churches with well-preserved mosaics, and explore the great contribution of Bernini to the appearance of the city.

The sixth walk is outside the downtown along the best-known of all Roman roads, the Via Appia Antica, parts of which are still intact after more than 2,000 years of use. The seventh walk explores some macabre points of interest, including a park said to be haunted by the Emperor Nero. The next couples Trastevere's atmospheric backstreets with the romantic viewpoints of the Janiculum. Lastly, there is a tour of churches and ancient ruins on, and around the tranquil, leafy Aventine.

Choosing a Walk

The Nine Walks
The routes of eight of the walks are marked on the larger map, which also shows the main sightseeing areas of Rome. The smaller inset map shows the location of the Via Appia walk in relation to the central area.

Tombs, Legends, and Artists (pp288–9)

Via Giulia (pp278–9)

Bernini (pp284–5)

Mosaics (pp282–3)

Trastevere and Janiculum (pp290–91)

Tiber (pp276–7)

Triumphal Arches (pp280–81)

Aventine (pp292–3)

Via Appia Antica (pp286–7)

Key

•••• Walk routes

— City wall

0 kilometers 1
0 miles 0.5

◀ Cobbled street leading to the Pantheon

A Two-Hour Walk by the Tiber River

Rome owes its very existence to the Tiber; the city grew up around an easy fording point where a marketplace developed. The river could also be a hazard; shallow and torrential, it flooded the city every winter up to 1870, when work began on the massive Lungotevere embankments that run along both sides of the river. These provide many fine views from points along their avenues of plane trees. The walk also explores the neighborhoods along the riverside, in particular the Jewish Ghetto and Trastevere, which have preserved much of their character from earlier periods in the colorful history of Rome.

From the old port of Rome to Via dei Funari

Starting from the church of Santa Maria in Cosmedin ① (see p204), cross the piazza to the Temples of the Forum Boarium ② (see p201). This was the cattle market that stood near the city's river port. The river here has preserved two less obvious structures from ancient Rome: the mouth of the Cloaca Maxima ③, the city's great sewer, and one arch of a ruined bridge, known as the Ponte Rotto ④. In Via Petroselli stands the rather extraordinary medieval Casa dei Crescenzi ⑤ (see p201), decorated with fragments of Roman temples. Passing the modern Anagrafe (public records office) ⑥, built on the site of the old Roman port, you come to San Nicola in Carcere ⑦ (see p153).

You are now in the Foro Olitorio, Rome's ancient vegetable market. To the east stand the ruins of a Roman portico and the medieval house of the Pierleoni family. Head for the massive Theater of Marcellus

Arch of the Ponte Rotto ④

Santa Maria in Cosmedin ①

⑧ (see p153); go and look at the three Corinthian columns of the Temple of Apollo beside it. Turn into Piazza Campitelli and walk up to Santa Maria in Campitelli ⑨ (see p153). The church honors a miraculous image of the Virgin credited with halting the plague in 1656. The 16th-century piazza was the home of Flaminio Ponzio, its architect, who lived at No. 6. Take Via dei Delfini to Piazza Margana, where you should look up at the 14th-century tower of the Margani family ⑩. Retrace your steps, then go up Via dei Funari (Street of the Ropemakers) to the 16th-century facade of Santa Caterina dei Funari ⑪.

The Ghetto

From Piazza Lovatelli take Via Sant'Angelo in Pescheria, which leads to the ruined Portico of Octavia ⑫ (see

p154) in the Jewish Ghetto (see p154). The Roman portico, once Rome's fish market, houses the church of Sant'Angelo in Pescheria. Find the marble plaque on the facade: fish longer than this slab were given to the city's *conservatori* (governors). Turn into the Ghetto: two column stumps belonging to the Portico stand in front of a patched-up doorway made of fragments of Roman sculpture. The cramped buildings and streets around Via del Portico

Main altar of Santa Maria in Campitelli ⑨

d'Ottavia are typical of old Rome: see the Casa di Lorenzo Manilio ⑬ *(see p154)*, and turn down Via del Progresso, past Palazzo Cenci ⑭ *(see p154)*, toward the river. On Lungotevere walk past the Synagogue ⑮ *(see p154)* to the small church of San Gregorio ⑯. Here stood the Ghetto's gates, which were locked at sundown.

Across the river to Trastevere

Crossing to Tiber Island *(see p155)* by Ponte Fabricio, with its two ancient stone heads on the parapet, you can enjoy a

Classical relief of Medusa above the doorway of Palazzo Cenci ⑭

Piscinula and the surrounding streets retain much of the spirit of old Trastevere. Walk up to the start of Viale di Trastevere at

As you go down Via della Lungaretta to Piazza Santa Maria in Trastevere, don't miss the old-fashioned pharmacy at No. 7. The piazza itself, in front of the magnificent church of Santa Maria in Trastevere ㉒ *(see pp214–15)*, has a cheerful atmosphere, and the fountain steps are a favorite meeting place. Go back a little way to Via del Moro. This leads to Piazza Trilussa, dominated by the fountain of the Acqua Paola ㉓, where you emerge onto the bank of the river again. Note the lifelike statue, near the fountain, of Roman poet Trilussa, who wrote in the local dialect. From Ponte Sisto ㉔ *(see p212)*, look back to Tiber Island and, beyond it, to the medieval bell tower of Santa Maria in Cosmedin, set against the pine trees on the summit of the Palatine.

Fountain of the Acqua Paola ㉓

0 meters   250

0 yards   250

Key

••• Walk route

good view of the river in both directions. On the island itself, you should not miss the Pierleoni Tower ⑰ or the church of San Bartolomeo all'Isola ⑱.

Trastevere

As you cross into Trastevere, you can see the medieval house of the powerful Mattei family ⑲, with its fragments of ancient sculpture. Beyond it, Piazza in

Piazza Belli. After crossing the road, look back at the medieval tower of the Anguillara ⑳ and the statue honoring the poet Gioacchino Belli ㉑ *(see p207)*.

Piazza in Piscinula, old Trastevere

Tips for Walkers

Starting point: Piazza della Bocca della Verità.

Length: 2 miles (3.5 km).

Getting there: The 23, 44, 81, 160, 280, 628, 715, and 716 buses stop near Santa Maria in Cosmedin.

Best time for walk: This walk can be very romantic in the evening but is enjoyable at any time.

Stopping points: Piazza Campitelli and Piazza Margana have elegant restaurants, and Via del Portico d'Ottavia has many restaurants and a bakery. Tiber Island has a bar and the famous Sora Lella restaurant *(see p314)*. In Viale Trastevere there are bars and pizzerias. Piazza Santa Maria in Trastevere has lively bars and restaurants with outdoor tables.

For map symbols *see back flap*

A One-Hour Walk along Via Giulia

Laid out by Bramante for Pope Julius II in the early 16th century, Via Giulia was one of the first Renaissance streets to slice through Rome's jumble of medieval alleys. The original plan included new law courts in a central piazza, but this project was abandoned for lack of cash. The street is now dominated by antique shops and furniture restorers. On summer evenings, hundreds of oil lamps light the street, while cloisters and courtyards provide romantic settings for a special season of concerts.

Baroque capital on the facade of Sant'Eligio degli Orefici ⑦

From Lungotevere to Largo della Moretta

Starting from Lungotevere dei Tebaldi ① at the eastern end of Via Giulia, you will see ahead of you an archway ② spanning the road. This was the start of Michelangelo's unrealized project linking Palazzo Farnese and its gardens (see p149) with the Villa Farnesina (see pp220–21) on the other side of the river.

Just before you reach the archway, you will see to your left the curious Fontana del Mascherone ③, in which an ancient grotesque mask and granite basin were combined to create a Baroque fountain.

Beyond the Farnese archway on the left is the lively Baroque facade of the church of Santa Maria dell'Orazione e Morte ④ (see p149). A bit farther along on the same side of the road stands Palazzo Falconieri ⑤, enlarged by Borromini in 1650. Note its two stone falcons glowering at each other across the width of the facade. On the other side of the road you pass the yellowish facade of Santa Caterina da Siena ⑥, church of the Sienese colony in Rome, which has pretty 18th-century reliefs. The figures of Romulus and Remus

Relief of Romulus and Remus on Santa Caterina da Siena ⑥

symbolize Rome and Siena – there is a legend that the city of Siena was founded by the less fortunate of the twins. After passing the short street that leads down to Sant'Eligio degli Orefici ⑦ (see p150) and the facade of Palazzo Ricci ⑧ (see p151), you come to an area of half-demolished buildings around the ruined church of San Filippo Neri ⑨, called Vicolo della Moretta. If you look to the left down to the river, you can see Ponte

Fontana del Mascherone ③

Mazzini and the huge prison of Regina Coeli on the other side of the Tiber. At this point you may like to make a small detour to the right to the beginning of Via del Pellegrino, where there is an inscription ⑩, defining the *pomerium*, or boundary, of the city in the time of the Emperor Claudius.

From Largo della Moretta to the Sofas of Via Giulia

Farther on, facing the narrow Vicolo del Malpasso, are the imposing prisons, the Carceri

Nuove ⑪, built by Pope Innocent X Pamphilj in 1655. When first opened, they were a model of humane treatment of prisoners, but they were replaced by the Regina Coeli prison across the river at the end of the 19th century. The buildings now house offices of the Ministry of Justice, and a small Museum of Crime.

At the corner of Via del Gonfalone, a small side street running down to the river, you

Key

• • • Walk route

0 meters   250

0 yards   250

Farnese archway across Via Giulia, built to a design by Michelangelo ②

originates from the traditional distribution of bread to the poor that took place on the saint's feast day.

On the corner there are more travertine blocks belonging to the foundations of Julius II's projected law courts, known because of their curious shape as the "Sofas of Via Giulia."

The Florentine Quarter

Your next stop should be the imposing Palazzo Sacchetti at No. 66 ⑮. Originally this was the house of Antonio da Sangallo the Younger, the architect of Palazzo Farnese, but it was greatly enlarged by later owners. The porticoed courtyard houses a 15th-century Madonna and a striking Roman relief of the 3rd century AD. Just opposite Palazzo Sacchetti, note the beautiful late Renaissance portal of Palazzo Donarelli ⑯. The 16th-century house at No. 93 is richly decorated with stuccoes and coats of arms ⑰. No. 85 is another typical Renaissance palazzo with a heavily rusticated ground floor ⑱. There is a tradition that, like

Plaque honoring Antonio da Sangallo on Palazzo Sacchetti ⑮

many houses of the period, it once belonged to Raphael. Palazzo Clarelli ⑲ was built by Antonio da Sangallo the Younger as his own house. The inscription above the doorway bears the name of Duke Cosimo II de' Medici, whose family later bought the palazzo.

This whole area used to be inhabited by a flourishing Florentine colony, which had its own water mills built on pontoons along the Tiber. Their national church is San Giovanni dei Fiorentini ⑳ *(see p155)*, the final great landmark at the end of Via Giulia. Many Florentine artists, and architects had a hand in its design, including Sangallo, and Jacopo Sansovino.

Coat of arms of Pope Paul III Farnese on the facade of Via Giulia No. 93 ⑰

Tips for Walkers

Starting point: Lungotevere dei Tebaldi, by Ponte Sisto.
Length: 1,100 yd (1 km).
Getting there: The 116 goes to and along Via Giulia, or you can take 46, 62, or 64 to Corso Vittorio Emanuele II, then walk down Via dei Pettinari, or take a 23 or 280 along Lungotevere. Best time for walk: On summer evenings, oil lamps often light the street. At Christmas, there are nativity scenes in many shop windows.
Stopping points: There are bars in Via Giulia, at Nos. 18 and 84. Campo de' Fiori has better bars, with outdoor tables, and a wide choice of places to eat. These include a fried fish bar in Piazza Santa Barbara dei Librari (closed Sun).

can see part of the foundations of Julius II's planned law courts. Just down the street stands the small Oratorio di Santa Lucia del Gonfalone ⑫, which is often used for concerts.

The next interesting facade is Carlo Rainaldi's 17th-century Santa Maria del Suffragio ⑬ on the left. On the same side is San Biagio degli Armeni ⑭, the Armenian church in Rome. It is often referred to by local people as San Biagio della Pagnotta (of the loaf of bread). The nickname

Detail on the side of the door of Santa Maria del Suffragio ⑬

For map symbols *see back flap*

A 90-Minute Tour of Rome's Triumphal Arches

Rome's greatest gift to architecture was the arch, and the Roman people's highest tribute to its victorious generals was the triumphal arch. In Imperial times, arches were erected to honor an emperor's campaign victories almost as a matter of course, promoting his personal cult and ensuring his subsequent deification. Spectacular processions passed through these arches. Conquering generals, cheered by rapturous crowds, proceeded in their chariots to the Capitol, accompanied by their legions bearing spoils from their campaigns.

Part of the Via Sacra, once spanned by the Arch of Augustus ③

Relief of barbarian captives on the Arch of Septimius Severus ①

Arches of the Forum

This walk through the Forum and around the base of the Palatine takes in Rome's three great surviving triumphal arches and two arches of more humble design that were used simply as places of business. It starts from the Arch of Emperor Septimius Severus ① and his sons Geta and Caracalla (see p85) in the Forum. Erected in AD 203, it celebrates a successful campaign in the Middle East. Eight years later, when Caracalla had his brother killed, all mention of Geta was removed from the inscription.

Look up at the reliefs showing phases of the campaigns. Set in tiers, they are probably the sculptural counterparts of the paintings illustrating the general's feats that were borne aloft in the triumphal procession. On the right, the inhabitants of a fortified city surrender to the Romans' siege machines. Below are smaller friezes showing the triumphal procession itself.

Heading east, make your way through the Forum to the ruins

of the Temple of Julius Caesar ②. The temple was built by Augustus in 29 BC, on the site where Caesar's body was cremated after Mark Antony's famous funerary oration. A nearby sign marks the ruins of one of the arches dedicated to Augustus ③, spanning the Via Sacra between the Temple of Castor and Pollux ④ (see p86) and the Temple of Caesar. This arch, erected after Augustus defeated Mark Antony and Cleopatra, was finally demolished in 1545, and its materials were used in the new St. Peter's. From here, proceed uphill toward the elegant Arch of Titus ⑤ (see p89). Compared with Septimius Severus's arch, it shows an earlier, simpler style. Look up at the beautiful lettering of the inscription before you examine the inner bas-reliefs. These show Roman legionaries carrying the spoils looted from the conquest of Jerusalem, heralds holding plaques with the names of vanquished peoples and cities, and Titus riding in triumph in his chariot.

The medieval Frangipane family turned the Colosseum into a vast, impregnable stronghold and incorporated the Arch of Titus into their fortifications. Notice the

Capital from Temple of Castor and Pollux ④

Key

• • • Walk route

0 meters	250
0 yards	250

wheel marks scratched on the inside walls of the arch by generations of carts; they indicate the steady rise in the level of the Forum floor before it was eventually excavated in the 18th and 19th centuries. Many of the carts that passed through the arch would have been

Arch of Titus in a 19th-century watercolor by the English artist Thomas Hartley Cromek ⑤

hectic battle scenes just above the smaller arches, sculpted in AD 315. In the curious dwarflike soldiers, you can see the transition from Classicism to a cruder medieval style of sculpture.

Now take Via di San Gregorio, which runs the length of the valley between the Palatine and Celian hills. This was the ancient route taken by most triumphal processions. Passing the entrance to the Palatine ⑧ and the well-preserved arches of the Claudian Aqueduct ⑨ on the right, you come to Piazza di Porta Capena ⑩, named after the gate that stood here to

Four-sided Arch of Janus in the Forum Boarium ⑬

take shelter from the sun or rain when discussing business. Like the Arch of Titus, it became part of a fortress built by the Frangipane family during the Middle Ages.

Tucked away beside the nearby church of San Giorgio in Velabro ⑭ (see p204) is what looks like a large rectangular doorway. This is the Arco degli Argentari, or Moneychangers' Arch ⑮. Look up at the inscription, which says that it was erected by local silversmiths in honor of Septimius Severus and his family in AD 204. As in the emperor's triumphal arch, the name of Geta has been obliterated by his brother and murderer, Caracalla. Geta's figure has also been removed from among the portraits on the panels inside the arch. Triumph in Imperial Rome could be very short-lived.

Arches of Domitian's extension to the Claudian Aqueduct ⑨

carrying building materials quarried from the Forum's many ruined monuments.

Arch of Constantine

Leave the Forum by heading down the hill toward the Colosseum ⑥ (see pp94–7) and the nearby Arch of Constantine ⑦ (see p93). This arch, hastily built to commemorate the emperor's victory over his rival Maxentius in AD 312, is a patchwork of reliefs from different periods. Stand on the Via di San Gregorio side and compare the earlier panels at the top (AD 180–193) with the

mark the beginning of the Via Appia (see p286). After rounding the back of the Palatine, follow Via dei Cerchi, which runs alongside the grassy area that preserves, in an oval outline, all that remains of the Circus Maximus ⑪ (see p207).

Arches of the Forum Boarium

When you reach the church of Sant'Anastasia ⑫, turn right up Via di San Teodoro, then first left down Via del Velabro. Straddling the street is the four-sided Arch of Janus ⑬ (see p204), erected in the 3rd century AD. This is not a triumphal arch but a covered area where merchants could

Tips for Walkers

Starting point: The Roman Forum, entrance Largo Romolo e Remo, on Via dei Fori Imperiali.
Length: 1.5 miles (2.5 km).
Getting there: The nearest Metro station is Colosseo on line B. Buses 75, 85, 87, 117, 175, 186, and 810 stop in Via dei Fori Imperiali, near Forum entrance.
Best time: Any time during Forum opening hours (see p84).
Stopping points: Several bars and restaurants overlook the Colosseum. There is a marvelous *pasticceria* on the corner of Via dei Cerchi and Via di San Teodoro, and an organic market (Sun) at the start of Via di San Teodoro. For a meal, try Alvaro al Circo Massimo (closed Mon) in Via di San Teodoro.

For map symbols *see back flap*

A Three-Hour Tour of Rome's Best Mosaics

In imitation of the audience chambers of Imperial palaces, Rome's early Christian churches were decorated with colorful mosaics. These were pieced together from cubes of marble, colored stone, and fragments of glass. To create a golden background, gold leaf was placed between pieces of glass. These were then heated so that they fused. The glorious colors and subjects portrayed gave the faithful a glimpse of the heavenly court of the King of Kings. This walk concentrates on a few of the churches decorated in this wonderful medium.

Apse mosaic in the Chapel of Santa Rufina ③

Obelisk and side facade of San Giovanni in Laterano ②

San Giovanni

Start from Piazza di Porta San Giovanni, where you can visit the heavily restored mosaic of the Triclinio Leoniano (see p181). Originally in the banqueting hall of Pope Leo III (795–816) ①, it shows Christ among the Apostles. On the left are Pope Sylvester and the Emperor Constantine, on the right, Pope Leo and Charlemagne just before he was crowned Emperor of the Romans in AD 800. Inside the basilica of San Giovanni in Laterano ② (see pp182–3), the 13th-century apse mosaic shows Christ as he appeared miraculously during the consecration of the church. In the panels by the windows, look for the small figures of two Franciscan friars; these are the artists Jacopo Torriti (left) and Jacopo de Camerino (right).

Leave by the exit on the right near the splendid 16th-century organ and head for the octagonal Baptistry of San Giovanni ③, where the Chapel of Santa Rufina has a beautiful apse mosaic, dating from the 5th century. In the neighboring Chapel of San Venanzio, there are golden 7th-century mosaics, showing the strong influence of the Eastern Church at this time.

Santo Stefano Rotondo to San Clemente

Leave the piazza by the narrow road that leads to the round church of Santo Stefano Rotondo ④ (see p187). One of its chapels contains a 7th-century Byzantine mosaic honoring two martyrs buried here. Farther on, in Piazza della Navicella, is the church of Santa Maria in Domnica ⑤ (see p195). It houses the superb mosaics commissioned by Pope Paschal I, who gave new impetus to Rome's mosaic production in the 9th century. He is represented kneeling beside the Virgin. On leaving the church, notice the facade of San Tommaso in Formis ⑥, which has a charming mosaic of Christ flanked by two freed slaves, one black and one white, dating from the 13th century.

Ceiling mosaic, Baptistry of San Giovanni ③

Interior of Baptistry of San Giovanni ③

From here, head up the steep hill, past the forbidding apse of Santi Quattro Coronati ⑦ *(see p187)*, to the fascinating church of San Clemente ⑧ *(see pp188–9)*. Its 12th-century apse mosaic shows the cross set in a swirling pattern of acanthus leaves. San Clemente also has a fine 12th-century Cosmatesque mosaic floor.

The Colle Oppio
Passing the old entrance to the church, cross Via Labicana and walk up the hill to the small Colle Oppio park ⑨. This has fine views of the Colosseum and contains the ruins of the Domus Aurea ⑩ *(see p177)* and the Baths of Trajan ⑪. Across the park lie San Martino ai Monti ⑫ *(see p172)*, which has a 6th-century mosaic portrait of Pope St. Sylvester near the crypt, and Santa Prassede ⑬ *(see p173)*. Here the Chapel of St. Zeno contains the most important Byzantine mosaics in Rome, reminiscent of the fabulous mosaics of Ravenna. Pope Paschal I erected the chapel as a mausoleum for his mother Theodora.

in the nave depict Old Testament stories, while the triumphal arch has scenes relating to the birth of Christ, including one of the Magi wearing striped stockings. In the apse there is a *Coronation of the Virgin* by Jacopo Torriti (1295).

On leaving Santa Maria, pass the obelisk ⑮ in the piazza behind the church and go downhill to Via Urbana and Santa Pudenziana ⑯ *(see p173)*. The figures in the apse mosaic, one of the oldest in Rome (AD 390), are remarkable for their naturalism. The two women with crowns are traditionally identified as Santa Prassede and Santa Pudenziana. When you leave the church, you can either retrace your steps to Santa Maria Maggiore or walk down Via Urbana to Via Cavour Metro station.

Mosaic saint in Santa Prassede ⑬

11th-century frieze above the doorway of Santa Pudenziana ⑯

The apse and triumphal arch of the church itself also have fine mosaics. When you move on to Santa Maria Maggiore ⑭ *(see pp172–3)*, go to the column in the center of the piazza in front of the church to see the beautiful 14th-century facade mosaics by Filippo Rusuti. Inside, the 5th-century mosaics

Key

••• Walk route
—   City Wall

0 meters   250
0 yards   250

Tips for Walkers

Starting point: Piazza di Porta San Giovanni.
Length: 2 miles (3.5 km).
Getting there: The nearest Metro station is San Giovanni, on line A, in Piazzale Appio, just outside Porta San Giovanni. The 16, 81, 85, 87, 218, and 650 buses and the 3 tram stop in front of San Giovanni in Laterano, while 117 stops around the corner on Piazza San Giovanni in Laterano.
Best time for walk: Go in the morning, in order to appreciate the mosaics in the best light.
Stopping points: The bars and restaurants in Piazza del Colosseo are popular with tourists. In the Parco del Colle Oppio there is a café kiosk with tables. There are several bars around Santa Maria Maggiore, some with outdoor tables.

A Two-Hour Walk around Bernini's Rome

Gian Lorenzo Bernini (1598–1680) is the artist who probably left the strongest personal mark on the appearance of the city of Rome. Favorite architect, sculptor, and town planner of three successive popes, he turned Rome into a uniquely Baroque city. This walk traces his enormous influence on the development and appearance of the center of Rome. It starts from the busy Largo di Santa Susanna just north of Termini station, at the church of Santa Maria della Vittoria.

Bernini's Fontana del Tritone ②

Through Piazza Barberini
Santa Maria della Vittoria ① (see p257) houses the Cornaro Chapel, the setting for one of Bernini's most revolutionary and controversial sculptures, *The Ecstasy of St. Teresa* (1646). From here, take Via Barberini to Piazza Barberini. In its center is Bernini's dramatic Fontana del Tritone ② (see p256), and at one side stands the more modest Fontana delle Api ③ (see p256). As you go up Via delle Quattro Fontane, you catch a glimpse of Palazzo Barberini ④ (see p257), built by Bernini and several other artists for Pope Urban VIII. The gateway and cornices are decorated with the bees that made up part of the Barberini family crest. Next, make your way to the crossroads, decorated by Le Quattro Fontane ⑤ (see p164), to enjoy the splendid views in all four directions.
  Passing the diminutive San Carlo alle Quattro Fontane ⑥

(see p159), built by Bernini's rival Borromini, take Via del Quirinale. The long wing of the Palazzo del Quirinale ⑦ (see p160), nicknamed the *Manica Lunga* (long sleeve), is by Bernini. On the other side of the road is the facade of Sant'Andrea al Quirinale ⑧ (see p163), one of Bernini's greatest churches. When you reach the Piazza del Quirinale ⑨, note the doorway of the palazzo, attributed to Bernini. From the piazza, go down the stairs to Via della Dataria, and into Vicolo Scanderbeg, which leads to a small piazza with the same name ⑩. Scanderbeg was the nickname of the Albanian prince Giorgio Castriota (1403–68), the "Terror of the Turks." His portrait is preserved on his house.

The Trevi Fountain
Go along the narrow Vicolo dei Modelli ⑪, where male models waited to be chosen by artists, then turn toward the Trevi Fountain ⑫ (see p161). Its energy is clearly inspired by Bernini's work, a tribute to his lasting influence on Roman taste.

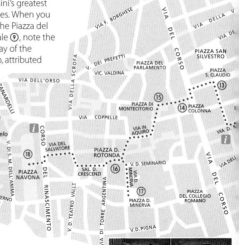

Facade of Santa Maria in Via ⑬

Leave the piazza along Via delle Muratte, where the composer Donizetti lived at No. 77, and turn into Via di Santa Maria in

Neptune Fountain at the north end of Piazza Navona ⑱

Via, where the church ⑬ has a fine Baroque facade by Bernini's follower Carlo Rainaldi. At the top of this street, turn left down to Via del Corso. On the other side of the road, you will see the towering Column of Marcus Aurelius ⑭ *(see p117)* in Piazza Colonna. Beyond this is Palazzo Montecitorio ⑮, begun in 1650 by Bernini, and now the home of the Italian parliament *(see p116)*.

Statue of the Nile River from the Fontana dei Quattro Fiumi

Key

• • • Walk route

central fountain, the Fontana dei Quattro Fiumi *(see p122)*, was by Bernini, though the figures symbolic of the four rivers were sculpted by other artists. The central figure in the Fontana del Moro, however, is by Bernini himself. Bernini's contemporaries were fascinated by the innovative use of shells, rocks, and other natural forms in his fountains, and his expert handling of water to create constant movement.

An Extended Walk

More energetic walkers may like to head toward the river to see the Ponte Sant'Angelo and its Bernini angels, and then on to St. Peter's *(see pp228–31)*, where they can admire Bernini's great colonnaded piazza in front of the church, the papal tombs, his altar decorations, and the bronze baldacchino.

Angel on Ponte Sant'Angelo

Pantheon to Piazza Navona

Via in Aquiro leads you to the Pantheon ⑯ *(see pp114–15)*. Refusing Pope Urban VIII's request for him to redecorate the dome, Bernini said that although St. Peter's had a hundred defects, the Pantheon did not have any. From the Pantheon, make a small detour to Piazza della Minerva where you can see the obelisk, supported by Bernini's small, bizarre elephant, by the church of Santa Maria sopra Minerva ⑪ *(see p112)*. Then retrace your steps, and take Salita dei

Crescenzi to reach the fabulous Piazza Navona ⑱ *(see p122)* which was remodeled by Bernini for Pope Innocent X Pamphilj. The design for the

Tips for Walkers

Starting point: Largo di Santa Susanna.
Length: 2 miles (3.5 km).
Getting there: Take Metro line A to Repubblica or any bus to Termini, then walk. Buses 61, 62, 175, and 492 stop in Via Barberini.
Best time for walk: Go either between 9am and noon for good lighting conditions in the churches, or between 4 and 7pm.
Stopping points: The Piazza Barberini and Fontana di Trevi areas have lots of bars, and pizzerias. The many elegant cafés en route include the famous Caffè Giolitti (see p113), and outdoor cafés and restaurants are plentiful around Piazza della Rotonda, and Piazza Navona.

⑩ A 90-Minute Walk Along the Via Appia Antica

Lined with cypresses and pines as it was when the ancient Romans came here by torchlight to bury their dead, the Via Appia is wonderfully atmospheric. The fields are strewn with ruined tombs set against the picturesque background of the Alban hills to the south. Although the marble or travertine stone facings of most tombs have been plundered, a few statues and reliefs survive or have been replaced by copies.

Tomb of Sixtus Pompeus the Righteous ⑨

Capo di Bove

Start from the Tomb of Cecilia Metella ① (see p268). In the Middle Ages, this area acquired the name Capo di Bove (ox head) from the frieze of festoons and ox heads still visible on the tomb. On the other side of the road you can see the ruined Gothic church of San Nicola ②, which, like the Tomb of Cecilia Metella, was part of the medieval fortress of the Caetani family.

Gothic windows in the church of San Nicola ②

Proceed to the crossroads ③, where there are still many original Roman paving slabs, huge blocks of extremely durable volcanic basalt. Just past the next

The ruined church of San Nicola ②

turn (Via Capo di Bove), you will see on your left the nucleus of a great mausoleum overgrown with ivy, known as the Torre di Capo di Bove ④. Beyond it, on both sides of the Appia, are other tombs, some still capped with the remains of the medieval towers that were built over them. On the right, after passing what remains of a thermal complex, you come to a military zone around the Forte Appio ⑤, one of a series of forts built around the city in the 19th century. On the left, a little farther along, stand the ruins of the Tomb of Marcus Servilius ⑥, showing fragments of reliefs excavated in 1808 by the Neo-Classical sculptor Antonio Canova. He was one of the first to work on the principle that excavated tombs and their inscriptions and reliefs should be allowed to remain in situ. On the other side of the road stands a tomb with a relief of a man, naked except for a short cape, known as the "Heroic Relief" ⑦. On the left of the road are the ruins of the so-called Tomb of Seneca ⑧. The great moralist Seneca owned a villa near here, where he committed suicide in

Key

• • • Walk route

0 meters   250
0 yards   250

Artist's impression of how the mausoleums and tombs lining the Via Appia looked in the 2nd century AD

Section of the Via Appia Antica, showing original Roman paving stones

AD 65 on the orders of Nero. The next major tomb is that of the family of Sixtus Pompeus the Righteous, a freed slave of the 1st century AD ⑨. The verse inscription records the father's sadness at having to bury his own children, who died young.

From Via dei Lugari to Via di Tor Carbone

Just past Via dei Lugari on the right, screened by trees, is the Tomb of Pope St. Urban (reigned 222–230) ⑩. Set back from the road on the left stands a large ruined podium, probably part of a Temple of Jupiter ⑪. The next stretch was excavated by the architect Luigi Canina early in the 19th century. On the right is the Tomb of Caius Licinius ⑫, followed by a smaller Doric tomb ⑬ and the imposing Tomb of Hilarius Fuscus ⑭, with five portrait busts in relief of members of his family. Next comes the Tomb of Tiberius Claudius Secondinus ⑮, where a group of freedmen of the Imperial household were buried in the 2nd century AD.

Passing a large ruined columbarium, you reach the Tomb of Quintus Apuleius ⑯

and the reconstructed Tomb of the Rabirii freed slaves (1st century BC) ⑰. This has a frieze of three half-length figures above an inscription. The figure on the right is a priestess of Isis. Behind her you can see the outline of a *sistrum*, the metal rattle used at ceremonies of the cult.

The majority of the tombs are little more than shapeless stacks of eroded brickwork. Two exceptions in the last stretch of this walk are the Tomb of the Festoons ⑱, with its reconstructed frieze of festive putti, and the Tomb of the Frontispiece ⑲, which has a copy of a relief with four portraits. The two central figures are holding hands.

When you reach Via di Tor Carbone, the Via Appia still stretches out ahead of you in a straight line and, if you wish to extend your walk, there are many more tombs and ruined villas to visit along the way.

Tips for Walkers

Starting point: Tomb of Cecilia Metella.
Length: 2 miles (3 km).
Getting there: Reach the tomb by taxi, or take the Archeobus (see p390), the 118 from Piazzale Ostiense, or the 660 from Colli Albani on Metro Line A.
Best time: On Sunday, when the road is closed to traffic. Go fairly early, before it gets too hot.
Stopping points: There is a bar on the corner of Via Metella and a pleasant picnic area in the grounds of a thermal complex just beyond Vicolo di Tor Carbone. There are also several restaurants on the first stretch of the Appia, including the Cecilia Metella, Via Appia Antica 129, tel 06-512 6769 (closed Mon).

Figure on the Tomb of the Heroic Relief ⑦

A Two-Hour Tour of Roman Tombs, Legends, and Artists

The northern half of central Rome with its air of mystery is a great place for families to explore. Following this trail of creepy places and famous deaths interspersed with glimpses of the city's historic artists' center, visitors can see Imperial mausoleums, a death mask, and a crypt decorated with monks' bones. This is also a Rome where art isn't just in the museums – it's everywhere – so you'll see working art studios, pass Rome's Gallery of Fine Arts, and wander down the famous "artists' row."

Castel Sant'Angelo, site of the Emperor Hadrian's tomb ①

Imperial Tombs

Begin at Emperor Hadrian's tomb, deep in the heart of the papal Castel Sant'Angelo ① *(see pp250–51)*. From the castle's riverside entrance, turn left then left again along the star-shaped walls, before turning right into Piazza Cavour, surrounded on the south by the huge, ostentatious Palazzo di Giustizia ② *(see p249)*, slowly sinking under its own weight since 1910. Turn right down Via Colonna to cross the Tiber on Ponte Cavour. Once across the busy Lungotevere, turn left to go into the church of San Rocco ③ *(see p143)*. Just beyond it lies the Mausoleum of Augustus ④ *(see p143)*, sprouting a miniature grove of cypresses. To its left sits the ancient altar, Ara Pacis ⑤ *(see p142)*.

Frieze from Ara Pacis

Camporese. On the right, at the corner of Via Canova, is the church of Santa Maria Portae Paradisi ⑦, designed in 1523 by Antonio Sangallo the Younger with a 1509 *Madonna and Child* by sculptor Sansovino. The octagonal interior dates to 1645. Turn right down Via

Canova (named after the sculptor Antonio Canova) to see the exterior of his studio ⑧ at No. 16, a corner building studded with ancient statues and carvings. Turn left onto Via del Corso ⑨, Rome's "Main Street." This is just under a mile (1.5 km) of *palazzi*, and shops that has hosted parades, carnivals, races, and processions for centuries, and still functions as the main drag for Rome's evening stroll, the *passeggiata*. As you pass San Giacomo on your left (once the church of a hospital founded in 1339 as a

The Tridente

Continue heading north up Via di Ripetta. On your left is the graffiti-covered courtyard of the Accademia di Belle Arti ⑥, Rome's fine art academy, designed in 1845 by Pietro

0 meters   200
0 yards   200

Key

• • • Walk route

Baroque magnificence inside the Chiesa di Gesù e Maria ⑩

The Piazza di Spagna, and the famous Spanish Steps, usually busy with visitors but quiet on rare occasions ⑱

Tips for Walkers

Starting point: Castel Sant'Angelo.

Length: 2.2 miles (3.6 km).

Getting there: Take bus 30, 34, 40, 49, 62, 70, 87, 130, 186, 224, 280, 492, 913, 926, or 990.

Best time for walk: Go in the afternoon, when the area starts to come alive.

Stopping points: Piazza del Popolo is flanked by two great Roman cafés with clear political affiliations – leftist Rosati (see p321) on the west side, right-wing Canova on the east. The Spanish Steps area has some great eateries as well as the usual fast food chains (see pp315–17).

hospice for pilgrims), you'll see on the right Chiesa di Gesù e Maria ⑩, Carlo Rinaldi's 1675 Baroque masterpiece. Farther along, at No. 18, is the Casa di Goethe ⑪ (see p138). The Corso ends in the dramatic Piazza del Popolo ⑫ (see p139).

from Old Master Madonnas to Modernist abstracts. Take the third left, then right onto quiet Via Margutta ⑯, home of artists' studios and galleries for centuries. Turn right again down Via Orto di Napoli to return to Via del Babuino, then left. On your right, reclining on a fountain, and surrounded by various graffiti, and placards, is one of the ugliest – and most respected – statues in Rome. The Babuino ⑰ (like the famous Pasquino, see p126)

Zuccari turned the door, and window frames of his Palazzetto Zuccari ㉒ into monsters. At the bottom of Via Gregoriana, turn left up to Via F. Crispi, then right down Via Sistina into Piazza Barberini ㉓, noting Bernini's fountain (see p254). Turn left up the square, cross Via V. Veneto, and left again. A few dozen paces up on the right is the staircase to the church of Santa Maria della Concezione. To finish off, stop at the first landing to enter the creepy Capuchin Crypt ㉔ (see p256), where there are four chapels decorated with mosaics, and skeletal displays. When you leave the crypt, head for Piazza Barberini, and the Metro station.

The square is named after the church on its north end, Santa Maria del Popolo ⑬ (see pp140–41). The church, which is full of art treasures, is called "St. Mary of the People" because it was built to help exorcise the ghost of Nero from a walnut grove on this site, once Nero's family estate where the disgraced emperor was secretly buried. The estate once continued up the slopes of what are now the Pincio Gardens ⑭ (see p138), above the piazza to the east, and locals declare that the ravens' screams are those of the dead emperor. Leave Piazza del Popolo from the southeast corner to stroll down Via del Babuino ⑮, lined with art galleries hawking everything

has served as a soapbox for political, and social dissent for centuries. Via del Babuino ends in Piazza di Spagna ⑱ (see p135), usually thronged with tourists. The pink house to the right of the Spanish Steps is the Keats-Shelley Memorial House ⑲ (see p136). Take a look inside to see Keats' death mask.

The Spanish Steps to the Capuchin Crypt

Go up the famed Spanish Steps ⑳ (see p136–7) to Trinità dei Monti ㉑ (see p137). Turn right down Via Gregoriana to No. 28, where painter Federico

Bones, and skulls from monks in the Capuchin Crypt ㉔

For map symbols see back flap

A Two-Hour Walk around Trastevere and Janiculum Hill

This walk begins in the warren of cobbled, medieval streets of Trastevere, which is becoming ever more popular, and shows you the neighborhood's hidden gems rather than its major sights. In the morning, enjoy the mosaics and frescoes in the local churches before pausing for lunch in central Trastevere. Then go for a gentle climb up the Gianicolo, or Janiculum Hill. This long crest parallels the Tiber and is blessed with the best panoramic views in Rome. At sunset, couples find it a romantic place to go for a stroll.

The high altar of San Benedetto ③

Southern Trastevere

Start at Santa Cecilia in Trastevere ① *(see p213)*, a church that hides its best – the basement excavations of St. Cecilia's house and Pietro Cavallini's sole surviving Roman fresco inside the cloistered convent – behind a bland 18th-century interior. Turn left out of the church, left again onto Via dei Salumi, then right on Via in Piscinula into Piazza in Piscinula ②, named for the remains of a bathing pool underneath. On the piazza's south side, below an 11th-century bell tower, sits the tiny church of San Benedetto in Piscinula ③ (ring the doorbell for entry). It contains parts of a beautiful Cosmati mosaic pavement, 13th-century frescoes, and the saint's cell. Head west along Via della Lungaretta and cross the Viale di Trastevere to visit the excavations of a 5th-century basilica and fragments of its later frescoes below San Crisogono ④ *(see p212)*.

Central Trastevere

Turn left out of the church and left again to continue along Via della Lungaretta to Piazza Santa Maria in Trastevere ⑤,

a communal outdoor parlor, busy with cafés, guitar-strumming backpackers on the fountain steps, and visitors to the gorgeous Santa Maria in Trastevere ⑥ *(see p214–15)*. Exit the square on the south side into tiny Piazza San Callisto, and take the right fork down Via di San Cosimato into the large triangular Piazza di San Cosimato ⑦, bustling (until 2pm) with an open-air food market. Backtrack to Piazza Santa Maria in Trastevere. Along the square's north side you'll see a tiny street called Fonte d'Olio, entrance into the twisting maze of alleys and ivy-covered buildings at the heart of Trastevere. The street bends sharply left, then turn right onto Vicolo del Piede to arrive at the diminutive Piazza de' Renzi, lined with medieval houses. Turn left to follow Via della Pelliccia, then left again at the pedestrian intersection. This will bring you into the elongated triangle of Piazza di Sant'Egidio ⑧, alive with cafés and bars. A short

staircase at No. 9 leads to the Museo di Roma in Trastevere ⑨ *(see p212)*, devoted to the history of everyday Roman life. Exit the piazza at the northwest corner and cross Vicolo del Cedro to continue straight on Via della Scala, past shops and

Piazza Santa Maria in Trastevere and its enchanting church ⑤

Raphael's *Galatea* in the Villa Farnesina ⑬

0 meters 150
0 yards 150

of frescoing the Villa Farnesina ⑬ *(see pp220–21)*, just up Via della Lungara, he spent so much time with his lover that, unlike the famed *Galatea* in the dining room, the "Raphael" work in the Loggia of Cupid and Psyche was executed largely by his assistants. Across from the Farnesina squats the Palazzo Corsini and the Galleria Nazionale d'Arte Antica ⑭ *(see p222)*. Tucked behind the gallery – accessible by backtracking down Via della Lungara and turning right on Via Corsini – are the Botanical Gardens ⑮ *(see p222)*.

The Gianicolo

Continue back south on Via della Lungara through the Porta Settimiana, and turn right up Via G. Garibaldi to climb Janiculum Hill. After the road makes a sharp left turn, veer right up a set of steps to San Pietro in Montorio, home to Bramante's Tempietto ⑯ *(see p223)*. Go on up Via G.

Tips for Walkers

Starting point: Santa Cecilia in Trastevere.
Length: 2.9 miles (4.7 km).
Getting there: Take bus 23, 44, or 280.
Best time for walk: Weekdays (to see the Cavallini fresco in Santa Cecilia), starting mid morning while the churches of southern Trastevere are still open.
Stopping points: Trastevere is the most restaurant-intensive district in Rome, so it has plenty of eateries and bars *(see pp317–19)*.

Garibaldi to the broad basin of the Fontana dell'Acqua Paola ⑰ *(see p223)*. Continue along Via G. Garibaldi to the 1644 Porta San Pancrazio ⑱, which had to be rebuilt in 1849 due to cannon damage *(see pp38–9)*. Turn right onto Passeggiata del Gianicolo to enter the park, where the first wide space with a panoramic vista over Rome is Piazzale Garibaldi with its equestrian

Key

• • • Walk route

bars into Piazza della Scala, where the Carmelite convent of Santa Maria della Scala ⑩ *(see p212)* has an ornate interior.

Northern Trastevere

The far northern part of Trastevere, between the Gianicolo and the river, is where the artist Raphael dallied with a baker's daughter at the Casa della Fornarina ⑪ *(see p212)*, on the right just before the Porta Settimiana ⑫ *(see p222)*. Instead

Steps at the tranquil Botanical Gardens ⑮

monument to the general ⑲ *(see p222)*. Here, paths are lined with marble busts of other Risorgimento heroes. When you reach the Lighthouse of Manfredi ⑳ *(see p218)*, the dome of St. Peter's appears to the north. Continue down the steps at the Passeggiata's first bend to see the 400-year-old remains of Tasso's Oak ㉑ *(see p218)*. At the foot of the steps, rejoin the Passeggiata. Beyond it, a few steps up, finish at the lovely church of Sant'Onofrio ㉒ *(see p223)*. From Viale Aldo Fabrizi you can catch bus No. 870 back downtown.

A Two-Hour Walk Around the Aventine

Rising just across the Circus Maximus from the Palatine, the residential Aventine Hill has served as a leafy haven of villas and mansions since Imperial times. This southernmost of Rome's legendary seven hills is still an oasis where traffic noise all but disappears. Yet few visitors walk here – despite the lure of fine old churches, lovely city panoramas, and rarely visited ancient ruins. You'll also explore Testaccio, a fine area for authentic restaurants, and see a Roman pyramid.

The gymnasium at the northwest side of the Baths of Caracalla ①

The Aventine

Begin at one of Rome's most magnificent ancient sites, the massive Baths of Caracalla ① *(see p199)*, where plebeian, and patrician alike once bathed (and, much later, where the poet Shelley found inspiration for *Prometheus Unbound*). Just outside the Baths' entrance sits the church of SS Nero e Achilleo ② *(see p196)*, with 9th-century mosaics. Across Viale delle Terme di Caracalla lies tiny San Sisto Vecchio ③, first home of the Dominican nuns *(see p195)*. Turning northwest up Viale delle Terme di Caracalla, take the first right onto Via di Valle delle Camene, a tree-lined avenue parallel to the main road. Angle right up Salita di San Gregorio, and ascend the imposing staircase of San Gregorio Magno ④ *(see p194)* for great views of the Palatine. Look for the third-century marble table (in the St. Barbara chapel, on the left side of the church) at which St. Gregory the Great shared meals with the poor and, once,

an angel in disguise. Turn left down Via di San Gregorio, and cross wide Piazza di Porta Capena, keeping the long, dusty oval of the Circus Maximus ⑤ *(see p207)* on your right. At the start of Viale Aventino you'll see the modernist bulk of FAO ⑥, originally intended to be the Ministry of Italian Africa when Mussolini was launching his ill-fated conquest of the Horn of Africa. Since its 1952 completion, it has housed the UN's Food and Agriculture Organization.

Across the Aventine

Turn right on Via del Circo Massimo, and immediately left onto Via della Fonte di Fauno to start climbing the Aventine Hill. This leads you to a small piazza before the church of Santa Prisca ⑦, built in the third century atop the house where the martyred saint's parents hosted

The apse of Santa Prisca ⑦

St. Peter. The current church dates largely to a Renaissance-era remodeling, and includes a Passignano altarpiece. Continue north up Via di Santa Prisca, angle left through Largo Arrigo VII, turn left on Via Eufemiano, and immediately right onto Via Sant'Alberto Magno. This leads right into Parco Savello ⑧, a garden of orange trees with a panoramic river view over Trastevere. Leaving the park, turn right onto Via di Santa Sabina to the gorgeous basilica of Santa Sabina ⑨ (see p206), where its rare, 5th-century wooden doors incorporate one of the earliest Crucifixion representations. Continue along Via di Santa Sabina to see the fine Cosmati work in SS Bonifacio e Alessio ⑩ (see p206). The street ends in the Piazza dei Cavaliere di Malta ⑪ (see p206), where you get a tiny view of St. Peter's dome through the keyhole at number 3. Turn left down Via di Porta Lavernate,

Keats' gravestone at the Protestant Cemetery on Via Caio Cestio ⑮

that have long burrowed into its flanks to take advantage of the terra cotta's constant, cool temperature for storing wine. Turn left through Piazza Orazio

Giustiniani to continue skirting the hill along Via di Monte Testaccio. Across the street, you'll see the blind arcades of the Ex-Mattatoio ⑭, a defunct abattoir whose workers were paid, in part, with the day's offal. They would carry this *quinto quarto* (fifth quarter) of the animal across the street to one of Testaccio's early eateries,

Tips for Walkers

Starting point: The Baths of Caracalla entrance on Viale delle Terme di Caracalla 52.

Length: 3 miles (5 km).

Getting there: You can walk from the Circo Massimo Metro stop, or take bus 118 or 628.

Best time for walk: Start in the morning, timing your walk so that you can eat lunch in Testaccio.

Stopping points: There are many options, since fantastic, and authentic local eateries abound in, and around Piazza Testaccio, from cheap pizza places to traditional Roman restaurants.

where it would be turned into such (now) classic Roman delicacies as oxtail stew, and *pajata* (calf intestines). Continue along Via di Monte Testaccio, which becomes Via Caio Cestio, to the Protestant Cemetery ⑮ (see p207) where such luminaries as Keats and Shelley lie in peace. At Via Marmorata, turn right to pass the Porta San Paolo ⑯, a city gate dating to AD 402. As you walk through the remains of the Aurelian Wall into Piazzale Ostiense, you can't miss on your right the Pyramid of Caius Cestius ⑰ (see p207). The final leg is a long stroll down Via Ostiense or, alternatively, hop on the bus (Nos. 23, 271, or 769) to see the wonderfully weird Centrale Montemartini ⑱, an early Industrial Age power plant now stuffed with ancient sculptures (see p269). Bus numbers 23 and 769 will take you back to within walking distance of Piramide Metro.

Key

••• Walk route

passing the facade of Sant'Anselmo ⑫. Built in 1900, the church houses a 3rd-century mosaic scene of Orpheus found during excavations. From Piazza dei Servili, turn right on Via Asinio Pollione to go down off the Aventine.

Testaccio and South

Cross Via Marmorata and continue down Via Galvani. As you cross Via Nicola Zabaglia, you see Testaccio market ahead on your right, while the ground on your left rises to form Monte Testaccio ⑬ (see p206), an ancient garbage dump made up entirely of potsherds. It is lined with various restaurants

Ancient sculptures on display in the Centrale Montemartini ⑱

For map symbols see back flap

TRAVELERS' NEEDS

WHERE TO STAY

Rome has been a major tourist centre since the Middle Ages, when pilgrims from all over Europe came to visit the home of Catholicism and its relic-packed churches. The nostalgic can still sleep in a 15th-century hotel, or stay around the Campo de' Fiori market, where visiting ecclesiastics were entertained by courtesans in the Renaissance era. Those who prefer their history a little less raffish could opt for an ex-monastery or convent, or stay in a still-functioning religious house. Romantics can sleep in the house once occupied by Keats, while stargazers can stay in former palaces graced by celebrities of the past and present. Rome can offer the full range of accommodations, mostly in historical buildings, very little purpose-built. *Pensione* (guesthouse) no longer refers to a specific type of establishment, but in practice many retain the name and more personal character that has made them so popular with travelers. Other possibilities include hostels, residential hotels and self-catering accommodation.

Hotel listings *(pp300–303)* are organized according to their theme and area, with DK Choice entries highlighted – see Recommended Hotels on p298–9 for more information.

Hotel Prices

Prices are set by the state, and hotels should display the official rate on the door of each room. VAT (IVA in Italian) is usually included, and has been taken into account in the price categories on page 300.

Hotels in Rome generally have low and high season rates. April to June, September and October are high season. Double-check tariffs when booking hotels at other times of year as you may initially be quoted the higher rate. Excepting Christmas and New Year, there are some real bargains to be had between November and February, and also in July and August. Many hotels also offer special Internet booking deals, especially if made far in advance, or at the last minute. Discounts for long-stay visitors, and groups are often negotiable. Rooms without a bathroom can cost about 30 per cent less. Single travelers are badly catered for, and though it is possible to find a single room for 60 per cent of the price of a double, on average you'll pay as much as 70 per cent, and occasionally even more.

Hidden Extras

Even if the price of your room includes service, you are frequently expected to tip bellboys and for room service.

Rates are often not inclusive of breakfast, especially at some luxury hotels, where it may cost up to €50. Hotels usually add hefty surcharges to international phone calls, and may charge for parking and air conditioning. The cost of drinks in minibars can also be high.

All hotels, B&Bs and campsites in Rome must add a city tax *(contributo di soggiorno)* to the final bill. At present this tax is for the first ten days of any stay and is fixed at €1 per day per person for campsites, €2 for establishments up to and including three-star hotels, and €3 for four- and five-star hotels. Children under ten are exempt, as are visitors staying in youth hostels.

Facilities

Internet access, air conditioning and bathrooms with hair dryers are common in most mid-range hotels, and phones in middle- to lower-price rooms, although budget travellers staying in cheaper hotels shouldn't expect much more than a clean room.

Because most hotels occupy historic buildings, room sizes can vary dramatically even within the same establishment (and this is often reflected in the pricing), so do ask to see your room before you check in. Swimming pools are rare, but roof terraces or gardens are common across the range of hotels.

Top-class hotels will usually have some soundproofing; otherwise noise levels can be dreadful, in which case ask for a room facing away from the road.

The Verdi Room in Via Veneto's Majestic Hotel *(see p302)*

◀ One of the many charming restaurants in Rome

Grand Hotel de la Minerve *(see p302)*

Parking in central Rome is a problem, though a few hotels have a limited number of parking spaces of their own.

Business visitors to the capital are well catered for, with practical hotel facilities such as conference rooms.

Making Reservations

It is best to book through the hotel website, by phone or email. You should do this at least two months in advance if you want a particular hotel during peak season. If you require any particular features, such as a view, insist on confirmation in writing to ensure that you get what you have been promised.

If a deposit is required you can usually pay by debit or credit card. Under Italian law a booking is valid as soon as the

The Portoghesi Hotel *(see p300)*

deposit is paid, so you could lose money if you pull out. Double-check bookings prior to departure. Many hotels have a fierce cancellation policy and there is every chance that you will be charged for at least one night, even if you don't stay. Another reason for checking bookings is that some hotels deliberately overbook and then offer unsatisfactory alternative accommodation.

If you arrive by train, touts may descend on you at the station with offers of hotels. They can be of some use if you are looking for a budget hotel, but exercise the usual caution. A better bet if you have not booked in advance is to head for one of the tourist board offices *(see p299)*, where staff will reserve you a room within the price range you specify.

Checking In and Out

Italian hoteliers are legally obliged to register you with the police, which is the reason they always ask for your passport. Everyone in Italy is supposed to carry with them some sort of identification.

In some of Rome's cheaper *pensioni*, do not be surprised if you are asked to pay on arrival. Mention in advance if you intend to pay by credit card. A common tax dodge by many hotels is to ask for payment in cash; you are entitled to refuse.

Disabled Travelers

Provision for disabled travelers is poor. Hotels that occupy parts of buildings often start their rooms up several flights of stairs, while others can only accommodate disabled guests on the ground floor. Ramps, wide doorways and bathroom handrails are rare.

Contact the hotel entries in the listings directly, before booking, to check whether they are wheelchair accessible and can provide any other specific requirements (for more information *see p368*).

There is a useful website (Roma Pertutti) dedicated to

Villa San Pio garden *(see p300)*

mobility within Rome, while the Lazio region provides advice on accessibility farther afield (800 27 1027). Public transportation authority **Bus Abile** offers a pick-up service and bus tourism for travelers with disabilities and must be reserved in advance.

Traveling with Children

Italians love children and they are usually welcome across the range of hotels. Most hotels can provide cribs or small beds, but high chairs, children's meals, and babysitting services are rare.

Many hotels do not have special rates for children and charge a standard rate if you require an extra bed in a room, whether for a baby or an adult, which can add anything from a few euros to 40 percent onto the price. For a family with older children, two-room suites are sometimes available.

Contact the hotel in advance of booking for more information on family rates and children's facilities.

Bed & Breakfast

A popular option for visitors to Rome is bed & breakfast accommodations. This can be anything from a spare room in an apartment to something more like a small hotel. The type of breakfast can also vary depending on the owner. Contact the **Bed & Breakfast Association** of Rome for details, or visit Rome's tourist board website *(see p299)*.

Residential Hotels

If you want the comfort and privacy of your own apartment coupled with the services of a hotel, you could opt to stay in a residence. Prices range from around €300 to over €3,000 for a week in a room with two beds, though some residences are only available for two-week or one-month rentals.

A full list of residential hotels is available from tourist board offices; some of the most central are listed in the directory on page 299.

Religious Institutions

If you do not mind an early curfew, quite a few religious institutions take in paying guests. All religions are welcome, and you do not have to be a practicing Catholic. Reserve well in advance, since all of the following places cater to groups of students and pilgrims. **Casa Il Rosario** convent is located near the Colosseum, while **Nostra Signora di Lourdes**, and the **Casa di Santa Brigida** are in the center of Rome. Prices are in the same range as for the cheaper hotels.

Budget Accommodations

Even if you are traveling on a shoestring, it is possible to find a decent room in Rome. More and more midrange options are now available, and dormitory accommodations can be found at rock-bottom prices in simple establishments, such as the Ottaviano. Youth hostels are also a good option. At the **Alessandro Palace**, bed, breakfast, and shower can all be had at a reasonable cost. **Fawlty Towers** has good facilities for the price, including a roof terrace; like **Stargate**, it is located near Termini station.

Women can get rooms at the **Foresteria Orsa Maggiore** in Trastevere or at the **Young Women's Christian Association (YWCA)** near Termini (those arriving in Termini at night should be careful). There are also several

The reception area of the Regina Hotel Baglioni *(see p302)*

downtown budget hotels offering clean rooms, and often a free breakfast. See websites like www.venere.com and www.eurocheapo.com for more options.

Self-Service Apartments

Independent apartments are a good alternative and allow you more freedom. Apartments range from luxury locations with a daily cleaning service to smaller basic facilities. Most come equipped with cooking utensils, towels, and bed linens. **RetRome Bed & Breakfast** provides apartments at various locations around town.

Camping

Camping has come a long way since the simple tent and trailer. Campsites around Rome offer everything from fully equipped cabins (with private bath) to Jacuzzis and on-site discos. Most campsites are located quite far out of

Bedroom at the Residenza Cellini *(see p303)*

town but offer a shuttle service, as well as airport transportation; **Flaminio Village** is one exception, at only 4 miles (6 km) north of the downtown. Like many sites, it has a pool, coffee bar, restaurant, and Internet access.

Tourist Boards

Provincial and city tourist boards can provide advice on accommodations. Hotel Reservation is a booking service with offices at Termini station, as well as both of the city's airports.

Recommended Hotels

The hotels recommended on pages 300–303 are listed under five categories: Boutique, Budget, Historic, Luxury, and Pensions and B&B. Boutique hotels are smaller and designed with an artistic eye, whether it be modern or ancient in style. Budget accommodations, while the least expensive option, are not limited to hostels and B&Bs. Surprisingly, Rome has some great options for frugal travelers who know where to look. The city is also full of historic accommodations, since many Renaissance palaces and villas have been turned into hotels. Antique furniture and exposed architectural elements make them the most romantic choices. Luxury hotels provide 5-star service and facilities, most with stunningly beautiful rooms, panoramic rooftop terraces, and award-winning restaurants.

Pensions and B&Bs may provide more basic facilities, but are often full of character at an affordable price.

Our hotels are divided into five geographical areas. In Central Rome, from Piazza Navona to the Jewish Ghetto and southward as far as the Tiber, you will find a plethora of hotels for all budgets. Many exclusive boutique hotels can be found here, as well as a number of mid-range options. Ancient Rome, from the Colosseum to the Esquiline Hill, including the Lateran and the Aventine, offers varied accommodations, including a number of budget options, particularly near Termini station. Most of the luxury hotels can be found in the Spanish Steps and Via Veneto neighborhoods, categorized under Spagna, Veneto, and Around, which

The pool in the Aldrovandi Palace garden *(see p303)*

also includes the Quirinal Hill. Trastevere and Around, including the Vatican and Janiculum areas, offer some great historical choices and many B&Bs. The Farther Afield section covers hotels outside the downtown and in nearby Tivoli.

Throughout the listings, certain hotels are highlighted as DK Choice. These offer a special experience – superlative service, beautiful interiors, cutting-edge amenities or gadgets, an excellent restaurant, or a combination of these.

DIRECTORY

Disabled Travelers

Bus Abile
Tel 800-469 540
(call between 9am and 1pm Mon–Fri).
W atac.roma.it

Roma per Tutti
W romapertutti.it

Bed & Breakfast

Bed & Breakfast Association of Rome
Via A. Pacinotti 73.
Tel 06-5530 2248.
Open 10am–2pm, 3–7pm Mon–Fri.
W b-b.rm.it

Rome Bed & Breakfast
Tel 1-800 872 2632.
W romebandb.com

Residential Hotels

Di Ripetta
Via di Ripetta 231, 00186.
Tel 06-323 1144.
W ripetta.it

In Trastevere
Vicolo Moroni 35–36, 00153. Tel 06-808 3375.
W romerenting.com

Residence Mallia
Via Damiano Chiesa 8, 00136. Tel 06-301 98.
W mallia.it

Vittoria
Via Vittoria 60-64, 00187.
Tel 06-679 7533.

Religious Institutions

Casa di Santa Brigida
Piazza Farnese 96, 00186.
Tel 06-6889 2596.

Casa Il Rosario
Via Sant'Agata dei Goti 10, 00184. Tel 06-679 2346.

Nostra Signora di Lourdes
Via Sistina 113, 00187.
Tel 06-474 5324.

Budget Accommodations

Alessandro Palace
Via Vicenza 42, 00185.
Tel 06-446 1958.
W hostelsalessandro. com

Associazione Italiana Alberghi per la Gioventù
(Youth Hostels Association)
Via Cavour 44, 00184.
Tel 06-487 1152.
W aighostels.com

Fawlty Towers
Via Magenta 39, 00185.
Tel 06-445 0374.
W fawltytowers.org

Foresteria Orsa Maggiore
Via di San Francesco di Sales 1A, 00165.
Tel 06-689 3753.
W casainternazionale delledonne.org

Ottaviano
Via Ottaviano 6, 00192.
Tel 06-3973 8138.
W pensioneottaviano. com

Stargate
Via Palestro 88, 00185.
Tel 06-445 7164.
W stargatehotels.com

YWCA
Via C. Balbo 4, 00184.
Tel 06-488 3917.
W ywca-ucdg.it

Self-Service

RetRome Bed & Breakfast
Tel 06-9555 7334.
W retrome.net

Camping

Flaminio Village
Via Flaminia Nuova 821, 00189. Tel 06-333 2604.
W campingflaminio. com

Tourist Board

Rome City Tourist Board
Termini Station 00185.
Tel 06-0608.
Open 8am–7.30pm daily.
W 060608.it

Terminal 3 (arrivals), Leonardo da Vinci Airport, Fiumicino.
Open 8am–7.30pm daily.

Where to Stay

Boutique

Ancient Rome

Canada €€
Via Vicenza 58, 00185
Tel *06-445 7770* **Map** 6 E2
🌐 hotelcanadaroma.com
Rooms vary at this above-average three-star; some have canopy beds. Free Wi-Fi.

Domus Aventina €€
Via di Santa Prisca 11b, 00153
Tel *06-574 6135* **Map** 8 E3
🌐 hoteldomusaventina.com
Simple but elegantly decorated rooms open directly onto a lush, quiet courtyard.

Hotel Celio €€
Via dei Santi Quattro 35/c, 00184
Tel *06-7049 5333* **Map** 9 A1
🌐 hotelcelio.com
Elegant three-star with a touch of whimsy. Reproduction artwork is found in every room.

San Anselmo €€
Piazza Sant'Anselmo 2, 00153
Tel *06-570 057* **Map** 8 D3
🌐 aventinohotels.com
A romantic choice, San Anselmo offers four-poster beds and claw-foot tubs for a memorable stay.

Villa San Pio €€
Via Santa Melania 19, 00153
Tel *06-570 057* **Map** 8 E3
🌐 aventinohotels.com
This quiet and secluded hotel is located just a stone's throw from downtown. Free parking and breakfast.

Fortyseven €€€
Via Luigi Petroselli 47, 00186
Tel *06-678 7816* **Map** 8 E1
🌐 fortysevenhotel.com
Stellar views of the ancient city from this retro-style hotel that prides itself on its hospitality.

Central Rome

Campo de' Fiori Hotel €€
Via del Biscione 6, 00186
Tel *06-6880 6865* **Map** 11 C4
🌐 hotelcampodefiori.com
Romantically decorated rooms with charming details and views of rooftops and domes.

Hotel Santa Chiara €€
Via di Santa Chiara 21, 00186
Tel *06-687 2979* **Map** 12 D3
🌐 albergosantachiara.com
Well-located hotel with an impressive, spacious lobby and simply furnished rooms.

Contemporary interior of the Babuino181 hotel

Portoghesi €€
Via dei Portoghesi 1, 00186
Tel *06-686 4231* **Map** 11 C2
🌐 hotelportoghesiroma.it
A good-value hotel nestled in a quiet cobbled alley. It has a lovely breakfast terrace.

Teatropace33 €€
Via del Teatro Pace 33, 00186
Tel *06-687 9075* **Map** 11 C3
🌐 hotelteatropace.com
Charming hotel decorated in ornate Baroque style with an excellent price/quality ratio.

Locanda Cairoli €€€
Piazza Benedetto Cairoli 2, 00186
Tel *06-6880 9278* **Map** 12 D5
🌐 hotelcairoliroma.com
Centrally located and comfortable hotel with a cozy family-style breakfast room. Quirky and eclectic furnishings.

Sole al Pantheon €€€
Piazza della Rotonda 63, 00186
Tel *06-678 0441* **Map** 12 D3
🌐 solealpantheonrome.com
Nice rooms with unparalleled views of the Pantheon. Can be noisy.

Spagna, Veneto, and Around

Art €€
Via Margutta 56, 00187
Tel *06-328 711* **Map** 4 F1
🌐 hotelart.it
While the art-inspired public spaces may be overdone, the rooms are sleek.

Deko Rome €€
Via Toscana 1, 00187
Tel *06-4202 0032* **Map** 5 C1
🌐 dekorome.com

Price Guide
Prices are based on one night's stay in high season for a standard double room, inclusive of service charges and taxes.

€ up to €120
€€ €120 to 300
€€€ over €300

Small but comfortable rooms in minimalist style. Spacious and luxurious bathrooms.

Parlamento €€
Via delle Convertite 5, 00187
Tel *06-6992 1000* **Map** 12 E1
🌐 hotelparlamento.it
Simple but romantic rooms with whimsical touches. Roof-top terrace with a lovely view for breakfast.

Piranesi €€
Via del Babuino 196, 00187
Tel *06-328 041* **Map** 4 F1
🌐 hotelpiranesi.com
This tiny hotel exudes quiet elegance and is in an ideal location. Facilities include a small gym.

Babuino181 €€€
Via del Babuino 181, 00187
Tel *06-3229 5295* **Map** 4 F1
🌐 romeluxurysuites.com
A Renaissance palace remodeled with a sleek, modern look and luxurious details.

Portrait Suites €€€
Via Bocca di Leone 23
Tel *06-6938 0742* **Map** 5 A2
🌐 lungarnocollection.com
Stylish hotel owned by Salvatore Ferragamo. Individually decorated rooms.

Trastevere and Around

Domus Tiberina €
Via in Piscinula 37, 00153
Tel *06-581 3648* **Map** 8 D1
🌐 hoteldomustiberina.it
A quaint hotel on a picturesque, vine-covered alleyway. Steps away from the Tiber.

Hotel Ponte Sisto €€
Via dei Pettinari 64, 00186
Tel *06-686 3100* **Map** 11 C5
🌐 hotelpontesisto.it
Comfortable rooms with panoramic views and a delightful roof terrace.

Palazzo Cardinal Cesi €€
Via della Conciliazione 51, 00193
Tel *06-684 0390* **Map** 3 C3
🌐 palazzocesi.it
Former cardinal's palace with original moldings, coffered ceilings, and a romantic garden.

San Francisco €€
Via Jacopa de' Settesoli 7, 00153
Tel *06-5830 0051*   Map 7 C2
W hotelsanfrancesco.net
An unassuming entrance hides
a gem of a hotel. San Francesco
has tasteful rooms and a chic
rooftop bar.

Sant'Anna €€
Borgo Pio 134, 00193
Tel *06-6880 1602*   Map 3 C3
W santannahotel.net
Modern convenience with an
old-fashioned feel. Exquisite
courtyard provides respite from
the busy street.

Budget

Ancient Rome

Blue Hostel €
Via Carlo Alberto 13, 00185
Tel *340-925 8503*   Map 6 D4
W bluehostel.it
The accommodations are an
excellent buy at this impressive,
spotless hostel.

Hostel des Artistes €
Via Villafranca 20, 00185
Tel *06-445 4365*   Map 6 E2
W hostelrome.com
Friendly and clean hostel with
dorm accommodations. Simple
private rooms are also available.

DK Choice

The Beehive €
Via Marghera 8, 00185
Tel *06-4470 4553*   Map 6 E3
W the-beehive.com
This gem of a hotel is owned
by an American couple and
offers both private rooms
and small dormitories.
Accommodations are basic, but
clean and comfortable. There are
many extras available, such as
yoga lessons, massage sessions,
and a café serving freshly baked
bread and organic coffee. An
excellent choice for frugal
travelers, but reserve early.

Central Rome

Mimosa €
Via di Santa Chiara, 61, 00186
Tel *06-6880 1753*   Map 12 D3
W hotelmimosa.net
Affordable accommodations with
basic rooms that are comfortable,
clean, and air-conditioned.

Palazzo Olivia €
Via dei Leutari 15, 00186
Tel *06-6821 6986*   Map 11 C3
W palazzo-olivia.it

Set in a 17th-century palace.
Self-service apartments, each
named after an opera character.

Spagna, Veneto and Around

Hotel Grifo €€
Via del Boschetto 144, 00184
Tel *06-487 1395*   Map 5 B4
W hotelgrifo.com
The compact, functional rooms
are kept immaculately clean.
Breakfast is served on a cozy
terrace with a charming view.

Trastevere and Around

**Casa Internazionale
della Donna** €
*Via di San Francesco di Sales 1A,
00165*
Tel *06-6889 2465*   Map 4 D5
W casainternazionaledelle
donne.org
Basic and inexpensive
accommodations in a quiet but
central area. For women only.

Centro Diffusione Spiritualità €
Via dei Riari 44, 00153
Tel *06-6880 6122*   Map 11 A5
W villariari.it
Rock-bottom prices at this
religious center located on a
quiet street. It has a lovely garden.

Hotel Ottaviano €
Via Ottaviano 6, 00192
Tel *06-3973 8138*   Map 3 C2
W pensioneottaviano.com
This simple but central hostel is a
backpacker's paradise. Just steps
away from the Vatican museums.

Hotel Trastevere €€
Via Luciano Manara 24a, 00153
Tel *06-581 4713*   Map 7 C1
W hoteltrastevere.net
A good buy for the area, with
basic service and large and bright,
though unimaginative, rooms.

Historic

Ancient Rome

Hotel Forum €€€
Via Tor de' Conti 25, 00184
Tel *06-679 2446*   Map 5 B5
W hotelforum.com
Dark wooden floors and rich
fabrics evoke an old-world feel.
Stunning views of ancient Rome.

Palazzo Manfredi €€€
Via Labicana 125, 00184
Tel *06-7759 1380*   Map 9 B1
W palazzomanfredi.com
Converted Renaissance palace
with elegantly decorated rooms.
The Colosseum is just steps away.

Central Rome

Sole al Biscione €
Via del Biscione 76, 00186
Tel *06-6880 6873*   Map 11 C4
W solealbiscione.it
This functional but charming
hotel claims to be the oldest in
Rome. Fantastic rooftop terrace.

Casa di Santa Brigida €€
Via Monserrato 54, 00186
Tel *06-6889 2596*   Map 11 C4
W brigidine.org
Not the cheapest convent in
town, but the location and
rooftop terrace are worth it.

Due Torri €€
Vicolo del Leonetto 23, 00186
Tel *06-6880 6956*   Map 11 C1
W hotelduetorriroma.com
Converted Renaissance palace
with small but well-appointed
rooms and friendly service.

Teatro di Pompeo €€
Largo del Pallaro 8, 00186
Tel *06-6830 0170*   Map 11 C4
W hotelteatrodipompeo.it
This simple but evocative hotel
was built on the ruins of Pompey's
ancient theater. Attentive staff.

Warm and inviting room at the Due Torri hotel

For more information on types of hotels *see pp296–7*

Spagna, Veneto, and Around

Locarno   €€
Via della Penna 22, 00186
Tel *06-361 0841*   **Map** 4 F1
Ⓦ hotellocarno.com
Many classic movies have been shot on the exquisite rooftop terrace of this Art Deco masterpiece.

Trastevere and Around

Bramante   €€
Vicolo delle Palline 24, 00193
Tel *06-6880 6426*   **Map** 3 C3
Ⓦ hotelbramante.com
On a quaint and cobbled back-street in the shadow of St. Peter's Basilica. Quiet and tasteful rooms.

Relais Casa della Fornarina €€
Via di Porta Settimiana 7, 00153
Tel *06-6456 2268*   **Map** 11 B5
Ⓦ casadellafornarina.com
Set in the house where Raphael's muse, the famous baker's daughter, lived. Busy area at night.

DK Choice

Donna Camilla Savelli   €€€
Via Garibaldi 27, 00153
Tel *06-588 861*   **Map** 7 B1
Ⓦ hoteldonnacamilla
savelli.com
This restored monastery still belongs to the nuns of the original order, but is now a four-star hotel. It was recently voted among the top 100 hotels in the world. All rooms are decorated with antique furniture, and some have Jacuzzi tubs. The cloister is an oasis in the heart of the city.

Luxury

Ancient Rome

Hotel Mediterraneo   €€
Via Cavour 15, 00184
Tel *06-488 4051*   **Map** 6 D3
Ⓦ romehotelmediterraneo.it
This four-star boasts Art Deco design, comfortable rooms, and a terrace with sweeping views.

Kolbe Hotel   €€€
Via di San Teodoro 48, 00186
Tel *06-679 8866*   **Map** 8 E1
Ⓦ kolbehotelrome.com
Modern furnishings mix with ancient architectual elements. Some rooms look directly over the Forum.

Radisson Blu ES   €€€
Via Filippo Turati 171, 00185
Tel *06-444 841*   **Map** 6 E4
Ⓦ radissonblu.com

A magnificent rooftop pool, cutting-edge design, and breath-taking views make for an unforgettable stay.

Central Rome

Grand Hotel de la Minerve €€
Piazza della Minerva 69, 00186
Tel *06-695 201*   **Map** 12 D3
Ⓦ grandhoteldela
minerve.com
Postcard views from nearly every room and an unbeatable rooftop terrace. Luxurious service and decor.

Hotel St George   €€€
Via Giulia 62, 00186
Tel *06-686 611*   **Map** 11 B4
Ⓦ stgeorgehotel.it
Discreet, romantic hotel with a rooftop terrace offering *aperitivo* (apértifs) and river views.

Nazionale   €€€
Piazza di Monte Citorio 131, 00186
Tel *06-695 001*   **Map** 12 E2
Ⓦ hotelnazionale.it
Antique furniture and rich fabrics at this elegant four-star. Ask for the Jacuzzi with a view.

Raphael   €€€
Largo Febo 2, 00186
Tel *06-682 831*   **Map** 11 C2
Ⓦ raphaelhotel.com
World-class service, a panoramic terrace, and gorgeous decor make for a romantic stay.

Spagna, Veneto, and Around

Boscolo Aleph   €€€
Via di San Basilio 15, 00185
Tel *06-422 901*   **Map** 5 B2
Ⓦ aleph-roma.boscolo
hotels.com
Modern opulence reigns at this five-star. Elegant conference rooms and a luxurious spa.

Boscolo Exedra   €€€
Piazza della Repubblica 47, 00185
Tel *06-4893 8012*   **Map** 5 C3
Ⓦ exedra-roma.boscolo
hotels.com

Lavish, modern five-star hotel with an award-winning spa and a rooftop infinity pool.

De Russie   €€€
Via del Babuino 9, 00187
Tel *06-328 881*   **Map** 4 F1
Ⓦ hotelderussie.it
Spectacular gardens surround this Renaissance villa-turned hotel. It has a fully-equipped spa.

Eden   €€€
Via Ludovisi 49, 00187
Tel *06-478 121*   **Map** 5 B2
Ⓦ edenroma.com
Outstanding service and an award-winning rooftop terrace restaurant at this elegant hotel.

DK Choice

Hassler   €€€
Piazza Trinità Dei Monti 6, 00187
Tel *06-699 340*   **Map** 5 A2
Ⓦ hotelhasslerroma.com
Impeccable service, plush furnishings, and incomparable views have made this legendary hotel the favorite Roman *pied-à-terre* for many celebrities. Each room is individually styled, and every possible comfort is available for a price. It is enviably located atop the Spanish Steps.

Hotel d'Inghilterra   €€€
Via Bocca di Leone 14, 00187
Tel *06-699 811*   **Map** 5 A2
Ⓦ hoteldinghilterrarome.com
Sumptuous accommodations in an enviable location. There is a candlelit rooftop terrace.

Majestic   €€€
Via Veneto 50, 00187
Tel *06-421 441*   **Map** 5 B2
Ⓦ hotelmajestic.com
Luxurious fabrics, antique elements, and a colorful, eclectic style at this high-end hotel.

Regina Hotel Baglioni €€€
Via Veneto 72, 00187
Tel *06-421 111*   **Map** 5 B2
Ⓦ baglionihotels.com

Impressive lobby of the Grand Hotel de la Minerve

Key to prices *see p300*

Charming touches at the inviting Pantheon View

A gem of Liberty-style decor, and architecture, with opulent furnishings and every comfort.

St Regis Hotel €€€
Via Vittorio Emanuele Orlando 3, 00185
Tel *06-470 91* **Map** 5 C3
W starwoodhotels.com
Extravagant decor at this over-the-top palace hotel. There is an on-site spa and fitness center.

Villa Spalletti Trivelli €€€
Via Piacenza 4, 00184
Tel *06-4890 7934*
W villaspalletti.it
Understated elegance and impeccable taste at this villa nestled in a lush garden setting.

Westin Excelsior €€€
Via Veneto 125, 00187
Tel *06-470 81* **Map** 5 B2
W westinrome.com
A favorite with honeymooners; the perfect spot to indulge in *la dolce vita*.

Farther Afield

Grand Hotel Duca d'Este €€
Via Tiburtina Valeria 330, 00019, Tivoli
Tel *07-743 883*
W ducadeste.com
Comfortable business hotel with a well-equipped wellness center. Near the famous thermal baths.

Aldrovandi Palace €€€
Via Ulisse Aldrovandi 15, 00197, Villa Borghese
Tel *06-322 3993* **Map** 2 D4
W aldrovandi.com
Spectacular five-star with airy rooms, a poolside restaurant, and views of the Borghese gardens.

Pension and B&B
Ancient Rome

La Casa di Amy €
Via Principe Amedeo 85A, 00185
Tel *06-446 0708* **Map** 6 D4
W lacasadiamy.com

Funky decoration and a friendly atmosphere at this family-run B&B. Bright, spotlessly clean rooms.

Paba €€
Via Cavour 266, 00184
Tel *06-4782 4902* **Map** 5 B5
W hotelpaba.com
Proximity to the Forum makes Paba a convenient budget option. Rooms are simply furnished.

Piccolo Principe €€
Via Giovanni Giolitti 255, 00185
Tel *32-0699 3110* **Map** 6 E4
W bebromatermini.it
Brightly painted rooms with basic funishings and clean bathrooms. Located near the Termini station.

Central Rome

DK Choice

Pantheon View €
Via del Seminario 87, 00186
Tel *06-699 0294* **Map** 12 D3
W pantheonview.it
This pension offers the comforts of a hotel, in addition to details such as wood-beamed ceilings, exposed brickwork, chandeliers, and copper faucets. Most rooms have Pantheon views.

Casa Banzo €€
Piazza del Monte di Pietà 30, 00186
Tel *06-683 3909* **Map** 11 C4
W casabanzo.it
Impressive details and period-style furniture make this low-priced option quite enjoyable.

Spagna, Veneto, and Around

Panda €
Via della Croce 35, 00187
Tel *06-678 0179* **Map** 5 A2
W hotelpanda.it
Simply furnished rooms are warmed by terra-cotta-tiled floors and wood-beamed ceilings.

DK Choice

Casa Howard €€
Via di Capo le Case 18, 00187 and Via Sistina 149, 00187
Tel *06-6992 4555* **Map** 12 F1
W casahoward.com
This B&B inspired by E. M. Forster's novel *Howard's End* has 10 unique rooms. What it lacks in round-the-clock service, it makes up for in style and character. Some rooms do not have private baths, but kimonos are provided for convenience.

Hotel Julia €€
Via Rasella 29, 00187
Tel *06-488 1637* **Map** 5 B3
W hoteljulia.it
A well-priced three-star with simple, comfortable rooms. The staff are friendly.

Hotel Suisse €€
Via Gregoriana 54, 00187
Tel *06-678 3649* **Map** 5 A2
W hotelsuisserome.com
Great value and warm service at this well-appointed and superbly located pension.

Oceania €€
Via Firenze 38, 00187
Tel *06-482 4696* **Map** 5 C3
W hoteloceania.it
Plenty of old-world charm and eccentric details at this simple but tasteful hotel.

Residenza Cellini €€
Via Modena 5, 00184
Tel *06-4782 5204* **Map** 5 C3
W residenzacellini.it
Spacious rooms with basic furnishings. Some bathrooms have Jacuzzi tubs.

Trastevere and Around

Arco del Lauro €€
Via dell'Arco de' Tolomei 27, 00153
Tel *06-9784 0350* **Map** 8 D1
W arcodellauro.it
A tiny hotel with simple but lovely rooms in a picturesque medieval location.

Farther Afield

Palazzo Maggiore €
Via Domenico Giuliani 89, 00019, Tivoli
Tel *39-3104 4937*
W palazzomaggiore.com
This sweet B&B with cozy, individually decorated rooms is the perfect base to explore Tivoli's incredible villas.

For more information on types of hotels *see pp298–9*

WHERE TO EAT AND DRINK

In Rome, eating out can be both a joy and an entertainment. On warm summer evenings, tables spill out into every conceivable open space, and diners dedicate long hours to the popular social activity of people-watching (and of being noticed and admired themselves) in a confusion of passers-by, buskers, rose sellers, and traffic. Although Romans have always loved to linger at the table, the lavish feasts of ancient Rome have slimmed down, and today's cooking is based on simplicity, freshness, and good-quality local ingredients in what is essentially a seasonal cuisine. Fast food is available, but it is fundamentally alien to the Roman temperament and way of life.

The restaurants reviewed in this chapter have been selected from the best that Rome can offer across all price ranges. Their descriptions, including the highlighted DK Choice entries, will help you narrow down your choice and enjoy a variety of cuisine types. The section on *Light Meals and Drinks* on pages 320–25 has details of recommended cafés, pizzerias, wine bars, and other places for more casual eating.

Types of Restaurants

In general, a *trattoria* is a family-run establishment with good home cooking, while a *ristorante* is more upmarket, more elegant, and thus more expensive.

Some eating places – where paper tablecloths give a clue to low prices – simply have no name. They offer excellent, basic home cooking. A number of them offer a great deal more than that, and your chances of finding authentic Roman cooking are higher in the best of these establishments than in expensive restaurants.

There will probably be times when you do not want a large meal, and Rome offers a huge variety of places for more casual eating (see pp320–25). One type of place offering snacks or more substantial dishes is the *enoteca*, which doubles as a well-stocked wine shop for browsers and connoisseurs.

Other places for a sit-down, informal lunch or dinner are *birrerie*, which are not only for beer drinkers, but also offer pizzas and even four-course meals.

There is always interesting take-out food for sale – *pizza rustica* or *pizza al taglio* (pizza by the slice) is available all over the city. For the best full-size pizzas, choose places with wood stoves (*forno a legna*). Other take-outs such as a whole roast chicken, or *pomodori al riso* (tomatoes stuffed with rice), can be found at a *rosticceria*. A self-service *tavola calda* will serve an impressive array of hot food and is ideal for lunchtime.

Fresh artichokes, a Roman specialty

Vegetarian Food

Purely vegetarian restaurants are few and far between in Rome, but everywhere you will find pasta and rice dishes (*risotto*). Most menus include an extensive list of vegetable-based side dishes (*contorni*), which could be anything from artichokes (stewed – *alla Romana* – or fried – *alla giudia*) to grilled or au gratin vegetables to sautéed spinach, chard, or chicory. Vegetables stuffed with rice then baked in the oven are also menu staples. Most menus are adaptable, as dishes are prepared to order. Tell your waiter that you are *vegetariano* (female: *vegetariana*) and he will advise accordingly.

The Price of a Meal

What you pay will depend on your choice of establishment. In a *tavola calda* or Roman pizzeria, for example, you can still eat for as little as €15 a head. A local *trattoria* costs perhaps €25, while in a fancier restaurant, plan on around €30 and up. Bottled wine, as opposed to a jug or carafe of house wine (*vino della casa*), will cost more but should offer a more interesting range of tastes (see p308). House wine can be a hit-or-miss affair.

Reading the Menu

The waiter will often tell you the day's specialties (*piatti del giorno*), usually not mentioned on the menu but almost always worth ordering. Or, ask for *la lista* (the menu) and allow yourself to be guided.

A meal could begin with *antipasti* (appetizers) or *primi*

Interior of a hotel restaurant

piatti – the latter consisting of *pasta asciutta* (pasta with some kind of sauce), *pasta in brodo* (clear broth with pasta in it), *pasta al forno* (baked pasta), risotto, or a substantial soup. You then move on to the *secondi*, the main meat or fish course, for which you will usually need to order vegetables *(contorni)* separately. Afterward you have *formaggi* (cheeses), *frutta* (fruit), or *dolci* (desserts). Romans do not usually eat cheese as well as a sweet dish. Strong espresso coffee, and perhaps a liqueur *(amaro or digestivo)* rounds off the meal *(see p309).* You may want to skip the first course, or prefer to choose a salad or vegetable dish. Pasta alone is not seen traditionally as a full meal.

Opening Times

Restaurants are generally open from about noon to 3pm and from 8pm to 11pm or later. The busiest times tend to be 9pm–9:30pm for dinner and 1pm–1:30pm at lunchtime. Dinner is generally the preferred time for relaxed eating, particularly in summer. Bars are open all day, often from the early hours, serving all kinds of drinks (alcohol can be sold at any time of day) and snacks. The quietest month is August, when many restaurant owners take their annual vacation (shown by *chiuso per ferie* signs).

Making Reservations

Reservations *(prenotazione)* are generally advisable. Sunday is the main lunchtime of the week

One of many Trastevere cafés

Outdoor café life in the piazza outside Santa Maria in Trastevere

when you should definitely book; the same usually goes for Saturday evening. Check the weekly closing day if you do not book. Many places are closed on Mondays, and Sunday evening can also be difficult.

In summer, try to reserve a shady table outside, since air conditioning is not universal.

Wheelchair Access

Rome is becoming more solicitous toward those in wheelchairs, but a call to the restaurant in advance will help secure the right table.

Taking Children Along

Children are made very welcome, particularly in family-run places. You can usually order half-portions, or just ask for an extra plate. High chairs *(seggioloni)* may also be available.

Smoking

Smoking is banned in restaurants, bars, and cafés.

Recommended Restaurants

Every area of Rome has its own culinary delights *(see Flavors of Rome pp306–7).* Our restaurants are divided into five geographical areas: Ancient Rome, Central Rome, Spagna, Veneto and Around, Trastevere and Around, and Farther Afield. Ancient Rome begins near the Forum, stretching past the Colosseum to encompass Testaccio, the Aventine Hill, the Lateran and the Esquiline Hill (where Termini station is found). Central Rome is the very heart of town, from

Piazza Navona and the Pantheon down to the river, including Campo de' Fiori and the Jewish Ghetto. Spagna, Veneto, and Around covers the heavily-trafficked areas from Piazza del Popolo to Piazza Barberini, as well as the Quirinal Hill and the gastronomically rich neighborhood of Monti. Trastevere and Around includes the Vatican and the foothills of the Janiculum as well. Farther Afield covers anything from areas just outside the downtown, like Monteverde and Parioli, to nearby cities Tivoli, and Fiumicino.

Each restaurant listed is given a cuisine category. Traditional Roman cuisine is hearty and meat-based, although vegetarian dishes do exist. Modern Italian restaurants use traditional recipes as a springboard to create new and modern dishes using unexpected ingredients. Every Italian region has its own local cuisine, and they vary drastically. Opt for a regional Italian restaurant to sample these varieties. Pizzerias abound, but keep in mind that some serve a range of other dishes, while others offer nothing but the beloved dough. The *enotecas* and *birrerias* listed offer food to go with drinks, from cheese platters to full meals. For an extraordinary meal, try a fine dining option, but be prepared for a hefty bill. Rome's international restaurants are great when pasta and pizza begin to get old.

Throughout our listings, we've marked recommended restaurants as DK Choice. We've highlighted these because they offer a special experience – either for the superb cusine, for enjoying a particularly Italian night out, for the excellent value, or a combination of these.

The Flavors of Rome

There are few more enduring pleasures than lingering over a leisurely alfresco meal in a piazza in the Eternal City. Roman food is tasty, nutritious, simple, and extremely varied. Menus tend to be seasonal, and there are even specialties eaten on specific days of the week. Traditionally, Thursday is *gnocchi* day, Friday is for salted cod *(baccalà)*, and Saturday for tripe. Food is redolent of aromatic herbs, olive oil, garlic, and onions, and there are many signature dishes, including pasta. But much authentic Roman cuisine is based on organ meats, and slow, inventive cooking transforms these tradtionally "poor" cuts into rich and flavorsome dishes.

Olives and olive oil

Pasta being made by hand in traditional style

Cucina Romana

Traditional Roman cuisine originated in the Testaccio area, near the old slaughterhouse, whose butchers *(vaccinari)* were paid partly in cash and partly in variety meats. The "fifth quarter" *(quinto quarto)* included head, trotters, tail, intestines, brain, and other unmentionable parts of the beast, which, when carefully cooked and richly flavored with herbs and spices, are transformed into culinary delight. These robust dishes, such as *coda alla vaccinara* (literally, "oxtail cooked in the style of the slaughterhouse butcher") still feature on the menus of many of Rome's top restaurants.

For more squeamish carnivores, lamb is popular, often served simply roasted. Veal is another specialty, as is piglet flavored with herbs. Authentic *cucina romana* also has roots in the Jewish cuisine of the Ghetto area. Local globe artichokes are fried whole in olive oil *(carciofi alla giudia)* or served *alla romana*, with oil, garlic, and Roman mint. Zucchini flowers are also deep-fried, as are Jewish-style salt cod fillets *(filetti di baccalà)*.

Seafood and fish restaurants are among the best in Rome,

Marinated artichokes · Roast peppers · Sun-dried tomatoes · Sweet baby peppers · Olives · Marinated mushrooms

Selection of delicious, typically Roman *antipasti* (appetizers)

Regional Dishes and Specialties

As an appetizer, *bruschetta* (Roman dialect for "lightly burned bread") may be topped with a selection of intense flavors. Other *antipasti* include crispy-fried or marinated vegetables. A favorite pasta dish is *bucatini all'amatriciana* – pasta tubes in a spicy tomato, and sausage or bacon sauce, sprinkled with grated tangy pecorino cheese. Veal is a great favorite and delicacies include *rigatoni alla pajata* (pasta with milk-fed veal intestines). Lamb is also very popular, in dishes such as *abbacchio al forno* (roasted milk-fed lamb) or *alla cacciatora* ("huntsman's style" with anchovy sauce). The word for organ meats is *animelle* (or *interiora*), and Roman delicacies include *cervella* (calves' brains), *pajata* (veal intestines), and *trippa* (tripe).

Bruschetta

Supplì These tasty fried rice croquettes are stuffed with mozzarella cheese that oozes out when they are cut.

Selecting fresh vegetables at a market in central Rome

La Dolce Vita

For those with a taste for "the sweet life," nuts, fruits, and versatile ricotta cheese are often combined in mouthwatering delicious sweets. Ice cream is an art form in Rome, where some parlors offer over 100 flavors of homemade *gelati*. Types vary from the classic *crema*, and *frutta* to *grattachecca* (water ice), from *semifreddo* (a half-frozen sponge cake, similar to *tiramisù* in consistency) to *granita* (ice shavings flavored with fruit syrups). Glorious *gelato* is one of the great pleasures here, to be enjoyed at any time of the day – or night.

although they can be very expensive. Everything is available, from sumptuous seafood platters to small fish caught off the Lazio coast, and served fried or used in soups, as well as superb sea bass cooked Roman-style with porcini mushrooms.

Pasta, Pasta

Pasta is the mainstay of the Roman meal, especially spaghetti. *Spaghetti alla carbonara*, made with *pancetta* (cured bacon) or *guanciale* (pig's cheek), egg yolks, and cheese, is a classic Roman dish, as is *spaghetti alle vongole*, with clams. Many menus also include *spaghetti cacio e pepe* (with pecorino cheese and pepper) and *bucatini all'amatriciana* (with a spicy tomato and bacon sauce). At a conservative estimate, there is

one type of pasta for every day of the year. Many have wonderfully descriptive or poetic names, such as *capelli d'angelo* (angel's hair), *strozzapreti* (priest chokers), or *ziti* (bridegrooms), whose shape is best left to the imagination.

Huge wheels of pecorino cheese ready to be cut and enjoyed

On the Menu

Abbacchio alla cacciatora Lamb simmered in Castelli Romani wine with anchovies, garlic, rosemary, and olive oil.

Bruschetta Toasted bread rubbed with garlic, drizzled with olive oil, may be served with a variety of toppings.

Gnocchi alla romana Little semolina dumplings served with a tomato or *ragù* sauce, or just with butter.

Pecorino romano The traditional Roman cheese, made from ewe's milk.

Spigola alla romana Sea bass with *porcini* mushrooms, shallots, garlic, Castelli Romani wine, and olive oil.

Spaghetti alla carbonara The creamy sauce thickens as the hot pasta mixes into the egg yolks and cheese.

Saltimbocca alla romana Veal slices are rolled with prosciutto and sage. Saltimbocca means "jump in the mouth."

Crostata di ricotta This rich, baked cheesecake is made using ricotta and flavored with Marsala and lemon.

What to Drink in Rome

Italy is one of Europe's most significant wine-producing countries, keeping up a tradition started in the hills around Rome over 2,000 years ago. Today, wine is usually drunk with meals as a matter of course, and knowing the difference between *rosso* (red) and *bianco* (white) may be all the vocabulary you need to get by. Beer is widely available, too, as well as good ranges of apéritifs and digestifs. Rome's drinking water, another debt to the ancient Romans, is particularly good, fresh, and sweet, and in abundant supply.

The vineyards of Frascati, southeast of Rome

Orvieto   Frascati

White Wine

Vines thrive in the warm climate of Lazio, the region around Rome, producing abundant supplies of inexpensive dry white wine for the city's cafés and restaurants. It is usually sold by the carafe. Of local bottled wines, Frascati is the best-known, but Castelli Romani, Marino, Colli Albani, and Velletri are very similar in style. All are made from one grape variety, the Trebbiano, though better-quality versions contain a dash of Malvasia for perfume and flavor. Other central Italian whites worth trying are Orvieto and Verdicchio. Quality white wines from all over Italy, including fine whites from Friuli in the northeast, are widely available in Rome.

Calcaia comes from Barberani, a reliable producer of Orvieto.

Bigi produces good-quality Orvieto, especially the single-vineyard Torricella.

Casal Pilozzo is an easy-drinking white wine from Frascati producers Colli di Catone. Choose the youngest vintage.

Colle Gaio, with its rich, fruity flavor, stands out among the dry white Frascatis.

Wine Type	Good Vintages	Good Producers
White Wine		
Friuli (Pinot Bianco, Chardonnay, Pinot Grigio, Sauvignon)	The most recent	Gravner, Jermann, Puiatti, Schiopetto, Volpe Pasini
Orvieto/ Orvieto Classico	The most recent	Antinori, Barberani, Bigi, Il Palazzone
Red Wine		
Chianti/ Chianti Classico/ Chianti Rufina	2007, 2006, 2001, 2000, 99, 97, 95, 90, 88, 85	Antinori, Castello di Ama, Castello di Cacchiano, Castello di Volpaia, Felsina Berardenga, Fontodi, Frescobaldi, Isole e Olena, Il Palazzino, Riecine, Rocca delle Macie, Ruffino, Vecchie Terre di Montefili, Villa Cafaggio
Brunello di Montalcino/ Vino Nobile di Montepulciano	2007, 2004, 2001, 99, 97, 95, 90, 88, 85	Altesino, Avignonesi, Biondi Santi, Caparzo, Case Basse, Lisini, Il Poggione, Poliziano, Villa Banfi
Barolo/Barbaresco	2006, 2004, 2000, 99, 98, 97, 95, 90, 89, 88	Aldo Conterno, Altare, Ceretto, Clerico, Gaja, Giacomo Conterno, Giacosa, Mascarello, Ratti, Voerzio

Red Wine

Though some local red wine is made, most of the bottled red wine in Rome comes from other parts of Italy. Regions like Tuscany, and Piedmont produce very good everyday drinking as well as top-class wines like Barolo. Price should reflect quality – try Dolcetto, Rosso di Montalcino, or Montepulciano for good-value reds.

Tuscan table wine   Barolo

Montepulciano d'Abruzzo, a rich and juicy red wine, is always a good buy. It is produced in the Abruzzi region east of Rome.

Chianti Classico Riserva is older and stronger than a normal Chianti Classico.

Torre Ercolana is produced in small quantities, and is generally regarded as one of Lazio's best red wines. It is made from Cesanese, and Cabernet grapes and requires at least five years' aging.

Reading the Label

Italy has a two-tier system for labeling quality wine. DOC *(denominazione di origine controllata)* means you can be sure the wine is from the region declared on the label and is made from designated grape varieties. A higher classification – DOCG *(denominazione di origine controllata e garantita)* – is given to top wines such as the reds Barolo, Barbaresco, Chianti Classico, and Brunello di Montalcino.

Chianti Classico

Apéritifs and Other Drinks

Bitter, herb-flavored drinks like Martini, Campari, or Aperol are the most popular apéritifs. (Ask for an *analcolico* if you prefer a non-alcoholic one.) Italians drink their apéritifs straight or with ice and soda. Strong after-dinner drinks, known as *digestivi* or *amari*, are worth trying, as is aniseed *sambuca*, served with coffee beans. Italian brandy, and grappa can be very fiery, and Italian beer is made in lager style.

Campari

Drinking Water

Unlike many Mediterranean cities, Rome benefits from a constant supply of fresh drinking water, piped down from the hills through a system of pipes, and aqueducts that has changed little from ancient Roman times. Only if there is a sign saying *acqua non potabile* is the water not safe to drink.

One of Rome's many fresh water drinking fountains

Soft Drinks

Italian fruit juices are good, and most bars squeeze fresh orange juice *(spremuta di arancia)* on the spot. Iced coffee, and fruit-flavored tea, such as peach, are popular.

Refrigerated storage for wine and beer

Coffee is almost more important to Roman life than wine. Choose espresso for strong black coffee at any time of day; milky cappuccino for breakfast or mid-afternoon; and caffè latte for extra milk.

Espresso

Cappuccino

Caffè latte

Where to Eat and Drink

Ancient Rome

0,75   €
Enoteca   **Map** 8 E1
Via dei Cerchi 65,
00186
Tel *06-687 5706*
Named for the size of a bottle
of wine, this friendly *enoteca*
offers a meal at almost any
time of day.

Angelina a Testaccio   €
Traditional Roman   **Map** 8 D4
Via Galvani 24a, 00153
Tel *06-5728 3840*
The gem of Testaccio, this
shabby-chic bistro offers
a tempting Sunday brunch.

Asmara   €
Ethiopian/Eritrean   **Map** 6 D2
Via Cernaia 36, 00185
Tel *06-481 4409*
A surprising combination
of flavors enliven the mostly
meat-based dishes; many
vegetarian options are
also available. Asmara has
a lively atmosphere.

Bibenda   €
Enoteca   **Map** 9 A1
Via Capo d'Africa 21,
00184
Tel *06-7720 6673*
The official wine bar of Rome's
most important sommelier
academy, Bibenda also offers a
wide selection of tasty snacks to
pair with white or red.

Da Oio a Casa Mia   €
Traditional Roman   **Map** 8 D3
Via Galvani 43,
00153
Tel *06-578 2680*
Friendly though unrefined
service at this family-style
restaurant serving traditional
Roman recipes. Do not miss the
lip-smacking oxtail stew.

Da Remo   €
Pizzeria   **Map** 8 D3
Piazza di Santa Maria
Liberatrice 44, 00153
Tel *06-574 6270*
Thin, crispy pizzas baked in
a wood-burning oven, plus
plenty of fried appetizers, are
offered here. Arrive early to
avoid the long lines.

Felice a Testaccio   €
Traditional Roman   **Map** 8 D3
Via Mastro Giorgio 29,
00153
Tel *06-574 6800*
Black-and-white checkered
floors and exposed brickwork
make a charming setting.
Roman cuisine, including plenty
of organ meat, is offered.

Hang Zhou   €
Chinese   **Map** 6 E5
Via Principe Eugenio 82,
00184
Tel *06-487 2732*
This is unanimously touted as
serving the best Chinese food
in town. The-all-you-can-eat
buffet is a steal, but generally
prices are higher than average.

I Clementini   €
Traditional Roman   **Map** 9 B1
Via di San Giovanni in
Laterano 106, 00184
Tel *06-4542 6395*
The chefs at this simple,
authentic, and traditional
restaurant take pride in using
their grandmothers' recipes.

Price Guide
Prices are based on a three-course meal
per person, with a half-bottle of house
wine, including tax and service.

€	under €40
€€	€40 to 75
€€€	over €75

Il Pentagrappolo   €
Enoteca   **Map** 9 A1
Via Celimontana 21b, 00184
Tel *06-709 6301*
A modern wine bar,
Il Pentagrappolo serves both
creative snacks and full
meals. Live jazz on most
weekend nights.

La Gallina Bianca   €
Pizzeria   **Map** 6 D4
Via Antonio Rosmini 9,
00184
Tel *06-474 3777*
Excellent pizza and much
more at this casual restaurant
with country-style decor. Do
not miss the tempting homemade desserts.

La Taverna dei 40   €
Traditional Roman   **Map** 9 A1
Via Claudia 24,
00184
Tel *06-700 0550*
Family-run establishment
serving classic Roman dishes.
Sit outside to see the
Colosseum in the distance.

Oasi della Birra   €
Birreria   **Map** 8 D3
Piazza Testaccio 39,
00153
Tel *06-574 6122*
The name says it all – this beer
oasis starts serving drinks and
food in the early afternoon, and
no guest leaves thirsty.

The bar area at 0,75, a trendy *enoteca*

Trattoria Monti €
Traditional Roman   **Map** 6 D4
Via di San Vito 13a,
00185
Tel *06-446 6573*
The daily specials at this
heavenly *trattoria* feature
seasonal ingredients that
are explained to guests in
detail by the brothers who
own the place.

Charly's Saucière €€
French-Swiss   **Map** 9 B1
Via di San Giovanni in
Laterano 270, 00184
Tel *06-7049 5666*
Hearty soups, warming au
gratin dishes, and fondue are a
few of the specialties available at
this popular restaurant.

Checchino dal 1887 €€
Traditional Roman   **Map** 8 D4
Via di Monte Testaccio 30,
00153
Tel *06-574 3816*
Hearty Roman dishes, lovingly
prepared, make Checchino dal
1887 a favorite spot for
discerning diners.

Da Danilo €€
Traditional Roman   **Map** 6 E5
Via Petrarca 13,
00185
Tel *06-7720 0111*
Typical Roman dishes are served
at this homey *trattoria* run by
mother and son. Also boasts
an impressive list of
artisanal beers.

Enoteca Provincia Romana €€
Enoteca   **Map** 5 B5
Largo di Foro Traiano 82-84,
00187
Tel *06-6994 0273*
Both the wine list and the
menu ingredients are
refreshingly local at this *enoteca*,
sponsored by the province
of Rome.

Flavio al Velavevodetto €€
Traditional Roman   **Map** 8 D4
Via di Monte Testaccio 97,
00153
Tel *06-574 4194*
Simple and satisfying Roman
pasta and meat dishes, plus a
few seafood options, all at
reasonable prices. Lots of
outdoor seating space in
good weather.

Maud €€
Modern Italian   **Map** 9 A1
Via Capo d'Africa 6,
00184
Tel *06-8956 2910*
Maud is a great choice for both
a creatively prepared meal and

Seating at the well-reviewed Checchino dal 1887

an after-dinner drink. Sleek,
modern decor, and useful for
people-watching.

Perilli €€
Traditional Roman   **Map** 8 D3
Via Marmorata 39,
00153
Tel *06-575 5100*
Generous portions of Roman
favorites are served here.
Authentic food, although the
prices are a bit high.

Tempio di Iside €€
Seafood   **Map** 9 B1
Via Labicana 50, 00184
Tel *06-700 4741*
Fish of all kinds, much of it raw,
including several varieties of
oysters. Romantic, candlelit
interior with exposed brickwork.

Trimani il Wine Bar €€
Enoteca   **Map** 6 D2
Via Cernaia 37b,
00185
Tel *06-446 9630*

Vibrant interior at the stellar
Agata e Romeo

Modern wine bar with a vast
selection of labels perfectly
paired with cold and hot
dishes, as well as a range of
Italian cheeses.

Agata e Romeo €€€
Fine Dining   **Map** 6 D4
Via Carlo Alberto 45,
00185
Tel *06-446 6115*
High-end dining with exceptional
taster menus. Even traditional
recipes have a sophisticated
twist. Cavernous wine cellar.

Aroma €€€
Fine Dining   **Map** 9 A1
Via Labicana 125,
00184
Tel *06-7759 1380*
A well-reviewed restaurant
with sleek interiors and
unequaled views of the
Colosseum. Seasonal menu
with regional favorites.

Central Rome

Acchiappafantasmi €
Pizzeria   **Map** 11 B3
Via dei Cappellari 66,
00186
Tel *06-687 3462*
This pizzeria, whose name means
"Ghostbusters," serves tasty and
crunchy ghost-shaped pizzas.

Baffetto €
Pizzeria   **Map** 11 C3
Via del Governo Vecchio
114, 00186
Tel *06-686 1617*
The thin, crisp Roman-style pizza
served here is considered by
many to be the best in Rome. Be
prepared for a long wait.

For more information on types of restaurants *see p304*

Diners at the cozy Nonna Betta, known for its authentic Jewish cuisine

Ba'Ghetto Milky €
Traditional Roman   Map 12 D5
Via Portico D'Ottavia 57,
00186
Tel *06-6830 0077*
Heavenly Jewish-Roman cuisine
served strictly kosher; only
vegetarian fare is available.
There is outdoor seating on a
bustling pedestrian street.

Cantina e Cucina €
Traditional Roman   Map 11 B3
Via del Governo Vecchio 87,
00186
Tel *06-689 2574*
You can rely on this *trattoria* to
provide a selection of all-time
favorites, such as *spaghetti alla
carbonara* with artichokes,
accompanied by great wines.

Capricci Siciliani €
Regional Italian   Map 11 B2
Via di Panico 83,
00186
Tel *06-4543 3823*
Elegant Sicilian food is served in
the heart of the historic city.
Specialties include swordfish
medallions and anchovy rolls.

Cul de Sac €
Enoteca   Map 11 C3
Piazza di Pasquino 73,
00186
Tel *06-6880 1094*
This narrow wine bar boasts
hundreds of labels as well as a
wide variety of tasty eats.

Da Pancrazio €
Traditional Roman   Map 11 C4
Piazza del Biscione 92,
00186
Tel *06-686 1246*
Dine here for a slice of history:
Da Pancrazio is set above the
ruins of Pompey's 1st-century
BC theater. Lovingly prepared
traditional Roman recipes
are offered.

Enoteca il Goccetto €
Enoteca   Map 11 B3
Via dei Banchi Vecchi 14,
00186
Tel *06-686 4268*
A casual wine bar that serves
top-quality bottles at fair prices;
delicious snacks are also
available. Popular with locals.

Enoteca il Piccolo €
Enoteca   Map 11 C3
Via del Governo Vecchio 74,
00186
Tel *06-6880 1746*
This tiny wine bar spills out onto
a busy piazza and boasts an
ample selection of Italian labels
at great prices.

Il Corallo €
Traditional Roman   Map 11 B3
Via del Corallo 10, 00186
Tel *06-6830 7703*
Located on a charming street,
simple yet imaginative dishes
are served by friendly staff. The
wine list is impressive.

DK Choice

Nonna Betta €
Traditional Roman   Map 12 D5
Via Portico d'Ottavia 16,
00186
Tel *06-6880 6263*
An authentic kosher restaurant
in the heart of the Jewish
quarter, the renowned
Nonna Betta specializes in
delectable Jewish-Roman
cuisine. The fried mozzarella
balls are highly recommended.
The ambience is warm
and cozy.

Old Bear €
Regional Italian   Map 11 C2
Via dei Gigli d'Oro 2–4,
00186
Tel *06-6821 0009*

Dark wood beams and low
ceilings create a warm, inviting
ambience. The Tuscan soup with
truffle oil is recommended.

Open Baladin €
Birreria   Map 11 C5
Via degli Specchi 6,
00186
Tel *06-683 8989*
Over 120 labels of craft beers,
as well as original all-natural
sodas, are available.

Osteria del Gallo €
Traditional Roman   Map 11 C2
Vicolo di Montevecchio 27,
00186
Tel *06-687 3781*
Classic Roman dishes and tasty
seafood options are served at
this informal spot with plenty
of outdoor seating on a
secluded piazza.

Osteria del Sostegno €
Modern Italian   Map 12 D2
Via delle Colonnelle 5, 00186
Tel *06-679 3842*
Tucked away in a tiny alley,
this charming little restaurant
creates inventive versions of
classic Roman recipes.

Pantha Rei €
Traditional Italian   Map 12 D3
Via della Minerva 19, 00186
Tel *06-8902 1922*
Traditional culinary flair is
combined with a romantic
atmosphere at Pantha Rei. The
menu includes a selection of
carpaccios and cooked scamorza
cheese dishes.

Polese €
Traditional Roman   Map 11 B3
Piazza Sforza Cesarini 40,
00186
Tel *06-686 1709*
Authentic traditional recipes
are served with a smile here.

Outdoor seating on a large square ensures a table even on a busy night.

Sora Margherita €
Traditional Roman **Map** 12 D5
Piazza delle Cinque Scole 30, 00186
Tel *06-687 4216*
This simple and authentic eatery whips up classic Italian fare. Do not expect English translations on the handwritten menu.

Vinando €
Enoteca **Map** 12 E4
Piazza Margana 23, 00186
Tel *06-6920 0741*
Great vegetarian options, as well as meat and fish dishes, are served at this chic wine bar. Open all day.

Vino e Camino €
Regional Italian **Map** 11 A2
Piazza dell'Oro 6, 00186
Tel *06-6830 1332*
Wine bottles line the walls and there is a working fireplace at this cozy restaurant with lovingly prepared food and excellent wine.

Al Duello €€
Traditional Roman **Map** 12 D2
Vicolo della Vaccarella 11, 00186
Tel *06-687 3348*
Hearty Roman fare is served in this *trattoria* named for the infamous duel in which the painter Caravaggio (1571–1610) killed his opponent.

Angolo Divino €€
Enoteca **Map** 11 C4
Via dei Balestrari 12, 00186
Tel *06-686 4413*
An intimate and romantic restaurant with an impressive wine list. Try the divine warm chocolate cake.

Armando al Pantheon €€
Traditional Roman **Map** 12 D3
Salita i Crescenzi 31, 00186
Tel *06-6880 3034*
Two brothers own and run this typical Roman *trattoria*. Classic dishes and some interesting vegetarian options available.

Camponeschi €€
Fine Dining **Map** 11 C4
Piazza Farnese 50/50a, 00186
Tel *06-687 4927*
World-class dining in the heart of the city. Try the tagliolini with lobster and black truffles. Wild game is the house specialty.

Casa Bleve €€
Enoteca **Map** 12 D3
Via del Teatro Valle 48, 00186
Tel *06-686 5970*
Vaulted ceilings and ceramic-tiled floors add a sense of occasion to any meal at this sophisticated wine bar. Ample buffet lunch.

Clemente alla Maddalena €€
Modern Italian **Map** 12 D2
Piazza della Maddalena 4, 00186
Tel *06-683 3633*
Imaginative takes on cuisines from all over Italy. Outdoor seating in a lovely square.

Da Giggetto €€
Traditional Roman **Map** 12 E5
Via Portico d'Ottavia 21/22, 00186
Tel *06-686 1105*
Dine in the shadow of ancient ruins at this famous Jewish-Roman eatery. The deep-fried artichokes are delectable.

Enoteca Capranica €€
Enoteca **Map** 12 D2
Piazza Capranica 99, 00186
Tel *06-6994 0992*
Numerous bottles line the walls of this large yet cozy wine bar. Mouthwatering dishes pair with excellent wines.

Convivial atmosphere at the popular Jewish-Roman Da Giggetto

Il Bacaro €€
Modern Italian **Map** 12 D2
Via degli Spagnoli 27, 00186
Tel *06-687 2554*
Specialties at this romantic and centrally located restaurant include the *trofie* with asparagus or beef *carpaccio* with chicory and truffles.

Il Convivio-Troiani €€
Fine Dining **Map** 11 C2
Vicolo dei Soldati 31, 00186
Tel *06-686 9432*
This elegant restaurant takes pride in its handmade products, from bread to pasta. Exquisite wine list.

Il Sanlorenzo €€
Seafood **Map** 11 C4
Via dei Chiavari 4, 00186
Tel *06-686 5097*
Pricy, but worth it for some of the best seafood in town. Try the tasting menu to make your money go farther.

DK Choice

La Pallacorda €€
Seafood **Map** 12 D1
Piazza Cardelli 5, 00186
Tel *06-683 4026*
This sophisticated restaurant excels at seafood dishes with a touch of imagination. Oysters are the house specialty and several varieties are available here, while the generous antipasto buffet boasts delicacies such as salmon tartare. Many pasta options are also on the menu, in addition to excellent desserts. A miniature chocolate cake with a liquid center makes the perfect end to a memorable meal.

Wine bottles adorning the walls of Enoteca Capranica

For more information on types of restaurants *see p304*

Charming outdoor seating and helpful staff at Piperno

Maccheroni   €€
Traditional Roman   Map 12 D2
Piazza delle Coppelle 44,
00186
Tel *06-6830 7895*
A Roman institution, this large
restaurant relies on tried and
true recipes, served in a rustic
and warm atmosphere by a
jovial staff.

Montevecchio   €€
Traditional Roman   Map 11 C2
Piazza Montevecchio 22/a,
00186
Tel *06-686 1319*
This is a tiny, sophisticated
restaurant where well-heeled
locals converse in hushed tones
over delectable pasta and
meat dishes.

Osteria del Pegno   €€
Traditional Roman   Map 11 C2
Vicolo di Montevecchio 8,
00186
Tel *06-6880 7025*
Small and intimate restaurant
with lovingly prepared staples
of the Roman tradition. A few
more inventive options also
feature on the menu. There is
an ample wine list.

Percento   €€
Modern Italian   Map 11 C4
Via del Pellegrino 160,
00186
Tel *06-6880 9554*
Diners at this modern restaurant
can watch the chefs at work in a
glass-enclosed kitchen while
enjoying the pan-Italian dishes.
The menu has a large selection of
international cheeses.

Pierluigi   €€
Modern Italian   Map 11 B4
Piazza de' Ricci 144,
00186
Tel *06-686 8717*
A sprawling outdoor seating
area in a cobbled piazza
enhances the heavenly and
imaginative inventions that come
out of Pierluigi's kitchen.

Piperno   €€
Traditional Roman   Map 12 D5
Via Monte de' Cenci 9,
00186
Tel *06-6880 6629*
Set in a pretty piazza, this place
serves traditonal Roman cuisine.
Large selection of seafood plus
excellent fried artichokes.

Roscioli   €€
Enoteca   Map 11 C4
Via dei Giubbonari 21,
00186
Tel *06-687 5287*
Roscioli is part wine bar and part
salumeria (delicatessen and
charcuterie). A drool-worthy
selection of meats and cheeses
accompanies a dizzying range
of wine labels.

Sangallo ai Coronari   €€
Modern Italian   Map 11 B2
Via dei Coronari 180,
00186
Tel *06-686 5549*
Time-honored recipes
from Rome and the area
immediately south of the city.
Tempting tasting menu and
helpful sommelier for wine
suggestions.

Settimio al Pellegrino   €€
Traditional Roman   Map 11 B3
Via del Pellegrino 117,
00186
Tel *06-6880 1978*
Knock if the door is closed at
this old-fashioned favorite
with locals. Simple food and
friendly service.

Sora Lella   €€
Traditional Roman   Map 8 D1
Via di Ponte Quattro Capi 16,
00186
Tel *06-686 1601*
Sora Lella has the distinction
of being the only restaurant on
the Isola Tiberina. This historic
trattoria has been in the same
family for generations and serves
lighter versions of Roman recipes.

Terra di Siena   €€
Regional Italian   Map 11 C3
Piazza di Pasquino 77, 00186
Tel *06-6830 7704*
Terra di Siena serves hearty
Tuscan dishes such as Florentine
steak and ribollita soup. Sit in a
cheerful dining room or on the
buzzing piazza.

The Library   €€
Modern Italian   Map 11 C3
Vicolo della Cancelleria 7,
00186
Tel *334 806 1200*
Located on a narrow back street,
this minuscule and romantic spot
has just a handful of tables. Great
wine and first courses.

Vitti   €€
Traditional Roman   Map 12 E1
Piazza di San Lorenzo in
Lucina 33, 00186
Tel *06-687 6304*
In good weather, be sure to
grab a table outside in one
of the most stylish piazzas in
town. The food is basic but the
location makes up for it.

Al Bric   €€€
Fine Dining   Map 11 C4
Via del Pellegrino 51,
00186
Tel *06-687 9533*
An impeccable wine list is
matched by the tempting
creations from the kitchen.
A warm, charming setting.

Hostaria dell'Orso   €€€
Fine Dining   Map 11 C2
Via dei Soldati 25c, 00186
Tel *06-6830 1192*

Intimate interior of the elegant
Al Bric restaurant

Inviting, traditional dining is raised to an art form. This legendary restaurant and nightclub has been welcoming guests for 500 years.

Il Pagliaccio €€€
Fine Dining **Map** 11 A3
*Via dei Banchi Vecchi 129,
00186*
Tel *06-6880 9595*
An unusual blend of pan-Asian and Mediterranean cuisines is offered at Il Pagliaccio. For true gourmands, the tasting menus have up to 12 courses.

La Rosetta €€€
Seafood **Map** 12 D2
Via della Rosetta 8/9, 00186
Tel *06-686 1002*
Top-quality seafood served right in front of the Pantheon. Be sure to reserve an outdoor table at this lovely restaurant.

Spagna, Veneto, and Around

Abruzzi ai SS Apostoli €
Regional Italian **Map** 12 F3
Via del Vaccaro 1, 00187
Tel *06-679 3897*
The wide selection of cold appetizers makes an excellent start to specialties from the Abruzzo region.

Ai Tre Scalini €
Enoteca **Map** 5 B4
Via Panisperna 251, 00184
Tel *06-4890 7495*
One of the hippest wine bars in town. Impressive wines, beers, and savory delicacies.

Antica Birreria Peroni €
Birreria **Map** 12 F3
Via di San Marcello 19, 00187
Tel *06-679 5310*
A casual spot that has been serving beer since 1906. All-Italian beef and pork dishes prepared on the grill.

Babette €
Modern Italian **Map** 4 F1
Via Margutta 1d, 00187
Tel *06-321 1559*
Inspired by the movie *Babette's Feast*, this large and boisterous restaurant whips up unusual versions of popular dishes from around the country. Reservations are recommended at this popular spot.

Baccano €
Modern Italian **Map** 12 F2
Via delle Muratte 23, 00184
Tel *06-6994 1166*

Retro decor dominates at this restaurant serving classic Italian dishes with alternative ingredients. Gourmet burgers and sandwiches are also available.

Cavour 313 €
Enoteca **Map** 5 B5
Via Cavour 313, 00184
Tel *06-678 5496*
Features a wood-paneled wine bar. The staff can help guests select a memorable vintage.

Colline Emiliane €
Regional Italian **Map** 5 B3
Via degli Avignonesi 22, 00187
Tel *06-481 7538*
Elegant *trattoria* serving hearty Bolognese specialties such as handmade tortellini and filling meat dishes.

Gusto €
Pizzeria **Map** 4 F2
Piazza Augusto Imperatore 9, 00186
Tel *06-322 6273*
Gusto has a unique factory-like setting with exposed brick and iron. Serves thick-crusted and chewy Neapolitan-style pizzas.

La Carbonara €
Traditional Roman **Map** 5 B4
Via Panisperna 214, 00184
Tel *06-482 5176*
This welcoming *osteria* serves hearty local fare including the pasta dish it was named for, a Roman favorite.

L'Asino d'Oro €
Regional Italian **Map** 5 B4
Via del Boschetto 73, 00184
Tel *06-4891 3832*
A reincarnation of a famous *trattoria* in Orvieto. Serves Umbrian specialties as well as Roman classics. Dishes are creative and tasty.

San Marco €
Pizzeria **Map** 5 C1
Via Sardegna 38D, 00187
Tel *06-4201 2620*
Also a wine bar and grill, San Marco is noted mostly for its excellent pizzas. The day's specials are listed on the chalkboard-covered walls.

Tati' al 28 €
Enoteca **Map** 4 F2
Piazza Augusto Imperatore 28, 00030
Tel *06-6813 4221*
Chic wine bar that also serves cocktails, tea, and coffee. Tasty snacks and lots of desserts available as well.

Taverna dei Fori Imperiali €
Traditional Roman **Map** 5 B5
Via della Madonna dei Monti 9, 00184
Tel *06-679 8643*
The whole family pitches in to make this inviting *trattoria* a favorite with locals and visitors alike. The burrata ravioli is simply divine.

DK Choice

Urbana 47 €
Modern Italian
Via Urbana 47, 00184
Tel *06-4788 4006*
This restaurant offers healthy and flavorful meals. Vintage furniture combined with designer pieces creates a funky and eclectic setting to enjoy local, seasonal, high-quality food at very reasonable prices. The menu is created by Michelin-starred chefs. Live music on weekends.

Exposed brickwork and subtle lighting at Gusto

For more information on types of restaurants *see p304*

Spectacular city views and romantic interiors at Imàgo

Canova-Tadolini Museum
Atelier   €€
Traditional Roman   **Map** 4 F2
Via del Babuino 150/a, 00187
Tel *06-3211 0702*
Dine amid dozens of artworks
at the studio of the legendary
18th-century sculptor Canova.

Cuoco e Camicia   €€
Modern Italian   **Map** 5 C5
Via Monte Polacco 2/4, 00184
Tel *06-8892 2987*
A cheerful eatery that prides
itself on using only the freshest
local ingredients. Interesting
tasting menu.

Doozo   €€
Japanese   **Map** 5 C4
Via Palermo 51, 00184
Tel *06-481 5655*
Courses in origami, a Bonsai
exhibit, and book presentations,
plus mouthwatering sushi,
feature at this restaurant and
Japanese cultural center.

Edoardo   €€
Regional Italian   **Map** 5 C2
Via Lucullo 2, 00187
Tel *06-486 428*
Taste delicious traditional dishes
from the Abruzzo region at this
elegant restaurant. Service is
refined. Live music on weekends.

Gaetano Costa   €€
Fine Dining   **Map** 5 B2
Via di San Basilio 15, 00187
Tel *339 801 8034*
Renowned chef Gaetano Costa
presents his exalted versions of
Italian mainstays at the luxurious
Boscolo Aleph hotel.

Hamasei   €€
Japanese   **Map** 12 F1
Via della Mercede 35/36, 00187
Tel *06-679 2134*

A minimalist black and white
setting with low tables for
authentic Japanese dining.
Ultra-fresh sushi and sashimi.

Il Palazzetto Wine Bar   €€
Traditional Roman   **Map** 5 A2
Vicolo del Bottino 8, 00187
Tel *06-69934 1000*
Sip excellent wine and dig into
classic Roman dishes on the tiny
roof terrace at the top of
the Spanish Steps.

La Campana   €€
Traditional Roman   **Map** 12 D1
Vicolo della Campana 18, 00186
Tel *06-687 5273*
Packed with Romans on any
night of the week, this quaint,
historic eatery dates back nearly
500 years.

Open Colonna   €€
Modern Italian   **Map** 5 B4
Via Milano 9/a, 00184
Tel *06-4782 2641*
Perched above the PalaExpo, this
modern, glassed-in open space
provides an airy setting to enjoy
tempting, creative dishes.

Papà Baccus   €€
Regional Italian   **Map** 5 C1
Via Toscana 36, 00187
Tel *06-4274 2808*
Every product used in this
Tuscan restaurant is selected
from trusted non-industrial
producers. Guaranteed fresh
and organic dishes.

DK Choice

Rhome   €€
Modern Italian   **Map** 4 F2
Piazza Augusto Imperatore 46,
00186
Tel *06-6830 1430*

As its name implies, the
objective of this restaurant is
to make its guests feel at
home. Plush couches and
overstuffed armchairs pull right
up to the table. The dining
experience here gives a whole
new meaning to the term
"comfort food." Carefully
prepared classic dishes mingle
with more daring recipes.

Vineria Il Chianti   €€
Modern Italian   **Map** 12 F2
Via del Lavatore 81, 00187
Tel *06-678 7550*
Elegantly arranged cheese
and salami platters are
followed by creative pan-Italian
appetizers and entrées.

Harry's Bar   €€€
Fine Dining   **Map** 5 B2
Via Veneto 150, 00187
Tel *06-474 2103*
Take a bite of *la dolce vita* at
this iconic bar and café serving
exquisite meals and the famous
Bellini cocktail.

Imàgo   €€€
Fine Dining   **Map** 5 A1
Piazza Trinità dei Monti 6,
00187
Tel *06-6993 4726*
Stellar dining with an exceptional
view from the top of the Spanish
Steps. Chef Apreda serves
creative Italian cuisine.

La Terrazza dell'Eden   €€€
Fine Dining   **Map** 5 B2
Via Ludovisi 49,
00187
Tel *06-4781 2752*
Special culinary events and
sensational tasting menus make
this award-winning rooftop
restaurant a special venue.

Le Jardin de Russie €€€
Fine Dining   Map 4 F1
Via del Babuino 9, 00187
Tel *06-3288 8870*
Delectable Mediterranean dishes served with flair and artistry in a refined and sumptuous setting.

L'Olimpo €€€
Fine Dining   Map 5 B2
Piazza Barberini 23, 00187
Tel *06-48 8931*
Dine high atop the Hotel Bernini Bristol, with its sweeping views of the entire city. Good deals at lunchtime.

Mirabelle €€€
Fine Dining   Map 5 B1
Via di Porta Pinciana 14, 00187
Tel *06-4216 8838*
Impeccable service and a panoramic view at this rooftop restaurant. Imaginative yet subtle Mediterranean dishes.

Osteria Margutta €€€
Modern Italian   Map 5 A2
Via Margutta 82, 00187
Tel *06-323 1025*
Historic restaurant on an idyllic vine-covered street. Serves classic Roman dishes with a modern twist.

Pipero al Rex €€€
Fine Dining   Map 5 C3
Via Torino 149, 00184
Tel *06-481 5702*
Sumptuous and meticulously prepared dishes are served at this magnificent restaurant.

Vivendo €€€
Modern Italian   Map 5 C3
Via Vittorio Emanuele Orlando 3, 00185
Tel *06-4709 2736*

Luxurious decor and fabulous Mediterranean cuisine. Wine tasting in the elegant cellar.

Trastevere and Around

Arian €
Persian   Map 4 D2
Via Tacito 54a, 00193
Tel *06-4544 1122*
Come here for authentic Iranian cuisine in a vibrant atmosphere. Live belly dancing Friday and Saturday night.

Arlù €
Traditional Roman   Map 3 C3
Borgo Pio 135, 00193
Tel *06-686 8936*
The most authentic restaurant in the busy Vatican area. A husband-and-wife team serve up delectable Roman cuisine.

Bir & Fud €
Birreria   Map 11 B5
Via Benedetta 23, 00153
Tel *06-589 4016*
Artisanal beers and microbrews from around Italy; perfect for washing down the crusty pizzas and gourmet potato chips.

Da Benito e Gilberto €
Seafood
Via del Falco 19, 00193
Tel *06-686 7769*
This small and friendly restaurant, run by a father and son, prepares classic pasta dishes and elaborate seafood delicacies.

Da Gildo €
Traditional Roman   Map 7 C1
Via della Scala 31, 00153
Tel *06-580 0733*

Try the simple and divine *gnocchi alla romana*. Quirky decoration and outdoor seating.

Fish Market €
Seafood   Map 7 C2
Vicolo della Luce 2/3, 00153
Tel *366 914 4157*
Choose the fish you like from the counter, tell the staff how you would like it cooked, and pick it up when it's ready. Loud, lively, and fun ambience.

In Vino Veritas €
Enoteca   Map 4 D5
Via Garibaldi 2a, 00153
Tel *06-5833 2012.0.*
A cozy and informal wine bar, with chess and other games in the tiny seating area.

Ivo a Trastevere €
Pizzeria   Map 7 C1
Via di San Francesco a Ripa 158, 00153
Tel *06-581 7082*
Delicious super-thin-crust Roman pizza has this simple eatery bustling with locals and the occasional celebrity.

Lo Scarpone €
Traditional Roman   Map 7 A2
Via di San Pancrazio 15, 00152
Tel *06-5814094*
Nestled in a lush garden with plenty of outdoor seating. The cozy interior has a working fireplace. The menu features lots of meat options.

Meridionale €
Regional Italian   Map 7 C1
Via dei Fienaroli 30a, 00153
Tel *06-589 7196*
Friendly and bright, this delightful restaurant specializes in fresh cuisine from southern Italy. Seafood options are particularly tempting.

Sushi and other Japanese delicacies laid out on a table at Doozo

For more information on types of restaurants *see p304*

Wine cellar at Spirito Divino, located within a 10th-century synagogue

Pizzeria L'Obitorio Panattoni €
Pizzeria   **Map** 7 C1
Viale di Trastevere 53, 00153
Tel *06-580 0919*
This pizzeria is nicknamed "the morgue" for its long marble-topped tables. Try the *supplì al telefono* (fried rice balls).

Rajdhani €
Indian   **Map** 8 D1
Via di Santa Cecilia 8, 00153
Tel *06-581 8508*
Tandoori chicken (cooked in a clay oven) and creamy *tikka masala* (spicy roasted chicken) are the specialties at this friendly spot. The set menu is a particularly good buy.

Roma Sparita €
Traditional Roman   **Map** 8 D1
Piazza di Santa Cecilia 24, 00153
Tel *06-580 0757*
Set in an enviable position in front of a gorgeous church, this traditional spot serves the best *cacio e pepe* (cheese and pepper pasta) in town.

Antica Pesa €€
Fine Dining   **Map** 7 B1
Via Garibaldi 18, 00153
Tel *06-580 9236*
The walls of this decadent restaurant are covered with murals by top international artists. Meals are served in a leafy courtyard in warm weather.

Antico Arco €€
Fine Dining   **Map** 7 A1
Piazzale Aurelio 7, 00152
Tel *06-581 5274*
Truffles, wild strawberries, and other such delights fill the menu. The vast wine list is equally tantalizing.

Da Cesare €€
Traditional Roman   **Map** 4 D2
Via Crescenzio 13, 00193
Tel *06-686 1227*
The owners of this local favorite are dedicated to using only local, seasonal, and non-industrial products.

Da Teo €€
Traditional Roman   **Map** 8 D1
Piazza del Ponziani 7a, 00153
Tel *06-581 8355*
Situated in a charming and quiet piazza, this casual yet elegant spot offers classic local recipes and flavorful marinated dishes.

Il Capriccio €€
Regional Italian   **Map** 7 C2
Via Roma Libera 19, 00153
Tel *06-581 6469*
Every meal can be served gluten-free at this jovial spot known for its traditional Sicilian cuisine. There are traditional music performances on weekends.

DK Choice

Isole di Sicilia €€
Regional Italian   **Map** 7 B1
Via Garibaldi 68, 00153
Tel *06-5833 4212*
This cheerful restaurant dishes up some of the best Sicilian food in town. Inspired by the native cuisine of the tiny islands surrounding Sicily, the elaborate dishes use delectable ingredients such as eggplant, capers, peppers, almonds, basil, and, of course, lots and lots of super-fresh fish. A vast antipasto spread kicks off a memorable meal. There is sidewalk seating on the tree-lined street in good weather.

La Gensola €€
Modern Italian   **Map** 8 D1
Piazza della Gensola 15, 00153
Tel *06-581 6312*
This sweet little *osteria* whips up excellent seafood and offers a surprisingly pleasant take on traditional Roman cuisine.

DK Choice

Spirito Divino €€
Modern Italian   **Map** 8 D1
Via dei Genovesi 31, 00153
Tel *06-589 6689*
An elegant, family-run establishment, housed in a 10th-century synagogue, but thoroughly modernized inside. The owner delights in describing to guests each exquisite dish on the ever-changing menu, while his wife lovingly prepares them in the kitchen. Take a peek into the 2,100-year-old wine cellar.

Taverna Angelica €€
Modern Italian   **Map** 3 C2
Piazza Amerigo Capponi 6, 00193
Tel *06-687 4514*
Creative seafood and meat specialties are popular at this cozy restaurant. The Sunday lunches are superb.

Taverna Trilussa €€
Traditional Roman   **Map** 4 E5
Via del Politeama 23, 00153
Tel *06-581 8918*
This bustling yet elegant spot serves classic Roman recipes, including delicious organ meats. Some pasta dishes are served in the pan they were cooked in.

Velando €€
Modern Italian Map 3 C3
Borgo Vittorio 26, 00193
Tel *06-6880 9955*
A fantastic, little restaurant,
Velando presents modern
takes on well-loved classic
dishes from Rome and beyond.
It pays much attention to detail.

Veranda €€
Fine Dining Map 3 C3
Via della Conciliazione 33, 00193
Tel *06-687 2973*
In a stunning setting inside a
frescoed palace with vaulted
ceilings and low lighting, this
elegant restaurant offers a
selection of finely tuned pasta,
meat, and fish dishes.

Glass €€€
Modern Italian Map 4 E5
Vicolo del Cinque 58, 00153
Tel *06-5833 5903*
This Michelin-starred, sleekly
modern restaurant offers
glorified Mediterranean
cuisine with a dash of
international flavor.

Farther Afield

Brasserie 4:20 €
Birreria Map 7 C3
Via Portuense 82, 00153
Tel *06-5831 0737*
Craft beers from around the world
are meticulously paired with
select dishes, particularly fish.

La Gatta Mangiona €
Pizzeria
Via Federico Ozanam 30, 00152
Tel *06-534 6702*
Creative toppings and daily
specials make this Monteverde
pizzeria popular with locals.

Vivi Bistrot €
International
Via Vitellia 102, 00152
Tel *06-582 7540*
Nestled in the sprawling grounds
of Villa Pamphil, Vivi Bistrot serves

American-style breakfast as well
as picnic options and *aperitivos*
on the grass in summer.

Ambasciata d'Abruzzo €€
Regional Italian Map 2 D3
Via Pietro Tacchini 26, 00197
Tel *06-807 8256*
Traditional Abruzzese dishes,
such as maccheroni with lamb
ragù, mingle with Roman
favorites in a convivial setting.

Avec 55 €€
Modern Italian
*Via Domenico Giuliani 55,
00019, Tivoli*
Tel *07-7431 7243*
A restaurant and culinary work-
shop combined. Chef Raoul Reperi
teaches amateur cooks how to
recreate his gastronomic feats.
The menu changes regularly.

La Sibilla €€
Regional Italian
Via della Sibilla 50, 00019, Tivoli
Tel *07-7433 5281*
Sweeping views of Villa
Gregoriana and Roman ruins
provide an unforgettable setting
for indulging in high-quality
regional cuisine.

DK Choice

Mò Mò Republic €€
Pizzeria
*Piazza Forlanini 10,
00151*
Tel *06-537 3087*
A 19th-century mansion
nestled in a leafy garden is the
setting for this modern and
trendy pizzeria. Oversized
chandeliers and parquet
floors add to the glamorous
ambience, yet prices are
surprisingly affordable. Large
round tables on the massive
terrace make it the perfect spot
for a big group of friends. In
summer, start with *aperitivos* on
the lawn. Pasta, meat, and fish
dishes are also available.

Osteria Flaminio €€
Modern Italian Map 1 B3
Via Flaminia 297, 00196
Tel *06-323 6900*
This restaurant, just north
of downtown, offers a range
of innovative and original
Italian dishes.

Osteria Scaloni €€
Traditional Roman
Via Carlo Mirabello 8, 00195
Tel *06-372 1593*
Simple, local cuisine is taken a
step further with unexpected
ingredients and creative touches
at Osterial Scaloni. The wine list
is excellent.

Bastianelli al Molo €€€
Fine Dining
*Via Torre Clementina 312,
00054, Fiumicino*
Tel *06-650 5358*
A vast terrace overlooking the
Tyrrhenian Sea is the setting for a
memorable meal of the freshest
seafood in Lazio.

DK Choice

La Pergola €€€
Fine Dining
*Via Alberto Cadlolo 101,
00136*
Tel *06-35 091*
Universally recognized as
Rome's finest restaurant, La
Pergola is also the only one to
earn the coveted three Michelin
stars. Chef Heinz Beck dazzles
diners with his exquisite
Mediterranean creations.
Perched atop Monte Mario hill,
the restaurant offers stunning
views of St. Peter's Basilica and
the entire city skyline. The award-
winning wine cellar boasts over
3,000 labels and more than
53,000 bottles, the oldest dating
to 1888. Reserve well in advance.

Oliver Glowig €€€
Fine Dining Map 2 D4
*Via Ulisse Aldrovandi 15,
00197*
Tel *06-321 6126*
This impressive poolside
restaurant serves rich
Mediterranean delicacies such
as scampi with artichoke hearts
and burrata cheese.

Settembrini €€€
Modern Italian
Via Luigi Settembrini 25, 00195
Tel *06-323 2617*
Talented chef Gigi Nastri serves
creative Italian cuisine that is
both well-presented and tasty.
The seafood options are
particularly delectable.

Seating amid bright flowers at Vivi Bistrot

For more information on types of restaurants *see p304*

Light Meals and Drinks

Rome can delight the most demanding gourmet and satisfy the biggest appetite, whatever the hour. An enticing array of *gelaterie, pasticcerie, pizzerie, enoteche, rosticcerie,* and *gastronomie* means that good food and drink are, literally, around the corner.

Hotel breakfasts often aren't very good, and you would be better off starting the day with a genuine Italian breakfast at your local stand-up bar: a cappuccino or latte with a hot *cornetto* (croissant) or *fagottino* (similar to a *pain au chocolat*). If you are in Italy during late winter, when blood-red oranges from Sicily are in season, order a *spremuta,* a freshly squeezed orange juice.

A heavy morning's sightseeing may leave you ready for a coffee or an apéritif in one of Rome's elegant 19th-century bars, followed by lunch at a wine bar or Roman-style fast food joint. Later, enjoy tea in a tearoom or coffee and cakes at a *pasticceria.* Once the sun starts to set, there are many places to sip a drink, linger over ice cream, and ponder another wonderful day in the city.

Pizzerias

Roman *pizzerias* are an obvious choice if you feel like an informal meal: they are noisy, convivial, and great fun. Many, however, open only in the evening. Look for the *forno a legna* (wood-burning oven) sign – electric ovens simply don't produce the same results. In the best *pizzerias* you can sit in view of the vast marble slabs where the *pizzaioli* flatten the dough and whip the pizzas in and out of the oven on long-handled pallets. The turnaround is fast and lines are common, so you may not be encouraged to linger after you have eaten.

The progression is fairly straightforward: you might have a *bruschetta* (toasted tomato or garlic bread) to start with, some *suppli* (fried rice croquettes), or *fiori di zucca* (zucchini flowers in batter, filled with hot mozzarella, and a single anchovy). Alternatively, try the *filetti di baccalà* (battered cod fillets) or perhaps a plate of *cannellini* beans in oil. Follow this with a crisp *calzone* (folded-over pizza) or the classic Roman pizza – round, thin, and crunchy – with a variety of toppings: the basic *margherita* (tomato, mozzarella), *napoletana* (tomato, anchovies, mozzarella), *capricciosa* (ham, artichokes,

eggs, olives) or anything else the *pizzaiolo* fancies. Draft beer or *birra alla spina* is the classic drink, but wine is always available, even if limited in choice and quality. You should expect to pay around €14 a head for a meal.

The most representative Roman *pizzerias,* from all points of view, are **Da Baffetto,** which can be easily found by looking for the line outside, and its offspring, **La Montecarlo. Da Remo** in Testaccio and **Dar Poeta** and **Pizzeria Ivo** in Trastevere, where tables line the road in summer, are also typically Roman. Another place not to be missed is **Panattoni – L'Obitorio,** where a huge variety of customers patiently wait for a sidewalk seat on Viale Trastevere in summer, or clamor for one of the marble-topped tables (which give it its nickname of "the mortuary") inside. For slick interiors and Neapolitan-style (high-rise) pizza, try **'Gusto,** but once again, be prepared to wait in line.

Enoteche

Enoteche or wine bars offer a very fine selection of wines, mainly from Italy, but often from around the world. Usually run by experts eager to share their

knowledge and advise on the best combinations of wine and food, many are simply shops for browsing, and buying wine. Others, such as **Achilli al Parlamento** (see p343) and **L'Angolo Divino** (see p354), offer the traditional *mescita* – wine, and champagne tasting by the glass, accompanied by snacks and canapés. Prices are fairly reasonable: about €3 for a glass on tap, €5 upward for a quality wine or for a *prosecco* or *spumante,* Italian champagne. **La Vineria** (see p342) in Campo de' Fiori is a typical spot for *mescita,* especially at night. Nearby, the beautiful **Il Goccetto,** with original painted ceilings, serves excellent wines and delicious food.

Some of the oldest wine bars are inside historic buildings, such as **Caffè Novecento,** which serves excellent food, mainly vegetarian. The prize for one of the most ancient must go to **La Curia di Bacco,** set in an atmospheric candlelit cave dating back to 70 BC.

For more substantial food for around €15–20 per head, try the bistro- or restaurant-style *enoteche,* open from lunch until late. Particularly recommended are the innovative **Cul de Sac, Trimani** (see p343), **Il Tajut** (serving specialties from Friuli), and **Cavour 313.** Food emporium **'Gusto** (see p343) has a wine bar with a gourmet cheese selection, while the specialty at **Al Bric** is *sarcofage bretone* – beef stroganoff with Barolo and a Jerusalem artichoke. The **Antico Forno Roscioli** is particularly creative, with great dishes such as pasta with *radicchio,* and orange peel and pear pastry with coconut.

Enoteche are often tucked away near famous sights or in unlikely places. **Vinando** is extremely convenient for the Capitol, the Tuscan **Vineria Il Chianti** is near the Trevi Fountain, and **Etablì** is behind Piazza Navona. Over in Testaccio, **Divinare** offers fine labels alongside top quality preserves and chocolate. There are a growing number of wine bars across the river. Crowds at **Enoteca Trastevere** spill on to the sidewalk outside, while **Friends Art Café** is a quieter venue with a reasonable evening menu. When night falls, try the lively **In Vino Veritas Art Bar** at the foot of the Janiculum Hill.

Birrerie

Roman *birrerie* or beer houses had their heyday in the early 1900s, often with sumptuous interiors and abundant stained glass. Although many subsequently closed, thanks to their growing popularity with most Italian teenagers they are today undergoing something of a revival. Many British- and Irish-style pubs have also opened. At German-style beer houses you can still enjoy beer and substantial snacks in traditional wood-paneled rooms. The **Old Bear** pub is a jewel inside a 17th-century convent, with romantic candlelight and excellent food and beer. **Löwenhaus** is bedecked in old oil paintings depicting typical Bavarian scenes, again with low lighting for a mellow evening. The ever-crowded **Antica Birreria Peroni**, serving classic beer-drinkers' fare, is also well worth a visit for its local beer and lovely decor. Attracting Italians and foreigners alike is the lively **Ma Che Siete Venuti a Fà** with its excellent range of well-selected ales. Across the river in Testaccio is the equally charming **L'Oasi della Birra**, which also serves good food. Other beer houses with a great atmosphere, food, and late closing times are **The Fiddler's Elbow**, often with live music, **La Pace del Cervello** (meaning "peace of mind" – or **Trinity College**, a favorite of expatriates and Romans.

Fast Food

The term "fast food" in Rome encompasses a cornucopia of choices. The most prolific establishments are *pizza a taglio* shops where slices of freshly baked pizza are available for €1 or €2 – these are sold by weight. Many of these places also sell spit-roasted chickens (*pollo allo spiedo*), *supplì*, and other fried fare. **Forno La Renella** in Trastevere is one of the finest. Figs and ham or potatoes and rosemary are typical pizza toppings. At **La Pratolina**, near the Vatican, pizza with sausage, potatoes, and truffles is on the menu. **Chagat**, in the Ghetto, prepares tasty kosher food, while **Rosticcerì**, with branches in Testaccio and near Piazza Navona, specializes in classic Roman carry-out with an inventive twist.

Rosticcerie and *gastronomie* also offer roast chicken and potatoes, as well as ready-made pasta dishes, cooked vegetables *sott'olio* (in oil), salads, and desserts – useful for picnics. Many also offer stools and narrow bars where you can devour your purchases on the spot. Near the Vatican are some of the finest, such as **Franchi** (*see p342*) and **Ercoli dal 1928**.

For a sit-down snack, bars with a *tavola calda* (hot table) have a similar selection, especially at lunchtime. One of the best is **Volpetti Più** in Testaccio. For unusual flavor combinations, head to **Pizza, Pere e Gorgonzola** near Piazza del Popolo. In the Galleria Alberto Sordi, opposite the Piazza Colonna, the excellent **Trevi e Tritone** offers hot and cold food until 10pm.

Most *alimentari* (food stores) or *salumerie* (delicatessens) will make you a *panino* (filled roll). Especially delicious are **Lo Zozzone's** hot plain pizza pockets stuffed with choices from the shop's counters, where you can also sip a glass of wine. Try a typical local specialty if you see the sign *porchetta* – whole aromatic roast pig with crackling, sliced into *rosette* (rolls) or thick country-bread sandwiches. A good place to try this is the **Antico Chiosco** in the small park in Viale Carlo Felice, near San Giovanni in Laterano. Alternatively, go to the hole-in-the-wall **Er Buchetto**, where you can sit down in (relative) comfort with a glass of wine.

For a really typical Roman snack, make a late-afternoon detour to **Filetti di Baccalà** serving, as the name suggests, fried cod fillets.

For cheese, go to **Obikà** near the Pantheon. This bar offers a vast choice of fresh buffalo and cow mozzarella; eat it as it should be – unadulterated – or prepared in a variety of creative ways.

Termini now has two good options for those waiting or rushing for trains – the self-service restaurant **Chef Express Gusto** or **Vyta** (*see p342*), which serves up gourmet sandwiches to go.

Bars, Cafés, and Tearooms

Roman bars are the city's lifeline: places to meet, eat, drink, buy milk or coffee, make phone calls, or find a restroom. Some are small, stand-up, basic one-counter bars for grabbing a quick *cornetto* and cappuccino; some may be more luxurious, doubling as a cake shop, ice-cream parlor, tearoom, or *tavola calda*; or a combination of all these. Most open early at about 7:30am and close late, particularly on weekends, at around midnight or 2am. If you sit down you will be served by a waiter and pay for the privilege. At busy times, or at popular bars, the crowds at the counter will be large and you will have to wait your turn. If you choose to stand, you pay for your drink at the register beforehand. A small tip (5 or 10 cents per drink) may increase your chances of speedy service. In summer, tables cover all available outdoor space, and the fight for a place in the shade is never-ending.

Traditionally elegant – and expensive – bars for people-watching are the admirably located **Rosati** and **Doney**, as well as **Caffè Greco**, the 19th-century haunt of artists, writers, and composers (*see p135*), or the carefully restored **La Caffettiera**, near the Pantheon. Other popular, and well-established bars are the **Antico Caffè della Pace** and **Café Romano**; both of these places are great for late-night drinks. **Zodiaco** on Monte Mario pulls in the crowds for its panoramic views, as does **Oppio Café** near the Domus Aurea. For sheer decadence, go to **Stravinsky** at the Hotel de Russie for wonderful martinis or a relaxed cup of coffee.

Tearooms are becoming increasingly popular. **Babington's Tea Rooms** (see p136) on Piazza di Spagna serves an outrageously expensive cup of tea and scones in genteel surroundings, while **Dolci e Doni** is more relaxed. Much better deals can be found at **Il Giardino del Te** and **Makasar**. For serious luxury, you can have a full afternoon tea at the **Grand Bar** in the St. Regis Grand (see p303).

Coffee fiends should try a *gran caffè speciale* at the counters of **Caffè Sant' Eustachio**, or one of Rome's best espressos at **La Tazza d'Oro** (see p106). Less familiar to tourists, however, are the excellent **Antico Caffè del Brasile** (see p343), **Bar del Cappuccino**, **Ciamei**, or **Spinelli**. **Ciampini al Café du Jardin**, with its garden setting and rooftop views, is unbeatable in summer, particularly at the apéritif hour, as is the **Caffè Parnaso** in Parioli. Gradually becoming common in Rome are bookshop cafés – **Caffè la Feltrinelli** and **Biblioteq** are two examples – and museum cafés. The **Caffetteria D'Art al Chiostro del Bramante** is in an art gallery on the upper loggia of a beautiful cloister. The bar at the Capitoline Museums has breathtaking views, if average food, while the café in the **Palazzo delle Esposizioni** (see p166) is open throughout the day with an attractive selection of snacks, and drinks.

Pasticcerie

On Sunday mornings you will often see Romans emerging from the local pastry shop or *pasticceria* with a beautifully wrapped package. This can contain dainty individual pastries, whole cakes or tarts, traditional Easter *colombe* (doves), or the Christmas *panettoni* – huge cakes with raisins and candied citrus peel – all for consumption by large gatherings of friends or family after lunch. The window displays of cake shops are often fantastic. These, and the aroma of brewing coffee, will tempt even those who claim not to have a sweet tooth. The selection is vast, from a hot *cornetto* or *brioche* in the early morning, a midday *pizzetta* or savory tart at lunch, or a choux pastry or fruit tart in the afternoon. **Cipriani** (see p339), open since 1906, has delicious biscuits, ricotta cake, and apple tart. Nearby **Regoli** has wonderful *mille feuilles* and *torta con crema e pinoli* (pine nuts). **Dagnino** prepares hundreds of Sicilian specialties every day, while **Boccione** specializes in traditional Roman-Jewish cakes. As well as cakes, numerous shops offer handmade chocolates. At some, such as **Rivendita di Cioccolata e Vino** (see p350), you can pause over a cup of coffee or glass of wine while deciding which you like best.

Gelaterie

Ice cream (*gelato*) is one of summer's main delights and at Rome's ice-cream parlors, you are certainly in for a lavish treat. Look for the word *artigianale*, if you want to savor the best. The choice is endless – water ices made with a phenomenal variety of fruit; lemon and coffee *granite* (crushed ice); as well as more exotic ice-cream specialties such as rice pudding, *zuppa inglese* (English trifle), *zabaglione*, and *tiramisù*. Choose as many varieties as the size of your cone or cup will hold, ask for an optional topping of cream (*panna*), and go for a sensation-filled stroll. Or take a seat and rest awhile – you will be served an obscenely sized creation at the table (at a price). *Gelaterie* are open all day, many until late at night, and are very much an integral part of Roman socializing. **Tre Scalini** in Piazza Navona is a famous spot for enjoying the pricy, yet so heavenly, chocolate *tartufo* (truffle), while a summer evening in EUR, especially with children, nearly always ends in a trip to **Giolitti**, a historic ice-cream name. The strategically placed, crowded original near the Pantheon deserves at least one visit too. Gourmet fans of *gelato* should not miss **San Crispino**, which offers homemade delicacies made with the best ingredients. Its *zabaglione* is made with 20-year-old barrel-aged Marsala. In summer, try the mouth-watering *susine* (yellow plum) flavor; in winter, the *arancia selvatica* (wild orange) should not be missed.

Adults may prefer to pick their nighttime treat at **Chalet del Lago**, again in EUR, while sitting beside the lake. If you come across a small kiosk with the sign *grattachecche* (most likely in Trastevere, and Testaccio), try one of Rome's oldest traditions: ice grated by a gloved hand on the spot, and enlivened with a variety of classic flavorings. Try **Sora Mirella**, near the Tiber Island.

Everyone has their own favourite flavors, and preferred *gelateria*, but the quest for perfection is an ongoing pleasure. For top *zabaglione*, try **Fiocco di Neve**, **Giolitti** of Via Vespucci, or **Petrini dal 1926**. **Palazzo del Freddo** makes an exceptionally wonderful rice pudding flavor, and its own *La Caterinetta* – one of the secret ingredients is honey. **Al Settimo Gelo**, a witty play on words (*settimo* is seventh, *cielo* is heaven and *gelo* is ice), creates exciting chestnut sorbet, chocolate with *peperoncino*, ginger and ice cream made from Greek yogurt. For those with dairy allergies, visit the Sicilian *gelateria* **Gelarmony**, which also uses soy milk and has 14 different flavors. At **Fior di Luna** in Trastevere, all ingredients are organic. Excellent ingredients also distinguish **Neve di Latte**, located near the MAXXI gallery (see p259), and the more central **GROM**.

DIRECTORY

Capitol

BARS, CAFÉS, AND TEAROOMS

Caffè Capitolino
Piazzale Caffarelli 4.
Map 12 F5.

Piazza della Rotonda

PIZZERIAS

Barroccio
Via dei Pastini 13.
Map 12 D2.

Er Faciolaro
Via dei Pastini 123.
Map 12 D2.

La Sagrestia
Via del Seminario 89.
Map 12 E3.

ENOTECHE

Achilli al Parlamento
Via dei Prefetti 15.
Map 12 D1.

Corsi
Via del Gesù 87/88.
Map 12 E3.

BIRRERIE

Trinity College
Via del Collegio Romano 6. **Map** 12 E3.

FAST FOOD

Obikà
Piazza Firenze 28.
Map 12 D1.

BARS, CAFÉS, AND TEAROOMS

Caffè Sant'Eustachio
Piazza Sant'Eustachio 82.
Map 12 D3.

La Caffettiera
Piazza di Pietra 65.
Map 12 E2.

Ciampini
Piazza S. Lorenzo in Lucina 29. **Map** 12 D1.

La Tazza d'Oro
Via degli Orfani 82/84.
Map 12 D2.

Teichner
Piazza San Lorenzo in Lucina 15–17. **Map** 12 D1.

Vitti
Piazza San Lorenzo in Lucina 33. **Map** 12 E1

GELATERIE

Fiocco di Neve
Via del Pantheon 51.
Map 12 D2.

Giolitti
Via degli Uffici del Vicario 40. **Map** 12 D2.

GROM
Via della Maddalena 30A.
Map 12 D2.

Piazza Navona

PIZZERIAS

Da Baffetto
Via del Governo Vecchio 114. **Map** 11 B3.

Da Francesco
Piazza del Fico 29.
Map 11 B2.

La Montecarlo
Vicolo Savelli 12/13.
Map 11 C3.

ENOTECHE

Caffè Novecento
Via del Governo Vecchio 12. **Map** 11 B3.

Cul de Sac
Piazza Pasquino 73.
Map 11 C3.

Etablì
Vicolo delle Vacche 9A.
Map 11 B2.

Giulio Passami l'Olio
Via di Monte Giordano 28.
Map 11 B2.

Il Piccolo
Via del Governo Vecchio 74–75. **Map** 11 C3.

BIRRERIE

Old Bear
Via dei Gigli d'Oro 62–4.
Map 11 C2.

FAST FOOD

Lo Zozzone
Via del Teatro Pace 32.
Map 11 B3.

BARS, CAFÉS, AND TEAROOMS

Antico Caffè della Pace
Via della Pace 5.
Map 11 C3.

Caffeteria D'Art al Chiostro del Bramante
Via della Pace. **Map** 11 C2.

PASTICCERIE

La Deliziosa
Vicolo Savelli 50.
Map 11 B3.

GELATERIE

Bar Navona
Piazza Navona 67.
Map 11 C3.

Da Quinto
Via di Tor Millina 15.
Map 11 C3.

Tre Scalini
Piazza Navona 28.
Map 11 C3.

Piazza di Spagna

PIZZERIAS

'Gusto Piazza Augusto Imperatore 9. **Map** 4 F2.

PizzaRé
Via di Ripetta 14.
Map 4 F1.

ENOTECHE

Antica Enoteca di Via della Croce
Via della Croce 76B.
Map 5 A2.

Buccone
Via di Ripetta 19.
Map 4 F1.

'Gusto
See Pizzerias.

Il Brillo Parlante
Via della Fontanella 12.
Map 4 F1.

BIRRERIE

Löwenhaus
Via della Fontanella 16B.
Map 4 F1.

FAST FOOD

Difronte A
Via della Croce 38.
Map 4 F2.

Fratelli Fabbi
Via della Croce 27.
Map 4 F2.

Pizza, Pere e Gorgonzola
Via Laurina 7. **Map** 4 F1.

BARS, CAFÉS, AND TEAROOMS

Babington's Tea Rooms
Piazza di Spagna 23.
Map 5 A2.

Café Romano
Via Borgognona 4.
Map 12 E1.

Caffè Greco
Via Condotti 86.
Map 5 A2.

Ciampini al Café du Jardin
Viale Trinità dei Monti.
Map 5 A2.

Dolci e Doni
Via delle Carrozze 85B.
Map 4 F2.

Rosati
Piazza del Popolo 5.
Map 4 F1.

Stravinsky Bar
Hotel de Russie, Via del Babuino 9. **Map** 5 A2.

GELATERIE

Venchi
Via della Croce 25.
Map 5 A2.

Campo de' Fiori

PIZZERIAS

Acchiappafantasmi
Via dei Cappellari 66.
Map 11 B3.

ENOTECHE

Al Bric
Via del Pellegrino 51.
Map 11 B3.

Antico Forno Roscioli
Via dei Giubbonari 21.
Map 11 C4.

La Curia di Bacco
Via del Biscione 79.
Map 11 C4.

Il Goccetto
Via dei Banchi Vecchi 14.
Map 11 B3.

L'Angolo Divino
Via dei Balestrari 12.
Map 11 C4.

Vinando
Piazza Margana 23.
Map 12 E4.

DIRECTORY

La Vineria
Piazza Campo de' Fiori 15.
Map 11 C4.

FAST FOOD

Chagat
Via Santa Maria del Pianto
66. **Map** 12 D5.

Da Benito
Via dei Falegnami 14.
Map 12 D4.

Filetti di Baccalà
Largo dei Librari 88.
Map 11 C4.

**Forno Campo de'
Fiori**
Piazza Campo de' Fiori 22.
Map 11 C4.

Pizza Florida
Via Florida 25. **Map** 12 D4.

**BARS, CAFÉS, AND
TEAROOMS**

Alberto Pica
Via della Seggiola 12.
Map 12 D5.

Bar del Cappuccino
Via Arenula 50.
Map 12 D4.

Bernasconi
Piazza Cairoli 16.
Map 12 D4.

Bibliotèq
Via dei Banchi Vecchi 124.
Map 11 B3.

Caffè la Feltrinelli
Largo Torre Argentina 5.
Map 12 D4.

PASTICCERIE

Boccione
Via del Portico d'Ottavia 1.
Map 12 E5.

La Dolceroma
Via del Portico d'Ottavia
20B. **Map** 12 E5.

GELATERIE

Blue Ice
Via dei Baullari 130 and
141. **Map** 11 C4.

Kosher Gelato
Via del Portico d'Ottavia 3.
Map 12 E5.

Quirinal

PIZZERIAS

Est! Est! Est!
Via Genova 32. **Map** 5 C4.

**Grazie a Dio è
Venerdí**
Via dei Capocci 1.
Map 5 C4.

ENOTECHE

Cavour 313
Via Cavour 313. **Map** 5 B5.

Monti DOC
Via Giovanni Lanza 93.
Map 5 C5.

Vineria Il Chianti
Via del Lavatore 81.
Map 12 F2.

BIRRERIE

The Albert
Via del Traforo 132.
Map 5 B3.

Antica Birreria Peroni
Via San Marcello 19.
Map 12 F3.

FAST FOOD

Er Buchetto
Via Viminale 2. **Map** 5 C3.

Fior di Pizza
Via Milano 33. **Map** 5 B4.

Trevi e Tritone
Galleria Alberto Sordi.
Map 12 E2.

**BARS, CAFÉS, AND
TEAROOMS**

**Antico Caffè del
Brasile**
Via dei Serpenti 23.
Map 5 B4.

La Bottega del Caffè
Piazza della Madonna dei
Monti 5.
Map 5 B5.

Il Giardino del Tè
Via del Boschetto 107.
Map 5 B4.

**Palazzo delle
Esposizioni**
Via Milano 15–17.
Map 5 B4.

Spinelli
Piazza del Viminale 18.
Map 5 C3.

Theatre Café
Largo Magnanapoli 157A.
Map 5 B4.

PASTICCERIE

Dagnino
Galleria Esedra, Via Vittorio
Emanuele Orlando 75.
Map 5 C2.

GELATERIE

San Crispino
Via della Panetteria 42.
Map 12 F2.

Termini

PIZZERIAS

Formula Uno
Via degli Equi 13.
Map 6 F4.

San Marco
Via Sardegna 38D.
Map 5 B1.

ENOTECHE

Enoteca Chirra
Via Torino 132–133.
Map 5 C3.

Trimani
Via Cernaia 37B.
Map 6 D2.

FAST FOOD

Chef Express Gusto
Galleria Termini – Exit Via
Marsala. **Map** 6 D3.

Vyta
Galleria Termini – Exit Via
Marsala. **Map** 6 D3.

Wok
Stazione Termini (Lower
Level). **Map** 6 D3.

**BARS, CAFÉS, AND
TEAROOMS**

Grand Bar
St Regis Grand Via Vittorio
Emanuele Orlando 3.
Map 6 C3.

Esquiline

BIRRERIE

The Fiddler's Elbow
Via dell'Olmata 43.
Map 6 D4.

Old Marconi
Via di Santa Prassede 9C.
Map 6 D4.

FAST FOOD

Panella
Via Merulana 54.
Map 6 D5.

**BARS, CAFÉS, AND
TEAROOMS**

Ciamei
Via Emanuele Filiberto 57.
Map 6 E5.

Oppio Café
Via delle Terme di Tito 72.
Map 5 C5.

PASTICCERIE

Cipriani
Via C. Botta 21. **Map** 6 D5.

Regoli
Via dello Statuto 60.
Map 6 D5.

GELATERIE

Palazzo del Freddo
Via Principe Eugenio
65/67. **Map** 6 E5.

Lateran

BIRRERIE

La Pace del Cervello
Via dei SS Quattro 63.
Map 9 A1.

ENOTECHE

Il Tajut
Via di San Giovanni in
Laterano 244–246.
Map 9 B1.

FAST FOOD

Antico Chiosco
Viale Carlo Felice.
Map 10 D1.

PASTICCERIE

Paci
Via dei Marsi 33. Off
Map 6 F4.

Pompi Tiramisú
Via Albalonga 7–11.
Map 10 D3.

GELATERIE

San Crispino
Via Acaia 56. **Map** 9 C4.

Aventine

PIZZERIAS

Da Remo
Piazza Santa Maria
Liberatrice 44. **Map** 8 D3.

BIRRERIE

L'Oasi della Birra
Piazza Testaccio 41.
Map 8 D3.

ENOTECHE

Divinare
Via Manuzio 13.
Map 8 D3.

FAST FOOD

Farinando
Via Luca della Robbia 30.
Map 8 D3.

Rosticcerì
Corso Rinascimento 83.
Map 11 C2.

Volpetti Più
Via Alessandro Volta 8.
Map 8 D3.

GELATERIE

Café du Parc
Piazza di Porta San Paolo.
Map 8 E4.

Giolitti
Via Vespucci 35.
Map 8 D3.

Trastevere

PIZZERIAS

Da Vittorio
Via di S. Cosimato 14A.
Map 7 C1.

Dar Poeta
Vicolo del Bologna 45.
Map 11 B5.

Panattoni – L'Obitorio
Viale Trastevere 53.
Map 7 C1.

Pizzeria Ivo
Via S. Francesco a Ripa
158. **Map** 7 C1.

ENOTECHE

Ferrara
Via del Moro 1A.
Map 7 C1.

Friends Art Café
Piazza Trilussa 41.
Map 11 B5.

Trastevere
Via della Lungaretta 86.
Map 7 C1.

BIRRERIE

**Ma Che Siete Venuti
a Fà**
Via Benedetta 25.
Map 11 B5.

FAST FOOD

Forno La Renella
Via del Moro 15.
Map 7 C1.

**BARS, CAFÉS, AND
TEAROOMS**

Ombre Rosse
Piazza Sant'Egidio 12.
Map 7 C1.

PASTICCERIE

Innocenti
Via della Luce 21A.
Map 7 C2.

Pasticceria Trastevere
Via Natale del Grande 49.
Map 7 C1.

**Rivendita di
Cioccolata e Vino**
Vicolo del Cinque 11A.
Map 11 B5.

GELATERIE

Fior di Luna
Via della Lungaretta 96.
Map 7 C1.

La Fonte della Salute
Via Cardinale Marmaggi
2–4. **Map** 7 C1.

Sora Mirella
Lungotevere degli
Anguillara (corner with
Ponte Cestio). **Map** 8 D1.

Janiculum

ENOTECHE

**In Vino Veritas
Art Bar**
Via Garibaldi 2A.
Map 11 B5.

Vatican

PIZZERIAS

L'Archetto
Via Germanico 105.
Map 3 C2.

Napul'è
Viale Giulio Cesare 91.
Map 3 C1.

ENOTECHE

Costantini
Piazza Cavour 16.
Map 4 E2.

Del Frate
Via degli Scipioni 118.
Map 3 C1.

Il Pane e Le Rose
Via Quirino Visconti 61A.
Map 4 E2.

BIRRERIE

Cantina Tirolese
Via Vitelleschi 23.
Map 3 C2.

Fonclea
Via Crescenzio 82A.
Map 3 C2

FAST FOOD

Ercoli dal 1928
Via Montello 26.
Off **Map** 1 A5.

Franchi
Via Cola di Rienzo 200.
Map 4 D2.

La Pratolina
Via degli Scipioni 248.
Map 3 C1.

**BARS, CAFÉS, AND
TEAROOMS**

Art Studio Café
Via dei Gracchi 187A.
Map 4 D2.

Faggiani
Via Ferrari 23. **Map** 1 A5.

Makasar
Via Plauto 33. **Map** 3 C3.

PASTICCERIE

Antonini
Via Sabotino 19–29. Just
off **Map** 1 A5.

Gran Caffè Esperia
Lungotevere Mellini 1.
Map 4 E1.

GELATERIE

Al Settimo Gelo
Via Vodice 21A. Just off
Map 1 A5.

Gelarmony
Via Marcantonio Colonna
34. **Map** 4 D1.

Via Veneto

PIZZERIAS

San Marco
Via Sardegna 38D.
Map 5 C1.

**BARS, CAFÉS, AND
TEAROOMS**

Café de Paris
Via Veneto 90.
Map 5 B2.

Cine Caffè
Largo M. Mastroianni 1.
Map 5 B1.

Doney
Via Veneto 141.
Map 5 B2.

EUR

ENOTECHE

La Cave des Amis
Piazzale Ardigò 27–29.

**BARS, CAFÉS, AND
TEAROOMS**

Palombini
Piazzale Adenauer 12.

GELATERIE

Chalet del Lago
Lake, EUR.

Giolitti
Casina dei Tre Laghi, Viale
Oceania 90.

Farther Afield

PIZZERIAS

Al Forno della Soffitta
Via Piave 62. **Map** 6 D1.

La Pantera Rosa
Piazzale del Verano 84. Off
Map 6 F4.

**BARS, CAFÉS, AND
TEAROOMS**

Caffè Parnaso
Piazzale delle Muse 22.
Map 2 E2.

Zodiaco
Viale Parco Mellini 88–92.
Off **Map** 3 A1.

PASTICCERIE

Mondi
Via Flaminia 468. Off
Map 1 A1.

GELATERIE

Neve di Latte
Via L. Poletti 6. **Map** 1 A2.

Petrini dal 1926
Piazza dell'Alberone 16A.
Map 10 F4.

SHOPS AND MARKETS

Rome has been a thriving center for design and cosmopolitan shopping since ancient times. In the heyday of the Empire, the finest craftsmen were drawn to Rome, and artifacts and products of all kinds, including gold, furs, wine, and slaves, were imported from far-flung corners of the Empire to service the needs of the wealthy Roman population. Shopping in Rome today in many ways reflects this diverse tradition. Italian designers have an international reputation for their luxuriously chic style in fashion, knitwear, and leather goods (especially shoes and handbags) as well as in interior design, fabrics, ceramics, and glass. The artisan-craftsman tradition is strong and the love of good design filters through into the smallest items. Rome is not a city for bargains (although there are often better buys here than Florence or Milan), but the joys of window shopping here will offer plenty of compensation.

Best Buys

Leather goods of all kinds, including shoes, and bags, are a strong point. Ready-to-wear Italian designer clothes are not cheap, but they are certainly less expensive than in other countries. Armani jeans are a good example (see p331). You are also likely to find designer lighting fixtures, for example, at lower prices here. Both modern, and traditional Italian ceramics, and handicrafts can be very beautifully made, and, if you have time to wander around the back streets, really unusual and individual gifts can often be found.

Sales

Bargain hunters may like to visit Rome during sale time (saldi), from mid-July to mid-September and the period from just after Christmas to the first week in March. Top designers (see p330) can slash prices by half, but their clothes are still very expensive even then. Good bargains can be found in the young designer-wear shops (see p331) and good-quality small and large shoe sizes are sold off very cheaply. In general, though, sales in Rome tend to offer moderate rather than huge discounts.

Both the original, and the sale price should be marked on each reduced item. Liquidazioni (closing-down sales) are usually genuine and can sometimes be worth investigating. However, other signs in shop windows such as vendite promozionali (special introductory prices) and sconti (discounts) are often only lures to get you into the shop. The sign on the door saying entrata libera means "browsers welcome."

When to Shop

Shops are generally open from 9am to 1pm and from 3:30pm

Antiques at Acanto (see p340)

to 7:30pm (4pm to 8pm in the summer months). Most downtown shops stay open all day from 10am to 7:30pm.

Most shops are closed on Sunday (except just before Christmas). Shops are also closed on Monday morning, apart from most food stores, which close on Thursday afternoons in winter, and Saturday afternoons in high summer.

August brings the city to a virtual standstill as Roman families flee the heat to the sea or the mountains, but this is gradually changing, with Romans taking shorter summer holidays. Most shops close for at least 2 weeks around August 15, the national holiday.

Shopping Etiquette

Apart from a few department stores, most Roman shops are

Flower stalls in Piazza Campo de' Fiori (see p344)

small, specializing in just one field. Browsing at leisure may at first seem daunting if you are used to large shopping centers. Customers will almost always receive better attention if they dress stylishly – the emphasis on *fare una bella figura* (making a good impression) is taken seriously.

Sizes are not always uniform, so it is wise to try clothes on if possible before buying, since refunds and exchanges are not always given.

Stylish leather gloves on display

How to Pay

Most shops accept all the major credit cards, whose signs are displayed in the shop window. Some will also accept foreign currency, though the exchange rate may not be good. When you make a purchase, you are bound by Italian law to leave the shop with a *scontrino fiscale* (receipt). You can try asking for a discount if paying cash, and you may be lucky, though many shops have a *prezzi fissi* (fixed prices) sign.

VAT Exemption

Value Added Tax – VAT (IVA in Italy) – is 21 percent of an item's price. Marked or advertised prices normally include the IVA. It is possible for non–European Union residents to obtain an IVA

refund for individual purchases that exceed €155, but be prepared for a long and bureaucratic process. The simplest method is to shop at a place displaying the "Euro Free Tax" sign. Present your passport when you make your purchase and ask for a tax refund check. On leaving Italy, show your new purchases, and receipts at customs, and get the check stamped. You can then collect your refund at Fiumicino airport by presenting the check at the **Global Blue** desk, where you will be reimbursed.

If you wish to buy something from a shop that is not part of the "Euro Free Tax" program, you must get an Italian customs agent to stamp the vendor's receipt at your departure, showing them the purchased article; then mail the receipt back to the shop, which should send you a refund.

Mercato delle Stampe *(see p344)*

Department Stores and Shopping Centers

Department stores, known as *grandi magazzini*, are few, and far between in Rome, but they tend to have longer opening hours than smaller shops. **La Rinascente**, and **Coin** are good for ready-to-wear clothes for both men, and women, household linens, and sewing notions, and have well-stocked perfume counters. The **Oviesse** and **Upim** chain stores offer moderately priced medium-quality clothes, and a variety of household goods.

Another alternative for the zealous shopper is to head for one of Rome's shopping malls. **Cinecittà Due Centro Commerciale**, built in 1988, offers around 100 shops

Bargains in Via Sannio *(see p345)*

plus bars, banks, and restaurants within easy reach of downtown by Metro (line A to Cinecittà).

DIRECTORY

Shopping

Cinecittà Due Centro Commerciale
Viale Palmiro Togliatti 2.
Tel 06-722 0910.

Coin
Termini Station. **Map** 6 D3.
Tel 06-4782 5909.

Piazzale Appio 7. **Map** 10 D2.
Tel 06-708 0020.

Via Cola di Rienzo 173. **Map** 3 C2.
Tel 06-3600 4298.

Global Blue
Terminal 3, Gate H1 and Terminal 5, Fiumicino airport.
Tel 00800 32 111 111 (toll free).
w global-blue.com

La Rinascente
Galleria Alberto Sordi. **Map** 12 E2.
Tel 06-678 4209.

Piazza Fiume. **Map** 6 D1.
Tel 06-884 1231.

Oviesse
Viale Trastevere 62. **Map** 7 C2.
Tel 06-5833 3633.

Via Appia Nuova 181–5.
Map 10 D2. **Tel** 06-702 3214.

Upim
Circonvallazione Gianicolense 78.
Map 7 A5. **Tel** 06-536 692.

Via Goberti 64. **Map** 6 D4.
Tel 06-446 5579.

One of many designer shops around Piazza di Spagna

Rome's Best: Shopping Streets and Markets

The most interesting shops in Rome are in the oldest part of the city, so shopping is easy to combine with sightseeing. Shops are often housed in medieval or Renaissance buildings, and their window displays can be exquisite. Just like shopkeepers in past centuries, traders tend to specialize in one type of merchandise. Street names often refer to the old tradesmen: locksmiths in Via dei Chiavari, leather jerkin makers in Via dei Giubbonari, and chairs in Via dei Sediari. Today, antiques merchants have taken over from the rosary sellers on Via dei Coronari. The top names in fashion and modern design dominate the Via Condotti area, and the artisan-craftsman tradition is still strong around Campo de' Fiori and Piazza Navona.

Via Cola di Rienzo
Situated close to the Vatican Museums, this long, wide street has the finest food shops and is also good for clothes, books, and gifts.

Via dei Coronari
Art Nouveau and antique collectors will love browsing in the shops that line this charming street just northwest of Piazza Navona. But be prepared for high prices, since most of the items are imported.

Via del Pellegrino
Book and art shops abound here next to working artisans in the historic downtown. Do not miss the mirror-lined alley near Campo de' Fiori.

Via dei Cappellari
This narrow, medieval street is a great place for watching furniture restorers and other artisans plying their trade in the open air.

Piaz
Spa

Pi
d
Ro

Vatican

Piazza
Navona

Janiculum

Can
de' F

Trastevere

Porta Portese
You can buy anything from antiques to a tin whistle at Trastevere's Sunday morning flea market. *(See p345.)*

Via Margutta
Upscale antique shops mix with genteel restaurants on this peaceful, cobbled street.

Via del Babuino
This street is renowned for designer furniture, lighting, and glass, as well as interesting antique and fashion shops.

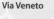

0 meters   500
0 yards   500

Via Veneto

Quirinal

Capitol

Forum

Palatine

Esquiline

Lateran

entine

Caracalla

VIA DELLA CROCE
D&G
VIA
VIA MARIO DE' FIORI
Missoni
Prada
PIAZZA DI SPAGNA
VIA DELLE CARROZZE
Giorgio Armani
BOCCA
Gucci
Trussardi
CONDOTTI DI LEONE
Valentino
PIAZZA MIGNANELLI
VIA
BORGOGNONA
VIA DEL CORSO
BELSIANA
VIA
VIA FRATTINA
Max Mara
VIA DELLA VITE
VIA DI PROPAGANDA
VIA DELLA MERCEDE

Designer Shopping

All the well-known stars of the Italian fashion scene, plus exclusive jewelers, gift shops, shoe designers, and tailors, are concentrated in this cluster of chic, and stylish shopping streets by the Spanish Steps *(see pp330–35)*. Romans love to stroll here in the early evening.

Testaccio Market
A visual feast of fruit and vegetables greets the eye in this lively market. *(See p344.)*

Via Borgognona
Crowds flock here to buy, or just gaze at, high-fashion clothes, shoes, leather bags, and other accessories.

Men's and Women's Fashion

Italy is one of the leading lights in high-class fashion, or *alta moda*. Many of the most famous designers are based in Milan, but Rome is home to a cluster of sophisticated and internationally distinguished fashion houses. There is also a wonderful selection of *alta moda* shops. Boutiques displaying an eclectic mix of designer goods rub shoulders with showrooms devoted to single collections. But even for those of us unable to splurge on genuine designer-wear, much fun can be gained from a stroll down the glittering streets that radiate out from the Piazza di Spagna, since some of the window displays are truly spectacular.

The "atelier" made-to-measure fashions are beyond most pockets, but the designers also offer ready-to-wear alternatives in their boutiques. These are not cheap, but cost far less than a tailor-made garment.

Women's High Fashion

Rome's most famous designer internationally is probably **Valentino**, who retired in 2008 but whose boutique on Piazza di Spagna is still a mecca for the younger fashionista. Just up the Spanish Steps, in chic Via Sistina, is the Rome branch of **Gattinoni**, which showcases the subtly extravagant haute couture, and ready-to-wear designs of Guillermo Mariotto.

The equally impressive **Fendi** occupies a 19th-century palazzo in Largo Goldoni. Fendi made its name with high-fashion furs, then branched out into leather goods, accessories, and ready-to-wear, collaborating with Karl Lagerfeld, who designed the coveted double-F logo that emblazons its very collectible products. Third-generation family members design the younger, less expensive Fendissime line.

For well over a decade, **Laura Biagiotti** has reigned as Rome's queen of discreet, conservative couture. From her headquarters in a castle just outside Rome, she designs a range of timelessly elegant knitwear and silk separates for women who don't want to sacrifice style for comfort. She is famous for her use of cashmere and white as well as her creative use of fabrics and quality of finish. Her flagship showroom in Via Mario de' Fiori stocks her complete collection, which now includes hosiery, perfumes, swimwear, and leather goods. Her scarves make wonderful presents, and are often reduced in price during sales; other items from previous collections are available in the shop all year at very good discounts. Meanwhile, in nearby Via Condotti, there is the temple to the creations of **Salvatore Ferragamo**.

Other internationally known Rome-based designers include **Renato Balestra**, who produces tailored suits and glamorous evening wear.

Milan's miraculous fashion house **Prada** has an alluring branch on Via Condotti, featuring clothes, shoes, and accessories in unmistakable style. The window display is always worth a look. Other luminaries of Italian fashion who have shops in Rome include **Gianni Versace**, **Trussardi**, and **Giada Curti**. Top designers **Giorgio Armani** and **Dolce & Gabbana** also have stores in the Via Condotti area.

An affirmed star in ready-to-wear is **Roberto Cavalli**, whose design team produces coolly imaginative, stylish collections.

If you're looking for clothes from more unconventional designers, **Gente** is the place to go – its Roman showrooms have exclusive rights to the original couture collections of avant-garde stylists such as Dolce & Gabbana, Moschino, and Jean-Paul Gaultier.

MaxMara also has a number of branches here. Chic suits and separates are the mainstays of this popular label. The quality of fabric and finish is superb and, with suits available for around €500, its prices are much lower than other *alta moda* couture designers' ready-to-wear lines.

Men's Tailors and Designer Wear

Italian men are every bit as fashion-conscious as the women, and there is no shortage of choice in Rome for the well-dressed man. Suits tend to begin at around €620, jackets €415, and pants €155.

Most of the "star" designers of women's *alta moda* have a shop for men, like **Salvatore Ferragamo**, **Prada**, and **Gianni Versace**. The designs are generally less dramatic than the women's, with the accent on understated sophistication and casual sportiness. **Valentino**'s distinctive monogrammed accessories are relatively affordable. **Battistoni** is probably the most prestigious designer

Valentino

One of the high priests of Italian fashion, **Valentino Garavani**, opened the doors of his Roman studio in 1959 to a distinguished clientele that included Sophia Loren, Audrey Hepburn, and Jackie Kennedy. Before retiring in 2008, Valentino created some of the most dramatic and flattering evening dresses of the last 50 years. In the 1970s he began designing ready-to-wear lines for both men and women alongside his *alta moda* collections, and you can now find his very distinctive "V" logo on a wide range of accessories. The Valentino brand is still based in a huge palazzo in Piazza Mignanelli, and there are separate ready-to-wear boutiques nearby (see p334).

concentrating on menswear. Giorgio Battistoni and family's fine custom-made shirts and suits have been in demand with movie stars and top society for over 50 years. **Etro** sells classically cut clothes, and accessories for men, and women in exotic Italian-designed printed fabrics.

Ermenegildo Zegna is housed in a Baroque palazzo setting. It offers elegant ready-to-wear, and the master tailor Gaetano will also make to measure. **Davide Cenci** has been a mecca for those in search of the English country gentleman look since 1926. **Brioni** offers traditional tailor-made and own-label ready-to-wear men's clothing, **Trussardi** sells beautifully tailored classics, and **Testa** has impeccably tailored suits that appeal to younger Romans. **Degli Effetti** stocks more avant-garde designers such as Romeo Gigli and Jean-Paul Gaultier.

Young Designer Wear

There is a huge choice for the young. Top designer Giorgio Armani offers his particular style translated into more affordable lines at **Emporio Armani** (Armani jeans are a good buy at around €100). **Fendi** has its Fendissime line, and **Ermanno Scervino** has a boutique on Via Borgognona. Aimed at the younger set, these are good places to pick up stylish, sporty clothes.

Timberland is another casual label very popular with young Italians. Average prices are in the region of €52 for a shirt and €210 for raincoats.

Energie is a big hit, and has some of the best window displays in Rome. Teenagers flock here for jeans and T-shirts, both the shop's own, and other labels. Trussardi's casual line is found at **Tru Trussardi**, and **Aria**, **Diesel**, and **SBU** are also very popular. **Eventi** represents the more avant-garde styles – *dark*, as they call it here – fusing Gothic, New Age, and punk influences, which can result in some outrageous window creations. For women, Via del

Governo Vecchio is the place to head for. **Arsenico e Vecchi Merletti**, **Luna e L'altra**, and **Maga Morgana** offer some unconventional designer clothes in a pleasant, friendly atmosphere.

Retail Fashion

Rome is not a good place to look for everyday wear, since there is a distinct lack of mid-price shops bridging the huge gap between the dazzlingly priced *alta moda* designer exclusives, and the ultra-cheap goods sold in markets *(see pp344–5)*. Lower-budget stores do exist, but quality is often poor. If you have the stamina, you may find a bargain along Via del Corso, Via del Tritone, Via Nazionale, Via Cavour, Via Cola di Rienzo, Via Ottaviano, or the Via dei Giubbonari.

The most convenient places to shop are department stores like La Rinascente, Coin, and Upim *(see p327)*. They may not sound exciting, but you can browse at leisure and occasionally find nice things. It is also worth trying shops mentioned under Young Designer Wear – particularly the *alta moda* designers' cheaper lines such as **Emporio Armani**. At the different branches of **Discount dell'Alta Moda** you can find end-of-season designer labels at 50 percent less than the boutique prices. **Ethic** is a chain selling interesting, fashionable clothes with an alternative touch. And while you don't need to come all the way to Rome to shop at **Benetton**, there are many branches here, which sell the authentic garments in their universal colors.

Knitwear

Knitwear is a particular strength in Italian design, and in Rome there are plenty of specialty shops. **Laura Biagiotti** is celebrated for her luxurious cashmere separates, and **Missoni** for spectacular kaleidoscopic patterns and colors. Krizia no longer has a shop in Rome, but

sophisticated knitwear can be purchased at **Liz**.

Other shops, such as the **Luisa Spagnoli** outlets, offer a wider selection, including lower-priced items, as does **Stefanel**, which has various branches in the city.

Lingerie

This is another Italian specialty excelling in both style and quality, with lines like La Perla exported worldwide. Lingerie is traditionally sold in top household linen shops *(see p337)* – **Cesari**, for example, has its own complete range. There are also boutiques specializing in lingerie and swimwear.

Marisa Padovan has a range of swimwear that's ideal for Italian beaches, as well as light, bright summer dresses. **Brighenti** is said to be where movie stars go for their lingerie. **Schostal** has more traditional underwear with a very good men's section. The popular chain **Intimissimi** has stores in most shopping areas and sells classy lingerie.

Secondhand Clothes

Those who are willing to browse will find a wide variety of secondhand clothes, whether inspired by a collector's interest in vintage clothes or by a tight budget. Apart from Via Sannio and Porta Portese markets *(see p345)*, which have many secondhand clothing stands, the mecca is Via del Governo Vecchio. Among the best shops in this ancient street near Piazza Navona is **Tempi Moderni**, which has mostly vintage leather coats, jeans, and some hats.

Le Gallinelle offers a marvelous selection of second-hand and vintage clothes, as well as their own line. At **Daniela e Francesca** in Via Mastro Giorgio, Testaccio, there is an excellent range of women's clothes, mostly with designer labels. Via del Pellegrino is also a good street for shops selling secondhand clothes, and for independent stores.

Shoes and Accessories

Italy's leather industry is renowned all over the world, and shoes, bags, and belts are a good buy in Rome. Accessories in general are not just an afterthought but an integral part of an outfit for the well-dressed Roman. The choice of stylish jewelry, scarves, ties, and other accessories is excellent.

Shoes

Rome is full of shoe shops, ranging from high-quality stores in the Via Condotti area (where prices tend to start at €170) to the more economical shops around the Trevi fountain, and every big market has bargain shoe stands on its fringes.

Probably the best-known shop is **Ferragamo** – one of the world's top shoe shops. It stocks classic yet fashion-conscious shoes, as well as women's clothing and leather goods. The silk signature scarves are famous.

Fratelli Rossetti is a close contender for the number one position. Founded by brothers Renzo and Renato some 50 years ago, this company produces classic men's shoes and beautiful, dressy low-heeled shoes for women that reflect the most up-to-the-minute trends. Along with shops like **Tod's** in Via Condotti, it represents the epitome of elegance. The prices, of course, are sky-high, but you can buy something small, and at least you'll have the bag!

Boccanera's retail outlets, over in Testaccio, offer the latest men's and women's shoe styles from top Italian and British designers, with prices to match.

Silvano Lattanzi is one of the longer-lived shoe shops in Rome, having been in business for almost two decades, but it can't compete with **Domus**, which opened in 1938. Silvano Lattanzi sells made-to-measure footwear for both men and women, particularly shoes for special occasions and to customers' personal specifications. Domus sells a selection of high-quality footwear, specializing in classic shoes for women. They also stock a limited range of

leather bags and accessories. **De Bach** has colorful shoe styles for women.

Via Frattina has several more great shoe shops, such as **Campanile**, which specializes in footwear for both men and women in trendy and imaginative styles. Native designer **Fausto Santini** stocks original, stylish, colorful designs for younger people. Beautiful, bright designs for both men and women can also be found at **Baldinini**.

Borini stocks simple and elegant, low-heeled designs. The **Mr Boots** chain of shops stocks a wide range of trendy boots and casual shoes for men and women, while **Nuyorica** sells quirky, chic footwear for women alongside its select clothes range. If comfort is your priority, head to the **Geox** flagship store on Via del Corso.

Leather Bags and Accessories

The most famous of Rome's leather shops is the super-trendy **Gucci**, a dandy's paradise selling shoes, suitcases, handbags, wallets, belts, and other accessories. It has a fashion boutique for men and women and is well-known for its silk ties and scarves. **Fendi** also has exquisite leather goods as well as some lower-priced lines in synthetic materials and a range of gift items. Although their famous "stripe" line of leather-finished synthetic handbags cost €130 (and their all-leather ones start at €155), they are at least cheaper to buy here than abroad. **Skin**, situated around the Via Sistina area, is also quite pricy. Located a short walk to the south of Skin, near the Trevi Fountain, is **La Sella**. It sells all things leather,

including a range of shoes, bags, purses, and belts.

Mandarina Duck's brightly colored fabric bags and range of luggage are very much in fashion and make an attractive (and vegetarian) alternative to the more traditional leather styles. For sleek, utterly fashionable handbags, check out the latest creations from **Furla** or go for one of **Alviero Martini**'s famous "map" bags.

For a more unusual men's present, try **La Cravatta** in Trastevere. In addition to their selection of classy handmade ties, they also manufacture ties to customers' specifications. You can choose the design, material, length, and shape of the tie to create the perfect gift.

Classic Jewelry

What Cartier is to Paris, Tiffany & Co. is to New York and Asprey's is to London, **Bulgari** is to Rome. This internationally revered jeweler has passers-by glued to the windows gazing at its large gemstones. These "windows" are rather curious small boxes inserted into a wall with one or two pieces of jewelry in each of them, which adds to the feeling of looking at precious items in a case at a museum. Bulgari's watches, especially the men's, are popular and very elegant, as are the famous mesh necklaces. It specializes in large, colorful stones in High Renaissance–style settings but also produces a selection of contemporary designs. This was one of Andy Warhol's favorite shops, and it is definitely the most palatial shop on Via Condotti. Inside, the shop's atmosphere is one of almost religious awe and contemplation.

Buccellati is an offshoot of the famous Florentine dynasty, which was begun by Mario Buccellati in the 1920s and patronized by the poet Gabriele D'Annunzio. Its delicately engraved designs are inspired by the Italian

Renaissance, and are real classics, displaying superb craftsmanship.

Ansuini designs are fashionable yet classic, with strong, imaginative themes being introduced for each new collection. **Massoni**, founded in 1790, is one of Rome's oldest jewelry houses. Its refined brooches and one-of-a-kind pieces are outstanding.

At **Moroni Gioielli** you will also find imaginative, unique pieces of the highest-quality workmanship.

Peroso is an old-fashioned shop that has been in existence since 1891 and specializes in antique jewelry and silverware. **Boncompagni Sturni** sells traditional designs with the emphasis on quality and craftsmanship. You have to ring the bell to be admitted to both of these shops, and they are extremely expensive.

Tiffany & Co. sells its classic designs in jewelry, watches, accessories, and gifts at an exquisite outlet on elegant Via del Babuino.

Costume Jewelry

For less conventional tastes, there are several shops selling innovative, avant-garde pieces, often using semiprecious metals and stones. **Granuzzo**, in Via dei Coronari, is worth trying.

Tempi Moderni has an interesting collection of Art Deco and Liberty (Art Nouveau) period jewelry, including Bakelite brooches. There is also a range of designer pieces from the fifties and sixties.

Danae makes interesting pieces using silver and precious stones, inspired by Coco Chanel, while **Paola Volpi** uses industrial materials and is one of the most interesting designers of modern jewelry in Italy.

Traditional Goldsmiths and Silversmiths

The mainstays of Rome's jewelry industry are still the traditional artisan goldsmiths and silversmiths, working to order in tiny studio workshops. These are concentrated in the old Jewish Ghetto area by the Tiber River, Campo de' Fiori, Ponte Sisto near Via Giulia, and in Montepietà (which is also where the city's pawnbrokers are situated).

Artisan jewelry can also be found in Via dei Coronari, Via dell'Orso and Via del Pellegrino. The jewelers create individual pieces to their own designs and have often learned their profession from their parents, and grandparents. They will also do repair work, or take old gold jewelry, melt it down, and make it into something new to the customer's specifications.

Gioie d'Arte produces some traditional artisan jewelry and always works to customers' commissions.

Gloves, Hats, and Hosiery

If you're looking for top quality, you will find an expensive line in gloves at **Di Cori**, and **Sermoneta**, both of which stock every imaginable kind.

To find stylish leather gloves to match your new shoes, and handbags, whatever their color, pay a visit to **Settimio Mieli** which is sure to have something suitable, and at a reasonable price.

Catello d'Auria specializes in gloves and hosiery. **Borsalino** is a good place to go for all sorts of hats, including its namesake.

Calzedonia has several branches in the city, and will provide you with almost any color or pattern of tights, and stockings that you could wish for.

Size Chart

For Australian sizes follow British and American convention.

Children's clothing

Italian	2-3	4-5	6-7	8-9	10-11	12	14	14+ (years)
British	2-3	4-5	6-7	8-9	10-11	12	14	14+ (years)
American	2-3	4-5	6-6x	7-8	10	12	14	16 (size)

Children's shoes

Italian	24	25½	27	28	29	30	32	33	34
British	7	8	9	10	11	12	13	1	2
American	7½	8½	9½	10½	11½	12½	13½	1½	2½

Women's dresses, coats, and skirts

Italian	38	40	42	44	46	48	50
British	8	10	12	14	16	18	20
American	6	8	10	12	14	16	18

Women's blouses and sweaters

Italian	81	84	87	90	93	96	99 (cms)
British	31	32	34	36	38	40	42 (inches)
American	6	8	10	12	14	16	18 (size)

Women's shoes

Italian	36	37	38	39	40	41
British	3	4	5	6	7	8
American	5	6	7	8	9	10

Men's suits

Italian	44	46	48	50	52	54	56	58 (size)
British	34	36	38	40	42	44	46	48 (inches)
American	34	36	38	40	42	44	46	48 (inches)

Men's shirts (collar size)

Italian	36	38	39	41	42	43	44	45 (cms)
British	14	15	15½	16	16½	17	17½	18 (inches)
American	14	15	15½	16	16½	17	17½	18 (inches)

Men's shoes

Italian	39	40	41	42	43	44	45	46
British	6	7	7½	8	9	10	11	12
American	7	7½	8	8½	9½	10½	11	11½

DIRECTORY

Women's High Fashion

Dolce & Gabbana
Via Condotti 51–52.
Map 5 A2.
Tel 06-6992 4999.

Fendi
Largo Goldoni 419.
Map 12 E1.
Tel 06-334 501.

Gattinoni
Via Sistina 44. **Map** 5 A2.
Tel 06-678 3972.

Gente
Via del Babuino 81.
Map 4 F1.
Tel 06-320 7671.
Also: Via Frattina 69.
Map 5 A2.
Tel 06-678 9132.

Giada Curti
Rampa Mignanelli 12.
Map 5 A2.
Tel 06-6979 7794.

Gianni Versace
Piazza di Spagna 12.
Map 5 A2.
Tel 06-678 0521.

Giorgio Armani
Via Condotti 77.
Map 5 A2.
Tel 06-699 1461.

Laura Biagiotti
Via Mario de' Fiori 26.
Map 12 F1.
Tel 06-679 1205.

Max & Co
Via Condotti 46.
Map 5 A2.
Tel 06-678 7946.

MaxMara
Via Frattina 28. **Map** 5 A2.
Tel 06-679 3638.

Prada
Via Condotti 92–95.
Map 5 A2.
Tel 06-679 0897.

Renato Balestra
Via Cola di Rienzo 9–11.
Map 3 C2.
Tel 06-482 1723.

Roberto Cavalli
Via Borgognona 25.
Map 5 A2.
Tel 06-6992 5469.

Salvatore Ferragamo
Via Condotti 73–74.
Map 5 A2.
Tel 06-679 1565.

Trussardi
Via Condotti 49–50.
Map 5 A2.
Tel 06-678 0280.

Valentino
Via Condotti 15.
Map 5 A2.
Tel 06-673 9420.

Men's Tailors, and Designer Wear

Battistoni
Via Condotti 61A.
Map 5 A2.
Tel 06-697 6111.

Brioni
Via Condotti 21A.
Map 5 A2.
Tel 06-678 3428.

Davide Cenci
Via Campo Marzio 1–7.
Map 4 F3 & 12 D2.
Tel 06-699 0681.

Degli Effetti
Piazza Capranica 79.
Map 4 F3 & 12 D2.
Tel 06-679 0202.

Dolce & Gabbana
Piazza di Spagna 93.
Map 5 A2.
Tel 06-669 1592.

Ermenegildo Zegna
Via Condotti 58.
Map 5 A2.
Tel 06-6994 0678.

Etro
Via del Babuino 102.
Map 5 A2.
Tel 06-678 8257.

Gianni Versace
Piazza di Spagna 12.
Map 5 A2.
Tel 06-678 0521.

Gucci
Via Condotti 8. **Map** 5 A2.
Tel 06-679 0405.

Salvatore Ferragamo
Via Condotti 65.
Map 5 A2.
Tel 06-678 1130.

Testa
Piazza Euclide 27.
Map 2 D2.
Tel 06-807 0118.

Trussardi
*See Women's High
Fashion.*

Young Designer Wear

Aria
Via Nazionale 239.
Map 5 C3.
Tel 06-48 44 21.

Armani Jeans
Via del Babuino 70A.
Map 4 F1.
Tel 06-3600 1848.

Arsenico e Vecchi Merletti
Via del Governo Vecchio 36.
Map 11 B3.
Tel 06-683 3936.

Diesel
Via del Corso 118.
Map 4 F3 & 12 E1.
Tel 06-678 3933.

Emporio Armani
Via del Babuino 140.
Map 4 F1.
Tel 06-322 1581.

Energie
Via del Corso 179.
Map 4 F2.
Tel 06-678 1045.

Ermanno Scervino
Via Borgognona 29.
Map 12 E1.
Tel 06-6920 0687.

Eventi
Via dei Serpenti 134.
Map 5 B4.
Tel 06-48 49 60.

Luna e L'Altra
Piazza Pasquino 76.
Map 4 E4 & 11 C3.
Tel 06-6880 4995.

Maga Morgana
Via del Governo Vecchio 27 & 98.
Map 4 E4 & 11 C3.
Tel 06-687 8095.

SBU
Via S. Pantaleo 68.
Map 11 C3.
Tel 06-6880 2547.

Timberland
Via del Corso 488.
Map 4 F2.
Tel 06-324 3363.

Tru Trussardi
Via Frattina 42.
Map 5 A2.
Tel 06-6938 0939.

Retail Fashion

Benetton
Piazza della Fontana di Trevi 91–94.
Map 12 F2.
Tel 06-6919 0919.

Discount dell'Alta Moda
Via di Gesù e Maria 14 & 16A.
Map 4 F2.
Tel 06-361 3796.

Emporio Armani
See Young Designer Wear

Ethic
Via Cola di Rienzo 265.
Map 3 C2.
Tel 06-322 4621.

Zara
Galleria Alberto Sordi.
Map 12 E2.
Tel 06-6992 5401.
Also:
Via del Corso 129–135.
Map 12 E2.
Tel 06-6992 3196.

Knitwear

Laura Biagiotti
See Women's High Fashion.

Liz
Via Appia Nuova 90.
Map 10 D2.
Tel 06-700 3609.

Luisa Spagnoli
Via del Tritone 30.
Map 5 A3–B3 & 12 F1.
Tel 06-6992 2769.
Also:
Via Vittorio Veneto 130.
Map 5 B1.
Tel 06-4201 1281.

Missoni
Piazza di Spagna 78.
Map 5 A2.
Tel 06-679 2555.

Stefanel
Via Frattina 31–33.
Map 5 A2.
Tel 06-679 2667.

Lingerie

Brighenti
Via Borgognona 27.
Map 5 A2.
Tel 06-678 3898.

Cesari
Via del Babuino 195.
Map 5 B3.
Tel 06-638 1241.

Intimissimi
Via Nazionale 227.
Map 5 B4.
Tel 06-487 1864.

Marisa Padovan
Via delle Carrozze 81–82.
Map 5 A2.
Tel 06-679 3946.

Schostal
Via Fontanella Borghese
29. **Map** 12 D1.
Tel 06-679 1240.

Secondhand Clothes

Daniela e Francesca
Via Mastro Giorgio 79B.
Map 8 D3.
Tel 06-5728 5208.

Le Gallinelle
Via Panisperna 61.
Map 5 B4.
Tel 06-488 1017.

Tempi Moderni
Via del Governo
Vecchio 108.
Map 4 E4 & 11 B3.
Tel 06-687 7007.

Shoes

Baldinini
Via del Babuino 150.
Map 4 F2.
Tel 06-3601 0347.

Boccanera
Via Luca della Robbia 36.
Map 8 D3.
Tel 06-575 6804.

Borini
Via dei Pettinari 86–87.
Map 4 E5 & 11 C5.
Tel 06-687 5670.

Campanile
Via Frattina 25.
Map 12 E1.
Tel 06-6994 0621.

De Bach
Via del Babuino 123.
Map 4 F1.
Tel 06-678 3384.

Domus
Via Belsiana 52. **Map** 4 F2.
Tel 06-67 8 9083.

Fausto Santini
Via Frattina 120.
Map 5 A2.
Tel 06-678 4114.

Ferragamo
Via Condotti 73–74.
Map 5 A2.
Tel 06-679 1565.
Also: Via Condotti 65.
Map 5 A2.
Tel 06-678 1130.

Fratelli Rossetti
Via Borgognona 5A.
Map 5 A2.
Tel 06-678 2676.

Geox
Via del Corso 444.
Map 4 F2.
Tel 06-6889 2720.

Mr Boots
Piazza Re di Roma 10.
Map 10 D3.
Tel 06-7720 8672.
Also: Via A Brunetti 2.
Map 4 F1.
Tel 06-321 5733.

Nuyorica
Piazza della Pollarola
36–7.
Map 11 C4.
Tel 06-6889 1243.

Silvano Lattanzi
Via Bocca di Leone 59.
Map 5 A2.
Tel 06-678 6119.

Tod's
Via Condotti 52–53A.
Map 5 A2.
Tel 06-699 1089.

Leather Bags and Accessories

Alviero Martini
Via Frattina 116.
Map 5 A2.
Tel 06-6992 3381.

La Cravatta
Via di Santa Cecilia 12.
Map 8 D1.
Tel 06-8901 6941.

Furla
Via Condotti 56.
Map 5 A2.
Tel 06-679 1973.
Also: Via Nazionale 54–55.
Map 5 C3.
Tel 06-487 0127.

Gucci
Via Borgognona 7D.
Map 5 A2.
Tel 06-6919 0661.
Also: Via Condotti 8.
Map 5 A2.
Tel 06-679 0405.

Mandarina Duck
Via Due Macelli 59F/G.
Map 12 F1.
Tel 06-678 6414.

La Sella
Via del Lavatore 56.
Map 5 A3 & 12 F2.
Tel 06-679 6654.

Skin
Via Capo le Case 41.
Map 5 A3 & 12 F1.
Tel 06-678 5531.

Classic Jewelry

Ansuini
Corso Vittorio Emanuele
151.
Map 4 E4 & 11 C3.
Tel 06-6880 6909.

Boncompagni
Via Vittoria 4A.
Map 4 F2.
Tel 06-321 3950.

Buccellati
Via Condotti 33.
Map 5 A2. **Tel** 06-679
0329.

Bulgari
Via Condotti 10.
Map 5 A2. **Tel** 06-696 261.

Massoni
Via Margutta 54A.
Map 4 F1.
Tel 06-321 6916.

Moroni Gioielli
Via Belsiana 32A. **Map**
4 F2. **Tel** 06-678 0466.

Peroso
Via Sistina 29A.
Map 5 B3.
Tel 06-474 7952.

Tiffany & Co.
Via del Babuino 118.
Map 5 A2.
Tel 06-679 0717.

Costume Jewelry

Danae
Via della Maddalena 40.
Map 12 D2.
Tel 06-679 1881.

Granuzzo
Via dei Coronari 193.
Map 4 E3 & 11 B2.
Tel 06-6880 1503.

Paola Volpi
Piazza dei Satiri 55.
Map 11 C4.
Tel 06-687 3366.

Tempi Moderni
Via del Governo
Vecchio 108.
Map 4 E4 & 11 B3.
Tel 06-687 7007.

Traditional Goldsmiths, and Silversmiths

Gioie d'Arte
Via de' Gigli d'Oro 10.
Map 4 E3 & 11 C2.
Tel 06-687 7524.

Gloves, Hats, and Hosiery

Borsalino
Piazza del Popolo 20.
Map 4 F1.
Tel 06-3265 0838.
Also: Via Sistina 58A.
Map 5 B2.
Tel 06-678 8821.

Calzedonia
Via del Corso 106.
Map 4 F2.
Tel 06-6992 5436.

Catello d'Auria
Via dei Due Macelli 55.
Map 5 A2 & 12 F1.
Tel 06-679 3364.

Di Cori
Piazza di Spagna 53.
Map 5 A2.
Tel 06-678 4439.

Fendi
See Women's High
Fashion.

Sermoneta
Piazza di Spagna 61.
Map 5 A2.
Tel 06-679 1960.

Settimio Mieli
Via San Claudio 70.
Map 5 A3 & 12 E2.
Tel 06-678 5979.

Interior Design

Italian design belongs to a long-established tradition based on the skills of the master craftsman, and some firms have a history going back hundreds of years. Rome's stylish interior design shops are worth seeking out, even if only to look around and enjoy the ambience. You might well pick up some design ideas for your home, or find some interesting or unusual things to buy. They are an excellent place to buy souvenirs, and presents to take home.

Furniture

Italy is well-known for its stylish, well-made furniture. Although there is no distinct area of Rome that is renowned for its furniture shops, many of the top stores are located to the north of the downtown.

In the heart of historic Rome, on Via della Scrofa, is **Arcon**. This airy outlet is packed with various slick furniture designs, particularly chairs, desks, and lighting, though there are some smaller, and more affordable household items.

Tucked in a side street off Via Giulia, **Sfera** displays a provocative blend of classic, and modern well-upholstered chairs, and divans matched with more minimalist designs.

Spazio Sette, near Largo Argentina, is worth visiting for the building itself. The store has a spectacular showroom on three levels in the Palazzo Lazzaroni, a former cardinal's palace. Spazio Sette is one of Rome's premier home furnishing stores and, as well as furniture, the shop stocks plenty of items that would make interesting gifts. The furniture, including modern, laminated stack-up chairs, and the vases, glass, bowls, and kitchen equipment are jumbled together in a fascinating display.

Nearby, on Piazza Cairoli, stands **Confalone**, a furniture shop that specializes in well-upholstered sofas and armchairs, though dining tables and chairs also crowd the display area. The shop's wide range of classical designs suits any interior.

Benedetti, which occupies a line of shops on the Via Marmorata, offers a range of fine modern wood furniture, while **Fattorini**, on Via Arenula, gives a modern Italian take on 1970s retro styling.

Light Fixtures

Light fixtures are one of the most popular and more easily transportable items, and there are several superb showrooms in Rome that are worth a visit.

Flos is a merger of two design houses whose Roman showroom displays its lights as if they were museum exhibits. The design style is chic, and minimalist, with plenty of black and white, chrome and steel.

Nearby **Artemide** is, like Flos, a design house in its own right, and is similarly well known abroad, above all for its classic anglepoise lamps in a variety of colors. Its showroom in Rome is elegant, with expensive, high-tech lighting design. Just across the road from the Palazzo delle Esposizioni, the **Targetti** store showcases their famous range: sleek, occasionally space-age designs that respond to any internal or external lighting requirement. **Borghini** sells less famous names, and is therefore more economical.

To see examples of light fixtures from all of Italy's leading producers, head to **Obor**, where high-tech items are displayed alongside more traditional designs.

Italian electrical equipment is designed for 220–240 volts. If you are going to use it in countries with lower voltage, always ask the shop whether the product needs a transformer, as this can depend on the model.

Light fixtures generally take standard screw-in light bulbs, but double-check before you buy.

Kitchens and Bathrooms

Although you won't be able to take one home with you, you may want to take a look at the ultra-modern high-tech kitchen designs in Rome.

For an overview of the latest in chic stainless steel designs, visit **Arclinea**, near Ponte Garibaldi, for its select display of state-of-the-art kitchens. Equally inspiring are the kitchens on display at **Emporio Cucina**, just off Piazza Navona.

Italian bathroom shops concentrate almost exclusively on modern designs, some of which are luxuriously decadent. **Ravasini** has very decorative floral fixtures with some matching accessories. **Materia** is another bathroom shop that sells all the latest styles.

Tiles

The Italian ceramic tile tradition is an ancient one. A great variety of tiles are displayed in kitchen and bathroom showrooms, but there are also one or two specialty shops.

Ceramiche Musa specializes in modern tiles incorporating decorative floral and ancient Roman motifs, which are popular, especially with foreign visitors.

Glass

Decorative glass objects are a popular buy in Rome. **Murano Più**, just behind Piazza Navona, sells Murano and other glass items at reasonable prices. This shop is one of the few that open on Sundays – which can be useful for visitors on short trips to Rome.

Archimede Seguso also specializes in Murano glass but includes smaller pieces, and also offers a range of gift-sized items. **Arteque** is a very beautiful shop that has a more traditional flavor.

For a wide selection of more affordable gifts, try **Stilvetro**. It is the ideal place for items such as pasta bowls, glass, and ceramics.

An added advantage is that shipment abroad can usually be arranged at any of these glass establishments, so you can make your purchase without worrying about transporting it home.

Fabrics

At **Aracoeli Home** you can find all manner of fabrics, some at bargain discount prices.

If you are looking for further bargains, take a walk around the old Jewish quarter, Il Ghetto, which runs from Largo Argentina down to the Tiber; the area contains numerous fabric shops such as **Paganini**. During sale times *(see p326)*, remnants of fabrics *(scampoli)* are always sold off cheaply, and if you are lucky you could find just the right fabric for just the right price.

Household Linen and Kitchenware

Shops selling household goods abound in Rome. For a selection of lovely sheets, and other bed linens, head to **Frette**.

If you enjoy designer kitchenware, don't miss **c.u.c.i.n.a.** which is tucked away in No. 65 Via Mario de' Fiori. The shop stocks kitchen utensils from all over the world, as well as pots, and pans in both rustic and sleek styles, and countless space-saving kitchen accessories.

Right next to Piazza Venezia, **Sorelle Adamoli** specializes in articles for the table, and kitchen, selling every accessory, and gadget imaginable.

The Roman pizzeria **'Gusto** *(see p323)* also offers an interesting range of kitchen utensils and essentials in its ground-floor shop.

Finally, there is **Limentani**, whose basement shop in the old ghetto area is well stocked with interesting gift ideas. Here, you will find an extraordinary array of household and kitchenware, including silver, china, and crystal items.

DIRECTORY

Furniture

Arcon
Via della Scrofa 104.
Map 12 D1.
Tel 06-6833 3728.

Benedetti
Via Marmorata 141.
Map 8 D3.
Tel 06-574 6610.

Confalone
Piazza Cairoli 110.
Map 12 D4.
Tel 06-6880 3684.

Fattorini
Via Arenula 55.
Map 12 D5.
Tel 06-6813 6615.

Sfera
Via delle Carceri 6.
Map 11 B3.
Tel 06-6889 2630.

Spazio Sette
Via dei Barbieri 7.
Map 4 F5 & 12 D4.
Tel 06-6880 4261.

Light Fixtures

Artemide
Via Margutta 107.
Map 4 F1.
Tel 06-3600 1802.

Borghini
Via Belsiana 87–89.
Map 4 F2.
Tel 06-679 0636.

Flos
Via del Babuino 84.
Map 5 A2.
Tel 06-320 7631.

Obor
Piazza San Lorenzo in Lucina 28.
Map 12 E1.
Tel 06-687 1496.

Targetti
Via Nazionale 193.
Map 5 B4.
Tel 06-474 4694.

Kitchens and Bathrooms

Arclinea
Lungotevere dei Cenci 4B.
Map 4 F5 & 12 D5.
Tel 06-686 5104.

Emporio Cucina
Piazza delle Cinque Lune 74. **Map** 11 C2.
Tel 06-6880 3685.

Materia
Corso Vittorio Emanuele II 189.
Map 11 C3.
Tel 06-686 1896.

Ravasini
Via di Ripetta 69–71.
Map 4 F2.
Tel 06-322 7096.

Tiles

Ceramiche Musa
Via Campo Marzio 39.
Map 4 F3 & 12 D1.
Tel 06-687 1204.

Glass

Archimede Seguso
Via dei Due Macelli 56.
Map 5 A2.
Tel 06-679 1781.

Arteque
Via Giulia 13.
Map 4 D4 & 11 A3.
Tel 06-687 7388.

Murano Più
Corso Rinascimento 43–45.
Map 4 E3.
Tel 06-6880 8038.

Stilvetro
Via Frattina 56.
Map 5 A2.
Tel 06-679 0258.

Fabrics

Aracoeli Home
Via Aracoeli 7.
Map 4 F5 & 12 E4.
Tel 06-6994 0872.

Paganini
Via Aracoeli 23.
Map 4 F5 & 12 E4.
Tel 06-678 6831.

Household and Kitchenware

c.u.c.i.n.a.
Via Mario de' Fiori 65.
Map 5 A2.
Tel 06-679 1275.
Via di Parione 21.
Map 4 E4.
Tel 06-324 3723

Frette
Piazza di Spagna 10.
Map 5 A2.
Tel 06-679 0673.

'Gusto
Piazza Augusto Imperatore 7.
Map 4 F2.
Tel 06-323 6363.

Limentani
Via del Portico D'Ottavia 48.
Map 12 E5.
Tel 06-6880 6949.

Sorelle Adamoli
Via del Plebiscito 103.
Map 12 E3.
Tel 06-679 4208.

Books and Gifts

Rome offers huge scope for gift buying, both in the well-established tourist stores in the *centro storico* (historic center) and in smaller shops in less frequented parts of the city. Seeking out the smaller shops can be an adventure in itself; many are in attractive parts of the city that you might not otherwise visit.

Unusual artisan ceramics, wonderful books on Italian art, and architecture, paper products, vintage Italian movie posters, beautiful prints of historic views of Rome, and specialty candies and cakes make ideal souvenirs to take home. While masterpieces by Michelangelo, Raphael, and Caravaggio are popular icons for T-shirts, statuettes, and postcards, religious artifacts are also readily available in the city that hosts the papal seat.

Bookshops

Rome is rich in bookshops, from the encyclopaedic to the very specialized. Italian books, both hardback and softback, are generally very attractive but also tend to be expensive.

As Italy's largest and most renowned bookshop chain, **Feltrinelli** dedicates its endless shelf space to both modern and classic Italian literature, and also houses a wide selection of non-fiction titles. **Feltrinelli International** on Via Emanuele Orlando has an excellent range of foreign-language fiction and specialty nonfiction, covering various subjects including art, cooking, travel, and history. It also stocks some superb photographic, art, and movie posters. Magazines, and stationery are available as well, and the noticeboard is a lifeline for information on rooms for rent and Italian language courses.

Specialty English bookstores include the **Anglo-American Book Co.**, which is located near Piazza di Spagna. In Trastevere, the **Almost Corner Bookshop**, though small, has probably the most extensive selection of English language fiction in the capital, as well as nonfiction titles – from ancient Rome to modern Italian culture, and politics.

The **Libreria del Viaggiatore** is jam-packed with maps and travel guides (some in English). The charming **Libreria Godel** is good for browsing, as is the more modern **Mel Bookstore**, which boasts two floors of books, stationery and DVDs, including a basement level full of secondhand titles. For prospective chefs, fantastic recipe books on Italian and international cuisine can be found at **Emporio Libreria 'Gusto** *(see p343)* in Piazza Augusto Imperatore.

As an alternative to traditional bookstores, there are lots of discount deals at the secondhand book stands in Via delle Terme di Diocleziano and in Largo della Fontanella di Borghese.

Multimedia and Music

The split-level **Feltrinelli** in Galleria Alberto Sordi on Via del Corso, and its sister store in Largo Argentina, represent the closest Rome gets to a multimedia megastore. At both these stores, in addition to their stock of fiction, and nonfiction titles, there is a reasonable selection of CDs and DVDs that cover mainstream tastes.

Stationery and Paper Crafts

Near the Pantheon, the Florentine **Il Papiro** sells a great range of illustrious paper-based products that include notebooks, diaries, envelopes, and beautiful seal-and-wax sets that make for an ideal gift. In a similar vein, a wide selection of pretty marbled notebooks, writing papers, and files and boxes in various sizes are also offered at **Laboratorio Scatole**. **Pineider**, stationery suppliers to the Roman gentry, will print sets of exquisite visiting cards for you. The more modern **Vertecchi** is filled with original paper gifts, including boxes of every shape and size, while **Fabriano** has its own fabulous line of stationery and notebooks.

Posters and Prints

Near Piazza Navona, **L'Image** has an extensive range of artistic, photographic, and movie posters for sale, as well as a decent range of stationery, souvenirs, and calendars. Geared more toward antiques, **Galleria Trincia** sells good-quality and reasonably priced prints of 17th-century panoramic paintings of Rome, as well as watercolors. It also undertakes restoration work.

For superb posters on past exhibitions as well as stylish souvenirs and postcards, visit Rome's museum shops – for example, **Il Chiostro del Bramante** near Piazza Navona, or **Complesso del Vittoriano** next to the Forum.

Artisan Handicrafts and Design

The central Via del Pellegrino is a street crammed with small specialty outlets such as **Le Tre Ghinee**, which sells ceramics and glass objects. **La Chiave** is a good choice for gifts, selling all things ethnic, with the emphasis on bright furnishings and original jewelry.

If you are more interested in contemporary design, visit the **Palazzo delle Esposizioni** *(see p166)*, where a wide range of objects by famous designers is available. For a really original gift, try **Bottega del Marmoraro**, a workshop that reproduces ancient Roman and Pompeian inscriptions on marble. The owner will recreate any design you choose to order.

Souvenirs and Religious Artifacts

Most of the tobacconists in central Rome sell postcards, stamps, and a variety of souvenirs. Cheap and sometimes appealingly kitsch souvenirs are also found at the mobile stands around the major tourist attractions.

Bookshops near the main basilicas, such as **Libreria Belardetti**, sell souvenirs and religious mementos. Other shops specialize in religious articles for both the clergy and the layperson. Facing the Vatican gates in Via di Porta Angelica there are several shops, such as **Al Pellegrino Cattolico**, selling artifacts to visiting pilgrims.

Candy and Cookies

In addition to the several bars and cafés that sell cakes and cookies to take our *(da portare via)*, there are a number of specialty stores in Rome well worth taking the time to visit.

Downtown near Piazza Navona, **La Deliziosa** *(see p323)*, though small, offers a great range of classic Italian desserts and cakes; the ricotta-based variety deserves a special mention. In the Galleria Esedra, near Piazza della Repubblica, **Dagnino** is renowned throughout the city as one of the best places for sugary Sicilian delicacies such as *cannoli* and *cassate*.

For a wonderful range of fresh and appetizing Italian cookies to suit all occasions and every whim, head for **Cipriani** *(see p322)* in Esquilino near Termini station, or **Innocenti**, a historic *pasticceria* famed for its elaborate cookies of the highest quality, prepared with varied ingredients including almonds, pine nuts, and honey. Innocenti is situated across the Tiber from the *centro storico* in Trastevere. Right next to the Circus Maximus, the renowned café **Cristalli di Zucchero** in Via San Teodoro has a wide range of marvelous mini-pastries

DIRECTORY

Bookshops

Almost Corner Bookshop
Via del Moro 45.
Map 7 C1.
Tel 06-583 6942.

Anglo-American Book Co.
Via della Vite 102.
Map 12 E1.
Tel 06-679 5222.

Emporio Libreria 'Gusto
Piazza Augusto Imperatore 7. **Map** 4 F2.
Tel 06-323 6363.

Feltrinelli
Largo Argentina 5A.
Map 4 F4. **Tel** 06-688 663 001. Also: Galleria Alberto Sordi 31–35.
Map 12 E2.
Tel 06-6975 5001.

Feltrinelli International
Via E. Orlando 84–86.
Map 5 C3.
Tel 06-482 7878.

Libreria del Viaggiatore
Via del Pellegrino 78.
Map 11 B3.
Tel 06-6880 1048.

Libreria Godel
Via Poli 45–46.
Map 12 F2.
Tel 06-679 8716.

Mel Bookstore
Via Nazionale 254–255.
Map 5 C3.
Tel 06-488 5405.

Multimedia and Music

Feltrinelli
See bookshops
W **lafeltrinelli.it**

Stationery and Paper Crafts

Fabriano
Via del Babuino 173.
Map 4 F2.
Tel 06-3260 0361.

Laboratorio Scatole
Via della Stelletta 27.
Map 12 D2.
Tel 06-6880 2053.

Il Papiro
Via del Pantheon 50 (leading to Via Degli Orfani).
Map 12 D2.
Tel 06-679 5597.

Pineider
Via dei Due Macelli 68.
Map 12 F1.
Tel 06-679 5884.

Vertecchi
Via della Croce 70.
Map 4 F2.
Tel 06-332 2821.

Posters and Prints

Il Chiostro del Bramante
Via della Pace 5. **Map** 11 C2. **Tel** 06-6880 9035.

Complesso del Vittoriano
Via San Pietro In Carcere.
Map 5 A5.
Tel 06-678 0664.

Galleria Trincia
Via Laurina 12. **Map** 4 F1.
Tel 06-361 2322.

L'Image
Via della Scrofa 67. **Map** 12 D2. **Tel** 06-686 4050.

Artisan Handicrafts and Design

Bottega del Marmoraro
Via Margutta 53B. **Map** 5 A2. **Tel** 06-320 7660.

La Chiave
Largo delle Stimmate 28.
Map 12 D4.
Tel 06-6830 8848.

Palazzo delle Esposizioni
Via Milano 15–17. **Map** 5 B4. **Tel** 06-4891 3361.

Le Tre Ghinee
Via del Pellegrino 90.
Map 11 B3.
Tel 06-687 2739.

Souvenirs and Religious Artifacts

Al Pellegrino Cattolico
Via di Porta Angelica 83.
Map 3 C2.
Tel 06-6880 2351.

Libreria Belardetti
Via della Conciliazione 4A.
Map 3 C3.
Tel 06-686 5502.

Candy and Cookies

Cipriani
Via C. Botta 21.
Map 6 D5.
Tel 06-7045 3930.

Cristalli di Zucchero
Via di San Teodoro 81.
Map 8 E1.
Tel 06-6992 0945.

Dagnino
Galleria Esedra,
Via Vittorio Emanuele Orlando 75.
Map 5 C2.
Tel 06-481 8660.

La Deliziosa
Vicolo Savelli 50.
Map 11 B3.
Tel 06-6880 3155.

Innocenti
Via della Luce 21A.
Map 7 C2.
Tel 06-580 3926.

Art and Antiques

Rome's art and antique shops range from exclusive establishments to contemporary art galleries. In response to a fashion for collecting early-20th-century artifacts, new dealers and galleries are springing up throughout Rome – Venini's Murano glass is popular, as are lighting and furniture. Many more sell general bric-a-brac and jewelry. Copies of antique prints can be picked up for a fraction of the original's price. Rome is not good for antique bargains, but it is worth looking in shops along Via dei Cappellari and Via del Pellegrino or going to the Porta Portese Sunday market *(see p345)*.

Antiques and Old Master Paintings

There are antique shops dotted all over the center of Rome, though the cream of the crop tend to be concentrated in distinct areas. Discreet haggling in the shops is accepted practice, but even if you get a reduction in price, make sure the dealer provides you with the relevant export documents.

The famous Via del Babuino, and to a lesser extent Via Margutta, which is better known for its art galleries, are home to around 30 of Rome's grandest showrooms for antique furniture, Old Master paintings, and *objets d'art*.

Cesare Lampronti is owned by the top dealer of that name. Aided and complemented by his partner Carlo Peruzzi, he sells 16th- to 18th-century European paintings, with an emphasis on Roman and Italian works in general.

Alberto di Castro, situated in Piazza di Spagna, is a fourth-generation dealer specializing in statues, paintings, and other precious objects from the medieval to the Neo-Classical periods. Nearby, **M Simotti-Rocchi** stocks Greek and Roman statuary, as well as more luggage-friendly coins and figurines.

Via Giulia *(see p155)* has over 20 high-quality antique shops to choose from. Definitely worth a visit is **Antichità Cipriani**, which is a temple to owner Paola Cipriani's love of simply elegant Neo-Classical furniture and paintings. She also sells the occasional modern piece. Another shop not to miss on Via Giulia is **Antiquariato Valligiano**. This is the only place in Rome where you can find 19th-century Italian country furniture, a rustic antidote to those overpowered by the grandiose Baroque.

Via Monserrato, running parallel, is worth scouring for slightly lower-quality pieces at more realistic prices. The area just to the north of Via Giulia is also a good hunting ground. **Mario Prilli**, on Via Banchi Nuovi, is tiny, but don't let that deter you. With every inch of space occupied by a wide variety of antiques, this fascinating shop is worth a look even if you are only browsing.

Via dei Coronari is largely devoted to antiques, with over 30 shops lining both sides of the street. Quality is very high – as are the prices. It is a good place for Baroque and Empire elaborate inlaid vases, secretaries, and consoles.

Ad Antiqua Domus is a treasure trove of antique Italian furniture. Pieces dating from ancient Rome through to the 19th century are for sale.

Liberty specializes in high-quality Art Nouveau (usually called *Liberty* here), while the **Art Deco Gallery** sells furniture and sculpture from that period.

Galleria dei Coronari has a superb collection of tapestries, clocks, paintings, and statuary. **Antichità Arredamenti** also specializes in Italian light fixtures and candlesticks.

Slightly farther away is Via della Stelletta, which is home to a handful of unusual, and fascinating shops. **Acanto** is an inexpensively priced Aladdin's cave with an eclectic mix of *objets d'art*. It is the perfect place to search for religious memorabilia, Italian curiosities, and prints.

Bilenchi is yet another specialist, this time in exquisite, early 20th-century lamps.

Another relatively undiscovered area is the one around Via del Boschetto and Via Panisperna. Shops around here tend to specialize in early 20th-century artifacts, with some English Victorian pieces thrown in. **Goffi Carboni** is more Asian in outlook, with Chinese, and Japanese ceramics, and prints alongside its 17th–19th-century European art collection.

Of course there are many perennial favorites apart from these streets. The best way to discover them is through word of mouth or just by chance as you stroll along. **Antichità Carnovale** is a shop full of interesting 19th- and 20th-century canvases, while **Agostini** is one of the oldest antique shops in Rome, and definitely one of the largest. It offers an impressive collection of European antiques.

Modern Art

Rome is rich in avant-garde galleries exhibiting paintings by recognized Modern Masters through to the up-and-coming generation of young, mainly Italian, artists.

Rome's art galleries are usually open 10am–1pm and 5–8pm Tue–Sat. Some open only in the afternoon; others also stay open on Monday afternoon. The best times to visit are afternoons, and early evenings.

As with Rome's antique shops, the art galleries tend to be concentrated in a couple of distinct areas. The largest of these covers the triangular area between Via del Babuino, and Via di Ripetta and adjoining streets, known locally as the Trident. Via Margutta is also home to several prestigious private galleries.

The **Galleria Valentina Moncada** exhibits contemporary Italian and international art, and also showcases 20th- century photography, while **Archeologia Monogramma Arte Contemporanea** deals with promising young artists from Italy and abroad. One of this area's highlights is the Via Margutta art fair *(see p345)*, which usually takes place around Christmas, and in springtime.

The enterprising **Fontanella Borghese** gallery shows works by foreign artists such as Sam Francis and Andy Warhol. Also on view at the gallery are Italian artists like Boetti, Festa, and Turcato.

Via Giulia and its surroundings is the next area to investigate: **Galleria Giulia** is a gallery/bookshop with works by artists such as Argeles, Boille, Cano, Cascella, Echaurren, Erba, and Lionni, as well as Bauhaus artists and German Expressionists. Fabio Sargentini at **L'Attico**

follows the latest trends in Italian art from Del Giudice to Corsini and Fabiani.

Another innovative downtown venture is **Galleria Bonomo** (owned by Alessandra Bonomo), which spotlights Italian and foreign painters such as Schifano, Boetti, Twombly, Nunzio, Tremlett, LeWitt, and Dokoupil.

On the other side of the Tiber, the **Galleria Lorcan O'Neill** showcases contemporary Italian and international art. Past exhibitions have included works by Tracey Emin, and Rachel Whiteread.

Antique Prints and Photographs

The justifiably celebrated **Nardecchia**, named after its erudite owner Plinio, is the cream of Rome's print dealers. Look out for originals by the 18th-century engraver Piranesi, as well as views of the city, and depictions of ancient Roman life.

Another Roman institution, **Casali**, has been trading for over 100 years. The family now runs two shops specializing in 16th- to 19th-century drawings and engravings of Roman scenes ranging from museum-standard Piranesi down to relatively inexpensive unknown and delightfully decorative floral scenes.

The Florence-based **Alinari** family is renowned for its old sepia photographs of Italy from 1890 onward, including shots of Rome a century ago. At its Roman outlet, prices of photographs from the original plates start at around €30 and mounted prints at €280. Larger sizes can be mounted on wood or posterboard.

Another place definitely worth heading for in search of that perfect print of old Rome, and some enjoyable, relaxing, and maybe persuasive browsing is the **Mercato delle Stampe** *(see p344)*.

DIRECTORY

Antiques and Old Master Paintings

Acanto
Via della Stelletta 10.
Map 4 F3 & 12 D2.
Tel 06-686 5481.

Ad Antiqua Domus
Via dei Coronari 41.
Map 4 E3 & 11 B2.
Tel 06-686 1186.

Agostini
Piazza Borghese 1. **Map** 12 D1. **Tel** 06-687 3632.

Alberto di Castro
Piazza di Spagna 5. **Map** 5 A2. **Tel** 06-679 2269.

Antichità Arredamenti
Via dei Coronari 218. **Map** 4 E3. **Tel** 06-6880 1254.

Antichità Carnovale
Via del Governo Vecchio 71. **Map** 11 C3. **Tel** 06-686 4850.

Antichità Cipriani
Via Giulia 122.
Map 4 D4 & 11 A3.
Tel 06-6830 8344.

Antiquariato Valligiano
Via Giulia 193. **Map** 4 E5 & 11 B5. **Tel** 06-686 9505.

Art Deco Gallery
Via dei Coronari 14.
Map 4 E3 & 11 C2.
Tel 06-686 5330.

Bilenchi
Via della Stelletta 17.
Map 4 F3 & 12 D2.
Tel 06-687 5222.

Cesare Lampronti
Via del Babuino 174–75 (also Via del Babuino 182).
Map 4 F1.
Tel 06-322 7194.

Galleria dei Coronari
Via dei Coronari 59.
Map 4 E3 & 11 B2.
Tel 06-686 9252.

Goffi Carboni
Via Margutta 109A. **Map** 5 A2. **Tel** 06-322 7184.

Liberty
Via dei Coronari 8. **Map** 11 C2. **Tel** 06-687 5634.

Mario Prilli
Via dei Banchi Nuovi 42.
Map 4 D3 & 11 A2.
Tel 06-686 8816.

M Simotti-Rocchi
Largo Fontanella Borghese 76. **Map** 12 D1. **Tel** 06-687 6656.

Modern Art

Archeologia Monogramma Arte Contemporanea
Via Margutta 57.
Map 5 A2.
Tel 06-3265 0297.

L'Attico
Via del Paradiso 41.
Map 4 E4 & 11 C4.
Tel 06-686 9846.

Fontanella Borghese
Via Fontanella Borghese 31. **Map** 12 D1.
Tel 06-687 3741.

Galleria Bonomo
Via del Gesù 62. **Map** 12 E3. **Tel** 06-6992 5858.

Galleria Giulia
Via della Barchetta 13.
Map 4 D4 & 11 B4.
Tel 06-686 1443.

Galleria Lorcan O'Neill
Vicolo dei Catenari 3.
Map 4 D4.
Tel 06-6889 2980.

Galleria Valentina Moncada
Via Margutta 54. **Map** 5 A2. **Tel** 06-320 7956.

Antique Prints and Photographs

Alinari
Via Alibert 16A. **Map** 5 A2.
Tel 06-679 2923.

Casali
Piazza della Rotonda 81A/82. **Map** 4 F4 & 12 D3.
Tel 06-678 3515. Also: Via dei Coronari 115. **Map** 11 B2. **Tel** 06-687 3705.

Nardecchia
Piazza Navona 25.
Map 4 E4 & 11 C3.
Tel 06-686 9318.

342 | TRAVELERS' NEEDS

Food and Drink

Having sampled the local cuisine during your stay in Rome, you may be tempted to take home some irresistible delicacies that are typical of Italy. The traditional Italian food stores, *alimentari*, offer an extensive range of goods, and are a great place to start. However, specialty shops are also well worth a visit. Shop around, and choose from many typically Italian products such as pecorino romano cheese, Parma ham, extra-virgin olive oil, dried porcini mushrooms, sun-dried tomatoes, olives, and grappa, as well as superb wines from Lazio, and elsewhere. If coffee or chocolate feature on your list, then there's plenty of opportunity to satisfy those cravings too.

Do bear in mind, however, that customs restrictions can apply to certain foodstuffs. Also, when on your shopping sprees, a decent pocket-sized dictionary can be very useful in helping you decipher the labels.

Alimentari

The well-stocked **Fratelli Fabbi**, near Piazza di Spagna, has an exceptional selection of delicious cold meats, and cheeses from every corner of Italy, as well as carefully chosen quality wines, and sparkling wines to accompany them. A few doors down Via della Croce, **Focacci** is a stiff competitor with its wonderful array of Italian delicacies, while nearby **Cambi** caters to its loyal clientele with similarly first-rate fare.

Elsewhere downtown, near Campo de' Fiori, **Roscioli** *(see p320)*, with a reputation for quality and friendly service, is a favorite among locals. In the Campo itself is the **Antica Norcineria Viola**, which is the place to go for an excellent range of sausages and salami.

Farther afield, **Franchi** *(see p321)* in Prati is recognized as one of the best delicatessens in the capital for its tempting window display of seafood platters, pâtés, regional cheeses, and cold meats that continue to pull in the crowds. The historic but expensive **Volpetti** in Testaccio is synonymous with great service, and uncompromising quality. Aside from specializing in unusual cheeses, olive oils, vinegars, and a fabulous selection of food hampers, it also stocks a variety of Italian lard and caviar – you can even try before you buy.

Nearby is the well-stocked **La Fromagerie**, though those who favor organic produce may prefer to head for **Canestro**.

In the vicinity of Via Veneto is **Carlo Gargani**, with its elaborate variety of food items.

A savior for commuters and tourists is **Vyta** *(see p321)*, inside Termini station; you can choose from a selection of appetizing sandwiches or wines by the glass *(alla mescita)* and enjoy them at the bar. An excellent weekend farmers' market, **Campagna Amica**, is tucked away behind the church of Santa Maria in Cosmedin, and is well worth visiting for organic, locally produced food and wine.

Rome's most impressive temple of food is inside the Ostiense station: **Eataly** offers four floors of excellent-quality Italian products – a dizzying experience for any gourmet.

Cheese Specialists

For the ultimate cheese lover, a wider choice of regional, and national cheeses, including the best buffalo mozzarella in town, can be found in a select number of specialty shops. In the Pinciano district, the **Casa dei Latticini Micocci** sells a comprehensive range of cheeses from even the most remote regions of Italy. While in Trastevere, the family-run store **Antica Caciara Trasteverina** also has a vast assortment of local and regional products, which include sheep's ricotta and the Piemontese *toma del fen*. Branches of **Cisternino** sell well-priced local cheeses.

Chocolate Specialists

The capital boasts a number of specialty shops designed to fulfill the needs of the ever-expanding luxury food market. In Santa Croce, **La Bottega del Cioccolato** is known for its creativity – try their chocolate Colosseums. Elsewhere, close to the Pantheon, the landmark **Moriondo e Gariglio** has been in operation since 1850, serving up strictly Piedmontese treats. Across the Tiber in Trastevere, **Dolce Idea** produces interesting concoctions such as white chocolate with lemon liqueur filling and dark chocolate laced with ginger. In San Lorenzo, **Said**, housed in a 1920s chocolate factory, has a café and shop selling homemade delicacies. **Rivendita di Cioccolata e Vino** *(see p322)* can also be recommended for its selection.

Enoteche

Although most *alimentari* and supermarkets stock a decent selection of reasonably priced Italian wines, Rome's many *enoteche (see p320)* represent a more characteristic, and gratifying alternative. As well as being wine bars and sometimes even restaurants, they also sell carefully selected wines, after-dinner liqueurs, spirits, and beers to take out.

Downtown, the cramped but friendly **Mr Wine** displays a superb range of mainly Italian and a few French wines, as well as a host of sparkling wines, whiskeys, grappa, rum, liqueurs, and some classic Italian food. **La Vineria** *(see p320)* in Campo de' Fiori, while maintaining its status as an institution for many bohemian drinkers, also successfully doubles as a well-stocked and competitively priced wine shop.

Better known for its Neapolitan pizza parlor, chic restaurant, and lively wine bar, **'Gusto** *(see* p320) offers an outstanding assortment of wines for sale too. Don't pass by the shop, either – it is full of designer kitchen accessories and specialty cookbooks with recipes for both Italian and international cuisine.

The central **Achilli Enoteca al Parlamento** (see p320) and **L'Angolo Divino** both warrant a visit for a refined alternative, especially if you want to relax with an apéritif while you select wines to carry home. **Ferrazza** in San Lorenzo and **Il Vinaietto** near Campo de' Fiori also deserve special mentions for

their extensive wine lists and memorable ambience.

In Trastevere, the well-stocked liquor store **Bernabei** has good deals, as does the family-run **Trimani** (see p320) near Termini, which has an astounding variety of wines and liquor.

Others that should not be overlooked include the **Costantini** in Piazza Cavour, the beer-oriented **Palombi** in Testaccio, and **Marchetti** in Pinciano, which is the wine experts' not-so-closely-guarded secret.

Coffee Specialists

Italian brand coffee has been internationally available for many years, but if you are looking for something rarer or more exotic, then make your way to **Antico Caffè del Brasile** (see p322) in Monti for four mouth-watering blends, from Brazilian gem (the 90 percent pure variety) to economy, and family mixes. In the shadow of the Pantheon, the historic **Tazza d'Oro** (see p106) also offers a fantastic selection of blends, including the Queen of Coffees and Jamaican Blue Mountain.

DIRECTORY

Alimentari

Antica Norcineria Viola
Campo de' Fiori 43.
Map 11 C4.
Tel 06-6880 6114.

Cambi
Via del Leoncino 30.
Map 12 D1.
Tel 06-687 8081.

Campagna Amica
Via di San Teodoro 74.
Map 8 E1. **Tel** 06-489 931.

Canestro
Via Luca della Robbia 12.
Map 8 D2.
Tel 06-574 6287.

Carlo Gargani
Via Lombardia 15. **Map** 5 B2. **Tel** 06-474 0865.

Eataly
Piazzale XII Ottobre 1492.
Map 8 F5.
Tel 06-9027 9201.

Focacci
Via della Croce 43.
Map 4 F2.
Tel 06-679 1228.

Franchi
Via Cola di Rienzo 200.
Map 3 C2.
Tel 06-687 4651.

Fratelli Fabbi
Via della Croce 28.
Map 4 F2.
Tel 06-679 0612.

La Fromagerie
Piazza Testaccio 35.
Map 8 D2.
Tel 06-5725 0185.

Roscioli
Via dei Giubbonari 21.
Map 11 C4.
Tel 06-687 5287.

Volpetti
Via Marmorata 47.
Map 8 D2.
Tel 06-574 2352.

Vyta
Galleria Termini
(Termini Station).
Map 6 D3.
Tel 06-4201 4301.

Cheese Specialists

Antica Caciara Trasteverina
Via San Francesco a Ripa 140a/b. **Map** 7 C1.
Tel 06-581 2815.

Casa dei Latticini Micocci
Via Collina 14–16.
Map 6 D2.
Tel 06-474 1784.

Cisternino
Vicolo del Gallo 18–19.
Map 11 C4.
Tel 06-687 2875.

Chocolate Specialists

La Bottega del Cioccolato
Via Leonina 82.
Map 5 C5.
Tel 06-482 1473.

Dolce Idea
Via San Francesco a Ripa 27.
Map 7 C1.
Tel 06-5833 4043.

Moriondo e Gariglio
Via del Piè di Marmo 21.
Map 12 E3.
Tel 06-699 0856.

Rivendita di Cioccolata e Vino
Vicolo del Cinque 11A.
Map 11 B5.
Tel 06-5830 1868.

Said
Via Tiburtina 135.
Map 6 F4.
Tel 06-446 9204.

Enoteche

Achilli Enoteca al Parlamento
Via dei Prefetti 15.
Map 12 D1.
Tel 06-687 3446.

L'Angolo Divino
Via dei Balestrari 12–14.
Map 11 C4.
Tel 06-686 4413.

Bernabei
Via San Francesco a Ripa 48. **Map** 7 C1.
Tel 06-581-2818.

Costantini
Piazza Cavour 16.
Map 11 B1.
Tel 06-321 3210.

Ferrazza
Via dei Volsci 59.
Map 6 F4.
Tel 06-490 506.

'Gusto
Piazza Augusto Imperatore 9.
Map 4 F2.
Tel 06-322 6273.

Marchetti
Via Flavia 28.
Map 5 C2.
Tel 06-474 1745.

Mr Wine
Piazza del Parlamento 7.
Map 12 E1.
Tel 06-6813 4141.

Palombi
Piazza Testaccio 38/41.
Map 8 D3.
Tel 06-574 6122.

Trimani
Via Goito 20.
Map 6 D2.
Tel 06-446 9661.

Il Vinaietto
Via Monte della Farina 37–38.
Map 12 D4.
Tel 06-6880 6989.

La Vineria
Campo de' Fiori 15.
Map 11 C4.
Tel 06-6880 3268.

Coffee Specialists

Antico Caffè del Brasile
Via dei Serpenti 23.
Map 5 B4.
Tel 06-488 2319.

Tazza d'Oro
Via degli Orfani 84.
Map 12 D4.
Tel 06-678 9792.

Street Markets

Rome's open-air markets are essential to visit if you are interested in soaking up the bustling atmosphere of Italian market-life. The markets can be incredibly colorful and vivid as Italian stallholders have raised the display of even the humblest vegetable to an art form.

The city is dotted with popular, small local food markets, and there are several fascinating well-established markets near the center of the city, along with the famous flea market over in Trastevere.

It is important to keep your wits about you in markets because pickpockets work with lightning speed in the bustling crowds. But that said, Roman markets provide a vibrant source of entertainment and it would be a shame to let such caveats deter you from joining in.

The street fairs that take place throughout the year are fun to go to, if they coincide with your visit, since they normally sell a good variety of local produce, handicrafts, and clothes. Seasonal fairs also occur, especially around Christmas, when you can stock up on Italian specialties.

Campo de' Fiori
Piazza Campo de' Fiori. **Map** 4 E4 & 11 C4. 40, 46, 62, 64, 70, 81, 116, 492, 628. 8. **Open** 7am–1:30pm Mon–Sat. *See p148.*

Right in the heart of the old city, Rome's most picturesque market is also its most historic. Its name, Campo de' Fiori, which translates as field of flowers, sometimes misleads people into expecting a flower market. In fact, the name is said to derive from Campus Florae (Flora's square) – Flora being the lover of the great Roman general Pompey. A market has actually been held in this beautiful piazza for many centuries. Every morning except Sunday, the piazza is transformed by an array of stands selling fruit and vegetables, meat, poultry, and fish. One or two stands specialize in beans, rice, dried fruit, and nuts, and there are also flower stands situated near the fountain. But the huge open baskets of broccoli and spinach, chopped vegetables, and freshly prepared green salad mixes are the main attraction for visitors. They provide a striking visual display as well as an edible feast.

The excellent delicatessens on the square, and bread shops nearby, complement the market. They make it a great place to stock up for an impromptu picnic if the weather is pleasant and you are tempted to do some alfresco dining in one of Rome's many parks. The market gets extremely busy on Saturdays, so be prepared to fight your way through the crowds.

Mercato delle Stampe
Largo della Fontanella di Borghese. **Map** 4 F3 & 12 D1. 81, 116, 117, 492, 628. **Open** 7am–1pm Mon–Sat.

This market is a veritable haven for lovers of old prints, books (both genuine antiquarian and less-exalted secondhand), magazines, and other printed ephemera. The quality varies, but it is a good deal more specialized than the *banche* or stands near Termini station, which are a more obvious tourist trap. Italian-speaking collectors can enjoy a field day leafing through back issues of specialty magazines. Other visitors might prefer the wonderful selection of illustrated art books and old prints of Rome. It is a good place to pick up that Piranesi print of your favorite Roman vista, ruin, or church – but be prepared to bargain hard.

Mercato dei Fiori
Via Trionfale. **Map** 3 B1. Ottaviano S. Pietro. 23, 51, 70, 490. **Open** 10:30am–1pm Tue.

Essentially a trade market, the Flower Market, just north of Via Andrea Doria, is open to the public only on Tuesdays. Housed in a covered hall, it has two floors overflowing with cut flowers upstairs, and all kinds of potted plants on the lower floor.

Anyone who has an interest in flowers will enjoy this wonderful array of Mediterranean blooms, which are sold at giveaway prices.

Mercato Andrea Doria
Via Andrea Doria. **Map** 3 B1. Ottaviano S. Pietro. 23, 70, 490. **Open** 7am–1:30pm Mon–Sat.

The market used to stretch the whole length of this wide avenue. It has now been transferred to a modern, covered state-of-the-art building. Apart from the magnificent displays of fruit and vegetables, it has numerous stands selling meat, poultry, fish, and groceries, as well as an interesting clothing, and shoe section. Situated northwest of the Vatican Museums, it is a little off the normal beaten track, and has remained very much a Roman market that caters to the needs of the large local population.

Nuovo Mercato Esquilino
Via Principe Amedeo. **Map** 6 E5. Vittorio Emanuele. 105. **Open** 7am–2pm Mon–Sat. *See p176.*

In the past, bustling Piazza Vittorio was perhaps the most Roman of the city's larger markets.

Rechristened, and housed in covered premises, it is still the place where bargain-hunting *popolari*, Rome's bustling shoppers, buy their food. Vendors offer cheap prices if you buy by the kilo (2.2 lb), but watch out for bad fruit.

This is also one of the city's more international markets, and features African and Asian food stands that cater to the area's many ethnic groups. Definitely a place to go to capture the atmosphere of a traditional but changing city.

Mercato di Testaccio
Between Via A. Volta and Via Galvani. **Map** 8 D3. Piramide. 23, 75, 280. 3. **Open** 7:30am–1:30pm Mon–Sat.

Filled with stands selling fresh produce of every kind, the local market for this most Roman of areas is a stage set of seductive colors and textures. Uniquely, it also houses the Roman remains found on the site during the construction of the present building; appropriately enough, archaeologists think that the ruins testify to a market that stood here in ancient times. Popular with local residents, who insist on high-quality produce at reasonable prices, the market also appeals to visitors for its relaxed and friendly atmosphere.

Porta Portese
Via Portuense & Via Ippolito Nievo.
Map 7 C3. H, 23, 44, 75.
3, 8. **Open** 6:30am–2pm Sun.

The *mercato delle pulci* or flea market is a relatively new market in Roman terms. Established shortly after the end of World War II, it is said to have grown out of the thriving black market that operated at Tor di Nona opposite Castel Sant'Angelo during those lean years. Vendors come from as far away as Naples and set up shop in the early hours of the morning – if you are strolling in that direction after a late night in Trastevere, it is well worth pausing just to watch them.

Anything and everything seems to be for sale, piled high on stands in carefully arranged disorder – clothes, shoes, bags, luggage, camping equipment, linen, towels, pots, pans, kitchen utensils, plants, pets, spare parts, cassettes, and CDs, old LPs and 78s.

Furniture stands tend to be concentrated around Piazza Ippolito Nievo along with what they call "antiques," though you may have to sort through an awful lot of junk before finding a real one. And then you will have to bargain for it. The technique is to offer them half the asked price, and then walk away. A lot of people go just for the fun of it and end up buying something.

There are also secondhand clothes – leather or sheepskin coats and jackets go for €10 – with many of the Via Sannio vendors relocating here for the Sunday market. In recent years, Porta Portese has become much frequented by customers belonging to the various immigrant groups in the capital. If you have a Sunday morning to spare, a visit to the market is now one of the most cosmopolitan experiences that the city offers.

Mercato di Via Sannio
Via Sannio. **Map** 9 C2. San Giovanni. 16, 81, 87. **Open** 8am–1pm Mon–Fri, 8am–6pm Sat.

In the 1960s and 1970s this used to be Italy's answer to London's Carnaby Street. Today, at first glance, it seems not to have anything special to offer – random stands selling inexpensive casual clothes, shoes, bags, belts, jewelry, toys, kitchen utensils, and music cassettes. But toward the end of the street there is a large covered section that extends back to the Aurelian Wall (*see p198*) with many stands piled high with second-hand clothes at very low prices for those who like to rummage. There is also a section that sells military-style goods plus some camping, and fishing equipment.

Some of these stands move their wares to Porta Portese on Sunday morning.

Local Markets
Generally Open 7am–1pm Mon–Sat.

Piazza delle Coppelle (**Map** 4 F3 & 12 D2), near the Pantheon, is probably the most picturesque of the food markets sprinkled around the city. A tiny market devoted to food, fruit, and flowers, it offers a charming splash of color in the heart of the city.

Piazza San Cosimato (**Map** 7 C1) in Trastevere hosts another lively local market with some tempting cheeses and salami.

There is a fairly big market on **Via Alessandria** (**Map** 6 D1) in Nomentana, and other smaller ones in **Via della Pace** (**Map** 4 E4 & 11 C3) near Piazza Navona, and in **Via Balbo** (**Map** 5 C4) and **Via Milazzo** (**Map** 6 E3) near Termini station.

All markets usually have at least one stand selling household goods, and basic Italian kitchen gadgets.

Street Fairs

A special and interesting feature of shopping in Rome is the street fair.

Neglected and under-exploited for most of the year, the lower banks of the Tiber come into their own in summer during the mid-June–early September **Lungo il Tevere** festival. This takes place daily from 6pm until after midnight on the stretch of river between Ponte Palatino and Ponte Sisto. Stands sell a variety of goods, from regional produce and ethnic bric-a-brac to books and confectionary. You can also take a break at one of the many bars and eateries lining the route.

There are various open-air antique markets held in the city throughout the year. One of the most central and best known is **La Soffitta sotto i Portici** (The Attic beneath the Porticoes), which is held 8am–7pm every other Sunday (except August) along the eastern edge of Piazza Augusto Imperatore. Professional and weekend sellers run stands offering antique (or simply retro) furniture, lamps, jewelry and *objets d'art*.

The **Via Margutta Art Fair** usually takes place around Christmas and in springtime. Set in one of the most charming and exclusive streets of the city, this is an event not to be missed, although it is more for browsing, since prices are very high.

The utterly glamorous **Spanish Steps Alta Moda Fashion Show** is a must for fashionistas but does not have a set date. The limited seating space is filled by invitation only. However, the public can squeeze in behind to enjoy this display of all-Italian designer fashion. So far it has been held mid-to-late July.

The traditional **Christmas Fair** held in Piazza Navona from mid-December until January 6 is now rather down-at-heel, but still fascinating for those who have not seen it before, or for children. Stands selling clay statues for nativity scenes and candies that look like pieces of coal are the main attraction.

Natale Oggi is a well-established event taking place near Christmas at the Fiera di Roma in the Portuense district, and worth visiting to take a look at the Italian Christmas treats.

Via Giulia hosts art fairs now and then, and open evenings when the antique and art galleries stay open late, offering food and wine to all visitors.

Every year Trastevere hosts its very own carnival, the **Festa de Noantri**, in late July, when Viale Trastevere is overrun with the typical *porchetta* stands (*see p347*), party lights, gift stands, and people.

The details given here may change, so consult the local listings, the tourist office, or the tourist call center (*see p369*).

ENTERTAINMENT IN ROME

There's a particular excitement attached to Roman entertainment. Soccer and opera, for example, are both worth experiencing for sheer atmosphere alone, whether or not you are a fan. The jazz scene is especially good, with international stars appearing alongside local talent. And concerts and movies take on an added dimension when performances take place beneath the stars in the many open-air arenas spread across the city.

Unexpectedly, given the general shutdown among shops and restaurants, the summer remains Rome's liveliest time for live music, and other cultural events. Rome's graceful Renaissance squares, vast parks, villa gardens, Classical ruins, and other open spaces host various major arts festivals. For those who prefer sports, or want to try out some Roman nightclubs, there's plenty available too.

Saxophonist at Planet Roma *(see p350)*

Practical Information

A good source of information about what's going on is *TrovaRoma*, the weekly Thursday supplement to *La Repubblica* newspaper. It has a day-by-day rundown of what's on where, and covers music, exhibitions, theater, movies, guided tours, restaurants, and children's entertainment. Daily newspapers like *Il Messaggero*, *Il Manifesto*, and *La Repubblica* usually list that evening's entertainment, but only in Italian.

The magazine *Wanted in Rome*, found at Via Veneto newsstands or English-language bookshops, provides less detailed listings in English, while the monthly *Where Rome*, available from reception desks of four- and five-star hotels, is a good source of information and up-to-date listings. Also worth getting hold of is *L'Evento*, a free booklet available from tourist information offices around the city *(see p369)*. Published every two months, it gives details in English of classical music, festivals, theater, exhibitions, and more in the city and surroundings. Up-to-date information can also be found on various websites.

Punctuality is not what Italians are renowned for, so don't be surprised if events start later than advertised.

Buying Tickets

Booking in advance is not part of the Italian lifestyle, though this is slowly changing. Two ticket agencies that will reserve tickets for some performances for you (for a small fee) are **Orbis**, and the Internet-based **Ticketeria**. Rome's **Tourist Info Line** also helps visitors book tickets for various events. Many theaters themselves do not accept phone bookings – you have to visit the box office in person. They will charge you a *prevendita* supplement (about 10 percent of the normal price) for any tickets sold in advance. The price of a theater ticket can be anything between €8 and €52.

Tickets for classical concerts are usually sold on the spot, and are sometimes for that night only, an arrangement

Stage at Caffè Latino *(see pp350–51)*

days before the performance. It is usually easier (and also a bit cheaper) to get tickets for the open-air summer performances.

The **Teatro dell'Opera** box office *(see p349)* handles face-to-face and online sales for both summer and winter seasons.

Tickets for most big rock and jazz events can be bought at **Orbis** and at larger record shops such as the Torre Argentina branch of **Feltrinelli**.

If you are trying to get hold of a ticket for a performance that has already sold out, you are unlikely to be able to obtain one from unofficial sources – there are very few ticket scalpers in Rome, except at major soccer games.

Member of contemporary dance group Momix *(see p349)*

that favors the last-minute decision to go. Opera is the exception. Tickets are sold months in advance, with just a few held back until two

Discount Tickets

Theaters and concert venues tend not to offer discounts directly, although there is a centralized service (**Last Minute Teatro**) offering up to

50 percent off seats on the day of the performance.

Movie theaters occasionally offer people over 60, and disabled people a 30 percent reduction on weekdays. Many theaters also have cheaper ticket prices for weekday afternoon screenings, and for all shows on Wednesdays.

Some clubs offer reductions: look for *due per uno* coupons in local bars that allow two people entrance for the price of one.

Summer night outdoor performance among Roman ruins

Facilities for the Disabled

Few Roman venues provide easy access for people with restricted mobility, and any disabled visitors and their companions are likely to find the lack of provisions for them very frustrating.

The situation does improve a little in summer, however, when a great many performances in the city are held at open-air venues. The classical concerts held in the beautiful gardens of Villa Giulia *(see pp354–5)* have wheelchair access.

Singers performing the *Barber of Seville*

For more general information on facilities for disabled people visiting Rome, see pages 368–9.

Open-Air Entertainment

Open-air opera, movies, and concerts fill the calendar from late June until the end of

The Teatro dell'Opera *(see p348)*

September. These outdoor performances can be wonderful, with spectacular settings and enthusiastic audiences. Some of them are grand affairs, but smaller events may be just as evocative – a recital in the grounds of the Theater of Marcellus *(see p153)*, for example, or jazz in the gardens of Villa Celimontana *(see p195)*.

Some movie theaters roll back their ceilings in summer for open-air screenings, or else move to outdoor arenas, and there are also annual open-air movie festivals. The Cineporto along the Tiber, and the Festival di Massenzio offer films, food, and small exhibitions in July and August. Theater, too, moves outside in summer. Greek and Roman plays are staged at Ostia Antica *(see p272)*, and other shows take place at the Anfiteatro del Tasso *(see p353)*.

The Basilica of Constantine and Maxentius in the Forum *(see p88)* hosts the Festa della Letteratura (mid-May–mid-Jun), with major international writers reading from their works. Hadrian's Villa *(see p271)* is the equally stunning setting for the Villa Adriana Festival of music and modern dance (Jun–Jul). Consult listings in newspapers, magazines, or websites *(see p346)*, or watch for posters around the city for the most up-to-date information.

More traditional is Trastevere's community festival, Festa de Noantri *(see p61)*, with music, fireworks, and processions. This religious festival begins on the Saturday after July 16, but celebrations continue into August. The Festa dell'Unità, run by the DS (the former Communist Party), but not limited to politics, is generally held in summer. The program includes games, stands, food, and drinks.

Finally, if you like your entertainment less structured, do as the Romans do and take part in the *passeggiata* (early evening stroll) – the city's favorite spots are Piazza Navona *(see p122)* and along Via del Corso.

DIRECTORY

Ticket Agencies

Feltrinelli
Largo Argentina 11. **Map** 4 F4.
Tel 06-6830 8596. Classical music, rock, pop, and jazz concerts, and some sporting events.

Last Minute Teatro
Via Bari 18 (off Piazza Salerno). **Map** 6 F1. **Tel** 06-4411 7799. **Open** 2–8pm Tue–Sat, 2–4pm Sun.

Orbis
Piazza dell'Esquilino 37.
Map 6 D4. **Tel** 06-474 4776.

Tourist Info Line
Tel 06-0608.

Useful Websites

W helloticket.it
W listicket.it
W ticketeria.it
W turismoroma.it

Classical Music and Dance

Classical concerts take place in a surprisingly large number of venues; tickets for opera premieres may be hard to get, but soloists, groups, or orchestras playing in gardens, churches, villas, or ancient ruins are more accessible. World-renowned soloists and orchestras make appearances all year round; past visitors have included Luciano Pavarotti and Placido Domingo, the Berlin Philharmonic, and prima ballerina Sylvie Guillem.

Programs are generally international in scope but sometimes you will find a festival dedicated to one of Italy's own, like Palestrina, the great 16th-century master of polyphonic church music, or Arcangelo Corelli, inventor of the Baroque *concerto grosso*.

Music in Churches

One of Rome's main attractions for classical music is the rich repertoire in the city's churches. Always sacred in theme (by decree of Pope John Paul II), music is mainly performed as concerts rather than during services.

Programs are posted around the city and outside the churches. You will often find very good musicians playing in the main churches, while the smaller, out-of-the-way churches frequently have young musicians, and amateur choirs as well.

St. Peter's *(see p228)* hosts one major RAI (national broadcasting company) concert on December 5, attended by the Pope and free to the general public. It has two established choirs. The Coro della Cappella Giulia sings at the 10:30am mass and 5pm vespers on Sunday. The Coro della Cappella Sistina sings whenever the Pope celebrates mass here, as on June 29 (St. Peter and St. Paul's Day).

Important choral masses also take place on January 25 in **San Paolo fuori le Mura** *(see p269)*, when the Pope attends, on June 24 in **San Giovanni in Laterano** *(p182)*, and on December 31 at the **Gesù** *(pp110–11)* where the *Te Deum* is sung. The church of **Sant'Ignazio di Loyola** *(p108)* is another favorite venue for choral concerts.

Plainsong and Gregorian chant can be heard in **Sant' Anselmo** *(p206)* every Sunday (Oct–Jul) at the 8:30am mass and 7:15pm vespers. Easter and the Christmas festivities are a great time for cheap (and chilly) concerts.

Orchestral, Chamber, and Choral Music

Up until the opening of the Renzo Piano–designed **Parco della Musica** on the Via Flaminia, with its three auditoriums and open-air arena, the **Auditorium Conciliazione**, and the **Teatro dell'Opera** had been Rome's two main auditoriums. All venues have their own resident orchestras and choirs, and offer varied seasons that include visiting groups, and soloists from all over the world. Rome's own Orchestra e Coro dell'Accademia di Santa Cecilia performs at the Parco della Musica throughout the year.

The season at the **Teatro Olimpico** usually offers good chamber music, some orchestral concerts, and ballet, with at least one concert a week.

Although a variety of classical concerts take place at the **Accademia Filarmonica Romana**, the emphasis is on chamber and choral music, with an internationally renowned series of concerts running from mid-October to mid-May. Performances take place in the Sala Casella, which seats around 180.

Ticket prices for classical concerts depend a lot on performers and venue. The **Auditorium del Foro Italico** sells tickets for most concerts for under €15; a ticket for the **Teatro Olimpico** costs between €15–€25, but seats for an important concert at **Teatro dell'Opera** may cost more than €80.

The Associazione Musicale Romana, dedicated to Renaissance and Baroque music, organizes three annual festivals in the **Palazzo della Cancelleria** *(see p151)*: the Festival Internazionale di Cembalo (harpsichord festival) in March; Musica al Palazzo in May; and the Festival Internazionale di Organo in September. Classical music fans should also watch for performances by the Orchestra di Roma e del Lazio at **Teatro Argentina** or **Teatro Valle** *(see p353)*.

It is always worth checking which musicians are due to be playing at the **Teatro Ghione**, the **Oratorio del Gonfalone,** and especially the **Aula Magna dell'Università La Sapienza**, which has one of the most innovative programs of classical, and contemporary music.

Open-Air Summer Concerts

In the summer, music lovers can enjoy concerts in cloisters, palazzo courtyards, and ancient ruins. Concerts can be one-time events or part of a festival program, regular fixtures or impromptu. Do as the Romans do: wait until the last moment and keep an eye on the posters and listings pages *(see p346)*.

Open-air opera, and dance have their summer home in the Baths of Caracalla, which provide a splendid backdrop to performances. Classical concerts are often part of festivals like Roma-Europa *(see p347)* but there are also open-air festivals, and concert series dedicated to classical music. Among the more interesting are those that take place in some of the city's historic churches. It is well worth checking out the summer programs for Sant'Ivo alla Sapienza *(see p124)* and San Clemente *(see p189)*.

The Associazione Musicale Romana organizes Serenate in

Chiostro – a lively and varied program of concerts during July in the cloisters of **Santa Maria della Pace** (see p123) with tickets at reasonable prices. The Concerti del Tempietto are a real summer treat with concerts held almost every evening from July to September in the **Area Archeologica del Teatro di Marcello** (see p153) or in the park of the Villa Torlonia.

Festival Villa Pamphilj in Musica, in July, is a series of concerts in the gardens of **Villa Doria Pamphilj** (see p269). Programs range from comic opera to jazz and 20th-century classical music.

Brass bands can be heard in the **Pincio Gardens** (see p138) on Sunday mornings from the end of April until mid-July – they usually strike up at around 10:30am.

Contemporary Music

The Parco della Musica and the Accademia Filarmonica Romana (usually at the **Teatro Olimpico**) often include contemporary pieces in their programs, but these are less popular than the classical pieces and there is no set venue with a regular contemporary program.

International names appear on festival programs, and at special concerts at the **Aula Magna dell'Università La Sapienza**. The most interesting contemporary music festival is organized by the Nuova Consonanza in the fall, while electronic, and digital music is showcased at the Dissonanze festival, which is generally held in May. Also worth keeping an eye out for are performances by scholars of the French Academy at **Villa Medici** (see p137).

Opera

Italy and opera are to many people synonymous. Critics will tell you (justifiably) that Rome's opera is not up to the standard of Milan's La Scala or Naples's San Carlo. But that doesn't mean it is not worth visiting – world-class singers do appear here (see p42), mainly in premières or solo recitals. However you judge the quality of the performances, the surroundings in which they take place are often incomparable. In summer the visual spectacle of Aida, say, performed in the open air, is quite magnificent.

The season starts late at **Teatro dell'Opera**, between November and January. In recent years, programs have concentrated on the great popular operas, rather than experimental productions. Tickets range from €17 to €130.

The Teatro dell'Opera moves outdoors in July and August to stage opera and ballet in the ancient Baths of Caracalla (see p199). Popular works by Verdi and Puccini are performed, and although the acoustics are not perfect, the unique setting makes up for it.

Ballet and Dance

Opportunities to watch ballet or contemporary dance can be limited in Rome. The opera house's resident company Corpo di Ballo del Teatro dell'Opera di Roma performs the great classics as well as Roland Petit–style modern choreographies. Performances are staged at **Teatro dell'Opera**.

Contemporary dance is best seen during the Parco della Musica's Equilibrio Festival in February or at summer festivals, but foreign companies also perform at **Teatro Olimpico**. American modern dance groups of the Moses Pendleton school – Pilobolus, Momix, ISO, and Daniel Ezralow – are popular visitors. **Teatro del Vascello** is another venue noted for its experimental dance performances.

In the fall, top visiting companies from all over the world perform during the **RomaEuropa Festival**.

DIRECTORY

For information about festivals and open-air concerts, see Trovaroma or similar listings (see pp346 & 367).

Orchestral, Chamber, and Choral Music

Accademia Filar-monica Romana
Via Flaminia 118. **Map** 1 A1. **Tel** 06-320 1752.
ⓦ filarmonicaromana.org

Auditorium Conciliazione
Via della Conciliazione 4. **Map** 3 C3. **Tel** 800-904 560. ⓦ auditorium conciliazione.it

Aula Magna dell'Università La Sapienza
Piazzale Aldo Moro 5.
Tel 06-361 0051.
ⓦ concertiiuc.it

Oratorio del Gonfalone
Via del Gonfalone 32A.
Map 4 D4 & 11 A3.
Tel 06-687 5952.

Parco della Musica
Viale de Coubertin 30.
Map 1 C2.
Tel 06-8024 1281 (for information);
Tel 892 982 (for credit card sales).
ⓦ auditorium.com

Sant'Anselmo
Piazza Cavalieri di Malta 5.
Map 8 D2. **Tel** 06-579 11.

Teatro Ghione
Via delle Fornaci 37.
Map 3 B4.
Tel 06-637 2294.
ⓦ teatroghione.it

Teatro Olimpico
Piazza Gentile da Fabriano 17.
Tel 06-326 5991.
ⓦ teatroolimpico.it

Opera

Teatro dell'Opera
Piazza Beniamino Gigli 1.
Map 5 C3. **Tel** 06-481 601.
ⓦ operaroma.it

Ballet & Dance

RomaEuropa Festival
Via dei Magazzini Generali 20A.
Tel 06-4555 3050.
ⓦ romaeuropa.net

Teatro Olimpico
Piazza Gentile da Fabriano 17.
Tel 06-326 5991.
ⓦ teatroolimpico.it

Teatro dell'Opera
Piazza Beniamino Gigli 1.
Map 5 C3. **Tel** 06-481 601.
ⓦ operaroma.it

Teatro Vascello
Via G Carini 78. **Map** 7 A2.
Tel 06-588 1021.
ⓦ teatrovascello.it

Rock, Jazz, Folk, and World Music

Rome's non-classical music scene is unpredictable and subject to vast seasonal changes, but there is a huge variety of music to be enjoyed at the many clubs and stadiums, with visiting foreign and homegrown stars. Summer months bring excellent open-air rock, jazz, and world music festivals.

The music sections of listings magazines *Trova-Roma* and *Roma c'è (see p346)* give a good idea of what's on, and ticket agencies at Orbis and Feltrinelli will have details of the latest tours. For smaller venues, you might need to buy a *tessera* (monthly or annual membership card) costing anything from €2 to €11, which often includes the entrance fee for smaller bands.

Rock Music

Big-name rock concerts are held in sports venues at the **Palalottomatica** and the legendary **Stadio Olimpico**, though it is also a good idea to keep an eye on who's performing at the **Atlantico**. The **Palladium** and Testaccio's **Villaggio Globale** at the Ex-Mattatoio (a converted abattoir) are other large-scale venues for concerts and other events, while the **Parco della Musica** also hosts top acts. Entrance can cost above €25, but there are plenty of opportunities for smaller budgets. If you're in Rome on May 1, join the crowds at the massive open-air concert that is usually held at Piazza San Giovanni. Bands also play for free during the European Festival of Music celebrations, on and around June 21. For all mega-concerts, it is always a good idea to show up an hour or so before the act gets under way to be sure of a good place. Not far from the Vatican, **Fonclea** is also worth checking out.

One of the city's most interesting venues is **Forte Prenestino**, a former prison taken over by squatters, and turned into a social center with a characteristically alternative feel. It now hosts rock concerts, debates, and art exhibitions. Meanwhile, **Locanda Atlantide**, with its low entrance fee and central location, is a place where many up-and-coming Roman bands, and soloists cut their teeth. **Init** is also worth checking out, as is **ConTestaccio**, whose live evenings focus on emerging talent.

Discos often double as live music venues, too, so check to see if there are any midweek surprises at **Piper** or weekend concerts at the **Circolo degli Artisti** and the slightly more alternative **Brancaleone**.

Jazz

Rome's taste for jazz has developed over the years as a result of visits from American and other foreign musicians. Miles Davis played one of his last concerts here, and other jazz gurus such as Pat Metheny, Michael Brecker, Sonny Rollins, and Joe Zawinul's Syndicate are all frequent visitors. On no account should *aficionados* miss a visit to the excellent **Casa del Jazz**. Top musicians also play at **Alexanderplatz** and Trastevere's **Big Mama** club, one of the city's legendary addresses for important names, offering everything from trad R&B to progressive jazz and rock. It is also worth checking out what's on at **Gregory's**, **Boogie Club**, and **Be Bop** jazz and blues club. **Planet Roma** is unique in offering separate concert halls, and interesting festivals featuring high-quality ensembles. Otherwise, check local listings to see what's on at **Caffè Latino** or **Caruso – Café de Orient**. Some of Rome's smaller venues, like **Charity Cafè**, also showcase formidable new talent.

If you want to mix music with your meal, then try **'Gusto**, a slick downtown pizzeria/ restaurant with live jazz performances on most nights. If Creole cuisine is more to your taste, then reserve a table in advance at Alexanderplatz.

Local names to look for include pianist Antonello Salis, who mingles jazz, and Caribbean rhythms, and respected soul-singer Fulvio Tomaino. Other leading lights on the blues scene are Roberto Gatto and Maurizio Gianmarco, frequent visitors at Big Mama.

The Roman summer abounds in jazz. The principal event is the Alexanderplatz Jazz Image festival in June and July, with nightly alfresco performances at the Villa Celimontana park, just behind the Colosseum. Tickets cost around €10, and are available at the park itself. Another important fixture is the yearly fall Roma Jazz Festival with big names from the Italian, and international jazz scene visiting the Parco della Musica.

Folk Music

Since the sad demise of Rome's historic Folkstudio, there is no single venue for folk aficionados in the city, though those prepared to scour the listings may uncover a country evening at **Four Green Fields**, an interesting acoustic set at **Caffè Latino**, or a soulful soloist at **Lettere Caffè**.

Traditional Roman folk music has been more or less reduced to tourist-diluted serenades at outdoor restaurants; besides, young locals tend to favor the folk music of other regions and countries. Many bands from various parts of Italy, such as Mau Mau and Agricantus, have found success by drawing on regional rhythms and singing in dialect. Italians' love of all things Irish also means that strains of the fiddle and drum can be heard in many of the Irish pubs dotted throughout the city. If you have to choose one, then make it the Guinness-enriched **Fiddler's Elbow** near Santa Maria Maggiore.

World Music

As the capital of a Latin country that has strong links with other Mediterranean cultures, Rome is a city where world music flourishes. Whether you are looking for South American salsa, African rhythms, or Arab cadences, you are unlikely to be disappointed.

Latin American music is no passing fad, as the well-established festivals, dance schools, and sellout tours by the likes of Brazilian mega-star

Caetano Veloso testify. Many venues offer opportunities to enjoy Latin American music throughout the year. **Arriba Arriba** serves up a choice menu of strictly spicy Latin rhythms. Also check what's on at **Caruso – Café de Oriente** in Testaccio, where you can enjoy a cocktail or two along with the predominantly Cuban music.

However, summer is the season when Latin American music really comes into its own. The two-month Fiesta festival at the **Ippodromo delle Capannelle** has become by far the most popular feature of the long list of Roman summer events, racking up in excess of a million ticket sales.

If your tastes are more eclectic, there's also the excellent "Roma Incontra Il Mondo." This summer festival of world music takes place at **Villa Ada**, a large park north of downtown, from mid-June to early August. Fans gather each evening to appreciate the talents of names like Angelique Kidjo and South African pianist Abdullah Ibrahim.

World music is also well served at the aptly named **Villaggio Globale**, which hosts regular concerts. For a somewhat more eclectic experience, try **Lettere Caffè**, Rome's first literary café, which offers occasional evenings of world music, with performances of anything from Australian aborigine to Greek syrtaki sounds.

DIRECTORY

Alexanderplatz
Via Ostia 9. **Map** 3 B1.
Tel 06-3974 2171.

Arriba Arriba
Via delle Capannelle 104.
Tel 06-721 3772.

Atlantico
Viale dell'Oceano Atlantico 271D, EUR.
Tel 06-591 5727.

Be Bop
Via Giulietti 14. **Map** 8 E4.
Tel 06-575 5582.

Big Mama
Vicolo San Francesco a Ripa 18. **Map** 7 C2.
Tel 06-581 2551.

Boogie Club
Via Gaetano Astolfi 63–65 (southeast of Stazione Trastevere).
Tel 06-6066 4283.

Brancaleone
Via Levanna 13 (in Monte Sacro). **Tel** 06-8200 4382.

Caffè Latino
Via di Monte Testaccio 96.
Map 8 D4.
Tel 06-578 2411.

Caruso – Café de Orient
Via di Monte Testaccio 36.
Map 8 D4.
Tel 06-574 5019.

Casa del Jazz
Viale di Porta Ardeatina 55. **Map** 9 A4.
Tel 06-704 731.

Charity Cafè
Via Panisperna 68. **Map** 5 C4. **Tel** 06-4782 5881.

Circolo degli Artisti
Via Casilina Vecchia 42.
Map 10 F1.
Tel 06-7030 5684.

ConTestaccio
Via di Monte Testaccio 65.
Map 8 D4.
Tel 06-5728 9712.

Feltrinelli
Galleria Alberto Sordi 31–35. **Map** 12 E2.
Tel 06-679 4957.

Fiddler's Elbow
Via dell'Olmata 43.
Map 6 D4.
Tel 06-487 2110.

Fonclea
Via Crescenzio 82A.
Map 3 C2.
Tel 06-689 6302.

Forte Prenestino
Via F. Delpino (east of city, along Via Prenestina).
Tel 06-2180 7855.

Four Green Fields
Via Morin 40. **Map** 3 B1.
Tel 06-372 5091.

Gregory's
Via Gregoriana 54D.
Map 5 A2.
Tel 06-679 6386
or 327 826 3770.

'Gusto
Via della Frezza 23.
Map 4 F2.
Tel 06-322 6273.

Init
Via della Stazione Tuscolana 133. **Map** 10 F3. **Tel** 06-9727 7724.

Ippodromo delle Capannelle
Via Appia Nuova 1245 (km 12). **Tel** 06-718 2139 or 06-5422 0870 (Roma Rock).

Lettere Caffè
Via San Francesco a Ripa 100. **Map** 7 C1.
Tel 06-9727 0991.

Locanda Atlantide
Via dei Lucani 22B (San Lorenzo district).
Tel 06-9604 5875.

Orbis
Piazza Esquilino 37.
Map 6 D4.
Tel 06-474 4776.

Palalottomatica
Piazzale dello Sport, EUR.
Tel 06-540 901.

Palladium
Piazza B. Romano 8 (to the south of Stazione Ostiense).
Tel 06-4555 3050.

Parco della Musica
Viale de Coubertin 15.
Map 1 C2.
Tel 06-8024 1281.
w auditorium.com

Planet Roma
Via del Commercio 36–38.
Map 8 D5.
Tel 06-574 7826

Stadio Olimpico
Viale dei Gladiatori (north-west of downtown, across the Tiber by Monte Mario).

Villa Ada
Via Salaria 197 (north of downtown).
Tel 06-4173 4712.

Villaggio Globale
Ex-Mattatoio, Lungotevere Testaccio 2.
Map 8 D4.
Tel 347 413 1205.

Movies and Theater

Going to the movies is a popular Roman pastime, with around 40 different films on show in any week. The excellent Casa del Cinema and high-profile International Festival of Cinema reflect the city's enduring love of the big screen.

The great majority of Roman movie theaters are *prima visione* (first run) and show the latest international movies in dubbed versions. The smaller arthouse theaters are more likely to show subtitled versions of foreign films.

Theater productions are performed in Italian whether the plays are national classics or by foreign playwrights. The main theaters offer a selection by great Italian playwrights. There are also performances of traditional cabaret, avant-garde theater, and dance theater. Theater tickets cost between €8 and €50 and can be bought in advance by visiting the theater box office, or through the last-minute booking service *(see p347)*.

Prima Visione

There are over 80 *prima visione* movie theaters in the city. The best ones for decor, and comfort are the **Fiamma** (two screens) and **Barberini** (three screens).

Foreign movies are usually dubbed. Films in the original language are shown at the **Nuovo Olimpia** (daily), on Mondays at the **Alcazar**, and occasionally at the **Greenwich**.

Tickets for new movies cost around €7, but a few theaters listed as *prima visione* charge less, namely **Farnese** and **Reale**. People over 60, and disabled people are normally entitled to a 30 percent discount on weekdays. Tickets are reduced in many theaters on weekday afternoons, and on Wednesdays. Check the newspaper or listings such as *TrovaRoma* or *Roma c'è* for details *(see p346)*.

Arthouse Movie Theaters

True film buffs flock to Rome in October for the International Festival of Cinema (www. romacinemafest.it) with events centering on the **Parco della Musica**.

There are two main types of art-house movie theaters in Rome: *cine-clubs* and *cinema d'essai*. Both are good if you're interested in catching older classics and new foreign films as well as movies by contemporary Italian directors.

The *d'essai* theaters now and then show films in the original

language (indicated by *v.o.* for *versione originale* in the listings). Try the **Azzurro Scipioni** (one of the few to be open throughout summer), **Filmstudio**, or Nanni Moretti's **Nuovo Sacher**. Some of the smaller theaters are called *cine-clubs* and require membership.

The **Palazzo delle Esposizioni** shows interesting series of international films, though you should head for the **Casa del Cinema** for the real arthouse experience.

Cartoons and children's favorites are shown at **Dei Piccoli**, in the leafy surrounds of the Villa Borghese.

English-Language Films

As well as occasional undubbed showings of American, British, and Australasian films in arthouse theaters and the **Nuovo Olimpia** and **The Space Cinema Moderno**, the excellent **Casa del Cinema** has a policy of screening all movies in their original language.

Summer Movies

Some Roman cinemas have roll-back ceilings that are in use during the summer, while the others close down. The **Nuovo Sacher** has an outdoor arena. Rome also has various summer film festivals: Cineporto and Massenzio, to name but two.

These show several films each night from 9pm until the small hours, with food and drinks for sale and often live music during intermissions. Cineporto takes place in the Parco della Farnesina nightly between July and September, but Massenzio moves around *(see listings)*.

Sci-fi enthusiasts should keep an eye out for the Fantafestival (early June), a science fiction, fantasy, and horror film festival. The Venezia a Roma event in September gives movie buffs a chance to see movies presented at the summer Venice Film Festival.

The listings pages *(see p346)* have details on retrospectives and avant-garde film seasons at the **Azzurro Scipioni** and the open-air arts festivals like RomaEuropa *(see p347)* and Festa dell'Unità *(see p347)*.

Mainstream Theater

The backbone of Rome's theatrical repertoire are Luigi Pirandello's dramas, and comedies by 18th-century Venetian Carlo Goldoni, 20th-century Neapolitan Eduardo de Filippo, and Nobel Prize winner Dario Fo. Major foreign playwrights are also performed from time to time.

The best classic productions are staged at the **Teatro Argentina**, **Teatro Quirino**, **Teatro Eliseo**, and **Teatro Piccolo Eliseo**. **Teatro Argentina** is state-owned and home of Rome's permanent theater company. Its sister theater, **Teatro India**, stages more innovative works. The historic **Teatro Ambra Jovinelli**, near Termini station, is the best place to go for comedy acts. Plays at the **Quirino** often feature famous Italian actors. The **Eliseo** and **Piccolo Eliseo** are among the city's best private theaters.

At **Teatro Sistina** and **Teatro Brancaccio** you can see hit musicals by visiting foreign companies and shows by popular Italian actors, while **Teatro Vittoria** goes in for plays by Noël Coward or Neil Simon.

Contemporary Theater

The home of contemporary theater is the ever-dynamic **Vascello**, the **Orologio**, and, beyond these well-known names, in a host of small theaters, ingeniously rigged up in cellars, garages, small apartments, or even tents.

The **Teatro Nuovo Colosseo** hosts some alternative fringe-type productions (known here as *teatro off*), while the **Palladium** and the **Vascello** tend to stage works by contemporary authors and occasional avant-garde productions. Some of them, like **Teatro India** and Orologio, also put on foreign-language productions.

Folk, Cabaret, and Puppet Theater

Roman and Neapolitan folk songs and cabaret can be enjoyed in Trastevere's tourist-trade restaurants, like **Meo Patacca**, while **Tina Pika Village** offers more alternative cabaret.

Puppet theater is another Roman tradition. Shows take place early in the evening on weekends, and sometimes during the week, at **Teatro Verde** and **Teatro Mongiovino**. In the Villa Borghese, the **Teatro San Carlino** also presents plays with the younger audience in mind. Among the most popular are the adventures of *Pulcinella* (the Italian Punch).

Open-Air Theater

The open-air summer theater season usually features Greek and Roman plays at **Ostia Antica** (*see pp272–3*).

The **Anfiteatro Quercia del Tasso** in the Janiculum Park takes its name from the oak tree under which 16th-century poet Tasso used to sit. Comedy shows are staged here in July to September, when the weather permits. In winter the company performs at the **Teatro Anfitrione**.

Nearby is a Neapolitan street puppet theater booth featuring *Pulcinella*. Shows are usually on in the afternoons, with morning shows on Sundays.

DIRECTORY

Prima Visione

Alcazar
Via Card. Merry del Val 14.
Map 7 C1. **Tel** 06-588 0099.

Barberini
Piazza Barberini 24.
Map 5 B3.
Tel 06-8639 1361.

Farnese
Piazza Campo de' Fiori 56.
Map 4 E5.
Tel 06-686 4395.

Fiamma
Via Bissolati 47. **Map** 5 C2.
Tel 06-4547 2090.

Greenwich
Via Bodoni 59. **Map** 7 C3.
Tel 06-574 5825.

Nuovo Olimpia
Via in Lucina 16. **Map** 12
E1. **Tel** 06-686 1068.

Reale
Piazza Sonnino 7.
Map 7 C1. **Tel** 06-5810 234.

The Space Cinema Moderno
Piazza della Repubblica 45.
Map 5 C3. **Tel** 892 111.

Arthouse Movie Theaters

Azzurro Scipioni
Via degli Scipioni 82. **Map** 3
C2. **Tel** 06-3973 7161.

Casa del Cinema
Largo M. Mastroianni 1.
Map 5 B1. **Tel** 06-423 601.
w casadelcinema.it

Dei Piccoli
Viale della Pineta 15.
Map 5 B1.
Tel 06-855 3485.

Filmstudio
Via degli Orti d'Alibert 1C.
Map 4 D4.
Tel 06-4543 9775.

Nuovo Sacher
Largo Ascianghi 1.
Map 7 C2.
Tel 06-581 8116.

Palazzo delle Esposizioni
Via Nazionale 194.
Map 5 B4.
Tel 06-3996 7500.
w palazzoesposizioni.it

Parco della Musica
Viale de Coubertin 30.
Map 1 C2.
Tel 06-8024 1281.
w romacinemafest.org

Mainstream Theater

Teatro Ambra Jovinelli
Piazza G. Pepe 43. **Map** 6
E4. **Tel** 06-8308 2620.

Teatro Argentina
Largo Argentina 56.
Map 4 F4. **Tel** 06-684 0001.
w teatrodiroma.net

Teatro Brancaccio
Via Merulana 244.
Map 6 D5.
Tel 06-8068 7231.

Teatro Eliseo
Via Nazionale 183. **Map** 5
B4. **Tel** 06-488 721.
w teatroeliseo.it

Teatro India
Via L. Pierantoni 6.
Map 7 C5.
Tel 06-684 0001.

Teatro Piccolo Eliseo
Via Nazionale 183.
Map 5 B4.
Tel 06-488 2114.

Teatro Quirino
Via delle Vergini 7.
Map 5 A4 & 12 F2.
Tel 06-679 4585.
w teatroquirino.it

Teatro Sistina
Via Sistina 129. **Map** 5 B2.
Tel 06-420 0711.

Teatro Vittoria
Piazza S. Maria Liberatrice 8.
Map 8 D3. **Tel** 06-574 0598.

Contemporary Theater

Palladium
Piazza B. Romano 8 (south
of Stazione Ostiense).
Tel 06-5733 2768.

Teatro Anfitrione
Via di San Saba 24.
Map 8 E3.
Tel 06-575 0827.

Teatro Nuovo Colosseo
Via Capo d'Africa 29A.
Map 9 A1.
Tel 06-700 4932.

Teatro dell'Orologio
Via dei Filippini 17A. **Map**
11 B3. **Tel** 06-687 5550.

Teatro Olimpico
Piazza Gentile da Fabriano
17 (off Via Guido Reni).
Map 1 A2.
Tel 06-326 5991.

Teatro Vascello
Via G. Carini 72. **Map** 7 A2.
Tel 06-588 1021.

Folk, Cabaret, Puppet Theater

Meo Patacca
P. dei Mercanti 30. **Map** 8
D1. **Tel** 06-581 6198.

Teatro Mongiovino
Via Genocchi 15.
Tel 06-513 9405.

Teatro San Carlino
Viale dei Bambini (Pincio).
Map 4 F1. **Tel** 06-6992
2117. w sancarlino.it

Teatro Verde
Circonvall. Gianicolense
10. **Map** 7 B4.
Tel 06-588 2034.

Tina Pika Village
Via Fonteiana 57
(Monteverde district).
Tel 06-588 5754.

Open-Air Theater

Anfiteatro Quercia del Tasso
Passeggiata del Gianicolo.
Map 3 C5. **Tel** 06-575 0827.

Nightlife

Rome's nightlife has never been as diverse or vibrant as it is today. The city has witnessed a sharp rise in the number of bar and club openings that cater to an ever more demanding clientele. Where once the choice was limited to the Irish theme bars near Termini, the few well-established but crowded bars in the downtown, and the hugely popular clubs in Testaccio, the capital now offers a wide range of options to satisfy all tastes and budgets. Depending on your mood, head first for a stylish pre-clubbing bar and then on to one of the exclusive clubs, or simply relax with friends and a bottle of good wine in an earthy wine bar in one of the historic downtown's breathtaking squares. For a memorable first stop, enjoy spectacular views with an apéritif from a rooftop terrace bar.

On the downside, despite the greater number of bars and clubs, prices have soared in Rome since the euro was introduced – today you can be charged up to €10 for a cocktail. For cheaper alternative nights out, away from the tourist traps, visit a bar in San Lorenzo.

What's On

As in any major city, Rome's nightlife is constantly evolving. Roman club-goers are an extremely varied group, and most clubs arrange different nights to appeal to the diverse range of tastes – so it is essential to keep up to date on what's happening by checking listings magazines (see p346) that hit the newsstands every Thursday.

Flyers for many nightclubs are handed out in some of the busier squares in and around the downtown, such as Campo de' Fiori and Piazza del Fico. They are also distributed inside the many pre-clubbing bars dotted around Testaccio, such as **33 Testaccio Lounge Bar**.

Practicalities

Preferred clubbing nights are Friday and Saturday, when the cars, and scooters of revelers clog the streets of the downtown. Lines at the most popular venues can be very long at peak entrance time (around midnight), so it is advisable to get there an hour or so earlier. However, if you are unable do so, and don't feel like waiting, try calling in advance and charming your way onto the guest list. Instead of an entrance fee, some smaller clubs require a *tessera*, a monthly or yearly membership card, which you can buy, and fill out on the spot. If you're paying just to get through the door that night, hold on to your entrance ticket as it usually entitles you to a free first drink (*la consumazione*); your second could be expensive, and cost as much as €15.

As a general rule, remember that all-male groups are rarely welcome, and in some exclusive clubs neither are unaccompanied men. Also, to enter any of the more select venues, you'll need both an introduction from one of the regulars, and clothes that aim to impress.

Bars

Despite increased competition, especially from the revitalized rustic wine bar **Il Nolano**, **La Vineria** (see p320) in Campo de' Fiori has maintained its cult status among Romans of all ages, and backgrounds for unpretentious, lively drinking at reasonable prices. Just around the corner, **L'Angolo Divino** (see p320) is less well-known, and consequently not as bustling. It nonetheless remains a perfect spot for socializing over great wines and heartwarming food. Another landmark in the *centro storico* (historic center), though for a more well-to-do and fashion-conscious crowd, is the in-vogue **Antico Caffè della Pace**, a popular choice near Piazza Navona for those who want to see and be seen. **Fluid**, on Via del Governo Vecchio, is much livelier, and has made its mark in the capital as the perfect venue to get you in the mood for late-night clubbing. A few doors down but really a world away, the comfortable and candlelit **Mimì e Cocò** is a great place to relax (alfresco or inside) and linger over subtle wines, served with a smile. Just off the top end of the same street, moving away from Corso Vittorio Emanuele II, is **Giulio Passami l'Olio**, a warm, welcoming, and animated *enoteca*, tucked away from the usual *passaggiate* (promenade) routes. Closer to Piazza di Spagna, the striking interior and extensive choice of wines by the glass make the **Antica Enoteca di Via della Croce** a favorite spot for wine connoisseurs. Although it's definitely not cheap, the impressive bar buffet is well worth sampling.

In Trastevere, too, the romantic streets are full of tiny bars aimed at diverse crowds. Find a table if you can outside **Ombre Rosse** in the wonderful Piazza Sant'Egidio and watch the world go by. If Ombre Rosse is too crowded, **Caffè della Scala**, just a few minutes' walk away, is a good alternative. Other bars in the area include the lively **Nylon** and **Friends Art Café**, which is a perfect spot to enjoy a refreshing, though expensive, apéritif with complimentary but elaborate snacks – a growing trend in the Eternal City. The simple, but vintage, **Bar San Callisto**, located just off Piazza Santa Maria, draws strictly nonconventional patrons.

Elsewhere in the city, the sophisticated **Ferrazza** (see p343), in San Lorenzo, serves up exceptional wines for more sophisticated customers, while the monumental student bar **Rive Gauche** does great business as the biggest pub in the area. The slick surf-bar **Duke's** in Parioli is slightly away from the center, but is worth it for star-spotting. Duke's has tried to curb its soaring popularity by closing on Saturday nights, but to no avail. It remains the number one place to be seen in north Rome.

Finally, and not just for hopeless romantics, breathtaking views of Rome can be enjoyed at the lavish rooftop terrace bars at hotel **Eden** (see p302), near Via Veneto, and the **Radisson Blu ES** hotel (see p302) near Termini. At dusk, particularly after a sunny day, these stunning venues offer a great place to start an unforgettable evening out. Not far from the Colosseum, **Caffè Propaganda** is a chic café whose interior is reminiscent of an early-20th-century Parisian bistro.

Clubs

To brush shoulders with TV starlets and parliamentary undersecretaries, head for **Gilda**. Its glitzy dance-floor and restaurant have made it a favorite with the Roman jet set and hangers-on. The famous Sixties nightclub, **Jackie O**, revamped in lavish style, with a lush interior, a piano bar, and an expensive eatery, draws an international, thirty-something crowd.

Bòeme is a safe option for commercial music among Roman twenty-somethings, though **Heaven** is slightly funkier with its marked preference for house. More challenging is the eclectic **Micca Club** with the chance to hear live sets, while the more traditional disco is at its best at **Piper**, which changes its look each season and organizes imaginative floor shows and other events. There are a few disco-pubs downtown that offer a compromise between a straightforward bar and an all-out club. **The Nag's Head** is one that is especially worth noting.

In and around Testaccio, the undisputed clubbing heart of Rome, you'll find it difficult to decide which club to visit. The stylish **Caruso – Café de Oriente** concentrates on Latin, R&B, and salsa sounds, while the multifunctional **Distillerie Clandestine** is the place for eating, drinking, relaxing, and dancing. **Caffè Latino** changes gear on weekends, with clubbers dancing to covers bands, while nearby are the trendy **La Saponeria** and **Neo**, a stronghold of underground music. Saturday night at **Big Bang** signifies all things dark and new wave, while at the equally alternative **Planet Roma**, you can drift between three rooms offering three completely different DJ sets. Last but by no means least, the legendary **Goa** remains the champion of Roman clubs, attracting the best of Italian as well as international DJs.

The wine bar at **'Gusto** offers live music, and the chance to explore the venue's various restaurant areas while enjoying a glass of wine from the vast selection available. On the other side of Corso Vittorio Emanuele, the select **La Maison** attracts a slightly older crowd with its less commercial music, and elegant ambience. However, if you're in the mood for a mainstream alternative that is free of charge, and easier to gain entry to, then head to the upbeat **Habana Café** for a continuous program of live music, and DJ sets every evening.

For something a little different, the **Radio Café** is a multifunctional venue with a lounge, café, disco, and meeting spaces frequented by a trendy media set.

Gay Scene

Rome is no longer the provincial backwater it once was. This is clearly reflected in both the rise in the number of gay bars, and clubs, and their increasing popularity. While some are exclusively gay, others attract a mixed clientele.

Across the river from the centro storico in Trastevere is the exclusive **Il Giardino dei Ciliegi**, a living-room-style bar that specializes in cocktails. It also stocks a wide variety of teas and serves exciting salads, and an excellent Sunday brunch – even on public holidays. For livelier social drinking, head for **Anfiteatro My Bar** and **Coming Out**, between San Giovanni, and the Colosseum, to mingle with a mixed crowd that usually spills out onto the street. Nearby, the men-only bar **Hangar** continues to pack them in.

When it comes to clubbing, the ever-growing number of gay one-nighters in both alternative and mainstream clubs in many ways present the best venues for drinking and dancing until the early hours. **Goa**, just off Via Ostiense, occasionally hosts gay nights such as the women-only Venus Rising once a month; Mucca Assassina (quite literally "homicidal cow") pulls in the crowds every Friday at the monumental **Qube** in Tiburtino; the rival Omogenic crew takes over the **Circolo degli Artisti** on the same evening, while **Planet Roma** hosts the Gorgeous I Am one-nighters every Saturday. These clubs are in addition to the justly famous gay-friendly disco **Alibi** in Testaccio with its explosive mix of house music, and retro classics.

Pride Week, a yearly event held at the end of June/early July, is a time when gay Romans hit the streets for seven days of nonstop partying. The program, and date change from year to year, so it is wise to consult listing magazines for full details.

In summer, as with most clubs, Rome's gay venues move outdoors in an attempt to beat the stifling heat.

Often the outdoor club nights are hosted at **Gay Village**, a summer-long outdoor party. This is yet another important indication that gay culture is finally beginning to be accepted on the mainstream entertainment scene.

Centri Sociali

Centri sociali, or illegally occupied buildings that have been converted into centers for the arts and entertainment, give an alternative edge to Rome's vivacious nightlife and cultural scene. While some centers are run on a professional basis and are able to successfully compete with many of the capital's swankier and

established venues, others have continued to maintain a staunch anti-establishment stance.

Top billing must go to **Brancaleone** in north Rome, which regularly features progressive Italian and international DJs for the very best in electronic and house tunes. This well-run establishment is also home to an organic café and shop, superb art exhibitions, and a cinema club.

Near the Baths of Caracalla, the **Angelo Mai Center** regularly organizes a multitude of cultural events, including exhibitions and showings of art house films – sometimes even in their original non-dubbed version. On weekends, the

venue dedicates its space primarily to club nights, covering a spectrum of tastes from underground and ethnic live bands to wild DJ sets. They also boast their own eatery.

Farther away from downtown, the abandoned fort, **Forte Prenestino**, is a magical maze of spooky rooms and endless corridors and represents the most bizarre of Rome's social center venues. Famous for its anti-establishment Labor Day concert – the official and free rock concert is held in Piazza San Giovanni in Laterano – it also holds theater productions, film festivals, and club nights throughout the year for a young but alternative crowd. Closer to the center, **Villaggio Globale**,

DIRECTORY

Bars

33 Testaccio Lounge Bar
Via Monte Testaccio 33.
Map 8 D4.
Tel 06-575 5142.

Angelo Mai
Viale delle Terme di Caracalla 55A.
Map 9 A2.
Tel 329 448 1358.

L'Angolo Divino
Via dei Balestrari 12–14.
Map 11 C4.
Tel 06-686 4413.

Antica Enoteca di Via della Croce
Via della Croce 76B.
Map 4 F2.
Tel 06-679 0896.

Antico Caffè della Pace
Via della Pace 3–7.
Map 11 C3.
Tel 06-686 1216.

Bar San Callisto
Piazza San Callisto 3–4.
Map 7 C1.
Tel 06-583 5869.

Caffè Propaganda
Via Claudia 15.
Map 9 A1.
Tel 06-9543 4255.

Caffè della Scala
Via della Scala 4.
Map 7 C1.
Tel 06-580 3610.

Duke's
Viale Parioli 200.
Map 2 D1.
Tel 06-8066 2455.

Eden
Via Ludovisi 49.
Map 5 B2.
Tel 06-478 121.

Ferrazza
Via dei Volsci 59.
Map 6 F4.
Tel 06-490 506.

Fluid
Via del Governo Vecchio 46/47. **Map** 11 C3.
Tel 06-683 2361.

Friends Art Café
Piazza Trilussa 34.
Map 4 E5.
Tel 06-581 6111.

Giulio Passami l'Olio
Via di Monte Giordano 28.
Map 11 B2.
Tel 06-6880 3288.

Mimì e Cocò
Via del Governo Vecchio 72. **Map** 11 C3.
Tel 06-6821 0845.

Il Nolano
Campo de' Fiori 11/12.
Map 11 C4.
Tel 06-687 9344.

Nylon
Via del Politeama 12.
Map 11 C5.
Tel 06-5834 0692.

Ombre Rosse
Piazza Sant'Egidio 12.
Map 7 C1.
Tel 06-588 4155.

Radisson Blu ES
Via Filippo Turati 171.
Map 6 D4.
Tel 06-444 841.

Rive Gauche
Via dei Sabelli 43.
Map 6 F4.
Tel 06-445 6722.

La Vineria
Campo de' Fiori 15.
Map 11 C4.
Tel 06-6880 3268.

Clubs

Big Bang
Via Monte Testaccio 22.
Map 8 D4.
Tel 392 901 1993.

Bòeme
Via Velletri 13.
Map 6 D1.
Tel 06-841 2212.

Caffè Latino
Via di Monte Testaccio 96.
Map 8 D4.
Tel 06-578 2411.

Caruso – Café de Oriente
Via di Monte Testaccio 36.
Map 8 D4.
Tel 06-574 5019.

Distillerie Clandestine
Via Libetta 13.
Tel 06-5730 5102.

Gilda
Via Mario de' Fiori 97.
Map 12 F1.
Tel 06-678 4838.

Goa
Via Libetta 13.
Tel 06-574 8277.

'Gusto
Via delle Frezza 23.
Map 4 F2.
Tel 06-322 6273.

Habana Café
Via dei Pastini 120.
Map 12 D2.
Tel 06-678 1983.

Heaven
Viale di Porta Ardeatina 119. **Map** 9 B5.
Tel 06-574 3772.

situated on a vast area of open space at the edge of Testaccio, has a very similar philosophy and range of services. In summer, it regularly hosts open-air concerts, occasionally beating out the competition to feature big-name Italian bands such as Tiromancino.

Jazz, Salsa, and African Sounds

Rome offers countless venues for jazz, from trad and swing to modern fusion (see p350). Several jazz and Latin American clubs combine live music with dancing, eating, and drinking. For South American style music, **Fonclea** and **Arriba Arriba** (see p351) or **Planet Roma** all pay

homage to Latin American and world music, although **Caffè Latino** in Testaccio is far and away the best place to check out on weekends.

Clubbing in Summer

At the height of the sweltering summer, when virtually everything closes down in the capital, **Art Cafè** in Villa Borghese stands out as the supreme club venue for the fun-loving, young, and hip. A number of smaller venues open up on the Tiber too, while some of the bigger clubs hit the coast from July through to December – most notably in Ostia and in Fregene, where the revamped **Janga Beach** is a

permanent fixture. Also worth checking out is the sophisticated **Singita** beach club, where they hold a special sunset ceremony accompanied by a DJ set.

After Hours

Most Roman clubs stay open until 2am or 3am. However, night owls may find one or two dance havens that see in the dawn, especially during the beach-party season. Before heading off to bed, you could join the other diehard clubbers for a final drink at one of the city's 24-hour watering holes, or else make for one of the early-morning bakers, and feast on sweet breakfast cornetti straight from the oven.

DIRECTORY

Jackie O
Via Boncompagni 11.
Map 5 B2.
Tel 06-4288 5457.

La Maison
Vicolo dei Granari 4.
Map 11 C3.
Tel 06-683 3312.

Micca Club
Via P. Micca 7A.
Map 6 F5.
Tel 06-8744 0079.

The Nag's Head
Via IV Novembre 138B.
Map 5 A4.
Tel 06-679 4620.

Neo
Via degli Argonauti 18 (to the south of Stazione Ostiense).
Tel 06-944 2526.

Piper
Via Tagliamento 9 (north of downtown).
Tel 06-855 5398.

Planet Roma
Via del Commercio 36/8.
Map 8 D5.
Tel 06-574 7826.

Radio Café
Via Principe Umberto 67.
Map 6 E5.
Tel 06-4436 1110.

La Saponeria
Via degli Argonauti 20 (to the south of Stazione Ostiense, off Via Ostiense).
Tel 06-574 6999.

Gay Scene

Alibi
Via di Monte Testaccio 39–44. **Map** 8 D4.
Tel 06-574 3448.

Anfiteatro My Bar
Via San Giovanni in Laterano 12. **Map** 9 A1.
Tel 06-700 4425.

Circolo degli Artisti
Via Casilina Vecchia 42.
Map 10 F1.
Tel 06-7030 5684.

Coming Out
Via San Giovanni In Laterano 8. **Map** 9 A1.
Tel 06-700 9871.

Gay Village
Phone or check website for venue. **Tel** 340-753 8396. **W** gayvillage.it

Il Giardino dei Ciliegi
Via dei Fienaroli 4.
Tel 06-580 3423.

Goa
See clubs.

Hangar
Via in Selci 69. **Map** 5 C5.
Tel 06-488 1397.

Planet Roma
See clubs.

Qube
Via di Portonaccio 212 (north of downtown).
Tel 06-438 5445.

Centri Sociali

Brancaleone
Via Levanna 11 (in Montesacro).
Tel 06-8200 4382.

Forte Prenestino
Via F. Delpino (in Prenestino).
Tel 06-2180 7855.

Villaggio Globale
Lungotevere Testaccio 2/ Via di Monte Testaccio 22.
Map 7 4C.
Tel 347 413 1205.

Jazz, Salsa, and African Sounds

Arriba Arriba
Via delle Capannelle 104.
Tel 06-721 3772.

Caffè Latino
Via di Monte Testaccio 96.
Map 8 D4.
Tel 06-578 2411.

Fonclea
Via Crescenzio 82A.
Map 3 C2. **Tel** 06-689 6302. **W** fonclea.it

Planet Roma
See clubs.

Clubbing in Summer

Art Cafè
Viale del Galoppatoio, 33 (Villa Borghese).
Map 5 A1.
Tel 06-3600 6578.

Janga Beach
Lungomare di Ponente 11, Fregene.
Tel 06-6656 0649.

Singita
Villaggio dei Pescatori Fregene.
Tel 06-6196 4921.

Sports

Do not be surprised if the peace of a Sunday afternoon in Rome is interrupted by the honking of cars and people shouting. It simply means that one of the home soccer teams has won at the stadium and the whole city appears to be celebrating the result.

Soccer is Italy's national sport, but other sports also attract a large following, and Roman sports fans have a varied choice of events and activites to watch or participate in.

You will find times and venues for most spectator sports listed in *TrovaRoma or (see p346)*, as well as the local sections of *La Gazzetta dello Sport* or *Corriere dello Sport*.

Soccer

An Italian soccer match is an experience not to be missed for the quality of the play and the fun atmosphere, though hooliganism has begun to raise its ugly head.

Rome has two teams, Roma and Lazio, and they take turns playing at the **Stadio Olimpico (CONI)** on a Sunday afternoon at 3pm, in the Campionato Italiano (Italian championship league).

Seats can be scarce, so get tickets in advance from the stadium (€15 to €80) from noon onward on the day itself, or through club websites (www.sslazio.it and www.asroma.it). The cheapest seats are in the Le Curve stand; the mid-price and most expensive are in Le Gradinate, and La Tribuna respectively.

On Wednesday evenings there may be international competitions – the UEFA Cup or the Coppa dei Campioni (European Championship Cup). In between these, teams battle it out for the national Coppa Italia.

Tennis

A major event, the International Championships go on at **Foro Italico** for two weeks in May. The world's top tennis stars thrash it out on clay courts at 1pm, and 8:30pm from Tuesday to Friday, and at 1pm only on weekends. Buy tickets in advance either directly from the Foro Italico or from a ticket agency.

If you wish to play yourself, there are now more than 350 tennis clubs in Rome. It is often essential to reserve at least a week in advance and there is usually a moderate court fee.

Clubs where membership is not required include **Tennis Club Nomentano** and the **Circolo Tennis della Stampa** in northern Rome and the **Oasi di Pace**, just off the Via Appia Antica. Large hotels offer tennis for a reasonable price. The **Crowne Plaza** requires a small annual membership fee on top of the court price, which includes the gym and the pool (in the summer).

Horse Racing, Trotting, and Leisure Riding

Important races include the Derby in May and the Premio Roma in November. There are both flat races and steeplechases at the **Ippodromo delle Capannelle**.

The International Horse Show, organized by the Federazione Italiana Sport Equestri (**FISE**), is held in May in Piazza di Siena, Villa Borghese *(see p350)*. It is one of the most important social, and sporting events in the calendar, and has a great setting.

Through the FISE, it may be possible to find a riding club that will take you on a trail ride in the countryside around Rome, but most do not accept short-term members.

Golf

Even the most elite golf clubs will accept a touring golfer with a home membership, and handicap. Many clubs close on Mondays and on weekends, when they host competitions and guests cannot play. Prices range from €55 to €100.

The **Olgiata Golf Club** is open to everybody, though it is best to call first if you want to play on the weekend, when demand and fees are much higher. **Country Club Castel Gandolfo** is the newest club and **Circolo del Golf di Roma Acquasanta** the oldest and most prestigious. Within the city's ring road is the course at the **Sheraton Golf Hotel** (closed Tuesdays).

One of the many important competitions on the various golf courses around Rome is the Circolo Golf Roma Coppa d'Oro (Gold Cup) in April.

Car and Motorcycle Racing

Formula 1 and Formula 3 races take place on Sundays at **Vallelunga**; be prepared for some expensive entrance fees. Frequently on Saturdays official trials are open to spectators, and on some non-racing Sundays Italy's car designers show new models.

Rugby

Rugby is becoming increasingly popular, thanks to Italy's participation in the Six Nations tournament. This means that in winter (usually Feb–Mar) there are a couple of international matches in Rome. The home team is drawn against two other member "nations" each year: France, England, Scotland, Ireland, or Wales.

Rowing

In mid-June, an Oxford/Cambridge crew challenges the historic Aniene crew to a race taking place alternately on the Tiber, and on the Thames in England. The best place to watch is between the Margherita and Sant'Angelo bridges. The race usually starts at around 6pm. Another event is the battle between the Roma, and Lazio crews, from Ponte Duca d'Aosta to Ponte Risorgimento, on the same variable date as the Roma-Lazio soccer derby.

Swimming

Swimming pools are scarce, and definitely not geared to the short-term visitor. It is often necessary to pay an expensive membership plus a monthly fee. Most pools also require you to produce a medical certificate assuring your good health, and have lane-only swimming. The state-owned pools can be slightly cheaper, but you still have to pay an initial membership fee.

The **Shangri-La Hotel** opens its pool to non-residents in the summer, as does the **Cavalieri Rome Hotel**, for an entry fee. The best deal is on a Sunday, when the sports club and swimming pool **La Margherita** opens to non-members 10am–1pm, for a reasonable entry fee. **Piscina delle Rose** is an Olympic-sized pool open from June to September 9am–5:30pm daily (to 7pm on weekends). For a swim with a view, reserve a chaise longue by the rooftop pool of the **Radisson Blue ES Hotel**.

Health Clubs

Like the swimming pools, Roman health clubs usually require both a membership fee and monthly payments. For a short stay in Rome, it is more sensible to try the facilities in your hotel, or, if you are willing to pay, head for one of the private clubs. Use of club facilities may be negotiable.

The **Roman Sport Center** welcomes daily members for a reasonable price (€30) and you can use the pools, the gym, and the sauna. The facilities are open 7am–10:30pm on weekdays (until 8:30pm Saturday, 9am–3pm Sunday). Any shorts worn must be made of Lycra.

Jogging and Cycling

Rome's perfect climate, and stunning scenery attract thousands of well-dressed joggers and cyclists into the city's many parks. Early on weekday mornings or at any time on a Sunday you'll find the more popular locations looking like high-speed fashion shows. Each March, however, serious runners take part in the Rome Marathon.

Villa Doria Pamphilj (see p269) is an extensive park situated above the Janiculum, where you can choose from various tracks, plenty of open spaces, and a network of paths. **Villa Borghese** (see p260) is another vast, popular place with a running track.

Alternatively, jog under the acacia trees and palms at Villa Torlonia, on the spotlit track at Villa Glori, or combine sports with culture by running the **Via Appia Antica** (see p267) branching off into Parco Caffarella. Other favorite places are Viale delle Terme di Caracalla, Circo Massimo, Parco degli Aquedotti, and Parco di Colle Oppio.

All of the above are also ideal for cyclists, and you can rent bikes from many places, including **Collalti** and **Treno e Scooter Rent**.

DIRECTORY

Soccer

Stadio Olimpico (CONI)
Via Foro Italico.
Tel 06-368 51.

Tennis

Circolo Tennis della Stampa
Piazza Mancini 19.
Map 1 A2.
Tel 06-323 2454.

Crowne Plaza
Via Aurelia Antica 415.
Tel 06-66420.

Foro Italico
Viale dei Gladiatori 31.
Tel 06-3272 3301.
w ctforoitalico.coni.it

Oasi di Pace
Via degli Eugenii 2.
Tel 06-718 4550.
w ct-oasidipace.it

Tennis Club Nomentano
Viale Rousseau 124.
Tel 06-8680 1888.
w clubnomentano.it

Horse Racing and Riding

FISE
Tel 06-8191 8628.
w fise.it

Ippodromo delle Capannelle
Via Appia Nuova 1255.
Tel 06-71 67 71.

Golf

Circolo del Golf di Roma Acquasanta
Via Appia Nuova 716A.
Tel 06-780 3407.
w golfroma.it

Country Club Castel Gandolfo
Via di Santo Spirito 13, Castelgandolfo.
Tel 06-931 2301.

Olgiata Golf Club
Largo dell'Olgiata 15.
Tel 06-3088 9141.

Sheraton Golf Hotel
Viale Salvatore Rebecchini 39. **Tel** 06-655 3477.

Car and Motor-cycle Racing

Vallelunga
Autodromo di Roma, Via Cassia km 34.5. **Tel** 06-901 5501. w vallelunga.it

Rugby

Federazione Italiana Rugby
Tel 06-4521 3117.
w federugby.it

Swimming

ARCA Swimming Club
Via Monti Tiburtini 511.
Tel 06-451 0552.

Cavalieri Rome Hotel
Via Cadlolo 101.
Tel 06-350 91.
w romecavalieri.com

Piscina delle Rose
Viale America 20.
Tel 06-5422 0333.
w piscinadellerose.com

Radisson Blue ES Hotel

Via Filippo Turati 171.
Map 6 D4.
Tel 06-444 841.

Shangri-La Hotel
Viale Algeria 141.
Tel 06-591 6441.

Health Clubs

Roman Sport Center
Via del Galoppatoio 33.
Map 5 A1.
Tel 06-321 8096.

Jogging and Cycling

Collalti
Via del Pellegrino 82.
Map 4 E4.
Tel 06-6880 1084.

Maratona di Roma
Tel 06-406 5064.
w maratonadiroma.it

Treno e Scooter Rent
Termini Station.
Map 6 D3.
Tel 06-4890 5823.

CHILDREN'S ROME

Italians love having children around, and you can be sure yours will be made welcome wherever they go. But there are few special facilities for children, and the heat, crowds, and lack of clean public restrooms mean that Rome is not an ideal city for a vacation with babies or under-sevens. It does, however, have plenty to offer slightly older children, especially those who like history or art.

The temptation may be to wear yourself and your children out by packing too many sights into one day. Plan in advance and leave plenty of time to wander around the city, looking at the quirkier fountains and monuments, watching knife-grinders at work in the markets, and spending hours agonizing over the choice of ice-cream flavors and special pizza toppings.

Practical Advice

If you are planning to bring your children to Rome, try to come in early spring or late fall, when the weather is good but not too hot. Easter is best avoided, as the city is more crowded than usual, and you're constantly jostled on packed buses and streets. Where you stay is crucial. A hotel near the Villa Borghese park will give your children an opportunity to relax and let off steam, though you may end up spending a lot of time and money to get to and from the downtown. A hotel in the old center is ideal, since you can easily stop back during the day for a rest and a clean bathroom. Because hygienic restrooms and changing facilities are rare within the city, it is really not advisable to bring a baby to Rome unless you are visiting friends or family. As with many historic cities, Rome may not instantly appeal to all children, but there is plenty to inspire their imaginations. Use this book to make the buildings and history come alive. Children might also enjoy learning a few Italian words and phrases so they can order food and buy things by themselves. If lingering over drinks on the café terraces is what you enjoy best, bring your offspring something to keep them busy once they finish their own treat: crayons and paper, a computer game, or an MP3 player. Alternatively, most

other adults are very tolerant of children running around and making noise while they relax and, if yours are reasonably outgoing, they could join in with the local children playing ball games in early evenings in piazzas like Campo de' Fiori.

If you feel the need for a total break, most hotels will be able to provide a babysitter or help you to contact a qualified babysitting agency.

If your child gets sick or injured, see pages 370–71 for information on what to do and a list of emergency numbers.

Getting Around

Bumpy cobbles, narrow streets without sidewalks, and overcrowded buses make pushing children around in strollers tiring work. Mothers with young

Fairground in the Villa Borghese park

children are, however, usually allowed to cut in line. Outside rush hours, the Metro is often less busy. Kids under 1 m (3 ft 3 in) tall travel free on mass transit.

Although the city is not good for cyclists, families with older children could rent bikes to ride along the Tiber on the cycle tracks to the north of the city, or to take on a regional train into the country. The bikes, tandems, and rickshaws for rent in Villa Borghese are good fun, and the bike rental hut in the Pincio gardens has free baby seats.

Eating Out

Children are normally warmly welcomed in neighborhood pizzerias and trattorias, and high chairs are often available for toddlers and babies. If there is no high chair, be prepared for the waiters to improvise for you with armloads of cushions or telephone

Children playing in the park at Villa Borghese

Families enjoying a sunny day in the Villa Borghese Gardens

napkins. Try deep-fried fruit and vegetables from Antico Forno Roscioli on Via dei Giubbonari *(see p323)* and *supplì al telefono*, rice croquettes with a gooey string of mozzarella inside, from *pizza al taglio* or *pizza rustica* outlets. A *tramezzino* comes quite close to a familiar sandwich, and if your kids are miserable without peanut butter, you can find it (and other foreign foods) at Castroni on Via Cola di Rienzo.

directories. Most places are perfectly happy to serve half portions, or to let children share meals.

In trattorias it can sometimes be difficult to be exactly certain what a certain dish contains (especially when there is no menu and the dishes of the day are reeled off, usually at top speed, by the waiter), so picky eaters are likely to be happier in pizzerias *(see pp320–21)*. Here they can choose their own topping (remember that *prosciutto,* which is usually translated in menus as ham, is cured). The most entertaining pizzerias for kids are the old-fashioned ones where they can watch the chefs pound, stretch, and flip the pizza dough.

Restaurants open in the evening at or soon after 7pm, and the best places get busy from around 8:30pm, so it is wise to go early to avoid having to wait in line.

Picnics

Picnics in the parks are ideal, and shopping for the food is often half the fun. There is no problem finding cartons of fruit juice and branded canned drinks, but these are expensive unless you go to a supermarket – various outlets are dotted around the center of the city.

Water from the drinking fountains is potable, so it is worth carrying plastic cups around with you.

As well as picnic food from bakeries and markets, there are lots of scrumptious carry-out foods. Many of them are appealingly messy, so it is wise to take paper

Ice Cream

Rome, of course, is famous for ice cream; you and your children are likely to be tempted at every turn.

Fontana della Barcaccia, Piazza di Spagna

Real ice-cream fans may even want to plan their day's sightseeing around one of the best *gelaterie (see pp322–5)*.

It is far cheaper to buy either a cone or tub of ice cream to eat in the street, but in some of the more traditional places it is worth paying to sit down, as the interiors can be fun and attractive to childen.

At Fassi, they have an old-fashioned ice-cream-making machine on display, and at Giolitti, you can enjoy gargantuan sundaes in the elegant parlor *(see p113)*.

If you are worried that your kids might have too much ice cream, look for places that sell the smaller *cono baby*.

Investigating some of the hundreds of Italian ice-cream flavors

Sightseeing with Children

Entrance to the Villa Borghese Zoo

General Tips

Rome does not have many museums with the kind of exciting hands-on exhibits that many other cities provide for children. However, Bernini's marble elephant (see p112), and the fat facchino, or porter (p109), tend to appeal to kids. The Capuchin crypt at Santa Maria della Concezione (p256), the catacombs (pp266–8), and the Mamertine Prison (p93) will capture more ghoulish imaginations, and children will also enjoy putting their hands into the Bocca della Verità (p204).

Keep your children's interest alive by looking for details like the dirty toenails on figures in Caravaggio's paintings; the Etruscan votives, which were offered to the gods, at the Villa Giulia (pp264–5); and the illusory collapsing ceiling in the Chiesa Nuova, as well as the fake dome of Sant'Ignazio di Loyola (see p108).

Museums your children will enjoy include **Museo Explora**, full of interesting hands-on exhibits for children, and the Museo delle Mura, which explores a short length of the Aurelian Wall (p198). Among the churches, St. Peter's (see p228) and San Clemente (see pp188–9) are the most fun.

At the Vatican, children will like the animal statues and mosaics in the Animal Gallery and also the Sistine Ceiling (p244), especially once they know that Michelangelo had to paint it hunched up on a scaffolding platform. Remember that Vatican dress etiquette (see p229) applies to kids too.

Ancient Ruins

The ancient ruins best appreciated by children are the Colosseum (see pp94–7), and Trajan's Markets (see pp90–91). You can still make out

what both these buildings looked like from their remains. The scant ruins of the Forum and Palatine, on the other hand, may not appeal so strongly. Ostia Antica, where the remains include a theater, shop, and 20-seater public toilet, is much more likely to interest them (see pp272–3).

Mosaics

There are scores of vivid, sometimes quirky, mosaics in buildings all over Rome.

Mosaic from the Vatican

Many of these are particularly appealing to children. Details in the mosaics range from brilliantly colored flowers, leaves, animals, and buildings (in the churches of San Clemente, Santa Prassede, and Santa Maria in Trastevere, see p188, p173 and pp214–15) to the debris of a banquet (in the Vatican's Museo Gregorio Profano, see pp232–3).

Entertainment

To find out what's going on for children in Rome, scour the movie pages of newspapers and the listings in Trova-Roma and Wanted in Rome, and entertainment websites (see pp346–7). Most theaters, and movie theaters have reduced entry fees for children, but shows are often only in Italian.

There are cartoons shown at Villa Borghese's Cinema dei Piccoli and traditional puppet shows every afternoon, except Wednesday, on Janiculum Hill. Located inside Villa Borghese, the **Casina di Raffaello** is a playhouse and mini-library

Miniature train in Villa Borghese

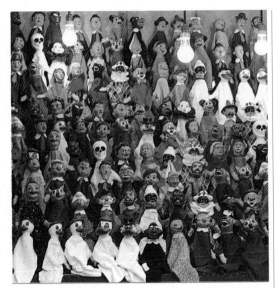

Stand at the Christmas toy fair on Piazza Navona

with toys and reading areas. It also organizes activities.

An appealing time for kids to be in Rome is over Christmas, when Piazza Navona hosts a Christmas toy fair, with stands selling toys and sweets.

Parks

Villa Borghese *(see p260)* has rowboats for rent; pony-cart rides; bikes to rent; a mini movie theater; a small fair; and a zoo. Villa Celimontana *(see p195)* has bike trails," and open-air theater performances in the summer. Technotown, a multimedia playhouse in the grounds of Villa Torlonia, is fun. In EUR *(see p268)* is the Piscina delle Rose, a swimming pool open in the summer *(see p359)*. The Bomarzo Monster Park, 60 miles (95 km) north of Rome, was built in the 16th century for a mad duke. Children can clamber over its giant stone monsters.

Toys

A visit to a Roman toy shop can be a lot of fun. **Città del Sole** sells educational toys and games, while the window display at **Al Sogno** is a delight for kids who love stuffed animals.

DIRECTORY

General Tips

Museo Explora
Via Flamino 82.
Map 1 C5.
Tel 06-361 3776 (book ahead).
W mdbr.it

Entertainment

Casina di Raffaello
Piazza di Siena, Villa Borghese.
Map 2 E5.
Tel 06-0608.
W casinadiraffaello.it

Toys

Al Sogno
Piazza Navona 53.
Map 4 E4 & 11 C3.
Tel 06-686 4198.

Città del Sole
Via della Scrofa 65.
Map 4 F3 & 12 D2.
Tel 06-6880 3805.

Children's Clothes

Benetton
Piazza della Fontana
di Trevi 91–94.
Map 12 F2.
Tel 06-6919 0919.

Lavori Artigianali Femminili
Via Capo le Case 6.
Map 5 A3 & 12 F1.
Tel 06-679 2992.

Rachele
Vicolo del Bollo 6–7
(off Via del Pellegrino).
Map 11 C4.
Tel 06-686 4975.

Children's Clothes

Italians adore dressing their children up, especially on Sunday afternoons. Many shops sell beautifully hand-crafted children's shoes and clothes. The downside is that they can often be expensive and impractical: dry-clean-only clothes are common and shoes are not made for mud.

Lavori Artigianali Femminili sells handmade silk and wool clothes for children up to the age of eight. **Rachele** offers top-quality handmade clothes for children, while **Benetton** has more wallet-friendly casuals.

Children enjoying pony-cart rides at Villa Borghese

SURVIVAL GUIDE

PONT·M

PRACTICAL INFORMATION

Romans often seem unconcerned by the priceless art treasures and ancient ruins that lie casually among the streets and buildings of their hectic 21st-century city. However, it's not always easy for visitors to make the most of these wonders; relaxed local attitudes make for dozens of variations in opening hours, and many places – including shops, banks, and offices – close for 2 or 3 hours over lunch, reopening in the late afternoon. On a more positive note, most of the main sights are within easy walking distance of one another. Start your day early and wear comfortable shoes. Rome can be a delightfully informal city to visit, but remember to observe dress rules and cover up in churches, since this is one area where regulations are strictly enforced.

Steps heading to Michelangelo's Piazza del Campidoglio

When to Go

Rome enjoys a Mediterranean climate, with hot, dry summers and mild-to-cold, rainy winters. From late March to June, and from September to October, the pleasant, sunny weather allows for plenty of time outdoors. Visitors can expect to pay more to stay during the high season, between March, and November. In hot August, most Romans are on vacation, and the smaller shops, and restaurants are closed, but all tourist sights stay open, the city is quieter, and you can find good hotel deals.

Visas and Passports

Italy is part of the Schengen agreement, which means travelers moving from one Schengen country to another are not subject to border controls, although there are occasional spot checks.

All visitors to Italy must register with the police within eight working days of arrival. If you are staying in a hotel, this will be done for you. Otherwise, you should contact the local *questura* (police station). European Union nationals, and citizens of the US, Canada, Australia, and New Zealand do not need visas for stays of up to three months.

Anyone wishing to stay for more than three months (eight working days for citizens from countries other than those mentioned above) will have to obtain a *permesso di soggiorno* (permit to stay). European Union citizens can apply for a permit at any main police station. Non-EU citizens must apply in advance in their home country for a permit to stay; it is very difficult for non-EU citizens to obtain a work permit. If you lose your passport, contact your embassy *(see p369).*

Customs Information

Duty-free allowances are as follows: non-EU citizens can bring into Italy 200 cigarettes or 50 cigars or 100 cigarillos or 250 grams of tobacco, 1 liter of spirits or 2 liters of wine, and 50 grams of perfume. EU residents do not need to declare goods, but random checks are often made to look for drug traffickers. To find out what you can take back from Italy to a non-EU country, contact that country's customs department. The refund system for Value Added Tax (IVA in Italy) for non-EU residents is very complex *(see p327).*

Tourist Information

Information kiosks run by the Comune di Roma are dotted around the downtown and have English-speaking staff who provide free maps, leaflets, and advice. Alternatively, call their **Rome City Tourist Office** for information in English. Rome Council's two useful websites have information on all the sights as well as on current exhibitions, events, and hotels in the city. A privately run company called **Enjoy Rome** has an informative website and offices close to the Termini train station. Note that admission prices, and opening times change often, and sights can be closed for long periods for restoration *(chiuso per restauro)* or because of a strike *(sciopero).*

Tourist information sign

Opening Hours and Admission Prices

Museums are generally open all day, although most close on Mondays and on some public holidays. Open-air sights such as the Forum are open daily year-round, closing 1 hour before sunset.

The three-day **Roma Pass** (€34) provides free travel within Rome, free entrance to two museums or archaeological sites, and discounts for various exhibitions, events, and services. National and city museums offer entrance free of charge to EU passport holders who are under 18 or over 65, and discounted entry for those between 18 and 25 with a valid student ID card.

Entrance to churches is free, and many contain extraordinary works of art: keep in mind that you may be charged a small fee to see a certain area, such as a chapel, cloister, or underground ruins.

Some of Rome's sights, such as Nero's Aqueduct, and the Vatican Gardens, are accessible only on personal application or by written appointment (see below). The Area by Area section of this guide has opening times for each sight, and states whether there is an admission charge.

During the Beni Culturali (Ministry for Culture, and Heritage) week in April, admission to state-run sites is free.

The weekly supplement of the daily paper La Repubblica, TrovaRoma (see p375), has a small English section with details of current exhibitions.

Sightseeing Permits

To visit certain sights in Rome, you need to obtain a written permit, and arrange your visit in advance, particularly for archaeological sites, which may sometimes be closed during excavations. Call the **Rome City Tourist Office** number on page 377, giving your name, the number of people in your party (individual visits are generally not possible), and when you would like to visit. You may then be asked to send written confirmation by email or fax.

Social Customs and Etiquette

Romans are generally courteous and friendly to foreign visitors. Italians are delighted at any effort to speak their language, so it is worth learning a few phrases (see p439). Italians tend to drink only with meals and are unlikely to be seen drunk – obvious drunkenness is frowned upon. Smoking is banned on public transportation, and in restaurants, bars, and cafés.

Visiting Churches

Many of Italy's churches are very dark, but they usually have electric, coin-operated light meters to illuminate chapels and works of art. Recorded information in several languages is also often available. Dress codes (see below) are firmly upheld in churches and should be respected. St. Peter's (see pp228–31) is especially strict – you cannot wear shorts.

Catholic Services

For many Catholics, a visit to Rome means an audience with the pope. General audiences are usually held every Wednesday at 10:30am either in St. Peter's Square, indoors at the Sala Paolo VI,

The altar in church of Santa Maria Maggiore

or at Castel Gandolfo. To attend an audience, call the **Prefettura della Casa Pontificia** (see p229) or go in person to the office through the bronze doors on the right of the colonnade in St. Peter's Square (9am–1pm). Travel agencies can also arrange an audience as part of a coach tour.

Mass is held daily in the main churches of Rome (High Mass is on Sunday). Confession is heard in St. Peter's (see pp228–31), San Giovanni in Laterano (pp182–3), San Paolo fuori le Mura (p269), Santa Maria Maggiore (pp174–5), the Gesù (pp110–11), Santa Sabina (p206), and Sant'Ignazio (p108). English-speaking Catholic churches include San Clemente (see p189) and Santa Susanna (see p257).

For details of non-Catholic services see p369.

Tipping

Service is sometimes included in the bill at restaurants, bars and cafés. Italians usually tip a few euros if the service was good. It is not necessary to tip taxi drivers – rounding up to the next euro is enough. Keep small change handy for sacristans, cleaners, doormen, and porters.

Access to Public Restrooms

Public restrooms are few and far between. There are clean ones by the Colosseum (with facilities for the disabled) and at St. Peter's. Most cafés will let you use theirs, but some will ask you to buy something.

Unacceptable dress in church: both sexes should cover torsos, upper arms, and legs

Disabled access sign at the Vatican

Travelers with Special Needs

Rome is not particularly well-equipped for disabled visitors. The **Disabled Customer Assistance** center at Termini station offers help, and advice on train travel. Disabled travelers needing assistance getting on and off the train should reserve a special lift service 12 hours in advance, stating the names of all the stations at which they require help. A limited number of buses and streetcars have wheelchair access, and only a few metro stations have elevators. Ramps, elevators, and modified restrooms are available in an increasing number of places, including Termini station, although you may find an elevator out of order or a ramp blocked by an illegally parked car. Some restaurants have wheelchair access to the dining area, but not to the restroom.

If you are traveling without an escort, consider a specially designed package tour, or contact an organization for disabled travelers before you go.

The Vatican Museums, Sistine Chapel, and St. Peter's are all accessible by wheelchair.

Senior Travelers

EU citizens over 65 have free entry to many museums, and discounts for *anziani* (elderly citizens) are available at most other sights and on some Trenitalia *(see p379)* tickets.

Student Information

If you are an EU passport holder, it is worth having an International Student Identity Card (ISIC) or a Youth International Educational Exchange Card (YIEE) because you will receive reduced admission prices to national museums. Non-EU members with an ISIC or a YIEE card can also benefit from discounts at some private museums.

Contact the **Centro Turistico Studentesco** for general student information. The **Associazione Italiana Alberghi per la Gioventù** (the Italian YHA) operates four hostels across the city.

International Student Identity Card

Gay and Lesbian Travelers

The main venue for Rome's gay community is the gay-friendly bar **Coming Out** *(see p355)*, near the Colosseum. The Gay Pride parade takes place in June. The two-month-long **Gay Village** event (one of Europe's largest gay festivals) begins in July. In Rome, displays of public affection between same-sex individuals are not common, and some violence against homosexuals has been reported in the past.

Rome Time

Rome is 1 hour ahead of Greenwich Mean Time (GMT). Examples of the time difference with Rome for other major cities are as follows: London: –1 hour; New York: –6 hours; Dallas: –7 hours; Los Angeles: –9 hours; Perth: +7 hours; Sydney: +9 hours; Auckland: +11 hours; Tokyo: +8 hours. These figures can vary slightly for brief periods during local changes in summer. For all official purposes, Italians use the 24-hour clock.

Electrical Adapters

Electric current in Italy is 220V AC, with two- or three-pin round-pronged plugs. Adapters can be bought in most countries. Most hotels of three or more stars have hair dryers and shaver outlets in all bedrooms.

Conversion Table

US to Metric
1 inch = 2.54 centimeters
1 foot = 30 centimeters
1 mile = 1.6 kilometers
1 ounce = 28 grams
1 pound = 454 grams
1 pint = 0.47 liters
1 gallon = 3.8 liters

Metric to US
1 centimeter = 0.4 inches
1 meter = 3 feet 3 inches
1 kilometer = 0.6 miles
1 gram = 0.04 ounces
1 kilogram = 2.2 pounds
1 liter = 2.1 pints

A Gay Pride march passing the Colosseum

Responsible Tourism

Rome is aware of the need to become more "green," and environmental initiatives are taking place across the city. Italian cooking has always placed an emphasis on local seasonal food, but Italians are also starting to understand the importance of reducing carbon emissions. Eating local is a good way to support the area's economy, as well as helping the environment.

Organic shops and restaurants are springing up across Rome. Buy regional food at **Spazio Bio**, inside the Città dell'Altra Economia, a large expo space dedicated to the promotion of an organic and sustainable lifestyle, fair trade, ethical tourism, and recycling (which is

Shady terrace at Rome's Bed & Breakfast Bio

gradually being introduced in Rome). Shops can also no longer use non-biodegradable plastic bags. Those dreaming of greener nights can book a room in one of the mini-boutique hotels and B&Bs offering an eco-friendly stay.

Two such establishments are **EcoHotel** and **Bed & Breakfast Bio**, both of which guarantee energy- and water-saving rooms, serve organic breakfasts, and offer free bicycles for rides in the surrounding parks and nature preserves.

DIRECTORY

Tourist Information

Enjoy Rome
Via Marghera 8A.
Map 6 E3. **Tel** 06-445 1843.
W enjoyrome.com

Rome City Tourist Office
Termini Station (Platform 24). **Map** 6 D3. **Tel** 06-0608.
W turismoroma.it and
W 060608.it

Opening Hours and Admission Prices

Roma Pass
Tel 06-0608.
W romapass.it

Embassies

Australia
Via A. Bosio 5.
Tel 06-85 27 21.
W italy.embassy.gov.au

Canada
Via Zara 30. **Tel** 06-85 444 2911. W canada.it

New Zealand
Via Clitunno 44.
Tel 06- 853 7501.
W nzembassy.com/italy

United Kingdom
Via XX Settembre 80A.
Map 6 D2.
Tel 06-4220 0001.
W ukinitaly.fco.gov.uk

United States
Via Veneto 119A/121.
Map 5 B2. **Tel** 06-467 41.
W italy.usembassy.gov

Religious Services

American Episcopal
St. Paul's, Via Napoli 58.
Map 5 C3.
Tel 06-488 3339.

Anglican
All Saints, Via del Babuino 153. **Map** 4 F2.
Tel 06-3600 1881.

Jewish
Sinagoga (Tempio Maggiore), Lungotevere Cenci. **Map** 4 F5 & 12 D5.
Tel 06-684 0061.

Methodist
Via del Banco di Santo Spirito 3.
Map 4 E3 & 11 A2.
Tel 06-686 8314.

Muslim
The Mosque (Grande Moschea). Viale della Moschea 85 (Parioli district). **Map** 2 F1.
Tel 06-808 2258.

Prefettura della Casa Pontificia
Città del Vaticano.
Map 3 B3.
Tel 06-6988 3114.

Presbyterian
St. Andrew's, Via XX Settembre 7.
Map 5 C3.
Tel 06-482 7627.

Travelers with Special Needs

Disabled Customer Assistance
Termini Station (Platform 1). **Map** 6 D3.
Tel 199-30 30 60.

Student Information

Associazione Italiana Alberghi per la Gioventù
Via Cavour 44. **Map** 3 D3.
Tel 06-487 1152.
Fax 06-488 0492.
W aighostels.com

Centro Turistico Studentesco
Via Solferino 6A.
Map 6 D3.
Tel 06-462 0431.

Piazza Sforza Cesarini 26.
Map 11 B3.
Tel 06-6880 3290.
W cts.it

Gay and Lesbian Travelers

Coming Out
Via San Giovanni, Laterano 8.
Map 9 A1.
Tel 06-700 9871.
W comingout.it

Gay Village
Parco del Turismo (EUR).
W gayvillage.it

Responsible Tourism

Bed & Breakfast Bio
Via Cavalese 28.
Tel 335-7151 749.
W bedandbreakfastbio.com

EcoHotel
Via di Bravetta 91.
Tel 06-6615 6920.
W ecohotelroma.com

Spazio Bio
Città dell'Altra Economia Largo Dino Frisullo.
Map 8 D4.
Tel 06-5730 0419.
W cittadellaltraeconomia.org

Personal Security and Health

On the whole, Rome is a safe, unthreatening place for visitors, but petty street crime is a problem. Do not carry more money than needed for the day, and leave other valuables or documents in a hotel safe. Cameras are less likely to be snatched if they are in a carrier bag rather than an obvious case. Take particular care in crowded places, such as train stations, or on full buses, and steer clear of bands of innocent-looking children – they may be skillful professional pickpockets.

Carabinieri in dress uniform

Police

There are several different police forces in Rome. The *polizia* (state police) wear blue uniforms with white belts and berets. They deal with all kinds of crimes and are the ones who issue *permessi di soggiorno* (residence permits) to foreigners and passports to Italian citizens (see p366).

The *vigili urbani* (municipal police) wear blue uniforms in winter and white in summer, and can issue heavy fines for traffic and parking violations. They can usually be seen patrolling the streets, enforcing laws or regulating traffic.

The *carabinieri* (military police) wear red striped trousers. They deal with everything from fine-art thefts to speeding tickets.

The *guardia di finanza* are the tax police and wear gray uniforms. They deal with tax evasion and with customs; you will see them at the airport, behind the "goods to declare" counter.

To report stolen or lost items, go to the nearest police station (*questura*) or *carabinieri* office. If you believe your car may have been towed away, you should

find a member of the *vigili urbani* on the streets or have the Comune put you through to them by calling 06-0606.

What to Be Aware of

Be wary of bag-snatchers on mopeds who operate in quiet streets. Carry your bag at your side away from the road, or carry a discreet money belt or a securely fastened, long-strapped shoulder bag across your body. Equipment like video cameras should be disguised. Pickpockets (sometimes children) adopt highly sophisticated distraction techniques with pieces of paper or newspaper while they part you from your possessions in seconds. Take extra care of your valuables in market places or on public transportation. Bus routes 40 and 64, which run between Termini station and the Vatican, are notorious for pickpockets.

Thefts from cars are also rife. Jackets or bags should never be left visible inside a car parked on Rome's streets. Do not carry luggage on a roof rack. The streets to the east and south of Termini station are well-known for prostitution and drug-peddling, and are seedy at night.

Women traveling alone (or even in small groups) may need to take extra care. Women without male escorts attract more attention than they do in much of the rest of Europe and North America.

Beware of unauthorized minicab drivers who are probably not insured and frequently overcharge. They operate in particular at the airport and Termini station, waiting to profit from new arrivals. Hotel touts and unofficial tour guides are also best avoided; instead, stick to the official tourist agencies (see p297 and p369).

In an Emergency

For emergency phone numbers, see the Directory. For other medical attention, contact the First Aid (*Pronto Soccorso*) department of a major hospital such as **Policlinico Umberto I**, or **Ospedale di Santo Spirito**, or check the Yellow Pages (*Pagine Gialle*) for a doctor (*medico*) or dentist (*dentista*). For children, the **Ospedale Pediatrico Bambino Gesù** is renowned. Emergency care in public hospitals is free, even for foreigners.

Municipal police officer
directing traffic

Poliziotto – a member
of the state police

Carabiniere – a member
of the military police

Police car

Ambulance

Fire truck

Lost Property

For items lost on a bus or on the Metro, contact the numbers in the Directory. Otherwise, ask at a police station. To make an insurance claim, report your loss to a police station and get a signed form. For lost passports, contact your embassy or consulate *(see p369)*; for lost credit cards or traveler's checks, contact the issuing company's office *(see p372)*.

Hospitals and Pharmacies

English-speaking doctors can be found at **Rome American Hospital** or by looking in the English Yellow Pages, which is available at some hotel receptions and international bookshops. For access to paediatricians, visit the **Ospedale Pediatrico Bambino Gesù**. The **Ospedale Odontoiatrico G Eastman** can help with serious dental problems.

Pharmacists display late-opening rosters (several stay open all night), and can usually supply the local equivalent of foreign medicines. The **Vatican Pharmacy** stocks some American and British pharmaceutical products. For minor problems, pharmacists can give advice and recommend over-the-counter medications.

Minor Hazards

No inoculations are needed for Rome, but take mosquito repellent and sunscreen in the summer. Be sure to wash your hands frequently if you use public transportation, especially in winter when colds and flu are rampant. The Tiber is polluted, but water from faucets, and potable street fountains is piped straight from the hills, and is fresh and palatable.

Travel and Health Insurance

All visitors should carry insurance for property and medical care. When buying airline tickets, ask if there are any waivers included in your particular ticket for medical problems, death in the family, or other emergencies.

Take out adequate property insurance before you travel (it is difficult to buy once you are in Italy), and look after your belongings while you are in Rome. Be particularly careful when using public transportation and when visiting crowded tourist sights, where pick-pocketing is common. If possible, leave valuables at your hotel instead of carrying them around with you. Some hotels provide personal safes in the bedrooms. You can set these with your own memorable number. (Do not use your date of birth; it is on your passport and registration slip.) To be prepared for all eventualities, it is advisable to keep a separate photocopy of vital documents, such as your passport and plane tickets, to minimize the problem of replacing them if they are lost or stolen. It is also useful to take along a spare passport-sized photograph or two.

Non-EU residents should purchase a primary medical travel insurance policy before leaving their home country. EU residents are officially entitled to reciprocal medical care, but the bureaucracy involved can be daunting. Before you travel, make sure you obtain the European Health Insurance Card (EHIC) from your department of health or a post office.

DIRECTORY

In an Emergency

Ambulance
Tel 118 (free from any telephone).

Fire
Tel 115 (free from any telephone).

General SOS
Tel 113 (free from any telephone).

Police
Tel 112 (Carabinieri); 113 (Police) (free from any telephone).

Samaritans
Tel 800-860 022. **Open** 1–10pm daily. w samaritansonlus.org

Traffic Police
Tel 06-676 91.

Lost Property

Buses and Streetcars
Tel 06-6769 3214.

Metro
Line A Tel 06-4695 7068.
Open 9:30am–12:30pm Mon, Wed, Fri. **Line B Tel** 06-4695 8165.
Open 8am–1pm Mon–Sat.
After 10–15 days:
Tel 06-6769 3214.

Hospitals and Pharmacies

Ospedale Odontoiatrico G Eastman
Viale Regina Elena 287B.
Map 6 F2. **Tel** 06-77 301.

Ospedale Pediatrico Bambino Gesù
Piazza S. Onofrio 4.
Map 3 C4. **Tel** 06-68 591.

Ospedale di Santo Spirito
Lungotevere in Sassia 1.
Map 3 C3. **Tel** 06-683 51.

Policlinico Umberto I
Viale del Policlinico 155.
Map 6 F2. **Tel** 06-499 71.

Rome American Hospital
Via E Longoni 69. **Tel** 06-225 51.

Vatican Pharmacy
Porta Sant'Anna, Via di Porta Angelica. **Map** 3 C2.
Tel 06-6988 9806.

Banking and Local Currency

ATMs are easily found across Rome. Many businesses will accept credit cards, but some smaller family-run establishments still only accept cash. Exchanging money and traveler's checks can involve a lot of paperwork. Banks and post office exchange rates are generally more favorable than those offered in travel agencies. Carry some small change, since coins are needed for tips and illuminating works of art and chapels in churches *(see p367)*.

The Banca d'Italia, Italy's central bank

Banks and Bureaux de Change

It is best to have a few euros when you arrive, so you won't have to change money immediately. However, ATMs are found everywhere, including the airports.

For the best exchange rates, change money at a bank (look for the sign *Cambio*). Exchange offices and hotels tend to give poor rates, even if they charge modest commissions. At the Vatican Museums *(see p233)*, you won't be charged any commission.

Lines in banks can be long and the paperwork involved in changing money can take up a lot of time. Take some form of identification with you, such as a passport. You may be asked to leave handbags, shopping bags, and metal objects in the small lockers outside the bank.

Post offices also give good exchange rates, but lines can be long here as well. Currency can only be changed at the main post offices, such as the one near Piramide Metro station.

Banks are usually open 8:30am–1:20pm and 3–4:30pm Mon–Fri, but opening times vary. They are always closed on public holidays.

Bureaux de change have more generous opening times, similar to store hours. The two exchange offices at Termini station *(see p378)* are also open on Sundays.

ATMs

ATMs (*Bancomat*) can be found throughout the city and accept a wide range of credit and debit cards. The daily limit for withdrawals is usually €250. A fee is charged for each withdrawal. ATM crime (mainly related to card cloning rather than to theft) has been reported in the past. Always use caution at an ATM machine: cover the hand that is typing the code with the other hand, and avoid withdrawing cash from any machine you are unsure about.

Credit Cards and Traveler's Checks

Credit cards are widely accepted in hotels, restaurants, and stores. All major credit and charge cards (American Express, MasterCard, Visa, Diners Club) are well known. Banks and cash dispensers are more likely to accept Visa cards for cash advances, but MasterCard is accepted by many retail outlets in Italy. Take both if you have them. Paying for anything in foreign currency will almost always be expensive.

Some restaurants and shops set a minimum expenditure level, below which they will not accept credit card payment. Ask first or make sure you have some cash just in case.

Traveler's checks are not as popular as they used to be, and tourists are finding it increasingly hard to cash or spend them. If you decide to use them, choose a well-known name such as American Express. Record the traveler's check numbers and refund addresses separately from the checks themselves in case they are stolen.

DIRECTORY

Banks and Bureaux de Change

Banca Intesa San Paolo
Piazza di Spagna 18. **Map** 5 A2.
Tel 06-6977 4711. **Open**
8:30am–1:30pm, 2:45–4:15pm
Mon–Fri; 8:30am–12:45pm Sat.

Banca Nazionale del Lavoro BNL
Piazza Venezia 6. **Map** 12 F4.
Tel 06-678 2979. **Open**
8:35am–1:35pm, 2:45–4:15pm
Mon–Fri.

Lost and Stolen Credit Cards

American Express
Tel 06-7290 0347 or 06-72282.

Diners Club
Tel 800-864 064 (toll free).

Visa and MasterCard
Tel 800-819 014 (toll free).

The Euro

The euro (€) is the common currency of the European Union. It went into general circulation on January 1, 2002, initially for 12 participating countries. Italy was one of those 12 countries.

The area comprising the EU member states using the euro as sole official currency is known as the eurozone. Several EU members have opted out of joining this common currency.

Euro notes are identical throughout the eurozone, each one including designs of fictional architectural structures. The coins, however, have one side identical (the value side), and one side with an image unique to each country. Notes and coins are exchangeable in all participating euro countries.

Euro Bank Notes

Euro bank notes (bills) have seven denominations. The €5 note (gray in color) is the smallest, followed by the €10 note (pink), €20 note (blue), €50 note (orange), €100 note (green), €200 note (yellow), and €500 note (purple). All notes show the stars of the European Union.

€5 note

€10 note

€20 note

€50 note

€100 note

€200 note

€500 note

€2 coin

€1 coin

50 cents

20 cents

10 cents

Coins

The euro has eight coin denominations: €1 and €2; 50 cents, 20 cents, 10 cents, 5 cents, 2 cents, and 1 cent. The €2 and €1 coins are both silver and gold in color. The 50-, 20-, and 10-cent coins are gold. The 5-, 2-, and 1-cent coins are bronze.

5 cents

2 cents

1 cent

Communications and Media

With the most recent advances in technology, it is easier and cheaper than ever to stay in touch with family and friends while overseas. Even if you don't have a cell phone with Internet capabilities, you'll find that Wi-Fi and Internet cafés are everywhere in Rome, and phone cards offering very reasonable call rates abound. You can stay abreast of global news through BBC World (most likely available in your hotel) or the English-language publications available at many newsstands in the center of Rome.

Telephone company logo

International and Local Telephone Calls

Privately owned "call centers" offer a convenient way of making private long-distance calls. They are equipped with several metered telephones in sound-proofed booths. An assistant will assign you a booth and meter your call. You pay at the desk when you are finished, so coins are not needed. Call centers tend to be open from early morning until late night, and many also offer fax, Internet, and photocopying facilities.

Reaching the Right Number

- The code for Rome is 06 (required also within the city).
- Multilingual directory assistance is at 1254 (press 2).
- Operator assistance is at 170. Collect calls and credit card calls are also accepted.
- Italian directory assistance is at 1254 (press 1).
- To reach the operator in your own country to place a collect or credit card call, dial 800 172, then: 444 for AT&T, US; 401 for Verizon, US; 405 for Sprint, US; 441 for the UK; 610 for Telstra, Australia; and 611 for Optus, Australia.

In the wake of the smart-phone revolution, demand for public telephones has decreased considerably. However, there are some pay phones around the city, mostly at train stations, metro stations, and other main hubs. From these you can dial long-distance and most international calls direct. The newest phones take coins; the older ones only take telephone cards (ask for a *scheda telefonica*), available in several denominations. Telephone cards are sold in shops and tobacconists *(tabacchi)*. Break off the marked corner, insert the card arrow first, and the value of the unexpired units will show in a display window. After your call, the card can be retrieved and reused until it expires.

Public telephone sign

International phone cards, such as the Europa card, are by far the cheapest option if calling overseas from Italy. They come in either €5 or €10 cards, which give 120 (or more) minutes of calling time. When using, dial the main number on the card, key in the PIN, and then dial the number required.

Any Italian landline telephone number needs to have the full area code (including the zero) dialed in front of it, even if you are calling within the same city. Cell phone number prefixes begin with a 3 and do not require a 0.

Keep in mind that telephone calls from hotel rooms are usually very expensive, sometimes marked up by as much as several hundred percent.

Cell Phones

If you are staying in Rome for a considerable period of time, it is probably worth buying an Italian SIM card, with its own unique telephone number, to use with your own cell phone. You must show an official ID (such as a passport) when buying a SIM card. There are five main mobile providers: Vodafone, TIM, Tre, PosteMobile, and Wind. The SIM cards cost around €15 and usually come with €5 of free credit. They can be purchased, and refilled, from various cell phone outlets throughout the city.

Once you have the SIM, you can also add credit with a scratch-off card *(ricarica)* bought at tobacconist's shops or some newsstands. Some tobacconist's shops have a computerized system where they enter your cell phone number and put the credit on your phone for you, which is easier and quicker than following the instructions on the scratch-off card.

Internet café sign

Internet Access

Many hotels offer an Internet connection or Wi-Fi so you can access the Internet and email with your own laptop (sometimes for an extra fee). There are some Internet cafés (Italians call them *Internet point*) where you can go online, such as **Interpoint Yex** in the central city. Those traveling

PRACTICAL INFORMATION | **375**

without their own laptop or smartphone can also use the Internet at one of the phone centers around Termini station.

Some Internet cafés offer headphones and webcams so customers can use Skype or other chat programs. Many Internet points have Wi-Fi so you can access the Internet through your own laptop with a password provided by the assistant. An anti-terrorism law requires Internet café staff to take your information from an official ID (such as a passport), so staff may want to take a photocopy before allowing customers to use the Internet on their computers. This does not apply to customers using their own laptops.

Many cafés and bars have wireless hotspots. You can also sign up to access free Wi-Fi for a couple of hours a day in select public spaces throughout Rome by registering at: www.romawireless.com.

Postal Services

Post offices are multifunctional in Italy, used not only for postal services, but also for paying bills, managing certain bank accounts, and more. Lines can be long and disorganized, so if you are just sending a regular letter or postcard, save yourself the exasperation and buy a stamp at a tobacconist's shop. Then drop your letter in one of the mailboxes on walls around the city; most are red, with a slot for mail within Rome (*Roma e provincia di Roma*) and one for mail outside Rome (*per tutte le altre destinazioni*). There are also some blue mailboxes exclusively for foreign destinations (marked *estero*).

Vatican post office sign

Vatican postage stamps

The mail itself is quite reliable and efficient, though it tends to be slower around Christmas time. For urgent items, use the post office's express or registered service.

The Italian post office offers a *poste restante* service, where letters and packages addressed to you can be picked up directly at the post office. Post should be sent care of (*c/o*) *Fermo Posta* and the name of the relevant post office. Print your last name clearly in block capitals and underline it to make sure it is filed correctly. To pick up your mail, you have to show your passport and pay a small charge.

Regular post office hours are generally from around 8:30am to 2pm (8:30am to noon on Saturdays and on holiday eves), but main offices stay open until well into the evening for some services (such as registered mail).

Post office sign

Newspapers, TV, Radio

Rome's main newspapers are *La Repubblica* and *Il Messaggero*. American and British newspapers are readily available, with the *International Herald Tribune* and the *Guardian* on sale on the day of issue. The *TrovaRoma* supplement in the Thursday edition of *La Repubblica* is generally considered the main guide to what's on in the capital. The magazines *Wanted in Rome* (www.wantedinrome.com) and

Vatican Post

The Vatican postal service costs the same as regular mail, but is faster. Buy cards and stamps at the post office near the Vatican Museums entrance, or in Piazza San Pietro. Letters bearing Vatican stamps can only be posted within the Vatican city.

Foreign papers at a newsstand

Where Rome (www.whererome.it) also have English listings. Some of these publications also have websites full of information.

The state TV channels are RAI Uno, Due, and Tre, matched by four private channels. Analog TV has been replaced by digital across the region, so all TVs must now have a digital decoder to pick up any channels; with the decoder, you can access these basic Italian networks, plus some other channels including BBC World in English.

Vatican Radio transmits on 93.3MHz and 105MHz (FM) and also broadcasts news in English.

DIRECTORY

Internet Cafes

Interpoint Yex
Piazza Sant'Andrea
della Valle 3.
Map 12 D4.
Tel 06-9727 3136.
Open 9am–9pm daily.

Post Offices

Termini Station,
Via Giolitti 14.
Map 6 E4.
Tel 06-488 8741.
Open 8am–7pm Mon–Fri,
8am–1:15pm Sat.

Piazza San Silvestro 19.
Map 5 A3.
Tel 06-6973 7205.
Open 8am–7pm Mon–Fri,
8am–1:15pm Sat.

GETTING TO ROME

Many national airlines, including Italy's Alitalia, fly direct to Rome from most European cities and several in North America. Fiumicino airport now has a high-security terminal, Terminal 5, for flights to the US, and Israel. Ciampino airport is smaller and mainly caters to low-cost airlines flying in from other European cities. Rome also has train and long-distance bus links with the rest of Europe. These take a lot longer than flights (about 24 hours from London, for example, compared with about 2½ hours by air), but tend to cost about the same, so are they are only really worthwhile if you want to travel overland. Trains are often crowded during the summer.

Arriving by Air

If you are flying from the United States, **Delta**, **American Airlines**, **US Airways**, and **Alitalia** operate regular direct scheduled flights to Rome, with services from New York. Flying time is about 8½ hours. **Air Canada** and **Qantas** operate from Canada and Australia, respectively. There are also direct flights from Boston, Atlanta, Miami, Philadelphia, and Toronto. However, it may be considerably cheaper for intercontinental travelers to take a budget flight to London, Paris, Athens, Frankfurt, or Amsterdam and continue the journey to Rome from there. **British Airways** both operate direct scheduled flights from London Heathrow to Rome (Fiumicino), and you can also fly from Gatwick. **Swiss** and **KLM** also fly to Rome from London, and other British cities. A plane change in Zurich or Amsterdam is usually involved.

Excursion fares generally offer the best value in scheduled flights, but you must purchase them well in advance. They are subject to penalty clauses if you

Part of the extension to Fiumicino airport

cancel, so it is advisable to take out insurance as soon as you buy your ticket.

In addition to BA and Alitalia, you can buy low-cost tickets direct from airlines **easyJet** and **Ryanair**, which have daily flights from London, and other locations to Rome. Hotels, and car rental can also be booked via these airlines' websites, and both offer their own privately chartered bus to transport incoming passengers from Ciampino airport to Termini.

Alitalia flight tickets

Regular charter flights from the UK to Ciampino airport run year-round. Most leave from Stansted, Gatwick, and Luton, but there are also flights that leave from Manchester, Glasgow, and Birmingham. The price of fares varies, peaking in summer and in Holy Week for the Pope's Easter blessing. In Rome, the American Express travel office (*see p369*) will also book flights.

Fiumicino Airport

Rome has two international airports. Leonardo da Vinci – known as Fiumicino – is the largest one and handles most scheduled flights, as well as several easyJet routes. It is located about 18 miles (30 km) southwest of the city and has four terminals: 1 for domestic flights, 2 for EU flights, 3 for international flights, and 5 for flights to the US or Israel. The vast shopping area inside the airport offers a variety of stores, selling the most important Italian brands.

From Fiumicino there are two types of trains to Rome: one (€8) runs every 15–30 minutes

Check-in area at Fiumicino, Rome's main international airport

(5:57am–11:27pm) to Fara Sabina station, stopping at Trastevere, Ostiense, Tuscolana, and Tiburtina, but not Termini. The other train, known as the "Leonardo Express," is faster and more expensive (€14), running nonstop to Termini every half-hour (6:37am–11:37pm). If the ticket office is not open, try the automatic ticket machine (you can choose to see the instructions in English). Remember to specify which train you want when buying your ticket.

Ostiense station is linked with Piramide Metro (Line B) where you can catch an underground train to the downtown from 5:30am until 11:30pm daily (to 1:30am Fri and Sat). It can be hard to find a taxi at Ostiense after 9pm, but there are buses (Nos. 63 and 30) to Piazza Venezia. At night there is a coach service from Fiumicino to Tiburtina station. Car rental is available from offices at the airport *(see p387)*.

Train linking Fiumicino airport to Stazione Termini

Ciampino Airport

The other airport that serves Rome is Giovanni Battista Pastine Airport, known as Ciampino. It is located approximately 12 miles (20 km) southeast of the city and used by the majority of charter flights and low-cost airlines. Ciampino airport is always busy and sometimes chaotic,

Check-in area at Rome's Ciampino airport

so it is advisable to arrive there well in advance of your departure time.

Major car rental firms have branches at the airport *(see p387)*, though you may find it less harrowing to travel into central Rome on public transportation or by taxi.

The fastest way to get to the center of Rome is by the private **Terravision**, **Atral/Schiaffini**, or **SITBusShuttle** bus services. Buses go direct to Termini station and tickets cost between €4 and €6 one way. You can buy them on board the bus. A cheaper option is by **COTRAL** bus to Anagnina Metro station, then by underground train to Termini. Tickets (€1.50, plus €1.50 for each large bag) can be bought on the bus. A local bus service also links the airport to Ciampino train station.

Airport Taxis

Always use the official white taxis with a "taxi" sign on the roof. They usually line up in the yellow TAXI lanes in front of the airports and stations. The Rome Comune has established a flat fee for taxi rides from, and to the airports: €48 to/from Fiumicino from/to anywhere downtown (inside the Aurelian walls) and €30 to/from Ciampino from/to downtown. The fare covers a maximum of four people with baggage included. If a taxi refuses to apply the flat fee, you should report the driver by calling 06-6710 70721 and stating the cab number, which is found on both the inside and the outside of the car.

DIRECTORY

Arriving by Air

Air Canada
w aircanada.com

Alitalia
w alitalia.com

American Airlines
w aa.com

British Airways
Tel 02-6963 3602.
w britishairways.com

Delta
w delta.com

easyJet
w easyjet.com

KLM
w klm.com

Qantas
Tel 848 350 010.
w qantas.com

Ryanair
w ryanair.com

Swiss
w swiss.com

US Airways
Tel 8488 13177.
w usairways.com

Fiumicino and Ciampino Airports

Atral (Ciampino)
Tel 0773 472 008.
w atral-lazio.com

COTRAL (both airports)
w cotralspa.it

SITBusShuttle (both airports)
Tel 06-5916 826.
w sitbusshuttle.it

Terravision (Ciampino)
Tel 06-9761 0632.
w terravision.eu

Arriving in Rome by Train, Bus, or Car

Any overland journey to Rome is fastest by train, though there are bus connections to most major European cities. Within Italy, journeys between large cities are usually also best done by train, but when traveling from towns that are not on the main Intercity rail routes, buses can be quicker. For drivers, the Italian Automobile Club *(see p379)* provides free assistance, and excellent maps to members of affiliated automobile clubs from all over the world.

A Eurostar train

The concourse at Stazione Termini

Stazione Termini

Stazione Termini, Rome's main train station, is also the hub of the urban transportation system. Beneath it is the only interchange between the city's two Metro lines, and outside, on Piazza dei Cinquecento, is the central bus terminus. Though it is one of Rome's most stunning 20th-century buildings, it also has some unsavory aspects, so don't linger longer than necessary at night.

If you do arrive here late, there are usually taxis available (go to the official taxi stand) even in the small hours, and many of the city's night buses start at Termini.

In summer, the station gets crowded, and you can expect long lines. Termini has baggage lockers, a police station, a bureau de change, and tourist, and travel information offices. Other facilities include many tobacconists and newsstands (where you can buy bus and Metro tickets), as well as various bars and restaurants on the mezzanine floor, with more eateries and shops, including a bookstore, on the lower Termini Forum level. A post office is adjacent to platform 24, as are car rental desks. There is only one waiting room, located next to platform 1.

Of Rome's other stations, four are most likely to be of interest to tourists. They are Ostiense and Trastevere, for trains to Fiumicino airport and Viterbo *(see p273)*; Tiburtina, for some of the late-night and high-speed trains on the north–south line through Italy; and Roma Nord, for trains to Prima Porta.

Traveling by Train

Trenitalia, the Italian state rail company, has several levels of service, including the Regionale trains. These stop at almost every station, often have no air conditioning, and are much cheaper than the other trains. On Regionale and Inter-regionale trains, sometimes first-class seats are "declassed" so second-class ticket holders can sit there. The Eurostar, a cleaner, faster train, offers a first- and second-class service. It runs between Rome and Milan, Turin, Genoa, Bari, Naples, and Venice, with an extra fast *(alta velocità)* service operating on the Naples–Rome–Milan and Venice–Rome lines, although it now faces stiff competition from the high-speed **NTV (Italo)** trains. You have to reserve a seat and you are charged hefty supplements for the privileges of speed and attendant services. Intercity trains, which are for fast long-distance journeys, also charge a supplement. First- and second-class tickets are available to larger cities. From Rome you can also take international or Eurocity (EC) trains to destinations all over Europe.

Reservations are required on all trains except those on

Trenitalia logo

Termini, the heart of Italy's rail network and Rome's transport system

Regionale and Inter-regionale routes. Tickets for immediate travel can be bought at the station, but you should allow plenty of time to wait in line.

The Trenitalia website *(see below)* is useful for planning trips, checking scheduled train times, and buying tickets. If you book in advance or are a family with a child, you may be able to get a cheaper rate. However, it is easiest to go to a travel agency when booking a discounted ticket because Trenitalia's offers and fares change all the time.

An Intercity train

Traveling by Bus

Long-distance coaches (buses) terminate at Tiburtina, which is the city's main coach station. Information and tickets for travel to European cities are available from the **Eurolines**, **Baltour**, or **Italybus** websites. The **Appian Line** offers regular services within Italy. Its itineraries include Florence, Naples, Capri, Sorrento, and Pompeii, and, in summer, Venice, and Assisi. Local buses, serving villages and towns within the Lazio region, are run by **COTRAL**. All bus stations used by COTRAL in Rome are linked to Metro stations. Tickets are purchased on the spot and cannot be booked in advance. Some day trips from Rome by bus are described on pages 270–73.

Machines for Trenitalia Rail Tickets

These machines are easy to use, and most have instructions on screen in a choice of six languages. They accept coins, bills, and credit cards.

1 Touch screen: choose destination, train, and ticket type, make seat reservations, and choose payment method.

2 Insert coins here.

3 Payment with credit card: touchpad with slot for card below.

4 Receive train tickets, seat reservations, and change here.

5 Insert bills here.

Traveling by Car

To drive your own car in Italy, you need your driver's license, an international Green Card (for insurance purposes), and the vehicle registration document. A translation of your driver's license, available at Italian tourist offices abroad, is useful. Wearing seatbelts is mandatory in Italy. Headlights must be turned on even during the day on freeways and outside of built-up areas. Heavy fines are imposed for using a cell phone while driving. You must also carry a warning triangle and a reflective orange or yellow vest to wear if you leave your car in case of breakdown. Main routes to Rome connect with the Grande Raccordo Anulare (GRA), Rome's "ring road" (bypass). Tolls are charged on most Italian freeways. You take a ticket when you enter a toll road, and pay on

exit. Tolls can be paid with cash, credit cards, or a prepaid ViaCard. The latter is widely available (even at highway rest stops), and the toll is deducted from the card on leaving the freeway. Prices vary according to road type.

Official speed limits are 30–50 km/h (equivalent to 18–30 mph) in town, 80–110 km/h (50–70 mph), on two-lane roads outside town, and 130 km/h (90 mph) on freeways.

Directory

Traveling by Train

NTV (Italo)
Ⓦ ntvspa.it

Trenitalia
Tel 89 20 21.
Ⓦ trenitalia.com

Traveling by Bus

Appian Line
Ⓦ appianline.it

Baltour
Ⓦ baltour.it

COTRAL
Ⓦ cotralspa.it

EUROLINES
Ⓦ eurolines.com

Italybus
Ⓦ italybus.it

Eurolines bus connecting Rome with the rest of Europe

Arriving in Rome

This map shows the main bus, rail, and Metro links used by travelers arriving in Rome. The connections between Rome's two airports and the center of the city are shown, as well as links between Rome and the rest of Italy, and international rail routes from neighboring European countries. Travel information, including details of trip times and service frequency, is listed separately in each box.

Local train connections
Links to Flaminio (Roma Nord station) from **Viterbo** (2 hr 30 min).

M Line A, northbound
Stops after Ottaviano S. Pietro are: Cipro, Valle Aurelia, Baldo degli Ubaldi, Cornelia, and Battistini (end station).

FS Coastal route from Northern Italy
Links with Termini and/or Ostiense stations. **Marseille** (11 hr), **Nice** (9 hr), **Turin** (7 hr 30 min), **Genoa** (6 hr), **Pisa** (3 hr 30 min).

Key
- ✈ Airport *see pp376–7*
- FS Railroad *see pp378–9*
- 🚌 Coach & Bus Link *see p397*
- M Metro *see p383*
- — Airport Link *see pp376–7*
- — State Rail Link *see pp378–9*
- — Metro Line A *see p383*
- — Metro Line B *see p383*
- ▪ ▪ Walkway
- — Tram 8

0 meters 500
0 yards 500

✈ Leonardo da Vinci (Fiumicino)
Direct train links to Ostiense, Tiburtina, and Termini.
FS Fiumicino–Fara Sabina
(via Trastevere, Ostiense, Tiburtina) every 15–30 minutes;
Fiumicino–Termini
Leonardo Express every 30 minutes. W **adr.it**

M Line B, southbound
Stops after Piramide are: Garbatella, Basilica San Paolo, Marconi, EUR Magliana, EUR Palasport, EUR Fermi, and Laurentina (end station).

Map labels: Flaminio, Lepanto, Spagna, Ottaviano S. Pietro, Piazza di Spagna, Barberini, Vatican, Piazza della Rotonda, Quirin, Piazza Navona, San Pietro, Campo de' Fiori, Capitol, Foru, Largo Argentina, Janiculum, Palati, Trastevere, Circo Massimo, Aventine, Piramide, Trastevere, Ostiense

For additional map symbols *see back flap*

Coach connections into Rome
National and inter-national bus links at the coach station in front of **Stazione Tiburtina**. Buses for the Lazio region link at **Lepanto**, **Anagnina**, or **Laurentina**.

Long-distance coach (bus) at Stazione Tiburtina

FS International and Northern Italy
Eurostar train links with Termini. Trains arriving after midnight terminate at Tiburtina. **Paris** (15 hr), **Vienna** (14 hr), **Geneva** (14 hr), **Basle** (13 hr), **Munich** (11 hr), **Verona** (7 hr), **Milan** (3 hr 30 min), **Bologna** (2 hr 20 min), **Florence** (1 hr 30 min).

M Line B1, northbound
Stops after Bologna are: Annibaliano, Libia, and Conca d'Oro (end station).

M Line B, northbound
Stops after Tiburtina are: Monti Tiburtini, Pietralata, Santa Maria del Soccorso, Ponte Mammolo, and Rebibbia (end station).

FS Eastern Italy
Links with Termini station. **Pescara** (4 hr 20 min), **L'Aquila** (3 hr 30 min).

FS Southern Italy
Links with Termini station. **Palermo** (12 hr), **Reggio Calabria** (9 hr 30 min), **Bari** (6 hr 30 min), **Naples** (1 hr 10 min).

Bologna — Policlinico — Castro Pretorio — Roma Termini — Tiburtina — Repubblica — Veneto — Vittorio Emanuele — Esquiline — Cour — losseo — Manzoni — Lateran — San Giovanni — Re di Roma — Ponte Lungo — aracalla — Tuscolana

M Line A, southbound
Stops after Ponte Lungo are: Furio Camillo, Colli Albani, Arco di Travertino, Porta Furba, Numidio Quadrato, Lucio, Sestio, Giulio Agricola, Subaugusta, Cinecittà, and Anagnina (end station).

Ciampino
Bus link every 30–60 min to Ciampino station (10 min) & Anagnina Metro station (Line A; 25 min). Both link with Termini station. Private coach services to Termini station are also available.
W adr.it

Termini Metro station

GETTING AROUND ROME

Rome's downtown is compact and, even though walking absolutely everywhere would be overambitious, it is a city in which you can spend much of your time on foot. Since the main streets in the central city are usually clogged with traffic, driving, and cycling are not recommended, but brave motorbike or scooter riders can have great fun buzzing around on a rented Vespa. Traveling by bus and streetcar can be very slow, so use overground transportation only when you have a long way to go. The Metro, designed to connect the suburbs with the downtown, has no stops in the historic city center near the Pantheon or Piazza Navona, though it is certainly the fastest way of crossing the city.

Green Travel

As the largest, and most advanced city of the ancient world, Rome was the first to face (and combat) air pollution from burning wood. The fight against smog continues today, as many Romans rely exclusively on their cars. Car-sharing programs, city-owned bicycles, and some (but not enough) bike lanes, **electric-car charging stations**, and car-free Sundays (in the springtime) are among the initiatives. Video cameras prevent unauthorized cars from entering the *centro storico*, where many bus lines (three of which are electric) cover almost everything there is to see. Though often busy and chaotic, public transportation is always a better option than driving, and some used bus tickets will buy you discounted entry to selected exhibitions (see instructions on the ticket itself). Walking around the downtown is pleasant, so if you want to enjoy the warm sunshine and avoid public transportation, make sure you wear sturdy, comfortable shoes.

Bus stop listing details of routes served

Buses and Streetcars

Rome's mass transit company is called **ATAC** (Azienda Tramvie e Autobus del Comune di Roma). Scores of buses and a few streetcars cover most parts of the city. Most run from early morning until midnight, meaning the last bus leaves from the end of the line at midnight. There are also a few night buses.

Apart from some small electric minibuses (like the 116 and 119), no buses can run through the narrow streets of the city's historic center. But there are plenty of bus routes to take you within a short walk of the main sights *(see inside back cover)*.

Bus stops list the details of routes taken by all buses using that stop. Night buses are indicated by an "N" before the number.

There are several streetcars in the city, but the only line of tourist interest is the 8, which runs from Torre Argentina to Casaletto, going through Trastevere and Monteverde.

Special Bus Services

There are two tourist bus services: the 110 Open and the Archeobus service. The 110 Open, a red, open-topped double-decker, is a hop-on/hop-off service that passes many of the city's tourist attractions. It leaves from Piazza dei Cinquecento every 15 minutes between 8:30am and 8:30pm (to 7pm in winter). Linking the downtown with the catacombs and the monuments on the Via Appia Antica, the Archeobus leaves Piazza Venezia every half-hour between 9am and 4:30pm.

Using Buses and Streetcars

The main terminus is on Piazza dei Cinquecento outside Termini station, but there are other major route hubs throughout the city, most usefully those at Piazza del Risorgimento and Piazza Venezia. Information on mass transit can be obtained from ATAC kiosks, the customer service office, or the ATAC website. Board the bus at the front or the back; the central door is reserved for people getting off. You must stamp your

A modern streetcar taking passengers through the city

One of Rome's red and gray ATAC buses

ticket in the yellow machine once you get on the bus. Timed tickets, *biglietto integrato a tempo* (BIT), can be used on all means of transportation.

Tickets

Tickets for buses, streetcars, and the Metro should be bought in advance, and stamped in the appropriate machine as soon as you start your trip. You can buy tickets at bars, some newsstands, and tobacconists, and Metro stations and bus terminals. There are automatic ticket machines at main bus stops, and Metro stations that take coins. Some

buses have a machine on board for buying tickets, but there is no way of knowing which buses have one, so purchase a ticket before you board.

BIT tickets are valid for 100 minutes, during which time you can take one Metro ride and as many buses, and streetcars as you like. If you are going to make four or more trips in one day, buy a daily (BIG) ticket. There are also three-day, seven-day, and monthly passes. To travel farther afield in Lazio, consider buying a regional BIRG ticket. Fare-dodging incurs a hefty on-the-spot fine.

Metropolitana

Rome's underground system, the Metropolitana, has two lines (A and B) that cross the city in a rough X-shape, converging at Termini station (*see inside back cover*). Line A (red) leads from Battistini in the west to Anagnina in the southeast of the city, from where buses go to Ciampino airport. Line B (blue) runs from Rebibbia in the northeast, branches off at Bologna station, then goes down to EUR in the southwest, where buses leave for the coast.

Metro logo

Stations are clearly marked by the Metro logo, a white M on a red background. Among the most useful stations are Colosseo, Spagna, San Giovanni, Ottaviano S. Pietro, and Piramide (for trains to Fiumicino). Both lines run from 5:30am until 11:30pm every day (to 1:30am Friday and Saturday). For more details, visit www.atac. roma.it. A third Metro line, C, is scheduled to open in 2015. A fourth line is also planned.

Useful Bus Routes

This map shows some of the buses that go through interesting parts of Rome with good views of major sights. The 40 Express is always full of tourists, since it goes from Termini to St. Peter's and the Vatican. The other routes are likely to be less crowded.

Walking

Wandering through Rome's old center is one of the most enjoyable aspects of the city. You can take in the architectural details, absorb the streetlife, take detours at will, and peek into any church, shop, or bar that catches your interest. You can easily visit several of the main tourist sights in a few hours.

Explore the city area by area, using public transportation when distances are too far. Although some parts of historic Rome are now pedestrianized, a street that is closed to cars may still be used by cyclists and, illegally, by scooter riders. There have been many plans to create more traffic-free zones, but imposing such measures on a population as insubordinate as Rome's is not easily done.

During the height of summer, you'll have a more enjoyable time if you follow the example of the Italians. Walk slowly on the shady side of the street; have a long lunch followed by a siesta during the hottest part of the day. Continue exploring in the late afternoon, when churches and shops reopen, and the streets are at their liveliest. Wandering at night is delightful, as the streets are cool, and many facades floodlit.

Crossing the Street

First impressions suggest that there can be only two kinds of pedestrians in Rome: the quick and the dead. Even if you cross

Passengers sightseeing on an open-top tour bus

roads at traffic lights, and pedestrian crossings strictly in your favor, there is sure to be some van or Vespa hurtling toward you with apparently homicidal intent. Fortunately, Roman drivers have quick reactions and accidents are relatively rare. The best tactic is to be as alert and confident as Romans. The roads are very busy. When crossing, you should try to leave as large a gap as possible between yourself, and oncoming traffic. Step purposefully into the road, making eye contact with approaching drivers, and don't hesitate or change your course. Once a driver sees that you are determined to cross, he will stop, or at least swerve. Pedestrians must take particular care at night, when the traffic lights are switched to a constantly flashing yellow, turning the crossings into free-for-alls.

Street Signs

Theoretically, although it may not always seem to be the case, pedestrians have right of way at crossings when the green *avanti* sign is lit up. The red sign *alt* means you must wait. Underground crossings are indicated by a sign reading *sottopassaggio*.

It is easy to get lost in the maze of streets and piazzas of the historic downtown. Until you know your way around, you can follow yellow signs marking routes between the sights and piazzas of particular

interest to tourists. Routes leading to other landmarks are indicated by signs on a brown or gray background.

Guided Tours

Several companies offer guided tours in English; these include the excellent **Walks of Italy**, **Green Line Tours**, **Context**, and **Carrani Tours**. Full-day city tours including lunch cost around €100; half-day tours around €40. Alternatively, the **110 Open Bus** passes many of the main sights on a 2-hour circuit. Tickets cost around €18, and the bus leaves from Termini every 15 minutes between 8:30am, and 8:30pm (to 7pm in winter); the website has further details as well as information on the Archeobus tours of the

Directions for walkers

Watch out for children

Pedestrian crossing

Nuns walking in downtown Rome

Avanti: go! Pedestrians have right of way

Alt: stop! Traffic has right of way

ancient monuments. Tour guides can often be hired at major sights, such as the Roman Forum (see pp80–89). Employ only official guides and establish the fee in advance; they usually charge at least €50 for a half-day tour.

Driving

Driving in Rome can be an extremely intimidating experience for visitors. The flamboyant aggression of Italian drivers is notorious, pedestrians step out into the roads without warning, and the one-way system operating in much of the downtown makes maintaining a sense of direction impossible. You'll also find drivers passing on the wrong side, while scooters, and Vespas zoom among the lanes of traffic and go the wrong way down one-way streets. One rule to remember is to yield to the right. Additionally, non-resident drivers cannot enter the central city's ZTL (Limited Traffic Zone) during the day and on some weekend nights. There are cameras at the entrance of the ZTL, and cars without a permit will incur a fine each time they pass in front of the camera. The cameras are very visible, and there is always an electronic sign saying whether access is open to everyone (varco aperto) or restricted (varco chiuso). You can call 06-57003 or check

No stopping

No parking

One-way street

No through road

www.atacmobile.it for ZTL times. Unless you are accustomed to driving in Italian cities and fully aware of the ZTL regulations and zones, leave your car at home – or, failing that, in a guarded parking lot.

Thefts from cars are rife in Rome, so never leave anything of value in your vehicle, even out of sight: areas such as Campo de' Fiori are patrolled by gangs on the lookout for anyone leaving cameras and other costly items in the car. You should also

remove the car radio and GPS if you can – you won't be the only person carrying these items around with you.

Take extra care if driving late at night. Not only do traffic lights switch to flashing yellow, but some drivers are astonishingly cavalier about driving under the influence of alcohol or drugs. In case of a breakdown, call the **ACI** (see pp386–7).

Parking

The most convenient parking lot is below the Villa Borghese. Much of the downtown is reserved for residents with permits, but there are around 2,000 metered parking spaces marked with a blue line (from 8am–8pm or 8am–11pm, depending on the area). If you do find a legal place to park, however, you may return to find you have been hemmed in by double-parked cars. Locations of some of the most useful parking lots are listed on page 387.

Beware of illegal parking attendants, found especially at night in busy areas where parking is free, who direct you to a space (sometimes even an unauthorized one) in exchange for some change. This practice is against the law, but Italians often pay, for fear the attendant will damage their car if they don't.

Gasoline

Gasoline is very expensive. As well as from regular garages, gasoline can be bought from roadside gas pumps, many of which are self-service, which is cheaper; these pumps take bills or debit/credit cards. Check whether your car uses unleaded gas (benzina senza piombo or benzina verde) or not. Late-night gas stations are listed on page 387. At night, most self-service stations are attended by illegal gas station attendants, who will put the gas in for you in exchange for a tip.

The state oil company logo

Illegal Parking

Rome's traffic police are vigilant. If you park illegally, your car may be clamped or (if it's causing an obstruction) towed away, so call 06-67 691 or 06-0606 before reporting it stolen. No-parking zones should be clearly marked, but check in case the sign is hidden by a tree.

zona rimozione fermata consentita per salita e discesa con conducente a bordo

Signpost for a tow-away area (zona rimozione)

A tow truck at work

Car Rentals

Major international firms (**Avis**, **Hertz**, **Europcar**) and **Sixt** have rental offices at the airports, Termini station, and in the city. However, you may get a better deal by reserving a car before you arrive through a travel agent or online, or by using a local firm (such as **Maggiore**). Make sure breakdown service and collision damage waiver are included. Prospective renters usually need to be at least 25 years old and have held a driver's license for at least a year. You will also need to leave a deposit – a credit card number is usually enough. Some firms also ask for an international license (available from your national automobile association).

Accident rates on Italian roads are high, so make sure you are fully insured against all eventualities. It is a good idea to join an internationally affiliated automobile association (such as the AAA in the US or the AA in Britain) so that if you do break down, the **ACI** (Italian Automobile Club) will tow your car without charging.

Details of road and traffic conditions (in Italian) are available from a special **Road Conditions** number. For more information on driving and parking in the city, as well as understanding road signs, and buying fuel, *see page 385*.

Moped and Bicycle Rental

Rome's narrow streets, and heavy traffic, combined with the seven steep hills on which it was built, make it a challenging place for even the most serious of cyclists. However, there are a few areas, such as the Villa Borghese, the banks of the Tiber, and some pockets in the historic downtown (around the Pantheon and Piazza Navona), where bike lanes make for a relaxing way to see the city.

Mopeds *(motorini)*, and scooters – like the classic Piaggio Vespa, meaning "wasp" – are good for getting through the traffic. You may want to stick to quiet streets to begin with, though.

Bikes and scooters can be rented from **Collalti**, **Bici & Baci**, and **Barberini Scooters for Rent**. There are also **Bike Rental** spots dotted around the city. Motorcyclists, scooter drivers, and their passengers must wear helmets by law; these can be rented from most rental shops. You may be asked to leave a credit card number or cash as a deposit when you pick up the vehicle *(see p359)*.

The **Roma Bikesharing** program is good for short rides in the central city. You must enrol and pay a €10 deposit for a "smartcard," which can be recharged. You then have access to bikes at stands across the city, though these may be few and far between.

Taxi on a busy street in downtown Rome

Taxis

Official taxis in Rome are white, say "Comune di Roma" on the side, and bear a "taxi" sign on the roof. Do not use the taxis offered by touts at stations and tourist spots; official taxi drivers do not solicit customers. Official taxis can be hailed at specially marked taxi stands or on the street (drivers are not supposed to stop in the street but many of them do). You can nearly always find them at the main tourist sights, airports, and stations (including Termini and Ostiense). Roman taxi drivers are not renowned for their friendliness and may even refuse to take you if you're going too far from the lucrative downtown or, conversely, if the ride is too short.

Taxis are not particularly cheap, so unless you have heavy luggage or screaming toddlers, public transportation is usually a better option. Taxi drivers charge supplements for more than one bag, night rides (10pm–7am), and travel on Sundays or public holidays.

Customers should make sure the meter is turned on and visible. The meter continues running while you are at a standstill, so traffic jams can become expensive. Some drivers may take suspiciously circuitous routes. Italians don't tip taxi drivers; they simply round up the fare to the nearest euro. You can call for a taxi (but you will pay from the time the driver gets the call from the switchboard) from: **Mondo Taxi**, **Radiotaxi 3570** or **La Capitale Radio Taxi**.

Motorbikes and scooters, a popular means of transportation in Rome

Taxi rides to and from the city's airports incur a flat fee for up to four passengers and their luggage (see p377).

River Tour

The summer service offered by **Battelli di Roma**, which usually runs from embarkation points near the Ponte Sant'Angelo and Tiber Island, is currently suspended due to damage to the boats. Call for the latest information.

Horse-Drawn Carriages

You can rent horse-drawn caleches (carrozzelle) for a gentle tour of the historic downtown. Carriages carry up to five people

Horse-drawn carriage offering tours from St. Peter's Square

and can be rented from many points: Piazza di Spagna, the Colosseum, Trevi Fountain, St. Peter's, Via Veneto, Villa Borghese, Piazza Venezia, and Piazza Navona. Trips last half an hour, an hour, half a day or a

day. They tend to be expensive, but prices for longer rides are negotiable; establish the price before you set off, and make sure you understand whether the rate is per person, or for the whole carriage.

DIRECTORY

Electric-Car Charging Stations

Via Cola di Rienzo.
Map 4 D2.
Piazza Mastai. **Map** 7 C1.
🔲 colonnineelettriche.it.

Buses and Trams

Atac
Piazza dei Cinquecento.
Map 6 D3. **Tel** 06-46951.
🔲 atac.roma.it

Traffic Info
Piazzale degli Archivi 40.
Tel 06-57003.
🔲 agenziamobilita.
roma.it

Guided Tours

Carrani Tours
Via V. E. Orlando 95. **Map** 5 C3. **Tel** 06-474 2501.
🔲 carrani.com

Context
Tel 06-9672 7371.
🔲 contexttravel.com/
city/rome

Green Line Tours
Via Amendola 32. **Map** 6 D3. **Tel** 06-482 7480.
🔲 greenlinetours.com

110 Open Bus and Archeobus
Piazza dei Cinquecento.
Map 6 D3.
Tel 800-281 281.
🔲 trambusopen.com

Walks of Italy
Tel 1-202 684 6916
🔲 walksofitaly.com

Parking Lots

Acqua Acetosa station.
Map 2 E1. Also: Lepanto Metro station. **Map** 4 D1.
Also: Villa Borghese.
Map 5 A1. Also: Piazzale dei Partigiani. **Map** 8 E4.

Useful 24-Hour Gas Stations

Portuense
Piazzale della Radio.
Map 7 B5.

Trastevere
Lungotevere Ripa.
Map 8 D1.

Car Breakdown Services

ACI Breakdown
Tel 803 116.

Road Conditions
Tel 1518.

Car Rental

Avis
Tel 199-100 133
(centralized booking).
Also: Ciampino airport.
Tel 06-7934 0195.
Also: Fiumicino airport.
Tel 06-6501 1531.

Also: Via Sardegna 38A.
Map 5 C1.
Tel 06-4282 4728.
🔲 avisautonoleggio.it

Europcar
Tel 199 307 030
(centralized free booking).
Also: Fiumicino airport.
Tel 06-6576 1211.
Also: Stazione Termini.
Map 6 D3.
Tel 06-488 2854.
🔲 europcar.it

Hertz
Via Gregorio VII 207.
Tel 06-3937 8807.
Also: Stazione Termini.
Map 6 D3.
Tel 06-474 0389.
Also: Fiumicino airport.
Tel 06-6501 1553.
🔲 hertz.it

Maggiore
Stazione Termini. **Map** 6 D3. **Tel** 06-488 0049.
Also: Via Po 8A. **Map** 5 C1.
Tel 06-854 8698.
🔲 maggiore.it

Sixt
Stazione Termini. **Map** 6 D3. **Tel** 06-4782 6000.
Also: Ciampino airport.
Tel 06-7934 0802.
Also: Fiumicino airport.
Tel 06-6595 3547.
🔲 sixt.it

Moped and Bicycle Rental

Barberini Scooters for Rent
Via della Purificazione 84.
Tel 06-488 5485.

Bici & Baci
Via del Viminale 5.
Map 5 C3.
🔲 bicibaci.com

Bike Rental
Piazza del Popolo.
Map 4 F1.
Also: Piazza di Spagna.
Map 5 A2.

Collalti
Via del Pellegrino 82.
Map 4 E4 & 11 C4.
Tel 06-6880 1084 (bikes).

Roma Bikesharing
Tel 06-57003.
🔲 bikesharing.roma.it

Taxis

La Capitale Radio Taxi
Tel 06-49 94.

Mondo Taxi
Tel 06-88 22.

Radiotaxi 3570
Tel 06-35 70.

River Tour

Battelli di Roma
Tel 06-9774 5498.
🔲 battellidiroma.it

STREET FINDER

Map references given with sights, hotels, restaurants, shops, and entertainment venues refer to the maps in this section (*see* How the Map References Work, *opposite*). A complete index of the street names and places of interest marked on the maps follows on pages 390–99. The key map below shows the area of Rome covered by the *Street Finder* only. This includes the sightseeing areas (which are color-coded) as well as the whole of central Rome with all the districts important for restaurants, hotels, and entertainment venues. Because the historic downtown is so packed with sights, there is a large-scale map of this area on maps 11 and 12.

How the Map References Work

The first number tells you which *Street Finder* map to turn to.

❼ Trevi Fountain

Fontana di Trevi. **Map 5** A3 & 12 F2. ⟨⟩ 52, 53, 61, 62, 63, 71, 80, 116, 119.

The letter and number give the grid reference. Letters go across the map's top and bottom; numbers on its sides.

The second reference refers to the large-scale maps of central Rome (11 & 12). It is read in exactly the same way as the first.

The map continues on map 8 of the *Street Finder.*

Key to Street Finder

- Major sight
- Places of interest
- **FS** Train station
- **M** Metro station
- Streetcar stop
- *i* Tourist information office
- Hospital with emergency room
- Police station
- Church
- Synagogue
- Train line
- Pedestrian street
- City walls

Scale of Map Pages 1-10

0 meters	250	
0 yards	250	1:12,000

Scale of Map Pages 11 & 12

0 meters	150	
0 yards	150	1:7,600

The key to the abbreviations used in the Street Finder is on page 390.

Street Finder Index

Key to Abbreviations used in the Street Finder

B.go	Borgo	P.	Piazza	S.	San, Sant', Santa
d.	di, del, dell', dello, della,	P.etta	Piazzetta	S. M.	Santa Maria
	dei, delle, degli	P.le	Piazzale	SS.	Santi, Santissima
Gall.	Galleria	Princ.	Principe	V.	Via
L.go	Largo	P.ta	Porta	Vic.	Vicolo
Lungot.	Lungotevere	P.te	Ponte	V.le	Viale
M.te	Monte	Reg.	Regina		

Q

R

General Index

Acknowledgments

Dorling Kindersley would like to thank the many people whose help and assistance contributed to the preparation of this book.

Main Contributors

Olivia Ercoli is an art historian and tour guide who has lived all her life in Rome. Bilingual in English and Italian, she lectures on art history and writes on a range of subjects for English and Italian publications.
Travel writer **Ros Belford** conceived the idea of the Virago Woman's Guides, of which she is now series editor, and wrote the *Virago Woman's Guide to Rome*. She has traveled widely in Europe and, as well as writing guide books, contributes to a variety of publications including *The Guardian*.
Roberta Mitchell heads the editorial section of the UN's Publishing Division in Rome, where she has lived for many years. An experienced writer and editor with extensive knowledge of the city, she has contributed to a number of guides to Rome including the *American Express Guide to Rome*.

Contributors

Reid Bramblett, Sam Cole, Mary Jane Cryan Pancani, Daphne Wilson Ercoli, Laura Ercoli, Lindsay Hunt, Adrian James, Leonie Loudon, Christopher McDowall, Davina Palmer, Rodney Palmer, Pardeep Sandhu, Debra Shipley. Dorling Kindersley wishes to thank the following editors and researchers at Websters International Publishers: Sandy Carr, Matthew Barrell, Siobhan Bremner, Serena Cross, Valeria Fabbri, Annie Galpin, Gemma Hancock, Celia Woolfrey.

Additional Photography

Max Alexander, Marta Bescos, Giuseppe Carfagna, Demetrio Carrasco, Andy Crawford, Peter Douglas, Mike Dunning, Philip Enticknap, Steve Gorton, John Heseltine, Britta Jaschinski, Neil Mersh, Ian O'Leary, Poppy, Rough Guides/James McConnachie, Alessandra Santarelli, David Sutherland, Martin Woodward.

Additional Illustrations

Anne Bowes, Robin Carter, Pramod Negi, Gillie Newman, Chris D. Orr.

Additional Picture Research

Sharon Buckley.

Cartography

Advanced Illustration (Cheshire), Contour Publishing (Derby), Euromap Limited (Berkshire), Alok Pathak, Kunal Singh. Street Finder maps: ERA Maptec Ltd (Dublin) adapted with permission from original survey and mapping from Shobunsha (Japan).

Cartographic Research

James Anderson, Donna Rispoli, Joan Russell.

Research Assistance

Janet Abbott, Flaminia Allvin, Fabrizio Ardito, Licia Bronzin, Lupus Sabene.

Revisions and Relaunch Team

Namrata Adhwaryu, Beverley Ager, Emma Anacootee, Jasneet Arora, Rupanki Arora Kaushik, Shruti Bahl, Meghna Baruah, Sreemoyee Basu, Marta Bescos Sanchez, Tessa Bindloss, Peter Bently, Vandana Bhagra, Subhashree Bharati, Hilary Bird, Divya Chowfin, Lucinda Cooke, Michelle Crane, Vanessa Courtier, Kristin Dolina-Adamczyk, Peter Douglas, Vidushi Duggal, Claire Edwards, Jon Eldan, Simon Farbrother, Emer FitzGerald, Karen Fitzpatrick, Anna Freiberger, Vanessa Hamilton, Marcus Hardy, Kaberi Hazarika, Christine Heilman, Sasha Heseltine, Sally Ann Hibbard, Paul Hines, Stephanie Jackson, Claire Jones, Steve Knowlden, Priya Kukadia, Rakesh Kumar Pal, Mary Lambert, Maite Lantaron, Jude Ledger, Janette Leung, Carly Madden, Shahid Mahmood, Nicola Malone, Alison McGill, Jane Middleton, Ian Midson, Fiona Morgan, Jane Oliver-Jedrzejak, Helen Partington, Catherine Palmi, Naomi Peck, Marianne Petrou, Carolyn Pyrah, Pete Quinlan, Salim Qurashi, Rada Radojicic, Pamposh Raina, Marisa Renzullo, Ellen Root, Collette Sadler, Sands Publishing Solutions, Mathew Baishakhee Sengupta, Jane Shaw, Azeem Siddiqui, Susana Smith, Solveig Steinhart, Clare Sullivan, Avantika Sukhia, Rachel Symons, Andrew Szudek, Alka Thakur, Stuti Tiwari, Daphne Trotter, Ajay Verma, Karen Villabona, Diana Vowles, Lynda Warrington, Stewart J. Wild.

Special Assistance

Dottore Riccardo Baldini, Mario di Bartolomeo of the Soprintendenza dei Beni Artistici e Storici di Roma, Belloni, Dorling Kindersley picture department, David Gleave MW, Debbie Harris, Emma Hutton and Cooling Brown Partnership, Marina Tavolato, Dottoressa Todaro and Signora Camimiti at the Ministero dell'Interno, Trestini.

Photography Permissions

Dorling Kindersley would like to thank the following for their kind permission to photograph at their establishments: Bathsheba Abse at the Keats-Shelley Memorial House, Accademia dei Lincei, Accanto, Aeroporti di Roma, Aldrovandi Palace, Alpheus, Banco di Santo Spirito at Palazzo del Monte di Pietà, Rory Bruck at Babington's, Caffè Giolitti, Caffè Latino, Comune di Roma (Ripartizione X), Comunità Ebraica di Roma, Guido Cornini at Monumenti Musei e Gallerie Pontificie, Direzione Sanitaria Ospedale di Santo Spirito, Dottoressa Laura Falsini at the Soprintendenza Archeologica di Etruria Meridionale, Hotel Gregoriana, Hotel Majestic, Hotel Regina Baglioni, Marco Marchetti at Ente EUR, Dottoressa Mercalli at the Museo Nazionale di Castel Sant'Angelo, Ministero dell' Interno, Plaza Minerva, Ristorante Alberto Ciarla, Ristorante Filetti di Baccalà, Ristorante Romolo, Signor Rulli and Signor Angeli at the Soprintendenza Archeologica di Roma, Soprintendenza Archeologica per il Lazio,

Soprintendenza per i Beni Ambientali e Architettonici, Soprintendenza per i Beni Artistici e Storici di Roma, Daniela Tabo at the Musei Capitolini, Villa d'Este, Villa San Pio, Mrs. Marjorie Weeke at St. Peter's.

Picture Credits

a - above; b - below/bottom; c - center; f - far; l - left; r - right; t - top..

Works of art have been reproduced with the permission of the following copyright holders: *Town with Gothic Cathedral*, Paul Klee © DACS, London 2011 239br.

The publishers are grateful to the following individuals, companies, and picture libraries for permission to reproduce their photographs:

Accademia Nazionale di San Luca, Rome: 162br; **AFE:** 59bc, 63cra; Sandro Battaglia 61c, 63bl, 63br, 328br; **Aeroporti di Roma:** 376bl, 377tr; **Agenzia Sintesi:** 370bl, 370br, 370cla; Marco Marcotulli 370bc; **AKG-Images:** Andrea Jemolo 10br; **Alamy Images:** Caro 151tr; CuboImages srl/Gimmi 387tr; Kathy DeWitt 307tl; Michele Flazone 44; Antonio J Galante - VWPics 261tl; Lautaro 194c; Prisma Archivo 241tl; Travel Division Images 310b; Travel Ink/Jim Gibson 374crb; Jozef Sedmak 200; Sklifas Steven 216; Superstock 64-5; John G. Wilbanks 274; Robin Wilkinson 371tl; Wilmar Topshots 252; AGF foto: 42–3c; **Aldrovandi Palace Hotel:** 299tr; **Alitalia:** 376cr; **Ancient Art and Architecture,** 20bl, 25tl,29bc, 38crb, 39tc, 48clb; **Artothek,** Städelsches Kunstinstitut Frankfurt, Goethe in the Roman Campagna by JHW Tischbein 138tr.

Babuino 181, Rome: 300tc; Baglioni hotels SPA: 298tr; Banca d'Italia: 372cla; Bed and Breakfast Bio: 369tr; **Biblioteca Reale,** Torino: 32–3c; Al Bric, Rome: 314br; **Bridgeman Art Library, London/New York:** 22br, 41tr, 164crb; Agnew & Sons, London 55tr; Antikenmuseum Staatliches Museum, Berlin 23bc; Bibliothèque da la Sorbonne 32c, British Museum, London 31cra; Christie's, London 97tr; The Fine Art Society, London 153tr, 281tl; Galleria degli Uffizi, Florence 35bl; Giraudon/Château de Versailles, France 37tr; Greek Museum, University of Newcastle-upon-Tyne 20br; Index/Bibliotheca Publica Episcopal, Barcelona 110bl, /Piacenza Town Hall, Italy/31br; King Street Galleries, London 37bc; Lauros-Giraudon/ Louvre 30br, 58br; Roy Miles Gallery, 29 Bruton St, London 248t; Musée des Beaux-Arts, Nantes 57tr; Museo e Gallerie Nazionali di Capodimonte, Naples, Detail from the predella of San Ludovico by Simone Martini 30tr; Musée Condé, Chantilly f.71v Très Riches Heures, 30tc; Museum of Fine Arts, Budapest 114br; Museo Archeologico di Villa Giulia 52cl; Palazzo Doria Pamphilj, Rome 109br; Private Collection 23br, 26bc, 28bc, 31tr, 181tl; Pushkin Museum, Moscow 115tc; Sotheby's, London 22bl; Vatican Museums & Galleries 45c, 235tr.

Capitoline Museums, Rome: 73cr; Enoteca Capranica, Rome: 313bl; **Cephas Picture Library:** Mick Rock 308tr; **Corbis:** Art on File 12bl; Alessandra Benedetti 367tr;

Bettmann 8-9; epa/Ettore Ferrari 100cla; Owen Franken 306cla; Robert Harding World Imagery/Bruno Morandi 258; Ken Kaminesky 156; Bob Krist 307c; Araldo de Luca 70tr; Checchino dal 1887, Rome: 311tr; Corpo Nazionale dei Vigili del Fuoco: 371cl; Croce Bianca Italiana: 371cla.

Il Dagherrotipo: 147tc, 327bl, 378cla; Stefano Chieppa 291bc, 292bc; Andrea Getuli 289tl; Stephano Occhibelli 290cla, 290br; Paolo Priori 206tr; Giovanni Rinaldi 198tr, 288cla, 288br, 289br, 292cla, 293br, 293tc, 383tl; **CM Dixon:** 21bl, 28c, 272bl, 273tr, 273cl; Dorling Kindersley: Courtesy of Basilica San Clemente 178; Courtesy of the Ministero della Pubblica Instruzione 263bc; **Dreamstime.com:** Avorym 13br; Bramble100 66; Danileon 12tr, 190; Dennis_ dolkens 107br; Krylon80 98; Luis007 294-5; Maui01 144; Monick79 167bl; Konstantinos Papaioannou 135clb.

Ecole Nationale Superieure des Beaux-Arts: 25cb, 26–7, 250tr; **ET Archive:** 18, 21tc, 21clb, 23tl, 23tc, 27t, 31clb, 35crb, 36br, 41bc; Eurolines: 379bl; **Mary Evans Picture Library:** 22cla, 27cb, 28cl, 33br, 34clb, 34bc, 35tl, 38cr, 38bl, 69br, 76tr, 83b, 93tc, 95br, 97tl, 137tr, 215bc.

Coraldo Falsini: 43tl, 346b, 347t, 347c; **Ferrovie dello stato:** 379cl, 379tr; **Werner Forman Archive:** 21cr, 24bc, 27crb, 27bl, 27br, 51ca, 177br; **Folklore Museum, Rome:** 212cra.

Garden Picture Library: Bob Challinor 175br; **Getty Images:** 42cb; AFP 61br; AFP/Andreas Olaro 368br; Sylvain Grandadam 171tc, 364-5; Andre Thijssen 368tl; Stone/ Richard Passmore 1c; Visions of our land 78; **Giraudon:** 19b, 32br, 40bc; Grandi Stazioni S.p.A: 378b; Grand Hotel de la Minerve, Rome: 302br; **Ronald Grant:** 56br.

Sonia Halliday: 23ca, 26br, 29cb; Laura Lushington 28bl; **Robert Harding Picture Library:** 27cra, 36bl, 81cr, 272c; Mario Carrieri 39tr; 347bl; G White 61bl; Hotel Due Torri, Rome: 301br; **Hulton Deutsch:** 59cr, 365c.

Imago, Hassler Roma: 316t.

Le Jardin de Russie, Rome: 317b.

Magnum: Erich Lessing 21tl, 91crb; **Mansell:** 23tr, 29bl, 30cb, 35ca, 58cl, 59cl, 77cla, 77c, 80cra, 94cb, 116c, 127tr, 134br, 135cr, 138bl, 141bl, 141bc, 174bl, 174bc, 176cl, 183crb, 198c, 212bl, 220bl, 247cb; Alinari 143bl, 256bc; Anderson 141crb, 165tl, 248crb; **Marka:** V Arcomano 37cr; D. Donadoni 11br; Lorenzo Sechi 10cla, 226bc; MAXXI: Roberto Galasso 261br; **Moro Roma:** 40cla, 41cl, 42bc, 43tr, 42br. Museo Nazionale Romano: Fabio Ratti 129cr, 129br, 165br.

National Portrait Gallery, London: 58tr, 59tr; **Grazia Neri:** Vision/Giorgio Casulich 116br, 158bc, Vision/Roberta Krasnig 126tr, 285tr; © **Nippon Television Network Corporation,** Tokyo 1999: 242bl and all pictures on 244-5; Nonna Betta, Rome: 312t.

Pantheon View, Rome: Gantcho Beltchev Photography 303tl.

Residenza Cellini: 298bc; **Rex Features:** Steve Wood 43crb.

Scala Group S.p.A: 51tr, 96tr, 127tl, 231tl, 280cl; Chiesa del Gesù 111tl, Galleria Borghese 36cla, 262tr, Galleria Colonna 159crb, Galleria Doria Pamphilj 50br, 107cr, Galleria Spada 50cl, Galleria degli Uffizi 20–21, 31bl, Museo d'Arte Orientale 177cl, Musei Capitolini 51br, Museo della Civiltà Romana 52tr, 52b, Museo delle Terme 25tr, Museo Napoleonico 53cr, Museo Nazionale, Napoli 25cl, Museo Nazionale, Ravenna 26cl, Museo del Risorgimento, Milano 40cb, 40–1c, Museo del Risorgimento, Roma 41tl, Palazzo Barberini 254bl, Palazzo Ducale 23cla, 25tr, Palazzo della Farnesina 220clb, Palazzo Madama 24cr, Palazzo Venezia 51cr, 68bl, San Carlo alle Quattro Fontane 37c, San Clemente 39clb, Santa Costanza 28–9c, Santa Maria dell'Anima 123tr, Santa Maria Maggiore 47tr, Santa Maria del Popolo 141tc, 141cra, Santa Prassede 30bl, 32clb, Santa Sabina 29ca, 33cb, Vatican Museums 23crb, 29tl, 29cr, 29cra, 31crb, 33tl, 33cr, 34cla, 35cr, 35br, 36c, 36clb, 45cra, 50cla, 52cr, 53bl, 226clb, 227cra, 233tl, 236 all, 238-9 all, 240 -1 all except 241tl, 243 all, 291tl; **Lourens Smak**: 11tl; Spirito Divino, Rome: 318t; STA Travel Group: 368c; Superstock: Tips images 208.

Trambus Open S.p.A: 384tr, **Topham Picture Source:** 42cl.

Vivi Bistrot, Rome: 319bl.

Zefa: 228cl, 229ca; Eric Carle 60ca; Kohlhas 229tl.

Thanks also to Dottoressa Giulia De Marchi of **L'accademia Nazionale di San Luca**, Rome for 162br, Rettore Padre Libianchi of **La Chiesa di Sant'ignazio di Loyola** for 108t, **Ente Nazionale per il Turismo,** and to **La Repubblica Trovaroma.**

Front Endpapers
Alamy Images: Jozef Sedmak Lfbr, Sklifas Steven Lfbl, Wilmar Topshotes Rtl; Corbis: Ken Kaminesky Rftl; Dorling Kindersley: Courtesy of Basilica San Clemente Rfbr; Dreamstime.com: Bramble100 Rtr, Danileon Rbc, Krylon80 Rfcrb, Maui01 Lfclb; Getty Images: Visions of our land Rfcr; Superstock: Tips Images Lbr.
Map Cover
Corbis: Arnaud Chicurel / Hemis
Jacket
Front main and spine top– **Corbis:** Arnaud Chicurel / Hemis

All other images © Dorling Kindersley.
For further information, see www.dkimages.com

Special Editions of DK Travel Guides
DK Travel Guides can be purchased in bulk quantities at discounted prices for use in promotions or as premiums. We are also able to offer special editions and personalized jackets, corporate imprints, and excerpts from all of our books, tailored specifically to meet your own needs.

To find out more, please contact:
in the United States **SpecialSales@dk.com**
in the UK **travelspecialsales@uk.dk.com**
in Canada DK Special Sales at **general@ tourmaline.ca**
in Australia **business.development@pearson. com.au**

Phrase Book

In an Emergency

Help!	**Aiuto!**	eye-**yoo**-toh
Stop!	**Fermate!**	fair-**mah**-teh
Call a	**Chiama un**	kee-**ah**-mah oon
doctor	**medico**	**meh**-dee-koh
Call an	**Chiama un'**	kee-**ah**-mah oon
ambulance	**ambulanza**	am-boo-**lan**-tsa
Call the	**Chiama la**	kee-**ah**-mah lah
police	**polizia**	pol-ee-**tsee**-ah
Call the fire	**Chiama i**	kee-**ah**-mah ee
department	**pompieri**	pom-pee-**air**-ee
Where is the	**Dov'è il telefono?**	dov-**eheel** teh-**leh**-
telephone?		foh-noh?
The nearest	**L'ospedale**	loss-peh-**dah**-leh pee-
hospital?	**più vicino?**	oovee-**chee**-noh?

Communication Essentials

Yes/No	**Sì/No**	see/noh
Please	**Per favore**	pair fah-**vor**-eh
Thank you	**Grazie**	**grah**-tsee-eh
Excuse me	**Mi scusi**	mee **skoo**-zee
Hello	**Buon giorno**	bwon **jor**-noh
Goodbye	**Arrivederci**	ah-ree-veh-**dair**-chee
Good evening	**Buona sera**	**bwon**-ah sair-ah
morning	**la mattina**	lah mah-**tee**-nah
afternoon	**il pomeriggio**	eel poh-meh-**ree**-joh
evening	**la sera**	lah **sair**-ah
yesterday	**ieri**	ee-**air**-ee
today	**oggi**	**oh**-jee
tomorrow	**domani**	doh-**mah**-nee
here	**qui**	**kwee**
there	**la**	**lah**
What?	**Quale?**	**kwah**-leh?
When?	**Quando?**	**kwan**-doh?
Why?	**Perchè?**	pair-**keh**?
Where?	**Dove?**	**doh**-veh?

Useful Phrases

How are you?	**Come sta?**	**koh**-meh stah?
Very well,	**Molto bene,**	**moll**-toh **beh**-neh
thank you.	**grazie.**	**grah**-tsee-eh
Pleased to	**Piacere di**	pee-ah-**chair**-eh dee
meet you.	**conoscerla.**	coh-**noh**-shair-lah
See you soon.	**A più tardi.**	ah pee-oo tar-dee
That's fine.	**Va bene.**	va **beh**-neh
Where is/are …?	**Dov'è/Dove sono…?**	dov-eh/doveh **soh**-noh?
How long does	**Quanto tempo ci**	kwan-toh **tem**-poh
it take to get to …?	**vuole per**	chee voo-**oh**-leh pair
	andare a …?	an-**dar**-eh ah…?
How do I	**Come faccio per**	koh-meh **fah**-choh
get to …?	**arrivare a …?**	pair arri-**var**-eh ah…?
Do you speak	**Parla inglese?**	**par**-lah een-**gleh**-zeh?
English?		
I don't	**Non capisco.**	non ka-**pee**-skoh
understand.		
Could you speak	**Può parlare**	pwoh par-**lah**-reh
more slowly,	**più lentamente,**	pee-oo len-ta-**men**-teh
please?	**per favore?**	pair fah-**vor**-eh?
I'm sorry.	**Mi dispiace.**	mee dee-spee-**ah**-cheh

Useful Words

big	**grande**	**gran**-deh
small	**piccolo**	**pee**-koh-loh
hot	**caldo**	**kal**-doh
cold	**freddo**	**fred**-doh
good	**buono**	**bwoh**-noh
bad	**cattivo**	kat-**tee**-voh
enough	**basta**	**bas**-tah
well	**bene**	**beh**-neh
open	**aperto**	ah-**pair**-toh
closed	**chiuso**	kee-**oo**-zoh
left	**a sinistra**	ah see-nee-strah
right	**a destra**	ah **dess**-trah
straight ahead	**sempre dritto**	**sem**-preh **dree**-toh
near	**vicino**	vee-**chee**-noh
far	**lontano**	lon-**tah**-noh
up	**su**	**soo**
down	**giù**	**joo**
early	**presto**	**press**-toh
late	**tardi**	**tar**-dee
entrance	**entrata**	en-**trah**-tah
exit	**uscita**	oo-**shee**-ta
restroom	**il gabinetto**	eel gah-bee-**net**-toh

free, unoccupied	**libero**	**lee**-bair-oh
free, no charge	**gratuito**	grah-**too**-ee-toh

Making a Telephone Call

I'd like to place a	**Vorrei fare**	vor-**ray far**-eh oona
long-distance call.	**una interurbana.**	in-tair-oor-**bah**-nah
I'd like to make	**Vorrei fare una**	vor-**ray far**-eh oona
a collect call.	**telefonata a carico**	teh-leh-fon-**ah**-tah ah
	del destinatario.	**kar**-ee-koh dell dess-
		tee-nah-**tar**-ree-oh
I'll try again later.	**Ritelefono più**	ree-teh-**leh**-foh-noh
	tardi.	pee-oo **tar**-dee
Can I leave a	**Posso lasciare**	**poss**-oh lash-**ah**-reh
message?	**un messaggio?**	oon mess-**sah**-joh?
Hold on	**Un attimo,**	oon **ah**-tee-moh,
	per favore	pair fah-**vor**-eh
Could you speak	**Può parlare più**	pwoh par-**lah**-reh
up a little, please?	**forte, per favore?**	pee-oo **for**-teh, pair
		fah-**vor**-eh?
local call	**la telefonata**	lah teh-leh-fon-**ah**-ta
	locale	loh-**kah**-leh

Shopping

How much	**Quant'è,**	kwan-**teh**
does this cost?	**per favore?**	pair fah-**vor**-eh?
I would like …	**Vorrei …**	vor-**ray**
Do you have …?	**Avete …?**	ah-**veh**-teh…?
I'm just looking.	**Sto soltanto**	stoh sol-**tan**-toh
	guardando	gwar-**dan**-doh
Do you take	**Accettate**	ah-chet-**tah**-teh
credit cards?	**carte di credito?**	**kar**-teh dee **creh**-dee-toh?
What time do	**A che ora apre/**	ah keh or-ah
you open/close?	**chiude?**	**ah**-preh/kee-**oo**-deh?
this one	**questo**	**kweh**-stoh
that one	**quello**	**kwell**-oh
expensive	**caro**	**kar**-oh
cheap	**a buon prezzo**	ah bwon **pret**-soh
size, clothes	**la taglia**	lah **tah**-lee-ah
size, shoes	**il numero**	eel **noo**-mair-oh
white	**bianco**	bee-**ang**-koh
black	**nero**	**neh**-roh
red	**rosso**	**ross**-oh
yellow	**giallo**	**jal**-loh
green	**verde**	**vair**-deh
blue	**blu**	bloo
brown	**marrone**	mar-**roh**-neh

Types of Shops

antique dealer	**l'antiquario**	lan-tee-**kwah**-ree-oh
bakery	**la panetteria**	lah pah-net-tair-**ree**-ah
bank	**la banca**	lah **bang**-kah
bookshop	**la libreria**	lah lee-breh-**ree**-ah
butcher shop	**la macelleria**	lah mah-chell-eh-**ree**-ah
cake shop	**la pasticceria**	lah pas-tee-chair-**ee**-ah
department store	**il grande**	eel **gran**-deh
	magazzino	mag-gad-**zee**-noh
delicatessen	**la salumeria**	lah sah-loo-meh-**ree**-ah
fishmonger	**la pescheria**	lah pess-keh-**ree**-ah
florist	**il fioraio**	eel fee-or-**eye**-oh
greengrocer	**il fruttivendolo**	eel froo-tee-**ven**-doh-loh
grocery	**alimentari**	ah-lee-men-**tah**-ree
hairdresser	**il parrucchiere**	eel par-oo-kee-**air**-eh
ice cream parlor	**la gelateria**	lah jel-lah-tair-**ree**-ah
market	**il mercato**	eel mair-**kah**-toh
newsstand	**l'edicola**	leh-dee-koh-lah
pharmacy	**la farmacia**	lah far-mah-**chee**-ah
post office	**l'ufficio postale**	loo-**fee**-choh pos-**tah**-leh
shoe shop	**il negozio di**	eel neh-goh-tsioh dee
	scarpe	**skar**-peh
supermarket	**il supermercato**	su-pair-mair-**kah**-toh
tobacconist	**il tabaccaio**	eel tah-bak-**eye**-oh
travel agency	**l'agenzia di viaggi**	lah-jen-**tsee**-ah dee
		vee-**ad**-jee

Sightseeing

art gallery	**la pinacoteca**	lah peena-koh-**teh**-kah
bus stop	**la fermata**	lah fair-**mah**-tah
	dell'autobus	dell **ow**-toh-booss
church	**la chiesa**	lah kee-**eh**-zah
	la basilica	lah bah-**seel**-i-kah
garden	**il giardino**	eel jar-**dee**-no
library	**la biblioteca**	lah beeb-lee-oh-**teh**-kah
museum	**il museo**	eel moo-**zeh**-oh
tourist	**l'ufficio**	loo-fee-choh
information	**turistico**	too-**ree**-stee-koh
train station	**la stazione**	lah stah-tsee-**oh**-neh

closed for the public holiday	chiuso per la festa	kee-oo-zoh pair lah fess-tah

Staying in a Hotel

Do you have any vacant rooms?	Avete camere libere?	ah-veh-teh kah-mair-eh lee-bair-eh?
double room	una camera doppia	oona kah-mair-ah doh-pee-ah
with double bed	con letto matrimoniale	kon let-toh mah-tree-moh-nee-ah-leh
twin room	una camera con due letti	oona kah-mair-ah kon doo-eh let-tee
single room	una camera singola	oona kah-mair-ah sing-goh-lah
room with a bath, shower	una camera con bagno, con doccia	oona kah-mair-ah kon ban-yoh, kon dot-chah
porter	il facchino	eel fah-kee-noh
key	la chiave	lah kee-ah-veh
I have a reservation.	Ho fatto una prenotazione.	oh fat-toh oona preh-noh-tah-tsee-oh-neh

Eating Out

Do you have a table for …?	Avete un tavolo per … ?	ah-veh-teh oon tah-voh-loh pair …?
I'd like to reserve a table.	Vorrei riservare un tavolo.	vor-ray ree-sair-vah-reh oon tah-voh-loh
breakfast	colazione	koh-lah-tsee-oh-neh
lunch	pranzo	pran-tsoh
dinner	cena	cheh-nah
The check, please.	Il conto, per favore.	eel kon-toh pair fah-vor-eh
I am a vegetarian.	Sono vegetariano/a.	soh-noh veh-jeh-tar-ee-ah-noh/nah
waitress	cameriera	kah-mair-ee-air-ah
waiter	cameriere	kah-mair-ee-air-eh
fixed price menu	il menù a prezzo fisso	eel meh-noo ah pret-soh fee-soh
dish of the day	piatto del giorno	pee-ah-toh dell jor-no
appetizer	antipasto	an-tee-pass-toh
first course	il primo	eel pree-moh
main course	il secondo	eel seh-kon-doh
vegetables	il contorno	eel kon-tor-noh
dessert	il dolce	eel doll-cheh
cover charge	il coperto	eel koh-pair-toh
wine list	la lista dei vini	lah lee-stah day vee-nee
rare	al sangue	al sang-gweh
medium	al puntino	al poon-tee-noh
well done	ben cotto	ben kot-toh
glass	il bicchiere	eel bee-kee-air-eh
bottle	la bottiglia	lah bot-teel-yah
knife	il coltello	eel kol-tell-oh
fork	la forchetta	lah for-ket-tah
spoon	il cucchiaio	eel koo-kee-eye-oh

Menu Decoder

apple	la mela	lah meh-lah
artichoke	il carciofo	eel kar-choff-oh
baked	al forno	al for-noh
beans	i fagioli	ee fah-joh-lee
beef	il manzo	eel man-tsoh
beer	la birra	lah beer-rah
boiled	lesso	less-oh
bread	il pane	eel pah-neh
broth	il brodo	eel broh-doh
butter	il burro	eel boor-oh
cake	la torta	lah tor-tah
cheese	il formaggio	eel for-mad-joh
chicken	il pollo	eel poll-oh
clams	le vongole	leh von-goh-leh
coffee	il caffè	eel kah-feh
dry	secco	sek-koh
duck	l'anatra	lah-nah-trah
egg	l'uovo	loo-oh-voh
eggplant	la melanzana	lah meh-lan-tsah-nah
fish	il pesce	eel pesh-eh
French fries	patatine fritte	pah-tah-teen-eh free-teh
fresh fruit	frutta fresca	froo-tah fress-kah
garlic	l'aglio	lahl-yoh
grapes	l'uva	loo-vah
grilled	alla griglia	ah-lah greel-yah
ham	il prosciutto	eel pro-shoo-toh
cooked/cured	cotto/crudo	kot-toh/kroo-doh
ice cream	il gelato	eel jel-lah-toh
lamb	l'abbacchio	lah-back-kee-oh
lobster	l'aragosta	lah-rah-goss-tah

meat	la carne	la kar-neh
milk	il latte	eel laht-teh
mineral water	l'acqua minerale	lah-kwah mee-nair-ah-leh
sparkling/still	gasata/naturale	gah-zah-tah/nah-too-rah-leh
mushrooms	i funghi	ee foon-gee
oil	l'olio	loll-yoh
olive	l'oliva	loh-lee-vah
onion	la cipolla	lah chee-poll-ah
orange	l'arancia	lah-ran-chah
orange/lemon juice	succo d'arancia/ di limone	soo-koh dah-ran-chah/ dee lee-moh-neh
peach	la pesca	lah pess-kah
pepper	il pepe	eel peh-peh
pork	carne di maiale	kar-neh dee mah-yah-leh
potatoes	le patate	leh pah-tah-teh
rice	il riso	eel ree-zoh
roast	arrosto	ar-ross-toh
roll	il panino	eel pah-nee-noh
salad	l'insalata	leen-sah-lah-tah
salt	il sale	eel sah-leh
sausage	la salsiccia	lah sal-see-chah
seafood	frutti di mare	froo-tee dee mah-reh
shrimp	i gamberi	ee gam-bair-ee
soup	la zuppa, la minestra	lah tsoo-pah, lah mee-ness-trah
steak	la bistecca	lah bee-stek-kah
strawberries	le fragole	leh frah-goh-leh
sugar	lo zucchero	loh zoo-kair-oh
tea	il tè	eel teh
herbal tea	la tisana	lah tee-zah-nah
tomato	il pomodoro	eel poh-moh-dor-oh
tuna	il tonno	ton-noh
veal	il vitello	vee-tell-oh
vegetables	i legumi	ee leh-goo-mee
vinegar	l'aceto	lah-cheh-toh
water	l'acqua	lah-kwah
red wine	vino rosso	vee-noh ross-oh
white wine	vino bianco	vee-noh bee-ang-koh
zucchini	gli zucchini	lyee dzoo-kee-nee

Numbers

1	uno	oo-noh
2	due	doo-eh
3	tre	treh
4	quattro	kwat-roh
5	cinque	ching-kweh
6	sei	say-ee
7	sette	set-teh
8	otto	ot-toh
9	nove	noh-veh
10	dieci	dee-eh-chee
11	undici	oon-dee-chee
12	dodici	doh-dee-chee
13	tredici	tray-dee-chee
14	quattordici	kwat-tor-dee-chee
15	quindici	kwin-dee-chee
16	sedici	say-dee-chee
17	diciassette	dee-chah-set-teh
18	diciotto	dee-chot-toh
19	diciannove	dee-chah-noh-veh
20	venti	ven-tee
30	trenta	tren-tah
40	quaranta	kwah-ran-tah
50	cinquanta	ching-kwan-tah
60	sessanta	sess-an-tah
70	settanta	set-tan-tah
80	ottanta	ot-tan-tah
90	novanta	noh-van-tah
100	cento	chen-toh
1,000	mille	mee-leh
2,000	duemila	doo-eh mee-lah
5,000	cinquemila	ching-kweh mee-lah
1,000,000	un milione	oon meel-yoh-neh

Time

one minute	un minuto	oon mee-noo-toh
one hour	un'ora	oon or-ah
half an hour	mezz'ora	medz-or-ah
a day	un giorno	oon jor-noh
a week	una settimana	oona set-tee-mah-nah
Monday	lunedì	loo-neh-dee
Tuesday	martedì	mar-teh-dee
Wednesday	mercoledì	mair-koh-leh-dee
Thursday	giovedì	joh-veh-dee
Friday	venerdì	ven-air-dee
Saturday	sabato	sah-bah-toh
Sunday	domenica	doh-meh-nee-kah